FAMILIES IN GLOBAL PERSPECTIVE

FAMILIES IN GLOBAL PERSPECTIVE

Edited by

JAIPAUL L. ROOPNARINE

Syracuse University

UWE P. GIELEN

St. Francis College

Boston ■ *New York* ■ *San Francisco*
Mexico City ■ *Montreal* ■ *Toronto* ■ *London* ■ *Madrid* ■ *Munich* ■ *Paris*
Hong Kong ■ *Singapore* ■ *Tokyo* ■ *Cape Town* ■ *Sydney*

Senior Editor: Jeff Lasser
Series Editorial Assistant: Sara Owen
Senior Marketing Manager: Krista Groshong
Editorial-Production Service: Omegatype Typography, Inc.
Composition and Prepress Buyer: Linda Cox
Manufacturing Buyer: JoAnne Sweeney
Cover Administration: Joel Gendron
Electronic Composition: Omegatype Typography, Inc.

For related titles and support materials, visit our online catalog at www.ablongman.com.

Library of Congress Cataloging-in-Publication Data

CIP data not available at time of publication.

ISBN 0-205-33574-8

Printed in the United States of America

10 9 8 7 6 5 4 3 2 1   09 08 07 06 05 04

CONTENTS

PREFACE   ix

PART ONE
INTRODUCTION   1

CHAPTER 1   FAMILIES IN GLOBAL PERSPECTIVE: AN INTRODUCTION   3
Jaipaul L. Roopnarine and Uwe P. Gielen

CHAPTER 2   FAMILIES: AN EVOLUTIONARY
ANTHROPOLOGICAL PERSPECTIVE   14
Bobbi S. Low

CHAPTER 3   (POST)MODERN FAMILIES   33
Louise B. Silverstein and Carl F. Auerbach

PART TWO
ASIA AND OCEANIA   49

CHAPTER 4   THE FAMILY IN MAINLAND CHINA:
STRUCTURE, ORGANIZATION, AND
SIGNIFICANCE FOR CHILD DEVELOPMENT   51
Xinjin Chen and Yunfeng He

CHAPTER 5   THE CHANGING JAPANESE FAMILY:
A PSYCHOLOGICAL PORTRAIT   63
Takashi Naito and Uwe P. Gielen

CHAPTER 6   CHANGING PATTERNS OF FAMILY LIFE IN INDIA   85
Pittu Laungani

CHAPTER 7   FAMILIES IN INDONESIA   104
Sarlito Wirawan Sarwono

CHAPTER 8   FAMILY DEVELOPMENT IN TWO ISLAND
CULTURES IN THE CHANGING PACIFIC   120
Mary Martini

PART THREE
THE MIDDLE EAST   149

    CHAPTER 9   EGYPTIAN FAMILIES   151
    Ramadan A. Ahmed

    CHAPTER 10   CONTEMPORARY TURKISH FAMILIES   169
    Diane Sunar and Güler Okman Fisek

    CHAPTER 11   FAMILISM, POSTMODERNITY,
    AND THE STATE: THE CASE OF ISRAEL   184
    Sylvie Fogiel-Bijaoui

PART FOUR
EUROPE   205

    CHAPTER 12   FAMILIES IN GREECE   207
    James Georgas, Tsabika Bafiti, Kostas Mylonas,
    and Litsa Papademou

    CHAPTER 13   THE ITALIAN FAMILY: PAST AND PRESENT   225
    Anna Laura Comunian

    CHAPTER 14   THE GERMAN FAMILY: FAMILIES IN GERMANY   242
    Heidi Keller, Ulrike Zach, and Monika Abels

    CHAPTER 15   NORWEGIAN FAMILIES FROM A PSYCHOCULTURAL
    PERSPECTIVE: A CHALLENGE TO THERAPEUTIC
    THEORY AND PRACTICE   259
    Wencke J. Seltzer

    CHAPTER 16   THE RUSSIAN FAMILY   277
    Eric Shiraev and Julia Gradskova

PART FIVE
THE AMERICAS   291

    CHAPTER 17   MARRIAGES AND FAMILIES IN THE UNITED STATES   293
    Brent C. Miller, Spencer C. Leavitt, Junius K. Merrill,
    and Kyung-Eun Park

CHAPTER 18 **CARIBBEAN FAMILIES IN ENGLISH-SPEAKING COUNTRIES: A RATHER COMPLEX MOSAIC** 311
Jaipaul L. Roopnarine, Pauline Bynoe, Ronald Singh, and Rommel Simon

CHAPTER 19 **FAMILIES IN BRAZIL** 330
L.-A. Rebhun

PART SIX
AFRICA 345

CHAPTER 20 **FAMILIES IN CENTRAL AFRICA: A COMPARISON OF BOFI FARMER AND FORAGER FAMILIES** 347
Hillary N. Fouts

CHAPTER 21 **FAMILY LIFE IN SOUTH AFRICA** 363
Engela Pretorious

INDEX 381

PREFACE

Historians and anthropologists teach that throughout recorded history and in all present-day societies, families have formed the basic cells of the social fabric of society. No other institution, it seems, is similarly adapted to fulfill the combined economic, emotional, and sexual needs of adults while simultaneously responding to the fundamental requirements of infants, children, and adolescents for sustenance, nurturance, and guidance. At the same time, a wealth of family forms that, additionally, are rapidly changing in the face of world-wide economic and technological transformations, has evolved within societies. It is the purpose of this book to document and explain family life in all its varieties from a global and dynamic point of view.

For several decades, cross-cultural and developmental psychologists, family researchers, anthropologists, feminist scholars, and other social scientists have been busy observing and cataloging the division of household labor, parent–child relationships, marital and childbearing patterns, beliefs about childrearing and socialization goals and practices, kinship and nonkinship networks among other processes, within and external to the family, in diverse cultural systems worldwide. Each step of the way, these efforts have led to a better understanding of how the family as the basic unit of society marshals its economic, social, cultural, and psychological resources to execute filial, marital, parenting/childrearing, economic, and other roles in an ever-changing global community. Simultaneously, we have witnessed the emergence of more culturally and cross-culturally oriented theoretical frameworks on family functioning that have their origins in diverse academic disciplines (e.g., ethnic studies, evolutionary biology, feminist and postmodern thinking, cultural psychology).

At the dawn of the new millennium, we are at an interesting juncture in the study of "the family." Within academia and the global community at large, there is a need to focus increasingly on the diverse family configurations that exist within preindustrial, industrial, and postindustrial societies, their constantly changing internal dynamics, and the ecological, sociodemographic, and economic factors that are essential shapers of family life. Along these lines, up-to-date knowledge about families across the globe is needed if we are to build a foundation for understanding the human family in all of its many representations, similarities and differences, and cultural prescriptions for successfully carrying out diverse familial functions and roles. Such knowledge seems necessary for students in the social sciences (e.g., anthropology, sociology, family studies, psychology, ethnic studies), family professionals, clinicians in the psychological sciences, and professionals at social service agencies who work or are planning to work with culturally diverse groups and communities worldwide.

This volume provides the reader with a profile of families in different cultural milieus. The authors of the chapters comprise a group of distinguished scholars from many disciplines, who practice their respective crafts in different regions of the globe. They have conducted research on the family within their cultures for sustained periods of time, often contributing groundbreaking new ideas and information about patterns of social organization, parent–child relationships, and childhood socialization and care in the context of diverse cultural belief systems. The information is quite rich, and organized around a set of themes that weave the content of the volume together: sociohistorical and demographic information about families, religious and cultural beliefs tied to family practices, husband–wife/partner roles and responsibilities within the family, parent–child socialization and possible developmental outcomes, and in some cases policy initiatives. As the chapter authors make clear, the family is far from being static in even the most traditional of societies. Furthermore, as social scientists aim to extricate the meaning behind the changes in family configurations and roles, the families themselves must muster the needed cognitive, emotional, and sociocultural know-how and strengths to meet head-on the challenges of a rapidly changing economic and technological world.

The chapters in this book capture some of the changes that are occurring in family organization and socialization patterns in preindustrial, developing, fully industrialized, and postmodern information societies. An introductory chapter provides a succinct overview of the general substance of the book, whereas Chapters 2 and 3 provide a basis for examining family changes and organization patterns from evolutionary and postmodern perspectives. Placing these three chapters at the beginning sets the stage for understanding the structure and functions of families in societies ranging from preindustrial to postindustrial configurations. There is a considerable range of chapters on Asian and Oceanic families residing, respectively, in China, Japan, India, Indonesia, the Marquesas Islands, and the four autonomous island states making up the Federated States of Micronesia. In some of these families, religious edicts, filial piety, and economic/political factors have variously affected current male–female roles and the socialization of children (Chapters 3, 4, 5, 6, 7, and 8). There follows a group of chapters on the changing and often complex cultural belief systems that govern family life in Egyptian and Turkish families, and on the meaning of familism in Israeli families (Chapters 9, 10, and 11). Next, a block of chapters on Greek, Italian, German, Norwegian, and Russian families chronicles the diverse family forms in several European postindustrialized societies as well as those that are witnessing dramatic sociopolitical and ideological transitions (Chapters 12, 13, 14, 15, and 16). Special care has been taken to include chapters on U.S., Caribbean, and Brazilian families, where marital norms and the family context for bearing and raising children are not only quite different from each other but also diverge from those in other parts of the world (Chapters 17, 18, and 19). To round out the book, two chapters on African families (Chapters 20 and 21) deal, respectively, with the complexities of life in a preindustrial culture, the Bofi farmers and Bofi foragers of the Central African Republic, and the diverse ethnic groups that exist in the newly constituted South Africa.

We hope you not only find this book informative in your college coursework, but are able to turn to its content as reference material to guide your own professional understanding of the diverse family configurations and practices that govern the lives of people around the world.

The editors express appreciation to the University Seminars at Columbia University for assistance in the preparation of the manuscript for publication. Material drawn from this work was presented to the University Seminar on Moral Education.

J. L. R.
U. P. G.

FAMILIES IN GLOBAL PERSPECTIVE

PART ONE

INTRODUCTION

CHAPTER 1

FAMILIES IN GLOBAL PERSPECTIVE
AN INTRODUCTION

JAIPAUL L. ROOPNARINE
Syracuse University

UWE P. GIELEN
St. Francis College

With an eye toward universalistic concerns about the human rights and welfare of children and families (see United Nations Development Program, 2001; United Nations General Assembly, 1989), today scientific discourses and investigations of families worldwide have become more focused on the cultural underpinnings of human behavior in general and interpersonal relationships more specifically, the changing ecology of childhood and family relationships, schooling, the reproductive health of young people, transnational or hybrid identities, and other pressing issues that affect the pulse of family life (Arnett, 2002; Comunian & Gielen, 2001; Gielen &

Comunian, 1998, 1999; Shweder et al., 1998; Super & Harkness, 1997). Witness, for example, the research emphasis on convergences and divergences in adolescent experiences and development in different regions of the world (Booth, 2002; Brown, Larson, & Saraswathi, 2002), father–child relationships in diverse ethnic and cultural groups (Lamb, 2004), cultural and cross-cultural views on childrearing and childhood socialization (Chao, 1994; Gielen & Roopnarine, 2004; Shweder et al., 1998; Super & Harkness, 1997), within- and between-region population movements and acculturation and transnational identities (Adler & Gielen, 2003; Tomlinson,

1999), changes in family composition—fertility rates and size, marital rates, age of entry into marriage, separation and divorce rates, life expectancies (Arnett, 2002)—changes in life stage markers (e.g., entrance into adulthood, marriage), cultural practices and traditions including religious prescriptions and family law (Nsamenang, 2002), and conceptual frameworks defining biological and social parenthood (Coley, 2001; Roopnarine, 2004).

Despite these laudable attempts and the fact that modern understanding of different dimensions of family relationships has profited tremendously from scholarly inquiries in such diverse disciplines as anthropology, psychology, child development and family studies, history, sociology, demography, economics, medicine, social work, education, and family therapy, there is still much speculation about families in diverse cultural groups. And seamless explanations of universalistic patterns of behaviors are often grounded in thin databases (e.g., Caribbean, Latin America, the Muslim world in general). The latter has contributed, in part, to misguided or controversial academic treatment of and sometimes harsh criticisms by different policy and political groups about the merit of different family structural arrangements (see Sigle-Rushton & Mclanahan, 2002, for a discussion) and cultural childrearing scripts (e.g., harsh discipline) for healthy childhood outcomes (Baumrind, Larzlere, & Cowan, 2002). As the twentieth century flows into the twenty-first, we remain bewildered by some very basic questions about families and their cultural scripts about specific roles: What constitutes a family in different cultures? How are paternal and maternal roles and responsibilities defined and exhibited in different cultures? How do sociocultural and religious belief systems or ethnotheories influence family organization patterns and the structuring of social and cognitive experiences for children? Do families across societies have common goals and expectations for childhood? Are developmental milestones and periods of transition from one life stage to the next expanding or compressing? How are families and children affected by increasing globalization?

Noting the ubiquity of globalization, factors that impel structural and processural changes in families (e.g., economic activities, migration, delayed marriage and cohabitation, increased schooling and educational attainment of women and children, maintaining traditional values), and the challenges families face in order to maintain key aspects of fairly established cultural traditions and practices as they become increasingly immersed in global consciousness (Arnett, 2002), this volume presents a representative sample of family systems that currently exist and the social-psychological, cultural, religious, economic, and demographic forces that govern their very organizational patterns and varied functions in diverse cultures around the world. An increasingly prominent view is that a better understanding of family social and structural organization patterns, division of household and childrearing functions, and family socialization practices can only be achieved through empirical knowledge guided by multiple conceptual and theoretical frameworks and research methodologies established in wide-ranging disciplines. This volume capitalizes on the multidisciplinary approach—which we believe is at the heart of defining the very nature of families, and cataloging, describing, and interpreting how families carry out their diverse roles in everyday settings. As such, we draw on the work of distinguished anthropologists, evolutionary biologists, psychologists, child development experts, education experts, family sociologists, cultural psychologists, and family therapists who have conducted basic research on families in different parts of the world. This volume includes a treatment of families in preindustrial cultures (e.g., Bofi farmers and foragers in the Central African Republic), families in societies that have experienced extreme transformations either in economic and/or political ideology within the last fifteen years (e.g., Russia, South Africa, China, Brazil, Micronesia), families in developing societies that are seemingly perpetually immersed in economic, political, and social adversities (e.g., Egypt, Indonesia, Caribbean), and families in postindustrial societies (e.g., Japan, Germany, Italy, Norway, the United States). There are several threads that weave the current volume together: a multidisciplinary approach that taps into both qualitative (e.g., participant observation, narrative) and quantitative research information, demographic and sociohistorical accounts of families in the various cultures, basic religious and cultural beliefs, family structural arrangements and the division of household labor, socialization practices and their implications for childhood development, and family policies. Against this backdrop, the goal is to provide a pan-cultural understanding of family relationships without making blanket injunctions about their internal dynamics or functioning.

In organizing this volume, it seemed appropriate to consider up front two major and sometimes contrasting perspectives on the family—evolutionary and post(modern). After all, we need to know how familial roles—husband–wife/partner, childrearing, and so on—evolved over time and whether there are patterns to variations across human societies. Having said that, a somewhat futuristic view of the family might encourage us to confront the complexities embedded in viewing "families" in all of their varied forms in diverse cultural systems, and, as noted already, the challenges and triumphs that families experience in executing their daily roles in an ever-increasing global community. The next two chapters accomplish this goal by providing a general basis for contextualizing the rest of the material presented in the book—from societies in which traditional familial roles are extremely differentiated to those in which the social organization and division of functions appear more egalitarian and where social parenthood and biological parenthood are not isomorphic. More important, Low's chapter on families from an evolutionary anthropological perspective (Chapter 2) points to specific patterns in the diversity of family life across a broad variety of societies, while Silverstein and Auerbach's chapter (Chapter 3) lays bare family forms (e.g., lesbigay families; technological families; visiting unions, common-law) that are only now garnering greater scientific attention. To be sure, Low argues that families across human societies have some common elements—caregivers, offspring, and other individuals who are influenced by the same ecological and evolutionary rules. Yet there is great diversity in mating (e.g., monogamous and polygynous) and marriage systems (socially accepted spousal arrangements).

Before moving on to an examination of some of the major themes of this book, a few other general remarks are necessary. It goes without saying that an integration of data from related disciplines might add greater explanatory power and subsequently depth to the sociocultural meanings of adaptive and maladaptive familial practices and their developmental implications for individual family members (Arnett, 2002; Comunian & Gielen, 2001; Gielen & Comunian, 1998, 1999; Tamis-LeMonda & Cabrera, 2002). Previous excursions into family life across cultures, whether anthropological or sociological (e.g., Nauck & Schoenpflug, 1997), have remained fragmentary. The same can be said for psychological studies of families in different cultural settings, which have often approached cultural diversity in family functioning and belief systems from the point of view of family therapy (e.g., Gielen & Comunian, 1998, 1999; McGoldrick, Giardano, & Pearce, 1996). A number of multicultural works on family life have explored "ethnic" families in the United States (e.g., Mindel, Habenstein, & Wright, 1999; Taylor, 1998), but have not aspired to a more global perspective.

Needless to say, attempts to present disparate sources of knowledge on families in different cultural contexts from different academic disciplines can serve to unify our understanding of domain- and behavior-specific symmetries and asymmetries in family life both within and across cultures.

True to the mission of providing an overview of families around the world through different academic lenses, chapter authors have utilized research information situated in theoretical frameworks and the diverse methodologies of anthropology (e.g., Fouts, Martini, Rebhun, Seltzer), psychology (e.g., Chen; Keller, Zack, & Abels; Georgas, Bafiti, Papademou, & Mylonas), and sociology (e.g., Fogiel-Bijaoui; Miller, Leavitt, Merrill, & Park), but with comparably rich and diverse theoretical perspectives on parenting and childhood socialization practices rooted in perspectives articulated in cultural and cross-cultural psychology (Chao, 1994; Greenfield, 1997; LeVine, in press; Shweder et al., 1998; Super & Harkness, 1997). Their varied nature aside, all told, the overall objectives of these chapters are the same: to describe the structural dynamics and intimate transactions of families in cultural contexts, their developmental trajectories, and the forces that possibly drive them. It is now appropriate to turn to some core concepts explored in this book.

SOCIODEMOGRAPHIC CHANGES IN FAMILIES

By the end of the twentieth century, several societies had undergone key changes in the structural arrangements and organization of families over prior decades (e.g., the rise in single-parent families in postindustrialized societies; declines in marriage rates; an increase in percentage of nuclear families because of drastically reduced fertility rates). Depending on the culture, family size and household composition have been affected by governmental policies (e.g., the one-child policy in China), movement of young people from rural to urban areas in search of better economic conditions, increasing educational and economic opportunities for women, changing gender roles, attitudes toward childbearing and childrearing, challenges to the traditional Confucian notion of filial piety, aging, postponement of marriage, decrease in arranged marriages, increase in divorce rates in developing societies, sustained schooling (e.g., compulsory education), movement toward or away from orthodox religious values (e.g., in Muslim countries), and global consciousness (Arnett, 2002; Booth, 2002; Friedman, 2000). Moreover, families are not static entities; as Keller et al. (this volume) point out, "families are composed, decomposed, and recomposed again with new members," with the traditional family serving as a life-phase transition to other family arrangements. Frequently, transformations in family structure do precipitate changes in familial, institutional, and community practices. These changes and the accompanying functional dynamics that they set in motion are complex and manifest themselves differently over the life span of the family.

Consider, for example, the delayed timing of transitions to particular familial roles (e.g., parenthood, marriage) (Arnett, 2002) and the impact of gender ratios on out-of-marriage births around the world (Barbour, 2000). Almost all of the chapters in this volume provide a sociohistorical basis for understanding contemporary changes in family structures and organizational patterns. It is difficult to imagine that placing families in "traditional" and "(post) modern" categories or in terms of structural arrangements without factoring in emotional closeness or "jointness," will suffice in capturing the "patchwork of family forms" and the metamorphoses (e.g., possible "degendering") occurring within them in the twenty-first century.

Not surprisingly, what emerges from the discussions of families that follow is that in different regions of the world family structures and organizational patterns fall along a continuum: though changing slightly, some remain rigidly planted in "traditional," patriarchal mores and religious edicts with heterosexual marriages as the cornerstone to family life (e.g., Egypt, Turkey), while in most developed societies (e.g., the United States, Israel, Italy, Japan, Germany, Norway) there is an admixture of family forms (e.g., single-parent, cohabiting, reconstituted, nonresidential-father households, extended households, lesbigay, etc.—see also Gore & Gore [2002]), with high or at least increasing divorce rates the norm and high out-of-wedlock births (50 percent of all births to unmarried women in Oslo, Norway, in 2001; 33 percent in the United States in 1999; 27 percent in Russia in 1999). These developed societies have given rise to the "traditional modern nuclear family"—suggesting that heterosexual couples struggle to redefine familial roles in the context of "the new fatherhood," "the dual-earner or co-breadwinner family," and the "mommy track" (nuclear families range from 33 percent in Germany to 43 percent in Belgium and France). Simultaneously, these families are faced with the legal, social, and moral legitimacy of "nontraditional" family arrangements that have become more acceptable over time. (To counteract these developments, the United States has recently proposed a promotion of heterosexual marriage policy).

Broadly speaking, in most societies considered, there appears to be some form of family "extendedness." Families may engage in functional extendedness, living nearby and offering mutual support and aid to cognates (Tulananda & Roopnarine, 2001). In some developed societies, such as Greece, extended families flourish, and they constitute significant numbers in others (e.g., in Japan and Italy). In Turkey, extendedness may mark a "transitional phase" after the son's marriage, and in Indonesia, it is given more importance than the nuclear family or individual members. Multigenerational units are also common in a number of developing countries (e.g., China, India), Polynesian Island cultures (e.g., Marquesas), preindustrial societies, and in those in which there is quite a bit of mate-shifting (Caribbean), where men and women have children from several "baby mothers" and "baby fathers" and "shift" children to be raised by collateral kin (e.g., neighbors in the yard or compound) or affinal relatives. As will be deduced, the role of extended members may include such diverse and highly significant functions as "childminders/caregivers," doting grandparents (e.g., China), and providing economic assistance and shelter for children whose parents migrate to the developed world to seek better economic opportunities and permanent residency (e.g., Caribbean parents).

The existence of multiple family forms calls into question notions of monogamy, two-parent heterosexual unions, and marriage as primordial to family formation. Regardless of family arrangements, the ability to execute different familial roles in these diverse cultural systems amidst political, social, and economic transitions globally will determine the stability of societies and their ability to raise children who are more likely than not to develop multiple cultural identities (Arnett, 2002). There is a good bet that attaining these objectives will in large measure rest on the quality of parenting skills and human capital, adequate support for childrearing, and other family processes and sociodemographic variables rather than family structure or composition per se.

Nevertheless, sociodemographic changes affecting family life have occurred on a worldwide basis during recent decades. Average life expectan-cies for both women and men have increased steadily in all societies not affected by war, revolutionary political changes, and/or high rates of HIV infection. This phenomenon has contributed to a steady "aging process," especially in the industrialized countries (e.g., Germany, Italy, Norway, Japan). Furthermore, women's fertility rates have been declining on a worldwide basis and to such an extent that in almost all industrialized countries they have now reached a level far below the "population replacement level." All of these demographic changes have drastic implications for the structure and functioning of families: Families begin to shrivel in size, extended families become the exception, mothers leave home in order to work, young people defer marriage or do not get married at all, and middle-aged adults (especially women) are asked to take care of their vulnerable aging parents. These and many other phenomena are intertwined with additional changes brought about by industrialization, the information revolution, the ensuing rise in education levels, increased consumerism, a more individualistic outlook on life, redefined gender roles, and the simple fact that having children is now becoming a very expensive proposition for prospective parents. Increasingly, children lose their utilitarian value to the family, a value that had been obvious to everybody in former centuries. Furthermore, many of these demographic and cultural changes are now becoming increasingly visible among the middle classes in the more successful developing countries such as Turkey, Mexico, and even India.

HUSBAND–WIFE ROLES AND HOUSEHOLD AND CHILDCARE WORK

Perhaps one domain in which families appear more resistant to change is in their assumption of household and childcare roles. It is fair to say that, whether it is in the postindustrialized, developing, or preindustrial societies, in heterosexual marital and nonmarital unions, women bear the brunt of childcare and household labor—engaging in the "second shift" if you will (Hochschild, 1989), and their participation in these activities is not appreciably different in single- or dual-earner families (see Wilkie, Ferree, & Ratclif, 1998, for an exception in the United States). Likewise, in a majority of societies considered in this volume, beliefs about familial roles are still largely aligned and anchored in patriarchal values, to the point where roles have been characterized as "duofocal" in Turkey or are defined by paradoxical cultural codes such as *familism,* where men still have the upper hand in the family (e.g., Israel). One may reasonably ask then: How convincing are the claims about the "new and emerging fatherhood" (Lamb, 2004; Tamis-LeMonda & Cabrera, 2002), and shifts toward more egalitarian roles between husbands and wives or mating partners? And what about the tenets of modernization theory proposing that with increasing industrialization and economic prosperity, people should reject and shed traditional values and move in lockstep toward modern values and individualism? What roles do religion and cultural beliefs play in the maintenance of so-called traditional values?

Though not consistent across societies, there is some indication that authoritarian family values are on the decline or that families are torn between traditional (e.g., *ie* in Japan; *familism* in Israel tied to Rabbinical Court Law-1953 and Druze Religious Courts Law-1962) and modern democratic structures. While customary marriage remains a major prerequisite to family formation and procreation and men are depicted as the head of the family in most societies, there is an increase in premarital sex and early entry into sexual activities, a decrease in arranged marriages and emphasis on bridewealth (*ilobolo; dowry, mehr or mihir*) and movement toward romantic or love marriages (e.g., Turkey, Japan), a partial replacement of polygamy by concubinage in a few societies (e.g., South Africa), a rise in the number of women in the labor force throughout the world which has led to greater expectations of more role sharing by men/fathers, the implementation of maternity and paternity leave policies, and a decline in paternal authority due to father absence and the questioning of traditional parental authority by children. All of this is compounded by the fact that "modern" parents are less desirous of hierarchical relationships between spouses/partners and with children. However, the latter may not be so for multiethnic, stratified societies (e.g., Israel), where a symbiosis is thought to exist between religion and "state" (Fogiel-Bijaoui, this volume), for rural, agricultural families with less educational attainment, and for families who are wed to religious and other ideological beliefs (e.g., Egyptians, Indians) that strongly endorse the superiority of men through religious edicts and religious laws (e.g., religious courts in Indonesia). Even here there is a lack of uniformity. The Minangkabau, a Muslim group in West Sumatra, do not subscribe to a patriarchal system—undoubtedly a rare exception. The point is that there is a feeling that overall familial practices are becoming less rigidly organized along conservative gender-differentiated lines and in developing societies as women utilize diverse strategies to establish psychological power and to ease the grip of male control on them, while in some (e.g., Japan and perhaps in other Confucian-origin cultures), mothers lavish more attention on children when they perceive emotional distance from their husbands—resulting in what some psychologists term "emotional matriarchy" (Naito & Gielen, this volume). Arguably, the economic, educational, and sociopolitical gains made by women around the world have had some impact on the assumption of household work by men. However, as can be gleaned from the different chapters, men in most cultural settings have changed minimally in this regard and tend to hold on to "traditional internal working models" about gender roles. So far, men's participation in childcare in countries that have liberal paternal leave policies (e.g., many European societies, Japan) has been somewhat disappointing, and in developing societies, migration to find employment (Egyptians to oil fields in the Middle East, Caribbean men as fruit pickers in the United States, rural fathers to the cities and towns of India [Gielen, 1993]) means that husbands are away from family members for extended periods of time. This phenomenon ("wage-father") is likely to multiply in the global workplace and in all likelihood will further alienate men from their families, place more childcare and household responsibilities on women's shoulders, and encourage grandparents to take care of their grandchildren.

PARENT–CHILD RELATIONSHIPS— SOCIALIZATION BELIEFS, GOALS, AND PRACTICES

It has been proposed that families may have similar expectations for children across the world: to develop the instrumental competencies and skills necessary to successfully navigate and meet the requirements of life within a given culture and to ensure the reproductive success of offspring. There are general agreements that, across societies, in some behavioral and cognitive domains parents share common goals when it comes to the socialization of children (e.g., health and survival of offspring, language competence, reproductive success of offspring, etc.). But research evidence also indicates that parents have different belief systems about what is important for raising competent children (Super & Harkness, 1997; Sigel & MiGillicuddy-De Lisi, 2002), varied expectations about how children should behave, the psychological and institutional value of children to the family at different stages of development, diverse family rituals and initiations (e.g., bar mitzvah in Israel; co-sleeping in India; Zulu ritual of seclusion among boys; Pedi and Tsonga seclusion of girls). And they voluntarily or involuntarily prioritize socialization goals (e.g., nutritional, safety versus early childhood education and stimulation; social versus technological skills) in concert with the demands of the physical environment, and the efficient employment of time-tested cultural scripts that parents and other adult members have come to embrace in the process of childrearing (LeVine, 1974, in press; Shweder et al., 1998; Martini, this volume).

This book builds on the decades of cultural and cross-cultural research on childhood socialization conducted by others (see Shweder et al., 1998; Berry, Dasen, & Saraswathi, 1997; Super & Harkness, 1997; Whiting & Whiting, 1963, to name a few), by returning to some rudimentary questions about how childrearing and child training goals, beliefs, and practices are instituted and carried out, and about potential changes that are occurring in family socialization as cultural groups increasingly come face to face with one another—a practice that at once brings our similarities to the surface but magnifies differences as well. An important difference between the current volume and those that have appeared before is that we have included a number of cultures that have been relatively ignored in the family literature (e.g., Brazil, Caribbean, Egypt, Indonesia, South Africa). From what has been said so far, these chapters should assist in charting, within the wide parameters of childrearing, the areas in which cultures around the world share common socialization beliefs, goals, and practices and those in which they diverge.

We hope you keep in mind the remarkable transformations that are taking place in family life across the globe (e.g., delocalization, marginalization, migratory patterns, economic modes of production, challenges to paternal power and cultural traditions, etc.) (Adler & Gielen, 2003; Arnett, 2002; Gielen & Roopnarine, in press; Tomlinson, 1999) that are bound to affect the very notion of how we view core concepts of childrearing in diverse societies. In this vein, it would be prudent to accept the possibility that childhood socialization goals, practices, and beliefs may not be identical in single-parent, extended and multigenerational households, biological two-parent households, co-habitant or same-sex family arrangements within, much less across societies. On the other hand, there are societies that appear as more "individualistic" (e.g., West European societies, the United States) than "collectivistic" (e.g., China, Japan) in their orientation (see Greenfield & Cocking, 1994), in valuing indulgence—especially those with prolonged infancy periods (e.g., India), in emphasizing obedience training and other conservative childrearing strategies such as strict discipline (see Value of Children [VOC] study; Kagitçibasi, 1996), in sharing similarities with others in the expectation that children will care for their aging parents (e.g., Japan, Caribbean, Turkey), in engagement in sibling care, and in their emphasis on interpersonal relationships within the family.

Before presenting a brief synopsis of similarities and differences in socialization patterns across cultures, it behooves us to indicate that in a number of societies that continue to experience ongoing shifts toward political and social freedoms (e.g., Russia, South Africa) and in those that face constant economic woes (e.g., Caribbean, Indonesia, Brazil), emphasis appears to be on ad-hoc childrearing strategies that are geared toward assisting children to develop coping mechanisms to deal with life amidst unpredictable social and economic conditions (e.g., street children in Brazil, Indonesia). Among Russians, Germans who lived in the former East Germany, and non-White South Africans, there is a dramatic shift away from "state" regulation of family life. In Israel, a multiethnic society, "religious law serves as a 'national asset'," but collides with the individualism inherent in capitalist development (Fogiel-Bijaoui, this volume). The uncertainty about the stability of family practices, however, may not be limited to these societies. From her clinical work, Seltzer opined that troubling social-psychological problems exist among young children in Norway due to multiple transient parental relationships and ambiguity surrounding the family nomenclature (Whom do I belong to? Who are my family members?)—problems that are seen in other European and some developing societies (e.g., Caribbean). In Japan, gaps have been identified between the lifestyles of parents and children (Naito & Gielen, this volume), and in South Africa, the Caribbean, and Egypt, there are concerns about the impact of prolonged father absence on childhood development. At the same time, in some parts of the world children experience and live with daily threats of violence (e.g., Israel).

Accepting the premise that parenting and parent–child relationships are constantly evolving as adults confront the task of raising children in a (post)modern world, we undertake the risky business of identifying similarities in socialization processes across cultures that are strongly demarcated along the lines of ideological and religious beliefs. It has already been mentioned that families have common goals with respect to the survival and well-being of their offspring. Beyond surface similarities, finding an adequate method of analyzing commonalities in the range of socialization practices across cultures is much more difficult. A primary concern is with assumptions of cultural equivalence in origin(s) and meanings of behaviors and practices. This notwithstanding, like other family processes outlined above, childrearing tendencies range from more autocratic methods of control and power assertion to relaxed reciprocity across cultures and families. Noteworthy is the appearance that Western industrialized societies lean toward the overarching belief in autonomy or independence training early in the child's life, instituting more "child-centered" approaches to childrearing that are embedded in "individualism." These societies have increasing numbers of immigrants (e.g., Germany, Italy) from other parts of the world, and in some (e.g., Israel, the United States) that have diverse populations, it has been demonstrated that parenting styles are hardly uniform and expectations of children may resemble those that have been observed in the natal cultures (see Roopnarine et al., this volume). For instance, English-speaking Caribbean immigrants in the United States maintain their beliefs in harsher forms of discipline, and Chinese immigrant parents in the Los Angeles area exercise more control in governing (*guan*) their children's lives than European Americans (Chao, 1994). Diversity in parenting styles and practices is perhaps also present in European countries that have accepted migratory workers and increasing numbers of immigrants from different parts of the world.

However, cultural common ground in parenting is evident in obedience training, loyalty, and unilateral respect for adults in quite a few societies (e.g., Indonesia, Caribbean, Turkey, India, China), and sibling care is not atypical in a few of them. It is tempting to say that these societies are more authoritarian in their childrearing techniques. This would constitute an egregious error, however. In cultures that are more "collectivistic" in their orientation, variability has been documented in the changing ecology of parenting (e.g., China, India, Japan). Thus, not unlike European and North American countries, parenting and parent–child relationships represent diverse strategies and practices in "collectivistic" societies—

which are becoming more child-centered than parent-centered as couples/partners reassess notions of love, companionship, marital norms, the value of children, and the meaning of childhood, and as children question and resist more autocratic methods of parental control. Nevertheless, some societies are steadfastly wed to archaic beliefs about the "child's place" in the family and society.

To summarize, childrearing/child training in different societies reflects diverse practices, goals, and expectations that are in the process of changing even in those societies that have clung to more authoritarian family organization patterns. Simply grouping societies as having a "collectivistic" or "individualistic" orientation would not do justice to describing the multiple childrearing practices that are in place in a given culture. Quite possibly, notions of dependence and independence training as well as other childrearing mechanisms are becoming blurred as families in different corners of the world are bombarded with images of parenting and childhood in other cultures. This does not mean that deep cultural differences do not exist in childrearing. To the contrary! As you will encounter, not only do societies place different emphases on what is important to family relationships, they have different developmental expectations and profiles of children and utilize different behavioral strategies in attaining the skills and competencies they believe are important for survival in their culture and to varying degrees in the world community.

FAMILY AND POLICY ISSUES

Whether it is the adoption of the United Nations Bill of Rights for Children or the religious courts of Indonesia, societies around the world have implemented policies that affect the lives of families and children. Some have recently attended to domestic violence and family violence issues (e.g., Caribbean), abolition of physical punishment (e.g., Sweden), the rights of Lesbigay families in the military (e.g., "Don't Ask, Don't Tell" policy in the United States), the one-child policy in China, human dignity (South

Africa), prevention of child abuse and the protection of vulnerable people in the family (e.g., Israel), and paternal leave policies, to name a few. The general goal of these policies is to bring order to and/or regulate family life, offer protection to basic human rights, and help to maintain dignity in the lives of families and children so that they can grow and live in productive and rewarding ways. In asking each chapter author to include a piece on family policy where appropriate, we intended to inform you, the reader, about the legal and political attempts being made around the world to address the needs of families and children who live under diverse social, political, religious, legal, and economic circumstances.

GENERAL SUMMARY

This book covers a diverse array of information on families in different cultural systems around the world. Recording caregiving patterns and strategies for socializing boys and girls, parent–child arrangements, allocation of resources, division of labor, and other aspects of family life embedded in different mating and marriage systems across societies should increase our acceptance, interpretation, and understanding of broad definitions of family life today. The call to unravel the cultural underpinnings of human behavior has taken on greater meaning in a globally conscious world that, at the moment, is attempting to come to grips with differences in family beliefs and practices, religious and linguistic differences, enormous economic disparities between and within nations, and social and political oppression. At this point, it is probably impossible to know the true extent of the impact of speeded-up globalization on family relationships in different societies. Clearly, technological advances in communication augmented by increased interpersonal contact, and questions posed at the individual, family, and societal levels about longstanding family structures/ roles, traditions, religious edicts, and family laws will continue to influence changes in family functioning and childhood socialization in covert and overt ways worldwide.

REFERENCES

Adler, L., & Gielen, U. (Eds.). (2003). *Immigration, emigration, and migration in international perspective.* Westport, CT: Greenwood.

Arnett, J. J. (2002). The psychology of globalization. *American Psychologist, 57,* 774–783.

Barbour, N. (2000). On the relationship between country sex ratios and teen pregnancy rates: A replication. *Cross-Cultural Research, 34,* 26–37.

Baumrind, D., Larzlere, R. D., & Cowan, P. A. (2002). Ordinary physical punishment: Is it harmful? *Psychological Bulletin, 128,* 580–589.

Berry, J., Dasen, P., & Saraswathi, T. S. (Eds.). (1997). *Handbook of cross-cultural psychology. Vol. 2: Basic processes and human development.* Boston: Allyn & Bacon.

Booth, M. (2002). Arab adolescents facing the future: Enduring ideals and pressures for change. In. B. B. Brown, R. Larson, & T. S. Sarsawathi (Eds.), *The world's youth: Adolescence in eight regions of the globe* (pp. 207–242). New York: Cambridge University Press.

Brown, B. B., Larson, R. & Sarsawathi, T. S. (Eds.). (2002). *The world's youth: Adolescence in eight regions of the globe.* New York: Cambridge University Press.

Chao, R. (1994). Beyond parental control and authoritarian parenting style: Understanding Chinese parenting through the cultural notion of training. *Child Development, 72,* 1832–1843.

Coley, R. (2001). (In)visible men: Emerging research on low-income unmarried, and minority fathers. *American Psychologist, 56,* 1–11.

Comunian, A., & Gielen, U. (Eds.). (2001). *International perspectives on human development.* Lengerich, Germany: Pabst.

Friedman, T. L. (2000). *The Lexus and the olive tree: Understanding globalization.* New York: Anchor.

Gielen, U. P. (1993). Gender roles in traditional Tibetan cultures. In L. L. Adler (Ed.), *International handbook on gender roles* (pp. 413–437). Westport, CT: Greenwood.

Gielen, U. P., & Comunian, A. L. (Eds.). (1998). *The family and family therapy in international perspective.* Trieste, Italy: Lint.

Gielen, U. P., & Comunian, A. L. (Eds.). (1999). *International approaches to the family and family therapy.* Padua, Italy: UNIPRESS.

Gielen, U. P., & Roopnarine, J. L. (Eds.). (in press). *Childhood and adolescence in cross-cultural perspectives and applications.* Westport, CT: Praeger.

Gore, A., & Gore, T. (2002). *Joined at the heart: The transformation of the American family.* New York: Henry Holt.

Greenfield, P. (1997). Culture as process: Empirical methods for cultural psychology. In J. Berry, P. Dasen, & T. S. Saraswathi (Eds.), *Handbook of cross-cultural psychology. Vol. 1: Theory and method* (pp. 301–346). Boston: Allyn & Bacon.

Greenfield, P. M., & Cocking, R. R. (Eds.). (1994). *Cross-cultural roots of minority child development.* Hillsdale, NJ: Erlbaum.

Hochschild, A. (1989). *The second shift.* New York: Viking.

Kagitçibasi, Ç. (1996). *Family and human development across cultures: A view from the other side.* Mahwah, NJ: Erlbaum.

Lamb, M. E. (Ed.). (2004). *The role of the father in child development* (4th ed.). New York: Wiley.

LeVine, R. (1974). Parental goals: A cross-cultural view. *Teachers College Record, 76,* 226–239.

LeVine, R. (in press). Challenging expert knowledge: Findings from an African study of infant care and development. In U. P. Gielen, & J. L. Roopnarine (Eds.), *Childhood and adolescence in cross-cultural perspective.* Westport, CT: Greenwood Press.

McGoldrick, M., Giardano, J., & Pearce, J. K. (Eds.). (1996). *Ethnicity and family therapy* (2nd ed.). New York: Guilford.

Mindel, C. H., Habenstein, R. W., & Wright, R., Jr. (Eds.). (1999). *Ethnic families in America: Patterns and variations* (4th ed.). Upper Saddle River, NJ: Prentice Hall.

Nauck, B., & Schoenpflug, U. (Eds.). (1997). *Familien in verschiedenen Kulturen* [Families in different cultures]. Stuttgart, Germany: Ferdinand Enke Verlag.

Nsamenang, B. (2002). Adolescence in Sub-Saharan Africa: An image constructed from Africa's triple inheritance. In B. B. Brown, R. Larson, & T. S. Sarsawathi (Eds.), *The world's youth: Adolescence in eight regions of the globe* (pp. 61–104). New York: Cambridge University Press.

Roopnarine, J. L. (2004). African American and African Caribbean fathers: Levels, quality, and meaning of involvement. In M. E. Lamb (Ed.), *The role of the fa-*

ther in child development (4th ed., pp. 58–97). New York: Wiley.

Shweder, R., Goodnow, J., Hatano, G., LeVine, R., Markus, H., & Miller, P. (1998). The cultural psychology of development: One mind, many mentalities. In R. Lerner (Vol. Ed.), *Theoretical models of human development. Vol. 1: Handbook of child psychology* (pp. 865–937). New York: Wiley.

Sigel, I., & McGillicuddy-De Lisi, A. (2002). Parental beliefs as cognitions: The dynamic belief systems mode. In M. Bornstein (Ed.), *Handbook of parenting* (Vol. 3, 2nd ed.). Mahwah, NJ: Erlbaum.

Sigle-Rushton, W., & McLanahan, S. (2002). *Father absence and child well-being: A critical review.* Paper presented in the Maxwell School, Syracuse University, Syracuse, NY, October 25.

Super, C., & Harkness, S. (1997). The cultural structuring of child development. In J. Berry, P. Dasen, & T. S. Saraswathi (Eds.), *Handbook of cross-cultural psychology. Vol. 2: Basic processes and human development* (pp. 1–39). Boston: Allyn & Bacon.

Tamis-LeMonda, C., & Cabrera, N. (Eds.). (2002). *Handbook on father involvement: Multidisciplinary perspectives.* Mahwah, NJ: Erlbaum.

Taylor, R. L. (Ed.). (1998). *Minority families in the United States: A multicultural perspective* (2nd ed.). Upper Saddle River, NJ: Prentice Hall.

Tomlinson, J. B. (1999). *Globalization and culture.* Chicago: University of Chicago Press.

Tulananda, O., & Roopnarine, J. L. (2001). Mothers' and fathers' interactions with preschoolers in the home in Northern Thailand: Relationships to teachers' assessments of children's social skills. *Journal of Family Psychology, 14,* 676–687.

Whiting, B., & Whiting, J. W. M. (1975). *Children of six cultures: A psycho-cultural analysis.* Cambridge, MA: Harvard University Press.

Wilke, J. R., & Ferree, M. M., & Ratcliff, K. S. (1998). Gender and fairness: Marital satisfaction in two-earner couples. *Journal of Marriage and the Family, 60,* 577–594.

United Nations Development Programme. (2001). *Human development report.* New York: Oxford University Press.

United Nations General Assembly (1989, November). Adoption of a convention on the rights of the child (U.N. Doc. A/Res.44/25). New York: United Nations.

CHAPTER 2

FAMILIES
AN EVOLUTIONARY
ANTHROPOLOGICAL PERSPECTIVE

BOBBI S. LOW
University of Michigan

A recent *New Yorker* cartoon shows a mailbox; on the mailbox it says: "Kim, Bill, Ned, Mary, Fred, Miki, Nels, Phaedra, Lenore, Spike, and Linda . . . a non-traditional family." Ask the next ten people you meet for a definition of "family." I just did this, and the results of this (highly unscientific) survey were that seven of ten gave some version of "mommy, daddy, and baby" (in anthropological terms, neolocal monogamy), two gave somewhat inclusive definitions of the "consenting domestic partners" sort (household-based), and one said "whatever one

wishes." Perhaps I need a bigger sample, but even this tiny sample reflects the diversity inherent in any concept of "family."

What constitutes a family? There is no singular answer, although differences in our individual concepts of "family" can lead to intense debate, and even (as recently in Utah) legal proceedings (e.g., Altman & Ginat, 1996). The 1950s in the United States provided one sort of answer: Beaver Cleaver (and Dennis the Menace). This rather restricted sense of "family" may well have led to family policy decisions in the United States that linger today (Luker, 1996; Coontz, 1992). At the other extreme, think of Gene Hackman, playing a conservative U.S. senator in drag, in the movie *The Bird Cage,* leading a motley assortment of drag queens out of an alternative nightclub, singing "We Are Family." Both these showed up in my unscientific survey. Variation in the definition of "family" is not a new thing. Look in the *Oxford English Dictionary,* and you'll find these definitions, among others: one's household servants, the retinue of a nobleman or grandee, the staff of a military officer, the members of a household.

There is some coherence. Two recurring themes are genetic relatedness (in surprisingly few formal definitions), and co-residence in a household. From a biological and ecological point of view, relatedness is absolutely central for making and testing predictions about familial behavior (Hamilton, 1964). On the other hand, demographers and historians tend to focus on households, often not even asking about relatedness (Flandrin, 1979; Wrigley & Schofield, 1981). Few of the dictionary definitions actually are restricted to the genetic relatives of a nuclear family; this highlights, I think, our human emphasis on social and cultural meanings for "family." Other chapters in this volume will demonstrate convincingly the diversity of families around the world; here I hope to lay the groundwork for that diversity, suggesting that, while it is clearly cultural and social, it is grounded in ecological and evolutionary conditions.

ECOLOGICAL INFLUENCES ON FAMILY LIFE IN OTHER SPECIES

Despite all diversity, there is pattern in the variations of family life one finds, both across human societies and even among nonhuman species. For a biologist, despite great diversity in particulars across species, "family" always has elements of (1) a dependent offspring, plus (2) one (usually the mother) or more adult caretakers. Whether there are one or more caretakers, whether mother, mother and father, and/or others, depends in part on the species and in part on ecological factors. The diversity is not random, but patterned. Perhaps most interesting and important,

the same ecological and evolutionary rules apply to human and nonhuman families, despite all the diversity (e.g., Emlen, 1997). In fact, the rules help create the diversity we see.

Consider briefly the diversity that exists among other species. One ecological constraint is paramount: whenever females can raise offspring successfully alone, the likely outcome is polygyny, and "family" will mean simply a female and her dependent offspring. Females will be able to raise offspring alone when the offspring are precocial (as in chickens and many other bird species), or when she can provide for an altricial (helpless) child by herself, as in many primates (in which the mother nurses, carries, and protects the infant, and the father is often nearby and may occasionally play with the infant, but is mostly concerned with his own status and rank among males). When these conditions are met, the result is female specialization in parental effort and male specialization in mating effort. Thus, across most species, a mother and her offspring comprise family.

Family structure is influenced by other ecological forces: ecological conditions set the stage for the particulars of solitary-versus-group living, the kind of group (relatives or not), and the mating system. About half of primate species live in multifemale groups.[1] Females tend to distribute themselves in response to predation and food pressures, and males, in turn, tend to distribute themselves around female distributions. So, even among primates in which females and their young can be an independent ecological/economic unit, there is still much variation (e.g, see Low, 2000a, chap. 4, for an overview). Whether one, or several, males join the females depends, again, on ecological conditions. When predation pressure is high and food is rich, the likeliest result is multimale, multifemale groups, as in savannah baboons. Several males can defend against predators better than a single male can. Whenever males can get away with it, single-male harems (with lower costs to the resident male in protecting his status) are common.

Monogamous, single-pair primates are rare; they tend to live in heavy cover. There are three hypotheses about the evolution of monogamy in primates (Reichard, 2003). One simply argues that when two-parent care is markedly more effective than maternal care alone, monogamy will evolve (Wright, 1984; Kurland & Gaulin, 1984). The second suggests that monogamy arises when mated males are able to protect their infants from infanticide by other males in the group (van Schaik & Dunbar, 1990; van Schaik, 1996). The third suggests that for primates, as for many other species, ecological factors influence a male's ability to monopolize more than one female (Mitani, 1984). There are few tests, but I suspect the last is the strongest hypothesis.

Perhaps the most unusual primate family forms occur among some tamarins. In these species, females give birth to twins, who grow rapidly. One female can't carry both offspring soon after birth. But tamarins are polyandrous: females mate with two males, and both males help care for the offspring, carrying, playing, and protecting. So in these tamarins, two males, a female, and her offspring comprise a family.

Ecological forces shape the form of family in primates; in turn, family form shapes other aspects of life—things we would not imagine to be connected to family forms. Pair-living monogamous, single-male polygynous, and multimale polygynous species differ in extraordinary ways. Males in single-male group-living species face high-risk, high-gain challenges from other males to fight for control of the females; they are physically much larger than females and have very large canines, as in gorillas. Males in multimale group-living species have a subtler problem as well: other males are always about, and sometimes in shifting coalitions. Sneak matings by other males in the group are, like overt fights, a serious problem. Males in such species are bigger than females (though not so strikingly as the single-male species), have large canines, but also have extremely large testes. Here competition between males exists not only between individuals, but carries down to the level of sperm competition. Males in pair-living species are not much larger than females and have relatively the smallest canines, the smallest testes. The ecology of group living influences male–male competition—and thus body size, canine size, and testes size.[2]

Among other species, when are males most likely to be devoted fathers? The ecological conditions that favor great male expenditure of offspring-specific effort include: (1) relatively safe adult life (low mortality) combined with conditions that (2) allow adults to extend that safety to their offspring (e.g., species such as geese), and (3) greatly enhanced offspring success under care by more than one parent. Under these conditions, we tend to see monogamous and polyandrous family systems, and behavioral (even physical) convergence between the sexes.[3] The less the two sexes specialize and the more they do the same things, the more alike they will be. So gorilla males and females are vastly different in size; tamarins and humans are not. Sex differences vary among environments, among mating systems, and even among cultures as a result of more subtle cultural influences.

DEFINING MATING, MARRIAGE, AND INHERITANCE

We humans are extraordinary in ways most of us never consider. For example, family forms, as we have just seen, are related to mating systems; these tend to be relatively defined for any particular species. But across human societies, we can find: mother-and-child families; monogamous families that live with the husband's parents, the wife's parents, other relatives, or in a new location (neolocal); polygynous families in which men marry sisters, marry nonsisters, capture women from other groups, in which co-wives live in the same household, or live apart; and polyandrous families in which brothers marry one woman. This degree of within-species diversity is unknown in any other species.

This within-species diversity is, again, nonrandom, but it is complex, and some definitions are necessary. *Mating systems* are not the same as *marriage systems,* and the differences in their meanings highlight selective issues of family life. Biologists and evolutionary anthropologists use the terms *monogamous* and *polygynous* to focus on the ways sexual selection shapes mating systems: what is the relative variance in reproductive success between the two sexes? When male variance is higher than female variance (a common condition), a few males will have many offspring, and many males will fail to reproduce at all. Polygynous systems result. Monogamy is rare among mammals; it is accompanied by extensive male parental care. Such male care is associated with circumstances in which the care of two (or more) adults significantly enhances offspring success.

Human *marriage systems,* in contrast, concern socially acceptable familial arrangements. *Monogamy* means, to cultural anthropologists, for example, social rules that prohibit more than one spouse at any time; or social rules that may permit more spouses, combined with ecological conditions that make it difficult to have multiple spouses. So the !Kung, for example, are classified among anthropologists as monogamous, with the description that only about 5 percent of men have more than one wife! Biologically, the !Kung have mild polygyny.

Societies such as Western industrial nations today that impose a one-spouse-at-a-time rule would be called "monogamous" or "serially monogamous" if one were interested in social rules. Most such societies, however, have, as a result of sex differences in remarriage (more men remarry than women) and fertility in second and subsequent marriages (men have children in these unions more than women), much greater variance in male than female reproductive success. A behavioral ecologist would call them functionally polygynous.[4]

The differences arise from a focus on different aspects of family life. Biological definitions of monogamy and polygyny predict much about parental care patterns, and the intensity of sexual selection. In contrast, marriage system definitions are about social rights. In most socially monogamous societies, wealthy and powerful men have always had more sexual access (and until very recently, higher fertility as a result) than other men. In polygynous societies, these forces interact. There can be great variance in men's reproductive success; whenever men can acquire resources, these are used to enhance reproduction. Women in polygynous societies typically control fewer resources, and resources have

less impact on women's reproduction. The result? Inheritance across polygynous cultures tends to be male-biased (Hartung, 1982, 1983, 1997; Dickemann, 1981, 1997).

Inheritance patterns across cultures are thus affected by family forms (Altonji, Hayashi, & Kotlikoff, 1997). In addition to the examples above, consider the concept of bastardy; we seldom think about it in the context of family structure—but we should; the concept of bastardy is really about inheritance rights (Betzig, 1997). Even in socially monogamous systems, inheritance patterns are related to the ecology of male and female reproduction, and the drive to consolidate resources in one's family. Men tend to leave bequests to their spouses, but women to their children (Judge & Hrdy, 1992; Judge, 1995). Why? Men remarry more often than women, and women have less certainty of their bequests through their husbands actually reaching their children; men have far fewer such worries, and their widows have more difficulty providing for the children (Dupâquier et al., 1981; Low, 1993, 2000a, b; Low, Clarke, & Lockridge, 1992).

The different options open to men and women in marriage also make a difference in how boys and girls are trained across cultures. The more polygynous the society (the higher the reproductive payoffs, and the greater the risk of failure), the more boys are taught to strive, but this is true only in nonstratified societies in which striving can make a reproductive difference (Barry, Bacon, & Child, 1957; Barry et al., 1976; Low, 1989). And, related to the differences in anthropological versus biological definitions of polygyny, some (anthropologically) monogamous societies have very intense training to strive; these are typically the societies that are (biologically) polygynous.

ECOLOGY OF MARRIAGE AND FAMILY SYSTEMS

There are some surprising ecological correlates to family patterns of polygyny, monogamy, and polyandry. Monogamy is associated with relatively poor resource bases: whenever children require so much care that men actually profit from foregoing additional matings (as in polygyny) in favor of child care, it is true that these conditions, and monogamy, are relatively rare. Polyandrous societies are very rare, and associated either with poor resource bases (the Lepcha of northern India: Gorer, 1967), or the desire of wealthy families in otherwise poor-resource-base societies to concentrate their resources among very few grandchildren (Tibetan polyandry: Peter, 1963). In all known cases, a woman marries brothers, rather than any men she chooses.

The degree of polygyny (usually measured as the percent of men and women married polygynously) has ecological correlates similar to those of polygyny in nonhuman species. Patterns of parasite risk, rainfall seasonality, irrigation, and hunting explain 46 percent of the observed patterns in human polygyny. The most powerful ecological correlate of the degree of polygyny found so far is perhaps a surprising one: pathogen stress—a major source of environmental unpredictability (Low, 1988a, b, 1990a, b, 2000a). Why should this be so? There are good, though perhaps not obvious, ecological reasons. Environmental unpredictability may make it difficult to "track" best phenotypes for an environment; in this case, the most successful parent will be one who produces offspring with genotypes likely, in turn, to produce new genetic combinations.[5] Across polygynous societies, men tend to marry sisters (sororal polygyny); sisters argue less, divorce is less frequent, and co-residential households are common. But when pathogen stress is high, men tend to marry nonsisters, and are quite likely to capture women from neighboring groups. All of these patterns mean that men are making mate choices that create genetically variable offspring in the face of pathogen stress, compared to the norm. In high-pathogen areas, women, too, face altered costs and benefits: is it better to be a second (or later) wife of a healthy, nonparasitized man, or the only wife of a parasitized man?

In some ways, marriages in traditional societies were less variable than those in modern societies. Most families were patrilocal, living with the husband's kin; most marriages in many societies were

of first cousins. This is perhaps surprising to those of us in Western societies, in which close relatives are typically forbidden to marry; however, this pattern also has ecological correlates with resources. Four kinds of first-cousin marriages are possible. A man could marry (1) his father's brother's daughter (FBD), (2) his mother's brother's daughter (MBD), (3) his father's sister's daughter (FZD), or (4) his mother's sister's daughter (MZD). Anthropologists also distinguish "parallel" (FBD, MZD) and "cross" (FZD, MBD) cousin marriage patterns. These combinations have very different implications for resource control and coalitions, and inheritance. Despite a great deal of complexity, some patterns emerge in the way resources and kin coalitions influence the choice of mates among cousins. FBD strengthens reciprocity and nepotism among male paternal kin; it is associated with patrilocal residence, and men have relatively great social power and resource control in such societies (Aswad, 1971; Barth, 1956; Alexander, 1979; see review by Flinn & Low, 1986). MBD (which strengthens reciprocity and nepotism among male maternal kin) is associated with matrilocal and avunculocal residence (Alexander, 1979; but see Flinn, 1981). FZD marriage allows high-status men to keep control of resources even in matrilocal societies, and is often practiced by such men (Fathauer, 1961; Flinn, 1981; Flinn & Low, 1986). MZD could enhance reciprocity and nepotism among female kin; perhaps because women so seldom control significant heritable resources, it is virtually unknown.

Throughout history, subsistence and marital locality have influenced family forms. From medieval times in Europe, land was a central resource, and structured much of family life (e.g., Mitterauer & Sieder, 1982; Laslett, 1965; Netting, 1993; Gies & Gies, 1989; Rotberg & Rabb, 1980). Male kin in landowning families tended to stay nearby, so most families lived patrilocally. Extended families tended to live together; both for working the land and proto-industrial production, the family was also an economic unit. Inheritance developed geographical patterns: the "Mediterranean" pattern, in which one child (typically the oldest living son) inherited virtually everything, while later-born children more or less fended for themselves, and the "European" pattern of more equal inheritance (Goody, 1988). Even within regions, variation could occur. In Sweden, for example, during the nineteenth century, families in the south (with smaller, more productive farms, and market penetration) tended to divide land among children, while in the mid-regions and the north, most land tended to go to the oldest son (Low & Clarke, 1992). Family forms, as well as inheritance patterns, also changed with the coming of the Industrial Revolution to Europe.

New work connects family and environment at an even more fine-grained level. When individuals perceive that their environment is relatively risky, and they cannot control it, a number of things happen. When life expectancy is short, women tend to have their first child earlier than otherwise—even when other conditions (e.g., socioeconomic status) are controlled for (Wilson & Daly, 1997; Geronimus, 1996a, b, 1997; Geronimus et al., 2001). First births are likely to be nonmarital, and single motherhood is not uncommon (Anderson & Low, 2002; Luker, 1996). People's perceptions of these difficulties also matter: when people perceive uncertainty, they are more likely to take life-threatening risks, and less likely to "attach" securely to a mate or child (Hill & Low, 1991; Hill, Ross, & Low, 1997). Although these may have racial correlates, the clear drivers are resource richness and predictability. Thus, life expectancy (and perceived life expectancy) can predict much about patterns of age at first marriage, risk taking (including in some cases drug and alcohol abuse; Hill, Nord, & Blow, 1992; Hill et al., 1994), family form (e.g., proportion of single motherhood), and even, perhaps, attachment style.

UNUSUAL ASPECTS OF HUMAN FAMILY SYSTEMS

The ways in which males compete, and females choose, vary ecologically. Among nonhuman species, if males can control resources useful to females, resource-based polygyny will exist. When control-

lable resources are lacking, males are reduced to trying to control females or to scramble competition (see Low, 2000a, chap. 3, for summary; classics: Emlen & Oring, 1977; Borgia, 1979; Alexander & Borgia, 1978). When resources can be accumulated and defended, they are seldom distributed equally among individuals, and when resources are unequally distributed, so typically is reproductive success.

This ecological variation in other species in how families are formed is nothing compared to the within-species variation in humans. We are quite peculiar in the enormous variation within our species. Some of this great variation, of course, is cultural—and that is far from trivial. But there are ecological, cost–benefit variations in the structure of family as well. Here, to set the stage for the great feast of variation that follows in upcoming chapters, let us explore some of that variation.

Although a large proportion of married people alive at this moment are monogamously married, that is because there are a few very large, socially monogamous societies. Most human societies have polygynous marriage. A count of societies in Murdock's *Atlas of World Cultures* (1981) and *Ethnographic Atlas* (1967) reveals that more than 90 percent of the societies listed are polygynous. In this, we are fairly typical mammals, for all the reasons given above. In another way, humans are highly unusual in our polygyny. First, as noted, we have many different forms of polygyny across societies, as well as monogamy and polyandry. Second, in other species, typically males compete and females choose. But "third-party" influences in humans extend to matters of mate choice. In many societies, others—the bride's and groom's fathers, for example—not the bride-to-be, make the choice (e.g., Whyte, 1978, 1979).

When societies lack rules of inheritance, suggesting that there is little to inherit, men typically do not exchange goods for women, but more commonly exchange women;[6] similarly, when there are no societal rules about wealth or hereditary class stratification, men are more likely to exchange women than goods. But even in such societies, resources are relevant to the pattern of exchange.

When men can use resources to gain mates, they do so (and inheritance is male-biased, and rules about bastardy exist). When men purchase wives (bridewealth societies), younger (higher reproductive value) women are worth a higher bride price.[7] The currency of choice varies: sometimes women are purchased with cattle, as among the Kanuri people (Cohen, 1967); sometimes with sheep, as among the Yomut Turkmen (Irons, 1975); sometimes with pigs, as among the Tsembaga-Maring (Rappaport, 1968); or a combination. When large surpluses can be stored and men control important resources, wealthy men can negotiate for more wives than others.[8] When men can accumulate resources, the variability in how many wives they can afford increases; when men cannot, and they exchange women, they have less variance.

In some societies, a bride's family pays a dowry, reflecting an interesting twist on the sexual utility of resources. Dowry is fifty times more common in monogamous, stratified societies than in polygynous or nonstratified ones; in these societies, males vary greatly in their status and wealth, and women married to wealthy, high-status men will benefit reproductively. So it may pay a bride's father to compete, bargaining for a wealthy man. In some of these societies, it appears that poorer women's families must pay more dowry than wealthy women's families—a striking ecological economic (Gaulin & Boster, 1990, 1997).[9] Insofar as poorer families are unable to do this, stratification is intensified. One example of dowry as female competition is that in modern rural India. Since about 1950, demographic shifts have resulted in a decline in potential grooms for potential brides of marriageable ages—and dowries have risen steadily. By 1990, a dowry was likely to be over 50 percent of a household's assets. Women from poor families, able to pay less in dowry, may be less likely to marry; if they marry, they have a high risk of spousal abuse (Rao, 1993a, b).[10]

In historical and modern societies, in which monogamy is socially imposed, resource control (particularly by men) still matters. The common pattern is that wealthier men marry daughters of wealthier men, marry younger women, and have more children. Even today, when birth control means that sexual activity is disconnected from fertility, powerful men have more sexual access if they want it.[11]

When men's sources of power are unpredictable, and women have sufficient resources to be independent, men cannot always control women. In such societies, "serial monogamy," really a sort of temporal polygyny, can result (just as in other polygynous systems) in high variance in men's reproductive success. This is the case among the Ache (Hill & Hurtado, 1996) and the Cuna (Nordenskiold, 1949) Indians. Ache men and women have perhaps ten spouses in a lifetime, the Cuna four or five. Among the Ache, children often have several social fathers, those who are or have been associated with the mother; but the Ache also keep track of who is the probable biological father.

WOMEN AND CHILDREN IN POLYGYNOUS FAMILIES

Successfully polygynous men are always reproductively better off than their nonpolygynous competitors; that's why it is worth all the cost and all the risk. But the situation is more complicated for women. Sometimes ecological factors (e.g., pathogen stress) mean that a woman is better off as a wealthy, healthy man's second spouse than as the monogamous wife of a poor or ill man. Sometimes polygynous marriage with a high-status man appears to be preferred by women or their families, even when there are no apparent reproductive benefits (e.g., see Hames, 1996; and Chagnon, 1979, 1982, 1988, 1997).

Nonetheless, women and their children often suffer in polygynous systems: in a number of societies, second and subsequent polygynous wives have lower fertility than monogamous wives, or than first wives in polygynous households.[12] In some societies, children are likely to survive less well in polygynous households (Dorjahn, 1958), and cross-culturally a major cause of divorce in polygynous societies is conflict among co-wives (Betzig, 1989, 1996; Strassman, 1997, 2000).

A variety of proximate factors undoubtedly interact: for example, men may be older when they marry their "later" wives; women who are not considered desirable are likely both to marry late (and thus have low reproductive value) and to be a later wife. Nonetheless, the net result is that within a polygynous society, a woman's (or her family's) choice between an already married man and a not-yet-married man may be complicated.

DIVISION OF LABOR IN FAMILY LIFE

Fathers and mothers tend to have quite different roles in families across cultures. These divisions of labor almost certainly relate to our mammalian heritage: to women's requirements of pregnancy and child care, and to the differential return curves of largely female parental effort, versus the high-risk, high-gain opportunism of typically male mating effort. Women are more likely to do activities that require daily attention, do not require long absences from home, are not life-threatening, do not require total concentration, and can be easily resumed after an interruption (e.g., Murdock & Provost, 1973). In most societies, throughout much of our evolutionary history, small children were likely to die if their mother died. Under most ecological conditions, the patterns we see were simply efficient and made ecological sense.[13]

Mothers, more than fathers, face conflicts of getting versus allocating resources. Among the South American Ache, Hiwi (Hurtado, Hawkes, & Hill, 1985; Hurtado et al., 1992), and Ye'kwana (Hames, 1988), nursing women can forage less than others. In some societies, other children, usually siblings, help with child care (see Children Raising Children, below), and the availability of such children can have an impact on a mother's lifetime fertility. It seems likely that the sexual division of labor, interacting with ecological factors, generates additional patterns of interest. Across societies, some have extended-family households; others do not. Women, as noted, almost universally have responsibility for child care. When women are also responsible for tasks that are really incompatible with effective childcare, extended-family households show up. Sometimes this is associated with agriculture, but it need not be (Ember & Ember, 1983, chap. 5).

UNUSUAL ASPECTS OF FAMILIES: THE ECOLOGY OF PARENTAL INVESTMENT

Human family arrangements show additional ecologically influenced complexities, and many of these are centered about parent–child arrangements. Again, the variations we see are complex, but not random. There are ecological, and of course cultural, influences. Further, complex interactions sometimes produce unexpected results, such as inequitable treatment as a result of intended equity (Hertwig, Davis, & Salloway, 2002).

Step-Parents

Step-parenting is very rare under natural conditions, for parents who show discriminative parental solicitude (favoring their genetic offspring over nonrelated children) garner more fitness benefits than others (Daly & Wilson, 1988). In other species, step-parenting occurs under predictable circumstances (Rohwer, 1986; Rohwer, Herron, & Daly, 1999).

In humans there are two very important things to know about step-parenting. First, consider the old proverb, "When you would court the mother, pay attention to the child." Indeed, in many (biologically polygynous, socially monogamous) societies, step-parenting (step-fathering, at least) looks like mating effort.[14] When young (high-reproductive-value) women have no mate, but do have existing children, a man's demonstration of willingness to invest in her existing children can be a powerful attractant. Yet the (biological) interests of the mother, her existing child, and a potential new mate are in conflict—more conflict than between genetic parents in monogamous or polygynous societies, or adopting parents who have together decided to adopt a child of no relation to either of them.

The second important thing to note is that the likelihood of safe, caring step-parenting, versus danger of neglect, underinvestment, even infanticide, depends on the relative costs of step-parenting. In many traditional societies (depending on the length and exclusivity of marriage), men may commonly invest in others' children. Cross-culturally, the effects of such step-parenting and blended families vary enormously. Among Aka pygmies, men frequently are social fathers even when they are not genetic fathers (Hewlett, 1991a). Similarly, among the Ache of Paraguay, where marriage comprises sleeping together in camp for a week or more, children are often counted to have several fathers—a primary (genetic) father, and other investing social fathers (Hill & Hurtado, 1996).

In contrast, when children require great investment for success, investing in others' offspring may be a real life cost. Divorced women with children are less likely than childless women of the same age to be able to marry. In modern North America, where childraising is a relatively costly affair, step-parents (whose reproductive interests do not coincide with the child's) are more likely to abuse or neglect children than genetic parents, and, regardless of the old fairy tales, step-fathers are more likely to commit infanticide than step-mothers. Even when such extremes are not evident, step-fathers in expensive-child environments tend to invest less in their step-children, compared to their genetic offspring, and to invest less in step-children's education. The step-children showed negative effects, including lower adult income; this varied with the length of time a step-father was co-resident to help parent.[15]

The conflicts of interests arising from the presence of a step-parent can affect household composition and stability. It is not unusual to find, as did Mark Flinn in Trinidad, that women's daughters leave the household at an earlier age when there is a resident step-father (Flinn, 1988).

I suspect the variation in kinds of step-parenting, like the other variable aspects of family life, also has resource connections. A testable hypothesis is that step-parents should be a positive influence and take on the role most willingly when investment is low and generalizable, or costs are defrayed. In contrast, when children are costly to rear for both parents, we should not be surprised if step- and foster-parents typically invest less than genetic parents. We see more neolocal blended families today than in past Western societies, and in conditions in which children do not defray much of their costs (e.g., Bumpass, Raley, & Sweet, 1995; Cher-

lin & Furstenburg, 1994; see also Hewlett, 1992). These patterns should be of interest to all of us who think about family life and family forms.

Adoption

In other species, there is virtually no adoption in the sense that we humans do so extensively. Remember that in most species, a female and her offspring are the family; females do not "adopt" nonrelated young under normal circumstances. One can trick a female sometimes (as do ranchers with an orphaned lamb), but it is typically difficult. Some ants raid the nests of other species and steal eggs and larvae; however, they do so not to care for the young, but to acquire nonreproductive slaves. We do see temporary and low-cost adoption when it has benefits. In African elephants, for example, the dominant female of a group controls access to valuable localized resources such as waterholes. A subordinate female may "adopt" the young of the dominant; by doing so, she gains far more access to the water (Dublin, 1983). However, these cases are few and far between.

Human adoption can be quite common, especially in Oceania and the Arctic; it tends to fall into a limited number of categories. Some human adoption is very like the elephant case: lower-status families adopt children from high-status families, and gain some benefits (Kottak, 1986 [in Madagascar]). In most cases, adoptive parents are close kin (grandparents, aunts, etc.), and the adoption arises because the genetic parents cannot, for some reason, manage to raise their children (Silk, 1980). Formal adoption of unrelated and unknown children, through agencies, is a new and evolutionarily novel condition.

Wet-Nursing and Other Delegated Mothering

Other situations in which nonparents give surrogate parental care also often create problems for children. A dramatic example is given by anthropologist Sarah Hrdy, who found that in eighteenth-century Paris, interbirth interval, fertility, and infant mortality all varied with the mother's status (Hrdy, 1992, 1999). The richest women had very short interbirth intervals, very high fertility, and low infant mortality; a linear relationship between the cost of the wet nurse and infant survivorship meant that the richest women, who could afford the best wet nurses, fared best in terms of fertility. But wet nursing had unintended consequences.[16] Among the bourgeois, complexities created more variation in pattern. Poor women had long interbirth intervals, low fertility, and high infant mortality; and the wet nurses fared worst of all, with very long interbirth intervals, very low fertility, and very high infant mortality.

Children Raising Children

In a variety of societies, older siblings (usually daughters) do much of the child care. This affects attitudes of children—children who do much child care quickly take on dominance in training. Both boys and girls are called across societies, but boys rarely engage in child care after about age 7 (e.g., Whiting & Edwards, 1988: 274–275). The availability of such children can have an impact on a mother's lifetime fertility. On the Pacific island of Ifaluk, for example, a woman's lifetime fertility is correlated with the sex of her first two children: women whose first two children are girls have greater lifetime fertility than others. Daughters assist in child care on Ifaluk, so mothers whose first children are daughters defray some costs and have more children (Turke, 1988).

Other Effects of Brothers and Sisters

In societies in which there are goods to inherit, sibling rivalry can be more than a playground affair. For example, in nineteenth-century Sweden, a man's fertility was related to his wealth, including land. Although inheritance was legally mandated to be equal in Sweden after the early 1840s, the oldest surviving son almost always got most of the land. Indeed, landowning men had higher fertility than their non-landowning brothers, and for men, a good predictor of later fertility was the number of brothers a man had (Low, 1991; Low & Clarke, 1991, 1992). In con-

trast, women were often drawn into child and parent care, and for them the total number of siblings was a better predictor. Across societies, the number and composition of a family's sibship has multiple effects (Bergerhoff-Mulder, 1998). And, surprisingly, parental attempts at equal allocation may have quite perverse results (Davis, Hertwig, & Sulloway, 1999; Davis, Todd, & Bullock, 1999).

Infanticide, Abortion, Abandonment, and Neglect

Parents seldom kill their children. After all, even though a parent's interests are not identical to a child's, an infant's death means the loss of considerable parental investment. Indeed, in most species infanticide is typically committed by reproductive competitors rather than parents; for example, in lions (Packer & Pusey, 1983, 1984), langurs (Hrdy, 1974, 1978, 1979), howler monkeys, and gorillas (Watts, 1989), when a male takes over a harem he is likely to kill all babies under a certain age (see also Struhsaker & Leland, 1987, Table 8.4). The mother becomes sexually receptive, and the male profits both by eliminating an offspring with a competitor's genes, and by gaining a mating.

Human parents, like parents in other species, therefore do commit infanticide and abort and abandon their infants. When is infanticide not pathological, but adaptive? Once again, we must remember the trade-offs: if each infant requires great investment, parents must apportion their effort, and parental investment biases, even to the extent of infanticide, can be reproductively profitable—for example, if the mother is alone and without family or resources to help with care, or if the child is unlikely to be successful.[17] Cross-culturally, deformed or seriously ill newborns are killed most often, and there is evidence that some cultural conceptions of "ill omens" leading to infanticide are real reflections of low newborn quality (Hill & Ball, 1996). Similarly, mothers are more likely to commit infanticide when external circumstances reduce their chances of successful investment; too-close births, twins, lack of an investing mate or stable pairbond—all increase the likelihood of infanticide or neglect (Bugos & McCarthy, 1984).[18]

Historical studies of child abandonment also reflect such considerations: a mother's ability to invest in the child (including her own health, familial resources, economic conditions), and the child's health, legitimacy, and sex. In France (Fuchs, 1984), Spain (Sherwood, 1988), and Russia (Ransel, 1988), infanticide was related to economic factors and a mother's abilities. Similarly, although he failed to discern any pattern, historian John Boswell's overview of child abandonment reveals that 46 percent (29/63) of cases he examined were, despite great variation in time, country, and other circumstances, related to maternal ability to invest. When resource allocation problems (16/63; 25.5 percent) and offspring quality (4/63; 6.3 percent) were considered, selective reasons were apparent in 49/63 cases, or 77 percent (Boswell, 1990).

Abortion, too, appears more common in circumstances in which the birth of a child is likely to reduce the mother's lifetime reproductive success (Hill & Low, 1991; Torres & Forrest, 1988). As women age, and their reproductive value declines (future reproductive opportunities wane), they are less likely to seek abortion (Betzig & Lombardo, 1991). Even attitudes toward abortion in our society are related to the proportion of women in any group who are "at risk" of unwanted pregnancy.

Of course, none of these behaviors, or attitudes about them, are set or in any way "determined"; they can be influenced not only by an individual's own condition, but by the attitudes of those around him or her. For example, in the United States today, a woman is likely to favor abortion if she is still fertile and thus potentially vulnerable to unwanted pregnancy (Betzig & Lombardo, 1991). Opinions on abortion also become political as individuals and party leaders influence each other. From 1972 to 1994 in the United States, Democratic and Republican Party positions on abortion have changed gradually (as reflected by House and Senate votes); as this has occurred, individual voters have switched party alliances to align with their own attitudes about abortion (Adams, 1997).

The Ecology of Sex Preference

Abortion, infanticide, and abandonment are extreme withdrawals of parental care. But biases in education, inheritance, even medical care are widespread. What lies beneath these differences?

In many societies, parents prefer sons—they give them better care, more inheritance—because sons under many conditions can turn parental investment into grandchildren more effectively than daughters. Not so among the Mukogodo of Kenya. Mukogodo parents appear to respond to the different costs and benefits of sons and daughters in several ways—but among the Mukogodo, daughters are preferred. The Mukogodo sit at the bottom of a regional socioeconomic hierarchy and are somewhat stigmatized by their neighbors. And this fact has had curious social and health consequences (Cronk, 1989, 1991a, b, c, d, 1993, 2000). As in many pastoral societies, the groups in this region use livestock for bridewealth. Because the Mukogodo are so poor, Mukogodo men have little chance of raising the bridewealth required to marry a woman from a neighboring group. It also means that as Mukogodo daughters are married to men of neighboring groups, the Mukogodo acquire cattle, sheep, and goats from bridewealth.[19] Daughters are more valuable than sons in important ways.

Mukogodo mothers nurse their daughters longer than their sons (the opposite of typical human and other mammalian patterns). Mukogodo caregivers (mothers and others) stay closer to girls than boys, and hold them more. Parents take their daughters more frequently than their sons to the dispensary and clinic for treatment, and enroll their daughters more in the local Catholic mission's traveling baby clinic. Non-Mukogodo parents do not show these biases. Probably because of the biased care, girls show better growth than boys: better height for age, weight for age, weight for height.

The general point, when we look at sex preference in investment (even to the point of abandonment and infanticide), is that when the two sexes have different futures (an economist would call these differential reproductive returns on investment), parents typically invest more in the sex that can use the investment to return more lineage profit. A Mukogodo son grows up and marries, usually a Mukogodo woman. A daughter may marry a Mukogodo man, but if she can marry a wealthier neighbor, he has to pay bridewealth, and she will bring wealth to her family (which may be used to help any brothers marry). Interestingly, the Mukogodo, living among societies that have a strong male preference, claim, if you ask them, to prefer sons to daughters—but their actions show a clear preference for daughters. Parents among the Mukogodo, as those in a number of societies, appear to favor the more profitable sex in their children.

CONCLUSION: PATTERNED VARIATION IN FAMILY LIFE AND FORM

The remaining chapters will take you, reader, on a fascinating tour of families today across many cultures. I hope this introduction has caused you to consider the wide varieties of family life and form, not only in primates in general, but in societies both traditional and modern; and to consider both ecological influences and interactions in creating the rich and varied pattern we see.

The diverse family forms we see have ecological roots: monogamy, polygyny, polyandry, extended or nuclear family, remarriage patterns, step-parenting, adoption, inheritance. Resource richness, predictability, and economic defensibility affect family forms. So too do men's and women's relative ability to acquire and use resources in family formation. Pathogen stress appears to affect women's costs and benefits in choosing whether or not to become a polygynous wife, and to affect men's choice of wives (endogamy versus exogamy). Sex differences in ability to use resources for family also affect inheritance patterns. And so, on to chapters that will characterize the diversity in human families around the world today.

NOTES

1. Avoiding predation through "selfish herd" groups, and defense of food by multifemale groups are two major hypotheses for the formation of primate groups. On food defense and female bonding, see Wrangham (1980 , 1987), van Schaik (1989, 1996), Barton, Byrne, and Whitten (1996); on predation, see Cheney and Wrangham (1987).
2. For body size, testis size, and canine size comparisons, see Harvey and Harcourt (1984). Humans fit, in this comparison, in the multimale polygynous group portion of the continuum (male body size moderately large, testes very large). Note that large body size may confer additional advantages in species such as gorillas and orangutans, in which males coerce females into copulations (Watts, 1989; Wrangham & Peterson, 1996).
3. This is true among mammals. There is an interesting difference in polyandry between mammals and birds, which highlights evolutionary aspects of family forms. The few polyandrous primates, including a very few human societies, appear to have come to polyandry through a combination of resources and effectiveness of parental care; either the environment is very harsh and the mother alone is unlikely to raise offspring successfully, or (in some human societies) the family concentrates wealth in few grandchildren. Among birds, polyandry often appears to be derived from monogamy (as in arctic sanderlings, in which monogamous and polyandrous pairs are in the same populations). In these cases, it is often a short and uncertain-length season for brood raising that seems to foster intense care, and re-nesting when the season permits. In some birds, such as jacanas, there is simple sex-role reversal: females are larger than males, and males give all the parental care.
4. Such societies are what Alexander et al. (1979) termed "socially imposed monogamous" systems: socially monogamous but biologically polygynous.
5. This argument is, of course, a major focus for work on the evolution of sexual reproduction itself (see Low, 2000a, chaps. 3, 4). The difficulty lies in defining the sort of uncertainty that will favor the advantages of sex, or variable offspring, to a degree sufficient to compensate for the loss of genetic representation. W. D. Hamilton and his colleagues (classic: Hamilton, 1980; reviews: Ebert and Hamilton, 1996; Low, 2000a) have argued cogently that pathogen stress is one of the few, perhaps the only, environmental uncertainty that will meet the criteria.
6. This is a highly significant relationship ($p = 0.00001$) (Flinn & Low, 1986).
7. Borgerhoff-Mulder's (1988a, b, 1997) study is the most detailed; she found that younger (higher reproductive

value) women commanded higher bride prices (see chap. 7).

8. For example, Native American societies of western North America (Jorgensen, 1980: 167). If variance in men's number of wives arises from choice of men (by women or their families) based on the men's resource control, then men's use of resources in reproductive effort should correlate with the degree of polygyny. Indeed, the use of some payment by men (e.g., bridewealth or bride service), rather than exchange of women or payment of dowry, is strongly associated with the degree of polygyny (Low, 1988b).

9. Gaulin and Boster's model of dowry is strong in predicting when dowry is unlikely to occur, but less powerful in predicting when it will occur (62 percent of stratified, and nonpolygynous societies lack dowry; Lang, 1993). Betzig (cited in Gaulin and Boster [1997:374]) makes an important point: the conjunction of stratification and non-polygynous marriage may well make female competition for wealthy males worth it; what is at stake is not protection from co-wives, but protection from inheritance claims of co-wives' children.

10. Further, domestic violence and spousal abuse have correlated with these increases in dowry worth; although alcohol is one causative factor, "insufficient dowry" is the second (Rao, 1997).

11. On historical societies, see Voland (1990), Voland, Siegelkow, and Engel (1990), Voland and Dunbar (1995), Low (1991), and Low and Clarke (1991, 1992). On modern societies and sexual access, see Betzig and Weber (1993), and Pérusse (1993). Modern life is complex because of novelties such as birth control, so that with regard to wealth or income and fertility, some studies find positive (e.g., Tasiran, 1995), and some negative (e.g., Kaplan et al., 1995), relationships (for review, see Low, 2000a, chap. 15; Low, 2000b).

12. For costs to women, see e.g., Chisholm and Burbank (1991), Strassmann (1997, 2000). For relative fertility of first and other wives, see e.g., Dorjahn (1958), Smith and Kunz (1976), Daly and Wilson (1983), Bean and Minneau (1986), Garenne and van de Walle (1989), Pebley and Mbugua (1989), and Sichona (1993). However, in at least some societies, these differences disappear after a generation (Josephson, 1993).

13. Of course, I am not saying anything whatsoever about women's work today. I do not think that past patterns dictate extra current utility, or individual choice.

14. That is, caring for a woman's existing child(ren) increases a man's probable success of getting her as a mate (e.g., Alexander and Borgia, 1978; Freeman-Gallant, 1997; Rohwer, 1986; Rohwer et al., 1999).

15. On human abuse, see Daly and Wilson (1984, 1985, 1987). Step-fathers, like langurs taking over a harem (Hrdy, 1974, 1978, 1979), reduce not only their costs for raising a nonrelative, but reduce the potentially competitive investment by the mother; and women may be less able to prevent a spouse's abuse than a man. On relative investment by step-fathers and fathers: Lancaster and Kaplan (2000), Anderson (2000).

16. These women experienced unanticipated costs. For example, the very-high-fertility women "endured a range of problems ranging from chronic anemia to prolapsed uteruses" (Hrdy, 1992).

17. See e.g., Hughes (1988), and Daly and Wilson (1988). Hill and Ball (1996) suggest that cultural "ill omens," as well as overtly biological cues, may be used.

18. For an overview, see Daly and Wilson (1984, 1988), or Hrdy (1992). Daly and Wilson (1984) compared sixty cultures in the Human Relations Area files to identify causal circumstances; Hrdy (1992, Table 1) compared infanticide rates in a set of traditional societies for which there are relatively good data.

19. Interestingly, this income does not appear to make these women's brothers, for example, able to marry more. So favoring daughters is not a matter of local resource enhancement.

REFERENCES

Adams, G. D. (1997). Abortion: Evidence of an issue evolution. *American Journal of Political Science, 41*(3), 718–737.

Alexander, R. D. (1979). *Darwinism and human affairs.* Seattle: University of Washington Press.

Alexander, R. D., & Borgia, G. (1978). On the origin and basis of the male-female. In M. F. Blum & N. Blum (Eds.), *Sexual selection and reproductive competition in insects* (pp. 417–440). New York: Academic Press.

Alexander, R. D., Hoogland, J. L., Howard, R. D., Noonan, K. M., & Sherman P. W. (1979). Sexual dimorphism and breeding systems in pinnipeds, ungulates, primates, and humans. In N. A. Chagnon & W. Irons (Eds.), *Evolutionary biology and human social be-*

havior: An anthropological perspective (pp. 402–435). North Scituate, MA: Duxbury.

Altman, I., & Ginat, J. (1996). *Polygamous families in contemporary society.* Cambridge, UK: Cambridge University Press.

Altonji, J. G., Hayashi, F., & Kotlikoff, L. J. (1997). Parental altruism and inter vivo transfers: Theory and evidence. *Journal of Political Economics, 105,* 1121–1166.

Anderson, K. G. (2000). The life histories of American stepfathers in evolutionary perspective. *Human Nature, 11*(4), 307–333.

Anderson, K. G., & Low, B. (2002). Nonmarital first births and women's life histories. In J. Rogers & H. P. Kohler (Eds.), *The biodemography of human reproduction and fertility* (pp. 57–86). Boston, MA: Kluwer.

Aswad, B. (1971). *Property control and social strategies in settlers in a Middle Eastern plain.* University of Michigan Museum of Anthropology, Anthropological Papers No. 44.

Barry, H., III, Bacon, M. K., & Child, I. L. (1957). A cross-cultural study of some sex differences in socialization. *Journal of Abnormal and Social Psychology, 55,* 327–332.

Barry, H., III, Josephson, L., Lauer, E., & Marshall, C. (1976). Traits inculcated in childhood. 5. Cross-cultural codes. *Ethology, 15,* 83–114.

Barth, F. (1956). *Models of social organization.* Occasional Paper No. 23, Royal Anthropological Institute, London.

Barton, R. A., Byrne, R. W., & Whiten, A. (1996). Ecology, feeding competition, and social structure in baboons. *Behavior, Ecology and Sociobiology, 38,* 3211–329.

Bean, L. L., & Minneau, G. P. (1986). The polygyny-fertility hypothesis: A re-evaluation. *Population Studies, 40,* 67–81.

Betzig, L. (1989). Causes of conjugal dissolution: A cross-cultural study. *Current Anthropology, 30*(5), 654–676.

Betzig, L. (1996). Not whether to count babies, but which. In C. Crawford & D. Krebs (Eds.), *Handbook of evolutionary psychology: Ideas, issues, and applications* (pp. 265–274). Hillsdale, NJ: Erlbaum.

Betzig, L. (Ed.). (1997). *Human nature: A critical reader.* Oxford, UK: Oxford University Press.

Betzig, L., & Lombardo, L. H. (1991). Who's pro-choice and why. *Ethology and Sociobiology, 13,* 49–71.

Betzig, L., & Weber, S. (1993). Polygyny in American politics. *Politics and the Life Sciences, 12,* 45–52.

Borgerhoff-Mulder, M. (1988a). Reproductive success in three Kipsigis cohorts. In T. H. Clutton-Brock (Ed.), *Reproductive success* (pp. 419–435). Chicago: University of Chicago Press.

Borgerhoff-Mulder, M. (1988b). Kipsigis bridewealth payments. In L. Betzig, M. Borgerhoff Mulder, & P. Turke (Eds.), *Human reproductive behavior: A Darwinian perspective* (pp. 65–82). Cambridge, UK: Cambridge University Press.

Borgerhoff-Mulder, M. (1997). Marrying a married man: A postscript. In L. Betzig (Ed.), *Human nature: A critical reader* (pp. 115–117). Oxford, UK: Oxford University Press.

Borgerhoff-Mulder, M. (1998). Brothers and sisters: How sibling interactions affect optimal parental allocations. *Human Nature, 9,* 119–162.

Borgia, G. (1979). Sexual selection and the evolution of mating systems. In M. F. Blum & N. Blum (Eds.), *Sexual selection and reproductive competition in insects* (pp. 19–80). New York: Academic Press.

Boswell, J. (1990). *The kindness of strangers: Abandonment of children in Western Europe from late antiquity to the Renaissance.* New York: Vintage Books. (First published by Pantheon, 1988.)

Bugos, P. E., & McCarthy L. M. (1984). Ayoreo infanticide: A case study. In G. Hausfater & S. B. Hrdy (Eds.), *Infanticide: Comparative and evolutionary perspectives* (pp. 503–520). New York: Aldine de Gruyter.

Bumpass, L., Raley, R. K., & Sweet, J. A. (1995). The changing nature of stepfamilies: Implications of cohabitation and nonmarital childbearing. *Demography, 32,* 425–436.

Chagnon, N. (1979). Is reproductive success equal in egalitarian societies? In N. A. Chagnon & W. Irons (Eds.), *Evolutionary biology and human social behavior: An anthropological perspective* (pp. 374–401). North Scituate, MA: Duxbury.

Chagnon, N. (1982). Sociodemographic attributes of nepotism in tribal populations: Man the rule-breaker. In Kings' College Sociobiology Group (Eds.), *Current problems in sociobiology* (pp. 291–318). Cambridge, UK: Cambridge University Press.

Chagnon, N. (1988). Life histories, blood revenge, and warfare in a tribal population. *Science, 239,* 985–992.

Chagnon, N. (1997). *Yanomamö* (5th ed.). Fort Worth, TX: Harcourt Brace.

Cheney, D., & Wrangham, R. W. (1987). Predation. In B. B. Smuts, D. L. Cheney, R. M. Seyfarth, R. W.

Wrangham, & T. T. Struhsaker (Eds.), *Primate societies* (pp. 227–239). Chicago: University of Chicago Press.

Cherlin, A. J., & Furstenberg, Jr. F. F. (1994). Stepfamilies in the United States: A reconsideration. *Annual Review of Sociology, 20,* 359–381.

Chisholm, J., & Burbank, V. (1991). Monogamy and polygyny in southeast Arnhem Land: Male coercion and female choice. *Ethology and Sociobiology, 12,* 291–313.

Cohen, R. (1967). *The Kanuri.* New York: Rinehart and Winston.

Coontz, S. (1992). *The way we never were: American families and the nostalgia trap.* New York: Basic Books.

Cronk, L. (1989). Low socioeconomic status and female-biased parental investment: The Mukogodo example. *American Anthropologist, 91,* 414–429.

Cronk, L. (1991a). Human behavioral ecology. *Annual Review of Anthropology, 20,* 25–53.

Cronk, L. (1991b). Wealth, status, and reproductive success among the Mukogodo of Kenya. *American Anthropologist, 93*(2), 345–360.

Cronk, L. (1991c). Intention versus behavior in parental sex preferences among the Mukogodo of Kenya. *Journal of Biosocial Science, 23,* 229–240.

Cronk, L. (1991d). Preferential parental investment in daughters over sons. *Human Nature, 2,* 387–417.

Cronk, L. (1993). Parental favoritism toward daughters. *American Scientist, 81,* 272–279.

Cronk, L. (2000). Female-biased parental investment and growth performance among Mukogodo children. In L. Cronk, N. Chagnon, & W. Irons (Eds.), *Adaptation and human behavior: An anthropological perspective* (pp. 203–221). Hawthorne, NY: Aldine de Gruyter.

Daly, M., & Wilson, M. (1983). *Sex, evolution, and behavior* (2nd ed.). Boston: Willard Grant.

Daly, M., & Wilson, M. (1984). A sociobiological analysis of human infanticide. In G. Hausfater & S. B. Hrdy (Eds.), *Infanticide: Comparative and evolutionary perspectives* (pp. 487–502). New York: Aldine de Gruyter.

Daly, M., & Wilson, M. (1985). Child abuse and other risks of not living with both parents. *Ethology and Sociobiology, 6,* 197–210.

Daly, M., & Wilson, M. (1987). Children as homicide victims. In R. J. Gelles & J. B. Lancaster (Eds.), *Child abuse and neglect: Biosocial dimensions* (pp. 201–214). New York: Aldine de Gruyter.

Daly, M., & Wilson, M. (1988). *Homicide.* Hawthorne, NY: Aldine de Gruyter.

Davis, J. N., Hertwig, R., & Sulloway, F. J. (1999). *Parental investment and the inequality of equality.* Paper presented at the 1999 Evolution and Human Behavior meetings, Salt Lake City.

Davis, J. N., Todd, P. M., & Bullock S. (1999). Environmental quality predicts parental provisioning decisions. *Proceedings of the Royal Society, London B: Biological Sciences, 266,* 1791–1797.

Dickemann, M. (1981). Paternal confidence and dowry competition: A biocultural analysis of purdah. In R. D. Alexander & D. W. Tinkle (Eds.), *Natural selection and social behavior* (pp. 417–438). New York: Chiron.

Dickemann, M. (1997). Cleo unveiled. In L. Betzig (Ed.), *Human nature: A critical reader.* Oxford, UK: Oxford University Press.

Dorjahn, V. R. (1958). Fertility, polygyny, and their interrelations in Temne society. *American Anthropologist, 60,* 838–860.

Dublin, H. T. (1983). Cooperation and reproductive competition among African elephants. In S. K. Wasser (Ed.), *Social behavior of female vertebrates* (pp. 291–313). New York: Academic Press.

Dupâquier, J., Hélin, E., Laslett, P., Livi-Bacci, M., & Sogner, S. (Eds.). (1981). *Marriage and remarriage in populations of the past* (pp. 163–175). New York: Academic Press.

Ebert, D., & Hamilton, W. D. (1996). Sex against virulence: The coevolution of parasitic diseases. *TREE (Trends in Ecology and Evolution), 11,* 79–82.

Ember, M., & Ember, C. R. (1983). *Marriage, family, and kinship.* New Haven, CT: HRAF Press.

Emlen, S. T. (1997). Predicting family dynamics in social vertebrates. In J. R. Krebs & N. B. Davies (Eds.), *Behavioural ecology* (4th ed., pp. 228–253). Oxford, UK: Blackwell Scientific.

Emlen, S. T., & Oring, L. W. (1977). Ecology, sexual selection, and the evolution of mating systems. *Science, 197,* 215–223.

Fathauer, G. (1961). Trobrianders. In D. Schneider & K. Gough (Eds.), *Matrilineal kinship* (pp. 234–269). Berkeley: University of California Press.

Flandrin, J. L. (1979). *Families in former times: Kinship, household, and sexuality.* (Trans. by Richard Southern). Cambridge, UK: Cambridge University Press.

Flinn, M. V. (1981). Uterine versus agnatic kinship variability and associated cousin marriage preferences. In

R. D. Alexander & D. W. Tinkle (Eds.), *Natural selection and social behavior* (pp. 439–475). New York: Chiron.

Flinn, M. V. (1988). Parent-offspring interactions in a Caribbean village: Daughter guarding. In L. Betzig, M. Borgerhoff Mulder, & P. Turke (Eds.), *Human reproductive behavior: A Darwinian perspective* (pp. 189–2000). Cambridge, UK: Cambridge University Press.

Flinn, M. V., & Low, B. S. (1986). Resource distribution, social competition, and mating patterns in human societies. In D. Rubenstein & R. Wrangham (Eds.), *Ecological aspects of social evolution* (pp. 217–243). Princeton, NJ: Princeton University Press.

Freeman-Gallant, C. R. (1997). Parentage and parental care: Consequences of intersexual selection in Savannah Sparrows? *Behavior, Ecology, and Sociobiology, 40,* 395–400.

Fuchs, R. (1984). *Abandoned children: Foundlings and child welfare in nineteenth-century France.* Albany: State University of New York Press.

Garenne, M., & van de Walle, E. (1989). Polygyny and fertility among the Sereer of Senegal. *Population Studies, 43,* 267–283.

Gaulin, S. J. C., & Boster, J. S. (1990). Dowry as female competition. *American Anthropologist, 92,* 994–1005.

Gaulin, S. J. C., & Boster, J. (1997). When are husbands worth fighting for? In L. Betzig (Ed.), *Human nature: A critical reader* (pp. 372–374). Oxford, UK: Oxford University Press.

Geronimus, A. T. (1996a). Black/white differences in the relationship of maternal age to birthweight: A population-based test of the Weathering Hypothesis. *Social Science and Medicine, 42*(4), 589–597.

Geronimus, A. T. (1996b). What teen mothers know. *Human Nature, 7*(4), 323–352.

Geronimus, A. T. (1997). Teenage childbearing and personal responsibility. *Political Science Quarterly, 112*(3), 405–430.

Geronimus, A. T., Bound, J., Waidmann, T. A., Colen, C. G, & Steffick, D. (2001). Inequality in life expectancy, functional status, and active life expectancy across selected Black and White populations in the United States. *Demography, 38*(2), 227–251.

Gies, F., & Gies, J. (1989). *Marriage and the family in the Middle Ages.* New York: Harper & Row.

Goody, J. (1988). *The development of family and marriage in Europe.* Cambridge, UK: Cambridge University Press.

Gorer, G. (1967). *Himalayan village* (2nd ed.). New York: Basic Books.

Hames, R. B. (1988). The allocation of parental care among the Ye'kwana. In L. Betzig, M. Borgerhoff Mulder, & P. Turke (Eds.), *Human reproductive behavior: A Darwinian perspective* (pp. 237–251). Cambridge, UK: Cambridge University Press.

Hames, R. B. (1996). Costs and benefits of monogamy and polygyny for Yanomamö women. *Ethology and Sociobiology, 17,* 181–199.

Hamilton, W. D. (1964). The genetical evolution of social behavior I, II. *Journal of Theoretical Biology, 7,* 1–52.

Hamilton, W. D. (1980). Sex versus non-sex versus parasite. *Oikos, 35,* 282–290.

Hartung, J. (1983). In defense of Murdock: A reply to Dickemann. *Curent Anthropology, 24*(1), 125–126.

Hartung, J. (1982). Polygyny and the inheritance of wealth. *Current Anthropology, 23,* 1–12.

Hartung, J. (1997). If I had it to do over. In L. Betzig (Ed.), *Human nature: A critical reader.* Oxford, UK: Oxford University Press.

Harvey, P., & Harcourt, A. H. (1984). Sperm competition, testis size and breeding systems in primates. In R. L. Smith (Ed.), *Sperm competition and the evolution of animal mating systems* (pp. 589–600). New York: Academic Press.

Hertwig, R., Davis, J. N., & Sulloway, F. J. (2002). Parental investment: How an equity motive can produce inequity. *Psychological Bulletin, 128*(5), 728–745.

Hewlett, B. S. (1991a). *Intimate fathers: The nature and context of Aka Pygmy paternal infant care.* Ann Arbor: University of Michigan Press.

Hewlett, B. S. (1991b). Demography and childcare in preindustrial societies. *Journal of Anthropological Research, 47,* 1–37.

Hewlett, B. S. (1992). *Father-child relationships: Cultural and biosocial contexts.* New York: Aldine de Gruyter.

Hill, C. M., & Ball, H. L. (1996). Abnormal births and other "ill omens": The adaptive case for infanticide. *Human Nature, 7,* 381–401.

Hill, E. M., Blow, F., Young, J., & Singer, K. (1994). Family history of alcoholism and childhood adversity: Joint effects on alcohol consumption and dependence. *Alcoholism: Clinical and Experimental Research, 18*(5), 1083–1090.

Hill, E. M., & Low, B. (1991). Contemporary abortion patterns: A life-history approach. *Ethology and Sociobiology, 13,* 35–48.

Hill, E. M., Nord, J., & Blow, F. C. (1992). Young-adult children of alcoholic parents: Protective effects of positive family functioning. *British Journal of Addiction, 87,* 1167–1690.

Hill, E., Ross, L. T., & Low, B. S. (1997). The role of future unpredictability in human risk-taking. *Human Nature, 8*(4), 287–325.

Hill, K., & Hurtado, A. M. (1996). *Ache life history: The ecology and demography of a foraging people.* New York: Aldine De Gruyter.

Hurtado, M., Hawkes, K., & Hill, K. (1985). Female subsistence strategies among Ache hunter-gatherers of eastern Paraguay. *Human Ecology, 13,* 1–28.

Hurtado, M., K. Hill, Kaplan, H., & Hurtado, I. (1992). Tradeoffs between food acquisition and child care among Hiwi and Ache women. *Human Nature, 3,* 185–216.

Hrdy, S. B. (1974). Male-male competition and infanticide among the lemurs (*Presbytis entellus*) of Abu Rajasthan. *Folia Primatologia, 22,* 19–58.

Hrdy, S. B. (1978). Allomaternal care and the abuse of infants aomg Hanuman langurs. In D. Chivers & P. Herbert (Eds.), *Recent advances in primatology,* Vol. 1. New York: Academic Press.

Hrdy, S. B. (1979). Infanticide among animals: A review classification and implications for the reproductive strategies of females. *Ethology and Sociobiology, 1,* 13–40.

Hrdy, S. B. (1992). Fitness tradeoffs in the history and evolution of delegated mothering with special reference to wet-nursing, abandonment, and infanticide. *Ethology and Sociobiology, 13,* 409–442.

Hrdy, S. B. (1999). *Mother nature.* New York: Pantheon Books.

Hughes, A. L. (1988). *Evolution and human kinship.* Oxford, UK: Oxford University Press.

Irons, W. (1975). *The Yomut Turkmen: A study of social organization among a Central Asian Turkic-speaking population.* Museum of Anthropology, University of Michigan, Anthropological Paper 58.

Jorgensen, W. (1980). *Western Indians.* San Francisco: Freeman.

Josephson, S. C. (1993). Status, reproductive success, and marrying polygynously. *Ethology and Sociobiology, 14,* 391–396.

Judge, D. S. (1995). American legacies and the variable life histories of women and men. *Human Nature, 6,* 291–323.

Judge, D. S., & Hrdy, S. B. (1992). Allocation of accumulated resources among close kin: Inheritance in Sacramento, California, 1890–1984. *Ethology and Sociobiology, 13,* 495–522.

Kaplan, H., Lancaster, J. B., Bock, J. A., & Johnson, S. E. (1995). Fertility and fitness among Albuquerque men: A competitive labor market theory. In R. I. M. Dunbar (Ed.), *Human reproductive decisions* (pp. 96–136). London: St. Martin's Press, in association with the Galton Institute.

Kottak, C. (1986). Kinship modeling: Adoption, fosterage, and fictive kinship among the Betsileo Malagasy. In C. P. Kottak, J. A. Rakotoarisoa, A. Southall, & P. Vérin (Eds.), *Madagascar: Society and history* (pp. 277–298). Durham, NC: Carolina Academic Press.

Kurland, J. A., & Gaulin, S. J. C. (1984). The evolution of male parental investment: Effects of genetic relatedness and feeding ecology on the allocation of reproductive effort. In D. M. Taub (Ed.), *Primate paternalism* (pp. 259–306). New York: Van Nostrand Reinhold.

Lancaster, J. B., & Kaplan, H. (2000). Parenting other men's children: Costs, benefits, and consequences. In L. Cronk, W. Irons, & N. Chagnon (Eds.), *Adaptation and human behavior: An anthropological perspective* (pp. 179–201). New York: Aldine DeGruyter.

Lang, H. (1993). Dowry and female competition: A Boolean reanalysis. *Current Anthropology, 34,* 775–778.

Laslett, P. (1965). *The world we have lost—Further explored.* London: Routledge.

Low, B. S. (1988a). Measures of polygyny in humans. *Current Anthropology, 29*(1), 189–194.

Low, B. S. (1988b). Pathogen stress and polygyny in humans. In L. Betzig, M. Borgerhoff Mulder, & P. Turke (Eds.), *Human reproductive behavior: A Darwinian perspective* (pp. 115–128). Cambridge, UK: Cambridge University Press.

Low, B. S. (1989). Cross-cultural patterns in the training of children: An evolutionary perspective. *Journal of Comparative Psychology, 103,* 311–319.

Low, B. S. (1990a). Human responses to environmental extremeness and uncertainty: A cross-cultural perspective. In E. Cashdan (Ed.), *Risk and uncertainty in tribal and peasant economies* (pp. 229–255). Boulder, CO: Westview.

Low, B. S. (1990b). Marriage systems and pathogen stress in human societies. *American Zoologist, 30,* 325–339.

CHAPTER 3

(POST)MODERN FAMILIES

LOUISE B. SILVERSTEIN
Yeshiva University

CARL F. AUERBACH
Yeshiva University

For two social constructionists, contemplating writing a chapter about "the modern family" was daunting. Thus we changed our topic from "modern" to "(post)modern," and from "family" to "families." Before beginning our discussion, we offer a few brief definitions in order to orient the reader in terms of the way that we think about families.

We define a family as two or more people who are in a relationship created by birth, marriage, or choice. Some families have legal protection and privileges, while others do not. One could argue that any family structure currently existing is "modern," that is, a modern version of itself. This would include families as diverse as polygynous hunting-gathering families in the Kalahari desert, polyandrous families in the mountains of Nepal, lesbigay families in the Netherlands, and non-gay step-families in Brooklyn, New York.

In an effort to demarcate the kinds of families that we will talk about in this chapter, we differentiate traditional, modern, and postmodern families. We realize that our categories are arbitrary. However, we are using them for heuristic rather than definitive purposes. We think of the "traditional" family as the heterosexual two-parent nuclear family with a husband/breadwinner and a wife/homemaker; and the "modern" family as a dual-earner family in which men and women both work outside the home, but only women are responsible for childcare and housework. From this perspective, the "modern" family is a dual-earner family, but not a role-sharing family. These families have not yet transformed the gendered division of labor or the gendered distribution of power. Therefore, we refer to dual-earner families as "modern," rather than postmodern.

"Postmodern" families, in contrast, represent a deconstruction or transformation of at least one aspect of the traditional family. For example, lesbigay couples and single mothers by choice would be examples of postmodern families in that they have deconstructed the cultural gender ideology that a healthy family requires two parents, specifically two parents of opposite sexes. Families conceiving children using new reproductive technology, e.g., egg implantation or maternal surrogates, would be another example of deconstructing our culture's insistence on the importance of a biological relationship between parent and child. Transnational families would be examples of families that violate the usual characteristic of household co-residence, because these families exist across national and cultural borders.

In an effort to narrow the scope of the chapter, we will be talking primarily about families in the United States, since that is the culture we know best. However, many of the trends we identify are present in other countries, especially other Western developed countries.

In our view, incredibly rapid social change is the single most important characteristic defining postmodern family life. In this chapter, we will discuss several of the changes that families underwent in the twentieth century. Again, we realize that our choice of four major trends is arbitrary, and an oversimplification of the enormous complexity of human families. The four changes in family life that we will focus on are: from homogeneity to diversity; from stability to change; from gendered parenting to transgendered families; and from male dominance toward more egalitarianism. We will try to see into the future, predicting what we think we can predict, and outlining what we know we do not know.

FROM HOMOGENEITY TO DIVERSITY

The most concrete evidence of change is the proliferation of many different types of family forms. In earlier historical periods in the West, there was more homogeneity in family forms. Both the patrilineal economic distribution of property and the presence of religious sanctions pressured the vast majority of people to establish and maintain a heterosexual, married lifestyle. Thus the two-parent heterosexual family was the ideal, if not the norm. Family structures that differed from that norm, such as the never-married, mother-headed family and the divorced family were considered deficit family forms. By 2001 non-nuclear families had not only increased dramatically in number, they were no longer as stigmatized as they once were.

In contrast to the hegemony of the nuclear family in previous historical eras, there has been an overall decline in marriage rates in Europe and the United States. People are waiting longer to get married for the first time, not marrying at all, divorcing more frequently, and not remarrying after divorce.

This combination of trends, combined with lower fertility rates, has resulted in smaller families in all developed countries. For example, in the United States the percentage of family groups with children that had four or more children decreased from 17 percent in 1970 to 6 percent in 2000. Overall, fertility patterns for U.S. women in 1998 were at 2.0 children per woman, slightly below the replacement level of 2.1 (Bachu & O'Connell, 2001). In the 1990s, when the fertility rates of other Western European countries were falling to or below replacement levels, only Swedish couples continued regularly to have three children (Hoem, 1995).

With the decline of legal marriage, the increase in unmarried couples with children (both gay and straight), and the increase in both divorce and remarriage, social scientists are struggling to develop the nomenclature to describe the different family compositions.

Cohabitation and Childbearing

In the United States, Scandinavia, and other Western European countries, many couples have chosen to live together, either as a prelude to legal marriage, or as a substitute for it. Sweden has often acted as a demographic trendsetter, and this is true in terms of the decrease in marriage and the increase in cohabitation.

In Sweden, the decision about whether or when to get married has varied by class (Hoem, 1995). Students tend to establish consensual unions at a young age. These unions seem to reflect a practical solution to the high cost of living, rather than a relationship commitment. Thus they are typically unstable. For middle-class employed women, consensual unions are more stable and long-lasting.

Both students and middle-class women typically have been unwilling to have children without the benefits of marriage. Thus, pregnancy usually converts a consensual union into a legal marriage for these groups. Working-class couples, in contrast, have been more likely to have children in the context of a consensual union that is not followed by marriage. Across all social classes in Sweden, the decision to get married without first living together has virtually disappeared.

These trends are similar for middle-class couples in Northern European countries. For example, in France over the course of only fifteen years (1970–1985), the proportion of first unions begun outside of marriage increased from an average of 20 percent to an average of 75 percent (Leridon & Toulemon, 1995)! Similarly, the mean age at first marriage for women in France has been slightly greater than 25 since 1988.

In addition to living together rather than getting married, large numbers of middle-class young people are also choosing to delay marriage until after the birth of their first child. In France, 40 percent of all first births in 1990 occurred outside of marriage (Leridon & Toulemon, 1995). This decision is so common in Scandinavia that wedding dresses are now made with bodices that allow a mother to breastfeed her infant during the wedding ceremony.

In Southern Europe, Italy and Spain share the trend of increased age at first marriage. However, cohabitation rates are lower than those in Northern European countries, and the birth of the first child in these two countries continues to be linked to mar-

riage (Pinnelli & De Rose, 1995; Delgado, 1995). The centrality of marriage in Spain and Italy may reflect the continuing strong influence of the Catholic church on family formation patterns.

In the U.S. middle class, the increase in cohabitation reflects the fact that both women and men are delaying marriage and childbirth while pursuing higher education and employment experience. In the United States the average age of women at first marriage is now 25, up from 20 in 1960; for men the average age is 27, up from 22 in 1960 (Fields & Caspar, 2001). In 1970, about 16 percent of all women aged 25–29 were unmarried; whereas by 1998, 45 percent were unmarried. Unmarried couples now constitute 9 percent of all couples (Terry-Humen, Manlove, & Moore, 2001).

Extramarital childbearing in the United States has often mistakenly been associated primarily with African American families and other families of color. However, in the 1990s, nonmarital birth rates have declined among Latino and African American couples. In contrast, white couples accounted for 50 percent of nonmarital births in the early 1990s, an increase from 33 percent in the 1980s (Terry-Humen, et al., 2001). Overall, the percentage of childbearing women who remained unmarried increased in all age categories, and across all ethnic groups.

For poor families in the United States, the trend for the birth of the first child to precede marriage has been generated by a different social and economic reality, i.e., a low ratio of marriageable men to women caused in large measure by the poor quality of education available in most inner cities and many rural communities.

Prior to the 1950s, when the United States had a large number of low-skilled jobs available, African American men were able to achieve a high level of employment. They were therefore able to fulfill the traditional fathering role, i.e., providing material resources to their families. In that context, African Americans had a higher rate of marriage than that of the white population (Walker, 1988). However, in the last half of the twentieth century, the economy changed so that there were many fewer low-skilled jobs. This absence of employment opportunities and the continuing underinvestment in high-quality education for the majority of African American children left them unable to compete for good jobs in a high-technology economy. Thus, a large majority of African American men are unemployed or under-employed.

Research in both the United States (Stier & Tienda, 1993) and across many other countries (Barber, 2000) has shown that men who do not have jobs, and thus cannot fulfill the provider role, are less likely to marry, and less likely to pay child support if they are not married.

In societies with low sex ratios (i.e., fewer available men than women of marriageable age), both men and women tend to lose interest in marriage. Women have difficulty finding husbands who can contribute to their economic security; and available men have so many women to choose from that they tend to be reluctant to marry and thus cut off other mating opportunities (Barber, 2000). Barber (2001), using United Nations data for forty-two countries, found that a low sex ratio increased out-of-wedlock births, and was also the strongest predictor of teen births.

The inferior education available to poor women further exacerbates these trends, because without access to high-quality education (one that will improve their economic prospects), there is no advantage to delaying childbirth in order to complete more education. Women in the United States who had not graduated from high school had the highest level of nonmarital childbearing in 1998 (60 percent), compared to 38 percent among women who had graduated from high school (Bachu & O'Connell, 2001). Thus, limited educational opportunities for poor young women and men of color, combined with the absence of available men due to incarceration or death, result in high rates of unmarried childbearing.

Because of the absence of economic incentives, many of these young men and women do not marry and often do not establish cohabiting households. A study of unmarried parents in sixteen urban centers indicated that nearly three out of ten fathers were unemployed, and about half of the couples lived apart at the time of their child's birth (Fragile Families Research Brief, 2001).

In our research, we found that many of the mother–baby dyads lived with the mother's family or in foster-care agencies, while the fathers lived alone or with their own families (Edwards, 2001). This postmodern "bi-nuclear" family structure of two isolated family frameworks tends to be unstable, in part because it has no legal, religious, or socially sanctioned support networks.

It is important to note that in the United States, the issue of family composition has become so politicized that census statistics have been used to proclaim both "the demise" and "the return" of the nuclear family. Those who want to emphasize the decrease in the number of two-parent married families cite statistics such as: the rate of marriage among unmarried women declined from 73.5 per 1,000 in 1960 to 52.3 in 1993; or the divorce rate more than doubled during the last half of the twentieth century (Mclanahan & Carlson, 2001).

Those who want to argue that the trend away from nuclear families has not increased have pointed out that the proportion of children under the age of 18 being raised with two married parents has remained stable at about 70 percent (Dionne, 2001). However, this statistic includes step-families as nuclear families when they are usually considered blended families. Others have cited a slight (from 34.8 percent in 1995 to 38.9 percent in 2000) increase in African American children living in two-parent, married-couple homes (Blankenhorn, 2001) as evidence that the nuclear family is being revived among African American families.

Given these conflicting perspectives, identifying exactly what the trends are in the United States can be difficult. From our perspective, the terrorist attack of September 11, 2001, is responsible for this dramatic shift in the "family values" discourse in the United States. Prior to the attack, there was consternation on the political right about the negative impact on society of the increase in unmarried childbearing and divorce. Subsequent to the attack, the same social commentators who trumpeted the "crisis of fatherlessness" (Blankenhorn, 1995) suddenly began to emphasize the fact that "the trend of family fragmentation that many analysts had assumed to be unstoppable . . . suddenly stopped in its tracks in about 1995" (Blankenhorn, 2001).

We believe that the need to couch the U.S. war on terrorism as a battle between good and evil has made it necessary to stop characterizing trends in American family formation as morally bankrupt. Thus we now hear about "the good news on the family" (Dionne, 2001). However, from our point of view, the trends of a decline in marriage, an increase in cohabitation and nonmarital childbirth, and a 50 percent divorce rate have not reversed themselves.

Lesbigay Families

In addition to the changes in heterosexual families, the gay civil rights movement has resulted in a proliferation of lesbigay families. In previous historical periods, most gay men and women who wanted to have children got married and hid their gay identity, sometimes even from themselves. Men and women who lived an openly gay lifestyle rarely had children. Most lesbigay families were childless couples.

In the past fifteen years, particularly in the United States, there has been a lesbian baby boom. Most recently, openly gay men have also begun to form families with children, either through adoption, surrogacy, or in partnership with a lesbian or nongay woman. The 2000 Census reported that 594,391 families were headed by same-sex couples (Associated Press, 2001). This figure is probably an underestimate, because many lesbigay parents may be reluctant to report their lifestyle because of discrimination. Patterson and Freil (2000) estimated a range of between 800,000 and 7 million lesbigay parents raising between 1.6 and 14 million children.

Thus, just as heterosexual families now come in a variety of shapes and sizes, so too do lesbigay families. These combinations might occur in the same or multiple households. In our research on gay fathers, one family lived in a duplex, with the gay dad downstairs and the lesbian moms upstairs. The children had rooms in both apartments. Other gay and lesbian individuals choose to parent alone. Still others begin with one partner, "divorce," and re-couple, establishing a lesbigay step-family. Although lesbi-

gay families have traditionally been discriminated against in the legal system, some countries (e.g., The Netherlands, France, Denmark, Canada) and some states within the United States have made legal unions and child custody rights available to lesbigay families (Stacey & Bilbarz, 2001).

The (limited) body of research in the United States has almost uniformly reported no notable differences between children reared by heterosexual and homosexual parents (Patterson, 1995; Patterson & Chan, 1997). Much of this research has been motivated by the desire to show that, in contrast to the societal biases and institutionalized discrimination against lesbigay parents, there are no empirical data to suggest that homosexual parents are any less competent than heterosexual parents.

Stacey and Bilbarz (2001) have noted that this ideological pressure has constrained scholarly efforts to understand the complex similarities and differences between lesbigay and heterosexual parenting. In their reconsideration of twenty-one prior studies, they reframed the research question from "Does the sexual orientation of parents matter?" to "*How* does it matter?"

Their findings indicated that, on variables related to gender and sexuality, children raised by gay and lesbian parents do differ from children raised by nongay families. Lesbian mothers were less concerned with enforcing gender-"appropriate" activities, and, correspondingly, their children, especially daughters, more frequently exhibited attitudes and behaviors that did not conform to gender role norms. A significantly greater proportion of young adult children raised by lesbian mothers was open to the idea of same-sex relationships. Overall, being raised in a lesbigay family seemed to be associated with less gender-stereotyped behaviors.

Extended Families

Another version of the postmodern family is the resurrection of a family form that was the norm in earlier historical periods, the extended family. In the United States, this version of the family has emerged primarily when nuclear families are stressed to such an extent that they can no longer function without additional support. Because of the absence of governmental supports for families in the United States, extended family members must pitch in when families are stressed.

In the 2000 Census, 3.9 million families described themselves as multigenerational (Fields & Casper, 2001). The largest group was those where the grandparent was the householder and lived with both his or her children and grandchildren. The next largest group was grandparents living in the home of a child along with his or her children's children. A smaller group of families included grandparents and great-grandparents, as well as their children and grandchildren.

Thus the large number of children living with extended family in the United States deconstructs a cornerstone of conservative family ideology, that individual families can raise children alone, without the safety net of family benefits that all other Western industrialized countries provide their citizens. In this chapter we will discuss only two social factors that are increasing the numbers of extended families: immigration and AIDS.

Immigration.   In previous historical periods, immigration was most often a unidirectional process from a country of origin to a country of choice. In this earlier context, ties to the natal country were severely limited or severed completely. In postmodern societies, however, there is much more diversity in the relations families establish for themselves with both their natal country and their host country(ies) (Roopnarine & Shin, 2003). Some families form communities in more than one country, traveling back and forth in a manner that, over time and across generations, blurs the concepts of natal and host country. These transnational families have unique challenges in terms of defining their ethnic identity, healing disrupted attachments caused by long and/or frequent separations, and establishing family cohesion.

The complicated process of immigration frequently demands that one parent travel alone to a new country, often illegally and at great cost. This parent may then have to spend several years establishing a "beachhead" before sending for the other parent and their children. This beachhead usually requires that the immigrating parent live with other extended-family members who had arrived in the host country earlier. When the children do finally arrive, the high cost of living means that both parents must work, and extended family is then needed to provide childcare.

This pattern of parts of families living at great distances from each other and astride multiple cultures can also occur within national borders when one or both parents immigrate from a rural setting to an urban center in search of work. When space travel becomes available in future decades, we will probably have families splintered between planets or between solar systems.

Thus one version of the postmodern family is a splintered family, one that crosses borders and cultures. When the family is reunited in the new country (planet), intrafamily culture clash often occurs. The member(s) who have been in the new country for some time are in the process of creating a new creolized culture, one that combines aspects of both the host culture and the culture of origin. The more recently arrived members, in contrast, arrive with the original culture more or less intact. These contrasting cultural perspectives inevitably generate family stress. The family stress is exacerbated if some members of the family regularly return to the country of origin, cementing their commitment to the natal culture, while others remain in the host country, becoming more acculturated to the new culture.

Inclan (2003) has written about how these cultural clashes are enacted in marital relationships. He has pointed out that middle-class Latino couples often espoused an egalitarian gender ideology, while their behavior reflected a more traditional patriarchal stance. This inconsistency between behavior and ideology generated marital conflict. Roopnarine and Shin (2003) reported similar relationship stress in that Jamaican men who had immigrated to New York City supported the sexual double standard and male dominance characteristic of Caribbean relationships, whereas Jamaican women expressed intolerance for that traditional way of life.

Inclan (2003) has pointed out that working-class Latino couples typically reported very traditional attitudes about gender roles. However, in these families wives must enter the paid workforce in order for the family to achieve economic stability. The wife's entrance into the workplace required the husband to take on more responsibility at home. Thus the couple often developed more role-sharing behaviors and a more egalitarian relationship, despite their gender-traditional ideology.

Similarly, we have studied Caribbean (Haitian, Dominican, and Puerto Rican) and Mexican fathers who are creating a creolized version of the fathering role. This new version of fathering combines elements of the traditional Haitian/Latino provider/disciplinarian with aspects of the more progressive U.S. nurturing father (Woldenberg et al., in preparation). These attempts to integrate two cultural traditions produce internal inconsistencies in attitudes and behaviors that in turn generate role strain in individuals and conflict in families. The intensity and pervasiveness of the strain of living *entre dos mundos* is indicated by the overrepresentation of immigrant and transnational families in the social service system (Roopnarine & Shin, 2003).

AIDS. AIDS is another social cataclysm that requires the support of extended family. As parents become ill and die, grandparents, aunts, and uncles have found themselves in the parenting role, raising grandchildren, nieces, and nephews. Foster families and institutional families (orphanages) have also proliferated because of the breakup of biological families caused by drugs as well as AIDS.

These families are often severely traumatized, initially by drugs, then by the prolonged physical suffering that AIDS causes, and finally by the death of a parent, sibling, and sometimes of young children who contracted the disease *in utero*. In many cases, the grandparents caring for the children are elderly and infirm. The repeated traumas, combined with the stress of caring for young children, further weaken them.

Thus extended families are the informal support systems that provide aid to families that are splintered and traumatized. In the absence of governmental supports, they are a family's last resort for dealing with external stress.

Technologically Enhanced Families

Upper-middle-class families in the West now have various technological advances—e.g., artificial insemination, egg implantation, *in vitro* fertilization—that enable them to have children in circumstances that would have been unimaginable during prior historical periods. These techniques not only allow heterosexual, married couples to solve their fertility problems, they also provide opportunities for single women and lesbigay individuals and couples to become families with children.

Technology has also changed other aspects of family formation strategies. Egg implantation has dramatically increased the age at which women can become pregnant. Techniques of sperm separation allow families to choose the sex of their children. Perhaps, most remarkably, transgender sex-change techniques now enable mothers to become fathers, and fathers to become mothers. These advances in childbirth technology and gender transformations have resulted in families with sperm donors, rather than fathers; father-headed families with surrogates, rather than mothers; and transgendered mothers who have penises.

We do not yet know the psychological impact that these technological changes will have on children. Family therapists have routinely assumed that it was important for individuals to trace their families of origin over several generations (e.g., Kerr & Bowen, 1989). This theoretical framework has assumed that it is the emotional, rather than the biological, relationships that are important. However, even in the case of adoption, family therapists have recommended that children also learn about, and often meet, their biological parents. This is not possible for all adopted children. It depends on the method of adoption and the kinds of records that have been maintained. Will this be possible for the children of sperm and egg donors? If this information is not available to children of the new technology, what impact will it have on children if they cannot learn their donor's motivation for selling his sperm or her eggs?

Just as current technological advances were previously unimaginable for most of us, it seems reasonable to assume that even more radical technological "enhancements" will be developed. We believe that at some point in the future children may be harvested exclusively in laboratory environments, rather than in women's (or men's) bodies. After carefully fertilizing an egg *in vitro,* it is much riskier to implant an embryo back into a human body that could become ill, have an accident, etc., than to enclose it in the controlled, i.e., protected, environment of the laboratory.

Ultimately, we presume that human society will have to struggle with the ethical dilemma of cloning, a process that dispenses with parents altogether. Similarly, we can imagine that the future may produce individuals who are partially human and partially mechanical. It is at this point that our imagination fails us. Unlike Marge Piercy (1995), we cannot yet imagine the emotional and sexual relationships of families composed of combinations of human beings and androids.

FROM STABILITY TO CHANGE

Not only are the forms of family structures within broader societies becoming more diverse, but change characterizes the lives of most individual families. In the past, because of social pressures, religious sanctions, and women's economic dependence on men, most couples stayed married. In many postmodern societies, about 50 percent of heterosexual couples now embark on a coupling/uncoupling journey that often continues across their life span. Most individuals spend some time living on their own, then choose a partner and live together, then get married (if that legal option is open to them). Some individuals may cohabit with several partners before getting married.

A high percentage of married couples (e.g., about half in the United States; 40 percent in France) then get divorced, with children sometimes changing residences over the course of their childhood. Divorced parents may live with another partner (and his or her children), and then remarry, sometimes more than once. Children grow up; move on; return home to live for a few years; move out again; and move back in because of their own divorce or separation. Elderly parents may also join nuclear families for some part of their final years.

Roopnarine (2001) has described similar family formation strategies for poor young men and women in the English-speaking Caribbean. Men and women commonly have a "marriage career" that spans several types of relationships and living arrangements. These progressive mating relationships, which include childbearing in multiple unions and child-shifting between unions, take place in the context of difficult economic circumstances, migration patterns, and acculturative stresses.

The first phase begins with a "visiting" relationship, i.e., young people who have their first child, but live with their own parents in an extended-family context. Approximately 25 percent of childbearing relationships in the Caribbean are visiting unions. The next phase is cohabitation, i.e., at the birth of a subsequent child, young people typically choose to live together, either with the same partner or with a new partner, who may come with children from a previous relationship. Both visiting and cohabiting relationships are nonlegal unions, and comprise about 45 percent of the unions in the Caribbean. These types of relationships are more characteristic of Afro Caribbean than Indo Caribbean or Chinese Caribbean men.

Marriage usually occurs much later in life, often after some children have grown up and left home. For example, among Caribbean men over 50, 54.3 percent were married, 24.2 percent were in common-law relationships, and 8.9 percent were in visiting unions (Roopnarine, 2001). For men under 30, 9 percent were married, 41 percent were in common-law unions, and 45 percent were in visiting unions. Many women were single parents for at least some part of their lifetime. For example, 34 percent of households in Jamaica in 1997 were reported to be mother-headed. Similarly, in that same year 34 percent of households of Jamaican immigrant households in New York City were mother-headed.

In an earlier section, we talked about families that chose to live in an extended-family context in order to decrease the stress caused by immigration. However, there are other families that absorb periods of separation without an extended family to support them. For example, because of the need to pursue economic opportunities, fathers and mothers sometimes live in different cities for years at a time. Others are separated, even while living in the same house. This phenomenon is true of upper-class fathers (and some mothers) in high-technology industries who work 16-hour days 7 days a week and travel frequently.

We use the concept of elasticity to characterize these types of changes in individual families. Families contract and expand over the life span, depending on a variety of factors, particularly economic circumstances and developmental stages. Individuals can no longer assume that they will live in the same family constellation for the duration of their childhood.

FROM GENDERED PARENTING TO TRANSGENDERED FAMILIES

Role Sharing in Heterosexual Couples

Nancy Chodorow (1978) described how the traditional nuclear family, with its breadwinner/father and homemaker/mother, exemplified the expression of traditional gender ideology about parenting roles. As long as the gendered division of labor in the family existed, cultural gender ideology could claim that women were more biologically suited to nurture children, and men were more biologically suited to provide resources to the family. This ideology was contradicted by the existence of working-class and poor women, who have always worked for wages outside the home. However, it was not until large numbers of middle-class and upper-class women entered the workforce that cultural gender ideology about women's roles in the family expanded to encompass breadwinning as well as nurturing.

Although women have entered the workforce *en masse,* large numbers of men have not yet begun to share family work equitably. After an extensive review of the literature, Pleck (1997) concluded that the highest level of role sharing occurs in dual-shift families, where fathers are left alone with the children while mothers are at work. In this context of mother absence, fathers have no choice but to manage various aspects of childcare. Research has also shown that high paternal involvement is more likely when the mother's income is significant to the family's standard of living.

On average, Pleck (1997) found that fathers now assume approximately 30 percent of childcare duties. Although this represents an increase in role sharing over previous decades, men's involvement in childcare has been much slower to change than women's participation in paid employment. Pleck pointed out that research had not yet identified a single aspect of childcare in which fathers generally assumed primary parenting responsibility.

Hochschild (1989) called this uneven distribution of labor a "second shift" for mothers, and identified it as the most common cause of marital conflict. Deutsch (1999) and Dienhart (1998), in separate empirical studies, reported that the majority of dual-earner and dual-career couples in the United States continue to struggle with this inequality. Thus, although role sharing has increased somewhat, we cannot yet characterize most U.S. families as egalitarian. Similarly, in the early 1990s, Haas (1991) estimated that extensive role sharing actually exists in about 27 percent of Swedish families.

Degendering Parenting

In contrast to heterosexual families, in which the evolution toward role sharing has been slow, in our own research on gay fathers, we have found that these dads are de-gendering parenting in a number of ways (Benson, Silverstein, & Auerbach, in press; Schacher, Auerbach, & Silverstein, in preparation; Silverstein & Quartironi, 1996). Because gay dads live either alone or in a same-sex couple, there can be no gendered division of labor. The "new" gay fathers that we studied, i.e., men who established a gay lifestyle before having children, stated that they did not distinguish between "mothering" and "fathering." Rather, they thought only of "parenting." One of the dads called himself a "Mommy/Daddy" parent (Silverstein & Quartironi, 1996).

We also studied a sample of gay men who had children in the context of a heterosexual marriage, and only later established a gay identity (Benson, Silverstein, & Auerbach, in press). About 40 percent of our sample of twenty-one men reported that the process of coming out to their children transformed their relationships. This disclosure, because it involved talking about intensely personal issues including their sexuality, led to a deepened sense of intimacy with their children. The fathers reported that, after disclosure, there was nothing that could not be discussed between themselves and their children. Thus the intimacy was reciprocal: their children also became more open with their fathers, at least as reported by the fathers.

From our point of view, this level of intimacy between fathers and their children is more typical of mother–child relationships, and therefore represents a major reconstruction of the fathering role. In earlier research on heterosexual couples, "modern" fathers have been characterized as more emotionally intimate with their children, relative to their own fathers, or to fathers living with mothers who were not in the workforce. Thus the standard of comparison for the "new," or "nurturing" father has generally been other *men*. These gay fathers, in contrast, are comparable to *mothers* in terms of the intimacy they report having with their children. Thus we think of these gay postmodern fathers as transforming the fathering role beyond the "nurturing" father to the "intimate" father.

Just as gay dads are changing the gender ideology of families by "de-gendering" parenting, transsexual parents are reconstructing family roles in an even more dramatic way. The phenomenon of crossing gender boundaries entered mainstream U.S. culture with Demi Moore's portrayal of the only woman in an elite military unit in the movie *G.I. Jane.* At first, Moore suffered many of the traditional punishments for violating cultural gender norms, including being raped by a fellow soldier. However, her ultimate acceptance as "one of the guys" was symboli-

cally enacted in a later scene when she spontaneously exclaimed, "Suck my dick!" in the heat of an argument.

For many of us, that scene may have reflected a futuristic "elsewhere" where a single individual could transcend our binary definition of gender. However, for transsexual families, that elsewhere is the here and now. Ariel (2000) presented a videotaped interview of a couple (we will call them Leah and Sara) in which Sara, the person formerly known as the husband, was a male-to-female (MFT) transsexual. The wife, Leah, was pregnant with Sara's sperm. The transsexual process that Sara had undergone included breast implantation and hormone treatment, but stopped short of the genital operation. For Sara, becoming a woman and retaining a penis were not mutually exclusive.

Thus the couple had been transformed from a heterosexual couple into what appeared to be a same-sex couple, but which is more accurately defined as a transsexual couple. At one point in the interview, Ariel pointed out that their child was about to come into a family with two mothers. She then asked Sara what she planned to tell their child about being a mom with a penis. Sara calmly responded that she would explain that "some mothers have penises and others have vaginas."

Similarly, the *New York Times* described a lesbian family in which one of the partners decided to become a female-to-male transsexual (FMT). The couple already had one daughter, Hannah, and the "wife" was pregnant with their second child. The FMT member of the couple had undergone two mastectomies and had taken hormones, but decided to forego genital surgery—becoming a dad without a penis. The article reported that when a neighbor made a comment about her Daddy, Hannah replied, "He's not my Daddy. He was born a woman!" In two other families that we are familiar with in our private practices in psychotherapy, the fathers became male-to-female transsexuals during their children's adolescence. In each case, the children continued to call their male-to-female transsexual parent, "Dad."

Transsexual families place us on the cutting edge of cultural change. Our culture does not yet have the language with which to conceptualize the transformations these individuals will make in our thinking about families, about gender, and about sexuality.

FROM MALE DOMINANCE TOWARD A DISMANTLING OF PATRIARCHY

All human societies are male-dominant. Although some societies may have been matrilineal (property inherited through the mother's family), or matrifocal (married couples live with the wife's family), no human society has ever been matriarchal (women have institutionalized power over men).

However, from our perspective, many of the changes that we have outlined in this chapter reflect a lessening of male dominance in the postmodern era. For example, now that women in most countries are free to pursue higher education and can compete for well-paying jobs, they are no longer entirely dependent on men for the economic survival of themselves and their children. This economic independence has given them the power both to refuse to enter into, and to leave, unsatisfactory marriages. This power is a dramatic change from earlier historical periods, when the only means for leaving one's family of origin for most women was through marriage; and the only avenue for leaving one's marriage was death.

Because, on average, women's earnings now account for 40 percent of their family's income, we would expect women to have more power within the institution of marriage (Families and Work Institute, 1995). However, recent research on dual-earner families has indicated that the majority of U.S. men in dual-earner and dual-career marriages are not yet accepting an equal share of childcare and household responsibilities. These studies suggest that, despite the importance of the wife's income to the family's finances, in the majority of these families a realignment of power and privilege has not yet occurred (Deutsch, 1999; Dienhart, 1998; Bonney, Kelly, & Levant, 1999). Although these families talk the talk of egalitarian relationships, only a small number of them actually walk the walk. More typically, although fathers are definitely doing more childcare than in previous decades, mothers continue to have

that "second shift" to complete after returning home from paid employment.

Another fascinating finding in these studies was that the majority of couples did not deal directly with this problem. Both husbands and wives participated in denying the problem by overstating the amount of work the husbands did at home. Moreover, only a small percentage of the wives openly acknowledged the unfairness of the situation and tried to negotiate a more equitable arrangement. Most wives avoided dealing with their angry feelings.

We speculate that the unfairness of this arrangement, and the inability of the couples to deal with it directly, may be responsible for the fact that in the United States women now initiate two of three divorces. We hypothesize that women believe that they cannot win the battle for equality, so they are choosing to leave the marriage rather than to fight for equality within it.

If we add to those women choosing divorce the number of women who are choosing to have children without partnering with a man (e.g., single mothers by choice and lesbian mothers), the sheer numbers of men in families has lessened dramatically. As the numbers of heterosexual men in families has decreased over recent decades, the number of families headed by openly gay dads has increased. Thus, one result of the trends of diversity, change, and the degendering of parenting is the dismantling of the patriarchal family.

However, it is important to note that another important source of the dismantling of patriarchy is the minority of heterosexual men who have willingly relinquished some aspects of male power and privilege and established egalitarian, role-sharing families.

In our own research, we have found a variety of motivations underlying this change (Weinberg, 1996). Some of the men have been motivated by fairness. They realize that their wives work just as hard outside the home as they do, and they understand that it is unfair for her to have to shoulder more of the responsibility inside the home. They have been willing to relinquish male privilege out of a sense of justice. Others have been captivated by the warm, affectionate relationship they established with their children. They wanted to participate more in child-care because of the emotional gratification this interaction with their children provided.

Deutsch (1999) reported another group of husbands who participated in role sharing because they realized that they would not be able to have a positive relationship with their wives unless they assumed an equal share of childcare and household responsibilities. These men described their motivation as practical rather than ideological. There was so much work to be done, if they did not share it, their wives would be too preoccupied with childcare and too exhausted to be involved in the marital relationship.

We believe that this trend toward dismantling the patriarchal family, although slow, is inexorable. Although it is currently placing heterosexual men at the margins, rather than the center, of the majority of families, we see this marginalization as a transitional state. We think that more and more men will become motivated to establish authentically egalitarian relationships in order to enjoy the benefits of family life.

However, this egalitarianism requires dramatic changes, not just in women's and men's willingness to renegotiate married life, but also in societies at large. Major changes in both governmental policies for families and the culture of the workplace are also necessary. Changes in governmental policies have already occurred in most industrialized countries other than the United States. Countries such as Sweden and France already believe that the challenge of working and raising young children is a public, rather than a private, responsibility. Their generous family policies reflect this commitment. Governmental supports to families such as paid parental leave, subsidized high-quality day care, and flexible work hours are now routinely offered in most Western and Eastern European countries. Thus one could describe a postmodern family as a governmentally supported, rather than ruggedly individualistic, family structure.

Workplace reforms include: equal pay for equal work; the inclusion of women in nontraditional professions so that the majority of low-paying jobs are not held by women; job sharing so that women and men with young children can choose to work part-time; and a change in the chilly climate toward fathers who want to limit their commitment to paid work in order to share equal responsibility for childcare. These reforms have been less forthcoming than governmental family policies in most countries.

It is interesting to speculate as to why family support policies are commonplace, whereas workplace reforms are not. From our perspective, family support policies have emerged in most industrialized countries because they were necessary to enable women to continue to have children while also entering the workforce as replacements for the huge numbers of men who had been killed in World War II. The birth rate of European countries dropped precipitously at the same moment that women were needed as workers to fuel postwar economic recovery. Without governmental family policies, women would have had to choose either to work or to have families. Few could have accomplished both. Thus, the motivation for family support policies was to support societies that were male-dominant. These policies have resulted in economic independence for women, and ultimately are contributing to dismantling patriarchy, but their original motivation was quite different.

Reform of the workplace, in contrast, has as its explicit goal a leveling of the playing field for women. Like all dominant groups, men have been reluctant to relinquish power. Thus workplace reforms have been much slower to emerge, and probably will not become widespread until more women hold positions of power in economic and political spheres.

CONCLUSION

We have focused on the universality of change in constructing the lives of postmodern families. However, it is important to note that rapid social change generates societal anxiety—the sense that things are falling apart—and a corresponding change-back reaction (Kerr & Bowen, 1989). This change-back reaction also constructs contemporary family life.

In the United States, the pressure to change-back has emerged as a claim by the political right and religious fundamentalists that the heterosexual, married nuclear family is "the one right way" to raise children. In 2001, the U.S. Congress was contemplating an array of governmental initiatives to strengthen marriage and discourage divorce. These policies include reserving 5 percent to 10 percent of the national welfare budget for state programs such as premarital counseling, and a Covenant Marriage Act that requires couples to delay the decision to divorce while receiving counseling (O'Keefe, 2001). For example, West Virginia offered welfare recipients an extra $100 monthly if they get and remain married.

We and others have pointed out how these social policies fly in the face of social science research findings on marriage, divorce, father absence, and virtually every social problem that the policies are designed to address (Coontz, 1992; Silverstein & Auerbach, 1999; Stacy, 1996). The Fragile Families Project (2001) issued a report emphasizing the importance of steady employment, rather than marriage, to lifting unmarried single mothers out of poverty. However, despite the fact that neoconservative pseudo-scientific claims have been discredited, policy initiatives to privilege heterosexual married couples continue to emerge (Will, 2001).

In Ireland and Italy, one expression of the change-back reaction has been the government's refusal to embrace divorce as a viable social relationship. The result of this refusal has been that even fewer couples are getting married. We assume that efforts, such as the Covenant Marriage Act, that make divorce more difficult to obtain in the United States will backfire in a similar fashion.

We believe that the September 11, 2001, terrorist attack on the United States by fundamentalist muslims was an extreme version of the change-back reaction. Osama Bin Laden, the Saudi leader of the terrorist Al Qaeda network, has been quoted as saying that his motivation for attacking the West is to remove U.S. soldiers (and culture) from Saudi soil. We believe that fundamentalist Muslim culture, like fundamentalist Christian and Jewish cultures, is threatened by secular Western cultures primarily because these cultures represent the loss of male power and privilege. We speculate that Bin Laden is expressing the fear of loss of male dominance for the entire fundamentalist world. It is not an accident that he chose to live in Afghanistan, the most extreme version of male-dominant culture extant.

However, we believe as Stephanie Coontz (2000) has so eloquently pointed out, that "You can't put the toothpaste back in the tube." Thus, although the change-back reaction is inevitable, we predict that the changes we have identified as constructing postmodern families will persist and intensify. As Octavia Butler has so succinctly stated, "God is change."

REFERENCES

Ariel, J. (2000). Gay and lesbian interest group. A presentation at the annual meeting of the American Family Therapy Association, San Diego, CA.

Associated Press (2001, August 22). Gay couples found to head more homes. *The New York Times,* p. 22.

Bachu, A., & O'Connell, M. (2001). Fertility of American women. *Current Population Reports.* Washington, D.C: U.S. Census Bureau, U.S. Department of Commerce.

Barber, N. (2000). On the relationship between country sex ratios and teen pregnancy raters: A replication. *Cross-Cultural Research, 34,* 26–37.

Barber, N. (2001). On the relationship between marital opportunity and the sex ratio question. *Journal of Cross-Cultural Psychology, 32,* 259–268.

Benson, A. L., Silverstein, L. B., & Auerbach, C. F. (in press). From the margins to the center: Gay fathers reconstructing the fathering role. *Journal of GLBT Family Studies.*

Blankenhorn, D. (1995). *Fatherless America: Confronting our most urgent social problem.* New York: Basic Books.

Blankenhorn, D. (2001, October). Is the family structure revolution over? *American Values Reporter, 101.* Washington, D.C: Institute for American Values.

Bonney, J. F., Kelley, M. L., & Levant, R. F. (1999). A model of fathers' behavioral involvement in childcare in dual-earner families. *Journal of Family Psychology, 13,* 401–415.

Chodorow, N. (1978). *The reproduction of mothering.* Berkeley: University of California Press.

Coontz, S. (2000, June). Historical trends in family formation. Annual Conference of the American Family Therapy Association. San Diego, CA.

Coontz, S. (1992). *The way we never were.* New York: Basic Books.

Delgado, M. (1995). Trends in family formation: Spain. In H. P. Blossfeld (Ed.), *The new role of women. Family formation in modern societies* (pp. 191–210). Boulder, CO: Westview.

Deutsch, F. M. (1999). *Halving it all: How equally shared parenting works.* Cambridge, MA: Harvard University Press.

Dienhart, A. (1998). *Reshaping fatherhood: The social construction of shared parenting.* Newbury, CA: Sage.

Dionne, E. J. (2001, August 10). Return of the nuclear family. *The Washington Post,* p. A25.

Edwards, W. K. (2001). The parenting experiences of young African American fathers: A culturally relevant perspective. Psy.D. Research Project, Yeshiva University, Bronx, NY.

Families and Work Institute. (1995). *Women, the new providers.* New York: Whirlpool Foundation Study.

Fields, J., & Casper, L. M. (2001). American's Families and living arrangements. *Current Population Reports.* Washington, D.C: U.S. Census Bureau, U.S. Department of Commerce.

Fragile Families Research Brief. (2001). The fragile families update. Princeton, NJ: Center for Research on Child Wellbeing.

Haas, L. (1991). Equal parenthood and social policy: Lessons from a study of parental leave in Sweden. In J. S. Hyde & M. J. Essex (Eds.), *Parental leave and child care: Setting a research agenda* (pp. 375–405). Philadelphia: Temple University Press.

Hochschild, A. (1989). *The second shift.* New York: Viking.

Hoem, B. (1995). Trends in family formation: Sweden. In H. P. Blossfeld (Ed.), *The new role of women. Family formation in modern societies* (pp. 35–55). Boulder, CO: Westview.

Inclan, J. (2003). Class, culture, and gender contradictions in couples therapy with immigrant families. In L. B. Silverstein & T. J. Goodrich (Eds.), *Feminist family therapy: Empowerment and social location* (pp. 333–348). Washington, DC: American Psychological Association Books.

Kerr, M., & Bowen, M. (1989). *Family evaluation.* New York: Norton.

Leridon, H., & Toulemon, L. (1995). Trends in family formation: France. In H. P. Blossfeld (Ed.), *The new role of women. Family formation in modern societies* (pp. 77–101). Boulder, CO: Westview Press.

Mclanahan, S. S., & Carlson, M. (2001). Welfare reform, fertility and father involvement. Working Paper #01-13-ff. Princeton, NJ: Center for Research on Child Wellbeing.

O'Keefe, M. (2001, July 29). Politicians across the country are advocating marriage. *The Cleveland Plain Dealer,* p. A1.

Patterson, C. J. (1995). Lesbian mothers, gay fathers, and their children. In A. R. DeAugelli & C. F. Patterson (Eds.), *Lesbian, gay and bisexual identities over the lifespan* (pp. 262–290). New York: Oxford University Press.

Patterson, C. J., & Chan, R. W. (1997). Gay fathers. In M. E. Lamb (Ed.), *The role of the father in child development* (3rd ed., pp. 245–260). New York: Wiley.

Patterson, C. J., & Freil, L. V. (2000). Sexual orientation and fertility. In G. Bentley & N. Mascie-Taylor (Eds.), *Infertility in the modern world: Biosocial perspectives* (pp. 238–261). Cambridge, UK: Cambridge University Press.

Piercy, M. (1993). *He, she, it.* New York: Fawcett Books.

Pinnelli, A., & De Rose, A. (1995). Trends in family formation: Italy. In H. P. Blossfeld (Ed.), *The new role of women. Family formation in modern societies* (pp. 174–190). Boulder, CO: Westview.

Pleck, J. H. (1997). Paternal involvement: Levels sources, and consequences. In M. E. Lamb (Ed.), *The role of the father in child development* (3rd ed., pp. 66–103). New York: Wiley.

Roopnarine, J. L. (2002). Father involvement in English-speaking Caribbean families. In C. Tamis-Lemonda & N. Cabrera (Eds.), *Handbook on father involvement* (pp. 279–302). Hillsdale, NJ: Erlbaum.

Roopnarine, J. L., & Shin, M. (2003). Caribbean immigrants from English-speaking countries: Sociohistorical forces, migratory patterns, and psychological issues in family functioning. In L. L. Adler & U. P. Gielen (Eds.), *Migration, immigration and emigration in international perspectives* (pp. 123–142). Westport, CT: Greenwood Press.

Schacher, S., Auerbach, C. F., & Silverstein, L. B. (in press). Gay fathers. Degendering parenting. *Journal of GLBT Family Studies.*

Silverstein, L. B., & Auerbach, C. F. (1999). Deconstructing the essential father. *American Psychologist, 54,* 397–407.

Silverstein, L. B., & Quartironi, B. (1996). Gay fathers. *The Family Psychologist, 12,* 23–24.

Stacey, J. (1996). *In the name of the family.* New York: Beacon.

Stacey, J., & Bilbarz, T. J. (2001). (How) Does the sexual orientation of parents matter? *American Sociological Review, 66,* 159–183.

Stier, H., & Tienda, M. (1993). Are men marginal to the family? Insights from Chicago's inner city. In J. C. Hood (Ed.), *Men, work and family* (pp. 23–33). Newbury Park, CA: Sage.

Terry-Human, E., Manove, J., & Moore, K. A. (2001). *Births outside of marriage: Perceptions vs. reality. Research brief.* Washington, DC: Child Trends.

Walker, H. (1988). Black-white differences in marriage and family patterns. In S. M. Dornbusch & M. H. Strober (Eds.), *Feminism, children and the new families* (pp. 87–111). New York: Guilford.

Weinberg, N. (1996). Dual earner families. Psy.D. Research Project, Yeshiva University, Bronx, NY.

Will, G. F. (2001, June 7). Lethal Reticence. *The Washington Post,* p. A31.

Woldenberg, C. Z., Auerbach, C. F., Silverstein, L. B., Pegaro, A., & Tacher, S. (in preparation). Creolization. The evolution of fatherhood identities among Latino fathers.

PART TWO

ASIA AND OCEANIA

CHAPTER 4

THE FAMILY IN MAINLAND CHINA
STRUCTURE, ORGANIZATION, AND
SIGNIFICANCE FOR CHILD DEVELOPMENT

XINYIN CHEN
University of Western Ontario

YUNFENG HE
Shanghai Teachers' University

"Blood is thicker than water," an old Chinese proverb says.

The family may play a more important role in Chinese society than in most other societies in the world. Unlike Western cultures, Chinese culture views the family, rather than the individual, as the basic social unit. The achievement of an individual is evaluated mainly on the basis of the well-being and success of the family and the status of the individual in the family. Moreover, family structure and organization serve as a model for almost all other social groups, from peer friendship groups to formal government institutions. Understanding family functioning is fundamental to the study of Chinese society. Along with social, political, and economic transitions in China, Chinese families have experienced dramatic changes, especially since the establishment of the New China in 1949 and the initiation of the economic reforms in 1978. In this chapter, we will discuss social and cultural background for family functioning, and describe changes in the structure and organization of the family in mainland China.

We will also discuss how family context, including social-economic status and family relationships, may affect parenting beliefs and practices, and how socialization patterns in turn may play a role in child development in Chinese culture.

SOCIAL AND CULTURAL BACKGROUND

China has a total population of close to 1.3 billion people, the largest in the world. Most of the population (69.1 percent) lives in rural areas. The age distribution ranges from 25.4 percent for 0–14 years, 67.7 percent for 15–64 years, to 6.9 percent for 65 years and above (*Bulletin of China's Economic and Social Development,* 2000). There are fifty-six ethnic groups in China, with the Nan nationality representing about 91 percent of the population of the country. As individuals of different nationalities communicate and interact with each other (mostly with those in the Han nationality), interethnic marriages have become increasingly common. Consequently, minority ethnic families are similar to Han families in many aspects.

Chinese society is relatively homogenous in cultural background, with Confucianism serving as a predominant ideological guideline for family functioning and individual behavior. In addition to Confucian philosophy, Taoism, an indigenous religious belief system in Chinese culture, has exerted significant impact on values and lifestyles of Chinese people, especially in the group with no or little education. A general feature of Chinese culture is that individual behaviors are often interpreted and discussed in a broad context, in terms of their connections and interactions with social relationships, societal norms, and ecological factors. This holistic view is reflected in Taoist concern about how one lives in relation to one's natural conditions (e.g., climate, food, resources) and in Confucian notions about how one lives in one's social environment. Achieving and maintaining harmonious family functioning and relationships is particularly emphasized in Confucian doctrines.

Consistent with the holistic perspective, the Chinese collectivistic orientation is highly attentive to the order and stability of the society. The interests of the individual are considered to be subordinated to those of the collective. Selfishness, including seeking individual benefits at the expense of group interests and indifference to group interests, is regarded as a cardinal evil (Ho, 1986; King & Bond, 1985).

Accordingly, the acquisition of the well-being of the family is regarded as a major goal in human life. In addition to their duties in providing social and financial support to the family, for example, adults are required to focus on child education and training. It is important for parents, particularly the father, who has the most responsibility to maintain and enhance the reputation of the family, to help children achieve to the highest level (Ho, 1987). Child education and socialization are central themes in the organization of the Chinese family because achievement of the young generation is closely linked to the status of the family. The child's failure in social and academic performance may bring disgrace and shame to parents and ancestors (Luo, 1996). To facilitate the socialization process, children are encouraged to pledge obedience and reverence to elders, which is indicated in the traditional Confucian notion of filial piety. As an attitude of warmth toward elders, filial piety was considered the "root of all virtues" and served as a philosophical and moral basis for family organization, including childrearing (Ho, 1986).

THE CHANGING CHINESE FAMILY

China has been an agricultural society for thousands of years. Due to relatively limited resources, a large proportion of the population has lived under adverse conditions during most periods of its history. A traditional Chinese family is usually a large, joint family, consisting of three or four generations. In the feudal period of China, families were authoritarian and hierarchical, with dominance by elders and men (Lang, 1968). The hierarchy in the family was backed by legal and moral rules, such as filial piety for children and the "three rules of obedience" for women (an unmarried girl should obey her father; a married woman, her husband; and a widow, her son). While some conventions and rules of the feudal family, such as dominance of elders, are retained in contemporary China, the structure and organization of Chinese families have changed in the last century.

Economic, Educational, and Health Conditions

The living standard in most parts of China has improved significantly in the past fifty years, especially since the economic reforms started in 1978. According to China State Statistics ("Achievement of the Family Planning Programs in China," 2000), in comparison to the annual per-capita income of 100 and 50 yuan for urban and rural areas in 1949, the annual per-capita income was 2,987 yuan (approx. US$360) for rural residents and 5,889 yuan (approx. US$710) for urban residents in 1999. The total poverty-stricken population was still 250 million in 1978, but dropped to 43 million in 1998. The per-capita living area was 8.8 square meters space for urban residents, and 22.46 square meters for rural residents in 1998. There is a continuing movement of urbanization in China. Over the past two decades, with economic development, China has created nonagricultural jobs for more than 250 million people, with 130 million laborers having been transferred from the agricultural to nonagricultural sectors.

China is working toward nine-year compulsory education. As reported in the *Bulletin of China's Economic and Social Development in 1999* (*Bulletin*, 2000), the program has covered approximately 75 percent of the total population. The enrollment rate for school-age children was 99.1 percent at the elementary school level and 88.5 percent at the junior high school level. Illiteracy has declined rapidly in recent years (23.5 percent in 1978, 12.01 percent in 1997). Among the young and adults, illiteracy has been reduced to 5.5 percent. About 42.5 percent of the population aged 25 years or older has received a secondary education.

Health conditions have also been improved significantly. The death rate dropped from 33 per thousand in 1949 to 6.5 per thousand in 1998. The rate of individuals who suffered from contagious diseases was 20,000 per 100,000 in 1949, but was 203 per 100,000 in 1998. The mortality rate of pregnant women and women in labor was 1,500 per 100,000 in 1949, and 56.2 per 100,000 in 1997. Most children (63.5 percent in 1997) are now delivered in the hospital. The infant death rate was 200 per thousand in 1949, but dropped to 33.1 per thousand in 1997. The life expectancy has gone from 35 years 50 years ago, to 70.83 years in 1998 (73.11 and 69.36 for women and men, respectively).

Family Structure

First, due to some social-economic factors (e.g., limited housing area in the cities), large, or joint, families have decreased in number, and small, nuclear families have increased in number. Nevertheless, there are still many "medium-sized" families in China in which three generations (parents of husband or wife, husband and wife, and children—usually only one child) live together. About a third of families consist of three generations (Chen, 1998). Four- or five-generation families are rare now (less than 0.3 percent), because most people get married in their middle to late twenties. According to a recent survey (*Bulletin*, 2000), the average family size was 4.79 persons in 1985 and 3.58 persons in 1999.

Because of the cultural emphasis on interdependence among family members, most families have very close social and financial connections with the parents of the husband and wife. In many cases, parents provide financial support to the young family, and help with childcare and child education. However, some senior people (about 3 percent; Xu & Ye, 1999) need financial support from their children, especially in rural areas.

The divorce rate is generally low, but is growing in China (Liu, 1998). Particularly among the young generation with high educational levels, divorce is no longer regarded as shameful. The divorce rate has risen rapidly since 1980 (less than 5 percent in 1980, 11.4 percent in 1995, and 13 percent in 1997; Ni, 2000). It is higher in major cities such as Shanghai and Beijing, reaching 25 percent in 1997. Thus, in urban areas, the number of single-parent families has increased considerably in the recent past.

Since the late 1970s, China has implemented a one-child-per-family policy. This policy has apparently been highly successful, especially in urban areas. The birth rate has declined dramatically, from 33.43/1,000 in 1970 to 15.23/1,000 in 1999 ("Achievement," 2000). As a result, the majority of children (over 95 percent) in urban areas are "only" children. A "four-two-one" family structure (four grandparents, two parents, and one child) is the norm in urban areas. Although the only-child policy has not been so successful in rural areas, it is the case that most families do not have as many children as in traditional families.

MARITAL RELATIONSHIPS

Since the Communists took power in China, the first State Marriage Law was promulgated and took effect in 1951, and then was revised in 1980. According to the law, the convention of parental arrangement of marriage must be abolished. Men and women should be allowed to choose their own marriage partners. Monogamy is the only legitimate form of marriage partners. Husband and wife in the family should have equal social and financial status. Women's rights in education, employment, and social and political affairs are specified in other related policies and laws, which clearly have implications for family relationships. For example, it is stipulated that there is a 3-month maternal leave with full salary (an extra 15 days if the family decides to have only one child). In addition, the mother is allowed to have 1 hour for breastfeeding during work time in the first year of the child's life.

Status of Man and Woman in the Family

As a result of the effort to improve women's social, political, and economic status in the family and society, substantial changes have occurred in Chinese women's lives. According to the results of a recent survey (Xu & Ye, 1999), inconsistent with the traditional practice that marriage is controlled by parents, about 86 percent of marriages are now decided by the husband and wife, and only 14 percent are

arranged by parents. In general, almost all adult women work outside the home, and have almost the same level of salary as men. In 1997, for example, about 90 percent of women between the ages of 20 and 49 years in urban areas were employed; female workers accounted for 46.5 percent of total employed people (Ni, 2000).

In the family, women are now involved in decision making on major activities. In a study conducted among eight hundred families in Shanghai, Guan Su, Guangzhou, and Harbin (Xu & Ye, 1999), it was found that decisions about family affairs were made by the husband in about 31 percent of the families, by the wife in 16 percent of the families, and by both in 53 percent of the families. Interestingly, men and women appear to play different roles in specific family affairs. Whereas women were more likely to decide on family financial plans and activities, housework, leisure time arrangements, and social relationships with relatives and others, men were more responsible for decisions concerning child education and traditionally "men's" work such as renovating the house and repairing furniture. Men typically spent about 16 hours per week on household chores such as cooking, cleaning, and doing laundry. In contrast, women spent much more time, 28 hours per week, on housework. Nevertheless, most women (about 78 percent) believed that the housework assignment between wife and husband was very fair or relatively fair (Xu & Ye, 1999).

It should be noted that substantial differences exist in marital relationships between urban and rural areas. Many of the rights and privileges, such as maternal leave and equal salary for men and women for the same job, are provided to women only in the city. In rural areas, because of their physical disadvantages in farming, which still relies on manual labor and primitive techniques, a large proportion of women (over 60 percent) reported that they had to depend on their husband financially. As a result, it was found that men made major decisions in 51 percent of families, and only 18.3 percent of men shared daily housework duties with their wife (Xu & Ye, 1999). Compared with their counterparts in urban China, women in rural areas were less satisfied with their marital relationships because they were not respected by their husbands (Xu & Ye, 1999).

Affective Quality of Marital Relationship

The affective aspect of marital relationship has been largely neglected in traditional Chinese culture. The main purpose of marriage is for the continuation of the family, and, thus, intimacy in spousal relationship is discouraged because it may undermine the couple's commitment to the whole family. Marriage is maintained by requiring the husband and wife to take their hierarchical roles as prescribed by the culture, and by "showing politeness and admiration to each other (mostly wife to husband) like to a guest."

There is little empirical research on affect in marital relationship in Chinese families. In a longitudinal project we conducted in Shanghai (Chen, Rubin, Li, & Li, 1999), it was found that men and women reported a similar level of satisfaction with marriage ($M = 4.86$ and 4.74 on a 7-point rating scale). The highest spousal conflict was about child education, which indicated the importance of child-rearing and education in Chinese families. It was found that family income was not related to the quality of marital relationships. However, parental education, especially maternal education, was positively associated with, and predictive of, self-reported marital satisfaction and low level of spousal conflict. Interestingly, parental age was positively associated with marital conflict and dissatisfaction, although the magnitude of the associations was weak. According to Xu and Ye (1999), perceived equal status of husband and wife is a major predictor of satisfaction of marital relationship in Chinese families. The decline of marital satisfaction with age may indicate increased differences on social and financial status between husband and wife in the family as the man gradually acquires relatively higher achievement in his career.

New Challenges in Marital Relationships

As a result of the development of a market economy and the introduction of Western values to China, some salient phenomena concerning family organization have appeared in recent years. First, many women in urban areas were laid off. For example, among all workers who were laid off in 1997, women constituted 59 percent (Xu & Ye, 1999). In other words, 10.9 percent of women lost their jobs. In contrast, only 4.5 percent of men were laid off in that year. The changes in economic conditions for women may affect their status and rights in the society and in the family. A survey showed that violence between spouses was reported in 30 percent of the families, rising at a rate of 15–18 percent annually in the past 10 years, with women often being the victim ("Achievement," 2000), mainly because women's economic status declined in the family. Actual violence might be even higher than what the data indicated. Many violent incidents were not reported because they were considered private affairs within the family.

In addition to the rapid growth of the divorce rate, traditional conservative attitudes about sexual behaviors have changed. It was recently found that 8.2 percent of married adults had extramarital sexual relationships ("Achievement," 2000; Liu, 1998). Whereas this rate is still low compared with that in the West, it represents a significant change in Chinese society. Furthermore, it was found that 2.4 percent of men had an illegal "second wife" ("Achievement," 2000). The problem is particularly serious in parts of Southern China such as Guang Zhou and Sheng Zhen, perhaps because many men in these areas have become wealthy by doing business and can afford to raise two "families." Given the potential threat to the stability of the family and the society, the China People's Congress is currently discussing strategies to deal with legal disputes that are involved in this type of marital problem.

PARENTING GOALS AND PRACTICES

Socialization in Western cultures focuses on how individuals adjust to social and nonsocial environments. Based on the Darwinian notion of adaptation, most developmental theories such as Piaget's cognitive development theory and the ethological perspective on social relationships emphasize the acquisition of personal autonomy, competence, and psychological well-being as the primary goal of human development (Baltes & Silverberg, 1994; Steinberg, 1990). Since it is believed that a sensitive and inductive parenting approach may enhance children's independence, perceptions of self-worth, and "individuation" (Steinberg, 1990), parents are encouraged to be sensitive to their children's needs, to understand children's abilities and behaviors from a "child-centered" perspective, and to use low-power parenting strategies such as guidance and reasoning in childrearing.

The holistic perspective in Chinese culture emphasizes the importance of group context for individual development. It is believed, for example, that it may be difficult to achieve internal emotional stability and psychological well-being in a conflictual family or peer-group environment. Discord or disorganization in interpersonal relationships will eventually be reflected in individual adjustment. Consistently, collectivistic principles underlie the interests of the group, especially when they are in conflict with those of the individual. Pursuing personal needs and autonomy is considered selfish and anticollective and is thus discouraged (Cen, Gu, & Li, 1999). Given this background, it is not difficult to understand that the primary goal of socialization in Chinese culture is to help children develop behaviors that are beneficial for the harmony and welfare of the collective.

Parenting Styles

As required by the socialization goal, the main task of parents in China is to train their children to control individualistic behaviors and to display cooperative-compliant and interdependent behaviors. To help children understand collectivistic norms and values and learn group-oriented ideologies and behaviors such as conformity and self-control, maintaining parental authority is believed to be essential in childrearing in Chinese culture (e.g., Luo, 1996). According to the Confucian doctrine of filial piety, children must obey their parents, and parents in turn are responsible for governing or disciplining their children (e.g., Ho, 1986). Thus, the culture endorses parental use of high-power strategies and emphasizes

child obedience, and Chinese parents are encouraged to use restrictive and controlling childrearing strategies (e.g., Chao, 1994; Ho, 1986).

Because of the high emphasis on parental control and directiveness in the culture, Chinese parents may perceive affective involvement as relatively unimportant for children's social and cognitive development. Maintaining parental authority may require the control of emotional and affective reactions in parent–child interactions. As authority figures in the family, parents may find it difficult to engage in intimate communication and to express affection explicitly to their children. In Confucian philosophy, emotional expression during interpersonal interactions is generally viewed as socially inappropriate; highly expressive individuals may be regarded as poorly regulated and socially immature (Chen & Swartzman, 2001; Ho, 1986; Kleinman & Good, 1985).

Findings from several research programs appear to support the arguments about childrearing attitudes and practices in Chinese parents. Compared with Western parents, Chinese parents appear more controlling and power-assertive, and less responsive and affectionate to their children (e.g., Chao, 1994; Chen et al., 1998; Dornbusch et al., 1987; Kelley, 1992; Lin & Fu, 1990; Wu, 1981). For example, Chinese parents are highly concerned with children's behavioral and emotional control. They are less likely to use reasoning and induction and appear more authoritarian than Western parents. Chinese parents are also less likely to encourage their children to be independent, curious, and exploratory. Finally, it has been found that Chinese parents are less affectionate toward their children and more punishment-oriented than North American parents (Chen et al., 1998). Of course, like their counterparts in the West, Chinese parents are not identical. There are substantial individual differences in parental beliefs and behaviors within Chinese culture. Nevertheless, relative to parents in other cultures, Chinese parents, as a group, display distinctive patterns of parenting styles and practices, which may be shaped by culturally prescribed socialization goals and expectations.

Family Economic, Social, and Psychological Conditions and Parenting

Family capital resources including income and housing conditions generally have little impact on child-rearing styles and practices of Chinese parents. In a study conducted in Shanghai (Chen & Rubin, 1994), it was found that parents from families with relatively higher income were perceived by their children as *less* warm and sensitive. The results were inconsistent with those found in Western societies (e.g., Lempers, Clark-Lempers, & Simons, 1989). It should be noted that economic status was not associated with educational or occupational levels, at least in the early 1990s. Parental educational and occupational levels, which indicated family *social status* in China, have been found to be related to childrearing practices (e.g., Chen & Rubin, 1994; Chen et al., 2000a). In general, parents with higher educational and occupational levels report greater acceptance of the child, and they are more likely to use inductive reasoning in childrearing. Moreover, children of parents who have high social status perceive their parents as more affectionate, responsive, and understanding than children of parents with low social status. It is possible that parents with a high education are more likely to understand the importance of warm and inductive parenting for the development of positive parent–child relationships and competent behavior in children. In addition to parental acceptance, it has been found that parents who have a high education are likely to emphasize independence in childrearing and to encourage their children to be curious and exploratory. In contrast, parents with low educational and occupational status tend to value conformity and obedience (Chen et al., 2000a). Again, variations in these childrearing practices may be due to different parental beliefs and values about child independence and exploration.

Consistent with Western findings (e.g., Booth, Rose-Krasnor, McKinnon, & Rubin, 1994), family psychological conditions, such as the quality of the marital relationship, the availability of social support systems, and overall family functioning, are related to parenting practices in China. For example, we have found that parental reports of marital harmony, satisfaction, and cohesion are positively related to parental warmth and acceptance and parental supervision of the child. In contrast, parents who have a conflict-laden marriage tend to be rejecting and hostile in parenting (Chen & Rubin, 1994).

Parenting and Child Functioning

What are the relations between parental affection and power assertion and child behavior in Chinese culture? For example, is parental emotional responsiveness relevant to social and academic adjustment in Chinese children? Does parental power assertion reinforce or inhibit deviant behavior such as aggression? Investigation of these issues is important for our understanding of the meaning of parenting practices in a cultural context, as well as for the development of family-based prevention and intervention programs in China. For example, if high-power parenting is associated with child behavioral problems, it would be an important component of the remediation program to help parents change their controlling parenting attitudes and behaviors, even though high-power parenting may be endorsed by Chinese culture.

Researchers have argued that such parenting styles as parental warmth and parental authoritarianism were initially developed based on Western cultures (Baumrind, 1971). Given the specific values and norms about parental authority and child obedience in Chinese culture, these parenting constructs may have different functional "meanings" or may not be relevant to social, cognitive, and emotional functioning in Chinese children (Chao, 1994; Kleinman & Good, 1985; Steinberg, Dornbusch, & Brown, 1992). Inconsistent with this argument, however, our recent studies have clearly demonstrated that fundamental dimensions such as parental warmth are associated with child adjustment "outcomes" in a virtually identical fashion in Chinese and Western cultures (e.g., Chen, Dong, & Zhou, 1997a; Chen, Rubin, & Li, 1997b; Chen et al., 2000a). As suggested in the Western literature (Rohner, 1986), parental warmth and affection may constitute a social and emotional resource that allows children to explore their social and nonsocial environments and contribute to the development of social and cognitive competence. Moreover, parental warmth may be a protective factor that buffers against the development of socioemotional problems such as depression (Chen, Rubin, & Li, 1997b; Chen et al., 2000a).

Similarly, concerning Baumrind's typology of parenting styles (1971), it has been found that authoritarian parenting is associated positively with aggression and negatively with social competence, distinguished studentship, and school academic achievement. In contrast, parental authoritative style is associated positively with indices of social and school adjustment and negatively with adjustment problems (Chen et al., 2000a; Chen et al., 1997a). It is possible that coercive, power-assertive, and prohibitive strategies that authoritarian parents use in childrearing may lead to the child's negative emotional and behavioral reactions such as fear, frustration and anger, which in turn are associated with adjustment problems. Since authoritative parenting provides explanation, guidance, and communication of affect, it may help the child develop feelings of confidence and security in the exploration of the world and positive parent–child relationships, which, in turn, are associated with children's social and cognitive competence. Thus, it may be reasonable to argue that, regardless of cross-cultural differences between Chinese and North American parents in the average levels of authoritativeness and authoritarianism, the functional meanings of these parenting styles in Chinese culture are similar to those typically found in the Western literature (e.g., Baumrind, 1971; Maccoby & Martin, 1983).

Differential Roles of Mothers and Fathers in Socialization

In Western cultures, fathers and mothers differ, both quantitatively and qualitatively, in childcare, childrearing, and parent–child interactions. Typically, fathers spend significantly less time than mothers in routine caregiving and interacting with children (Lamb, 1987; Parke & Buriel, 1998; Russell & Russell, 1987). Moreover, whereas mothers are likely to

engage in a variety of activities including affection provision, verbal communication, daily life care, and helping with children's schoolwork, fathers are more actively involved in play activities (Parke & Buriel, 1998). During adolescence, whereas mothers are likely to help children develop communal and interpersonal skills, fathers may help them develop independence and autonomy by acting like a "peerlike" playmate (Parke & Buriel, 1998).

Like their Western counterparts (Larson & Richards, 1994; Parke & Buriel, 1998), Chinese mothers are regarded as important for providing care and affection to the child (Ho, 1987). Unlike Western fathers, who often interact with the child like a playmate, however, Chinese fathers engage in few play activities with children (e.g., Ho, 1987; Roopnarine, Lu, & Ahmeduzzaman, 1989). This may be due to the fact that children's play is perceived as unimportant for development, or a "waste of time," in Chinese culture. The role of the father in the family is mainly to help children achieve in academic areas, learn societal values, and develop appropriate behaviors (Ho, 1986).

In a study we conducted in Shanghai, China (Chen, Liu, & Li, 2000b), it was found that, according to child self-reports, mothers and fathers were equally warm and affective toward their children. However, parental warmth had differential contributions to children's adjustment in specific areas. Whereas maternal warmth significantly predicted later *emotional* adjustment, including feelings of insecurity, loneliness, depression, and perceived self-worth, paternal warmth significantly predicted later *social and school* adjustment, including social preference, peer- and teacher-assessed social competence, aggression-disruption, and academic achievement.

The differential contributions of maternal and paternal warmth to social, academic, and psychological adjustment were rather interesting. It is possible that parental warmth may be manifested differently in fathers and mothers' behaviors and in father–child and mother–child interactions. Compared with fathers, mothers may be more sensitive to the child's emotional well-being and problems (e.g., Ho, 1986). They are also more likely to provide social support and assistance when children experience psychological problems and emotional distress. As a result, maternal warmth may be helpful for children in coping with their emotional problems. Children whose mothers are insensitive and unresponsive to their emotions and feelings may develop negative self-regard and loneliness and depression. In contrast, although fathers are encouraged to participate in childrearing in Chinese culture, they may pay attention mainly to their children's performance and problems in social and academic areas, as required by the cultural conventions (Ho, 1987). Paternal warmth may be expressed as providing guidance and assistance to children in learning social skills, acquiring social status, and achieving in academic areas. Consequently, children of sensitive and warm fathers may become more competent socially and academically than children who have relatively cold or hostile fathers.

It was also found that paternal control, but not maternal control, might moderate the development of social and academic competence (Chen et al., 2000b). Paternal control positively predicted later social competence for children who were initially competent. At the same time, however, paternal control also positively predicted social problems for children who displayed problems. Thus, it appears as if paternal control may promote adaptive development for children who are well adjusted, but exacerbate behavioral problems for children who have difficulties. As argued by Chen et al. (2000b), paternal monitoring and control may be useful for children who have basic skills to achieve further social status and become more competent. However, for children who constantly experience frustration in social interactions and lack self-regulatory abilities, paternal control and restraint may increase negative emotional and behavioral reactions, which, in turn, may lead to rebellious and deviant behaviors. As a result, these children may develop further adjustment problems.

Finally, it was found in this study that paternal indulgence, but not maternal indulgence, had significant and negative contributions to the prediction of later leadership, social competence, and academic achievement. Furthermore, paternal indulgence significantly and positively predicted later aggressive-disruptive behaviors. Thus, children who had indulgent fathers tended to be less competent and more maladjusted than others in both social and academic areas. The results seem to suggest that maternal indulgence, lenience, and tolerance of child impulsive and self-centered behaviors are relatively "normative" and thus may not lead to adjustment problems in children. However, because fathers are usually expected to place requirements on children and train children (Ho, 1987), paternal indulgence may indicate a lack of parental coordination in childrearing and threaten the conventional role structure of the family for socialization. As a result, children who have indulgent fathers may not have adequate opportunities to learn social, behavioral, and learning skills such as self-control that are required for successful social and school performance (Chen et al., 2000b).

ONLY CHILDREN VERSUS SIBLING CHILDREN

The "one-child-per-family" policy has been implemented for over 20 years in China. An important issue concerning the impact of this program is how it affects parental behavior, which in turn affects children's social and behavioral development. Many parents and educators in China are concerned about whether "only" children are indulged or overindulged in the family (Jiao, Ji, & Jing, 1980; Tao & Chiu, 1985). Early reports from China tend to suggest that only children may have more negative behavioral qualities and adjustment problems, including impulsiveness, aggressiveness, selfishness, poor peer relationships, and high demand for immediate satisfaction (e.g., Jiao et al., 1980). More recent studies have indicated that, as a group, only children may not differ significantly from sibling children (e.g., Chen, Rubin, & Li, 1994). According to Falbo and Poston (1993), where differences are present, only children are taller and weigh more than sibling children, and only children have better verbal abilities. Similar findings have been reported by others (e.g., Rosenberg & Jing, 1996).

The discrepancies between results in early and recent studies concerning only children may be related to changes in childrearing and childcare conditions in China. Increased numbers of children have received preschool education and daycare in the past 20 years, particularly in urban areas. Many children in urban areas go to public nursery centers at a very young age because most parents work outside the home. Almost all children now enter kindergarten at the age of 4 or 5 years and primary school at about the age of 7 years. The same early out-of-home care experiences may weaken the different parental influences on only and sibling children. Participation in a variety of collective activities in public settings may compensate, to some extent, for the lack of sibling interactions for only children. Furthermore, it has been indicated that only children may have advantages in health and educational conditions; as a result, they may develop higher intellectual ability and social competence than children with siblings (Ho, Peng, & Lai, 2001).

CONCLUDING COMMENTS

In this chapter, we described structural and organizational characteristics of families in mainland China, and discussed the significance of family context for child development. Several issues need to be considered for further understanding of Chinese families. First, social and economic conditions differ dramatically across regions, particularly between urban and rural areas, which obviously affects family functioning. We have paid particular attention to potential effects of regional differences in our discussion. Because of practical restraints, however, most of the research programs described in the chapter have been conducted in urban samples. Generalization of the findings (e.g., the relations between parenting styles and child behavior) to different areas should be made with caution.

Second, China is a socialist/communist country under strict control of the central government. Family organization, interpersonal relationships, and individual behaviors are often influenced by official social, political, and economic policies such as the only-child population policy. Thus, it is important to understand the Chinese family in a larger social context.

Finally, traditional cultural values and ideologies play a major role in guiding and regulating the organization of Chinese families. Because of its enduring and resilient nature (Ho et al., 2001), the culture will probably continue to exert influence on family functioning for a long time. However, it should be noted that China is in transition toward a market economy. During this process, values and customs imported from other cultures, particularly Western cultures, constitute a serious challenge to the traditional pattern of family organization. It will be interesting to investigate, in the future, how Chinese families adapt to the changing circumstances.

ACKNOWLEDGMENTS

The preparation of the chapter was supported by grants from the Social Sciences and Humanities Research Council of Canada and by a Faculty Award from the William T. Grant Foundation.

REFERENCES

Achievement of the family planning program in China (2000, November 7). *The People's Daily (Overseas Edition)*, p. 1.

Baltes, M. M., & Silverberg, S. B. (1994). The dynamics between dependency and autonomy: Illustrations across the life span. In D. L. Featherman, R. M. Lerner, & M. Perlmutter (Eds.), *Life-span development and behavior* (pp. 41–90). Hillsdale, NJ: Erlbaum.

Baumrind, D. (1971). Current patterns of parental authority. *Developmental Psychology Monograph, 4*(1, Pt. 2).

Booth, L. C., Rose-Krasnor, L., McKinnon, J., & Rubin, K. H. (1994). Predicting social adjustment in middle childhood: The role of preschool attachment security and maternal style. *Social Development, 3*(3), 189–204.

Bulletin of China's economic and social development in 1999 (2000, February 29). Beijing: Xin Hua She.

Cen, G., Gu, H., & Li, B. (1999). *The new development of research on moral psychology.* Shanghai: Xue Lin Publication House.

Chao, R. K. (1994). Beyond parental control and authoritarian parenting style: Understanding Chinese parenting through the cultural notion of training. *Child Development, 65,* 1111–1119.

Chen, X. (1998). The changing Chinese family: Resources, parenting practices, and children's socio-emotional problems. In U. P. Gielen & A. L. Comunian (Eds.), *Family and family therapy in international perspective* (pp. 150–167). Trieste: Edizioni LINT.

Chen, X., Dong, Q., & Zhou, H. (1997a). Authoritative and authoritarian parenting practices and social and school adjustment. *International Journal of Behavioral Development, 20,* 855–873.

Chen, X., Hastings, P., Rubin, K. H., Chen, H., Cen, G., & Stewart, S. L. (1998). Childrearing attitudes and behavioral inhibition in Chinese and Canadian toddlers: A cross-cultural study. *Developmental Psychology, 34,* 677–686.

Chen, X., Liu, M., Li, B., Cen, G., & Chen, H. (2000a). Maternal authoritative and authoritarian attitudes and mother–child interactions and relationships in China. *International Journal of Behavioral Development, 24,* 119–126.

Chen, X., Liu, M., & Li, D. (2000b). Parental warmth, control and indulgence and their relations to adjustment in Chinese children: A longitudinal study. *Journal of Family Psychology, 14,* 401–419.

Chen, X., & Rubin, K. H. (1994). Family conditions, parental acceptance and social competence and aggression. *Social Development, 3*(3), 269–290.

Chen, X., Rubin, K. H., & Li. B. (1994). Only children and sibling children in urban China: A re-examination. *International Journal of Behavioral Development, 17*(3), 413–421.

Chen, X., Rubin, K. H., & Li, B. (1997b). Maternal acceptance and social and school adjustment in Chinese children: A four-year longitudinal study. *Merrill-Palmer Quarterly, 43*(4), 663–681.

Chen, X., Rubin, K. H., Li, B., & Li, Z. (1999). Adolescent outcomes of social functioning in Chinese children. *International Journal of Behavioral Development, 23,* 199–223.

Chen, X., & Swartzman, L. (2001). Health beliefs, attitudes and experiences in Asian cultures. In S. S. Kazarian & D. R. Evans (Eds.), *Handbook of cultural health psychology* (pp. 389–410). New York: Academic Press.

Dornbusch, S., Ritter, P., Leiderman, R., Roberts, D., & Fraleigh, M. (1987). The relation of parenting style to adolescent school performance. *Child Development, 58,* 1244–1257.

Falbo, T., & Poston, D. L. (1993). The academic, personality, and physical outcomes of only children in China. *Child Development, 64,* 18–35.

Ho, D. Y. F. (1986). Chinese pattern of socialization: A critical review. In M. H. Bond (Ed.), *The psychology of the Chinese people* (pp. 1–37). New York: Oxford University Press.

Ho, D. Y. F. (1987). Fatherhood in Chinese culture. In M. E. Lamb (Ed.), *The father's role: Cross-cultural perspectives* (pp. 227–245). Hillsdale, NJ: Erlbaum.

Ho, D. Y. F., Peng, S. Q., & Lai, A. C. (2001). Parenting in mainland China: Culture, ideology, and policy. *International Society for the Study of Behavioural Development (ISSBI) Newsletter, 38*(1), 7–9.

Jiao, S., Ji, G., & Jing, Q. (Ching, C. C.). (1986). Comparative study of behavioural qualities of only children and sibling children. *Child Development, 57,* 357–361.

Kelley, M. L. (1992). Cultural differences in child rearing: A comparison of immigrant Chinese and Caucasian American mothers. *Journal of Cross-Cultural Psychology, 23,* 444–455.

King, A. Y. C., & Bond, M. H. (1985). The Confucian paradigm of man: A sociological view. In W. S. Tseng & D. Y. H. Wu (Eds.), *Chinese culture and mental health* (pp. 29–45). New York: Harcourt Brace Jovanovich—Academic Press.

Kleinman, A., & Good, B. (1985). *Culture and depression: Studies in the anthropology and cross-cultural psychiatry of affect and disorder.* Berkeley: University of California Press.

Lamb, M. E. (1987). *The father's role: Cross-cultural perspective.* Hillsdale, NJ: Erlbaum.

Lang, O. (1968). *Chinese family and society.* New Haven, CT: Yale University Press.

Larson, R., & Richards, M. H. (1994). *Divergent realities: The emotional lives of mothers, fathers and adolescents.* New York: Basic Books.

Lempers, J. D., Clark-Lempers, D., & Simons, R. L. (1989). Economic hardship, parenting, and distress in adolescence. *Child Development, 60,* 138–151.

Lin, C. C., & Fu, V. R. (1990). A comparison of child-rearing practices among Chinese, immigrant Chinese, and Caucasian-American parents. *Child Development, 61,* 429–433.

Liu, D. (1998). *Changes of Chinese marriage and family.* Beijing: China Social Sciences Publisher.

Luo, G. (1996). *Chinese traditional social and moral ideas and rules.* Beijing: The University of Chinese People Press.

Maccoby, E. E., & Martin, C. N. (1983). Socialization in the context of the family: Parent–child interaction. In E. M. Hetherington (Ed.), *Handbook of child psychology: Vol. 4. Socialization, personality and social development* (pp. 1–102). New York: Wiley.

Ni, S. (2000, November 3). How should we revise the Marriage Law? *The People's Daily (Overseas Edition),* p. 5.

Parke, R. D., & Buriel, R. (1998). Socialization in the family: Ethnic and ecological perspectives. In N. Eisenberg (Ed.), *Handbook of child psychology: Vol 3. Social, emotional, and personality development* (pp. 463–552). New York: Wiley.

Rohner, R. P. (1986). *The warmth dimension: Foundation of parental acceptance-rejection theory.* Newbury Park, CA: Sage.

Roopnarine, J. L., Lu, M., & Ahmdezzaman, M. (1989). Parental reports of early patterns of caregiving play and discipline in India and Malaysia. *Early Child Development and Care, 50,* 109–120.

Rosenberg, B. G., & Jing, Q. (1996). A revolution in family life: The political and social structural impact of China's one child policy. *Journal of Social Issues, 52*(3), 51–69.

Russell, G., & Russell, A. (1987). Mother–child and father–child relationships in middle childhood. *Child Development, 58,* 1573–1585.

Steinberg, L. (1990). Autonomy, conflict, and harmony. In S. Feldman & G. Elliot (Eds.), *At the threshold: The developing adolescent* (pp. 255–276). Cambridge, MA: Harvard University Press.

Steinberg, L., Dornbusch, S., & Brown, B. B. (1992). Ethnic differences in adolescent achievement: An ecological perspective. *American Psychologist, 47*(6), 723–729.

Tao, K., & Chiu, J. (1985). The one-child-per-family policy: A psychological perspective. In W. Tseng & D. Y. H. Wu (Eds.), *Chinese culture and mental health* (pp. 153–165). New York: Harcourt Brace Jovanovich—Academic Press.

Wu, D. H. (1981). Child abuse in Taiwan. In J. E. Korbin (Ed.), *Child abuse and neglect: Cross-cultural perspectives* (pp. 139–165). Los Angeles: University of California Press.

Xu, A., & Ye, W. (1999). *Research on marital quality in China.* Beijing: Social Sciences Publication House.

CHAPTER 5

THE CHANGING JAPANESE FAMILY
A PSYCHOLOGICAL PORTRAIT

TAKASHI NAITO
Ochanomizu University

UWE P. GIELEN
St. Francis College

THE WATANABE FAMILY

Together with their 14-year-old daughter Akiko and 16-year-old son Michio, Mr. and Mrs. Watanabe ("Everybody") live in a small town in the Chiba prefecture, on the outskirts of Greater Tokyo. Each morning, Mrs. Watanabe gets up first and prepares the family's breakfast. After hurrying through his meal, Mr. Watanabe dashes off for his bus and later tries to catch his train for Central Tokyo. Altogether, it takes him well over an hour to reach his office—no wonder, since the Tokyo–Yokohama zone makes up the largest urban conglomeration on earth.

The children, in turn, are off to their juku, *a tutorial cramming school. Hopefully this will help them pass the highly competitive entrance examinations for a good college. With everyone else gone, Mrs. Watanabe begins to clean the apartment, only to leave a few hours later for her part-time job.*

Mr. Watanabe returns to his home quite late in the evening, even though nominally he is supposed to work only 8 hours a day. All too often, however, he has dinner and some drinks at a restaurant with his colleagues or with employees of related companies—both for the sake of friendship and of good business. On some weekends, he plays golf with customers. On other Sundays, when he stays home, he is tired and spends much of his time watching TV on the sofa.

Mrs. Watanabe has more time to talk with her children and understands them well. She is the primary disciplinary figure, though at times she asks her husband to admonish the children about some undesirable behavior. But Mr. Watanabe hesitates to do so, because he knows too little about his children and lacks confidence in his ability to be a good father.

Years before, Mr. Watanabe had been introduced to his future wife by one of his colleagues. Although she continued to work after the wedding, when she became pregnant, she left the company. Their relationship has changed over the years; for example, after their first child arrived, she began to call him "Daddy" (and she became "Mom"), a usage suggesting that the family revolves more around the children (and their education) than the marital relationship. At home, she is in charge of housekeeping and the family's finances, but Daddy plays a crucial role in deciding important questions such as the future of their son. They have time to talk together after the children have gone to bed but, at times, she feels that Daddy is uncommunicative. Nevertheless, husband and wife trust each other, even though they do not profess their love to each other in the Western style.

As a first son, Mr. Watanabe feels obligated to take care of his parents. He has heard, however, that in some families, conflicts have arisen between the wife and her mother-in-law once they are living in the same house. Consequently, Mr. Watanabe decided to live close to his parents, but in a separate home—a decision that evoked little opposition from his wife. Still, the two know that one day, his aging parents will live in their home so that they can be better cared for.

At first glance the Watanabe family might just as well be a Western family living in New York, London, or Stockholm rather than in Tokyo. The uncommunicative and exhausted father spending his Sunday afternoon as a TV-watching "couch potato" with a beer in his hand, the harried housewife holding a part-time job, the small family size, the central role of education in the lives of the two teenage children—all these are themes pervading the lives of numerous middle-class families residing in other industrialized countries.

But beneath the apparent cross-cultural similarities, a different family psychology makes itself felt.

Consider, for instance, the matter of divorce: the likelihood that Mr. and Mrs. Watanabe will divorce each other is small compared to the chance that Mr. and Mrs. Smith in New York will part company. In spite of some very real cross-cultural similarities, the cohesiveness of the Watanabe family is based on a different—if mostly implicit—social contract compared to that holding the Smith family together. To this day, the Japanese family remains a more stable and cohesive unit than the American, English, or Swedish family.

In this chapter, we consider the Japanese family from three perspectives. To begin with, the Japanese family constitutes the central institution of a unique, unusually homogenous, highly organized and integrated island society not to be found anywhere else on earth. At the same time, Japanese society continues to share many features with other Confucian-heritage societies with a Buddhist past, such as Taiwan, Mainland China, and Korea. Finally, Japan is one of the most modern "information societies" on earth and therefore shares many features with other information societies located mostly in Western Europe and North America.

Ethnically, linguistically, and culturally, Japan is more homogenous than any other major country. Some 99.4 percent of its inhabitants are citizens. Noncitizens include, for instance, the *Zainichi Kankokujin,* persons of Korean ancestry who were born and live in Japan. Among the "minority groups" are the *Hisabetsu buraku,* an indigenous group who in earlier times were treated as outcasts but whose status has been improving thanks to various efforts by the Japanese government. Standard Japanese is the official language and is understood by almost everybody, although many dialects of it exist. The country's literacy rate is close to 100 percent, a very large percentage of the population has undergone at least 12 years of rigorous schooling governed by society-wide standards, most Japanese feel themselves to be middle-class, and low crime rates demonstrate the success of most Japanese families in socializing their children. While economic inequalities are certainly important in the lives of Japanese families, they tend to be less visible and less destructive than those that can be encountered in Brazil, the United States, or France.

Because of the (relative) cultural homogeneity of Japanese society, this chapter emphasizes the common themes of, rather than the differences between, Japanese families. In this context, we pay less attention to the lives of the very rich or the very poor, but instead focus on the 90 percent of Japanese who see themselves as ordinary members of the middle class. We do, however, wish to underline two major sources of cultural differentiation. These include sharply delineated, though steadily changing, gender roles, as well as important generational differences with regard to attitudes, values, and behavior patterns. The pleasures and tensions of Japanese family life can only be understood if we take into account the myriad forces of rapid social change, as well as the strongly gender-typed nature of Japanese society.

In the following, and based on cross-cultural as well as indigenous investigations, we sketch the cultural context, historical evolution, and current situation, as well as some of the major problems of the Japanese family according to the findings of historical studies, developmental psychology research, sociological surveys, and investigations of pertinent folklore. Throughout much of the chapter, we have adopted a life-cycle approach ranging from the socialization of young children to the role of the elderly in the family system. Much emphasis is placed on the relentless nature of social change that has led to numerous structural and psychosocial changes in Japanese family life.

JAPANESE CULTURE AND THE EVOLUTION OF THE JAPANESE FAMILY

Given their relatively isolated geographic position on an "aircraft carrier of the eastern shores of Asia," the Japanese have developed a unique culture based on the intertwining of indigenous, Chinese, and Western influences as well as the relentless onslaught of the forces of modernization. From China came Confucianism, Buddhism (as modified by various Chinese traditions), a major portion of the Japanese writing systems (but not the language per se), as well

as many artistic traditions. Confucianism in particular has influenced many past and current Japanese beliefs about the central role of the family, its patriarchal composition, the importance of sharply differentiated gender roles, the traditional division of parental roles into "stern father–benevolent mother," the moral force of "filial piety" uniting ancestors, grandparents, parents, children, and future descendants, a heavy emphasis on the importance of duties, obligations, and loyalties, and many other aspects. Confucianism was especially important during the Tokugawa period (1603–1867) because at that time Japan was largely isolated from the rest of the world. It should be added that Confucian ideals, as propagated by the government, were not always reflected in actual family practices. Today, the influence of Confucianism continues in an attenuated and frequently invisible mode as the structure of the Japanese family is steadily transformed by economic and cultural changes.

Other religious influences include the native Shinto religion, several sects of Buddhism, Christianity, and a variety of "new religions," some of which have a special appeal to housewives. These religions have intermingled over the centuries and been "Japanized." For instance, it is not uncommon for a person to have been presented as a young child to the Shinto gods (*kami*), married according to a mixture of Shinto and Christian traditions, and be buried according to Buddhist rites. For many Japanese, religion means mostly the practice of family-related rituals and celebrations, rather than adherence to a tightly organized system of beliefs.

Following Japan's isolation during the Tokugawa period, the Meiji government (1868–1913) attempted to modernize Japan so that it could compete successfully with the Western nations. It strengthened the centralization of the political system and introduced unified laws for all of Japan. Before the Meiji restoration in 1868, a considerable variety of family systems existed across Japan. These were influenced by local as well as class differences, reflecting the tight class system made up of warriors, administrators, farmers, artisans, and tradesmen. During the Meiji era, a patrilineal family system based largely on Samurai norms was legally enforced. Furthermore, the government used the formal education system to spread patriarchal standards throughout Japan. In the newly constructed public schools, the students were taught traditional Confucian family virtues such as filial piety, as well as the fundamental importance of loyalty to the nation. For women, the Meiji policies reinforced the complementary roles of *ryosai kenbo* ("good wife, wise mother")—an emphasis that implicitly continues to influence modern policies as well as many social mores (Uno, 1993).

With the end of World War II in 1945, the antidemocratic social system adopted before the war was subjected to severe criticism and a democratic system based on the U.S. system was adopted. The new government abolished many aspects of the patrilineal system, and democratic principles were introduced into the legal system dealing with the family. For example, primogeniture was abandoned, and equal legal rights of succession for both sons and daughters, regardless of birth order, were stipulated. Since that time, the Japanese family has been changing, because of both the new legal system as well as the changing economic circumstances and evolving cultural traditions.

Japanese ideas concerning family and household structures have tended to oscillate between an emphasis on the traditional *ie* system and on modern, democratic family structures. The term *ie* refers to a supraindividual household group having economic, kinship, religious, and political functions. At birth, children's names are entered in the *ie* or family household registry, because individual birth certificates do not exist in Japan. The *ie* includes some immediate ancestors as well as several generations of living family members. The continuation of the family line is of utmost importance, and the family is organized hierarchically.

Traditionally, the *ie,* more than the Shinto shrines or Buddhist temples, formed the center of religious practice, with *ie* officials presiding over their own rituals. Even today, for many Japanese, the immediate ancestors remain an important focus of religious practice. Although to some, the ancestors have ascended to a sacred realm and perhaps lost their individuality, others think that they continue to serve as protectors of, and advisors to, the family, especially in the rural areas. Japanese beliefs about the afterlife (if any) are varied, fluid, and at times quite vague. It should be added that, in contrast to the old Chinese and Korean family system, the Japanese concern for ancestors is typically focused on those who were personally known to some of the surviving family members. Such a practice lends a certain interpersonal warmth and immediacy to the relationships between the deceased and those still living.

If no suitable child (especially no son) exists to continue the *ie,* a variety of adoptive options may be considered. In many cases, a younger son from another family will be adopted. He is taken into the new *ie* after marrying one of the daughters of his new family, whose name he will adopt. His psychological position in the new home, however, is often difficult, because he is dealing with a group of people who have already lived together for many years and formed bonds of mutual affection and interest.

In theory at least, the traditional family hierarchy placed the father at the top, with the heir-presumptive (most often the oldest son) next, followed by the other males according to descending age. Below them ranked the females in order of age. Especially among the wealthy and powerful, extended family groupings (*dozuku*) played an important role during the course of history. These included the central stem as well as satellite "branch houses," who owed loyalty and services to the main branch. Today, *dozuku*-like though modernized family conglomerations continue to be of some importance in the upper echelons of society, where they serve to protect economic and political interests as well as maintaining the social status of the family. The common people, in contrast, were more likely to live in smaller and less hierarchically ordered family groupings (Kumagai, 1995; Passin, 1968). In this context, Kawashima (1950) and others have suggested that traditionally, most Japanese families functioned in a less structured and "Confucian" way than might be concluded from the official and patriarchal government edicts and pronouncements. These were intended to increase government control over the population, but were not always followed at the village level, where most people lived.

Although the *ie* lost many of its functions and legally enshrined prerogatives after World War II, it continues to be of some importance in modern Japan, though typically in modified and attenuated form. In contrast to the hierarchic organization of the *ie*, modern families place greater emphasis on the equal rights of the family members. A national poll of the NHK Institute of Opinion Research (1984) confirmed, however, that many Japanese continue to feel a bond with their ancestors, such as the fathers of their grandparents: 59 percent of the respondents agreed with the statement, "I feel a profound connection to my ancestors," and 68.5 percent of the interviewees confirmed that "I often visit our ancestors' graves during the *Bon* Lantern Festival and the equinoctial week."

To the Japanese, authority relations in the family have "provided a model for authority relations in non-kinship groupings. The terms *oya* (parent) and *ko* (child), for example, have been extended in meaning to indicate supervisors and inferiors" such as "employer and employee, leader and follower" (Passin, 1968, p. 240). Familism, then, has been a pervasive influence in Japanese society, and family-like relationships and groupings continue to persist in shops, companies, landlord–tenant relations, and even in organized crime. Japanese gangster movies, for instance, may depict *oyabun–kobun* (godfather–crime family soldier) relationships somewhat similar to those portrayed in the U.S. *mafioso* movie, *The Godfather.* Similarly, youngsters wishing to establish a career in the world of traditional Japanese arts often become apprentices in a family-like environment organized according to the principle of *iemoto*. The principle demands loyalty toward and dependence on a master, who, in turn, guides his disciples in a paternalistic way.

Whether democratic, egalitarian, and modern, or more traditional and patriarchal, or most likely a complex mixture of the foregoing, families are expected to play a key role in the lives of everyone. For instance, a study showed that 46.7 percent of Japanese adults selected "families" as the most important factor influencing juvenile delinquency when compared to other factors such as a person's general social environment and his or her character (Prime Minister's Office, 1995). Above all, families are expected to play a central role in the enculturation and socialization of children. However, the demographic, psychosocial, and culturally complex (and sometimes contradictory) structures of the Japanese family system are undergoing major changes, which, in turn, are giving rise to a variety of family and societal problems.

DEMOGRAPHIC DESCRIPTION OF JAPANESE FAMILIES

In this section, we describe some current demographic aspects of the Japanese family based mainly on the source book of the National Institute of Social Security and Population Problems (1999).

The total population of Japan in 1998 was 126 million, and the average life expectancy was 77.2 years for males and 84.0 years for females. These are the highest life-expectancy figures in the world, and by the year 2015 one in four Japanese will be an elderly person. The age distribution of the population is depicted in Table 5.1. It shows that the percentage of children is comparatively small. This situation is not due to high childhood mortality rates, since these are now very low. For example, the infant below-one-year death rate was 0.36 percent in 1998. However, birth rates have declined dramatically in recent decades: the total fertility rates were 3.65 per woman in 1950, 2.13 in 1970, and 1.34 in 2000. A rate of 1.34 is far below the population replacement rate of about 2.1 children for each woman, and it is doubtful that the slowly increasing but controversial immigration of persons mostly from other Asian countries will be able to stem a threatening future population decline. (By way of contrast, the present birth rate in the United States is 2.08 per woman. Many European countries, however, have fertility rates approximately as low as those of Japan.)

Women, who had been wives for 15 to 19 years, had an average number of 4.27 children in 1940,

Table 5.1   Age Distribution of Japan's Population in 1998

AGE (YR)	%
0–9	9.5
10–19	11.7
20–29	15.0
30–39	12.9
40–49	14.4
50–59	14.2
60–69	11.5
70–79	7.3
80–89	3.6

Source: Adapted from National Institute of Social Security and Population Problems (1999, p. 25).

2.20 children in 1972, and 2.21 children in 1997, respectively. The fact that the respective numbers of births per married female in 1972 and in 1997 were almost the same may seem to be inconsistent with the notion that the total fertility rate decreased dramatically from 1970 to 2000 (see above). However, the increase of single females and the later marriages of females can help to explain this apparent inconsistency: between 1970 and 1998, the mean age of first marriage increased from 26.9 years to 28.6 years for males and from 24.2 years to 26.7 years for females. Similarly, the percentage of single females 25–29 years old increased dramatically, from 18.1 percent in 1970 to 48 percent in 1995. The corresponding increase for males was from 46.5 percent to 66.9 percent. An increasing number of men find it difficult these days to convince a young woman to become their life partner, while others are themselves reluctant to start a family.

Family size has shrunk dramatically over time. For example, the average number of family members was 4.9 in 1920, 3.7 in 1970, and 2.9 in 1995. One may ask why the mean number of family members decreased in spite of the fact that the number of elderly has increased in the society. In this context, it should be noted that the elderly increasingly live apart from their children. For instance, the percentage of those persons who were at least 65 years old

and living with their son or daughter declined from 69.0 percent in 1980 to 50.3 percent in 1998.

The Japanese family type has been steadily changing since the end of the World War II, when the patriarchal system lost some of its power. The distribution of family types in 1970 and in 1995 is depicted in Table 5.2. As can be seen, the percentage of lineal families was 13.4 percent in 1970 but declined to 11.2 percent in 1995. The percentage of nuclear families was 58.7 percent in 1995 and this percentage has not changed much during the last 30 years, since in 1970 nuclear families already made up 56.7 percent of all families. In contrast, the proportion of singles and married couples without children increased over time. It should be added that traditional three-generation households can be found most frequently in the more conservative rural areas, where people live in larger homes and continue to follow somewhat more traditional life patterns.

Table 5.2   Percentage Distribution of Household Types in 1970 and 1995

MEMBERS OF FAMILY	1970	1995
Married couple; no children	9.8	17.4
Parents and a child or children	41.2	34.2
One parent and one child or more children	5.7	7.1
Total nuclear family	56.7	58.7
Married couple and their parent(s)	1.2	2.0
Married couple, their parent(s) and one child or more children	12.2	9.2
Total lineal family	13.4	11.2
Married couple, their parent(s) and other kin	0.8	0.3
Single	20.3	25.6
Others	1.1	3.3

Source: Adapted from National Institute of Social Security and Population Problems (1999, p. 125).

Will Japanese families abandon the lineal family system altogether in future years? As mentioned above, there are the current tendencies of late marriages, an increasing number of singles, more married couples without any children, and the many elderly who do not live with their children. However, many current parents still would prefer to live with their sons or daughters when they become older, a preference inconsistent with the nuclear family system. In a recent survey, 64.3 percent of all parents who had 0–15-year-old children said that they wanted to live with their children in their old age (Management and Coordination Agency, 1996), although not all of them will see their desires fulfilled. The corresponding percentages for parents in Korea, the United States, and England were 46.4, 8.9, and 5.1 percent, respectively, suggesting that modern East Asian parents are still far more likely to wish to live with their children when compared to Anglo-Saxon families.

Two additional aspects of Japanese family life should be mentioned. First, an increasing number of wives are working outside their family homes; thus, in 1999, the percentage of working mothers was 42.7 percent (this percentage did not include those active in agriculture, forestry, and fisheries). However, the rate of working mothers with children below the age of 3 was only 23.4 percent. In addition, the percentage of part-time workers (less than 35 hours per week) among women was 52.8 percent, and this percentage has been increasing rapidly in recent years: 37.4 percent of all female workers (more than 15 years old) are now part-time workers, and that percentage is three times the percentage of 1980.

The frequency of international marriages has also increased, even though their absolute number remains fairly small. The rate of intermarriage between Japanese and foreign persons in Japan was 0.5 percent in 1970, but 3.82 percent in 1998. Half of the marriages in 1998 were between Japanese and either Chinese or Koreans.

In general, these demographic data suggest that there exists now a greater variety of family styles than before. These include traditional nuclear families, families consisting of elderly parents living together with their sons and/or daughters, elderly couples, childless families, families with an adopted son, and others. However, in the interests of perpetuating society, many families continue to consider the socialization of their children as their main task.

THE SOCIALIZATION OF CHILDREN

Folk Beliefs about Children

Traditional Japanese nursing styles for young children have been described as permissive when compared to those found in Western societies such as the United States (e.g., Benedict, 1946). Even nowadays, many parents hold permissive attitudes toward young children. For instance, the Management and Coordination Agency (1996) compared the attitudes of parents in Japan, Korea, and the United States, finding that 38.6 percent of the Japanese parents, but only 8.2 percent of the U.S. parents, endorsed the statement, "Young children should be allowed to do what they want; only as they grow older should discipline be imposed."

Traditionally, the Japanese people subscribe to the belief that children, before the age of 7, are in the sphere of gods: that is, they belong to a sacred realm. In addition, the children are thought to be in an intermediate and unstable status between "the world of gods" and the visible world. Consequently, children's misbehavior was tolerated even if it took place in sacred spaces, for example, in front of the gods in Shinto shrines. Additionally, those children who had died before the age of 7 were not buried in graves, because they were expected to return to the world of gods. Thus, the Japanese people traditionally believed that children are influenced not only by parents, family, and the community, but also by the invisible presence of supernatural beings (Hara & Minagawa, 1996). Elderly persons, too, are seen as being close to the gods, because after death they will return to them.

From the foregoing, one may mistakenly conclude that the Japanese believe in the innate goodness of children because they regard them as staying close to the world of the gods. However, a large-scale cross-national survey did not show such a belief (Prime Minister's Office, 1973). Instead, the

Japanese were *more* likely to believe that human nature is bad than respondents from other nations including the United States, England, West Germany, France, Switzerland, Sweden, Yugoslavia, India, the Philippines, and Brazil. Thirty-three percent of all Japanese 18–24-year-olds agreed with the statement, "Human nature is fundamentally bad"; in contrast, only 16 percent of the U.S. adolescents agreed with it (Prime Minister's Office, 1973).

The Japanese believe that children are not innately morally good, because the gods' world from which the children are said to come is not an entirely moral world; the beliefs about children imply only that parents should accept their young children's actions as being pure rather than impure in nature, but not necessarily as moral rather than immoral.

Earlier folk beliefs continue to influence present-day family and socialization practices. In this context, one may note that many Japanese parents follow traditional rituals for children. For example, on November 15 (*shichigosan*), they pay visits to Shinto shrines with their 3- and 5-year-old boys as well as their 3- and 7-year-old girls. In addition, parents, especially in rural areas, may threaten their misbehaving children by citing the supernatural force of *Bachi,* a kind of "punishment by gods" (Naito, 1987). A nationwide Children's Day is observed on May 5.

An amusing example of how traditional beliefs continue to affect the Japanese is shown by the decrease of children born in the *hinoeuma* year (Hara & Minagawa, 1996). The year of 1966 was a special *hinoeuma* year, which occurs only once every 60 years. Females who are born in a *hinoeuma* year are believed to be strong-minded and difficult to deal with by their husbands. Sure enough, the number of births in 1966 was dramatically reduced when compared to the previous and subsequent years: the number of births in 1965, 1966, and 1967 was 1,824,000, 1,360,000, and 1,936,000, respectively (National Institute of Social Security and Population Problems, 1999).

Expectations Regarding Childrearing

According to the results of a comparative research project among parents from the United States, Japan, and Korea (Prime Minister's Office, 1982), Japanese parents, more than Korean and American parents, expect their children to be "considerate of other people," "to be cooperative," "to observe rules of conduct," or "to have a sense of civic responsibility." In contrast, they emphasize "leadership," "fairness," and "emotional stability" less than Americans, and "politeness" less than Koreans (see Table 5.3). These differences are consistent with the notion that the Japanese society is collectivistic in nature, placing a special emphasis on considerate, cooperative, responsible behavior in the context of group relationships. Other virtues consistently emphasized for Japanese children include endurance, diligence, empathy, and being a responsive, cheerful youngster.

Azuma, Kashiwagi, and Hess (1981) found that the Japanese mothers of 5-year-olds expected their children to learn to be obedient to adults and to be courteous at an earlier age than U.S. mothers. In contrast, U.S. mothers expected their children to master certain social interaction skills with other children, such as "verbal assertion of self." The Japanese mothers were less insistent on such skills. In general, Japanese children are indulged during their earliest years, but once school starts, society places increasingly stringent demands on the youngsters. Peer-group socialization, enculturation into clearly delineated gender roles, and deep immersion into one's school culture are also of great importance, thereby adding to the clearly delineated and collectivistic nature of Japanese socialization practices. From early on, the Japanese learn that to be a person means being a nexus in a series of human relationships.

Interactions between Children and Mothers

Caudill and Weinstein (1969) compared prevailing maternal care and infant behaviors in urban middle-class families in Japan and the United States. They observed interactions between mothers and 3–4-month-old infants, finding that the Japanese mothers held their infants more frequently but talked to them less frequently. In addition, the Japanese infants were less physically active. The Japanese mothers stayed with their infants longer, but were less encouraging

Table 5.3   Characteristics That Parents Desire for Their Children: Japan, United States, and Korea[a]

CHARACTERISTIC	JAPAN (%)	U.S. (%)	KOREA (%)
Polite	34	26	61
Observing rules of conduct or having a sense of civic responsibility	45	24	32
Is fair, has a strong sense of justice	11	32	10
Considerate of other people	62	27	9
Emotionally stable	5	29	15
Responsible	40	50	58
Patient or persevering	18	9	19
Cooperative	17	6	13
Ability to insist on his/her own opinion in the presence of others	30	15	28
Creative or original	8	18	8
Ability to plan ahead or do things without help	16	19	29
Leadership	3	25	11
Not wasteful of money and other things	12	14	6

[a]The numbers reflect percentages of characteristics selected by parents from a list of thirteen characteristics (multiple choices allowed).
Source: Adapted from Prime Minister's Office (1982, p. 49).

of their verbal and physical activities. Caudill and Weinstein suggested that from early on, Japanese infants acquire Japanese personality traits and virtues such as obedience and a collectivistic orientation, although their findings may also have been influenced by the fact that many Japanese families live in small apartments and houses.

Another study showed that Japanese mothers frequently refer to the feelings of other persons when controlling their children's behaviors. For instance, in a study by Hess et al. (1986a), Japanese mothers used "appeals to feeling" more frequently and "appeals to mother's authority" less frequently than U.S. mothers.

Whereas from early on U.S. mothers tend to elicit their children's verbal responses and expect frequent feedback from them, Japanese mothers focus on maintaining a symbiotic relationship between themselves and their children. In this they are unusually successful. Miyake (1993), for instance, reports that in experimental studies using the Strange Situation, Japanese infants do not exhibit avoidant attachment behavior. Instead, they attempt to prevent separation from their mothers in order to foster a deep bond of dependency.

The Japanese custom of children co-sleeping with others points to a very close mother–infant relationship. In this context, Caudill and Plath (1966) interviewed 326 families in Tokyo, Kyoto, and Matsumoto and found that 91 percent of the children below 6 years of age slept with some adult(s). Azuma et al. (1981) confirmed these results. They found that

20 percent of the 3-year-old children slept with mothers and 50 percent of them with parents, or parents and sibling(s), but a mere 4 percent of the children slept with their fathers only. In contrast, 91 percent of the U.S. children slept alone or with siblings. In addition, it was found that the co-sleeping did not depend on the number of rooms and spatial arrangements in the family home. These results suggest that Japanese families provide very close attachment opportunities for their children, although adolescents get their own rooms (or rooms shared with siblings): 67 percent of 13–18-year-olds have their own room and 23.2 percent of them have shared rooms with siblings (Prime Minister's Office, 1991).

Some sociologists and psychologists, especially those following the psychoanalytic tradition, have emphasized the mother's role in the upbringing of Japanese children and adolescents (e.g., Doi, 1973; Yamamura, 1971). Yamamura, on the basis of an analysis of TV programs presented between 1959 and 1967, suggested that the ideal image of the traditional mother has been that of one who devotes herself completely to her child (though not necessarily accepting all of her child's desires). As a consequence, the Japanese continue to feel a powerful debt of gratitude to their mothers throughout their lives—a debt that can never be repaid in full. This image of an ideal mother has been propagated since the Meiji era.

Doi (1973) argued that the indigenous concept of *amae,* which refers to feelings of attachment, the desire to be accepted, and needs for dependency and nurturance from a benevolent superior, sensitize the Japanese to the behaviors and feelings of others. Doi pointed out that the prototype of *amae* is the infant's desire to be "one with the mother" and to deny the fact that while they are together, they nevertheless are also independent of each other.

The close mother–child relationship has served as a model for some forms of psychotherapy originating in Japan, such as Naikan therapy. Inobu Yoshimoto originally developed it, and some correctional systems and therapeutic institutions have adopted it. In this kind of therapy, patients recollect and examine the memory of receiving care and benevolence from a particular person at a particular time, and then recollect memories of giving back to that person. Through this process, the patients are expected to become aware of the basic interdependency of their existence and to feel gratitude toward others. In this therapy, the mother has typically been the crucial reference person, because she is devoted to, and in close contact with, her child (Murase, 1986).

Ignoring the details of the descriptions by these authors, the mother's potent influence on the psychological development of her children may be summarized as follows.

1. The Japanese are orientated toward group harmony (*wa*) and caring for each other.

2. This emphasis derives from the prototype of a close mother–child bond.

3. Children and adolescents experience the dedication of their mother and will continue to feel a profound debt of gratitude to her throughout their lives. Consequently, they will be motivated to realize her expectations both during childhood and—in more subtle ways—throughout adulthood. In addition, the original attachment bond will influence their interactions with others throughout life.

4. Although Japanese society is highly patriarchal on the surface, many Japanese have a submerged psychic layer resulting from Japan's "emotional matriarchy." It encourages dependency feelings well into adulthood—and especially so in the case of men. In this regard, one may surmise that when young mothers feel isolated or discontent with their marital relationship, they may be even more motivated to establish a close bond with their child.

5. The close bodily interaction between mother and young child will, in the child's later life, induce longings to return to the early "paradise." For instance, quite a few Japanese teenagers, and even adults, report wistfully that they would like to be young children again.

6. Following psychoanalytic theory, we would expect that early experiences of merging physically-emotionally with one's mother will subsequently lead to an unusually vivid, physically tinged fantasy life emphasizing developmentally early psychosexual themes. These may find expression, for instance, by one's becoming interested in the widely dispersed *manga* (cartoon comics). Some *manga* read by teenage boys portray a lurid world of sex, bodily preoccupations, and violence directed against women. In contrast, the *manga* read by teenage girls are more likely to depict a highly imaginative world of romantic adventures and other encounters in faraway lands. The contrast between the vivid fantasy world of the *manga* and the restrained, orderly world of Japanese everyday life is quite remarkable (Schodt, 1983).

7. Because many early mother–infant interactions are physical, nonverbal, and empathic in nature, we may expect Japanese culture to emphasize the importance of feeling and body-oriented forms of interaction. This is indeed often the case. Great sensitivity to the feelings and implicit expectations of significant others, an emphasis on empathy as the cornerstone of Japanese interpersonal morality, some distrust of eloquent speech making, and the frequent use of subtle, indirect means of communication are common characteristics influencing interactions in small groups such as the family.

8. Traditionally, many families lived in small homes with paper-thin walls that facilitate close contact. Such living situations would appear to be compatible with a mother-centered childrearing style that emphasizes a kind of "emotional osmosis" across permeable boundaries rather than the importance of firm ego boundaries and individualistic self-assertion. More recently, however, many families have come to prefer Western-style habitations, whose thicker walls may possibly encourage a reduction of some forms of family interaction.

Interaction between Fathers and Children

Traditionally, Japanese fathers were expected to adopt stern attitudes toward their children. The "rigorous father" was one of the well-known ideal father types in the pre-World War II era (Shimizu, 1983), and such fathers continue to be admired. For example, according to the results of comparative research by the Prime Minister's Office (1982), 72.7 percent of all Japanese fathers and mothers who had 0–15-year-old children agreed with the statement, "What is most of all needed for a father is to be stern and to have decisive attitudes toward his children." To this question, 77.5 percent of the Korean parents but only 49.0 percent of the U.S. parents and 63.8 percent of the English parents agreed. In spite of this expectation for Japanese fathers, however, they are losing their authority in many families (Shimizu, 1983).

Fathers in Japan tend to spend less time with their children when compared with those in some other societies. This is especially true for mainstream "salaryman" families in the cities, although on the whole less true in some of the more traditional rural families. The Ministry of Education and Science (1994) conducted a comparative study about the amount of time fathers and mothers spend with their 0–12-year-old children during a typical weekday. Japanese fathers spent 3.32 hours per day with their children; this was the shortest amount of time when compared to Korea (3.62), Thailand (6.00), the United States (4.88), England (4.75), and Sweden (3.64). In contrast, Japanese mothers spend 7.44 hours per day with their children, compared to mothers in Korea (8.44), Thailand (8.06), the United States (7.57), England (7.52), and Sweden (6.49). It should be added that in Ishii-Kuntz's (1994) study, Japanese fathers spent less time with their sons than U.S. fathers, but almost the same amount of time with their daughters. The author interprets this result by pointing to the father's feeling that the daughter will soon be "taken away" by marriage.

There are also 480,000 cases of absentee-father families, the so-called *Tanshinfunin* (Tanaka, 1994). Typically, when a father is transferred and moves to a place near his office, his family may not move with him, especially if they believe that the new environment will lead to educational disadvantages for the children.

Some studies have suggested that many fathers have little chance to demonstrate their authority. For instance, the image of fathers selected by a group of 10–15-year-olds included characteristics such as "dedicated to his work" (57 percent) and "generous" (46 percent), whereas the concepts "strict" (26 percent) and "strong" (20 percent)—which appear to be more authority-related—were selected less frequently (Management and Coordination Agency, 1987). In addition, a study by the Prime Minister's Office (1993) showed that 33.7 percent of all 18–24-year-olds consult with their mothers about their problems, but only 18.8 percent with their fathers.

Several authors have explored the problems that Japanese families have in terms of their insufficient influence as agents of children's moralization (e.g., Central Education Council, 1998). As Shimizu (1983) argues, because many fathers cannot perform their traditional role as children's socializers in a satisfactory way, mothers are led to perform both of the parental roles, which formerly had been expected to be separate. The father's role was to introduce strict social norms to his children as the agent of society, whereas the mother should accept children with benevolence. In a study by the Management and Coordination Agency (1987), only 23.3 percent of the Japanese children aged 10–15 years selected their father as the figure of "the one who is strictest with you." In contrast, 47.1 percent of them selected their mother for this role, and 21.7 percent chose both parents. By way of comparison, 44 percent of U.S. children selected fathers for this statement, 34 percent selected mothers, and 14 percent selected both. Accordingly, Shimizu (1983) has argued that because Japanese mothers must adopt both roles, they may feel ambivalent and, as a result, anxious.

It should be added that many fathers working in nonmainstream occupations, e.g., on farms or in local stores, will see more of their children and wives than mainstream fathers sent overseas by their corporation to head a branch operation. In Japan as elsewhere, economic conditions are bound to have a major impact on family life.

ADOLESCENTS AND YOUTH

In Japan, a greater value is assigned to an individual's academic career than to his or her actual ability. Thus an emphasis on achieving a brilliant academic career through hard work is ingrained in the child throughout his or her upbringing, since a parent's desire for the child's happiness in life seems achievable only if the child successfully completes tertiary education. In fact, 67.5 percent of parents expect their sons to graduate from a university, and 39.6 percent of them expect it of their daughters (Management and Coordination Agency, 1996). Clearly, the pressure to succeed academically is greater on sons than on daughters, and so, many girls are sent to junior colleges that teach them to be "ladylike."

These high expectations are, however, not always attained. Among mothers, 26.6 percent answered "very much dissatisfied" and 31.6 percent answered "fairly satisfied" when asked about the school achievements of their third-grade middle-school children, although only 7.0 percent of mothers were "much dissatisfied" with their third-grade primary-school children. In contrast, only 16.8 percent of fathers felt dissatisfied with their third-grade middle-school children (Shimizu, 1983). Many teachers and researchers have pointed out that numerous children experience problems such as low self-esteem and a lack of commitment because of academic pressures to prepare for, and succeed in, the fiercely competitive entrance examinations. Some other children adamantly refuse to go to school or become the victims of school bullying (Kameguchi, 1998).

After graduation, when sons and daughters get their first jobs, they develop relationships with colleagues and superiors at their place of work. However, they continue to enjoy profound relationships with their parents. Typically, they attempt to live up to their parents' expectations. In a study conducted by the Department of Citizens' Lives of Metropolitan Tokyo (1977), 67.3 percent of 20–25-year-olds answered that their fathers had high hopes for them, and 63.4 percent wished to live up to their expectations; 73.9 percent of them said that their mothers placed high expectations on them, and 70.6 percent wished to fulfill them. These percentages were much higher than those corresponding to other reference persons such as "colleagues or friends" (33.4 and 25.9 percent, respectively). These results are consistent with the aforementioned notion that parents, and especially the mother, profoundly influence the moral character of their children and adolescents. It should be added that in many situations, parents—and especially mothers—may prefer to use an indirect, guilt-inducing style of conveying their expectations to their children, rather than giving them direct commands. Children (especially boys), in turn, may resist the socialization process and in some cases even hit their parents.

Nevertheless, surveys have repeatedly pointed to major gaps in lifestyle and values between parents and adolescents (e.g., Prime Minister's Office, 1973, 1993). It is not rare for Japanese adolescents to face internal conflicts between their wish to live up to their parents' expectations (because they feel deeply indebted to them) and their own convictions and lifestyle preferences. Consequently, some of the domestic violence perpetrated by sons, especially against their mothers, is thought to result from conflicts between internalized parental expectations and the son's own wish to achieve an independent identity. In this view, the son's violence represents an attempt to cut himself off from strong feelings of dependence on his parents.

In addition, sociologists and journalists have recently uncovered "parasite singles," that is, daughters who, for many years, depend on their parents financially and in other ways, to support their single lifestyle. They frequently live at home. These supposedly "parasitic" singles may go abroad to learn a foreign language, attend college to learn additional skills, become counselors, immerse themselves in the world of fashion, and so on. They know that if they marry, they will be expected to spend quite a few hours engaged in housekeeping tasks. Should a child arrive, they probably will feel they should abandon their full-time job. Consequently, some of these single women may prefer to live their own, independent lives rather than follow the traditional path of becoming wives and mothers (Orenstein, 2001). That society feels deeply ambivalent about these singles becomes clear when we consider the derogatory nature of the label used by some journalists and others to refer to them. Others, however, look at them in a more positive light and consider them to be the pioneers of a more independent, creative, self-assertive, individualistic, and less gender-typed lifestyle.

The aforementioned findings and trends suggest that in the future, Japanese adolescents will need to strike a new balance between feelings of dependency on their parents, the desire to gain independence, their attitudes toward gender roles, and the shifting expectations of their peer group, the world of work, and the larger society (White, 1993).

MARRIAGE

After graduation from high school or college, most young men and women get jobs. As many as 70 percent of 20–30-year-old females find employment (Department of Women in the Ministry of Labor, 2000). They enter the "life stage for marriage" as traditionally defined. *Miai-kekkon* (traditional arranged marriage) was the most common marriage style until the early 1960s. For instance, in the 1930s, 69.0 percent of all marriages were arranged (National Institute of Social Security and Population Problems, 1998).

In contrast to modern "love marriages," *miai* are based on observing traditional formalities, rely on the initiative of others, do not depend on premarital interaction, and do not presume that romantic love is a precondition for marriage. It is expected that love—or at least some kind of respectful attachment—will follow rather than precede the tying of the marriage knot. The marriage partners tend to emphasize that respect between husband and wife and the fulfillment of expected duties should take priority over more transitory feelings, sexual satisfaction, and mere companionship. The families involved tend to be especially concerned about their honor, their status, and their position in a network of stable community relationships (Blood, 1967). When, in the 1960s, Blood compared arranged marriages with love marriages, he found that, on the whole, both wives and husbands tended to be more satisfied with arranged marriages. Because modern love marriages place a greater emphasis on emotional infatuation and involvement, they introduce an element of instability, given the transitory nature of many human feelings. Consequently, traditional mature persons may believe that the pervasive modern trend toward love marriages furthers immature dependence on unrealistic expectations as well as an individualistic (egotistical) disregard for the wider interests of the community, the extended family, and the needs of children for a stable home.

Miai (arranged meetings) were typically set up by respected and knowledgeable women of the community, such as wives of rental-house owners and wives of superiors in the workplace. These go-betweens (*nakodo*) would gather detailed information about marriageable young women and arrange meetings with the intention of finding a marriage partner for them.

The percentage of arranged marriages has decreased sharply over the years and was a mere 9.9 percent between 1995 and 1997. Instead, modern men are becoming acquainted with prospective marriage candidates mainly in the workplace (33.6 percent in 1997) or on the basis of friends' or brothers' introductions (27.1 percent) (National Institute of Social Security and Population Problems, 1998). The decline of *miai* has been linked to the increased chance of meeting prospective partners at the workplace, the increasingly individualistic outlook on life emphasized by modern education, and the paucity of traditional go-betweens as a result of the increasing diversity and fragmentation of traditional communities. Nevertheless, some young people find it difficult to meet suitable marriage partners, as may be the case for young men working in computer systems or oil companies, where they are unlikely to meet female colleagues. Consequently, many companies now provide go-between services, an industry that has come to mean big business. It should be added that go-betweens such as family friends, relatives, or mentors are frequently employed in love marriages as well, where they can be helpful in arranging delicate negotiations between the families involved. Consequently, some differences between "love marriages" and arranged marriages may be more apparent than real.

Weddings frequently blend Eastern and Western customs and symbols. They often include a traditional Shinto ceremony, in which the bride and the groom wear beautiful kimonos. This may be followed by a Christian-style observance where the participants appear in formal Western attire. Even in the case of love marriages, a go-between couple is likely to serve as witnesses during the marriage ceremony, because the marriage is expected to cement relationships not only between the couple, but also between their families of origin. Some well-to-do families stage elaborate and expensive weddings culminating, for instance, in a laser show during which the couple emerges dramatically from a gondola. Many weddings nowadays take place in hotels or wedding halls, the high point typically being the *hiroen* ("public banquet"), during which the new couple are celebrated in speeches and an elaborate dinner is held in their honor. Much of the attention throughout the whole proceedings focuses on the bride, since it is understood that she, more than anybody else, is undergoing a fundamental change in status, residence, and lifestyle. However, some weddings are deliberately of a much simpler and less formal nature.

HUSBAND AND WIFE

After the wedding, the physical and psychological situation of the new couple leads to many changes—especially if they live together with the husband's parents. Consequently, one sometimes reads about conflicts between the wife and her husband's mother or sister in the newspaper advice columns. Some of the problems reported occur because of the differences between the "culture" (*kafu*) the wife brought with her when she left her family of origin and the culture of the husband's family. In a related fashion, conflicts may arise between the hopes and expectations of the new couple and the norms endorsed by the rest of the husband's family.

The traditional role assignments for husbands and wives have become more flexible and collaborative in recent decades, but in many families they remain firmly in place. According to Yuzawa (1995), the belief that "husbands should work outside the home and wives should take care of the home" was confirmed by 80.1 percent of women in Tokyo in 1982, but by only 55.6 percent in 1992. According to a survey by the Prime Minister's Office (1992), most of the work in homes is assigned to wives rather than to husbands (or the whole family): cleaning (84.5 percent versus 11.6 percent), preparing dishes (90.0 percent versus 5.1 percent), caring for young children (63.4 percent versus 17.9 percent), teaching the children (48.7 percent versus 24.7 percent). Whereas many wives in the survey said they decided daily family finances (70.5 percent), husbands tended to hold greater decision-making power in other important areas such as buying a house (53.2 percent). As a whole, when asked which person had the real decision-making power in their family home, 61.0 percent of the respondents said "father," 11.6 percent answered "mother," and 19.1 percent said "both."

The divorce rate decreased from 1882 to 1960 but has increased since then. For instance, the divorce rates were 0.7 percent in 1960 and 1.94 percent in 1998 (Tokuoka, 1981; National Institute of Social Security and Population Problems, 1999). Tokuoka (1981) explains the changes by noting that whereas the traditional type of divorce has decreased over time, the modern type of divorce has increased since 1960. The former type of divorce occurred when a wife could not adapt successfully to the enlarged family, and the latter type occurs because of a psychological mismatch between husband and wife in a context where the rapidly changing family system leads to divergent and sometimes contradictory role expectations and norms for family life. It should be kept in mind, however, that in spite of some recent increases in the divorce rates, they remain well below the rates found in most other industrialized countries.

Children frequently command a central position in the family. For example, from the arrival of the first-born child, Mr. Watanabe began to be called "Daddy" by his wife, while he began to call her "Mom." In the future, with the advent of grandchildren, Mr. Watanabe will become "Grandfather" for his wife, and he will refer to her as "Grandmother."

In 1998, 40.4 percent of divorced couples had no children, although only 5 percent of all married couples were estimated to have no children (National Institute of Social Security and Population Problems, 1998). The data are consistent with the Japanese proverb, "The child is an iron clamp to [hold together] parents." However, it is uncertain whether having children would decrease the likelihood of divorce. In addition, it is easy to point out covariates of divorce, such as the couple's respective ages: younger married couples who tend to have no children and enjoy better chances of getting jobs to support them after their separation divorce more frequently than older couples.

Masuda (1981) pointed out that the image of the relationship between husband and wife in traditional families is unclear when compared to the more definite image of good parent–child relationships. He argued that in the traditional family, the relationship between wife and husband is not well delineated because the total family system is focused on the parent–child relationships. In addition, because of rigid traditional norms for male–female interactions, the couple is unlikely to express their love to each other even in the home.

The spheres of many couples' lives do not overlap all that much. They may have few mutual friends and are unlikely to attend many social functions together. Quite a few marriages are arranged for the sake of convenience, and conjugal love is not necessarily the crucial ingredient of a successful Japanese marriage. Furthermore, even if the early phases of the marriage were characterized by sexual passion and romantic attachment, these can easily evaporate over time—a process that in most cases does not endanger the stability of the marriage. Some wives agree with the ironic phrase that appeared some dozen years ago as part of a TV commercial: it is nice that the husband is fine and out of the home. In contrast, other wives may resent the merciless demands made by their husband's company on his time and energy. The resentment may be fueled as much by the wife's concern that he plays too little a role in the upbringing of the children as by her desire for his companionship. Still other wives may be tempted to start an extramarital affair, possibly with a man they met in the course of their part-time work. Extramarital affairs and sexual encounters, however, have traditionally been the prerogative of men, who, if so inclined, can easily avail themselves of the services of women working in the extensive sex and entertainment industry. Men may also be expected by their companies to frequent hostess clubs "after" work, where they engage in drinking, singing, joking with each other, and suggestive sexual talk with the hostesses (Allison, 1994).

As is the case in the Watanabe family, the relationship between many spouses tends to have a slightly "cool" quality so that they take each other for granted. In addition, they relate to each other not so much as partners having different qualities, personalities, and opinions, but rather as two halves of a unit. They may try to avoid discussions in which different perspectives are revealed, preferring instead to act as a functional unit held together by tacit understandings and a mutual concern for the welfare of the children and the home. Some men, in particular, distrust "rational" discussions and would rather rely on unspoken agreements; or else they might attempt to avoid discussions of family problems by staying away from the family much of the time. Masuda (1981), for instance, cited the findings of the NHK Research Center, which asked the husbands, "What are you for your wife?" Many of them answered "breadwinner of the family" (40.6 percent), "like a friend" (17.7 percent), or "something like air or water" (11.9 percent)—that is, a person who is tacitly taken for granted in a relaxed, smooth relationship. To the corresponding question about husbands, wives answered "friend" (25.9 percent), "like air or water" (22.3 percent), "breadwinner of the family" (18.9 percent), or "like a mother" (9.5 percent).

Because of increased life expectancy rates, married couples are now spending more and more years with each other. This raises, among other things, the question of how the Japanese are dealing with the graying of their society, the changing roles of the elderly in the family, and the ongoing redefinition of family roles and relationships in the postretirement phase.

THE ROLE OF THE ELDERLY IN THE FAMILY

Whereas much research on families has focused on the relationship between parents and young children,

very few studies have investigated relationships between aged persons and other family members (Kawai, 1988).

The status of older persons in the family is an important theme in Japan because the number of elders is increasing steadily, although their status is often ambiguous because of the changing nature of the Japanese family. Different generations may hold different beliefs: the elderly frequently hope to live with their son's family, but, as in the case of the Watanabe family, the younger generation may feel more ambivalent about living together with their parents.

According to Yuzawa (1995), in 1990, 34.5 percent of persons at least 64 years old lived with their married sons or daughters and grandchildren, 13.7 percent with their single son(s) and/or daughter(s), 24.2 percent with their husbands or wives, and 15.2 percent alone or in institutions. According to statistics provided by the National Institute of Social Security and Population Problems (1999), the percentage of persons aged 65 and above who live with their family was 86.8 percent in 1960, decreased to 55.9 percent in 1995, and has since declined even further. These percentages are far higher than those found in the United States (1.3 percent in the case of persons at least 60 years old in 1960).

Once the Japanese grow older, many face the problem of how best to live with their son's family. In the traditional three-generation family, the grandfather gradually hands over his role to his sons. Hasegawa (1981) describes how this process occurred among farming families living near Osaka. At first, the grandfather handed over financial responsibilities, such as managing the family budget, to his sons, and later allowed them to become the final decision makers in the family. Finally, the oldest son was officially registered as the head householder. In contrast, the daughters-in-law became responsible for most of the housekeeping tasks soon after they entered the family. The grandmothers took on or continued with complementary roles in housekeeping. The new wives were expected to obey the family patriarchs—typically their fathers-in-law—and to devote themselves completely to their new families. The older generation kept their status as householders until a certain age, which varied with the profession and other considerations, until they retired from active life.

Minoura (1987) discussed the status of wives within families living in a farming area. In interviews, many older women stated that they had been treated cruelly by their mothers-in-law, but nowadays, they must accept that their daughters-in-law are becoming much more assertive. Minoura explained this new assertiveness in the following way. To begin with, there were only a few women who wanted to marry farmers, and this situation raised the wives' bargaining position while weakening the traditional family system. Moreover, they were increasingly going out into the workplace to earn their own salary. Finally, as the frequency of arranged marriages declined, in which the women were asked to join an *ie* rather than simply marrying a husband, the wives adopted new attitudes toward their marriage. Increasingly, they felt a greater obligation toward the marital relationship, rather than the family at large. It should be added that in recent years, farming families have been forced to look for potential wives for their sons in other Asian countries such as the Philippines—a surprising development for the Japanese, who like to emphasize the racial integrity of their society.

A much-discussed potential problem concerns the relationship between the wife and her mother-in-law. Sodei (1977) examined the contents of advice columns in various newspapers over a period of 10 years. She found that more than 30 percent of those problems involving aged persons revolved around tensions between wives and their mothers-in-law. Kawai (1988) pointed out that typical conflicts occurred when the beliefs of wives clashed with those of their mothers-in-law, who, in turn, wanted to assert their traditionally superior role. It is also likely that, for the husbands, there was the further conflict between their deep-seated feeling of dependence on their mothers and the modern emphasis on the equal rights of all family members. Hence, husbands may find it difficult to side with their wives rather than their mothers, even if they agree with modern notions of the nonhierarchical nature of the family.

An additional problem concerns the nature of the relationship between grandparents and grandchildren. Japanese tend to believe that grandparents spoil their grandchildren, labeling such (supposedly) selfish and poorly disciplined children "grandfather's (or grandmother's) children." Accordingly, grandparents may tend to favor their grandchildren because they see them as the heirs to the family name. At the same time, they struggle to adhere to conventional family norms governing the grandparent–grandchildren relationship.

In a collaborative study of three-generation families living in Osaka, Fujimoto (1981) argued that grandparents have come to be placed in an ambivalent status in the current transitional period of the lineal family system and the nuclear family system. The results of the study showed that most grandparents had intimate relations with their grandchildren, but one-third of them refrained from acting as childrearing authority figures for them. They came to accept the idea that only their sons and daughters should have the responsibility to educate their grandchildren.

In today's fast-paced world, grandparents often find it difficult to teach their grandchildren, who are being prepared to live in a society quite different from that in which the grandparents themselves grew up. The grandparents can, however, offer affection, care, and general guidance. Thus they may play a supplementary role to the parents by, for instance, teaching their grandchildren by example what it means to become older and to face death. In this respect, the current elders have the task of redefining their role in the socialization of their grandchildren within the new family system.

There is the further question about the role of the family in caring for aged members, such as bedridden aged persons and persons on their deathbed. According to Yuzawa (1995), bedridden elders increasingly wish to be taken care of by their spouses, social helpers, or institutions rather than by their daughters-in-law. These changes in attitude will further weaken the lineal family system. It should be pointed out that in 2000 the Japanese government introduced a new social insurance system providing financial support for the time when aged persons need in-home care.

These developments mean that the aged persons must learn to adapt to the contract nature of being cared for in an institution or in their home by trained personnel who are strangers rather than family members.

Many companies adhere to the policy that their employees must retire at age 60. However, many employees will retire from their posts, but stay on in the company or a related company as part-time workers receiving a reduced salary. The Ministry of Labor (2000) has published statistics showing the following percentages for working persons: 94.5 percent for 55-year-old persons, 73.8 percent for 60-year-olds, and 55.8 percent for 65-year-olds, indicating a gradual decrease of work involvement with advancing age.

Many retirees are contemplating changes in their lifestyle and spend more time at home: in the aforementioned survey, 87.1 percent of the men in their sixties said that they usually have dinner with their wives, although only 59.7 percent of the men in their thirties gave the same reply. However, a mere 37.0 percent of the elderly indicated that they discussed their troubles and concerns with their partners. That percentage was practically the same as that for the men in their thirties (38.3 percent).

Furthermore, many of the elderly experience anxieties about their health status. In a survey by Yuzawa (1995), 52.3 percent of the elderly indicated that they sometimes or always felt anxious about their health, 31.1 percent said they felt lonely or isolated, and 28.4 percent were worried about their social relationships.

Altogether, it seems clear that many of the elderly need to redefine their relationship with each other and how to spend their free time. Many books are now being published that discuss how newly retired persons can find new purposes in their everyday lives.

CONCLUSION

In the foregoing, we have portrayed the Japanese family as moving steadily away from the traditional, hierarchically ordered, more or less extended, patrilineal stem family model exemplified by the *ie* as well as from less hierarchically ordered forms of traditional family life. Over the course of the twentieth century, the family has shrunk dramatically in size, become more nuclearized, lost some of its former economic foundations, grown increasingly diversified, and become more egalitarian in nature. Higher levels of education, a dramatic rise in life expectancies, ongoing redefinitions of gender roles, consumerism, a greater awareness of other ways of life, and the recent rise of a more individualistic outlook on life among the younger generation all suggest that Japanese society must strive for new balances between the demands of family life, the demands of the world of work, and the individual's striving for a fulfilling and meaningful life.

Many of the structural changes that the Japanese family system has undergone during the last hundred years are paralleled by corresponding changes in other modern societies, including some Eastern societies such as Singapore and practically all Western societies. Nevertheless, the psychosocial interior of the Japanese family remains distinct in many ways. Rothbaum et al. (2000), for instance, have argued that the development of close relationships in Japan follows the "path of symbiotic harmony," whereas in the United States the preferred path is that of "generative tension." The modern Western path of generative tension revolves around the process of individuation and is characterized by themes such as autonomy, expressiveness, self-assertion, and exploration. In contrast, the ideal Japanese path, from infancy on, emphasizes the themes of empathy, tacit nonverbal communication, interpersonal connectedness, and feelings of loyalty, care, and commitment, all in an atmosphere of symbiotic harmony. The family constitutes the central institution that prepares children for their respective paths through life.

Along these lines, the Japanese infant is expected to develop feelings of complete dependence on the mother, which, in time, become the prototype for the *amae*-based, interdependent, symbiotic relationships of later childhood and adulthood. For the mother, the traditional cultural model prescribes self-sacrifice and perfect devotion to her children. In contrast, the father cuts a more shadowy figure within the family and tends to remain tangential to the inner circle of intimacy between the mother and her children. Instead, he is expected to devote himself completely to his work, thereby ensuring the economic welfare of his family. In spite of the dramatic effects of industrialization and urbanization on Japanese society that intensified after World War II, the underlying value system regulating many aspects of this family system remained intact for many years.

More recently, however, the nuclearization of the Japanese family has advanced so rapidly that basic Japanese values emphasizing strivings for interpersonal harmony, self-effacement, and responsiveness to the expectations of others are moving in the direction of an increased emphasis on individualistic strivings for self-fulfillment. This process is intertwined with the ongoing cultural change in gender roles that is likely to shape the future of the Japanese family—and thereby the whole of Japanese society.

Consider, for example, the previous discussion surrounding the phenomenon of "parasite singles." More than half of all Japanese women these days are still single at the age of 30. Frequently ambivalent about the choices that Japanese society has to offer, they defer (and sometimes forgo) marriage, the bearing of children, and financial dependence on husbands in favor of flaunting their quality of being *wagamama* (selfish, willful). More generally, Orenstein (2001, p. 21) interprets their behavior as representing an "unconscious protest against the rigidity of both traditional family roles and Japan's punishing professional system." Clearly, a major conflict has been brewing between women following their traditional destiny—to immerse themselves in the task of raising children—and their desire to pursue a more modern and independent lifestyle.

In Japan, even more so than in other countries, it is very difficult for women to combine a professional career with having children. As a result, the birth rate has plummeted and Japan's population has been aging more rapidly than any other on earth. These changes are so dramatic that some have even argued for the unthinkable: Japanese society may (literally!) need to replenish itself by opening its doors to extensive immigration—or else shrink in size and economic strength. It is doubtful, however, that even such a revolutionary policy change would truly be able to solve Japan's problems, which are predominantly cultural in nature.

It seems, then, that the new century will pose difficult challenges to Japanese society and its families. Some traditionalists have argued that the solution to Japan's demographic problems is a return to the traditional family. In other words, men should continue to clock innumerable hours at work, while their wives stay home to raise the children. The needs of the company should take priority over the needs of the family, and gender roles should follow suit. It seems doubtful to us, however, that such a stale, patriarchal recipe will be successful in the new century. Instead, Japanese society will need to create a more egalitarian gender-role system together with the clear expectation that, in the future, the physical and emotional needs underlying a healthy family life will be more fully recognized and integrated with the demands of the world of work than has been true in the past. The rigidities of traditional gender and family roles together with the rigidities of Japan's professional system need to be dissolved. At a time of economic stagnation and crisis, one may well ask: Is Japanese society prepared to face such a fundamental challenge?

REFERENCES

Allison, A. (1994). *Nightwork: Sexuality, pleasure, and corporate masculinity in a Tokyo hostess club.* Chicago: University of Chicago Press.

Azuma, H., Kashiwagi, K., & Hess, R. D. (1981). *Hahaoya no taidoto kodomonochitekihattatsu* [Attitudes of mothers and the cognitive development of children]. Tokyo: Tokyodaigakushuppankai.

Benedict, R. (1946). *The chrysanthemum and the sword: Patterns of Japanese culture.* Boston: Houghton Mifflin.

Blood, R. O. (1967). *Love match and arranged marriage: A Tokyo–Detroit comparison.* New York: The Free Press.

Caudill, W., & Plath, D. W. (1966). Who sleeps by whom? Parent-child involvement in urban Japanese families. *Psychiatry, 29,* 344–366.

Caudill, W., & Weinstein, H. (1969). Maternal care and infant behavior in Japan and America. *American Psychiatry, 32,* 12–43.

Central Education Council. (1998). *Atarashii jidaiokizukukokoroosodaterutameni* [Fostering the mind which creates new times: An interim report]. Tokyo: Unpublished report.

Department of Citizens' Lives of Metropolitan Tokyo (1977). *Daitoshiseinen no sekatsu kachikannikansuruchousa* [Research on the life and values of adolescents in a large city]. Tokyo: Unpublished report.

Department of Women in the Ministry of Labor (2000). *White paper on the labor of women.* Tokyo: The 21st Century Occupation Foundation.

Doi, T. (1973). *The anatomy of dependence.* Tokyo: Kodansha International.

Fujimoto, N. (1981). Sofubo to mago [Grandparents and grandchildren]. In T. Kamiko & K. Masuda (Eds.), *Nihonjinnokazokukankei* [Family relationships of the Japanese: A cross-national comparison] (pp. 167–194). Tokyo: Youhikaku.

Hara, H., & Minagawa, M. (1996). From productive dependents to precious guests: Historical changes in Japanese children. In D. W. Shwalb & B. J. Shwalb (Eds.), *Japanese childrearing: Two generations of scholarship* (pp. 9–30). New York: Guilford.

Hasegawa, A. (1981). Roujin to kazoku [Aged persons and their families]. In T. Kamiko & K. Masuda (Eds.), *Nihonjinnokazokukankei* [Family relationships of the Japanese: A cross-national comparison] (pp. 195–218). Tokyo: Youhikaku.

Hess, R. D., Azuma, H., Kashiwagi, K., Dickson, W. P., Nagano, S., Holloway, S., Miyake, K., Price, G., Hating, G., & McDevitt, T. (1986a). Family influences on school readiness and achievement in Japan and the United States: An overview of a longitudinal study. In H. Stevenson, H. Azuma, & K. Hakuta (Eds.), *Child development and education in Japan* (pp. 147–166). New York: Freeman.

Ishii-Kuntz, M. (1994). Paternal involvement and perception toward fathers' roles. *Journal of Family Issues, 15*(1), 30–48.

Kameguchi, K. (1998). Family therapy with Japanese families. In U. P. Gielen & A. L. Comunian (Eds.), *The family and family therapy in international perspective* (pp. 243–256). Trieste, Italy: Lint.

Kawai, C. (1988). Sansedai kankei [Intergenerational relationships between three generations]. In T. Okadou, S. Kunitani, K. Sugitani, H. Hasegawa, N. Hiraki, & A. Hoshimo (Eds.), *Kouza Kazokushinrigaku 6* [Lectures on the psychology of the family] (Vol. 6, pp. 98–124). Tokyo: Kanekoshobou.

Kawashima, T. (1950). *Nihonshyakaino kazokutekikousei* [Family construction in Japanese societies]. Tokyo: Nihonhyouronshya.

Kumagai, F. (1995). Families in Japan: Beliefs and realities. *Journal of Comparative Family Studies, 26,* 135–163.

Management and Coordination Agency (1987). *Nihonno chichioyato kodomo* [Fathers and children in Japan]. Tokyo: The Printing Office of the Ministry of Finance.

Management and Coordination Agency (1996). *Kodomotokazokunikansurukokusaic-hosahoukokusho* [Report of a cross-cultural study about children and families]. Tokyo: The Printing Office of the Ministry of Finance.

Masuda, K. (1981). Fuufukankei [The relationship between husband and wife]. In T. Kamiko & K. Masuda (Eds.), *Nihonjinnokazokukankei* [Family relationships of the Japanese: A cross-national comparison] (pp. 53–78). Tokyo: Yuhikaku.

Ministry of Education and Science (1994). *Kateikyoiku-nikzansurukokusaihikakuchousa* [International comparison of education in the family]. Tokyo: Unpublished government report.

Ministry of Labor (2000). *Roudou hakusho* [White paper on labor]. Tokyo: Nihon roudou kenkyu kikou.

Minoura, Y. (1987). Katei [Family]. In T. Sofue (Ed.), *Nihonjin wa doukawattanoka* [How do the Japanese change?] (pp. 69–92). Tokyo: Nihon housou shyuppan kyoukai.

Miyake, K. (1993). Temperament, mother–infant interaction, and early emotional development. *Japanese Journal of Research on Emotions, 1*(1), 48–55.

Murase, T. (1986). Naikan therapy. In T. Sugiyama Lebra & W. P. Lebra (Eds.), *Japanese culture and behavior: Selected readings* (rev. ed., pp. 388–397). Honolulu: University of Hawaii Press.

Naito, T. (1987). Children's beliefs of immanent justice and style of discipline. *Research in Social Psychology, 3,* 29–38 (in Japanese).

NHK Institute of Opinion Research (1984). *Nihonjin no shyuko isiki* [Japanese awareness of religion]. Tokyo: Nippon Housou Kyokai.

National Institute of Social Security and Population Problems (Eds.). (1998). *Nihonjinnokekkonto shyussan* [Marriage and childbirth in Japan]. Tokyo: Kousei tokei kyokai.

National Institute of Social Security and Population Problems (Eds.). (1999). *Jinko no doko 1999* [Population trends in 1999: Japan and the world]. Tokyo: Kousei tokei kyokai.

Orenstein, P. (2001). Parasites in Prêt-à-Porter. *The New York Times Magazine,* July l, pp. 31–35.

Passin, H. (1968). Japanese society. In D. L. Sills (Ed.), *International encyclopedia of the social sciences* (Vol. 8, pp. 236–249). New York: Macmillan & The Free Press.

Prime Minister's Office (1973). *Sekaino seinen and Nihonno seinen* [Adolescents in the world and in Japan]. Tokyo: The Printing Office of the Ministry of Finance.

Prime Minister's Office (1982). *Seishonen to katei* [Children, adolescents and families: A report of comparative research about adolescents and children, and families]. Tokyo: The Printing Office of the Ministry of Finance.

Prime Minister's Office (1991). *Seishonennoyujinkankei* [Friendship of children and adolescents: A report of a cross-national study of friendship of children and adolescents]. Tokyo: The Printing Office of the Ministry of Finance.

Prime Minister's Office (1992). *Danjyobyoudou ni kansuru yoronchyousa* [Opinion survey regarding the equality of both sexes]. Tokyo: Unpublished government report.

Prime Minister's Office (1993). *Sekaiseinenishikichosa* [Survey of adolescents in the world]. Tokyo: The Printing Office of the Ministry of Finance.

Prime Minister's Office (1995). *Shounenhikounikansuruseronchyous* [Public opinion poll about delinquency]. Tokyo: Unpublished government report.

Rothbaum, F., Pott, M., Azuma, H., Miyake, K., & Weisz, J. (2000). The development of close relationships in Japan and the United States: Paths of symbiotic harmony and generative tension. *Child Development, 71*(5), 1121–1142.

Schodt, F. L. (1983). *Manga! Manga! The world of Japanese comics.* Tokyo: Kodansha.

Shimizu, Y. (1983). *Kodomo no Shitsuke to Gakkouseikatsu* [The discipline of children and school life]. Tokyo: Tokyo University Press.

Sodei, T. (1977). Problems of aged persons in daily life. *Social Gerontology, 7,* 3–23.

Tanaka, Y. (1994). Review of work-induced family separation (*Tanshifunin*) studies. *Japanese Journal of Educational Psychology, 42,* 104–114.

Tokuoka, H. (1981). Rikontokodomo [Divorce and children]. In T. Kamiko & K. Masuda (Eds.), *Nihonjinnokazokukankei* [Family relationships of the Japanese: A cross-national comparison] (pp. 79–106). Tokyo: Youhikaku.

Uno, K. S. (1993). The death of "Good Wife, Wise Mother?" In A. Gordon (Ed.), *Postwar Japan as history* (pp. 293–322). Berkeley: University of California Press.

White, M. (1993). *The material child: Coming of age in Japan and America.* New York: The Free Press.

Yamamura, Y. (1971). *Nihonjin to haha* [The Japanese and the mother]. Tokyo: Toyokan Shuppansha.

Yuzawa, Y. (1995). *Zusetsu Kazokumondai no genzai* [Current problems of families]. Tokyo: Nippon hoso kyokai.

SUGGESTED READINGS

Azuma, H., & Hara, H. (1974). *Shitsuke* [Discipline]. Tokyo: Koubundo.

Bacon, A. M. (2000). *Japanese girls and women.* London: Kegan Paul International.

Becker, C. B. (1998). Aging, dying, and bereavement in contemporary Japan. *International Journal of Group Tensions, 28* (1–2), 59–83.

Bowlby, J. (1969). *Attachment and loss. Vol. l. Attachment.* New York: Basic Books.

Bumiller, E. (1996). *The secrets of Mariko: A year in the life of a Japanese woman and her family.* New York: Random House.

Cheng, S.-J., & Miyake, K. (1987). Japanese studies of infant development. In H. Stevenson, H. Azuma, & K. Hakuta (Eds.), *Child development and education in Japan* (pp. 135–146). New York: Freeman.

Cherry, K. (1987). *Womansword: What Japanese words say about women.* Tokyo: Kodansha.

Coleman, S. (1991). *Family planning in Japanese society: Traditional birth control in a modern urban culture.* Princeton, NJ: Princeton University Press.

Gielen, U. P., & Naito, T. (1999). Teaching perspectives on cross-cultural psychology and Japanese society. *International Journal of Group Tensions, 28* (3–4), 319–344.

Gilligan, C., & Wiggins, G. (1987). The origins of morality in early childhood relationships. In J. Kagan & S. Lamb (Eds.), *The emergence of morality in young children* (pp. 277–305). Chicago: University of Chicago Press.

Hamabata, M. M. (1991). *Crested kimono: Power and love in the Japanese business family.* Ithaca, NY: Cornell University Press.

Hardacre, H. (1993). The New Religions, family, and society in Japan. In M. E. Marty & R. S. Appleby (Eds.), *Fundamentalisms and society Reclaiming the sciences, the family, and education* (Vol. 2, pp. 294–310). Chicago: University of Chicago Press.

Hess, R., Holloway, S., McDevitt, T., Kashiwagi, K., Nagano, S., Miyake, K., Dickson, W. P., Price, G., Hatano, G., & McDevitt, T. (1986b). Family influences on school readiness and achievement in Japan and United States: An overview of a longitudinal study. In H. Stevenson, H. Azuma, & K. Hakuta (Eds.), *Child development and education in Japan* (pp. 147–166). New York: Freeman.

Hirayama, H., & Hirayama, K. K. (1986). The sexuality of Japanese Americans. Special issue: Human sexuality, ethnoculture, and social work. *Journal of Social Work and Human Sexuality, 4,* 81–98.

Imamura, A. E. (1995). *Urban Japanese housewives: At home and in the community.* Honolulu: University of Hawaii Press.

Iwao, S. (1992). *The Japanese woman: Traditional image and changing reality.* New York: The Free Press.

Jeremy, M., Robinson, M. E., & Hoichi, U. (1989). *Ceremony and symbolism in the Japanese home.* Honolulu: University of Hawaii Press.

Joshi, M., & MacLean, M. (1997). Maternal expectations of child development in India, Japan, and England. *Journal of Cross-Cultural Psychology, 28,* 219–234.

Kamiko, T. (1981). Nihonnokazoku [Japanese families]. In T. Kamiko & K. Masuda (Eds.), *Nihonjinnokazokukankei* [Family relationships of the Japanese: A cross-national comparison] (pp. 1–22). Tokyo: Youhikaku.

Kawai, H. (1986). Violence in the home: Conflict between two principles—maternal and paternal. In T. Sugiyama Lebra & W. P. Lebra (Eds.), *Japanese culture and behavior: Selected readings* (rev. ed., pp. 297–306). Honolulu: University of Hawaii Press.

Kojima, H. (1987). Child rearing concepts as a belief-value system of the society and the individual. In H. Stevenson, H. Azuma, & K. Hakuta (Eds.), *Child development and education in Japan* (pp. 39–54). New York: Freeman.

Lebra, T. S. (1984). *Japanese women: Constraint and fulfillment.* Honolulu: University of Hawaii Press.

LeTendre, G. K., & Rohlen, T. P. (2000). *Learning to be an adolescent: Growing up in U.S. and Japanese middle schools.* New Haven, CT: Yale University Press.

Ministry of Education and Science. (1999). *Japanese government policies in education, science, sports and culture.* Tokyo: The Printing Office of the Ministry of Finance.

Naito, T., & Gielen, U. P. (1992). Tatemae and honne: A study of moral relativism in Japanese culture. In U. P. Gielen, L. L. Adler, & N. A. Milgram (Eds.), *Psychology in international perspective: 50 years of the International Council of Psychologists* (pp. 161–172). Amsterdam: Swets and Zeitlinger.

Ono, S. (1962). *Shinto: The kamiway.* Tokyo: Charles E. Tuttle.

Reischauer, E. O. (1988). *The Japanese today* (2nd ed.). Tokyo: Charles E. Tuttle.

Sengoku, T. (1998). *Nihon no koukousei* [Japanese high school students]. Tokyo: Nihonhousoukyoukai.

Shwalb, D. W., Imaizumi, N., & Nakazawa, J. (1987). The modern Japanese father: Roles and problems in a changing society. In M. E. Lamb (Ed.), *The father's role: Cross-cultural perspectives* (pp. 247–269). Hillsdale, NJ: Erlbaum.

Smith, R. J. (1987). Gender inequality in contemporary Japan. *Journal of Japanese Studies, 13*(1), 1–25.

Takahashi, K. (1987). The role of the personal framework of social relationships in socialization studies. In H. Stevenson, H. Azuma, & K. Hakuta (Eds.), *Child development and education in Japan* (pp. 123–134). New York: Freeman.

Wagatsuma, H., & DeVos, G. A. (1984). *Heritage of endurance: Family patterns and delinquency formation in urban Japan.* Berkeley: University of California Press.

Yamamoto, J., & Kubota, M. (1983). The Japanese-American family. In G. J. Powell (Ed.), *The psychological development of minority children* (pp. 307–329). New York: Brunner/Mazel.

CHAPTER 6

CHANGING PATTERNS
OF FAMILY LIFE IN INDIA

PITTU LAUNGANI
Manchester University

> *Happy families are all alike, every unhappy family is unhappy in its own way.*
>
> —Leo Tolstoy

Since it is impossible to visualize family life without the presence of children, let us start with a truism: children are children are children, the world over. They are all born helpless and defenseless and need care, comfort, food, and shelter for their biological survival. Their biological survival also runs parallel with their cognitive, linguistic, and emotional development, which is indispensable in order for them to become part of the society and the culture into which they are born. Without human care and guidance, it would be impossible for children to acquire the above human characteristics. Several remarkable opportunistic case studies have shown that in the case of abandoned infants who were brought up in the "wilds" by wolves, when brought back into human society, they failed to acquire any of the positive human emotions, such as smiling, laughing, or any physical attributes such as being able to walk on their feet, being able to use implements and tools with their hands, nor indeed the most rudimentary linguistic skills. Further studies, such as those of Bowlby, Wayne and Dennis, Ainsworth, Sluckin, and others, in keeping with an ethological perspective, have also demonstrated the deleterious effects of deprivation on children brought up in orphanages and in homes where their care has been minimal or virtually nonexistent. In recent years, similar findings have been reported in studies of refugee children from Romania, Bosnia, Serbia, and other Eastern European countries (Bill Young, 1999, personal communication).

It is obvious, therefore, that the biological, social, linguistic, emotional, and cultural development of children is totally dependent on their being nurtured and cared for by humans in a human society. That is the only way by which they can become "humanized." It need hardly be emphasized that the most powerful influences on the growth and development of a child are those of the child's family members (or, in their absence, the child's caregivers).

Families vary along several characteristics and dimensions: size, affluence, levels of education, occupation, intelligence, attitudes, beliefs, values, and so on. Families also undergo change, which is often brought about by demographic factors, industrialization, urbanization, economic depression, war, famine, natural disasters, and so on. (United Nations, 1996).

A family is a microcosm of a wider section of our community, which, in turn, is a microcosm of the society and the culture in which each family lives. Society provides us with a structure, which regulates our lives, our beliefs and practices, so that we are able to make sense of ourselves, of our own lives, of others, of our own culture, and of the world around us. We tend to see society in tangible terms because it consists of a group of people who occupy a given territory and live together.

It needs to be emphasized that the terms *society* and *culture,* although related, are not synonymous. The term *culture,* like many such global terms, is best understood as an umbrella term, which includes a variety of meanings and perspectives. It is a historically created system of beliefs, attitudes, values, and behaviors of people enjoined by a common language (or several languages) and religion, and occupying a given geographic territory or region (Parikh, 2000). These factors allow individuals living in that society to structure their lives in accordance with the established norms and values of that society. It also allows them to regulate their individual and collective lives (Barnlund & Araki, 1985; Brislin, 1990; Kakar, 1979/1992; Laungani, 1998, 2000, 2001b; Roland, 1988; Segall, Dasen, Berry, & Poortinga, 1999; Smith & Bond, 1993; Triandis, 1972, 1994; White, 1947; Whiting, 1963).

Notwithstanding the fact that all children all over the world need human care for their growth and development, there are significant variations both within and between cultures in the manner in which children are cared for and socialized.

Even within a single culture, people vary along a variety of dimensions, including skin color, language, dietary preferences, religious beliefs, attitudes, and practices, to name but a few. As one learns to make sense of one's culture, one notices that differences also extend into political, social, economic, physical, and other environmental domains. Despite the differences, however, there is a sense of "belongingness," a feeling of oneness with people of one's own culture. This occurs when one understands that all the diverse groups in one's society are to a large extent united by a set of core values. Value systems have a significant bearing on a variety of factors, including childrearing techniques, patterns of socialization, development of identities, kinship networks, work habits, social and familial arrangements, and the religious beliefs and practices of people of that society.

In order to put Indian family life into a meaningful perspective, it is useful to identify certain Western markers against which the Indian family can be compared.

FAMILY SIZE AND STRUCTURE IN WESTERN CULTURES

In the not too distant past—less than half a century ago—a family unit consisted of the father, the mother, their two to three children, and even the grandparents. The father was seen as the patriarch and the proverbial "bread winner." He had no role to play in the day-to-day bringing up of children, which was left largely in the hands of the women at home. Day-to-day life revolved around the family.

In the last three to four decades, however, the situation has changed, so much so that the concept of what constitutes a family has become difficult to define with any degree of accuracy (Levin, 1990; Trost, 1990). This is due to several factors. Formalized marriage has lost its status in many Western societies (Dumon, 1992). Cohabitation without marriage has increased. The rate of divorce has been rising in most European countries, including Britain. It is estimated that at least one-third of all British families are single-parent families, headed by a female. More than 25 percent of the population lives alone. Other extraneous factors such as changes in demographic trends, economic recessions, wars, famines, migrations, technological innovation, urbanization, and widening opportunities for women also account for the changes that have taken place.

The changes in the size and the structure of families, combined with high levels of social and occupational mobility, may have "destabilized" society, creating a sense of loss of community life, particularly in the urban metropolitan cities (United Nations, 1996). From a psychological point of view, major changes have occurred in collective values, particularly those that support individualism, in which the needs of an individual take priority over the needs of the family and the group. Although the family is recognized as the basic unit—the microcosm of society—changes in society have altered the roles and functions of both men and women in families. It is clear that the "traditional" role of the family as a self-sustaining, self-contained unit has changed almost beyond recognition. What impact a nuclear or a one-parent family (or a family of "changing" parents due to living with different partners or remarriage), combined with increasing occupational, physical, and social mobility, has on the future growth and development of the child is still an open question. However, in such a changing family situation, the child is more than likely to be de-

nied a sense of continuity and familiarity, not just in terms of being brought up by the same parents, but also in terms of friends and acquaintances.

It has been argued that families in Western countries, particularly the United States, have been unable to develop positive ways of adjusting to these rapid changes, and "the speed of change alone is a major factor of stress in families" (World Bank, 2000).

FAMILY SIZE AND STRUCTURE IN INDIA

Indian (Hindu) society, not unlike other Eastern societies, is a family-based and community-centered society (Basham, 1966; Flood, 1996; Kakar, 1981; Klostermaier, 1998; Koller, 1982; Lannoy, 1976; Laungani, 1997, 1999; Lipner, 1994; Mandelbaum, 1972; Sharma, 2000; Zaehner, 1966).

In non-Western cultures, particularly in India, Pakistan, Bangladesh, and several other countries in Southeast Asia, including Malaysia and Indonesia, the size of the average family tends to be large. In China, although the present population is in the region of 1.27 billion, concerted attempts are being made by the government to restrict and control family size to one child per family. The projection figures tend to show that by 2010 China's population will rise to 1.357 billion, and in 2020 it is expected to reach 1.433 billion (Encyclopaedia Britannica, 2003).

Non-Western cultures even today follow a pattern of extended family networks, which often include the child's parents, grandparents, uncles, aunts, sisters-in-law, nieces, nephews, and other siblings in the household. In many affluent Indian homes, there is also a retinue of faithful and long-serving servants (or "faithful retainers," to use a Victorian phrase) involved in the care and the upbringing of children (Laungani, 2001b; United Nations, 1996). Thus a child learns from an early age to be tended by a variety of persons of different ages in the household. The child also learns the nature of his or her individual relationships with different members in the family.

From my personal experience, I can point out that even at a rough count there were over twenty members in my household, not counting the retinue of servants, who, so far as I can remember, had always been around. And far from a decline in numbers, the number of members staying at home rose regularly as a result of more children being born into the family. One of the obvious consequences of such a cultural arrangement is a sense of continuity and permanence that is created in the mind of the growing child. Even after thirty years of living in the West, a return to India, to the decaying ancestral family home, creates a sense of sameness, which I find far more reassuring than the changes wrought by time in that country. The same faces—many of them wizened, lined, bent, and even arthritic—create an (albeit false) sense of permanence.

Given the large number of members in the family, children of course become the beneficiaries of multiple caregivers. The child in an Indian home is likely to be subjected to a variety of influences (both contradictory and complementary) in the process of socialization. In other words, a growing child is also likely to acquire a variety of role models in the course of socialization.

The sense of sameness and permanence is also perpetuated by the fact that divorce is rare in India. It is not unheard of, but the rates are extremely low, particularly among Hindus, who comprise 82 to 84 percent of the total Indian population. Nowhere, not even in large urbanized metropolitan cities, do they reach the kind of epidemic proportions found in the West.

Marriage in India (particularly among Hindus, Catholics, Sikhs, and Parsis) is seen as a sacred religious ceremony, and the couple is expected to remain together until "death do them part." That is the socially accepted view, which contains more than a tinge of moral righteousness. The putative sacredness of a Hindu marriage is often seen as the standard against which marriages in Western countries are judged—*and found wanting.* Reality, however, does not in many cases reflect such high-sounding moral claims. A strong and pernicious social stigma is associated with divorce—particularly for the female, who in most cases is economically and socially dependent on the husband, his family members, and their network of relations *(baradari).* She is not even in a position to countenance the idea of a divorce, let alone take any steps toward achieving it. The serious

consequences—e.g., loss of status, the possible loss of custody of her children, homelessness, the threat of poverty, the danger of being referred to as a "loose" woman (and thus "easy game")—conspire to exert the required pressures to keep the marriage institution intact. So strong and powerful are the social pressures that most women, even under the most appalling domestic conditions (maltreatment, violence, abuse, lack of independence, subjugation at home, overwork, lack of political and legal awareness and recognition of their "rights," etc.), elect to stay within the confines of a tyrannous family as silent sufferers rather than break away.

FEATURES OF EXTENDED FAMILIES IN INDIA

Westerners in general tend to construe extended families in India largely in structural terms. It has been argued that the extended family network in India, particularly in the large metropolitan cities, is gradually breaking down and is beginning to undergo change, even giving way to a Western-style nuclear family structure.

It is doubtless true that some families in the larger cities of India have adopted a nuclear family network; one can in many instances see a replica of the "2.4-family-member structure," to which we referred earlier. But these exceptions notwithstanding, it needs to be stressed that Indian family life operates predominantly in an extended family network.

The misconception is based on how the term "extended" family is defined. In the West an extended family is generally understood in "structural" terms, viz., all members of the family, living together, sharing jointly, the kitchen, the income, and other resources. The patriarch in most instances is seen as the head of the family, and the other members within the family are expected to defer to the wishes, the authority, and even the dictates of the head of the family. In some instances, his authority remains absolute. This type of a family is best referred to as a *joint family.*

An extended family, however, although sharing most of the above characteristics, may not always live under the same roof and share all the resources. Thus, not all extended families are joint families (see Chapter 12 on Greek families for somewhat similar considerations). While the system of joint families still prevails in many parts of India, particularly in rural areas, monumental changes have taken place in the large cities. A desperate attempt to escape from the evils of debt, poverty, starvation, disease, lack of medical care, caste-related exploitation, and so on, has led to massive migrations from the rural to urban sectors in India. This of course has resulted in large cities being choked for space, fresh air, and accommodation. Only a few of the migrant families manage to put a roof over their heads. And the slums in which they live are often so small and cramped as to make it impossible for the entire family (of, say, eight persons) to live in them. The rest of the migrants survive by the roadside, next to a bus stop, on the pavements, in the lee of a boundary wall of a building, under a tarpaulin sheet tied to overhanging branches of a tree, or in illegally constructed mean hovels, which are often razed by the police, the local municipal authorities, or the lashing rains during the monsoons. What these families subsist on can only be left to conjecture. How they manage to survive under these indescribable conditions is in itself a miracle. It is estimated that over 40 percent of the urban dwellers in large metropolitan cities live by the roadside! These factors have led to a physical separation of families, but such a state of affairs has by no means led to an erosion of the normative power of the extended family system.

In addition to its "structural" features, the extended family needs to be understood in its psychological and functional terms as well. For a start, the patterns of relationships tend largely to be intrafamilial. Family life is organized along age- and gender-related hierarchical lines, with male elders being accorded a privileged position and a position of power. Each member—right from childhood—learns to understand and accept his or her own position within the family hierarchy. Who can take "liberties" with whom, who can shout at whom, who will defer to whom, who will seek comfort and solace from whom, who can confide in whom, are subtle emotional patterns of expressions one soon learns in an extended family network.

Since relationships play a central role in extended families, it is worth pointing out that in India, each relationship has a specific name attached to it. For instance, the words brother-in-law and sister-in-law can mean any one of three relationships in English. Without further information, the westerner cannot know which of the following three persons is being referred to by the term *brother-in-law*:

ENGLISH TERM	INDIAN (HINDI) TERM
My wife's brother	*Salaa*
My sister's husband	*Bhanoi*
My wife's sister's husband	*Saandu-bhai (or Jeejaji)*

The same difficulties arise for the word *sister-in-law*. She could be:

My wife's sister	*Saali*
My brother's wife	*Bhabhi*
My wife's brother's wife	*Saali*

Each of these six relationships in most Indian languages is identified by a specific name. The above examples refer to fairly easy-to-understand relationships. Complex relationships, such as *my mother's brother's, daughter-in-law's, son* are easily identifiable because of a specific name attached to it. Such, as one can see, is not the case in the English language. It is clear from this that specific words have been invented because of their functional importance within the cultural system. It does not take long for children to learn not only the exact nature of such complex relationships, but also the range and types of feelings and emotions that they may or may not be allowed to express within their large extended family network. These are common lessons that children of both sexes learn at home.

GENDER DIFFERENCES IN SOCIALIZATION OF CHILDREN IN INDIA

There are significant differences in socialization processes between boys and girls. Male children enjoy a more privileged position than their female siblings. The elders in the family allow a male child to "get away" with behaviors they would find hard to condone in a female child (Kakar, 1981). The privilege also extends to food, clothing, toys, and play. In an impoverished home or a home of less than adequate means, a larger share of food is given to the male children; they may also be fed first by the family members. The needs of the female child seldom or never take precedence.

In accordance with ancient Hindu scriptures, the birth of a male child in a family is considered to be a blessing, for a variety of reasons (Laungani, 1997). First, it ensures the perpetuation of the family name. Second, the son is seen as an economic asset and on marriage will "bring in" a handsome dowry. Third, he will also be expected to support and look after his parents when they become old and frail. Fourth, it is the son who, upon the death of his parents, is expected to perform all the funeral rites and also to light the funeral pyre, to ensure the safe passage and the eventual repose of their souls.

The birth of a daughter, on the other hand, is treated with mixed feelings and even with some misgivings. As Kakar (1981) points out, the daughter in a Hindu family hardly ever develops an identity of her own. Upon birth, she is seen as a daughter; she is expected to remain chaste and pure; on reaching marriageable age she may be seen as an economic liability because of the dowry she is expected to take with her to her husband's home. Upon entering her married home, her status changes. She is seen as a wife, as a daughter-in-law, as a sister-in-law in the new home, and then as a mother, a grandmother, and should her husband predecease her, as a widow. Like a snake casting off its skin, the daughter on marriage is shorn of her own name. She acquires a new persona and is given a new name by which she is addressed in future. While the snake's discarding of its old skin and acquiring a new skin is a natural event, which has certain biological and evolutionary advantages, the Hindu bride, on entering her new home—her own feelings notwithstanding—is expected to bury her past, which includes her identity, and start her life with a new identity that is *ascribed* to her by her husband and her in-laws. Such a stag-

gering metamorphosis confers no biological or evolutionary advantages. On the contrary, it reinforces the defenseless if not subjugated role that she is expected to play after marriage. Thus, her maiden name Geeta may be turned into Seeta, and Mohini to Rohini, Rajini to Sajni, and so on. She appears to have no individual identity other than the changing identities she acquires through reflected role relationships. Her private persona remains largely submerged within these changing and conflicting identities. Right from birth to death, she does not possess an identity of her own. However, it is important to stress that several enlightened parents look on the birth of a girl as "a gift of the gods" and see it as their sacred duty, which is part of Hindu *dharma* to have their daughter(s) handsomely and "happily" married.

Despite the seemingly pitiful nature of the daughter-in-law's position in her husband's family home, there are compensatory psychological and power-related dramas that are played out in extended families in India. Imagine a scenario: three brothers with their respective wives living in an extended and joint family network. The oldest daughter-in-law (the oldest daughter-in-law is referred to as *jethani*), by virtue of being married to the oldest son, is often in an extremely dominant position to exercise power—delegating cooking, cleaning, washing, and such other household tasks to the two younger sisters-in-law (the younger sister-in-law is referred to as *derani*)—even the care of her own children may be relegated to her younger sisters-in-law. The power exercised can in certain instances be extremely tyrannical. The second sister-in-law can exercise a certain amount of power over the youngest sister-in-law, and so on, moving down along age-related hierarchical lines. However, the power structure can change dramatically in a variety of subtle ways, which often remain unnoticed to an outsider. For instance, the eldest sister-in-law may be childless, or may not have produced a male child, while the younger sisters-in-law may have produced sons; they may also have come from affluent homes, and may also be highly educated, or their respective husbands may have a far superior earning capacity than their oldest brother, and so on. The balance of power is by no means fixed; it is flexible, subtle, and changes from time to time. However, all three sisters-in-law are expected to defer to the unquestionable power of their mother-in-law, who often rules the house.

Upon the death of the mother-in-law, the balance of power shifts quite dramatically. Covert (and sometimes not so covert) battles may be fought by the three daughters-in-law, with each jockeying for a position at the top. At times, the husbands too may be brought into the fray, leading to severe turmoil within the family, until the dust settles and the family situation reaches a new equilibrium.

Such subtle psychological dynamics are difficult if not impossible to investigate objectively; even the idea of using any of the qualitative methods of social research—handing out a questionnaire, for instance—is too ludicrous to demand serious consideration. One would need to be part of the ongoing family drama to arrive at some understanding of the problems and the intrigues involved and the manner in which they are handled.

Several writers (Flood, 1996; Kakar, 1981; Klostermaier, 1998; Koller, 1982; Lannoy, 1976; Laungani, 1997, 1999; Mandelbaum, 1972; Roland, 1988) on this subject have pointed out that, despite a large number of persons involved in the socialization of children, the part played by the mother in the bringing up of children is of paramount importance, particularly in her relationship with her son—a special relationship develops between the two. Whether this relationship can be construed in Oedipal terms is arguable, although several writers, including Kakar, Lannoy, and Roland, and others operating from within a Freudian framework, have asserted that this is often the case. The male child is indulged, pampered, protected, and as far as possible, is denied very little. While the mother may attempt to strike a balance between the male and female children's demands, it often transpires that the male child's impulsive wishes, wants, and desires take precedence over the needs of the female child. The father, on the other hand, tends to remain detached from the day-to-day cares related to the upbringing of the child, male or female. His role, at least during the first few years, tends to be minimal.

It is generally after the sacred thread ceremony of the male child that the father may start to take a keen interest in the son's education, socialization, and the acquisition of those qualities and behavior patterns that will turn him into a model Hindu as prescribed in the ancient Vedic scriptures.

While boys are pampered and accorded privileges, girls are often brought up on a relatively strict regime. A girl is made aware of the role she is expected to play both at home, during adolescence, and more importantly, after her marriage. Verily are virtue and virginity venerated. To convey the concept of virtue, the children are taught lessons from ancient Hindu texts, including the two Indian epics, the *Ramayana* and the *Mahabharata*. Glorious stories of the virtuous and religious acts performed by Hindu women are held up as the ideal to which the female child is expected to aspire. Virtue consists of obedience (initially to parents and then to the husband and to the husband's family), doing one's duty, truthfulness, prayer, and ensuring the health and security of the husband and family. She is also trained in the necessary culinary and other domestic skills so that when she is married no criticisms befall her and she is looked upon as an ideal wife, a dutiful daughter-in-law, a compliant sister-in-law, and when she has children of her own, a loving and caring mother and indulgent grandmother.

DEVELOPMENT OF IDENTITY

One of the features—and there are several such features—that distinguishes Indian families from Western families is in the manner in which children develop their identities. In the West, as is well known, the development of individual identity is generally seen in socio-psycho-cognitive terms. The process of identity formation starts in infancy and, according to received wisdom, passes through several critical stages, from childhood, to adolescence, and into adulthood. To acquire an appropriate identity that asserts one's strengths, is located in reality, separates the individual from others and is thereby kept distinct from those of others, reflects one's true inner being, and leads to the fulfillment or the realization of one's potential is by no means easy. It often results in conflict that, if unresolved, leads to severe stress, and in extreme cases to an identity crisis (Camilleri, 1989; Erikson, 1963; Maslow, 1970, 1971; Rogers, 1961, 1980). In other words, the individual concerned has to "work" toward achieving an appropriate identity.

First, living as people do, in an extended family network, there are no clear demarcating boundaries between "I" and "thou." Boundaries merge. Thus, living together in a confined physical area, combined with the fact that most day-to-day activities are done jointly and are shared, the need for psychological and physical space and privacy, which is of such paramount importance to Westerners, does not have the same value among Indians. It might be true to say that people walk in and out of each other's rooms—even lives—without qualm, without any fears or sense of intrusion. One might even go as far as to argue that one acquires a *collective* identity, which reflects all the norms and values shared by the family, their caste, and subcaste members.

Let me illustrate this with a personal example. On each of my trips to India, one of the things I found irritating was the fact the people walked into my room without knocking. There was little I could do to change ancient family customs; I accepted them as a long-suffering martyr. However, I thought I might have some success with our servants, particularly our cook, who has been with us for over forty years. One morning, as he barged into my room with a cup of tea, I suggested to him as gently as I could that he should knock, and wait for my response before entering my room. He seemed genuinely bewildered by my request. He scratched his head, thought for a minute or two, and replied, "But, Sahib, I *know* you are in your room. What is the purpose of knocking?" I was chastened by his innocent good humor and never repeated my request for privacy—an idea that made no sense to him, whatever. The notion of privacy, the desire to seek it, the fear of intruding on another person's privacy, does not in general have the same functional value as it does for people in most Western countries (Laungani, 1999, 2000).

Second, in India, identity to a large extent is *ascribed* and, to a lesser extent, *achieved*. To a large extent one's identity is *ascribed* at birth. One is born into one of the four hereditary castes (this applies mainly to Hindus, who comprise over 82 percent of the total population of India) and one is destined to stay in it until death. An upward movement from a lower to a higher caste is virtually impossible. It is possible for an individual to fall from a higher into a lower caste, but to a large extent, people tend to be rooted to their caste origins and consequently their internalized attitudes, beliefs, and values, their familial and social behaviors, are also caste-related.

There are advantages and disadvantages in such traditional arrangements. On the one hand, the individual in an Indian family setup does not have to pass through the critical stages in the process of developing an identity, as is normally the case with children in Western individualistic cultures. On the other hand, an ascribed identity tends to restrict the choices open to the individual. While personal choice is central to an individualistic society, it is seen as an exception in a communalistic society. The growing child may be denied the opportunity of "experimenting" with multiple identities, as is possible in Western societies.

The question is, how does caste influence the acquisition of identity and a variety of other enduring psychological and behavioral characteristics in the individual?

THE HINDU CASTE SYSTEM

Although in many respects Indian society is similar to that of most other Eastern societies, its unique distinguishing feature lies in its caste system. The caste system is construed in different ways by different scholars; in varying ways, it is seen as a form of institutionalized inequality, an instrument of social assimilation, an extension of the joint family system, a system of graded relationships, and so on. Its origin dates back to over 3,500 years ago. The four castes in their hierarchical order are as follows:

Brahmins: the learned and the educated elite; the guardians of the Vedas; the priests

Kshatriyas: the noble warriors; defenders of the realm

Vaishyas: the traders, businessmen, farmers, money lenders

Sudras: their main function is to serve the needs of the upper three

Members of the upper three castes are known as the "twice born" because their male members have undergone an initiation. It is after the sacred thread ceremony that marks their "second birth"—the rites of passage—that they are allowed to read and learn from the Vedas and to participate in all religious ceremonies. This rite separates the three highest castes from the Sudras, who are not permitted such an initiation. The Sudras are further subdivided into "touchables" and "untouchables." Sudras are normally expected to engage in occupations that are considered by the upper three castes to be demeaning and polluting: garbage collector, crematorium attendant, barber, masseur, cleaner, cobbler, tanner, butcher, water carrier, and so on. For the members of the upper three castes to engage in any of the above activities results in their being "spiritually polluted." In some cases, to allow any members of the lowest caste into one's home results in pollution of the house. One would then need to engage in a variety of religious practices to ensure the purification of one's home. In the past, many homes in India used to be constructed in a manner that permitted a "sweeper" (a lavatory attendant) to enter the lavatory through a side entrance, without ever entering the house through the front door. Although such practices have declined significantly, they have not disappeared entirely. Many educated, modernized Indians look on this ancient practice with feelings of revulsion but, despite their valiant attempts, have failed to put an end to such humiliating practices. They can be observed in certain parts of India, particularly in the rural areas in Uttar Pradesh, Madhya Pradesh, Bihar, Orissa, Bengal, Tamil Nadu, and a few other states. It is clear that one's caste origins are so strongly ingrained in the Hindu psyche that it is difficult for most to renounce such appalling practices.

THE UBIQUITOUS POWER OF THE CASTE SYSTEM

Hinduism, unlike Islam and Christianity, is not a proselytizing religion. But such is the awesome power of the caste system that variants of the system have spread to other religious groups, including Muslims, Catholics, and Sikhs, in certain parts of India. Although in theory these religious groups would consider the very idea of caste as anathema to their own religious beliefs, caste and caste relations creep into social practices in subtle ways. In India, it is not uncommon to notice that many Catholics, in addition to their own Christian names, also use Hindu names, and operate in a *de facto* caste system. Hindu names such as Prabhu, Shankar, Ashok, or Harish may be followed by Catholic (Portuguese) surnames, such as Periera, Fernandes, Correa, Colaco, Torcato, or D'Silva. Many Muslims, too, operate on a similar basis: their names are also often indistinguishable from Hindu names. A person unacquainted with Indian names would find it difficult to tell from surnames such as Bahadur, Bhat, Bhatti, Bhimji, Chamar, Choudhary, Dalal, Darzi, Ghani, Kanji, Kamal, Mehta, Mistry, Nawab, Nayak, Patel, Raja, Ramji, Sutaria, Shah—to name but a few—whether the persons referred to are Hindus, Christians, or Muslims. Even within Sikhism, which is a theoretically caste-free religion, many Sikhs operate in a *de facto* caste system in certain parts of India and in Britain.

THE SACRED AND THE SECULAR

In Western countries there is a clear distinction between the sacred and the secular, but in Hinduism there are no sharp distinctions between the sacred and the secular. The lines are blurred. This can be observed even in the most mundane day-to-day activities, such as washing one's hands, having a bath, carrying out one's morning ablutions, accepting drinking water or food from others, or offering it to others. Although seemingly trivial, they have deep-rooted religious connotations. To a Westerner unversed in the day-to-day ritualistic practices of Hindus, such behaviors may seem strange and even quite bizarre. To a Hindu, however, they fall within the orbit of necessary religious ablutions, which he or she has internalized from childhood and performs automatically. So much of day-to-day Hindu behavior is influenced by religious beliefs that it is virtually impossible to identify behaviors that might be seen as secular (Pandey, 1969).

Since the majority of rituals performed either privately or collectively have a religious connotation, it is clear that ritual activity is addressed to sacred beings, such as gods or ancestors. Ninian Smart (1996) refers to such rituals as *focused rituals,* where the focus is on worship. Rituals therefore are forms of personal communication with gods. Communication itself may serve different purposes: worship, giving thanks, asking for favors, expiation, and atonement. Smart adds that a variant of the religious ritual is the yogic ritual, in which the performance of yogic exercises is seen as a means by which a person seeks to attain a higher state of consciousness.

The efficacy of rituals is believed to rest on their repetition; their meticulous performance provides a source of comfort to those practicing them. Failure to perform the rituals leads to a form of spiritual pollution. Flood (1996) points out that it is ritual action that anchors people in a sense of deeper identity and belonging.

Although varying numbers of rituals are recorded in different texts, the rituals appear to be organized in a sequence that expresses the Hindu social order, or *dharma.* The most important rituals are those related to birth, the initiation ceremony, marriage, which signals the beginning of the householder's life, and the final funeral rites and after-death rites.

The day-to-day religious and secular behaviors of Hindus make sense when seen within the context of purity and pollution. Hindus view purity and pollution largely in spiritual terms and not in terms of hygiene (Filippi, 1996; Fuller, 1992). The status of a person in India is determined by his or her position in the caste hierarchy and by the degree of contact with the polluting agent. Proximity to a polluting agent may constitute a permanent pollution. This means that certain occupations are permanently polluting. Such a form of pollution is collective—the entire family remains polluted. It is also hereditary.

Pollution may be temporary but mild, severe, and permanent. One is in a state of mild impurity on waking up in the morning, prior to performing one's morning ablutions, when one has eaten food, when one has not prayed. Mild states of pollution are easily overcome by appropriate actions, such as baths, prayers, wearing clean, washed clothes, and engaging in appropriate cleansing and purification rituals.

Severe pollution occurs when high-caste Hindus come into physical and/or social contact with persons of the lowest caste, or when they eat meat (particularly beef), or when the strict rules governing commensality are abrogated. Commensality is concerned with hospitality, with extending and receiving hospitality. To overcome this form of pollution it is necessary for the polluted individual (in some instances the entire family may be polluted) to perform a series of appropriate propitiation rites, rituals, and religious ceremonies under the guidance of their family priest.

Permanent pollution occurs when a Hindu belonging to the highest caste (Brahmin) marries a person from the lowest caste, thereby breaking the principle of endogamy that has always been regarded as one of the cementing factors holding the caste system together. Endogamy—marrying within one's own caste and subcaste—was seen as a desired course of action in India. The Brahmins, in interpreting the Vedas, claimed that it was essential for persons to marry within their own caste. Such a form of marriage was considered to be sacred. An endogamous marriage enabled the parties involved in matrimony to retain the ritual purity of their caste and avoid any form of intercaste contamination. It also ensured the perpetuation of the caste system.

It is notable that over the centuries, the principle of endogamy has not been swept aside: it has continued to retain its stronghold over Hindus all over India, particularly in the rural areas of the country, and to a large extent, even among ex-patriot Hindus in Britain. Marriages are still arranged and organized by the parents of prospective spouses. Although the style of arranged marriages has undergone a modest change within Indian society—particularly among the affluent members of society in the urban sectors of the country—arranged marriages are still the norm.

Furthermore, what binds families in India is the fact that virtually all the major social and religious festivals and activities, such as christenings, betrothals, marriages, pilgrimages, are performed together. Most social relationships tend to be family-oriented. Visiting cousins, uncles, aunts, staying with the family, are an integral part of family life. Even an illness striking a family member tends to be transformed into a family problem (Kakar, 1981; Laungani, 2000, 2001b; Mandelbaum, 1972; Pandey, 1969), and attempts are made to find a joint solution to the problem.

For instance, in the case of a severe health-related problem affecting one family member, the entire family "takes over." Illness is like a magnet, which draws families together. Each member volunteers his or her own diagnosis of the illness, its causal factors, and cures and remedies, which he or she will urge the patient to follow regardless of their appropriateness. The entire family may resort to several conflicting strategies in dealing with the patient's illness. Special prayers are held for the speedy recovery of the patient; acts of piety and generosity, such as feeding the poor and the needy, are performed. The women in the household undertake fasts and prayers; and the family members get together to discuss and assess the patient's condition on a day-to-day basis. The patient is seldom left alone. Neighbors and other relatives are informed of the situation, word spreads, and visitors flock in at all hours to spend time with the patient. The fact that the patient might need to be left alone to rest, regain strength, and recover is not seen as an important consideration. Such overwhelming concern for the patient's health to a large extent needs to be seen within the context of social and cultural expectations and not necessarily in terms of "overflowing" love and affection for the patient. Not to visit a sick relative—close or distant—is likely to earn social disapprobation.

Interestingly enough, there is a paradox when it comes to a person in the family suffering from a psychological or psychiatric disorder. Attempts are made to conceal the disorder from relatives, friends, and the outside world because of the fear of social stigma befalling the entire family (Laungani, 2004). From a cultural point of view it is worth noting that the fear of social stigma related to mental disorders often leads to a conspiracy of secrecy. Many parents have been known to keep a severely disturbed member of the family "in hiding," concealed from the outside world, confined to a room. In such situations the family will go to great lengths to conceal a problem to prevent it being discovered and leading to social censure, which may also have an adverse effect on the marital prospects of the girls in the family.

The onset of a physical illness is often attributed to the workings of the law of karma—whether the patient recovers from (or succumbs to) the illness. It was fated. It was written. It was kismet. It was destined. It was karma. But psychological disorders are often explained in terms of "bad blood"—the family concerned having inherited "bad blood" from its ancestors.

The law of karma, as an all-embracing model, plays a vital explanatory role in the life of a Hindu right from birth to death at individual, familial, social, caste-related, and cultural levels.

THE LAW OF KARMA

The law of karma, in its simplest form, states that all human actions lead to consequences. Right actions produce good consequences and wrong actions produce bad consequences. At first sight, the law of karma seems to be identical with the law of universal causation, which asserts that every event has a cause, or that nothing is uncaused. Though seemingly identical, there are significant differences between the two laws. Unlike the law of universal causation, the law of karma is not concerned with consequences in general, but with consequences that affect the individual—the doer of the action. Second, the law of karma applies specifically to the moral sphere. It is therefore not concerned with the general relation between actions and their consequences, but "rather with the moral quality of the actions and their consequences" (Reichenbach, 1990, p. 1). Third, what gives the law of karma its supreme moral quality is the assertion that the doer not only deserves the consequences of his or her actions, but is unable to avoid experiencing them (Prasad, 1989). It should be made clear that the actions of the doer may have occurred in his or her present life, or in his or her past life. Similarly, the consequences of the doer's actions may occur during the person's present life or in his or her future life. The main point is that it is impossible to avoid the consequences of one's actions.

In his analysis of the law of karma, Hirayana (1949) explains that the events of our lives are determined by their antecedent causes. Since all actions lead to consequences, which are related to the nature and the type of action, absolute justice is our lot, in the sense that good actions lead to happiness and bad actions to unhappiness.

The doctrine of karma is extremely significant because it offers explanations not only for pain, suffering, and misfortune, but also for pleasure, happiness, and good fortune. Each of us receives the results of our own actions and not another's. Thus, the sins of our fathers are not visited on us. The deterministic belief that one's present life is shaped by one's actions in one's past life (or lives) allows Indians to explain and accept a variety of misfortunes (and good fortunes) that befall them through the course of their journey through life. It engenders within their psyche a spirit of passive, if not resigned, acceptance of misfortunes, ranging from sudden deaths within the family to glaring inequalities of caste and status, disease and illness, poverty and destitution, exploitation and prejudice.

Interestingly, the law of karma does not negate the notion of free will. As Von Fürer-Haimendorf (1974) has pointed out, in an important sense karma is based on the assumption of free will. The theory of karma rests on the idea that an individual has the final moral responsibility for each of his or her actions and hence the freedom of moral choice.

The law of karma stands out as the most significant feature of Hinduism. Although there is no basis for establishing its empirical validity, Hindus in general have an unswerving faith in the workings of the law of karma. It has shaped the Indian view of life over centuries. One might even go to the extent of saying that the Hindu psyche is built around the notion of karma (O'Flaherty, 1976, 1980; Reichenbach, 1990; Sharma, 2000; Sinari, 1984; Zaehner, 1966).

The influence of the law of karma manifests itself at every stage in a Hindu's life: at birth, in childhood, during adolescence and adulthood, in marriage, in illness and health, in good fortune and misfortune, in death, and bereavement, and after death.

A belief in determinism is likely to engender in the Indian psyche a spirit of passive, if not resigned, acceptance of the vicissitudes of life. This prevents a person from experiencing feelings of guilt—a state from which Westerners, because of their fundamental belief in the doctrine of free will, cannot be protected. It often leads to a state of existential despair, and in certain instances, moral resignation, compounded by a profound sense of inertia. One does not take immediate proactive measures; one merely accepts the vicissitudes of life without qualm. While this may prevent a person from experiencing stress, it does not allow the same person to make individual attempts to alleviate his or her unbearable condition.

A belief in the unending cycle of birth and rebirth, a belief that one's life does not end at death but leads to a new beginning, and that one's moral actions in one's present life or past lives will lead to consequences in one's future life, may create in the Hindu psyche a set of psychologically protective mechanisms in the face of death. A belief in an afterlife helps to reduce the terror of death and the fear of extinction.

The unshakable belief that on one's death one's indestructible spirit (*atman*) will survive the body and at some point during the individual's karmic cycle of birth and rebirth find abode in another body (hopefully a more pious and august one) makes the acceptance of death less painful.

Finally, the belief in the cycle of birth and rebirth creates an aspiration of hope. Hindus "know" that they need to engage in meritorious acts of piety. In so doing they will reap the rewards of their actions in their present life or in a future life by being born into a "better" family and into a higher caste in another birth.

The teachings from the *Gita,* which among other things is concerned with the law of karma, play a major role in the socialization of children. Since the law of karma explains virtually any and every human experience—success, failure, illness, brightness, dullness, love, depression, sorrow, happiness, wealth, poverty, glaring differences in society, one's physical appearance—it is invoked with such unremitting regularity that it becomes, as Sinari (1984) has argued, part of one's psyche. Even chance events are explained by resorting to the law of karma.

Knowledge of the law of karma, even in its most rudimentary form, exists all over India. Several years ago, when I lived in India, I used to notice a group of street urchins who, along with their parents, had taken shelter a few doors away from a palatial mansion, with electronic iron gates that swung open when the owner drove past in his chauffeur-driven Mercedes. Upon seeing the gates swinging open, the urchins would run to the gate, and as the car drove past them, would salute the owner, who from time to time threw a few coins from the open car window. In my misplaced reformative zeal, I felt a sense of outrage at the condescending and patronizing manner of the owner. One day, on an impulse, I rounded up the urchins, about a dozen of them—they were hungry little creatures, illiterate, emaciated, unkempt, dirty, between the ages of 5 and 13. When I questioned them, they explained, in their own limited way, that they felt no rancor, no anger, no animosity toward the owner when the coins came flying through the car window. In fact, they were proud to be associated with such a great man, the *Burra Sahib!* He must have performed deeds of great virtue in his past birth to achieve such an eminent position in his present life! It turned out that he had become their role model. They were convinced that if they too engaged in righteous and virtuous actions in their present life, they would reap the fruits of their endeavors in their future lives. So convinced were the children in their beliefs that one of them, using an old Indian proverb, boasted that when God decided to give him wealth, it would come hurtling through the roof! Such a view allowed them to accept their own destitution, if not with equanimity, certainly without rancor. It also allowed them to sustain the hope of a better life in their next life. The belief in the munificence of God cuts across all castes and classes in India.

THE CONTEMPORARY SCENE

We saw earlier that, in Indian thinking, it is difficult to separate the religious from the secular. Similarly, it is difficult, if not impossible, to separate the past from the present: they reside (often uneasily) side by side. India's past is like a dormant volcano, which from time to time erupts into the present, which then has an impact on its future. In the past it might have been possible to describe Indian family life in terms of (1) traditional families, (2) transitional families, and (3) Westernized families. The defining characteristics of traditional families would have been their being rooted in ancient Indian traditions and their ignorance of or indifference to the changes imposed by modernity. Transitional families might be construed as those that are in the process of change and adaptation to modernism. Westernized families are best referred to as those that have acquired Western education, tend to see themselves as being modernized, Westernized, and have imbibed many of the Western value systems, including liberalism, secularism, individualism, and so on. But the reader must bear in mind that these are convenient abstract categories; whether they have a basis in reality is an open question.

It is not often recognized that over 72 percent (Manorama, 2002) of the total Indian population (1.01 billion) lives in villages. In recent years, due largely to rapid industrialization and globalization in the country, there have been massive migrations of younger people from the rural sectors into the urban areas of India. As indicated earlier, squatter settlements, shanty towns, and slums have grown and sprawled everywhere and have extended even beyond the recognized urban limits. It has been estimated that about 40 percent of the urban population lives in slums, or squatter settlements, or on streets, in wretched poverty. Their living arrangements are devoid of basic amenities such as safe water, electricity, sewerage, and health care. The departure of the young migrants from the rural to the urban areas has created an age-related imbalance in the rural areas of India, with a high percentage of the elderly living in the rural areas, which of course makes it even more difficult for them to survive without the help of their children. The lines between urban areas and rural sectors in many instances have blurred, making it difficult to tell where an urban area ends and the rural sector begins, and vice versa.

The age-related imbalance between the rural and the urban areas, the economic imbalance in the urban areas between those who live below the poverty line on the streets and in the slums, and those who live in houses, with relative economic and financial security, militates against describing an Indian family in terms of urban and rural differences. The elderly who live in villages feel alienated from their children who have migrated to urban areas; in turn, the young migrants live in abject poverty, possess limited levels of literacy, have inadequate occupational skills, and hardly any preparation for urban life (United Nations, 1996).

All Indian families, regardless of where they live, are part of the politico-legal system of India. They are all subject to the rule of law. They all share a common codified written Constitution, which among other things emphasizes the rule of law, secularity, freedom of worship, freedom of movement, occupation, area of residence, and so on. From a philosophical and cultural point of view, all Indian families are the "inheritors" of the ancient Indian traditions, which are enshrined in the *Vedas,* the *Puranas,* the *Upanishads,* the great Indian epics, including the *Ramayana* and the *Mahabharata,* and of course the *Gita,* which forms an integral part of the *Mahabharata.* The ancient Indian traditions also consist of myths, legends, metaphors, proverbs, and folklore, which over the centuries have become part of the Indian psyche. Plays depicting scenes from the *Ramayana* and other ancients texts are played out all over the country during festive seasons, Whether one sees crude, hastily put together village performances of the *Ram-Leela* or the Dasera festivals, or the ones professionally enacted in the National Centre for Performing Arts in Mumbai, the "theme" of the plays and the emerging moral messages of the performances remain unchanged. Stories from the *Ramayana,* the *Mahabharata,* tales from the *Jatakas* (former lives of the Buddha), stories of bravery, valor, self-discipline, obedience, performance of austerities, prayer, bravery, revenge,

and forgiveness form the basis of socialization of children.

As noted earlier, rituals play an important role in the daily life of a family in India. Rituals surrounding family-related events such as adolescence, marriage, and death help to ease life cycle transitions for the individuals, while simultaneously embedding them more firmly in their kinship units. They cement an individual's identity within the confines of his or her family.

Again, it is difficult to understand family life in India fully without taking into serious consideration the role that religion plays in daily life. Most Hindu homes have a shrine (which may consist of a framed picture of a Hindu god, or a clearly demarcated sacred place of worship), at which prayers are offered day and night. Whether the entire family joins in the prayers—particularly the *arti*—or they are left to the women in the house to perform, is related to the importance given by the family members to such daily rituals. Children are generally encouraged to participate in such daily offerings and prayers. On festive occasions (of which there are scores in a year), the entire family is expected to join in the prayers and offerings. The elders in the family—the grandparents, an aged aunt—often develop a special relationship with the growing children. Since the elders are often seen as the repositories of knowledge, virtue, and wisdom, they often take it on themselves to read from the scriptures to the children, in order to "inculcate" the desired values of obedience, reverence, honesty, and self-discipline in the young children at home.

In addition to the gods worshipped at home and in the daily or weekly visits to temples, Indians also visit their own gurus—or, as a cynic has remarked, their "designer" gurus. They do so at regular intervals, seeking their blessings in whatever social, spiritual, economic, commercial, marital, and health-related endeavors in which they are engaged. It is not at all unusual to see several specially chartered planeloads of Indians from abroad, coming to India to participate in a religious "jamboree" arranged by the gurus(s) they all worship. To be looked on as a guru who has magical, if not divine, powers is to be accorded the highest accolade. (Many of my own extended family members who live abroad undertake such organized chartered trips every year, spending weeks on end in an *ashram.*) Asking "favors" of gods and gurus is a custom hallowed by tradition. It often operates on a "barter" system: One tries to do a deal with God. "God, if You grant me this favor, I'll do this for You," which could mean undertaking a long, extensive, and expensive pilgrimage to the holy cities in India, the feeding of hundreds of mendicants, special prayers being performed by a team of Brahmin priests either at home or on the banks of the Ganges, and other acts of piety, all of which form part of the "barter" system. And given the multiplicity of gods and gurus in India, changing or swapping gods and gurus should the favors go unanswered is also a custom hallowed by tradition. Since heresy is a meaningless concept in Hinduism, it is not at all sacrilegious to abandon one set of gods for another.

In recent years, the worship of gurus appears to have become a thriving commercial enterprise. The commercialization (or even more appropriately, the industrialization) of the guru cult and its spread in the West—*a la Rajneesh* and *Mahesh Maharishi Yogi* (the giggling guru of The Beatles' fame)—will not have gone unnoticed by many a Western reader. Many gurus appear to enjoy a higher status and following than is characteristic of film stars and other celebrity icons. To Indians, God is not merely a metaphysical abstraction—which to a large extent tends to be the case in the West—on which profound discourses can be held, tomes written, books published. There is within the Indian psyche a staunch, unshakable belief—impervious to any critical reasoning—in the reality and the benevolent powers of God.

The desire to follow gurus, to sit at their feet, and have a *darshan* (the sighting of a guru is seen as a beatific experience!) is a desire that drives rich and poor alike to wherever their guru holds a religious meeting.

It is now clear that, notwithstanding the urban–rural differences, differences in levels of education and affluence, differences in caste and class, differences in occupations, language, diet, and so on, there is a core set of values that Indians, regardless of which part of India they live in or come from, tend to share in common, which have a direct bearing on family life in India. The major value systems comprising Indian culture and that distinguish Indian cul-

ture from Western cultures have been described and elaborated elsewhere (e.g., Laungani, 1997, 1998, 1999, 2000, 2001a, 2001b, 2002).

CONTEMPORARY INFLUENCES ON FAMILY LIFE IN INDIA

Colossal changes have taken place in India over the last two decades, as a result of industrialization, massive foreign aid and foreign investments, globalization, and a revolution in information technology. When one sees e-mails being sent through mobile telephones from impoverished villages, one is apt to believe that the old order has changed, yielding to the new. But in the next breath one notices that water is still being drawn from a well, and beside it sits a man from the lowest caste, waiting for a high-caste Hindu to pour water into the Untouchable's pot. (In certain parts of India members of the Untouchable caste may be denied access to wells because of their hereditary "polluting" characteristics and for fear of spiritually "contaminating" the well.) One notices that the villagers still plough their fields with their own hands, using antiquated instruments, where safe water is an undreamt of luxury, and villagers carry their *lota* (metal pot) into the fields to wash themselves after their early-morning ablutions. And only a few miles away, on the outskirts of a small town, we can see workmen using pickaxes to dig up ridges to lay fiber-optic cables for advanced telecommunication systems. When such contradictions etherize one's senses, one has to concede that the new order has by no means replaced the old. The old and the new, the ancient and the contemporary, the backward and the advanced, the superstitious and the rational, the religious and the secular, live higgledy-piggledy, in an uneasy relationship. Trying to classify families into traditional families, transitional families, and modern families seems a meaningless exercise—an old romantic dream that has too little basis in reality.

However, cultures are living, breathing organisms, pulsating with life. Like all living organisms, they grow, evolve, change, progress, and a few, like the ancient dinosaurs and mammoths, decay, die, and become extinct. Why some cultures develop, progress, thrive, and assert their will, values, and power over the rest of the world cultures is due to several reasons, not the least of which are those related to economic, political, industrial, technological, literary, artistic, and other considerations. Although a discussion of these factors is well beyond the scope of this chapter, there is one issue—globalization—that needs to be examined because of its dramatic and unpredictable impact on the underdeveloped and the developing countries around the world. Let us briefly concern ourselves with this issue, but bearing in mind that our main concern is with family life in India.

THE IMPACT OF GLOBALIZATION ON FAMILY LIFE IN INDIA

One needs only to consider the impact of industrialization on Western society in the nineteenth century to realize how it radically transformed the very structure of Western society. The postindustrialization period in the West led to dramatic changes in religious beliefs, family structures, family size, work ethic, morals, economics, education, literature, health, politics, human rights, medical and scientific research, and several other areas of human concern.

Changes have also begun to emerge in the developing countries, including India. As to what the long-term impact of these changes will be, what benefits they might confer, or what "threats" they might forebode, one cannot predict with any degree of accuracy. Whether developing countries will also "go the Western way," or will adopt their own cultural and indigenous means of coping and adjusting to these changes, remains for the time being an unanswered question. We do not have a precise instrument by which we can measure the quantity and the quality of such changes. Nonetheless, by using broad-based economic, social, political, and other markers, it might become possible to articulate and preempt the likely future changes in the country as a whole.

It has been argued that globalization will lead to a process of Westernization and modernization and that all the developing countries will eventually come to imbibe the Western values of individualism, rationalism, humanism, empiricism, and secularism, thus becoming ultimately indistinguishable from the West-

ern countries. Since the West will set the "gold standard," all developing countries, including India, will aspire to achieve such a standard, thus completing the process of homogenization. The East shall no longer be East, and the West, West, as Rudyard Kipling remarked many years ago; in fact, the twain will meet and become culturally unified and homogenized.

That certain Western values, as a result of globalization, will impinge on the people of Asian cultures is inevitable. Insofar as economic affluence is concerned, this is already evident by the significant changes that are noticeable in India. Affluent Indians in the urban areas of India have begun to adopt Western ways of living, including living in luxurious high-rise blocks, condominiums (with swimming pools and tennis courts), furnishing their homes in modern Westernized styles, membership in exclusive Western-type clubs, Western culinary preferences, modes of dress, artistic and other esthetic preferences, driving imported luxury cars, increasing use of communication and information technologies, and last but not least, foreign travel. Conspicuous consumption of "new" money appears to carry the same hallmark as it does in many Western countries.

The West, in that sense, is certainly having a major commercial and economic impact in developing countries. It is interesting to note that there are over 35 million cable television homes—more than all of Latin America—in India (Das, 2002). English is also fast becoming the language that is spoken in the large metropolitan cities of India. However, the spoken English is a curious mixture of Indian languages, particularly Hindi. Indian English is referred to as Hinglish (Hindi and English). It has been predicted that by 2010, "India will become the largest English speaking nation in the world, overtaking the United States" (Das, 2002, p. 19). Even the "Bollywood" film industry has turned "native" in the Western sense of the word! In addition to Western types of sets, Western forms of dancing, English and Hindi dialogues, with a bewildering variety of Indianized English accents, continue to assault puritan ears.

Insofar as the family life of Westernized, affluent Indians living in large metropolitan cities is concerned, a change is beginning to become noticeable in young children from the age of 6 onwards. The major change, to a large extent, is noticeable at a consumer level: preference for fast foods offered by McDonalds and other multinational outlets, designer clothes, footwear, mobile phones, computers, digital televisions, camcorders, and other such consumer goods. To all outward appearances, there are hardly any differences between an Indian child and an American child.

However, as soon as one starts to dig deeper and observe the day-to-day lives of families at home, the picture changes; the observable similarities, so easily noticeable from the outside, seem merely cosmetic—not unlike a new, conspicuous patchwork on an ancient family heirloom. The house, although furnished in modern Western style, is still dominated by a temple or a shrine. The family members, one finds, usually eat their meals together, the home-cooked food often conforms to the families' indigenous regional culinary habits, family life still tends to operate on a hierarchical order. Although children "enjoy" a certain degree of latitude in expressing their views and opinions, and although the children are not any less indulged than they were in the past, deference to the views of the elders to a large extent is taken for granted and remains unquestioned. Collective activities, in which all family members are expected to participate—visiting relatives, entertaining relatives, performing prayers and *pujas,* participating in all the religious rituals (e.g., the mundan ceremony [tonsure ceremony], the sacred thread ceremony, betrothals, marriages, and festivities), are still an integral part of family life.

One of the most important factors that distinguishes Indian families from Western (English or American) families is the fact that children (sons), upon reaching maturity, are *not* expected to leave home and set up their own lives, so to speak. Any departure from this norm causes distress, but over the years, such a departure has come to be accepted with resigned equanimity. Married sons may choose to live separately, but the general trend is to live close to one another—even in the same block of flats, if that is possible. In many such homes, cooking is centralized: meals play a central role in uniting the families.

Indian society has displayed the ability and the tenacity to survive through centuries of foreign invasions and occupations. It is therefore questionable that globalization in all its magnitude and economic power will completely transform the ancient value systems of Indian society, and lead to a process of "cloning." At a superficial level it might seem as though the East is beginning to become indistinguishable from the West. But the cosmetic changes in India must not lull one into believing that the bell has already started to toll, proclaiming the demise of values in India.

In terms of physical distance, the West has crept closer to the East. But in terms of fundamental cultural values, it remains as distant as it ever was.

Or perhaps, a little less so!

REFERENCES

Appadurai, A, (1990). Disjuncture and difference in the global cultural economy. *Theory, Culture and Society, 7,* 295–310.

Barnlund, D. C., & Araki, S. (1985). Intercultural encounters: The management of compliments by Japanese and Americans. *Journal of Cross-Cultural Psychology, 16,* 9–26.

Basham, A. L. (1966). *The wonder that was India.* Bombay: Rupa.

Brislin, R. (Ed.). (1990). *Applied cross-cultural psychology.* Newbury Park, CA: Sage.

Camilleri, C. (1989). La communication dans la perspective interculturelle. In C. Camilleri & M. Cohen-Emerique (Eds.), *Chocs de Cultures: Concepts et Enjeux pratiques de l'interculturel* [Culture shocks: Concepts and intercultural applications]. Paris: L'Marmattan.

Das, G. (2002). *The elephant paradigm: India wrestles with change.* Delhi: Penguin Books.

Dumon, W. (Ed.). (1992). National family policies in EC-countries in 1991. Luxemberg: Commission of European Countries.

Encyclopaedia Britannica (2003). *India: Book of the year 2003.* New Delhi:The Hindu.

Erikson, E. (1963). *Childhood and society.* London: Penguin.

Filippi, G. G. (1996). *Mrtyu: Concept of death in Indian traditions.* New Delhi: D. K. Printworld.

Flood, G. (1996). *An introduction to Hinduism.* Cambridge, UK: Cambridge University Press.

Fuller, C. J. (1992). *The camphor flame: Popular Hinduism and society in India.* Princeton, NJ: Princeton University Press.

Hirayana, M. (1949). *The essentials of Indian philosophy.* London: Allen & Unwin.

Kakar, S. (Ed.). (1979/1992). *Identity and adulthood.* New Delhi: Oxford India Paperbacks.

Kakar, S. (1981).*The inner world—A psychoanalytic study of children and society in India.* New Delhi: Oxford University Press.

Kakar, S. (1982). *Shamans, mystics and doctors.* Mandala Books. London: Unwin Paperbacks.

Klostermaier, K. K. (1998). *A short introduction to Hinduism.* Oxford: One World.

Koller, J. M. (1982). *The Indian way: Perspectives.* London: Collier Macmillan.

Lannoy, R. (1976). *The speaking tree.* Oxford, UK: Oxford University Press.

Laungani, P. (1988). Accidents in children—An Asian perspective. *Public Health, 103,* 171–176.

Laungani, P. (1997). Death in a Hindu family. In C. M. Parkes, P. Laungani, & W. Young (Eds.), *Death and bereavement across cultures* (pp. 52–72). London: Routledge.

Laungani, P. (1998). The changing pattern of Hindu funerals in Britain. *Pharos International, 64*(4), 4–10.

Laungani, P. (1999). Death among Hindus in India and England. *International Journal of Group Tensions, 28*(1/2), 85–114.

Laungani, P. (2000). Cultural influences on the development of identity: India and England. In J. Mohan (Ed.), *Personality across cultures: Recent developments and debates* (pp. 284–312). New Delhi: Oxford University Press.

Laungani, P. (2001a). Hindu spirituality in life, death, and bereavement. In J. Morgan & P. Laungani (Eds.), *Cross-cultural issues in the care of the dying and the grieving.* Vol. 1. Amityville, NY: Baywood.

Laungani, P. (2001b). The influence of culture on stress: India and England. In L. L. Adler & U. P. Gielen (Eds.), *Cross-cultural topics in psychology* (2nd ed., pp. 149–170). Westport, CT: Praeger.

Laungani, P. (2002). The Hindu caste system. In G. Howarth & O. Leaman (Eds.), *The encyclopedia of death and dying.* London: Routledge.

Laungani, P. (2004). *Asian perspectives in counselling and psychotherapy.* London: Routledge.

Levin, J. (1990). How to define family. *Family Reports, 1*(17), 7–18.

Lipner, J. (1994). *Hindus: Their religious beliefs and practices.* London: Routledge.

Mandelbaum, D. G. (1972). *Society in India.* Vol. 2. Berkeley: University of California Press.

Manorama. (2002). *Manorama Yearbook.* Kottayam, India: Malayala Manorama Co. Ltd.

Maslow, A. (1970). *Motivation and personality* (2nd ed.). New York: Harper & Row.

Maslow, A. (1971). *The farther reaches of human nature.* New York: McGraw-Hill.

O'Flaherty, W. D. (1976). *The origins of evil in Hindu mythology.* Berkeley: University of California Press.

O'Flaherty, W. D. (1980). *Karma and rebirth in classical Indian traditions.* Berkeley: University of California Press.

Pandey, R. (1969). *Hindu Samskaras: Socio-religious study of the Hindu sacraments.* Delhi: Motilal Banarasidass.

Parikh, B. (2000). *Rethinking multiculturalism: Cultural diversity and political theory.* New York: Palgrave.

Prasad, R. (1989). *Karma causation and retributive morality: Conceptual essays in ethics and metaethics.* New Delhi: Indian Council at Philosophical Research/Munshiram Manoharlal Publishers Pvt. Ltd.

Prasad, R. C. (1995). *The Sradha.* Delhi: Motilal Banarasidass.

Reichenbach, B. R. (1990). *The Law of Karma: A philosophical study.* Honolulu: University of Hawaii Press.

Rogers, C. (1961). *On becoming a person.* Boston: Houghton Mifflin.

Rogers, C. (1980). *A way of being.* Boston: Houghton Mifflin.

Roland, A. (1988). *In search of self in India and Japan.* Princeton, NJ: Princeton University Press.

Segall, M. H., Dasen, P. R., Berry, J. W., & Poortinga, Y. H. (1999). *Human behavior in global perspective: An introduction to cross-cultural psychology* (2nd ed.). Boston: Allyn & Bacon.

Sharma, A. (2000). *Classical Hindu thought: An introduction.* New Delhi: Oxford University Press.

Sinari, R. A. (1984). *The structure of Indian thought.* Delhi: Oxford University Press.

Smart, N. (1996). *World philosophics.* London/New York: Routledge.

Smith, P. B., & Bond, M. H. (1993). *Social psychology across cultures: Analysis and perspectives.* Hemel Hempstead, England: Harvester, Wheatsheaf.

Stiglitz, J. (2002). *Globalization and its discontents.*

Tnest, J. (1990). Do we mean the same by the concept of family? *Communication Research, 17*(4), 431–443.

Triandis, H, C. (1972). *The analysis of subjective culture.* New York: Wiley.

Triandis, H. C. (1994). *Culture and Social Behavior.* New York: McGraw-Hill.

United Nations (1996). *Family: Challenges for the future.* New York: United Nations Publications.

Von Fürer-Haimendorf, C. (1974). The sense of sin in cross-cultural perspective. *Man, 9,* 539–556.

White, L. A. (1947). Cultural versus psychological interpretations of human behavior. *American Sociological Review, 12,* 686–689.

Whiting, B. B. (1963). *Six cultures: Studies of child rearing.* Cambridge, MA: Harvard University Press.

World Bank. (2000). Global economic prospects and the developing countries 2000. Washington, DC: World Bank.

Zaehner, R. C. (1966). *Hinduism.* New Delhi: Oxford University Press.

CHAPTER 7

FAMILIES IN INDONESIA

SARLITO WIRAWAN SARWONO
University of Indonesia

Indonesia is a former Dutch colonial territory that gained independence in 1945. It is an archipelago spread out between the Philippines and Australia, and between the Indian Ocean and Papua New Guinea. Its area is equal to the whole of Western Europe or the mainland United States (See Table 7.1). The population is approximately 208,200,000 (Table 7.2); 59 percent of the people live on the island of Java, which, however, consists of only 7 percent of the nation's land (Table 7.3).

According to the anthropologist Koentjaraningrat (1981), there are 151 ethnic groups in Indonesia living under 33 areas of *adat* (traditional) law and speaking their distinct native languages. However, the national language, Bahasa Indonesia (the "Indonesian

language") is spoken by almost everybody, because it is the language of instruction in schools and universities. In the past, the government recognized only five religions, namely, Islam (the most dominant), Roman Catholicism, Protestantism, Hinduism, and Buddhism. Other religions, such as Confucianism and Judaism, were banned for more than 30 years because of political reasons. However, since 1988—the new era of reformation—religious restrictions no longer exist in Indonesia (See Table 7.4).

MARRIAGE AND THE EXTENDED FAMILY

Like many other Eastern cultures, Indonesia follows a tradition in which the extended family is as important,

Table 7.1 Geographic Profile of Indonesia

Location	Between Asia and Australia
Total width	9.8 million square kilometers
Water	7.9 million square kilometers (80.60%)
Land	1.9 million square kilometers (19.38%)
Number of islands	17,500
Five biggest islands	Sumatera, Java, Kalimantan, Sulawesi, Irian (Papua)
Climate	Tropical
Temperature	23–28° C
Number of provinces	27

Source: PKBI, 2000, pp. 5–6.

Table 7.2 Demographic Profile of Indonesia

NO.	POPULATION	1997	1998[a]	1999[b]
1	Total (million)	201.8	205.1	208.2
1a	Male (million)			103.6
1b	Female (million)			104.6
2	Under poverty line (million)	22.5	79.4	49.5
2a	Urban poverty (%)	9.7	28.8	21.9
2b	Rural poverty (%)	12.3	45.6	25.7

[a]Peak of monetary crisis.

[b]Recovery from monetary crisis.

Source: Central Bureau of Statistics, National Manpower Survey (1997, 1998, 1999), cited in Wahono, 2000, p. 13; PKBI, 2000, p. 6.

Table 7.3 Comparative Demographic Profile of Java and Other Islands

Population of Java	59% of total population
Width of Java	7% of total land width
Density of Java	1,000 per square km
Density of Jakarta (national capital)	14,000 per square km
Population outside Java	41% of total population
Total width outside Java	93% of total land width
Density outside Java	100 per square km
Density of Irian (Papua)	5 per square km

Source: PKBI, 2000, p. 7.

if not more important, than the nuclear family, and the family is more important than its individual members. The tradition itself is very complex and differs from one ethnic group to another. In most provinces, a mixture of religions is practiced, making for very unusual combinations. In North Sumatra, for example, the local ethnic culture is divided into two subcultures, the Islamic subculture predominant in the South of the province among the Mandailing, and Christianity, which prevails among the Batak in the North. Originally, however, the two ethnic-religious groups traced their descent from the same ancestor and followed the same tradition and family system. This meant, for example, that cousins from the same *marga* (surname) could not marry. In addition, the bridegroom's *marga* is considered to have a higher status than the bride's *marga*. That is why, among the Mandailing and Batak, a son is given more value than a daughter. Parents will not stop having children before the birth of a son. However, since the Mandailing and the Batak people follow different religious practices, it is much easier and more acceptable for a Batak person to marry a non-Batak Christian than it is for a Mandailing or Muslim Batak. Similarly, it is easier and more acceptable for a Mandailing to marry a non-Mandailing Muslim than for a Batak or Christian Mandailing.

On the other hand, the Minangkabau, a Muslim ethnic group in West Sumatra, do not follow the patriarchal system of Islam as it is practiced by the Mandailings. The Minangkabau, who are also called the Minang or Padang, endorse a matrilineal system, in which the mother is the dominant authority figure in the family. The uncle on the mother's side, however, is the head of the household, and the family lineage derives from the mother's side. In a Minang marriage, the parents of the bride are supposed to ask

Table 7.4   Population by Religion in Selected Provinces

RELIGION	YOGYAKARTA (1962)		WEST JAVA (1965)		BALI (1930)		SOUTH SULAWESI (?)		AMBON (1968)		NORTH SUMATRA (1968)	
	No.	%	No.	%	No.	%	No.	%	No.	%	No.	%
Islam	497,358	98.67	19,344,622	98.26	16,942	1.56	?	90	36,631	46.16	1,353,716	51.26
Catholic	6,300	1.25	24,072	0.12	—	—	Christian (including Protestant?)	10	—	—	115,867	4.39
Protestant	256	0.05	65,000	0.33	—	—	—	—	31,165	39.27	1,013,085	38.39
Hindu	—	—	2,500	0.01	1,062,805	97.33	—	—	—	—	192	0.00
Buddhist	—	—	43,128	0.22	—	—	—	—	—	—	21,326	0.81
Others	151	0.03	207,609	1.05	12,160	1.11	—	—	11,568	14.57	136,892	5.18
Total	504,065		19,687,531		1,091,957		?		79,314		2,641,078	
Notes					In 1971: 2,130,338		? = not available					
Author	Kodiran		Harsoyo		I Gusti Ngurah Bagus		Matulada		Subyakto		Payung Bangun	
Article	Javanese culture		Sundanese culture		Balinese culture		Bugis-Makasarese cultures		Ambonese culture		Batakese culture	
Page no.	330		324		289		281		186		113	

Source: Koentjaraningrat, 1997.

for the hand of the son of the other family, and not the other way around as is more common. If the request is granted, then the bride's family will pay an amount of money or goods, called *mahar* or *mas kawin* (bride price), to "buy" the son.

Problems occur, for example, when a Minang wants to marry a Javanese (Central and East Java) or a Sundanese (West Java). Although most of the Javanese and Sundanese are also Muslims, the two ethnic groups follow a bilateral family system. Both ethnic groups are not accustomed to the use of surnames, and many of their people have only one name such as Sukarno or Suharto, the first two presidents of Indonesia. However, in terms of marriage customs, the Javanese and the Sundanese are more similar to the Mandailing and the Batak, for example, in terms of the *mahar* custom. In big cities such as the nation's capital, Jakarta, Medan (capital of North Sumatra), Bandung (West Java), and Surabaya (East Java), where the possibility of interethnic and interreligious marriage is great, the problem is usually solved by having a third party, such as another family, act as a mediator, and by the use of a neutral place, such as another person's house, a restaurant, or another public place, to conduct interfamily negotiations.

However, constraints do not arise only with regard to distinct interethnic marriages. Problems exist in marriages between culturally similar ethnic groups and even in intraethnic marriages. For example, the Javanese and the Sundanese have very similar traditions in that both adopt a bilateral family system and most are Muslims. However, they speak different languages even though their languages are rooted in the same old Javanese language, Kawi. Culturally and religiously, there should be no problems in terms of intermarriage between the two ethnic groups. However, a constraint exists because of their belief in a mythological story about a Javanese king who wanted to marry a Sundanese princess. The king's real motivation was territorial expansion, which made the Sundanese king angry, leading to a war between the two kingdoms. Even today, traditional parents of both ethnic groups who live in villages (not in cities) are reluctant to have their son or daughter marry someone of the other ethnic group.

As for Javanese culture itself, since the Javanese comprise the largest population in Indonesia (for further reading on Javanese culture, refer to Koentjaraningrat, 1994), there are subcultures within the group. The Javanese living in the inland areas of Yogyakarta and Solo, the most central of the former Javanese kingdoms, are mainly Muslims, but are also strongly influenced by Hinduism and animism. Consequently, their religion has many syncretic features. In contrast, the Javanese Muslims living on the northern coast of the island and in the province of East Java are not strongly influenced by these belief systems. Problems might arise when a Yogyakarta or Solo person wants to marry a Javanese person from the other areas, because the inland Javanese marriage ceremony is very elaborate and laden with traditional religious symbolism, whereas the marriage ceremony among the coastal Muslim Javanese is much simpler. In an inland-aristocratic-traditional Central Javanese marriage, for instance, the parents of the bridegroom are not allowed to witness the wedding (the religious and traditional ceremony), and they can only join the festivities when the reception begins. Usually they have to wait in a neighbor's house until the bride's parents send some members of the family to invite them. In contrast, in a coastal Muslim Javanese marriage, both the bride's and the bridegroom's parents are expected to be present and witness the whole wedding ceremony.

Likewise, a marriage between a Hindu-influenced Javanese and a pure Hindu from Bali will not be problem-free. Since sons are expected to inherit Hinduism and maintain the religion for the next generation, Balinese families, who are mostly Hindu, are very reluctant to allow their sons to marry non-Hindu women, unless the women convert to Hinduism. However, if the intermarriage involves a Balinese girl, the family will not be very reluctant. The parents of a Balinese girl who is about to be married will expect that, according to their tradition, the family of the boy will assume all the wedding costs. The reason for this is that the groom's family has taken away their daughter, particularly if the daughter is required to convert to the groom's religion. The problem is that in the Javanese tradition, it is always the bride's family who is responsible for the costs of the wedding ceremony. Consequently, if a Balinese girl is going to marry a Javanese boy, both families have to decide at the onset who will be responsible for planning the ceremony and how much each family will contribute financially.

The above indicates that the extended family has a very important role in making decisions concerning marriage, including wedding procedures and the choice of mates for daughters and sons. In the past, the offspring did not even have the right to have relationships with the opposite sex, but had to wait until the parents chose their mates.

The influence of the extended family was even stronger in the past when people lived in the "big house" (*rumah gadang*), which is a long house inhabited by the whole extended family, sometimes including three or even four generations. These would include grandparents, uncles, aunts, nephews, nieces, children, and grandchildren, and up to one hundred persons might live in a single house. In such a house, most decisions, including those related to marriages and intranuclear family affairs, were made by the entire extended family, with the senior members acting as leaders. At present, some "big houses" still exist, for instance, among the Dayak people in Kalimantan.

Today, in the era of globalization, the rules relating to family practices and marriage are becoming less conservative. For example, boys and girls form relationships at schools, at social meetings, public places, sporting and recreational activities, and most of them develop serious relationships with partners of their own choice. However, the extended family still makes the final decision. A serious relationship may or may not lead to marriage, depending on the agreement or lack of agreement of the families involved, particularly the parents. Decisions about marriage still encounter complications and difficulties, and divorce is a problem as well.

RELIGION

Islam came to Indonesia in the seventh century, brought by Muslim merchants from Gujarat, India, at a time when Java and the southern part of Sumatra were ruled by the Hindu kings of the Majapahit and Srivijaya kingdoms, who in turn had succeeded Buddhists rulers (*Ensiklopedia Islam,* 1993, vol. 2, pp. 214–215). This is the reason why there are many Hindu and Buddhist temples in Central Java, including the world-famous Buddhist Borobudur temple. Currently, there is a Buddhist community near the Borobudur temple as well as the whole Hindu population, who retreated to the island of Bali after the Muslims had defeated them. Today, Islam, which is influenced by diverse local ethnic cultures, is the major religion of Indonesia, comprising of 80–90 percent of the population, particularly in the western part of Indonesia, which includes the islands of Sumatra, Java, Kalimantan, and part of Sulawesi.

The Christian religions of Roman Catholicism and Protestantism were brought to Indonesia by the Dutch, who ruled Indonesia for 350 years, and also by the Portuguese through their missionaries. Some people in Java and Sumatra, particularly the Chinese descendents, converted to Christianity because they attended good, privileged schools that were run by missionaries during the colonial era. Rich Chinese families had the money to pay the requisite expensive tuition fees. People in other islands, mostly in the eastern part of Indonesia such as Flores, Timor, Papua, North Sulawesi, and Maluku, were converted to Christianity by missionaries, who frequently traveled aboard the ships that carried soldiers and traders to Indonesia. Today, Christianity predominates in the eastern Indonesian islands.

Regardless of religion, religious practices are very dominant among Indonesian families. Some religious practices are mixtures of different religions. In Java, for example, after the death of a family member, the rest of the family, including the extended family, will recite some religious prayer (*selametan*) on the 3rd, 7th, 40th, and 100th days after the date of the death, regardless of the religion practiced by the families. Muslim families observe these religious practices in an Islamic way, and Christians follow Christian traditions. The motivation underlying the prayer is the ancient Javanese animistic belief that the soul of the dead will not be released to heaven before the family engages in prayer for the dead on those particular days. Another example of the commingling of cultural tradition and religion in family life is the *Idul Fitri,* which occurs at the end of the fasting month celebrated by Muslims. At the end of the month of Ramadan in the Islamic lunar calendar, the Muslims terminate their month-long fasting (i.e., no food, drinks, or cigarettes during daylight) with a celebration on the first and second days of the following month of *Syawal,* which are national holidays. The entire celebration is called *Idul Fitri,* which means the day of the winners, because the Muslims have triumphed over their own bodily passions.

On the morning of the first *Syawal,* beginning at 7:00 a.m., people engage in mass praying for about 30–45 minutes in mosques or in open spaces such as football fields or town squares. Following this, they gather in their homes to celebrate with their own families, neighbors, and friends. Special food is served and shared with close relatives. During the *Idul Fitri,* people ask for forgiveness from others, particularly from parents and the elderly, for whatever mistakes, whether intentional or unintentional, they had committed during the last year, and people customarily forgive each other. At the end of the *Idul Fitri* feast, also called *lebaran* and lasting for at least one week, people feel clean, because they are now free from the errors and transgressions they may have committed in the past.

Lebaran, which is unknown in the original Islamic teachings, is obviously centered around the family. One week before *lebaran* and during the fasting month, people begin traveling from their homes to their original hometowns and villages. Many of them travel in groups of families including infants or friends, for hundreds of kilometers. They use any form of transportation, such as private vehicles, buses, trains, ships, and airplanes, and cause traffic jams and overload public transportation. This is particularly true when they are on their way to the hometowns of the Javanese majority in Central and East Java (see Table 7.5).

The tradition of family gatherings is also observed by Indonesian Christians during the Christmas and New Year's holidays and by Hindus during Galungan, but since the number of gatherings is not

Table 7.5   Profile of Lebaran Travelers (from Jakarta to Home Villages/Towns)

Destination	
Central Java & Yogyakarta	46%
West Java	36%
East Java	11%
Sumatra	6%
Others	1%
Income	
< Rp. 200,000 per month	35%
Rp. 200,000–Rp. 400,000 per month	38%
> Rp. 400,000 per month	27%
Length of stay in Jakarta	
<10 years	73%
10–20 years	62%
20–30 years	48%
30–40 years	41%
40–50 years	34%
>50 years	14%

Source: Kompas, 1996.

high, their social and economic impact is not readily observed. In contrast, the social and economic impact of the *lebaran* is tremendous. For example, in Jakarta, many offices and shops are closed for more than two weeks. The streets are desolate, and many families who remain in Jakarta have to do their own housework because all servants return to their villages, although some families choose to stay at hotels during the *lebaran* holidays. Although this tradition has been criticized as being too consumptive, uneconomical, and too much trouble, it persisted even during the periods of economic crisis in 1998 and 1999.

Religion influences sexual relationships. Based on religious norms, sexual intercourse is forbidden before marriage. However, as a result of higher standards of education and employment, the average age of newlyweds has increased from approximately 13–15 years old in traditional communities of the past to 16 years old for girls, 18 years old for boys (Marriage Law Act No. 1/1974), and even 25–30 years old among the upper-middle class in the big cities. The changes have increased the possibility of premarital sex. Consequently, an increasing number of people contract sexually transmitted diseases (STDs). There are more unwanted pregnancies, which usually lead to early marriages, illegitimate children labeled "sinful children" or *anak haram* by the society, and illegal abortions that place the mothers' lives at risk if they are not carried out professionally. Even abortions by physicians are illegal in Indonesia, except when performed for medical reasons.

Given the religious teachings, unmarried yet sexually active youths are ineligible for any services related to sex because they are not expected to engage in sexual relations, regardless of their ages. Consequently, they are not eligible for reproductive health services and sex education. Thus, it is very difficult for students, for example, to obtain condoms, not only because condoms are unavailable in stores, but also because students would feel embarrassed to ask store clerks for them.

Another example of the influence of religion on family life is the marriage regulation (Marriage Law Act No. 1/1974) that states that interfaith marriages will not be recognized officially by the government unless one of the partners converts to the religion of the other, prior to the marriage. This policy, which was originally influenced by politics, causes problems for couples who embrace different religions and are planning to marry. The problem is experienced by the nuclear and extended families on both sides, and frequently the wedding will be canceled by the families. Wealthier couples might decide to marry abroad to avoid these constraints. Less wealthy couples will marry informally, i.e., not in the eyes of the law, or they will undergo a pseudo-conversion simply to receive the legal marriage certificate and then continue to practice their original religions as soon as the wedding ceremony is over.

FAMILY PLANNING

Family planning was first introduced in Indonesia in the early 1950s. Under President Sukarno, the government's policy was pro-life. Parents were urged to have as many children as possible, because the country needed ample labor to develop. However, some prominent female activists saw the suffering of the majority of the mothers who had to sacrifice their

health, and even their lives, in childbirth at a time when the average number of children per couple was six. In 1958, the activists founded a nongovernmental organization (NGO) called the Indonesian Planned Parenthood Association/IPPA (Perkumpulan Keluarga Berencana Indonesia/PKBI) to help these at-risk women.

In its early years of operation, the IPPA's programs were focused on promoting the mother's health, mainly by preventing numerous births, in order to minimize the mother and child mortality rates (the mother mortality rate in the last decades has varied between 300 and 1,000 per 100,000 live births [*Kompas,* 2000]). But more than two decades later, in 1975, under President Suharto, the government took over the program and founded a government institute called the National Family Planning Coordinating Body/NFPCB (Badan Keluarga Berencana Nasional/BKKBN). Since then, family planning has been a national program and its focus has shifted from the mother's health to the family's welfare. It now emphasizes fewer children, decreasing expenses, increasing the quality of life, improving nutrition, offering better education, and so on. Population growth was reduced from 3.2 percent per year in 1979 to 1.64 percent in 1999 (Table 7.6). The International Planned Parenthood Federation/IPPF and the UN Fund for Population Activities/UNFPA have recognized this as the most successful family planning program in developing countries and singled out the Indonesian family planning program as a model for other developing countries to follow.

The target of the National Family Planning Program is limited to eligible couples (married people) only, because religious norms restrict unmarried people from such services. Consequently, adolescents and unmarried youth are excluded from the program, although many of them are sexually active. As a result, the IPPA took the initiative to provide sex education and information to unmarried youth in high schools and universities, to young workers, and even at reproductive health clinics, which were supported by other NGOs and NFPCB but were not mandated to target the youth program because of political constraints. Today, sex education and information are provided as a part of extracurricular activities at

Table 7.6 Family Planning Profile

Population growth in 1999	1.64%
Total fertility rate (TFR)	
National	2.78 per woman
Rural	2.98 per woman
Urban	2.40 per woman
Java & Bali	2.57 per woman
Outside Java & Bali	3.20 per woman
Median age of first marriage	
National	18.6 years
Rural	17.9 years
Urban	20.4 years
Married persons	
10–14 years: 1996	1.4%
1998	1.7%
15–19 years: 1996	62.1%
1998	62.7%
Predicted number of	
reproductive females (15–49)	
2000	58.9 million
2005	63.7 million
2010	66.1 million

Source: PKBI, 2000, pp. 7–8, 11.

schools, in public seminars, in articles, on TV talk shows, and so on. Additionally, counseling for unmarried youth via hotlines, by post, e-mail, and face to face is no longer taboo, and is increasingly provided not only by NGOs but also by professionals, school personnel, mass media, electronic media, and even religious organizations. Some of them are provided as independent services, while others are combined with multipurpose programs including home economics, family nutrition, drug abuse, STD, and HIV/AIDS prevention.

WOMEN'S ROLES

Compared to many other developing countries, the role of women in Indonesia is very advanced. The pioneer of the women's improvement movement was R. A. Kartini (1870–1904), who died at the age of 24, after delivering her first baby. She was the second wife of the *Bupati* or local aristocratic head of the county of Rembang, Central Java. As a daughter of another *Bupati* of Jepara (a neighboring county of

Rembang), Kartini had, according to the colonial rules, the right to receive a European education. However, she only completed her elementary European education locally.

After completing elementary school, Kartini wanted to attend a high school in the Netherlands, but instead was forced to marry the *Bupati* of Rembang. She became very frustrated, and in her frustration wrote a series of letters to her former school friend, then living in the Netherlands (published as a book entitled *Habis Gelap Terbitlah Terang* [There is a light after darkness]). The letters revealed Kartini's idealism with respect to improving the role and status of women in Indonesia. She carried out her ideas by educating girls and women living at the *Bupati*'s residence and nearby areas. Her effort is considered the trigger of the women's liberation movement in Indonesia.

Today there are minor gender differences in Indonesia regarding education and employment. Schools, universities, and most employment opportunities are open to both genders (Table 7.7).

Women's participation in the labor force is 33.0 percent, and some of the female working force include university professors, professionals, businesswomen, and government officials including ministers. A 3-month maternity leave with full pay is available to pregnant working women. When there are gender differences in employment, they usually exist because of practical reasons, such as jobs requiring extensive travel, or where an individual must remain away from the family for prolonged periods, work in remote and isolated areas, work the night shift, and so forth.

Subconsciously, the mostly conservative and religious Indonesians have not abandoned the traditional ideas, which emphasize the domestic role of women regardless of their level of education. In particular, males believe that a wife is expected to be her husband's partner and her task is to support his career. In a related fashion, a female police or military officer who marries another officer is not expected to exceed her husband's rank, although law does not support this. Housewife organizations in government institutions, the military, and the police forces are expected to be organized on the basis of the husbands' positions in these institutions. For

Table 7.7   Human Development Index, 1995

COUNTRY	LIFE EXPECTANCY (YEARS)		LITERACY (%)		SCHOOL ENROLLMENT (%)		HUMAN RESOURCE PARTICIPATION (%)	
	Female	Male	Female	Male	Female	Male	Female	Male
Indonesia	65.8	62.2	78.0	89.6	59.1	61.3	33.0	69.6
Developing countries	63.6	60.7	61.7	78.8	53.0	58.9	32.4	67.6
Developed countries	77.9	70.4	98.5	98.8	84.0	81.6	38.0	62.0

Source: UNDP, 1998, pp. 131–133.

example, the wife of a battalion commander will automatically be the chairperson of the housewife organization of the battalion regardless of her expertise and abilities, although law does not legitimize the practice.

Gender discrimination occurs in husband–wife relationships. Under the Marriage Law Act No. 1/1974, a husband is allowed to marry more than one woman, particularly when the wife is not able to conceive or she is terminally ill. Although this is a rare practice, the law is definitely considered unfair by most women, particularly feminist activists, because under similar conditions the wife is not allowed to have more than one husband. Government policy, aimed at continuously improving the status of women by establishing a Minister for Women's Affairs, is insufficient to reduce these gender differences when compared to the impact of the marriage law. Clearly, the law represents the predominant religious attitude of Muslims toward women. In practice, many women, though they may be well educated, terminate employment after marriage due to restrictions placed on them by their husbands or because they are too busy taking care of their children. Others choose to remain unmarried or at least delay marriage until they feel ready to do so, when they are already in their thirties.

CHILD WELFARE

Children are well protected under the Indonesian laws. The 1945 constitution states that the government is responsible for children's education. The Na-

tional Education Law (Act No. 2/1989) confirms the right of every Indonesian child to receive nine years of basic education, and the Child Welfare Act No. 4/1977 and Labor Law Act No. 25/1997 prevent any form of forced child labor. However, the government lacks adequate funding to provide for free basic education, and many families living in villages or among the urban poor cannot afford to provide adequate education for their offspring. Some schools and universities are run by private organizations (e.g., Muslim and Christian schools), which are relatively costly. Furthermore, most public schools are not well maintained, because of the government's limited budget. Thus approximately 1.5 million children drop out of schools, and 6.5 million are potentially unable to continue their education (Table 7.8).

In villages it is common for a child to help the parents from an early age. A 7-year-old girl, for example, is expected to take care of her younger siblings while her mother is working in the kitchen and her other brothers are taking care of the family's buffaloes. Furthermore, in villages, girls as young as 11 years old are frequently forced into marriage, although it is against the law. Yet the economic hardships encountered by the rural families (see Table 7.2) often lead them to follow this custom. The government has very limited control over this matter, since the marriage is usually performed by the local people and endorsed by local traditional leaders, including local religious leaders. Many practices are upheld, not because they are legal, but according to local customs and religious beliefs. Because of the *mahar* (bride

Table 7.8 Number of School Dropouts

	1997	1998
Elementary school	833.000	912.000
Junior high school		
Potentially unable to continue school		643.000

Source: Kompas, 2000.

price), the poor parents of the girl perceive marriage as a way to acquire money.

Among the urban poor (see Table 7.2), young children are also expected to help their families. Consequently, they work in the street, in the informal sectors: cleaning shoes, selling newspapers, renting umbrellas during the rainy season, or they are beggars. While some attend schools, others do not. There are street children who do not have families because they ran away from their families in the villages and do not have money to go back to their home villages. Some of the boys become criminals and some of the girls become street prostitutes. Another form of child labor can be seen in some factories or home industries, particularly in Java. Children are hired illegally as a source of cheap labor with the parents' consent because the children are earning money for the family, or at least for themselves.

PARENTING

As in most other Asian countries, Indonesian parents are generally authoritarian. During socialization, children are taught not to talk back to their parents and the elderly. An ideal child is obedient, respects his or her parents, and listens to them. Most parents will not encourage their children to be creative or ambitious, since these traits are perceived as being in opposition to social norms. However, some parents want to see their children excel in school and will not hesitate to pay a great deal of money to send their children to the best schools they can afford. The parents will also pay additional money for after-school tutoring, either to improve their children's academic performance or to enroll them in extracur-

ricular activities such as music lessons, dancing, and sports. Most parents want their children to be the best in their schools or neighborhoods, not merely for the benefit of the children themselves, but also for the interests of the parents.

For the better-educated parents, children's education is always paramount, and the parents' desire to see their children succeed is reflected in their strict rules. For example, children should study during particular hours, are not allowed to play outside or watch TV before finishing homework, and should cease any other activities if school grades fall, particularly in mathematics and the exact sciences. Usually the children are not happy with the strict discipline they receive from their parents, because they see on TV or even among their own friends that other children have more time for fun and do not have to study as hard. Consequently, *many children trick their parents and even their teachers in order to be able to go out with their friends.*

In spite of the strict discipline, parents are very protective of their children. If the children fail to earn good grades, some parents may dishonestly pay money to the teachers so they will give better grades to their children. Alternatively, if a child is about to repeat a grade, the parents will bribe the school principal and ask for better grades in order to discharge the child from the school and transfer him or her to a higher grade in another school. They do this because repeating a class is considered shameful, not only for the children, but also and especially, for the parents. Although most teachers and school principals are honest professionals, the tendency of most parents to engage (or try to engage) in bribery reveals the overprotective attitude of the parents.

The tendency toward overprotection is typical among Indonesian parents, and is not limited to the area of education. For example, parents will forbid their children from making friends with children in the neighborhood if they are not from the same social class. Such restrictions may also be associated with racial or religious prejudice. Even when the children are already attending university, seeking employment, or planning for marriage, the parents will continue to play a decisive role. In the eyes of Indonesian parents, children will always be children, even when they have become adults. For some young couples, this prevents them from gaining their full independence from their parents, but for others, especially middle-class couples who are working and already have young children, the presence of the parents and/or parents-in-law tends to be very helpful, because they can provide childcare while the young parents are at work. Some grandmothers live in the house with the young parents; others make daily visits to babysit grandchildren; and still others live in their own houses, but the parents take the children to the grandparents' house on their way to work and pick them up, on their way home.

In any case, privacy and independence are not easily acquired by young families in Indonesia—particularly by those who still live in homes (including the *rumah gadang*) consisting of two to four generations. The influence of the extended family is much stronger than that of the nuclear family. On the one hand, it means there is limited individual freedom, which is so highly regarded in the West, but on the other hand, particularly in the case of emergencies, the extended family is often able to protect the family against hardship and serves as an insurance system. Since a welfare system is lacking, the extended family has taken over this role.

However, many children from wealthier urban families are not too happy with the authoritarian form of parenting. The influence of a Western lifestyle leads them to prefer greater freedom and independence. Consequently, many children avoid staying at home as much as possible, choosing instead to walk around in shopping malls after school, loaf on the streets close to school, or stay at friends' houses. The youth subculture arises as a protest against the parents' strict discipline. The subculture is expressed in peculiar teenage slangs, unique styles of dress and ornaments, special music, and hairstyles. The teenagers demand freedom from authoritarian parents and some of them, in their efforts to seek more freedom, encounter a new world of sex and drugs. Others express their self-identity in inter-high-school street fighting (gangs), particularly in Jakarta. Many parents are confused and shocked about the intergenerational cultural differences. Au-

tomatically they become stricter with their children, which further increases the generation gap. Psychologists are frequently consulted by parents to overcome this problem.

ISLAMIC LAW

Although Indonesia is inhabited by the largest number of Muslims in the world, it is not officially an Islamic country. However, Islamic law does apply to its Muslim citizens particularly with regard to marriage, divorce, kinship relationships, inheritance, and recently, banking. Islamic law, which is based on the *Qur'an* and the prophet Mohammed's teachings, is enforced by a special court called the Religious Court (*Pengadilan Agama*). This court deals only with Islam. Consequently, if a Muslim couple is getting married, or some family members are in dispute about some inheritance, they go to the Religious Court, whereas non-Muslims go to the Civil Court (*Pengadilan Negeri*).

Some Islamic law is also a part of general civil law, such as the marriage law, and there are other statutes. However, most of the laws are recorded only in religious books, not officially recorded by the government, and yet they apply to particular citizens. The judges of the Religious Courts are civil servants, paid by the government, and have the same rights and obligations as their colleagues in the Civil Courts. They receive their education at the Faculty of Islamic Law (*syariah*) at the Institute of Islamic Science.

Differences between Islamic law and the civil law can be found, for example, in the marriage and inheritance laws. A Muslim man is allowed to marry more than one woman—although it is not commonly practiced—while a non-Muslim man is allowed to marry only one woman. Regarding inheritance, under Islamic law, a daughter will receive only one-third of a son's inheritance, while under the civil law, every child in the family will have equal rights unless stated differently by the testator. Under Islamic law, an adopted child is not regarded as a descendant of the parents, so he or she is not eligible to inherit. The child should receive the inheritance from the biological father. In case of marriage, an adoptive father is not allowed to marry off his adopted daughter, because under Islamic law only the biological father has this right. If the biological father is not available, his role will be taken over by the judge (*wali hakim*). In addition, an adopted child is prohibited from using the surname of the adopted father. The child should retain the biological father's name, or if it is unknown, the biological mother's surname. According to Islamic teachings, these rules are necessary to prevent intra-nuclear-family marriages from occurring by error. Since Muslim citizens are also subject to civil law, problems may arise when two disputing Muslim parties favor separate laws and consequently go to separate courts to solve their dispute.

THE CHINESE FAMILY

Originally, the Chinese in Indonesia were not a homogenous ethnic group. They came from two different provinces in China (Fukien and Kwangtung), and they spoke four distinct languages (Hokkien, Teo-Chu, Hakka, and Cantonese). The first migrants were Hokkienese, generally merchants, who arrived between the sixteenth and nineteenth centuries. Their skill as merchants was utilized by the Dutch colonial government and remains of use to the current Indonesian government and the *pribumi* (indigenous) people. They continue to play an important role in the Indonesian economic system because the *pribumi* consider merchants to have a lower status than government employees or highly educated professionals such as medical doctors or lawyers. Therefore, there were hardly any *pribumi* businessmen for a very long time (Vasanty, cited in Koentjaraningrat, 1997).

Today, most Chinese Indonesians (particularly in Java and West Sumatra) remain business people (only recently are there *pribumi* businessmen as well) who are economically better off than the average *pribumi*. The other Chinese ethnics were originally farmers and laborers, and they are scattered throughout the other main islands (Table 7.9).

Although originally the Chinese Indonesians consisted of four ethnic groups, in the eyes of the *pribumi* there are only two groups of Chinese. The first group was called the *totok,* and they consisted of indigenous (original migrant) Chinese. They were reluctant to adopt customs, tended to keep their Chinese language and traditions, and married women imported from the Chinese mainland. They looked down at the other Chinese as a lower-class group who were abandoning their original traditions and religion. The second group was called the *peranakan* and consisted of mixed Chinese-*pribumi* descendants. They did not speak Chinese, changed their religion, and married other *peranakan* or local *pribumi* women. Today we can find hardly any *totok* Chinese (except for new immigrants from China), because most of the Chinese have adjusted themselves to the new Indonesian social, economical, political, and cultural environments.

However, this does not mean that the prejudice of the *pribumi* toward the Chinese has ceased. To the

Table 7.9 Percentage of Chinese Population in Indonesia (1961)

AREA	CHINESE POPULATION	TOTAL POPULATION	PERCENTAGE
Java and Madura	1,230,000	63,059,000	2.0%
Sumatra	690,000	15,739,000	4.4%
Kalimantan	370,000	4,102,000	9.0%
Other areas	215,000	13,427,000	1.2%
Total	2,505,000	96,327,000	2.5%

Source: Skinner, G. W. (1963), The Chinese minority. In R. T. McVey (Ed.), *Indonesia*. New Haven, CT: Human Relations Area Files. Cited by Vasanty, P. (1997), Kebudayaan orang Tionghoa di Indonesia [The Chinese culture in Indonesia]. In Koentjaraningrat (Ed.) (1997), *Manusia dan Kebudayaan di Indonesia* [Man and culture in Indonesia] (p. 358). Jakarta: Djambatan.

contrary, it still exists, reflecting a long history of discrimination. The Indonesian government continues to discriminate frequently against the Chinese, although on paper laws supporting discrimination have been abolished since independence. Examples include not permitting Chinese Indonesians to enter the military and limiting their ability to enter state universities and other institutions. Such practices are causing many interethnic troubles in Indonesia, particularly in Java.

During the colonial era, there was a law that categorized the people into three classes: Europeans (a small minority that controlled the country), alien Easterners (including some Arabs, but mostly Chinese), and the *pribumi* or indigenous people (the majority). The law divided the three groups on the basis of daily social, economical, and political life. The Europeans (Caucasian) were treated as first-class citizens, enjoying the best facilities and full rights. The alien Easterners ranked second, and the *pribumi* were considered as the lowest among the three "castes" (except the aristocrats, who were given the same status as the Europeans).

The sharp status differences manifested themselves (among others) in educational facilities (only Europeans and the aristocrats were eligible for European schools, the Chinese were allowed to have their own schools, while most of the *pribumi* did not go to school at all), recreational facilities (special cinemas, restaurants, and clubs for the Europeans and the Chinese), social organizations (the Rotary Club was only for the Europeans and the Chinese), and religion (the Europeans and most of the Chinese were Protestants or Roman Catholics, while most of the *pribumi* were Muslims).

The Arabs, although they were also eligible for the better facilities and higher status, were (and still are) not considered as a distinct group by the *pribumi* due to their insignificant numbers and, more important, their Islamic religion. On the other hand, as a consequence of ethnic discrimination, much prejudice existed between the Chinese and the *pribumi*, and continues to exist today. The Chinese would consider the *pribumi* to be an uncivilized, lazy, unproductive, and dependent people, while according

to the *pribumi*, the Chinese were arrogant, rich, opportunistic, and lacking in social concern (Sarwono, 1997, pp. 269–275).

The opportunism of the Chinese was actually only a form of social adjustment. Being second-class citizens in the system, which formerly did not allow for any social mobility, the Chinese tried to adjust to their intermediate position between the higher and the lower classes (because they lived in the middle of the *pribumi* population). They adopted Christianity and the European education system, and the women often married European men in an effort to receive protection from the authorities. In relationship to the *pribumi*, they adopted their culture and language, which they mixed with their own language, resulting in a new and unusual dialect. In addition, they married *pribumi* women in order to maintain good relationships with the locals.

When a Chinese (or a *pribumi*) woman married a European man, she upgraded her status. Particularly if she had children and the father recognized his offspring as European by giving them European names and sending them to local European schools or to the Netherlands, the woman would be treated as being equal to other Europeans. In some cases, the woman would invite her mother to stay in the master's (*tuan*) house and the mother would then live in the servant's room, which was still much bigger and better than her original hut in the village. However, if the father did not recognize his children, the woman would remain a mistress (*nyai*) and her original status would not rise.

In the case of a Chinese man marrying a *pribumi* woman, usually the children would (and will) be recognized by the father, since the Chinese need local women to maintain and expand their families. Consequently, the woman would enjoy an upgrading of her status. Only in some cases did the *pribumi* remain a *nyai* who would not enjoy the status of a legal wife. This was particularly true if the Chinese man already had a wife.

As for the Chinese and European women, they were, and still are, not expected to marry men from the lower classes. Once a woman married a lower-class male, she would be downgraded to the husband's class. Even with respect to clothes, a European or a Chinese woman was not expected to wear *pribumi* dresses such as the *kebaya*. However, since the Chinese were more likely to adjust to the customs of *pribumi,* they developed their own mixed kind of dress (*kebaya encim*). Again, this did not apply to the men. European or Chinese men were very welcome to wear *pribumi* dress, because the *pribumi* felt honored. Traditional dress was especially worn at local parties, when the male guests were invited to dance with local female dancers.

Within the Chinese community itself there are some marriage restrictions. First of all, persons having the same *she* (surname) are not permitted to marry. Today, the restriction is less frequently enforced than before. Same *shes* are permitted to marry each other, as long as they are not close kin. In addition, a man is not allowed to marry a woman of an older generation (aunt, mother/father's cousin, etc.), even though the age of the woman is younger. However, a woman is allowed to marry a man from an older generation.

Another regulation is that a younger sister is not supposed to marry before her older sisters have married. The same regulation also applies to a younger brother and his older brothers. However, a younger sister is allowed to marry, even if there are still some older unmarried brothers. (Note: this tradition also applies among the Javanese.)

After marriage, the first son and his wife must live in his parents' house (patrilocal), since the first son must carry on the family's tradition. The next sons are free to choose their own houses, such as the house of the wife's family (uxorilocal) or a house of their own (neolocal).

A Chinese man is allowed to marry only one wife, but he is allowed to have more than one mistress. In the nineteenth century, it was usual for the mistress(es) and their children to live together in one house with the wife. The children were treated as the wife's own sons or daughters (particularly if the wife did not have a son), but the mistress became a servant in the household. Today, the custom does not exist any longer, because the wives refuse to live together with the mistress. Should the husband insist, the wife can then ask for a divorce.

THE REFUGEES

Since 1999, Indonesia has experienced political and social conflicts in some of its provinces outside the island of Java, such as the former East Timor, which became independent in 1999, Aceh, West Kalimantan, Ambon, and North Maluku. Thousands of people have been killed and many houses, shopping centers, vehicles, schools, mosques, and churches have been destroyed. As of August 2000, some of the conflicts have been controlled in West Kalimantan and the former East Timor, but in other areas such as Ambon, North Maluku, and Aceh, conflicts continue and thousands of refugees have left their residences in search of safer areas.

In March 1999, the present author, serving as a consultant to the chief of the Indonesian National Police, was sent to some of the areas of conflict in Ambon and West Kalimantan and had the opportunity to interview some of the refugees. Many of them were and are elderly persons, women, and children who had insufficient access to food and drinking water. They were living in tents in football fields or other open fields, military or police barracks, mosques, churches, and sport stadiums, with very limited sanitary facilities. They did not have any personal belongings except for the clothes they were wearing. They were and are sponsored by charities provided by the government, NGOs, international organizations, and so on, and all, including the adult males, were depressed and experiencing posttraumatic stress disorder (PTSD). Many of them had lost one or more members of their family, and none of the children could attend schools.

When the author returned as the Dean of the Faculty of Psychology at the University of Indonesia in Jakarta, he organized a crisis center, consisting of some faculty members and senior psychology students. The center then trained several teams to be sent, together with other teams from various organizations and institutions, to the troubled areas to help the refugees adjust to their critical situation and to provide alternative education for the children.

In the crisis center teams' reports and from my own observations, it is clear that the prolonged conflict has led to family fragmentation, with children suffering the most. Considering the government's, NGOs', and other institutions' limited resources, and the prolonged conflicts between the political elites in Jakarta, which is perceived as the main cause of the conflicts, it is very likely that there will be more victims in the near future. It is now too early to determine the future of the children; however, many have predicted that there will be a "lost generation." Such a generation will suffer the ill effects of inadequate nutrition, education, and affection, which may continue for 10–15 years. The "lost generation" will create many social problems in the future because of their inability to survive and their hostile attitude toward the society.

CONCLUSIONS

Indonesian families differ from Western families in several ways. First of all, the extended family is more dominant than the nuclear family, and the parents have a very strong influence on the individual family members. Second, Indonesian parents tend to be authoritarian and their parenting style tends to produce docile, obedient, respectful, and less aggressive children, which also means inhibited, less confident, and less creative children.

Schoolteachers, in general, have similar authoritarian attitudes rooted in Asian norms, which dictate that an individual's self-interest should not take priority over the interests of society. Consequently, a child is not supposed to develop too much initiative or to be too ambitious. In Bahasa Indonesia, the word "ambitious" has a negative connotation. Frequently, particularly among middle- and upper-class families, overambitious parents force their children to excel, causing the child to become both depressive and rebellious, leading to drug addiction and criminal or abusive sexual activity.

The traditional religious beliefs and age-old traditions are combined in different and unique cultures throughout the country, influencing the family and social life. There is a general perception that the female's status and role in the family are beneath that of the male's, although in society and in work their positions are slightly more equal.

The strong influence of religion is obvious in matters such as marriage, the marriage law, and premarital sex, and among the Muslim people, the Religious Court is expected to deal with marriage, kinship, and inheritance issues.

Child welfare laws protect children, but the government lacks adequate financial resources, staff, and institutions to enforce them. Combined with the poverty experienced in rural villages and among the urban poor, the governmental ineffectiveness easily leads to child abuse, forced child labor, youth crimes, and even child prostitution. However, the lack of a national social welfare system in Indonesia is frequently compensated for by the extended family, whose members function as a social security system, protecting each other in times of emergency.

In general, it can be concluded that the Indonesian family is undergoing a process of change. Although at present it remains predominantly traditional and religious, the family is moving toward more modern nuclear and individualistic forms, particularly among middle- and upper-class people living in big cities. This trend reflects the combined influence of better education, the mass media, and globalization. Such changes are unavoidable and are occurring in all developing countries. Unfortunately, in some places in Indonesia, the process of change is taking place too rapidly and in too drastic a fashion while being under the disruptive influence of political interests. The result is social unrest, which creates many victims in terms of fragmented families and a "lost generation."

REFERENCES

Koentjaraningrat (1981). *Pengantar Ilmu Antropologi* [Introduction to Anthropology]. Jakarta: Bhineka Cipta Sarana.

Koentjaraningrat (1994). *Kebudayaan Jawa* [The Javanese Culture]. Jakarta: Balai Pustaka.

Koentjaraningrat (1997). *Manusia dan Kebudayaan di Indonesia* [People and culture in Indonesia]. Jakarta: Djambatan.

Kompas (1996, February 23). *Pengumpulan pendapat tentang Mudik* [Public Opinion Polling on Lebaran Travelers], *Kompas,* Jakarta, p. 1.

Kompas (2000, August 22). *Laporan Pendidikan di Indonesia [Education in Indonesia], Kompas,* Jakarta, p. 1.

PKBI (Perkumpulan Keluarga Berencana Indonesia [Indonesian Planned Parenthood Association] (2000). *Draft Rencana Strategis PKBI 2001–2010* [Draft of PKBI strategic planning 2001–2010]. Paper presented at the PKBI National Conference, Jakarta, August 23–28.

Sarwono, S. W. (1997). *Psikologi sosial: Individu dan teori-teori psikologi sosial* [Social psychology: Individuals and the theories of social psychology]. Jakarta: Balai Pustaka.

UNDP (1998). *Human development report.* New York: Oxford University Press.

Wahono, F., SJ. (2000). *Ekonomi politik pendidikan: Antara kompetisi dan keadilan sosial* [The economics of educational politics: Between competition and fairness]. Paper presented at the National Seminar: "Quo Vadis the Indonesian Education?" sponsored by the University of Sanata Dharma, Kanisius Foundation, and Ford Foundation in Yogyakarta, August 21–23, 2000.

CHAPTER 8

FAMILY DEVELOPMENT IN TWO ISLAND CULTURES IN THE CHANGING PACIFIC

MARY MARTINI
University of Hawaii at Manoa

The purpose of this chapter is to review economic and political developments occurring in the Pacific in the past 30 years and to describe their effects on family life in two regions: (1) in the Federated States of Micronesia (four autonomous island states that are in a pact of free association with the United States); and (2) in the Marquesas Islands (six islands that are part of French Polynesia, an overseas territory of France). In both regions, family forms shifted from a predominance of collective, lineage-base extended family units to relatively self-sufficient, nuclear or conjugal family units.

This shift occurred in the Marquesas Islands in the early 1900s, as the islands became severely depopulated as a result of exposure to Western diseases. Clans lost many members, survivors lived in smaller and smaller units, and missionaries encouraged conjugal families to live apart to reduce spread of contagious diseases. By the late 1970s, when Martini and Kirkpatrick conducted fieldwork in the Marquesas, only 23 percent of the households in two valleys resembled the "traditional" extended family form of having two or more couples with their children residing and working together. Half of all households consisted of nuclear families (parents and their children alone), and another 27 percent included only one other extended family member (Kirkpatrick, 1983).

The shift to nuclear family forms occurred much later in Micronesia, in the 1970s, when the family economic base shifted from subsistence farming and fishing to wage labor (Hezel, 1992a; Hezel & Barnabas, 1992). In the two Pacific island groups, changes in family form occurred at different historical periods and under different conditions. They were accomplished in different ways and have had different effects on family members' adaptations. Examining variations in these shifts may provide useful background and perspective for public policy judgments and decisions about family lives and individuals' adaptations in the changing Pacific.

In this chapter I describe the effects of seven kinds of developments on family forms and on families' abilities to help their members adapt: (1) increased government spending on projects that provide paying jobs to islanders; (2) shifts in families' economic bases from subsistence farming and fishing to paid work; (3) shifts in predominant family forms from cooperative extended kin units to self-contained nuclear family units; (4) improved health care, education, transportation, communication, and sanitation; (5) increased expendable income and access to consumer goods, including intoxicants; (6) mandatory Western schooling; and (7) increased migration of islanders from rural to urban areas in search of work and money. I describe both positive changes (e.g., families' improved abilities to keep their children alive and healthy) and indicators of family destabilization (e.g., increased rates of alcoholism, divorce, child neglect, child and spouse abuse, and teen suicide).

Social scientists have studied family adaptations in each of these two areas, separately. This chapter contributes to that work by comparing influences on and effects of family changes in the two regions. Martini and Kirkpatrick conducted fieldwork in the Marquesas Islands in 1977–1979 (as reported in Kirkpatrick, 1981, 1983, 1987; Martini, 1994; Martini & Kirkpatrick, 1981, 1992). Andrea Guillory, who assisted in gathering data for this chapter, has worked in Micronesia as a public health specialist. Hezel (2000b, 2001a, 2001b) and participants in the Micronesian Seminar (see numerous citations), have carefully documented social changes in that region, year by year, from the late 1960s to today. Their work is drawn upon heavily in this chapter. And researchers at the Pacific Region Educational Lab (now Pacific Resources in Education and Learning, PREL) have evaluated the school systems and cultural conditions for learning for the past 15 years (e.g., Aka, 1993; Brown, Hammond, & Onikama, 1997; Busick & Inos, 1994a, 1994b; Gooler, Kautzer, & Knuth, 2000; Hammond, 2000; Hammond, Inos, & Busick, 1994; Inos & Quigley, 1995; Kawakami 1995a, 1995b, 1995c; Koki, 1996a, 1996b, 1999; Koki & Less, 1998; Koki, Van Broekhuizen, & Uehara, 2000; Miyasto, 1998; Onikama, Hammond, & Koki, 1998; PREL, 1996; Research & Development Cadre, PREL, 1995, 1998; Shigemoto, 1997; Simanu-Klutz, 1999; Uehara & Flores, 2000). Recent information on the Marquesas Islands is less complete. Leu (1996), Thomas (1990), Bolin (2000), and visitors to the islands have provided accounts of change in the past years.

Contemporary families in the two regions are similar in many ways. Subsistence farming, fishing, living close to the land, and spending time meeting both physical and social needs are important activities in both regions. Social relationships, sharing, being in contact with others, seeking status, committing to group efforts, and developing social safety nets for children continue to be valued processes in both regions. Both regions are marginal to world markets, but are strongly affected by political and economic trends. As fairly self-contained island cultures, both are strongly affected by population demographics. In both island groups, young people may be the most valuable economic resource (Barlow, 1996).

Traditionally, Marquesan and Micronesian islanders worked the land and sea to produce daily resources. Staple foods and food preparation in the two regions were similar. Diets consisted of breadfruit, fermented breadfruit ("popoi"), taro, sweet potatoes, fish, shellfish, citrus fruits, and domesticated animals such as chickens and pigs. Access to land was crucial in these subsistence cultures, and systems of land ownership developed in both regions. Extended families worked as coordinated groups under a lineage chief to fish, farm, build, clean, and cook. Extended families ate together in a common cooking house near a shared earth oven, but tended to sleep in nuclear family sleeping houses. Children were raised by the group and had "many laps to sit in." Authority relations in the extended family groups in both regions provided checks and balances, "safety valves," and forms of conflict resolution.

Families in the two regions have shifted from cooperative, lineage-based family units to nuclear-family economic units. The shifts have occurred at different times and in different ways and have had different effects on adaptation. Families in the two regions have reacted somewhat differently and to somewhat different economic and political developments in the past 30 years. Micronesian families currently exhibit both more signs of family destabilization (higher rates of alcoholism, child neglect and abuse, teen suicide, etc.) *and* more signs of enhanced opportunities for individuals (higher rates of high school completion, college attendance, salaried professional work, etc.). However, comparisons must be made with caution, since Micronesian families described in this chapter tend to live in peri-urban areas with high population density, geographic mobility, day-to-day access to consumer goods, and exposure to Western influence, while the Marquesans described in this chapter live in small valleys with low population density, low geographic mobility, sporadic access to consumer goods, and low day-to-day exposure to Western influences.

Differences in how families and their members have adapted may stem from the following differences in the regions (see Tables 8.1–8.4):

Table 8.1 Comparing Physical Features of the Federated States of Micronesia (FSM) and the Marquesas Islands

PHYSICAL ENVIRONMENT	FSM	MARQUESAS
Remoteness: Distance to nearest continent	1,000 mi	5,000 mi
No. of hours of jet travel from continent	<1 hr	4–5 hr
Size: land mass (in square miles)	270 mi^2	270 mi^2
Average daily temperature	80°F	77°F
Average yearly rainfall	100–300 in.	30–100 in.
Protective coral reefs?	Yes	No
Numerous navigable harbors?	Yes	No
Transportation between settlements easy?	Yes	No

- The Marquesas Islands are more remote, difficult to reach by sea or air, and less accessible than the Micronesian Islands.
- Historically, Marquesans experienced lower intensities and frequencies of Western contact (but suffered more extensive depopulation once exposed to Western diseases).
- The French territorial government pursues a policy of encouraging valley-level agricultural self-sufficiency in their overseas territories, including the Marquesas Islands.
- The U.S. government pursued a policy of developing human resources in Micronesia in the absence of viable plans for economic self-sufficiency.
- Basic education is provided in the Marquesas, but opportunities to pursue higher education or white-collar occupations are rare.

Table 8.2 Demographic Differences between the Federated States
of Micronesia (FSM) and the Marquesas Islands (MRQ)

POPULATION DEMOGRAPHICS	FSM 1980	MRQ 1980	FSM 2000	MRQ 1996
Number of people in region	85,500	5,000	105,500	8,064
Population density (people/square mile)	316	19	389	30
% of population who are female	9%		49%	47%
% of population 5 and younger		HM 23%	16%	12%
% of population 65 and older	3%	HM 2%	3%	3%
Crude birth rate/1,000	35 (1985)	HM 38.2		20.3
Crude death rate/1,000	5 (1985)	HM 4.8		2.6

HM = Valley of Hakamaii, Ua Pou.

Table 8.3 Health Indicators in Two Regions

HEALTH INDICATOR	FSM 1980	MRQ 1980	FSM 2000	FP 1996
Life expectancy for women	66 (1990)	72 (1990)[a]	70	75
Life expectancy for men	60 (1990)	67 (1990)[a]	66	70[a]
Infant mortality rate/1,000		18 (1990)[a]	37	10[a]

[a]French Polynesia figures, not MRQ.

Table 8.4 Education Indicators in Two Regions

EDUCATION	FSM 2000	MRQ 1996
No. of primary schools	140	28
No. of high schools	16	2
No. of community colleges/universities	4	0
% of 25+ who finished elementary school	60% (1994)	69%
Who finished high school	36%	3%
Who have had some college	18%	3%
Who have a college degree	5%	1%

- Widespread elementary, high school, and community college education are provided in Micronesia, and opportunities to pursue higher education and white-collar occupations are numerous.
- Nuclear families began to predominate in the Marquesas Islands in the early twentieth century as a reaction to epidemics and severe depopulation.
- Cooperative extended-family forms persisted in Micronesia through the 1960s, until subsistence farming and fishing began to be replaced by wage earning as the economic base.
- Marquesan families tend to live in small valley settlements, with low population density, low geographic mobility, and a high proportion of young, dependent children.
- Micronesian families tend to live in large peri-urban communities, with high population density, high geographic mobility, and a similarly high proportion of young, dependent children.
- Marquesans are only a few generations removed from a severe population "bust," in which their numbers were decimated as a result of exposure to Western diseases (only 1,200 Marquesans remained in 1920, from the estimated precontact population of over 20,000).
- Micronesians are experiencing the largest boom in their population in recorded history.

In this chapter I will sort out some of these influences and reactions to tell a story of contemporary family development from extended to conjugal forms in two island cultures in the Pacific. First I will review models of the relationship between family functions and structures. Then, for each set of islands I will:

1. Provide information on the physical, political, economic, and historical contexts in which families function and develop in that region
2. Describe typical family forms and functions in that area at the beginning of this period of change (in the 1960s–1970s)
3. Describe major political and economic developments that influenced family life in the region during the last 30 years
4. Describe positive and negative family adaptations to these changes

Then I will discuss possible reasons why families adapted in similar and in different ways in the two regions.

FAMILY FUNCTIONS AND RELATIONSHIP PATTERNS

LeVine (1974) posits that parents' major tasks are to provide, for all family members, the human needs outlined by Maslow (1987) in his "pyramid of human needs." At the base of the "pyramid of parental functions" (see Figure 8.1, adapted from LeVine) is the family's basic task of keeping family members alive, healthy, and out of danger.

In dangerous situations, parents will focus all attention on assuring survival, ignoring less essential needs (such as shelter in the case of fleeing refugees) that are "higher" on this pyramid. Beyond the need to avoid danger is the parental need to provide basic necessities—food, water, shelter, and clothing. Next in this hierarchy of family functions is the task of preparing offspring for economic and physical survival in their own futures, for when the parents are no longer present. Adults train children to adapt to environments that adults guess they will encounter as adults. They teach children the skills they will

FIGURE 8.1 Hierarchy of Parenting Tasks
Adapted from LeVine (1974).

need to survive once the parents are gone. A fourth family task is to provide a setting in which members feel they belong, have meaningful, contributing roles, and feel valued, supported, and safe. The top two levels of the pyramid of parent functions are to develop the child's social skills for future belonging: self-esteem for adaptive functioning, and individual potential.

LeVine points out that in difficult environments, parents focus all attention on tasks at the base of the pyramid, ignoring more esoteric tasks, such as helping the child develop self-esteem or individual potential. He notes that only in affluent societies can parents focus mainly on children's self-esteem and self-development.

In the next sections I will use this model to ask: (1) To what extent and how do families at each period and place succeed in fulfilling these family functions? (2) Which family functions are emphasized in different regions and at different times? (3) Which family functions are affected by economic and political changes? (4) Which family functions are targeted for support by various government policies? (5) Which family functions degenerate when families become destabilized? And (6) How do new family forms emerge to continue to perform these functions?

Families help their members adapt in many ways. Different roles, structures, routines, mutual expectations, and interaction styles arise to fulfill the needs of the members. In some families, members perform complementary roles to provide basic needs, to assure safety, and to train the young (such as fathers providing food, mothers nurturing; or fathers hunting, mothers farming). Gender-specific and rank-specific work roles are an example of complementary efforts that increase the efficiency of the unit. In other family forms, all members perform most functions, most of the time, without specialization and at the loss of some efficiency but with possible gain in relationship complexity and depth. In still other families, members have primary roles, but flexibly take on each others' roles whenever the need arises. Family relationship patterns typically include "checks and balances" (such as grandparents monitoring the severity of parents' discipline techniques), "safety valves" (such as relatives providing a home for an alienated teenager), and methods of resolving conflict in the group (such as neutral relatives intervening in a spouse conflict).

When in balance, families smoothly perform most of these functions to an adequate degree. When out of balance, family members may focus on one function (such as searching for a job or new mate) while completely ignoring others (such as making sure their toddler has been left behind in competent hands). Severely destabilized families may have trouble performing any of these functions well, resulting in high levels of neglect and abuse of vulnerable family members, escapist activities, substance abuse, homelessness, suicide, and so on. When out of synchrony, some families fall apart— the shared expectations, rules, routines, roles, checks and balances disintegrate rapidly. But the more common family dysfunction is rigidity or the tendency of family members to cling to old routines and roles that are no longer adaptive to new conditions and needs. Families facing extreme changes in economic, social, political, and physical condi-

tions tend to "destabilize" for varying periods of time in the process of coming up with new patterns that are better suited to these conditions. These models of family functions and patterns will be used to examine indicators of family breakdown in the Pacific (increased divorce, child abuse, neglect, suicide), to determine which functions have "broken down," and why and how families are repairing themselves.

Contexts of Family Life in Micronesia

Physical, political, economic, and historical features influence how families organize themselves and function. It is important to understand the contexts in which families function to understand family structures and shifts in structures. I will tell the story of shifts in family forms and functions, first for Micronesia (drawing heavily on the documentation and analysis of Hezel), and then for one island in the Marquesas Islands.

Geopolitical Context. The Federated States of Micronesia (population 103,251) are located due north of Australia and New Guinea, and between the Philippine Islands to the west, the Marshall Islands to the east, and Guam and the Northern Mariana Islands to the north (see Table 8.1). The 607 islands are scattered across more than a million square miles of the Pacific. The Federation consists of four states or sets of islands, which stretch more than 1,700 miles from West to East. These are: (1) Yap, the island group closest to the Asian mainland (about 1,000 miles) and consisting of 2 large, 5 small, and 134 very small islands, with a land area of 46 square miles and a population of 11,019; (2) Chuuk (consisting of 7 major island groups, with a land area of 49 square miles, and a population of 50,491); (3) Pohnpei, by far the largest island group, with a land area of 133 square miles and a population of 34,228; and (4) Kosrae (with 5 islands close together, 42 square miles, and the lowest population of 7,513) (Bank of Hawaii, 1995; Government of the Federated States of Micronesia, 2000).

Accessibility.   Compared to the Marquesas Islands, the Federated States are more accessible. They are relatively close to a continental landmass and have had more extensive contact with voyagers and colonizers than have had the Marquesas Islands. Repeated, early contact exposed islanders to foreign diseases for which they had no antibodies, causing general ill health, high childhood mortality, and short life spans. One advantage over time, however, was that Micronesians slowly built up antibodies against these diseases. This saved them from the decimation suffered by more remote Polynesian islands when voyagers arrived in large numbers in the Pacific in the 1800s, triggering epidemics.

Ease of Subsistence.   The Micronesian islands are well suited for subsistence farming and fishing. Geologically they range from high, volcanic islands to low coral atolls. The climate is tropical, with an average daily temperature of 85° F and heavy rates of rainfall (110–330 inches/year). Flat land is rare, so agriculture is limited to subsistence farming, with little cash cropping or exporting. Most islands are surrounded by coral reefs and have protected harbors—facilitating trade, transportation, and contact. Waters are warm, fish are plentiful, and fishing is relatively safe, in protected lagoons.

Cultural Patterns.   Micronesia is made up of a mix of people with at least eight major languages. Each state has its own language. The common language of commerce, education, and government is English. Settlement was believed to have occurred over 3,000 years ago from the western to eastern islands and by people speaking different root languages. Learning English at school is seen as functional for communicating with other Micronesians, not just as an academic task.

History of Contact.   Micronesia has been colonized by many nations, and cultural beliefs and practices of the colonizers have been assimilated in many ways into local cultural forms. However, as long as the economic base remained subsistence farming and fishing, traditional family structures and functions remained the same and islanders resisted cultural change, frustrating some missionaries and colonizers.

Spanish Jesuit missionaries arrived in the Mariana Islands, to the north, in 1668. American Protestant missionaries arrived and opened missions and schools on Ponape and Kosrae in the 1850s. Spanish colonial rule began in 1886 on Yap and then on Ponape and ended in 1898, when Germans took over ruling the islands. The Japanese then took control of the Western Pacific from 1914 to the end of World War II. Many Japanese people settled in the islands at this time and built roads, harbors, electrical plants, schools, and military bases. They managed farms for the export of foodstuffs to Japan (Bank of Hawaii, 1995).

After World War II, the United Nations granted the islands to the United States to administer, as protectorates. U.S. foreign policy through the 1950s was one of nonintervention. The government saw its role as standing guard, ready to protect the islands if they were invaded by other forces. The government intervened little in the internal workings of the islands, and was criticized by some countries for neglecting its protectorates.

Government Policy and Spending.   Economic theories influencing foreign policy shifted under President John F. Kennedy in the early 1960s. Economic advisers recommended a new policy of developing "human potential" in Third World countries as a mechanism for jump-starting economic development. The new model posited that economic development would proceed more quickly in a region if people were healthy, well educated, had money to spend on consumer goods, and had the skills and capital to govern themselves and to develop new forms of economic self-sufficiency. In response to this model, the United States doubled and then tripled its financial input into the islands, with the objective of improving health, education, and welfare (Bank of Hawaii, 1995).

The government invested $1.5 billion from the early 1960s to 1979 to fund large-scale infrastructure projects—to build roads, bridges, harbors, runways, power plants, water systems, sewage systems, schools, and clinics. It paid islanders as unskilled and skilled laborers for these projects, which were supervised by engineers and Peace Corps volunteers. Other Peace Corps volunteers were brought in to be the first wave of teachers and health workers. The plan from the beginning, however, was to phase out American workers and to hire islanders as soon as they could be trained. To this purpose, the school systems were jump-started to produce the needed government workers.

Health care and sanitation improved dramatically, and indicators of improved health rose. Many tropical diseases were brought under control—increasing quality of life for children and adults alike. Infant mortality and childhood death due to accidental injury were drastically reduced. Schooling became mandatory to age 16, and the literacy rate and proportion of the population with first an elementary, and later, a high school education jumped quickly. The standard of living, as measured by indices such as electricity and indoor plumbing in the home, hot water, motorized transport and electrical appliances, and steady wages, increased dramatically.

Political Autonomy.   In 1979 the nearby Marianas and Marshall Islands adopted constitutions of independence and entered into 15-year pacts of free association with the United States. The four Micronesia states joined together to form a federation, the Federated States of Micronesia (FSM), and gradually negotiated a pact of free association with the United States, which included the obligation that the U.S. government pay large sums until 2001, to gain free passage through the waterways while excluding other powers. The immediate problems involved in the region's failure to develop a self-sufficient economic base were avoided by negotiating regular U.S. payments to the Federation government. Through this process, the Federation government continues to be, by far, the major employer in the islands (Hezel, 1980).

Local government was modeled after U.S. forms, with a national government made up of a president and vice president; a state government

headed by a governor and lieutenant governor; and a municipal government headed by a local chief—head of the local lineage or clan (Petersen, 1997; Pinsker, 1997). From 1979 to 2001 another $1.5 billion was paid to the Federation, which mainly paid the salaries of teachers, health care workers, engineers, clerks, and administrators, and supported a burgeoning government bureaucracy.

Economic Dependency and Vulnerability.   The islands planned to use U.S. funds to develop economic self-sufficiency projects such as fish-processing plants and a tourism infrastructure, but these plans did not materialize (Bank of Hawaii, 1995). The FSM is no closer to economic self-sufficiency than it was in the early 1960s, but by now a broad base of Micronesians are well educated, want to continue in salaried and wage positions, and may migrate to the United States to do so if necessary (San Mateo County District College, 1997).

The Federated States of Micronesia has been a consumer economy for five decades, paid for by the United States. Modern communications, transportation, and utilities have been developed in the urban centers. Micronesians have become accustomed to working paying jobs, having expendable income, and having free access to Western goods. Many people have abandoned self-sufficiency farming and fishing. If the United States decreases the rent it agrees to pay for exclusive use of the waterways, then the standard of living in Micronesia will decrease precipitously. In anticipation of this event, hundreds of Micronesians have been leaving the country to settle in Hawaii and California (Bank of Hawaii, 1995).

FAMILY STRUCTURES AND FUNCTIONS IN MICRONESIA PRIOR TO GOVERNMENT INTERVENTIONS

Living and working in extended-family units was the norm in Pohnpei, Chuuk, and other Micronesian islands in the 1950s. The few nuclear households that were exceptions to these patterns were ridiculed at the time (Hezel, 1992b). Members of either a matrilineal (Chuuk) or patrilineal clan (Pohnpei) lived and worked together in a highly structured family group, on land held in common by the members of the lineage.

In Chuuk, all sisters in a lineage, their husbands, and their children lived together on one estate, along with other unmarried relatives (Hezel, 1992b). In Pohnpei, all brothers in a lineage, their wives, and children lived together on one estate, held in common (Hezel & Barnabas, 1992). In both areas, these collectives were led by a clan chief, typically the eldest competent male in the lineage.

Family Functions

These collective units effectively performed the following adaptive family functions.

Land Tenure/Secure Sense of Place. Title to land was and is held by the lineage members as a collective, but managed by the "chief." (Recent attempts by chiefs to sell off portions of a lineage's land have resulted in clan members forcing legislation that confirms and protects the rights of all members to a say in decisions about selling lineage land [Hezel, 1992a].) Family members gained a stable sense of belonging in a particular place. On Yap, villages were ranked, with different statuses, and a person's place of birth became a major component of that person's identity (Kirkpatrick & Broder, 1976).

Basic Needs. Members of the lineage worked the land and sea together and pooled products and proceeds (including money they earned from cash crops such as copra or coffee). Nuclear families and individuals "owned" certain breadfruit, coconut, and fruit trees (which, in some cases, had been planted by their parents at their births), and they picked from these trees freely. In general, however, all gathered food was distributed evenly across the members of the lineage, who cooked and ate together each evening. Members developed a strong sense of economic and social security and of belonging in a particular place.

Shelter. Nuclear families slept in separate thatched or plywood sleeping houses, with one or more unmarried relative(s). Sometimes two nuclear families shared a sleeping house. Sleeping houses were clustered around a common cooking house, earth oven, and meeting house. The clan meeting house was also used for feasts and served as the sleeping quarters for adolescent males of the lineage, who were forbidden from sleeping in their own families' houses, because of the presence of their teenage sisters. The shared earth oven, cook house, and meeting house were considered to be the heart of the lineage.

Sense of Purpose, Valued Roles, Meaningful Work. Lineage members worked together, daily, to produce food, under the leadership of the most senior male of the lineage (on Pohnpei, the grandfather or eldest brother; on Chuuk, the brother of the eldest woman of the lineage). Together, the adults fished, farmed, gathered fruits, gardened, hunted, cleaned, and cooked together. All food produced by the group was cooked, shared among the lineage members, and eaten together. Family members also worked communally to produce feasts, deal with emergencies, and do large-scale building. Labor resources were pooled on a daily basis and resources were distributed daily.

From the early days of shipping, copra became a cash crop in Micronesia, and was worked communally on these islands. Lineage groups, organized by the chief, gathered coconuts and scraped out the meat to produce sacks of copra. Payments received for these sacks were handed over to the lineage chief, who invested the capital in building materials or staples for the group.

Cooking tasks, prior to the wide availability of metal pots (Hezel, 1992a), were most efficiently completed as a group. The lineage members cooked in one earth oven that they prepared and used daily and over a central open fire. Extended family members ate together, as a large group, each evening. Canoe building and house construction also required group efforts. Indigenous house materials (pandanus mat walls, thatched roofs, bamboo poles, ridge poles, rafters, and ledgers) required the coordinated work of groups to prepare and raise (Rensel, 1997). Also, thatched houses required regular upkeep and frequent rebuilding. It was possible to handle Western materials (plywood, sheets of tin, nails) with two or three workers and these were more durable.

Working Efficiently. Complementary roles increased the efficiency of the groups. Women focused on women's tasks (cooking for the whole group, cleaning, fishing from shore, child care, and care of clothing). Men worked together on men's tasks (communal net fishing, net repair, fishing from canoes, building canoes and structures, planting and harvesting taro, picking and pounding breadfruit, preparing the earth oven, voyaging and hunting).

Social Belonging and Meaningful Roles for Children. Children were cared for communally, under the supervision of older children, teens, or one or two mothers. Children spent their days in large, cross-age groups of cousins and siblings, in which they contributed to work efforts. Adults spent their days among their adult siblings, cousins, aunts, uncles, and parents, while children played on the peripheries of these work groups or worked alongside. In this way, children lived on the periphery of adult activity and observed adults at work and at rest, but belonged to supportive peer groups and gained experience teaching and caring for younger children.

Multiple "Laps to Sit On." Children had many alternate parents in addition to their birth parents. In this way the children were raised, disciplined, cared for, and emotionally supported by a large group of caregivers. Children had "many laps" to sit on and were corrected, scolded, and punished by all competent family members. Children were also carried, cared for, slept with, and played with by available adults, and developed strong relationships with many adults and adolescents in the extended family.

Adoption/Fosterage. Children were not adopted in a formal sense of being taken from one set of parents and given to another. Instead, they had alternate sets of parents they could live with and go to in times of need. (See the following for detailed accounts of adoption in Polynesia: Carroll, 1970; Goodenough, 1970; Howard, 1970; Howard, Heighton, Jordan, & Gallimore, 1970; Kirkpatrick & Broder, 1976; Levy, 1970). Children chose which sleeping house to sleep in each night and wandered with their cousins and siblings from house to house. In this way, there was both vertical care, with older children caring for younger children, and horizontal care, with many relatives, young and old, caring for the child (Rubinstein, 1994).

Consistent Socialization, yet Protection. Children in Micronesian families faced a formidable united front of coordinated adults, who conveyed the same messages about expected behavior to the children. At the same time, children's rights to fair treatment were protected by several people in the system. Families had regular contact with their affines, or "other sides" of their families—in matrilineal Chuuk, with the father's lineage; in patrilineal Pohnpei, with the mother's lineage. These relatives, while living on different estates, stayed in frequent contact through ritual gift giving, feasts, and daily visits. The affines served as important checks on the childrearing done by the main lineage group. If adults in the main lineage mistreated children or spouses, the victims could seek refuge with their affines. These relatives would also intervene on their part to scold or shame the severe adults into less hurtful behavior. Ethnographic reports of childrearing in these lineage units in the 1950s emphasized gentle, calm treatment of children, with no reported instances of hitting, beating, yelling, or physical punishment (Hezel, 1992a; Hezel & Barnabas, 1992; Rubinstein, 1994).

Social Belonging and Meaningful Roles for Teens. The mother's brother, or chief of the lineage in Pohnpei, was a firm socializer of the teenage boys in the lineage. A major problem for families in all societies is how to transition autonomy-seeking adolescents into productive, constrained members of the family. In Micronesia, smooth transitions were accomplished in the following way. Adolescent boys were granted increasing autonomy from their families of origin. They slept together as an age group in the lineage meeting house and spent their free time together. They organized themselves as work groups but were told what to do by the chief of the lineage. They had meaningful and respected roles as hard workers. They were known for their fishing, canoeing, building, hunting, and farming skills. They were called on whenever speed, strength, or endurance were needed. They were revered for their youthful beauty and grace. As a work group they were of great service to the community. In their spare time, they were allowed to wander and entertain themselves as they wished (Hezel, 2000; Rubinstein, 1994; Kirkpatrick, 1987, describes similar patterns for the Marquesas Islands).

Prevention and Resolution of Conflict.

Teen boys' own fathers did not direct them. The lineage chief tended to be strict and decisive, but neutral with the boys. If the boys took offense with his level or style of control, they complained to their own fathers or to their affines, who supported them, treated them more leniently, and intervened, if necessary, to ensure fair treatment (Hezel & Barnabas, 1992). This process distributed the contradictory roles of disciplinarian and supporter to different members of the family. It preserved supportive ties between father and son while harnessing the energies of teenage boys for the good of the unit. Teenage girls, who showed less resistance to authority, worked side by side with their mothers and aunts, had valued roles as caregivers, cooks, and gardeners, and were treated as quasi-adults. Teens were carefully integrated into adult domains with respect for their autonomy needs.

Social Support.

Adults had many hands to help with daily work and with watching children. Adults helped each other out, and neutralized the potential intensity of the parent–teen relationship—avoiding many conflicts and resolving others. Young parents learned childrearing *in situ* from older parents. Biological parents had much autonomy in caring for and disciplining their young children, but the family unit helped out daily and particularly during difficult periods. Young parents, parents of teens, and parents under other stresses benefited, in particular, from this "safety net" of consistent, group care.

Family members had ample moral support—mothers talked, daily, to their sisters, aunts, brothers, and fathers, who also protected and supported them. Children sought refuge with grandparents, aunts, uncles, or their affines when they felt misunderstood or mistreated at home. Angry fathers took solace in talking with other fathers, and conflicts were often mediated in traditional ways by neutral parties (Hezel, 1989b; 1992a; Hezel & Barnabus, 1992; Rubinstein, 1994).

Opportunities and Constraints.

Multiple caregivers and foster parents gave children many laps to sit in. The parenting burden (caregiving, teaching, disciplining, supporting) was lifted off the shoulders of the two birth parents. The intensity of parent–child relations was lessened as children dealt with a large number of caregivers. Multiple disciplinarians neutralized the conflictual nature of family life. Extensive peer support for adults, teens, and children made family life less stressful. Family members also balanced each other—in their temperaments and skills. They played complementary roles and controlled for the unbridled anger, interests, or weaknesses of any one individual (Hezel, 1992a; Hezel & Barnabas, 1992).

However, individuals in this system were tightly controlled in terms of needing to conform with the group ways. Individuals were watched, commented on, and encouraged to conform. These constraints grated on some members constantly. Some adults, children, and particularly teens yearned to make their own decisions and felt constrained in this system (Levy, 1970, 1973). Members were tightly interdependent, and some had trouble making independent, decisions when they needed to. Levy (1973) found pervasive low levels of tension in family members' day-to-day relationships in tight extended units in Tahiti.

In conclusion, extended family provided safety, shelter, stable food sources, help with child care, daily company, a sense of meaningful, productive work and of belonging for all ages, and help with intense parent–child and spouse relationships. On the other hand, these mechanisms prevented nuclear family members from developing intense mutually dependent relationships and from exercising skills in independent judgment. Spouses did not rely solely on each other and children were not dependent on their set of two parents. Levy (1973) noted lack of depth and intensity in relationships. Relationships became conditional on desires of the moment and were not imbued with permanence.

DEVELOPMENTS IN U.S. FOREIGN POLICY IN MICRONESIA

From World War II to the 1960s, the United States did not invest a great deal of money in Micronesia. U.S. foreign policy at that time was to protect protectorates but not to intervene in internal affairs. In the 1960s, under President Kennedy, a major shift in foreign policy occurred (Hezel, 1973, 1992b; Bank of Hawaii, 1995). New economic models emphasized the development of human capital. They posited that economies would become stronger if consumers became better educated, better informed, healthier, happier, able to govern themselves and innovate new economies, and when they had money to spend.

Infrastructure

The United States began to spend a great deal of money in the region to improve infrastructure and to improve health, education, and welfare. A total of $1.5 billion was invested in the region between 1965 and 1979 to build water systems, sewers, roads, bridges, harbors, boat ramps, hospitals, clinics, schools, and electrical plants and to develop systems of communication and transportation to urban centers with hospitals and sources of wage labor. These improvements directly helped families care for their members' basic needs for safety and health and were warmly welcomed by the people.

Health

The U.S. government put into place a universal health system, which both directly improved health and provided more jobs. Universal health care included prenatal, birth, and first-year checkups, and childhood accident maintenance and dissemination of information on health, sanitation, and prevention. Information was disseminated in each of these areas, first by Peace Corps workers and later by trained Micronesians. The U.S. government funded the building and staffing of hospitals in urban areas, clinics in each rural area, and transportation systems to get to them (Hezel, 1987, 1992a).

Education

The government also targeted education as an area to be overhauled: schools were built and/or improved and were staffed. The policy was two-pronged: (1) to improve the educational process, and (2) to produce incentives (such as access to higher education and to jobs afterwards) so that a broad base of people would want to become educated. Peace Corps volunteers were the first wave of workers to implement these changes. They were trained to be project foremen, teachers, engineers, and transportation and communication specialists. Local youth began to prepare, however, for taking over these positions as teachers, health workers, postal clerks, radio operators, construction bosses, and so on (Hezel, 1979, 1987). These improvements supported families' efforts in two other important tasks, closer to the top of the "human needs pyramid": to prepare youth for economic sufficiency in a changing world and to help individual children develop their potential skills.

Schools were developed and classes taught—using U.S. curricula and textbooks and conveying American values of individualism, consumerism, and democracy (Hezel, 1975, 1984). Opportunities to continue education into high school and community college increased, first in Guam, then in Hawaii, and then in new community colleges and colleges in Micronesia (Hezel, 1989a; Hezel & Levin, 1989). The U.S. government funded more than twice the number of primary, secondary, and college-level schools (per 100,000 people) as had the French government.

In the 1970s policy changes increased opportunities for Micronesian students to pursue higher education. The U.S. government revised its policy on minority-student eligibility for college loans and scholarships to make Micronesian students eligible for minority-student scholarships (Hezel & Levin, 1990). At the same time, quota systems were established in U.S. universities to include minority students, and Micronesian students—even of average intelligence and achievement—began to be accepted and funded to go to mainland U.S. colleges. As early as 1977, 42 percent of high school graduates were college-bound (Hezel, 1979). By 1994, 60 percent of the population had completed elementary school; 36 percent had completed high school; 18 percent had had some college experience, and 5 percent had college or graduate degrees (Hezel, 2001a, b).

Early emigrating students sought technical, agricultural, fishing, and construction courses of study, to develop advanced skills in the techniques needed in daily life. Later high school graduates, however, were accepted into liberal arts colleges and went off to study history, government, languages, social work, and psychology. These occupational degrees were useful for the human services jobs provided by the U.S. government in Micronesia at the time. However, these jobs were filling fast, and forecasters predicted that liberal arts degrees and skills would be useless for the future economic self-sufficiency of the islands (Hezel, 1987, 1989a).

Forecasters worried about what these youth would do once the white-collar jobs had become filled in the islands. Three solutions, however, evolved. First, some college educated youth who were unable to find white-collar jobs in town put off the problem of employment by continuing on to graduate school, and upon return, these professionals picked off the best health, education, human services, and management jobs the island had to offer. Other college graduates did not leave the islands, as had been predicted, but returned to village life, in-

stead. These well-educated Micronesians had much less difficulty adjusting to subsistence farming and fishing and village life than forecasters had predicted. Many became innovative leaders at the village level, bonding with other college-educated youth in their areas to introduce initiatives. Migration to urban areas within Micronesia, and to Guam, Saipan, and New Zealand, did increase, as predicted, but consisted mainly of the migration of skilled and unskilled laborers who were unable to find construction work close to home and could not compete with high school and college graduates for other jobs.

Third, another change in U.S. policy enabled Micronesian youth not just to study in the United States, but also to work there. This provided an occupational safety valve for those youth who wanted to work in their field. The "brain drain" that many people feared has only begun to materialize with recent worries that the United States will drastically reduce the amount of rent it is willing to pay to the Federation for access rights in the 2001 renegotiations of the contract (Hezel & Levin, 1989, 1990; Hezel & McGrath, 1989).

Expendable Incomes and Access to Consumer Goods

U.S. intervention introduced expendable incomes, Western goods, and advertising. Increased access and consumerism fueled the desire for material wealth, not just for increased comfort and stimulation, but as a sign of achievement—a major value stressed in the new curriculum. Micronesians now had easy access to alcohol, cigarettes, and marijuana; canned, frozen, and processed food; designer clothing; sporting and driving equipment; modern appliances and entertainment electronics (Hezel, 1976, 1987, 2000b). Real-value, per-capita imports of alcohol almost doubled in eight years, from $13.49 in 1969 to $24.45 in 1977 (Hezel, 1981). Marijuana users were estimated at 8 percent of the population in 1983 (15 percent of males and 0.8 percent of females) (Hezel, 2001b). Alcoholism, poor diet, and indiscriminate leisure pursuits became new problems as new earners developed an appetite for material goods, bought on impulse, and in many cases, drove their families into debt. Lack of money led to insufficient provision of basic food and shelter, and to domestic violence stemming from parents' inability to cope (Hezel, 1976, 1981, 1989b, 1993, 2000b).

Effects of these Changes on Daily Life and the Family

Access to Paying Jobs.   The influx of paying jobs produced a number of changes in families. Early jobs went to skilled and unskilled laborers for construction. Nuclear families of men with jobs no longer needed to rely on the extended family for resources. They could buy food from grocery stores and pay for fish. Many bought building materials and, with the help of family members, built their own modern-style houses with kitchens and bathrooms.

Some men found work on nearby projects; others went to urban settings, leaving wives and children with the extended family. The collective work unit was disrupted when large numbers of men went to work for wages. The men no longer contributed labor to the group, and even those who remained in the area stopped sharing communal meals with the extended family. Wage laborers, their wives, and children began to eat separately in their own cook houses or in newly constructed kitchens. As fewer and fewer men worked in the collective unit, the clan chief lost power in directing group work and in making group decisions. Nuclear households, producing their own resources, now began to make their own decisions about how to use them (Hezel, 1992a; Hezel & Barnabas, 1992).

The Dissolution of Extended Family Units.   For a period after this slow breakup, families continued to share food on a regular basis. On certain days, for example, one family made popoi or procured fish and took the portions around to the separate households, and on other days other families did so (Hezel,

1992a). After a while, however, these daily food-sharing routines broke down as well. Extended families still cooperated to prepare feasts, make canoes, build houses, and entertain guests. And relatives visited with each other daily. But the group was no longer held together by a strong, shared goal of producing their own food and maintaining their collective resources.

The wives of wage earners also stopped contributing to group work during the day, and tended to their own households and children. They reasoned that they were no longer eating the communal food, so why help gather and prepare it? Similarly, children of wage earners withdrew to play near their own houses and were no longer cared for as a group near the adult work site. This shifted the burden of childcare onto relatively isolated mothers (Hezel, 1992a).

Loss of Family Supports.   Heads of nuclear families gained autonomy, freedom from being monitored by kin, freedom to make their own decisions, and geographic and social mobility. However, family members lost many supports when extended units fragmented. All members lost a sense of economic and social security and a sense of belonging in a viable group and place. Parents lost help caring for, training, and disciplining their children and now struggled to perform all family functions on their own. Children lost their "many laps to sit in," protection by extended family members from parental frustrations and attacks, and "escape valves" by which they could move in with relatives when they felt mistreated or misunderstood in their nuclear home. Teen boys, in particular, lost a structured situation in which their work was valued, their autonomy respected, and their peer tendencies supported (Rubinstein, 1994). The elderly lost positions of respect and security in their old age. And all members lost the checks and balances, reciprocal help, and emergency safety nets provided by group living (Rubinstein, 1994; Hezel 1992a; Hezel & Barnabas, 1992).

Reduced Interdependence.   In addition, traditional expectations concerning offering and asking for help broke down. Young people who had left extended family units were now hesitant to ask parents and elders for help. They had shunned family obligations and positions of deference and were now either ashamed to ask for help or wanted to maintain their autonomy. Young parents also hesitated to ask age-mates for help—they saw parallel nuclear family units as equally shaky as their own and did not want to impose. Parents, aunts, uncles, siblings, and grandparents hesitated to intervene to help or advise young nuclear families, even when they sensed they were in trouble. They had received the impression that the young people saw their offers of help as interference.

Migration, Instability, and the Loss of Support Networks. Migration to a new place exacerbated the destabilizing effects of leaving the extended unit. Islanders first worked labor jobs near home, but when these ended or filled, people had developed a taste for making their own money, and many people emigrated to urban centers where there were more jobs. The first wave of emigrants were young men who set up shifting households in shanty towns on squatters' land on the peripheries of cities. These households usually consisted of unrelated men and a few girlfriends. They bore little resemblance to traditional families and performed few of their supportive functions. They were rife with conflict, as unsettled, unfamiliar people moved into and out of them—trying to find jobs, stay sober, stay out of trouble. After a period of finding a job and stabilizing housing, workers sent home some earnings in the form of remittances. Many first-wave migrations were goal-specific—e.g., to make enough money for building materials for a new house back home—and many men returned home after 1–3 years (Hezel & Levin, 1989, 1990; Hezel & McGrath, 1989).

Wives and children of first-wave emigrants tended to stay in the home villages—if fortunate, among extended kin. Women left to care for numerous young children, on their own and relying mainly on remittances and their own subsistence work, often came up short, and child neglect and

abuse increased in villages during this period (Akin, 1985; Korbin, 1989; Rubinstein, 1994; Shewman, 1992).

Subsequent migrations involved men, women, and families, in search of wage-paying jobs. Many young couples migrated to urban settings, leaving their young children with aging grandparents or other relatives in the village. Child neglect often occurred when children were left with relatives too old and lacking in resources to care for them. Other families went to the city with their children. Island families found shanty-type housing where they could—if lucky, with relatives or neighbors from their villages. Stress was high and supports were weak. Divorce, child neglect and abuse, and spouse abuse, were significantly more prevalent in these unstable living situations. Overstressed parents took out their frustrations on children and each other. They had few supports, as they were out of contact with kin in their villages who would have helped, advised, relieved, and monitored them.

Access to Money and Consumer Goods. More people now had access to money, and to buying on credit in some urban areas. Improved transportation and trade facilities brought increasing numbers of consumer goods into even remote villages. Family members began to spend money on unhealthy habits: canned and packaged foods, high in sugars, salt, and fat; soft drinks, cigarettes, and, most destructively, alcohol. Alcoholism among men became a serious problem both in peri-urban areas and in home villages, and was associated with spouse and child abuse, indebtedness, unemployment, homelessness, suicide, and mental illness. Parents also began to run nuclear families into debt by purchasing appliances, clothing, and luxuries, spending beyond their means (Hezel, 1976). As people developed appetites for consumer goods and excess, they became dependent on wage-earning jobs and abandoned subsistence farming and fishing entirely.

Mandatory Schooling and Segregation of Youth. Compulsory schooling removed children from day-to-day integration in adult activities at home and taught them new values of independence, exploration, self-reliance, equality, materialism, and need for control. At school, children spent their days in age-segregated groups with children from all over the village or town. They were no longer integrated, day to day, in adult work, and spent less time caring for young siblings and working and learning, side by side, with their adult relatives. An increasing number of teens remained in high school. Prior to this, teen boys had done a large share of the fishing, farming, and building for the family unit. An increasing number of older teens chose to go on to trade school, community college, college in the territory, or college and graduate school abroad. Parents felt their immediate losses of labor and respect were well worth their children's new opportunities to develop themselves and to move beyond village horizons.

New Values. Micronesian schools were extremely effective in conveying new sets of values to a broad base of students and families. American schooling conveyed culturally valued ideas of democracy, egalitarianism, self-reliance, skepticism, questioning of authority and tradition, and the desire for individual control over one's own destiny (Hezel, 1973, 1975, 1976, 1989a). Many of these values ran counter to Micronesian ideals concerning social hierarchy, unquestioning respect of elders and tradition, and knowing one's place. Nonetheless, generations of Micronesian youth absorbed these values quickly, and elders did their best to tolerate the changes with equanimity. Compared to other colonial educational systems, U.S. educational policies maximized the relevance, accessibility, and influence of school ideas and habits of thinking on the everyday lives and thinking/working styles of a broad base of students (although many felt the system could do more [Samuels, 2000]).

Concern for broad-based, effective education. American school administrators and Micronesian successors have been unusually attentive to improving the fit between school, community, culture, and occupation possibilities—particularly when compared to the lack of efforts in these areas by school administrators in French overseas territories or in colonial school systems in the past.

Effects of these changes on families' abilities to help their members adapt. Improved infrastructure and health care helped parents save their infants from early death and their children from death or permanent injury from childhood accidents or disease. Improved health care reduced the prevalence of tropical diseases, increasing people's quality of life. These interventions targeted the basic-level needs in the "human needs hierarchy." However, new access to money, unhealthy foods, soft drinks, cigarettes, alcohol, and drugs introduced new health hazards and dangers to a stable lifestyle. Alcoholism, drug abuse, and their discontents grew to epidemic proportions (Hezel, 1981, 1993; Lindstrom, 1987).

The movement from a subsistence to a money economy, the dissolution of the extended family, and migration to stressful peri-urban environments threatened the ability of nuclear families to perform most family functions. Heads of new households needed to shoulder all responsibilities on their own, and they had little training in doing so (Akin, 1985; Gegeo & Watson-Gegeo, 1985; Hezel, 1976, 2000b). Many new families were unable to provide for basic needs, to protect children, to provide a sense of security and belonging, to enable members to contribute in meaningful ways, and to train children for future success (Hezel, 1992a; Hezel & Barnabas, 1992). Dramatic increases in divorce, spouse abuse, child neglect, child abuse, and teen suicide signaled this breakdown (Counts, 1989; Crawford, 2001; Hezel, 1992b, 1993; Korbin, 1989; Marshall, 1985a, b; Pan Pacific and Southeast Asia Women's Association, 1996; World Bank, 2000).

Teen suicides, for example, tended to be by boys who: were drunk, had recently quarreled with their fathers, felt belittled and devalued by their fathers, had few skills for discussing problems, had fathers with few skills for dealing with these conflicts, felt they had no way to elicit help from relatives, and saw no alternative plans of action, such as moving in with protective kin. Their suicide attempts (often carried out by leaning into a noose until they blacked out, fell, and hanged themselves) may have started as cries for help to their families, but because of isolation from monitoring others and drunken misjudgments, many attempts ended in death (Hezel, 1989; Rubinstein, 1994).

At the same time, education opportunities enabled an unprecedented number of islanders to finish elementary school, high school, and even college and to pursue white-collar occupations (Hezel, 2001a, 2001b; Hezel & Levin, 1990). These interventions helped parents offer children an unprecedented level of support in developing their individual potential.

Needs Targeted by U.S. Interventions. U.S. interventions in Micronesia appear to have bolstered processes at the very bottom of the human needs hierarchy (e.g., avoiding death due to disease) and at the very top (developing individual potential through extensive education) while inadvertently initiating family destabilization that threatened—at least for the time being—the middle-level family functions of assuring security, connectedness, purpose, and ability to contribute, which then also destabilized the provision of basic needs and safety.

CONTRAST: THE MARQUESAS ISLANDS

The Marquesas Islands provide a revealing contrast of a different transformation of family forms and functions and adaptive forms of coping. Government interventions in French Polynesia were based on different foreign policy goals for the overseas territories and contributed to different kinds of adaptations.

The Marquesas Islands are geographically much more isolated, difficult to access, and difficult to leave and return to than are the Federated States of Micronesia. The French government encourages local self-sufficiency by subsidizing agriculture and providing adequate infrastructure for healthy living. It discourages migration to Tahiti for wage work. Settlements are isolated and small, and even though families live in nuclear units, people interact extensively all day, every day. Informal support networks provide a social security net that prevents impoverishment, domestic violence, substance abuse, and

the dissolution of family structures and functions observed in some areas of Micronesia. Although daily life is more stable, opportunities to move beyond a subsistence fishing and farming existence are limited.

Contexts of Family Life in the Marquesas Islands

Geopolitical Context. The six Marquesas Islands are rugged, outlying islands of French Polynesia, about 5,000 miles west of South America. French Polynesia, an overseas territory of France, consists of over 130 islands in five archipelagos: (1) the six Society Islands, including Tahiti, with its capital city of Papeete; (2) the eighty atolls of the Tuamotus; (3) the six Marquesas Islands; (4) the Austral Islands; and (5) the Gambier Islands in the Southeast. Distances are extensive in the territory, as islands are scattered over nearly 2 million square miles (Bank of Hawaii, 2001).

Accessibility. The Marquesas Islands are considered to be the most isolated of all islands in the world. Even by jet, they are 4–5 hours from the nearest continent. Physical features of the islands make transportation difficult to and among the islands and valleys. The islands are mountainous, with no surrounding reefs or coastal plains. The valleys are separated by high ridges. There are few protected harbors, and until recently, transportation was arduous to the islands and between valleys and settlements on each island—such that each settlement remained isolated.

Ease of Subsistence. Conditions are less conducive for subsistence farming and fishing in the Marquesas Islands than in Micronesia. The climate is tropical with cooling trade winds (an average temperature of 77° F), but rainfall is inconsistent on the higher islands (e.g., about 30 inches a year on the leeward side of 'Ua Pou, compared to Micronesia's average of 110–330 inches per year). Fair weather and rich, volcanic soil enable good growing conditions on some islands. But other, drier islands suffer droughts (sometimes for 3–5 years) and have experienced famines in the past.

In contrast to Micronesia, islands in the Marquesas are not surrounded by protective coral reefs. Cold sea currents from Antarctica inhibit growth of coral. Fishing is limited to more difficult and dangerous deep-sea, line-fishing or spear-fishing forms. Highly productive, group net fishing in lagoons cannot be practiced in the Marquesas. The average daily time needed for subsistence farming and fishing for a family of six under favorable conditions in Micronesia is estimated to be 4 hours of work per day for one worker (Hezel, 2000a). This increases to an estimated need of about 6–8 hours per day for two workers in the Marquesas Islands.

Cultural Patterns. Polynesian settlement is believed to have proceeded from the western islands of Samoa and Tonga, to Tahiti, and then on to the Marquesas, about 2,000 years ago. From these more eastern centers voyagers then moved on to settle Hawaii and Easter Island (as cited in Martini & Kirkpatrick, 1992). Polynesian language and cultural forms pervade Marquesan life, language, and beliefs, but many cultural practices were prohibited by French Catholic missionaries in the 1800s and had disappeared until a recent cultural renaissance (Kirkpatrick, 1983; Leu, 1996).

Early Western contact descriptions are of energetic people in a heavily populated land. Population was estimated at 20,000 in 1798 or about 75 people per square mile (compared to fewer than 20 per square mile, today). Indigenous social organization consisted of chiefdoms within each valley. A particularly strong chief might rule all clans in a valley, but more typically, as in Micronesia as late as the 1960s, each lineage had its own chief and chiefs cooperated to coordinate valley life. Only one island, 'Ua Pou, had a centralized chief ruling the whole island (Kirkpatrick, 1983).

Traditional Social Organization. Chiefs were considered to be men and kinsmen, not gods. They became chiefs through their own efforts, the power of their clans, and through carefully organized marriages and adoptions. Land acquisition appeared to be by force between competing clans. Settlement of the many valleys on the islands and of the numerous islands appears to have occurred when one clan was driven out of its home valley by an invading clan and relocated to a new valley (Kirkpatrick, 1983; Leu, 1996).

Precontact Marquesans were reputed to be ferocious warriors. Elaborate cultural and technical practices were documented. Status within a clan and larger tribe had more to do with a person's traits and skills than his or her genealogy. Many Marquesan terms were developed to mark expertise in different crafts and arts (Bolin, 2000; Leu, 1996).

Traditional Family Patterns. Early family structure resembled the Micronesian pattern described above. Archeological finds show numerous hamlets scattered throughout the steep valleys. Each hamlet consisted of five or six stone house platforms, believed to be sleeping houses for conjugal families, with a common earth oven, cookhouse, and meeting house nearby (Leu, 1996).

Two aspects of Western contact in the 1800s drastically changed Marquesan family patterns from extended to nuclear forms: (1) depopulation as a result of disease decimated lineage units; and (2) missionaries prohibited numerous cultural practices and pressured people to live in separate conjugal units (in part as an effort to stem the devastating spread of disease).

History of Western Contact. French Polynesia was discovered by English and French explorers in the late 1700s. Between this time and rediscovery in the mid-1800s, when the French made the islands a protectorate, Marquesans experienced little contact with Westerners. The French did not see the islands as useful for naval posts or settlements, so ignored them while they developed the port town of Papeete, in Tahiti.

The French colonial period began in 1880 with the abdication of King Pomare V in Tahiti, similar to the U.S. takeover of the Hawaiian kingdom in 1893. French Catholic missionaries spread through the Marquesas Islands and discouraged traditional cultural forms of living, singing, dancing, and pagan religious rites. Generations later, Marquesans parroted missionaries' judgments that early Marquesans had been barbaric heathens (Kirkpatrick, 1983).

After 1842 the islands experienced much greater contact with trade and war vessels. Many sea battles were fought in the vicinity, and a large number of shipwrecked or fatigued sailors jumped ship to settle in the islands. Sailors and traders brought Western diseases (Leu, 1996).

Depopulation.   The Marquesas Islands suffered the most severe depopulation caused by exposure to Western diseases of all Pacific Islands. Indigenous people had lived in almost complete isolation for centuries and had built up few antibodies to protect them from introduced diseases. They had no access to Western medical care. Contagious diseases spread quickly through large families living in close contact with minimal sanitation. Once epidemics started, they tended to wipe out entire lineages, valley settlements, or even islands. (Even as late as 1951, a measles epidemic killed sixty people on 'Ua Pou [Kirkpatrick, 1983].)

First, syphilis and other venereal diseases introduced by sailors rendered many females infertile. Then, high infant mortality, resulting from unclean water and new Western diseases, inhibited population growth even further. Then, measles and smallpox decimated the remaining population. The Marquesan population dropped from a conservative estimate of 20,000 in 1798, to 10,000 in 1863; to 4,000 in 1904; to 2,890 in 1911; to 1,800 in 1920; and to a nadir of 1,200 in 1923. The 1798 population had been reduced by 94 percent in 125 years (Kirkpatrick, 1983; Leu, 1996).

Effects on Family Forms.   Entire chiefdoms and valleys were wiped out. Cooperative work units were not viable without the authoritative leadership of a clan chief. In some cases only a single nuclear household was left in a valley. Survivors tended to be members of families living far away from others.

During this period, French missionaries converted many Marquesans to Catholicism, strongly discouraged many cultural practices, and encouraged conjugal families to live apart from each other, in part to stem the spread of contagious diseases. Also at this time, the French colonial government imposed the French system of land tenure, by which family land is passed down in equal parcels to all surviving children. These events, the loss of clan leadership, and fears of disease undermined many reasons for Marquesans to live and work together in extended family units.

In the 1920s, during the childhood periods of the oldest informants of Kirkpatrick, the population began to rebuild, slowly (Kirkpatrick, 1983). Population increased to 2,000 by 1926; to 5,400 by 1970; to 7,350 by 1990; and to 8,064 by 1996. As late as 1951, 'Ua Pou suffered epidemics that wiped out many people. Today, the islands are still much less densely populated than the Micronesian Islands (20 people per square mile in the Marquesas versus 398 in Micronesia). By the late 1970s over half the Marquesan families in the two valleys we studied were living in nuclear family units. Another 27 percent had only one or two extended family members (such as an aging grandmother) living with them. Only 23 percent of the households followed the traditional extended family pattern (Kirkpatrick, 1983). Many of these actually consisted of young parents and their babies living in their own parents' household for a temporary first few years of union, and not the "ancient" form of adult siblings and families living together.

Government Policy.   The goal of the French government policy is to encourage self-sufficiency efforts, such as agriculture, at the valley level, in order to discourage mass migration to the urban centers. At the same time, the government funds enough infrastructure, health, and education projects at the rural valley level to provide adequate day-to-day services and enough supplemental income to valley families to enable them to continue to live tolerable rural subsistence lives. This policy is beginning to show results. In 1950, about 25 percent of the population of French Polynesia lived in urban areas (mainly Papeete, Tahiti). This rose to 64 percent by 1990 but had fallen off to 48 percent by 1996 (World Resources Institute, 1994). Decisions about law and public safety continue to be made in France, and the school system remains closely patterned after that in France—making these areas culturally quite disconnected from Marquesan everyday life (Bank of Hawaii, 2001).

To encourage geographic stability, the government subsidizes and stabilizes the market prices of copra and coffee, the main export crops. This gives families an incentive to continue to gather these crops. The territorial government funds experimental forms of farming, contracts to local farmers for food for boarding schools and government workers, and assures reliable ship transport to the islands. France also pays for obligatory primary schooling, voluntary secondary schooling, and the French University of the Pacific in Tahiti.

Comparative Investment in Human Capital.   French government investment in human development, however, has been weak in comparison to U.S. investment in Micronesia. The French government has funded less than half the number of schools per 100,000 people in French Polynesia as has the U.S. government in the FSM (Bolin, 2001; Hezel, 2001b). Opportunities for higher education, until the founding of the French University of the Pacific in Papeete in 1997, were almost nonexistent. Employment opportunities for college-educated islanders are rare in the Marquesas Islands.

Migration.   The French government is the main employer in French Polynesia, as the U.S. government was in the FSM, but funds flow mainly to Tahiti, not to the distant islands. In spite of government attempts to make village life more attractive, islanders from rural areas flocked to Papeete to seek work from the 1950s to the 1990s. The city expanded from holding 25 percent of the population of French Polynesia in 1950 to holding 70 percent in 1990 (Bank of Hawaii, 2001). Migration has slowed in recent years.

Marquesans who migrate to urban centers abandon subsistence fishing and agriculture and take up residence, usually with relatives or neighbors from home. They live in plywood shacks on squatters' land in shantytowns with no plumbing or electricity. Older people, wives, and children tend to be left in villages, where they continue subsistence practices and receive remittances. Settlers who stay on in the urban settlements develop more stable households, having their wives, children, and sometimes their own parents join them. Older people, however, prefer to stay in the home valleys. After 5 to 10 years of extreme disorganization, families often "right themselves" and set up viable lifestyles in Tahiti.

Education.   Foreignness and lack of utility of the content of school learning in everyday island life have been extreme, but the mismatch has not concerned French administrators enough to elicit school reform. Schooling in the islands follows much the same curriculum as schooling in Paris. In addition, there are few opportunities for continuing to high school and college, or for working white-collar jobs in the home valleys.

French language has limited utility in the islands, but is the sole language of instruction at school. Indigenous languages are used within island communities. Tahitian is used for cross-group communication, and French and Tahitian are the languages of commerce (Bank of Hawaii, 2001). In the late 1970s, much of the primary school content resembled that taught in Paris and appeared to have little relevance or application to valley life or to advancement beyond valley life.

Marquesan Family Life in the 1970s

The Marquesas Islands in the 1970s provide examples of family functions and forms that are intermediate between extended family and isolated nuclear family forms. Many nuclear families functioned as self-reliant economic units but *within supportive, interdependent networks*. Many features of their lifestyle, described below, reduced the possibility of alienation, anomie, and family dissolution described as existing in some areas of Micronesia. Marquesan nuclear families and their safety nets managed to provide smoothly for most human needs. Households managed their own resources and needs day to day, but nearby kin helped in times of emergency and provided social, psychological, and moral support. Members of these small communities passed around surplus food, goods, and labor whenever they had them. Depleting needed household resources through indiscriminate giving was seen as foolish, but hoarding surpluses was seen as stingy, short-sighted, and immature.

The few households in these valleys that could not support themselves were headed by old people or single mothers who relied on remittances and could not fish or farm adequately for subsistence. These households were considered defective by islanders' standards but were consistently supported without ill feeling or expectation of payback. The major problem was how to give to these families without shaming the members. Allowing people in need to go hungry or to be harmed through neglect or abuse was seen as a sign of lack of maturity or *kaoha* of the community, and residents saw themselves as mature and compassionate.

Families in these small communities exhibited many fewer signs of destabilization than did peri-urban families in Micronesia. On the other hand, they also had access to far fewer opportunities for individual development than did families in Micronesia.

The smaller valley had about 200 inhabitants, all Marquesan, and was geographically separated from other settlements by rugged ridges and a long walk or canoe trip. Marquesans, at that time, already preferred nuclear family forms. Houses were dispersed, set back from a major road or path. Marquesans stated explicitly that they valued distance between themselves and their neighbors, allowing them some freedom from others' observation and potential criticism (Martini & Kirkpatrick, 1992). However, they tended to live within sight of two or more relatives.

Half the households in the two valleys consisted of nuclear families—parents and their children. Most other households included only one extended family member, such as an elderly grandmother. On average, a household contained eight persons, most of whom were the children of the two parents. Most families had small plywood sleeping houses built on posts a few feet off the ground and their own cookhouses near the communal path (Kirkpatrick, 1983).

While Marquesans valued a degree of privacy and independence, they typically lived within sight of kin. Land was subdivided among sibling heirs according to French law. The three to five siblings' homes formed neighborhood groupings. Talk, borrowing, and informal cooperation usually linked nearby households. Many of young children's early social experiences were in kin-based neighborhoods, among siblings, cousins, aunts, uncles, and grandparents. (See Kirkpatrick [1981] and Marshall [1981b] for comparisons of adult sibling relationships in Polynesia and Micronesia.)

Daily Life. Economic and political developments had far fewer effects on the communal, interconnected daily life in these valleys than in Micronesia. Households and individuals were autonomous, but within a supportive safety net. Marquesans had been living in self-contained households for several generations and parents had developed methods for producing resources, raising children, and managing time, labor, goods, and ties with kin and neighbors. Most people profited from daily company, meaningful relationships, and moral and social affirmation. However, this was at the expense of being watched and analyzed regularly. Being monitored and gossiped about was a strong incentive to parents to manage family affairs properly. Perceived mistreatment of children, the elderly, or spouses was a heated topic of gossip.

Migration was limited to a particular stage of life (youth), and a complete shift of the family's economic base to wage labor was not an alternative for most families. Children who were left behind tended to be left in the care of competent householders. In the few cases in which children were left behind with less competent adults, the neighboring households kept these limping families going. Migration had a less widespread effect in this stabilized, small-town context, where alienation and anomie had not set in and people took responsibility for others' needs.

Interdependence.   All but a few households were economically self-sufficient, depending mainly on subsistence agriculture and fishing, but also on some wage labor (temporary public works jobs and paid work gathering and preparing copra). Some monetary work was done by emigrating young people, with money sent back as remittances.

Families worked for and protected their basic resources but were generous with surpluses. Families who returned from upland areas with sacks of avocados or citrus fruits distributed them freely among kin and nonkin. When a family slaughtered a cow or pig, meat was distributed freely. Goat hunters and fishermen distributed their catches generously. Adolescents who went lobster fishing at night, or looking for river shrimp, in part for sport, distributed their catches happily. When people began experimenting with growing "European" vegetables, they competed in growing the biggest items and delighted in giving these to neighbors to try. Families shared "windfall" work groups, as when numbers of their young adults returned home from Tahiti for a visit. Valley residents with boats provided rides to others, to the other valleys. They lent teens to canoe out to visiting yachts, and sent extra children to help the elderly.

The few families that had trouble supporting themselves (a small number of households headed by old people or single mothers who cared for young "left behind" children, and who lived on irregular remittances from Tahiti) were regularly given food, clothing, and other necessities. Marquesans went to great lengths to disguise these supports as casual, insignificant gifts and to preserve the dignities of the householders. Some informants expressed the view that it would be abhorrent to allow dependent people to suffer in their home valleys.

Synchrony in Daily Life.   While sleeping, eating, and working in nuclear family units, Marquesans were in contact with others in the valley many hours

a day. Marquesans in the smaller valleys all tended to do the same kinds of work for their households at the same time. Most people were on the same schedule, saw each other at these daily activities, and spent their afternoon leisure times sitting and talking to each other.

Daily life was organized around subsistence work for the household. Men and adolescent boys left in the early morning to go fishing in outrigger canoes. Women cleaned house, washed clothes, prepared breadfruit, worked in the garden, and (on some days) wove, ironed, or fished from shore. Children got up, fixed their own breakfasts of bread and coffee, did light chores, minded infants, and went to school. By late morning the men returned from fishing. Children returned from school and the family ate together (usually fish and breadfruit popoi) in their nuclear family cookhouse. The children played for a while, then returned to school until 3:30. Adults sat in their covered cooking areas, talked, visited neighbors in their cookhouses or at the valley bake shed, or slept for a while. In the mid- to late afternoons they worked in the upland gardens or did jobs around the house. In the evenings families mingled in cookhouses by the path or listened to the radio in their own sleeping houses. Household adults worked about 6 hours a day on subsistence food gathering, growing activities, or household upkeep, and teens appeared to work 3–5 hours a day (Kirkpatrick, 1983; Martini & Kirkpatrick, 1992).

Community Care.   Childcare was manageable even for single mothers during the work day. Older children were at school, and toddlers and preschoolers either played by themselves on the path near their houses or went down to the sea to play near the schoolyard. Men going out to fish and women in households nearby kept a general eye out on these young children and scolded them when they played on the boat ramp, in the surf, on high walls, or on dry-docked boats (Martini, 1994). Parents and teens had the unspoken right to scold children in any family, and some adults (such as the school teacher) had the right to punish them as well.

Meaningful Roles.   Adolescent boys who were old enough to leave boarding school returned to the valley to enjoy increased autonomy. Some slept in a separate, abandoned "young people's" house in the smaller valley—gaining autonomy. They fished, daily, for their own families and worked as a group, to complete larger building or gathering projects for relatives. In the evenings they roamed the valley, gathered in publicly lit areas, played guitar and ukulele, talked and sang. They experienced some autonomy from their families, while remaining a valued work force. They were called upon as a group to complete labor-intensive activities, such as moving a motor boat down to the water or paddling out to the monthly cargo ship (Howard, 1998; Kirkpatrick, 1983; Martini & Kirkpatrick, 1992).

Delimited Migration.   Young adult males left the island for 1–5 years to complete their military service and to work as laborers in Tahiti or other urban areas, sending home money as remittances. Most left with specific goals (such as earning enough money for housing materials) and returned to the island to marry and settle down. There were not enough jobs in local valleys to enable people to rely solely or even mainly on wage labor. The prospects of permanently settling in Tahiti seemed to be losing favor even by the late 1970s. Migration was seen as a temporary means of gathering capital for large projects.

Access to Consumer Goods.   Several French government policies protected the Marquesas from the rampant consumerism, alcoholism, and credit buying that have been destructive in Micronesia. The government limited access to wage labor to levels of supplementing subsistence work rather than replacing it. Expendable incomes were kept small. Buying on credit was regulated. Interisland transport was controlled by the government, and distribution, advertising, and retailing did not boom in the distant islands as was the case in Micronesia. Marquesans had access to most goods, but needed to work hard and pay dearly to get these sent. Time, distance, and difficulty controlled impulse buying. Catholic and Protestant deacons discouraged alcohol use, and strict laws discouraged drug use.

Limiting the Destructive Effects of Innovations.
Marquesans in at least one valley were pragmatically skeptical about the long-term benefits of innovations and were able to work as a concerted group to limit destructive effects. According to travelers' reports, when electric lines were finally strung into one valley in the 1980s, several households bought, first, washing machines, and then freezers. Young men then started fishing for long periods to gather and freeze fish for sale to the monthly trade ship. Within a few months, people started noticing a much lower daily yield of fish and began to suspect they were fishing out the bay. According to reports, the adult members of the valley met, discussed the problem, decided that people should stop fishing so persistently, and set some limits and consequences. Most valley members followed this injunction, and many families eventually abandoned their freezers when they started to need repairs.

Similarly, the introduction of telephones sent people into a month-long frenzy of talking to relatives on the other side of the island. When the first phone bills arrived, most families had their phones disconnected. VCRs and satellite television ran a similar course. According to reports, these completely destablized life for a few months in one valley. People retreated completely into their households, had little contact with each other or others, and watched television day and night, and long into the night. Adults and teens alike refused to get up to fish or work. School children refused to go to school on grounds of fatigue, women refused to cook meals during favorite programs, people became irritable, and babies and small children started to show signs of neglect. Again, according to reports, the valley called a general meeting and decided, as a group, to restrict television viewing.

Many Marquesans had an advantage over Micronesians in that they lived in small, tightly knit communities in which group decisions could be made and community opinion and injunctions provided incentives for constructive behavior.

Stable Developmental Careers.   An additional stabilizing factor was that an attractive developmental life course was clear and accessible to young people, and many said they would pursue this traditional course. Once young men returned to the home valleys, they tended to court a teen or young woman and, in time, settled down to live in either the woman's or man's parental home. They often lived like this for 1–3 years while their first and, in some cases, second children approached toddlerhood. In this protected setting, they learned to parent slowly and gradually took over the needed functions. Grandparents and the young parents' siblings cared for their first children, who then either remained with the grandparents or moved out with the young parents when they eventually married and moved into their own home. Marquesans then described a stable progression of adults becoming more and more responsible, supporting more and more dependents, exhibiting more and more *kaoha,* and finally reaching a stage of respected old age (Kirkpatrick, 1983; Martini, 1996). Many Marquesan youth expressed a preference for village life and this valued developmental course over city living. Urban living was good, but only for a period of youthful "wandering," and for building capital.

CONCLUSIONS: EFFECTS OF DEVELOPMENT ON FAMILY AND ADAPTATION IN TWO REGIONS OF THE PACIFIC

The Marquesas Islands provide an informative contrast to the effects of economic development in Micronesia. Marquesan families, at least in their home valleys, exhibit many fewer signs of destabilization than do Micronesian families in their home communities. Suicide rates, child abuse, child neglect, domestic violence, and criminality have not increased significantly in the past 20 years in rural areas and do not approach the rates found in Micronesia. At the same time, positive indicators of increased opportunities, such as standard of living, family income, literacy rates, and years of education have also not increased markedly nor at nearly

the fast pace seen in Micronesia. Opportunities for white-collar employment and lifestyles are available to a much broader base of people in Micronesia than in the Marquesas—particularly with new policies allowing Micronesians to work and settle in the United States.

U.S. foreign policy in Micronesia targeted supporting families as they met human needs at the very top and very bottom of the pyramid of human needs. Improved infrastructure and health care increased families' abilities to keep their children alive and healthy, while enhanced educational opportunities increased their opportunities for self-development. However, government interventions inadvertently affected the dissolution of stable extended families and the loss of many family supports. Many new families were unable to take on the support functions previously performed by members of the traditional extended family. At the same time that improved health care reduced infant mortality, easy access to money, processed foods, soft drinks, cigarettes, alcohol, drugs, and other consumer goods introduced other survival risks of equal magnitudes. At the same time that access to wage labor increased opportunities for autonomy and advancement, the dismantling of extended family supports threw many families into disarray. Many new parents were unable to shoulder all responsibilities of family life at the same time. Lack of skills in resource management, time organization, task management, teaching and disciplining children, money management, family communication, and conflict resolution sorely taxed household heads. All members suffered—children, teens, women, the elderly, and the wage earners themselves.

On the other hand, a much broader base of Micronesians today (and particularly in comparison to Marquesans) complete high school, graduate from college, earn graduate degrees, and return to the islands to take over major administrative and government roles. These young people, and the broad base of people they represent, have a much louder voice in self-government and in decisions affecting the future of the islands (Crocombe, 1991; Petersen, 1997; Pinsker, 1997). While many Micronesians have lost control of their lives at the local, day-to-day level, others have gained control in these higher functions.

French foreign policy in the Marquesas, in contrast, targeted the middle level of family tasks on the hierarchy of human needs. The policy aimed to maintain traditional family and social forms, to encourage valley-level subsistence activities, to enhance village life, and to reduce the attractions of moving to Tahiti. The government shored up existing family functions but did not offer many new lifestyle alternatives, except to the very few. In particular, educational investments and policies have restricted full educational development to a very small elite. While many Marquesans in rural areas have retained greater control over their day-to-day lives, fewer have benefited from opportunities to develop their individual potentials and to have an effective voice in government and administrative processes that will affect their futures.

ACKNOWLEDGMENTS

This chapter was prepared with the assistance of John Kirkpatrick, SMS Research, Inc. My thanks to Andrea Guillory, Department of Public Health, University of Hawaii at Manoa, for related discussions and for requesting Marquesas statistics. I would like to thank Mme. Nicole Cerf, Chef du Bureau d'Epidemiologie and de Statistiques Sanitaires, Direction de la Santé, Papeete, Tahiti, for providing current statistics and information on the Marquesas Islands, namely Brugiroux (1998); Froute (1997); Institut Territorial de la Statistique (2000); Ministère de l'Education (2000), Recensement General de la Population de Polynesie française du 3 septembre (1996).

REFERENCES

Aka, K. Y. (1993). *Developing effective educational partnerships: The why, what and how.* PREL Briefing Paper. Honolulu, HI: PREL (Pacific Resources for Education and Learning).

Akin, K. G. (1985). Women's work and infant feeding: Traditional and transitional practices on Malaita, Solomon Islands. In L. B. Marshall (Ed.), *Infant care and feeding in the South Pacific.* New York: Gordon & Breach.

Bank of Hawaii (1995). Federated States of Micronesia Economic Report. Honolulu, HI: Bank of Hawaii.

Bank of Hawaii (2001). French Polynesia Economic Report. Honolulu, HI: Bank of Hawaii.

Barlow, T. W. (1996). *America's youth: Managed care's most valuable population.* PREL Reports. Honolulu, HI: PREL (Pacific Resources for Education and Learning).

Bolin, A. (2000). *French Polynesia: Demographics and a historical perspective.*

Brown, Z. A., Hammond, O. W., and Onikama, D. L. (1997). *Language use at home and school: A synthesis of research for Pacific educators.* PREL Briefing Paper. Honolulu, HI: PREL (Pacific Resources for Education and Learning).

Busick, K. U., & Inos, R. H. (1994a). *Synthesis of the research on educational change: Overview and initiation phase.* PREL Reports. Honolulu, HI: PREL (Pacific Resources for Education and Learning).

Busick, K. U., & Inos, R. H. (1994b). *Synthesis of the research on educational change: Implementation phase.* PREL Reports. Honolulu, HI: PREL (Pacific Resources for Education and Learning).

Carroll, V. (Ed.). (1970). *Adoption in Eastern Oceania.* Honolulu, HI: University of Hawaii Press.

Counts, D. (1989). Domestic violence in Oceania. Special issue of *Pacific Studies, 13*(3).

Crawford, P. (2001). *Strategies for improved social protection in Asia: Child protection (theoretical background).* Presentation at the "Social Protection Workshop 4: Child Protection: Cost or Investment?" at the Asia and Pacific Forum on Poverty: Reforming Policies and Institutions for Poverty Reduction." Asian Development Bank, Manila, Philippines, February 5–9, 2001.

Crocombe, M. (1991). Polynesia in review: Issues and events, 1 July 1990 to 30 June 1991. *The Contemporary Pacific, 4*(1), 191–208.

Gegeo, D. W., & Watson-Gegeo, K. A. (1985). Kwara'ae mothers and infants: Changing family practices in health, work, and child-rearing. In L. B. Marshall (Ed.), *Infant care and feeding in the South Pacific.* Philadelphia: Taylor & Francis.

Goodenough, W. H. (1970). Epilogue: Transactions in parenthood. In V. Carroll (Ed.), *Adoption in Eastern Oceania.* Honolulu, HI: University of Hawaii Press.

Gooler, D., Kautzer, I. K., & Knuth, R. (2000). *Teacher competence in using technologies: The next big question.* PREL Briefing Paper. Honolulu, HI: PREL (Pacific Resources for Education and Learning).

Government of the Federated States of Micronesia (2000). General information on the Federated States of Micronesia.

Hammond, M., Inos, R. H., & Busick, K. U. (1994). *Synthesis of the research on educational change: Institutionalization and renewal phase.* PREL Reports. Honolulu, HI: PREL (Pacific Resources for Education and Learning).

Hammond, O. W. (2000). *Pacific mega-trends in education.* PREL Briefing Paper. Honolulu, HI: PREL (Pacific Resources for Education and Learning).

Hezel, F. X. (1973). The school industry. *Friends of Micronesia Newsletter, 3*(2),19–22.

Hezel, F. X. (1975). In search of a home: Colonial education in Micronesia. *Topics of Culture Learning, 3,* 125–131. East-West Center, Honolulu.

Hezel, F. X. (1976). The Micronesian dilemma: How to support expensive habits and still run the household. *Journal de la Société des Oceanistes* (Paris), 110–121.

Hezel, F. X. (1979). The education explosion in Truk (Chuuk). *Pacific Studies, 2*(2), 167–185.

Hezel, F. X. (1980). The new formula for self-reliance. *Pacific Perspective, 8*(2), 33–36.

Hezel, F. X. (1981). *Youth drinking in Micronesia.* Paper presented at the conference: Youth Drinking in Micronesia, Kolonia, Ponape, November 12–14, 1981, p. 26.

Hezel, F. X. (1984). Schools in Micronesia prior to American administration. *Pacific Studies, 8*(1), 95–111.

Hezel, F. X. (1987). The dilemmas of development: The effects of modernization on three areas of island life. In S. Stratigos & P. Hughes (Eds.), *The ethics of development: The Pacific in the 21st century.* Port Moresby, Papu, New Guinea: UPNG Press.

Hezel, F. X. (1989a). The price of education in Micronesia. *Ethnies: Droits de l'Homme et Peuples Autochtones, 8–10,* 24–29.

Hezel, F. X. (1989b). Suicide and the Micronesian family. *The Contemporary Pacific, 1*(1), 43–74.

Hezel, F. X. (1992a). The changing family in Chuuk: 1950–1990. In *Micronesian Seminar Discussion Paper,* Pohnpei, FSM.

Hezel, F. X. (1992b). In search of a talking point on human rights. *UMANIDAT, 3*(1), 111–116.

Hezel, F. X. (1993). Alcohol and drug use in the Federated States of Micronesia. In *Micronesian Seminar Discussion Paper,* Pohnpei, FSM.

Hezel, F. X. (2000). The cruel dilemma: Money economies in the Pacific. In *Micronesian Seminar Discussion Paper,* Pohnpei, FSM.

Hezel, F. X. (2001a). How good are our schools? In *Micronesian Seminar Discussion Paper,* Pohnpei, FSM.

Hezel, F. X. (2001b). Micronesian Seminar education statistics on Micronesia. In *Micronesian Seminar Discussion Paper,* Pohnpei, FSM.

Hezel, F. X., & Barnabas, S. (1992). Change in the Pohnpeian family: 1950 to 1990. In *Micronesian Seminar Discussion Paper,* Pohnpei, FSM.

Hezel, F. X., & Levin, M. J. (1989). New trends in Micronesian migration: FSM migration. *Pacific Studies, 19*(1), 91–144.

Hezel, F. X., & Levin, M. J. (1990). Micronesian emigration: The brain drain in Palau, Marshalls and the Federated States. In J. Connell (Ed.), *Migration and development in the South Pacific* (pp. 42–60). Canberra, Australia: Australian National University.

Hezel, F. X., & McGrath, T. B. (1989). The great flight northward: FSM migration to Guam and the Northern Mariana Islands. *Pacific Studies, 13*(1), 47–64.

Howard, A. (1970). Adoption on Rotuma. In V. Carroll, (Ed.). *Adoption in Eastern Oceania.* Honolulu, HI: University of Hawaii Press.

Howard, A. (1998). Youth in Rotuma, then and now. In G. Herdt & S. Leavitt (Eds.), *Adolescence in Pacific Island societies.* Pittsburgh: University of Pittsburgh Press.

Howard, A., Heighton, R. Jordan, C. E., & Gallimore, R. G. (1970). Traditional and modern adoption patterns in Hawaii. In V. Carroll (Ed.), *Adoption in Eastern Oceania.* Honolulu, HI: University of Hawaii Press.

Inos, R. H., & Quigley, M. A. (1995). *Synthesis of the research on educational change: The teacher's role.* PREL Reports. Honolulu, HI: PREL (Pacific Resources for Education and Learning).

Kawakami, A. J. (1995a). *Culture and learning at home and school: A study in Kosrae State.* PREL Briefing Report. Honolulu, HI: PREL (Pacific Resources for Education and Learning).

Kawakami, A. J. (1995b). *A study of risk factors among high school students in the Pacific Region.* PREL Reports. Honolulu, HI: PREL (Pacific Resources for Education and Learning).

Kawakami, A. J. (1995c). *Young children and education in the Pacific: A look at the research.* PREL Reports. Honolulu, HI: PREL (Pacific Resources for Education and Learning).

Kirkpatrick, J. (1981). Meanings of siblingship in Marquesan Society. In M. Marshall (Ed.). *Siblingship in Oceania: Studies in the meaning of kin relations.* Ann Arbor: University of Michigan Press.

Kirkpatrick, J. (1983). *The Marquesan notion of the person.* Ann Arbor, MI: UMI Research Press.

Kirkpatrick, J. (1987). *Taure'are'a:* A liminal category and passages to Marquesan adulthood. *Ethos, 15*(4), 382–405.

Kirkpatrick, J., & Broder, C. R. (1976). Adoption and parenthood on Yap. In I. Brady (Ed.) *Transaction in Kinship: Adoption and fosterage in Oceania.* Honolulu, HI: University of Hawaii Press.

Koki, S. (1996a). *New research on learning indicates need for cultural awareness among educators.* PREL Briefing Paper. Honolulu, HI: PREL (Pacific Resources for Education and Learning).

Koki, S. (1996b). *Promising practices in the Pacific region.* PREL Briefing Paper. Honolulu, HI: PREL (Pacific Resources for Education and Learning).

Koki, S. (1999). *Promising programs for school wide reform.* PREL Reports. Honolulu, HI: PREL (Pacific Resources for Education and Learing).

Koki, S., & Less, H. (1998). *Parental involvement in education: What works in the Pacific?* PREL Reports. Honolulu, HI: PREL (Pacific Resources for Education and Learning).

Koki, S., Van Broekhuizen, L. D., & Uehara, D. L. (2000). *Prevention and intervention for effective classroom organization and management in Pacific classrooms.* PREL Briefing Paper. Honolulu, HI: PREL (Pacific Resources for Education and Learning).

Korbin, J. (1989). *Hana'Ino:* Child maltreatment in a Hawaiian-American community. In D. Counts (Ed.), *Domestic violence in Oceania.* Special issue of *Pacific Studies, 13*(3).

Leu, R. W. (1996). *Surviving people and cultural change in the Marquesas Islands—A historical geographical case study of Fatuiva.* Paper presented at the Third Conference of the European Society for Oceanists: Pacific People in the Pacific Century: Society, Culture, Nature. Copenhagen, Denmark, 13–15 December 1996.

LeVine, R. (1974). Parental goals: a cross-cultural view. *Teachers College Record, 76,* 226–239.

Levy, R. I. (1970). Tahitian adoption as a psychological message. In V. Carroll (Ed.), *Adoption in Eastern Oceania.* Honolulu, HI: University of Hawaii Press.

Levy, R. I. (1973). *Tahitians: Mind and experience in the Society Islands.* Chicago: Univeresity of Chicago Press.

Lindstrom, L. (Ed.). (1987). *Drugs in Western Pacific societies: Relations of substance.* Lanham, MD: University Press of America.

Marshall, L. B. (1985a). *Infant care and feeding in the South Pacific.* New York: Gordon & Breach.

Marshall, L. B. (1985b). Wage employment and infant feeding: A Papua New Guinea Case. In L. B. Marshall (Ed.), *Infant care and feeding in the South Pacific.* New York: Gordon & Breach.

Marshall, M. (1981a). Sibling sets as building blocks in greater Trukese society. In M. Marshall (Ed.), *Siblingship in Oceania: Studies in the meaning of kin relations.* Ann Arbor: University of Michigan Press.

Marshall, M. (Ed.). (1981b). *Siblingship in Oceania: Studies in the meaning of kin relations.* Ann Arbor: University of Michigan Press.

Martini, M., & Kirkpatrick, J. (1981). Early interactions in the Marquesas Islands. In T. Field, A. Sostek, P. Vietze, & P. Leiderman (Eds.), *Culture and early interactions.* Hillsdale, NJ: Erlbaum.

Martini, M. & Kirkpatrick, J. (1992). Parenting in Polynesia: A view from the Marquesas. In J. L. Roopnarine & D. B. Carter (Eds.), *Parent–child socialization in diverse cultures.* Norwood, NJ: Ablex.

Martini, M. (1994). Peer interactions in Polynesia: A view from the Marquesas. In J. P. Roopnarine, J. E. Johnson, & F. H. Hooper (Eds.), *Children's play in diverse cultures.* Albany: State University of New York Press.

Maslow, A. H. (1987). *Motivation and personality* (3rd ed.). New York: Harper & Row.

Miyasato, E. (1998). *Setting the stage for dynamic use of distance learning technologies in education.* PREL Briefing Paper. Honolulu, HI: PREL (Pacific Resources for Education and Learning).

Onikama, D. L., Hammond, O. W., & Koki, S. (1998). *Family involvement in education: A synthesis of re-*

search for Pacific educators. PREL Briefing Report. Honolulu, HI: PREL (Pacific Resources for Education and Learning).

Pan Pacific and Southeast Asia Women's Association. (1996). *Women, the family and health: Proceedings of the Workshop of the Pan Pacific and Southeast Asian Women's Association, 19–20 April 1996,* Apia, Samoa.

Petersen, G. (1997). A Micronesian chamber of chiefs? The 1990 Federated States of Micronesia Constitutional Convention. In G. M. White & L. Lindstrom (Eds.), *Chiefs today: Traditional Pacific leadership and the postcolonial state.* Stanford, CA: Stanford University Press.

Pinsker, E. C. (1997). Traditional leaders today in the Federated States of Micronesia. In G. M. White & L. Lindstrom (Eds.), *Chiefs today: Traditional Pacific leadership and the postcolonial state.* Stanford, CA: Stanford University Press.

PREL (1996). *Languages open doors to success and wisdom.* PREL Reports. Honolulu, HI: PREL (Pacific Resources for Education and Learning).

Rensel, J. (1997). From thatch to cement: Social implications of housing change on Rotuma. In J. Rensel & M. Rodman (Eds.), *Home in the Islands: Housing and social change in the Pacific.* Honolulu, HI: University of Hawaii Press.

Research and Development Cadre, PREL (1995). *Remoteness and access to learning opportunities in the Pacific region.* PREL Reports. Honolulu, HI: PREL (Pacific Resources for Education and Learning).

Research and Development Cadre, PREL (1998). *Retention and attrition of Pacific school teachers and administration (RAPSTA) study (Kosrae State).* PREL Reports. Honolulu, HI: PREL (Pacific Resources for Education and Learning).

Rubinstein, D. H. (1994). Changes in the Micronesian family structure leading to alcoholism, suicide, and child abuse and neglect. In *Micronesian Seminar Discussion Paper,* Pohnpei, FSM.

Samuels, L. D. (2000). What should our schools be doing?: Educating Micronesians for Micronesia. In *Micronesian Seminar Discussion Paper,* Pohnpei, FSM.

San Mateo County College District. (1994). *The new Americans: Pacific Islanders* (video recording): KCSM-TV; San Mateo, CA: National Asian American Telecommunications Association [distributor].

Shewman, R. (1992). Neglect, physical abuse, and sexual molestation in Palau. In *Micronesian Seminar Discussion Paper,* Pohnpei, FSM.

Shigemoto, J. (1997). *Language change and language planning and policy.* PREL Briefing Paper. Honolulu, HI: PREL (Pacific Resources for Education and Learning).

Simanu-Klutz, F. (1999). *Language of instruction: Choices and consequence.* PREL Briefing Paper. Honolulu, HI: PREL (Pacific Resources for Education and Learning).

Thomas, N. (1990). *Marquesan societies: Inequality and political transformation in Eastern Polynesia.* Oxford, UK: Clarendon Press.

Uehara, D., & Flores, J. (with L. D. van Broekguizen & B. Collins). (2000). *Diversity in action: Improving educational research in the Pacific region.* PREL Reports. Honolulu, HI (Pacific Resources for Education and Learning).

World Bank (2000). Gender statistics, Summary gender profile; Basic demographic data; Population dynamics; Labor force; Education; Mortality and reproductive health on American Samoa; Federated States of Micronesia; Marshall Islands; Republic of Palau; French Polynesia.

World Resources Institute (1994). Statistics on French Polynesia. Website.

PART THREE

THE MIDDLE EAST

_____CHAPTER 9_____

EGYPTIAN FAMILIES

RAMADAN A. AHMED
Kuwait University and Menoufia University

**SOME BASIC DEMOGRAPHIC
INFORMATION ON FAMILIES**

Different Ethnic Groups/
Populations/Languages in Egypt

Egypt is a country occupying the northwestern corner of Africa, with a mountainous extension across the Gulf of Suez, and the Sinai Peninsula, which is usually regarded as part of Asia. Strategically situated at the crossroads between Europe and the Orient and between north Africa and Southeast Asia, Egypt is an almost square block of mostly arid land: 995,450 square kilometers to be exact. Its greatest extent is 1,024 kilometers south to north (from 22 to 32°N)

and 1,240 kilometers west to east (from 26 to 36°E). It is bounded on the north by the Mediterranean Sea, on the east by the Red Sea, on the South by the Sudan, and on the west by Libya. Most of its political borders are straight lines, drawn by the European colonial powers in the twentieth century; and all have been disputed since the time of their definition.

From the dawn of history, human habitation hinged on the Egyptian people's ability to harness the River Nile, which annually flooded its banks, depositing a fertile alluvium of silt brought down from Lakes Victoria and Albert and from the mountains of Ethiopia. The creation of a system of basin irrigation to capture the silt and store the floodwaters, and

151

of efficient devices to raise water from the channels and basins to the fields, was a prerequisite for the evolution of Egyptian agriculture between six and three millennia before the birth of Jesus Christ.

Egypt, which has pharanoiac ancestors and Arab fathers, had an estimated population of 65 million in 1999, which included 49.6 percent females, and 25 percent of the Egyptian population was less than 16 years old (*Al-Ahram,* August 28, 2000). More recent statistics (reported in *Al-Ahram,* January 18, 2002) indicate that in 2000, 32 percent of the Egyptian population was between 10 and 24 years old. In 1990, life expectancy for Egyptians was estimated as 60 years for males and 63 years for females (Radwan, 1997). More recent statistics (*Al-Ahram,* September 15, 2000) show that life expectancy rates in Egypt have been improving during the last 10 years. In the year 2000, they reached 67 years for males and 71 years for females. Moreover, statistics also show that the overall fertility, which was estimated in 1990 at 36.3 per 1,000, declined to 27.4 per 1,000 in 1999. Another recent report by the Central Agency for Public Mobilization and Statistics in Egypt (*Al-Seyassah,* August 12, 2001) shows that the number of children per family in the Nile Delta was 4.8 in 2000, while it reached 5.5 in the more rural areas of Upper Egypt. In Cairo and other larger cities such as Alexandria, it was only 4.

Religion plays a major role in Egypt today, and approximately 90 percent of the population are Sunni Muslims. There are several religious minorities, the largest of which is the indigenous Christian Coptic population. In 1990, estimates of the Coptic population ranged from 3 million to 7 million (or 5 to 11 percent of the population). For 1990, Ciaccio and El-Shakry (1993) estimated the Egyptian Christian population at 5 million (or 8 percent of the total population), while other Christians included approximately 350,000 followers of the Greek Orthodox Church, 175,000 Eastern and Latin Rite Catholics, and 200,000 Protestants. In addition, an estimated 1,000 Jews remained in Egypt as of 1990. The Jewish population represents a fragment of the community of 80,000 Jews who lived in Egypt before 1948.

Broad religious tolerance has been a hallmark of traditional Egyptian culture, and the Egyptian Constitution of 1971 guarantees freedom of religion, although tensions along religious lines have risen sharply since the 1970s. The centrality of religion in defining Egypt is deeply rooted historically. From the time of the Pharaohs, demigods in the eyes of their subjects, religion has played a central role in the life of the inhabitants of the Nile Valley. The priests of ancient Egypt, who presided over the cults that defined each province, made up a central part of the ruling class. Though religion among the Egyptians took different forms through a succession of foreign conquerors, it always remained a key element of the political culture.

By the end of the reign of the second Islamic caliph, Umar ibn al-Khattab (ruled 634–644), the expanding empire of Islam had succeeded in incorporating the Egyptian provinces of the Byzantine Empire. Ascendant Islam found fertile soil in Egypt. The Arab conquest gave the inherited religious bond a distinctive Islamic form. Islam ruled out any version of the old pharanoiac claim of the ruler as a "descendant of the Gods" and the notion of a closed caste of priests. Instead, the new faith impelled Muslims as a collective body to express their faith by founding a community of believers or *ummah.* The central moral precepts of Islam, expressed in the Qur'an and the traditions of the Prophet, have provided guidance for personal salvation, the moral basis for a good society on earth, and the central building block of this society, life in the family (Esposito, 1995).

The common language in Egypt is Arabic; however, English, French, German, Italian, and Spanish, in that order, are also known and spoken in many places, especially in the capital city, Cairo, and in the second largest Egyptian city, Alexandria. Egypt's culture incorporates a trend of open acceptance toward other cultures.

Egypt is the world's oldest continuous nation, with a recorded past of over six thousand years. Often invaded, conquered, and occupied by foreign armies, Egypt has never lost its identity. The Egyptians of today, although they have changed their language once and their religion twice, descend mainly from the Egyptians who built the Giza Pyramids and the Temple of Karnak, who served Alexander the Great and his heirs, who submitted to Augustus Caesar and grew much of the grain that fed the Roman Empire, who started Christian monasticism and the veneration of the Virgin Mary, and who advanced and sustained Muslim learning in what is now the longest-functioning university in the world, Al-Azhar University in Cairo (established in 969) (Gold Schmidt, 1994).

For centuries, the Byzantines established and reestablished their control of Egypt, until the Arab conquest of 639–642. For Egypt, the Arabs came as liberators. Early Muslim rule meant religious tolerance and lighter taxes, not forced conversion to Islam, which taught that God had spoken to a series of prophets, of whom the last was Mohammed, an unlettered Meccan merchant, to whom He had revealed the Qur'an, as earlier God had revealed the Torah to the Jews and the Gospels to Christians. Muslims therefore respected Jews and Christians as peoples who had received scriptures and who could live within the lands of Islam without being molested, let alone converted. Coptic Christianity remained the country's majority religion until the tenth century.

In 1517, Egypt, along with Syria and the Hijaz, became a part of the Ottoman Empire, the largest and longest-lasting Muslim state in history. From 1517 to 1798, even though nominally under governors appointed by the Ottoman Sultan, the real rulers of Egypt were the Mamluks. In June 1798, the French Armada commanded by Napoleon Bonaparte landed at Alexandria and for three years, the French ruled in Cairo.

In 1881 and 1882, Colonel Ahmed Urabi emerged as the first champion of Egypt's resistance to foreign control (especially Britain and France since 1879). The Urabist movement competed against the Europeans for mastery in Egypt, which led to riots and a devastating life in Alexandria. Finally, a British expeditionary force invaded the country and defeated Urabi's troops occupying Cairo on September 14, 1882.

On July 23, 1952, a group of army officers (called Free Officers) seized control of the barracks and the government, deposed the king, drove out the old-style politicians, and ended the British occupation. Thus, a new Egypt—freed from foreign control—emerged.

FAMILY IN THE EGYPTIAN TRADITIONS

Egyptian Constitutions of 1923, 1956, and 1971 emphasized the role of the family in building, developing, and enhancing the society. Article No. 9 of the 1971 Constitution stated that family is considered as the society's main backbone and is based on religion, morality, and patriotism.

Several studies of Egyptian culture have stressed the importance of the family in the development of the individual (Sanders, 1986). According to these investigations, the family constitutes the basic framework in which the life of the individual unfolds. One's first loyalty is to the family, on which reputation, well-being, and wealth depend. Family members exert considerable influence on the individual concerning education, employment, marriage, religious obligations, family honor, and to a certain extent, the management of family property.

Men hold authority in the Egyptian family:

From an early age, children are taught that males are inherently superior to females. Respect for masculine authority and seniority is stressed, and children are expected to show proper deference to their elders. The questioning of decisions or judgments made by superiors is considered neither permissible nor proper. The father—characterized as stern, severe, and authoritarian—is held in awe and respect. Considered strong yet somewhat nervous, he demands obedience from his wife and children. Although affection may exist between him and his children, its expression tends to be suppressed. In contrast to the father, the mother is portrayed as warm, loving, compassionate, self-sacrificing, sensitive, and patient. The children develop a greater affectionate relationship with their mother than with their father, and the love for the mother remains important even after marriage. (Sanders, 1986, pp. 459–460)

Most studies of the Egyptian family have relied on anecdotal accounts based largely on village populations or on personal observations and knowledge of popular literature. Only a few systematic studies using questionnaires and interviews are available, and they were conducted almost 30 years ago, as Sanders (1986) noticed. According to these studies, Egyptian secondary and university students, like their U.S. counterparts, expressed favorable attitudes toward their parents and viewed their families as relatively happy. Reported conflicts between Egyptian parents and children did not seem to be affected by Western or modern influences. Furthermore, the authors of these studies noted a gradual, albeit undramatic, movement toward liberalization and secularization in Egyptian attitudes toward family and parents. Presumably, resistance to change existed because of the authoritarian nature of Egyptian culture, as Melikian claimed in 1959 (cited in Sanders, 1986).

According to old Arab family traditions, the son is expected to take on the responsibilities of the head of the family upon his father's death or his own marriage. This could explain why education is considered worthwhile and necessary for boys, but somewhat less necessary or even positively harmful for girls. Families are often anxious about the effect of work on the morality of their daughters, presumably because they fear that their young women will enjoy their new role in the workforce at the expense of their traditional role in the home (Simmons & Simmons, 1994).

MARRIAGE

Islamic societies, including Egypt, have remained strictly marriage-oriented and conspire relentlessly to lead their youth into the matrimonial fold. Islam prohibits premarital relationships, and the Prophet Mohammed decreed that marriage is the only road to virtue. Even a nonreligious bachelor usually feels that he should marry because of his need for sons as security against old age, since most Islamic countries did not provide pensions until recently. Marriage is a Sunna (that is, one of the Prophet's practices and teachings). Islam also prohibits celibacy. The Prophet said, "There is no celibacy in Islam."

In 1926, Westermarck stated that "Marriage is rooted in the family rather than the family in marriage" (cited in Shoukry, 1985, p. 250), and this is particularly true for the Egyptians. They consider marriage to be the most important event in their lives because it means a moral way of providing psychological and physical satisfaction. Egyptians assume that marriage is the main method to protect youth from secret (or illegal) relationships; moreover, marriage reinforces society's relationships, because secret or illegal sexual relationships between men and women will produce illegal children, which is prohibited by Islam. Marriage is a religious obligation—many *Suras* of the Qu'ran as well as the Prophet Mohammed's instructions encourage Muslims to get married. Because marriage in many ways reflects a society's preferred behavioral patterns, thoughts, and feelings, it is useful to discuss some Egyptian marriage customs in the past and the present and their effects on society.

Ancient Egyptians were the first people to establish marriage laws. They regarded marriage as a religious, civil, and legal relationship. Their laws organized the marriage relations and specified the rights and duties for couples. Many of the old marriage contracts were registered and signed by three officers. Wives were respected, had high prestige, and were given the right to divorce as well as men.

Ancient Egyptians practiced engagement customs, and these are similar to those practiced in Egypt's countryside to this day. The process begins with the suitor's parents visiting his fiancée's house to get her family's approval for the marriage and reaching an agreement about three items: the dowry, called *Mahr,* to be paid by the fiancée's family to help the new couple acquire various household goods; the *Mu'akhr,* a sum set aside for the wife in case of divorce (Ciaccio & El-Shakry, 1993), and the valuable gift of gold called *Shabke,* given by the suitor to his fiancée. The value of the gift depends on the financial abilities and social level of the suitor's family. After the two families have reached an agreement, they fix an appointment for the engagement or wedding party, which will be attended by relatives and friends of both families.

Marriage customs in Egypt are still traditional. At the same time, they are deeply influenced by social and economic circumstances, such as the migration of about 2 million Egyptian workers to the oil-producing Gulf States in recent years (Ahmed, 2003).

As for the marriage home, the neolocal pattern is the common form in urban areas, while the bilocal pattern is frequently found in the rural areas, which allows the couple to be near their families (Al-Khouly, 1983).

According to the Central Agency for Public Mobilization and Statistics in Egypt, the number of marriage contracts in 1999 reached 520,000 (*Al-Seyassah,* August 12, 2001) and increased to 579,000 in 2000 (*Al-Watan,* January 13, 2002). Nevertheless, a tendency for delaying marriage, especially among the well educated, can be noticed. A survey (in Shehatta, 1999) showed that 49 percent of the individuals between 20 and 25 years old have never married. The figures for the ages 25–30 and 30–35 were 19 and 11 percent, respectively.

Mixed Marriage

Marriage between followers of different religions (Islam, Christianity, and Judaism) is very rare and socially not fully welcomed. In addition, marriage between Egyptians and other nationals was traditionally not accepted, although during the last three decades, a gradual increase has occurred in the number of marriages between Egyptians and other nationals, especially Arabs.

Secret Marriage

During the last three decades, and because of several social and economic hardships, official marriages and public weddings have become a major problem for young men and women. As a result, they have declined in frequency and instead, secret marriages (written or oral contracts between a man and a woman witnessed by two adults and not registered officially) are often seen as a solution. However, a secret marriage has many negative aspects and consequences—legally, socially, and for the family itself. Fortunately, statistics (*Al-Ahram,* March 12, 2001) show that the rate of secret marriages decreased during 1999–2000, and the official marriage rate, especially among blood relatives, increased during the same period.

Mate Selection

It is useful to mention here that the Prophet Mohammed advised his followers to chose their partners carefully because the family, from Islam's point of view, is the backbone of the society. Islam has clear instructions on establishing a family. In Egypt, the patterns of mate selection are, in general, traditional in nature. However, changes that are taking place in marriage customs today aim to improve a woman's chances of choosing her own husband, by allowing her to meet men and by easing the family's burden of providing a dowry. It is believed that this fully takes care of the modern woman's sexual needs since they are to be fulfilled only within marriage (Minai, 1981).

Because of the increasing divorce rate, as well as current economic hardships, choosing a future husband or wife has become a matter of great importance, especially for young people. Premarital sexuality is neither socially, legally, nor religiously accepted among Egyptians. Virginity is absolutely required for the bride who marries for the first time. Dating is neither welcomed nor accepted. There is, instead, a "marriage marketplace," which refers to a series of activities performed by men and women when sizing someone up as a potential mate. In this marketplace, each person possesses resources, such as social class, status, age, and physical attractiveness. People tend to choose partners whose overall rating is about the same as their own (Strong & Devalut, 1989). As in other places of the world, marital exchange in Egypt is based on gender roles. Men traditionally offer status, economic resources, and protection, while women are valued for their nurturance, childbearing ability, homemaking skills, and physical attractiveness. Recent changes in women's economic status (such as their increased participation in work and social life) give women more bargaining power, while the decline in the value of bearing and raising children, housekeeping, and the greater availability of female sexual partners give men more bargaining power.

Ahmed (1991) summarized several studies and surveys on patterns of mate selection and found that well-educated men in Egyptian urban areas prefer that their future wives have the following characteristics in this order: education, skills in housekeeping, and health. Men in rural areas have a different order of desirable characteristics: a "good" background, high moral standing, a good reputation, housekeeping skills, physical beauty, and the best education possible.

Additional studies on mate selection have been conducted in the last three decades, including various types and variables influencing it. Among these studies are those of El-Saati (1969); Mohammed (1986); Rizk (1989); Kasem (1988); and Shehatta (1992, 1999). Mohammed (1986) found that female university students preferred the following characteristics in their future husbands: vivid and good personality, a prestigious position or profession, intelligence and reason, goodness and kindness, a car, a respectful family, suitable age, respect for his wife, and a mother who is no longer living!

Rizk (1989) studied the mate-selection choices of 304 female university students and found that they preferred the following characteristics for choosing their future husbands: appropriate age, good personality, higher status or position, wealth, a prestigious or respected family, respect for his wife, and intelligence.

Shehatta (1992) studied the preferred characteristics of the future wives or husbands in a sample of male and female Egyptian university students and found that female respondents preferred for their future husbands to have: respect for his wife, religious commitment, the ability to satisfy his wife's needs as a woman, and seriousness in his manner. Males preferred the following characteristics in their future wives: obedience, helpfulness, religious commitment, loyalty to her husband, and a nonauthoritative attitude.

In a more recent study, Shehatta (1999) investigated mate selection among female academic workers (aged between 25 and 40 years), and single university students (aged between 19 and 21 years). Respondents were asked to rate: (1) thirty traits of desired husbands, and (2) seven items about length of engagement, failure of engagement, and the reasons why men do not want to marry. Analysis of the collected data revealed the following:

1. Female students have a higher engagement rate than female academic workers.
2. Female academic workers attributed the failure of their engagements to their ambition, intelligence, and rigidity, while female students attributed it to economic factors and the opinion of their families.
3. The image of a desired husband among female students included being a gentleman and a genius, while among academic workers, it was a man with a high income.

Kasem (1988) focused on the marriage motives among 145 Egyptian nonmarried girls and found that motherhood was the strongest motive for the girls to get married. Respondents considered motherhood as the best means to keep marital relations strong and healthy. The study also revealed many similarities between a girl's father image and the image of her future husband. This last result was also found in another study conducted in Egypt by Bena (1976).

Age of Marriage

Recent statistics (*Al-Ahram,* March 12, 2001) show that there are 3.5 million unmarried Egyptian women aged 30 years and older, a great many of whom are well educated. This situation has created great social concern, and some researchers are calling for a return of traditional matchmakers.

The average marriage age is higher in the urban areas than in the rural areas: 25–35 years for men and 20–30 years for women in the urban areas, and 20–25 years for men and 16–18 years for women in the rural areas (Adler, 2001; Ahmed, 1991). Reasons for the higher marriage age among urban men and women, compared to their rural counterparts, include the following: Urban men need first to finish their education and look for suitable work. Only then do most of them begin to think about forming their own family, which requires them to secure a suitable place (house) for marriage and the furniture and, moreover, the expenses for marriage requirements (*Shabka* and *Mahr*) and the marriage party. At present, young men—particularly in the urban areas—need from 5 to 10 years after their graduation before they can meet these responsibilities. Urban girls, in turn, prefer to finish their education and then wait until the right person comes along. He, in turn, should be able to provide his future wife with good *Shabka* and *Mahr,* a suitable apartment or house, have a solid profession, and enjoy a good income. In the rural areas, where marriage expenses are much less, the parents of both the groom and the bride usually provide their children with as much help as possible so they can marry.

Marriage Advertisements

In the last 30 years, advertisements have appeared in Egyptian newspapers and magazines in which women and men respectively seek husbands and wives. The advertisements highlight the tenacity of traditional notions of masculinity and femininity, which may have limited survival value today. These women and men, who almost always are well educated, search for husbands and wives in good circumstances. In particular, women want husbands with occupations that pay better than theirs for practical reasons. But they insist also on their future husbands being taller and older. Men invariably advertise for women who are younger, shorter, and less educated than they are (Adler, 2001; Ahmed, 1991).

One can observe that many female university graduates in Egypt are not married. Surveys have shown that the chief reason for their remaining unmarried was that the male graduates tended to prefer that their future wives be less educated, either from higher or lower secondary schools or even primary school (Adler, 2001; Ahmed, 1984, 1991). It is discouraging for women's education when these graduates, who are supposed to set an example, either avoid their duty or cannot get married (Ahmed, 1991).

Marital, Childcare, and Household Roles

Egyptian women are very children-oriented, but they suffer impediments to improving their present situation, such as illiteracy and die-hard traditions, which are difficult to eradicate (e.g., relative neglect, especially during the prenubial years).

PREGNANCY AND CHILDBIRTH: ATTITUDES AND PRACTICES

It is widely expected and hoped that every Egyptian woman will become a mother after marriage. This expectation is deeply rooted in Islamic cultural tradition, which places mothers at the highest level.

During the past periods of harem life, or because of ignorance and poverty, women were little more than sexual objects and childbearing machines. Related to that, and to the male image of women as weak and second best, it often seemed that pregnancy and childbearing became the only duties of a woman (in 1990, one-half of Egyptian women were in their childbearing years). That is a possible way for a married woman to keep the relationship with her husband very strong, and to avoid divorce. It may explain, at least partly, the high fertility rate (the annual rate of population growth was 2.8 percent in 1990), especially in rural areas, and particularly among uneducated married women. Recent statistics (Abdel-Atey et al., 2000) reveal that urban, well-educated, younger women (under 40) tend to have fewer children (two to four), than rural, uneducated or less educated, and older women (40 and older), who have an average of five to eight. It seems that women's employment opportunities affect their fertility: fertility tends to be lower for better-educated women, working women with high incomes, and women in larger cites (Ahmed, 1991). Studies summarized by Ahmed (1991) show that fertility tends to be higher in rural areas because of the characteristics of agricultural labor, which require and encourage large families; couples who work in the fields may wish for children, especially sons, to lessen their burden.

The high fertility rate is a function of many factors, such as the universality of marriage; the early age of marriage, especially for rural women; the cultural correlation between femininity and fertility; lack of social security for women, especially in old age;

the high rate of mortality among children (which was estimated in 1990 at 53 per 1,000 in the first year of life), especially in the rural areas. The high fertility rate is also due to the fact that parents prefer to have boys rather than girls, since the cultural pattern encourages the belief that fathers who have boys are immortal. Rural women in particular believe that their value depends on their ability to bear children, and especially boys. Traditionally, children are a source of prestige to rich families, and of income to poor families (Ahmed, 1991; Minai, 1981).

FAMILY PLANNING AND BIRTH CONTROL

Several Egyptian studies (summarized by Radwan, 1997) have shown a positive relationship between a woman's type of work and her method of family planning. Urban, well-to-do, and highly prestigious working women, in general, tend more than their rural, lesser educated, and semi- and nonskilled working counterparts to practice birth control and/or family planning. Other studies (Jacoup, 1974; Radwan, 1997) have also revealed a positive correlation between a family's socioeconomic status and the family's tendency to practice birth control and/or family planning.

INFANCY AND EARLY CHILDHOOD

Although the Qu'ran and the Prophet Mohammed himself recognized the equality of the sexes 14 centuries ago, and even though about 80 years ago the first Muslim feminist reasserted the equality of the sexes, girls in Egypt are still considered second-best.

Preference for Sons

Like many of their counterparts in other parts of the world, parents in Egypt prefer sons. It is said that a man with a son is immortal, whereas a girl is brought up to contribute to someone else's family tree.

There are many compelling economic reasons why parents prefer a boy. At least 70 percent of Egypt is rural. Here, sons are indispensable as muscle power on the land. Without their continued presence on family land, parents would have to look

forward to a miserable old age. Unlike girls, boys do not have to be supervised very closely, since their sexual behavior cannot dishonor the family or compromise their chance for marriage. If a girl survives infancy in the poverty-stricken areas in Egypt, she is saddled with work as soon as she can walk, and in many cases she cannot even attend a cost-free primary school (Ahmed, 1991).

Women's nurturing duties begin early in life, such as helping with babycare and kitchen duties, while frequently working with real farm equipment and weaving tools. Although not always counted in government surveys, girls are, in rural areas especially, economic assets from the start. They constitute a large labor force of usually unpaid workers and helpers to their parents. If they were counted along with their brothers, who hire themselves out as farmhands, sweatshop assistants, or peddlers, the prevalence of child labor would be staggering.

The picture is grim. Overall enrollment figures for elementary school children are perhaps a better indication of how many girls help their families survive. Only about 70 percent of the girls of school age are allowed to attend school, while the proportion for boys is 85 percent. The picture is far worse in the rural areas.

SOCIALIZATION IN EGYPTIAN FAMILIES

Egyptian families today are facing a variety of challenges, which influence the role of the family in socialization (*Al-Ahram,* September 25, 2000). The most important challenges are the following:

1. The family is no longer the only source for socialization. Many other institutions in the society, such as school, sports clubs, social and cultural associations, are sharing the same duty, but they do not work consistently in the same direction as the family. As a result, the family now has a defensive role and has to rebuild or correct ideas and behaviors acquired by children through these institutions, instead of being able to build upon the right ideas and behaviors.

2. Most current families are suffering from a lack of parenthood skills, which would enable them to raise their children in a healthy and positive way.

Raising children in current Egyptian families has become a mother's increasingly difficult duty, given that there is an increasing number of absentee fathers working abroad, a rising rate of divorce, and too many fathers who remove themselves from the burdens and responsibilities of raising their children, leaving this duty to the mothers (Ahmed, 2003).

3. Socialization is typically defined as a process during which children acquire psychological, social, and cultural values and traditions. However, today the socialization process must concentrate on teaching children how to cope with the shifting circumstances produced by globalization, rapid sociocultural change, and the resulting cultural conflicts. In short, socialization has to change from teaching children facts or knowledge to teaching them, instead, methods and ways of solving societal problems. Unfortunately, this new way of looking at socialization is unlikely to find widespread acceptance in the near future.

4. Contemporary Egyptian families are suffering from a severe imbalance between their incomes and their expenditures. Recent statistics by the Central Agency for Public Mobilization and Statistics in Egypt (reported in *Al-Ahram,* November 15, 2000) show that Egyptian families devote 56 percent of their incomes to food, 10 percent to housing, 9 percent to clothes, 7 percent to children's education, and only 4 percent to medical care. Such an imbalance can affect negatively the role of the family in the socialization process. So economically and sexually advantageous is a son to his father, that men—even those well informed about the latest findings of genetics—will get divorced and remarry repeatedly until one wife finally bears them a son (Minai, 1981).

Throughout Egypt, women are viewed as subordinate to men, but vital for nurturing; yet there are several ways to mold little girls to that ideal.

With premarital and extramarital sex being commonplace in spite of its being forbidden by the Qur'an, a very demanding task befalls the parents to safeguard their daughter's virginity while preparing her for her future role as mother. How this is accomplished varies from family to family according to its socioeconomic status (Bahensy, 1980; Minai, 1981; Sadek, 1979). Professionals and those who can af-

ford it do not have to depend on their son's work in old age, and so their wives feel less threatened if their baby should turn out to be a girl rather than a boy. The daughter is likely to receive a good education. This makes her fear divorce much less than her poorer sisters, who remain without education and thus without marketable skills.

From early on, parental expectations emphasize masculine behaviors for boys and feminine behaviors for girls. Such practices later result in the sexes having negative attitudes toward one another. At the same time, the primary school curriculum encourages and fosters the traditional sex-typed upbringing of boys and girls, which in turn is reinforced by the mass media and by films (Minai, 1981).

Several studies have focused on family socialization practices and their relation to children's personality traits. Among these studies are those of Abdalla (1980); Abdel-Majeed (1980); Al-Omeri (1981); El-Damerdash (1980); Bedani (1995); Musalem (1997); Sanders (1986); and Sobhey (1975). Abdalla (1980) found that conflicts between parents negatively affect their children's personality traits. Abdel-Majeed (1980) found a relationship between healthy socialization practices (such as emphasizing democracy, warmth, and love) and positive personality traits and value systems in children, while El-Damerdash's (1980) study revealed a positive correlation between a child's acceptance of his mother's role in the process of socialization and the child's psychological adjustment. More recent studies have found positive relationships between parental behavior and the children's achievement motivation (Musalem, 1997), and between socialization practices among working mothers and their children's social maturity (Bedani, 1995).

Sanders (1986) compared attitudes toward parents and family in Egyptian and American male and female university students, aged 17–23 years, by using a semantic differential technique. Both groups expressed a favorable attitude toward their parents and viewed their families as rather happy. Egyptians reported their parents to be relatively more patient and more relaxed, but also somewhat more serious than the Americans. The stereotypical negative portrayal of the Egyptian father as restrictive and authoritarian was not supported in this study.

The Unseen Father

During the last three decades, because of social and economic hardships, Egyptians began to move out, especially to some other Arab and Gulf oil-producing states, where they are seeking better conditions and trying to improve their lives. As a result, fathers must leave their families temporarily or permanently. In the interest of reducing expenses in the countries that receive the Egyptians, or as result of rules and laws in those countries, which sometimes do not allow immigrants to bring their families with them, or do not welcome this sort of reunion, many Egyptian migrants, especially fathers, have been negatively affected:

1. Wives of these migrant fathers and husbands became even more responsible simultaneously for caring for the children and for doing the household chores, which added an extra burden on their shoulders.
2. Negative changes have occurred in children's value systems and the structure of the family. Studies have shown that children of absent fathers are more likely to become aggressive and delinquent. For instance, El-Damerdash (1976) found that children deprived of their fathers have low and unrealistic self-concepts. A more recent study (Abou-elala, 1994) found that a father's/husband's absence negatively affects the psychosocial adjustment of both his wife and children. These findings were confirmed by Abou-el-Kheir (1998), who found a positive relationship between children's perceived father figure and their self-esteem.
3. When fathers are absent, their influence on their children weakens dramatically (Abdalla, 1988, 1992; Ahmed, 2003).

Marital Adjustment

During the last three decades, several Egyptian studies have been conducted to investigate marital adjustment and related variables. Examples of these studies are those of Daniel (1966); Serrey (1982); Abdel-Rahman and Dousseki (1988); Farag and Abdalla (1999); and Hashem (1999). Daniel (1966) studied the dynamics of marital adjustment, and reported that maladjustment among couples was the main reason for divorce or separation between husband and wife. Serrey (1982) investigated the relationship between psychological adjustment in samples of married and divorced female teachers, and some personality traits. Results revealed a positive correlation between general psychological adjustment and both self-concept and positive attitudes toward marriage, and a negative correlation between general psychological adjustment and both marital conflicts and neuroticism. It was also found that married female teachers, compared with their divorced counterparts, scored significantly higher on all dimensions of psychological adjustment (e.g., personal, social, marital, family, emotional and occupational adjustment). Abdel-Rahman's and Dousseki's (1988) study reported that higher educational level, religiosity, and a man's and a woman's good relationship with his or her parents are good predictors for a healthy marital adjustment. Another study (Hashem, 1999) showed that marital adjustment was higher among husbands and wives who were similar in educational level and socioeconomic status, and that long engagements, long marriages, and age differences between husbands and wives affected the marital adjustment positively. Husbands and wives who were higher in marital locus of control and marital comparison levels were higher on marital adjustment. The last result suggested that both the Marital Locus of Control Scale and Marital Comparisons Level Index could be used to predict marital adjustment. Farag and Abdalla (1999) studied the relationship between assertiveness and marital adjustment in 140 well-educated husbands and their wives. Results showed significant positive correlations between general assertiveness and marital adjustment, and between the levels of assertiveness among husbands and wives. Criticism and expression of admiration (as assertive skills) correlated positively with marital adjustment.

POLYGAMY

Islam did not introduce polygamy, but it was a common practice in many ancient societies because of certain social and humanitarian considerations, such as infertility, and in regions where the female population outnumbered the male population. Polygamy is not prohibited in Egypt. However, the polygamy rate is very low (below two per thousand), mainly due to economic reasons. Recent statistics (Abdel-Atey et al., 2000) show that the number of men who have more than one wife is constantly decreasing. Already in 1970, the proportion was only 3 per 1,000 for well-educated couples and 8 per 1,000 for uneducated couples.

As an alternative to banning polygamy, a Marital or Personal Status Law was issued in 1979, which required the husband to inform his current wife of his intention to marry another woman and to inform the future wife of his current marital status. Since secrecy facilitated polygamy, this measure presumably discouraged some men from taking additional wives. The first wife was entitled to a court divorce and possibly monetary compensation within a year, if she found out that her husband had married again without informing her first (Ahmed, 1991).

DIVORCE

A husband may divorce his wife simply by stating "I divorce you," three times, and there need not be any specific grounds for divorce. A wife, however, may ask for a divorce only under certain circumstances, some of which are:

- A husband's absence for a year or more
- A husband's imprisonment for three or more years
- Mental or physical illness (Ciaccio & El-Shakry, 1993, p. 52)

The rate of divorce in Egypt is fairly high. Al-Khouly (1983) reported that in the early 1980s the divorce rate in Egypt generally reached 2.1 per 1,000 of the married cases (the rate of divorce in rural areas was 1.7 per 1,000, while the rate of divorce in the urban areas was 2.6 per 1,000). Al-Khouly noticed that a large portion of divorced women were under the age of 20, while most of the divorced men were between the ages of 20 and 35 years. Recent studies (reported in *Al-Ahram,* March 12, 2001) showed that the

divorce rate in the first year of marriage has increased in the last 10 years. Other recent statistics (reported in *Al-Watan,* January 13, 2002) indicated that the number of divorce cases reached 68,000 in 2000, while the number of divorced men and women was estimated at 264,000, 76 percent of whom were females.

In March 2000, the Egyptian government revived an Islamic law, *Al-Khula,* which gives a married woman the right to ask the court to grant her a divorce if she feels that marital life with her husband is impossible to continue. A married woman must prove her claim, and the court carries on an investigation to clarify the matter. If the court is convinced by the woman's claims, a divorce issue will be declared together with special arrangements to determine the subsequent rights and duties of the couple.

Between March 2000 and March 2001, three thousand cases were filed in court by married women who wanted to be divorced according to the *Al-Khula* law. The husband's impotency and the repeated abuse of wives were the two most common reasons cited (*El-Resalet,* March 21, 2001).

ILLITERACY

Illiteracy is a major national problem in Egypt. An estimated 52 percent of the population aged 15 years and over are illiterate; among males the rate is 37.1 and among females, 66.2 percent (Ciaccio & El-Shakry, 1993). Recent statistics (reported in *Akhbar El-Yom,* November 25, 2000) showed a decrease of illiteracy in Egypt in 2000, which fell to 33.6 percent. The illiteracy rates in the rural areas were 36 and 63 percent for males and females, respectively, while the rates for urban males and females were 20 and 34 percent, respectively (*Al-Ahram,* January 18, 2002).

It has been estimated that between 1990 and 2000, the Adult Education and Illiteracy Eradication Project, which was established in the early 1980s, eradicated illiteracy among 1 million Egyptians, 70 percent of whom were females (Radwan, 1997).

EDUCATION

While education in Egypt is compulsory between the ages of 6 and 14 years, more males than females begin and continue their primary education. Although the percentage of females enrolled at all levels of the educational cycle has increased consistently since 1952, their enrollment still lags considerably behind that of males (Ciaccio & El-Shakry, 1993).

Nevertheless, Egypt has achieved reasonable progress in the field of education. In 1990, the rate of children at school age (6 years) who enrolled in the primary school was 96 percent for boys and 89 percent for girls (Abdel-Atey et al., 2000). That the education of girls has improved over the years can be seen in the number of enrolled girls, especially in primary schools: it was 36 percent of all enrolled pupils in 1960, 44 percent in 1990 (Radwan, 1997), and 47 percent in 2000 (*Akhbar El-Yom,* November 25, 2000). As for other educational levels, recent statistics show that girls make up 49 percent of all students enrolled in secondary schools and 46 percent in the universities.

WORK AND UNEMPLOYMENT

Women in Egypt have always worked, but as a result of industrialization today, they now have the right to enter the labor force on their own and accept jobs outside the home without the help or permission of their men.

Women started working outside their homes as a means of economic and social security, that is, in order to be financially independent and to increase the family income. Women began working before society was able to prepare suitable conditions to help them organize their household chores, care for their children, and plan their families. Initially, women's employment was limited to those whose provider had lost the ability to work for one reason or another. However, the activities in this category for women were restricted to some industries and housekeeping services (Ahmed, 1991).

In 1993, it was estimated that the number of working women and girls in Egypt was about 67.7 percent of the total number of females aged 6 years and up. Other statistics show that the number of working women reached 36–40 percent of the female population aged from 12 to 64 years. Statistics also show that the number of working women in rural areas is

about double that of their urban counterparts. It should be noted in this context that about two-thirds of the Egyptian working women are working at home and without pay (Radwan, 1997). Consequently, the number of working women who are paid for their services is not more than 13 percent of the total number of the Egyptian female population who are old enough to work (Abdel-Atey et al., 2000).

Seventy percent of the Egyptian working women were, in 1993, illiterate. As for the rate of unemployment, statistics for 1993 show that while the rate among males of working age was only 8 percent of the total number of Egyptian males aged 16–64 years, the rate of unemployment among their female counterparts was a very high 21 percent (Radwan, 1997).

Statistics (cited in Shend, 2000) show that working women constitute 31 percent of the total number of governmental employees. Most of these working women are concentrated in fields of pre-university education, health, and social affairs, and the majority of them can be found in the Greater Cairo area (48.9 percent of the total number of governmental employees).

Women also participate in other fields such as banking, university education (22 percent), and the general production sector, where their participation has been estimated at 11.1 percent.

The Impact of Unemployment

Unemployment is one of the most serious problems facing Egyptian society. The overall rate of unemployment increased during the last 10 years from 7 percent to about 15 percent (the rate of unemployment for males is now 8 percent and for females, 21 percent), due to a variety of economic, social, and political reasons. These include the return of more than 1 million Egyptians who had been working in Iraq and Kuwait, as a result of the first Gulf War in 1990–1991; an increasing number of university and secondary school graduates; a reduction of work opportunities; and the government's withdrawal of its obligation to appoint the new graduates of university and secondary schools.

As for the psychological well-being of the unemployed, especially the well-educated ones, several research studies have been conducted to assess the impact of joblessness (Al-Bakry, 1996; Al-Sharkawy & El-Qamah, 1993; Askar & Abdel-Razek, 1998; Mahmoud, 1989; Mourad, 1997; Mustapha, 1986, 1993).

Al-Bakry (1996) compared the relationship between unemployment and some personality traits between samples of working and nonworking well-educated men and women by using Spielberger's State-Trait Scale of Anxiety, a scale to assess feelings of loneliness, and the Cornell Index for Adjustment. He found that unemployment correlated positively with higher levels of state-trait anxiety, feelings of loneliness, and maladjustment. Similarly, Mourad (1997) found that unemployed, well-educated people, when compared to employed ones, scored higher on indices of frustration and aggression, but lower on a self-esteem scale. Additionally, a positive relationship between duration of unemployment and level of frustration was found.

Maternity Leave

Egyptian labor law was modified in 1971 to stipulate that during the 3 months of maternity leave (a postpartum leave), a woman is to receive her full salary, as stated in international agreements. Laws 47 and 48 (1978) pertain to the public sector and ensure women the right to 2 years' unpaid maternity leave for a maximum of three times and the right to paid maternity leave for 3 months. However, a woman is not entitled to have more than three leaves during the period of her employment. This modification has also given those women nursing their baby the right to take nursing breaks for 1 hour daily, for 1 year beginning after delivery. This additional daily 1-hour break is included in the working hours and entails no reduction in salary (Ahmed, 1991). Law 137 (1981), in turn, pertains to the private sector and grants women 50 days' paid maternity leave and 1 year's unpaid maternity leave. It also prohibits the employment of women in jobs "detrimental to their health or morals or in strenuous jobs." Finally, it requires employees to provide nursery facilities (Ciaccio & El-Shakry, 1993).

The Impact of Mother's Work on Children and the Family Structure

A fundamental problem facing Egyptian working women is that of childcare. Decree No. 68 of 1961 states that every employer who employs in one place at least 100 female employees must provide a day nursery for their children who are between the ages of 3 months and 6 years (Ahmed, 1991).

Several studies have been conducted to compare working and nonworking women and their children with regard to various personality traits (Kandeel, 1964; Muharram, 1973), to assess the socialization of working women's children (Abdel-Gawad, 1974; Abdel-Majeed, 1980; Bedani, 1995), to measure the levels of aspiration among working mothers' children (Mohammedian, 1996), and to compare the academic achievement of children of working and non-working mothers (Ahmed, 1982). Other research studies have focused on working women's self-image and their motives to work (Abdel-Fattah, 1967; Dousseki, 1980; El-Sayed, 1980; Kandeel, 1964), the problems of working mothers (Muharram, 1973), working women's psychological well-being (Abdel-Rahim, 1982, in Shend, 2000; Adam, 1980; Ahmed & Abdel-Bakey, 1985; Shend, 2000), job satisfaction in working women (Abdel-Majeed, 1975; Al-Khatib, 1986; Askar & Abdel-Razek, 1998; Shoukry, 1998), and women's leadership behavior (Abdel-Fattah, 1981).

In the following sections, examples of these studies will be briefly reviewed. In 1973, Muharram investigated the problems of working women, finding that they were suffering from work overload from outside and inside the home, high levels of role conflict, and husbands' negative attitudes toward their work. Yet working women tended, more than non-working ones, to solve their problem by using a rational style of thinking. Adam (1980) investigated working women's self-image and its relation to some personality traits in a sample of working mothers from different educational levels. It was revealed that well-educated and older working mothers tended, more than their less-educated and younger counterparts, to solve their conflicts in more positive ways and to have a positive self-image. Shoukry (1998) investigated the relationship between type A (high-strung, impatient, aggressive) and type B behavior (less driven, less aggressive, more relaxed), marital relations, and some work variables in a sample of married working women. Results showed that when compared to women classified as type B, women showing type A behavior were better educated, suffered more from excessive workloads, experienced more marital conflicts, and were less able to participate efficiently in family affairs and to communicate with their husbands and children. Furthermore, positive correlations were found between type A behavior in married working women and their husbands.

Other studies have focused on role conflicts that face working women, especially working mothers, and the impact of these conflicts on their own adjustment and that of their children. Among these studies are those of Abdel-Rahim (1982, in Shend, 2000), Khalil (1989), and Shend (2000). Abdel-Rahim (1982) studied the relationship between role conflict in working mothers and the personal and social adjustment of their children. Findings showed that working mothers were suffering, more than nonworking ones, from role conflict. Children of working mothers were found to be less well adjusted than the children of nonworking mothers. This finding was in line with the results of an earlier study conducted by Kandeel (1964). Khalil (1989) investigated psychological adjustment and its relation to role conflict and some personality traits in a sample of working mothers who continued their studies at the same time, versus nonworking mothers. It was found that working student mothers scored higher than nonworking mothers on indices of psychological and social adjustment, and self-image, while nonworking mothers were rated higher on family and emotional adjustment. In contrast, no differences were found between the two samples on indices of neuroticism, extraversion, and marital adjustment. In a recent study conducted by Shend (2000), scales for assessing anxiety, neurotic depression, role conflict, and psychological adjustment were administered to 400 full-time and part-time working mothers in Cairo. Results showed that full-time working mothers scored higher than their part-time counterparts

on indices of role conflict and neurotic depression, but lower on indicators of adjustment.

Taken together, the aforementioned studies suggest that in spite of the progress that has been achieved by Egyptian women in fields of education, work, marital and civil rights, and politics, and the positive consequences of woman's work (such as a greater sense of independence and increased participation in making family decisions), Egyptian women still are suffering from several negative effects resulting from their participation in work. Most likely, such negative effects occur because they do not receive proper cultural and social support for their work involvement.

Children's Work

Egypt is among the countries that have seen, especially during the last three to four decades, an increasing number of working children. In 1993, it was estimated that about 7 percent (or 1 million children) of all children aged 6–12 years went to work (Radwan, 1997). Several studies have been conducted during the last 10 years that focused on the social and psychological impact of children's work. Mahmoud (1997), for instance, compared working and nonworking children aged 10–16 years and found that working children experienced less satisfaction and exhibited poorer psychological adjustment. Mahmoud's results are in line with the results of an earlier study on children's work by El-Deba (1993).

OLD AGE

Improved health care conditions and working environments have resulted in an increasing number of elderly (60 years and above), who in 1999 constituted about 15 percent of the total population. In addition, the Egyptian Ministry of Social Affairs has established homes and clubs for the elderly in Cairo and Alexandria, as well as in other large cities. Furthermore, since the 1970s elderly people who were not governmental employees are entitled to receive monthly pensions (called Sadaat's pensions), which are given to both men and women.

INSTITUTIONS THAT OFFER SERVICES TO THE FAMILY

Several Egyptian institutions offer a variety of services to the family (Aly, 1999). Among these institutions are the following:

1. Centers for Motherhood and Childhood Care: These centers began for the first time in 1912 through charity societies. Currently, the number of these institutions has reached 250, spread all over the country. Their goals include reducing delivery risk, reducing the rate of mortality and disease among babies and preschool children, and caring for school children.

2. Offices for Family Counseling: These offices are located in Cairo and in most large cities. They provide two types of services: treatment and research. They aim to help families overcome crises and solve conflicts between husbands and wives, which could lead to a healthier atmosphere for raising their children. These offices assist the family courts.

3. Productive Family Project: This project aims to help poorer families to become a productive unit, by providing them with the raw materials, machines, tools, and training necessary for starting a small industry project in the family context. The project also provides productive families with marketing facilities.

4. Social Units: These units are located in several urban and rural settings and offer several services such as establishing nurseries, centers for family planning and birth control, clubs for youth and the elderly, and medical clinics.

5. Offices for Marriage Counseling: These offices are operating in Cairo, Alexandria, and other large cities and offer counseling and health services for persons planning to marry. The aim is to provide future families with necessary aids required for establishing healthy families, both psychologically and physically.

6. Foster Families Project: This project started in 1956 and is aimed at providing social, psychological, educational, and professional care for those children who, for many reasons, are deprived of a normal family life: illegitimate children, orphaned children, and children whose families were not capable of providing normal living conditions for them.

7. Day Nursery: This project was established in Egypt for the first time in 1933 to provide daily care with lower admission fees for the children of working mothers. At present, each neighborhood in larger cities in Egypt has its own Day Nursery.

8. Shelter Institutions: These institutions aim at providing normal health care for children 6–18 years of age who have lost their families through death, illness, and/or imprisonment.

9. SOS Villages: In 1977, the first SOS village was established in Cairo. Later, two other villages were set up in Alexandria and Tanta (Delta). They accept homeless children between the ages of 2 and 6 years. Enrolled children should not be psychologically or physically handicapped. SOS villages in Egypt provide children with psychological and medical care, and children can join the general education system until 18 years of age.

Egypt has more than 15,000 nongovernmental societies and associations that offer services to the different sectors of the population and cover a variety of activities (such as social, economic, and medical care). Additional new societies and associations have recently become active, among them the Center for Caring for Battered Women, which was founded in Cairo at the end of 2001 and has as its purpose to help battered women and reduce violence within the family (*Al-Ahram,* January 27, 2002).

SYNOPSIS

In Egypt, the family is an old institution. At the dawn of recorded history, Egyptians had established rules for marriage outlining the legitimate way to form a family. The rules considered both the rights of the couple and those of the larger family. Some ancient marriage traditions are still followed in contemporary Egyptian daily life. Marriage remains the only legitimate way of forming a family, and its forms continue to be strongly influenced by religion, traditions, and customs. However, in recent years, and as a result of social and economic hardships, the family's role has weakened. In response, the Egyptian government has issued several laws to protect the family as the basic social unit. Furthermore, for decades, efforts by governmental and nongovernmental organizations in Egypt have led to the establishment of various institutions, societies, and social service offices to support families and to avoid—or at least to minimize—the destructive effects of family breakups.

REFERENCES

Abdalla, J. G. (1980). *The impact of the relationship among parents on some personality traits of the child.* Unpublished master's thesis, Faculty of Arts, Ain Shams University, Egypt (in Arabic).

Abdalla, J. G. (1988). *The impact of father absence on the mental and psychological development in the early childhood.* Unpublished doctoral thesis, Faculty of Arts, Ain Shams University, Egypt (in Arabic).

Abdalla, J. G. (1992). Hostility as a function of father absence. *Psychological Studies,* Egypt 2(2), 351–369.

Abdel-Atey, E., Bayyumi, M., Hasan H. M., Omar, N., El-Ramekh, E., & El-Sayed, R. (2000). *Family sociology.* Alexandria: Dar el-Maarefa al-Gamaiaa (in Arabic).

Abdel-Fattah, K. I. (1967). *A study of women's work in Egypt: Motives and results.* Unpublished doctoral thesis, Faculty of Arts, Ain Shams University, Egypt (in Arabic).

Abdel-Fattah, S. (1981). *Patterns of leadership behavior among Egyptian working women.* Unpublished master's thesis, Faculty of Commerce, Ain Shams University, Egypt (in Arabic).

Abdel-Gawad, I. S. (1974). *Raising children by working and non-working women: A comparative study.* Unpublished master's thesis, Faculty of Arts, Ain Shams University, Egypt (in Arabic).

Abdel-Majeed, F. Y. (1975). *A comparative study of flexibility/rigidity among married working and non-working women.* Unpublished doctoral thesis, Faculty of Arts, Ain Shams University, Egypt (in Arabic).

Abdel-Majeed, F. Y. (1980). *Children's socialization and its relationship with children's personality traits and value systems.* Unpublished doctoral thesis, Faculty of Arts, Ain Shams University, Egypt (in Arabic).

Abdel-Rahman, M. E. & Dousseki, R. H. (1988). Marital adjustment prediction. *Proceedings of the 4th Annual Convention of the Egyptian Association for Psychological Studies (EAPS)* (pp. 671–694), Cairo, Egypt, January 25–27, 1988. Center for the Human Development and Information (in Arabic).

Abou-elala, M. A. A. M. (1994). *Father absence and its relation to the psychosocial adjustment of their mothers (wives) and children at the age of adolescence.* Unpublished master's thesis, Institute for Higher Studies on Childhood, Ain Shams University, Egypt (in Arabic).

Abou-el-Kheir, M. M. S. (1998). Perceived father figure and self-esteem among college students. *Psychological Studies,* Egypt, 8(2–3), 419–452 (in Arabic).

Adam, M. S. (1980). *Role conflict in working woman: A psychosocial study of working women's social role image and some personality traits.* Unpublished doctoral thesis, College of Girls, Ain Shams University, Egypt (in Arabic).

Adler, L. L. (2001). Women and gender roles. In L. L. Adler & U. P. Gielen (Eds.), *Cross-cultural topics in psychology* (2nd ed., pp. 103–114). Westport, CT: Praeger.

Ahmed, A. M. (1982). *The relationship between working mothers' anxiety levels and the academic achievement of their children.* Unpublished master's thesis, Faculty of Education, Assiut University, Egypt (in Arabic).

Ahmed, R. A. (1984). *Mate selection in Sudanese male and female university students.* Unpublished research study, Khartoum, Sudan, December 1984.

Ahmed, R. A. (1991). Women in Egypt and the Sudan. In L. L. Adler (Ed.), *Women in cross-cultural perspective* (pp. 107–133). New York: Praeger.

Ahmed, R. A. (2003). Egyptian migrations. In L. L. Adler & U. P. Gielen (Eds.), *Migration: Immigration and emigration in international perspective* (pp. 311–327). Westport, CT: Praeger.

Ahmed, S. K., & Abdel-Bakey, S. M. (1985). *A clinical study of woman's psychological structure.* Cairo: The Anglo-Egyptian Bookshop (in Arabic).

Al-Bakry, M. A. (1996). *Unemployment and its relation to some personality traits among university graduates.* Unpublished master's thesis, Faculty of Arts, Ain Shams University, Egypt (in Arabic).

Al-Khatib, R. A. (1986). *Job satisfaction among women employed in the governmental sector: An empirical and clinical study.* Unpublished doctoral thesis, Faculty of Humanities, Al-Azhar University, Egypt (in Arabic).

Al-Khouly, S. (1983). *Marriage and family relations.* Beirut, Lebanon: Dar el-Nahad el-Arabia (in Arabic).

Al-Omeri, M. A. (1981). *Differences in parental behavior as perceived by parents and children: A comparative study of parents from different educational levels.* Unpublished master's thesis, Faculty of Education, Ain Shams University, Egypt (in Arabic).

Al-Sharkawy, F. M., & El-Qamah, E. (1993). Unemployment among well-educated youth. *Journal of Contemporary Psychology,* Egypt, 2(6), 26–62 (in Arabic).

Aly, A. M. Y. (1999). *Lectures on population, family and childhood issues.* Alexandria: The Modern University Office (in Arabic)

Askar, A. E., & Abdel-Razek, I. A. (1998). Unemployment, anxiety state and depressive feelings among youth. *Proceedings of the 5th International Conference of the Counseling Center, Ain Shams University (Egypt), Counseling and Human Development, December 1–3, 1998* (pp. 27–73). (in Arabic)

Bahensy, F. A. H. (1980). *Parents' educational level and its relation with raising primary school children.* Unpublished master's thesis, Faculty of Education, Ain Shams University, Egypt (in Arabic).

Bedani, A. K. M. (1995). *Socialization of working and non-working mothers and its relation to social maturity in their male and female children at the intermediate educational level.* Unpublished master's thesis, Institute for Higher Studies on Childhood, Ain Shams University, Egypt (in Arabic).

Bena, N. E. (1976). *The extent of projecting one's parent image onto the husband and its relation to marital adjustment and spouse choice.* Unpublished master's thesis, College of Girls, Ain Shams University, Egypt (in Arabic).

Ciaccio, N. V., & El-Shakry, O. S. (1993). Egypt. In L. L. Adler (Ed.), *International handbook on gender roles* (pp. 46–58). Westport, CT: Greenwood.

Daniel, A. G. (1966). *Dynamics of adjustment in marital life: An experimental and psychological study.* Unpublished master's thesis, Faculty of Arts, Ain Shams University, Egypt (in Arabic).

Dousseki, I. M. (1980). *Woman's social role and its relation with her self-concept.* Unpublished master's thesis, Faculty of Arts, Ain Shams University, Egypt (in Arabic).

El-Damerdash, I. M. A. (1976). *Self-concept in children deprived of their father.* Unpublished master's thesis,

College of Girls, Ain Shams University, Egypt (in Arabic).

El-Damerdash, I. M. A. (1980). *The child's acceptance of the mother's role in the process of socialization and its relation with the child's psychological adjustment.* Unpublished doctoral thesis, College of Girls, Ain Shams University, Egypt (in Arabic).

El-Deba, N. R. S. (1993). *Children's work and its relation to psychological adjustment: A field study on a sample of working children.* Unpublished master's thesis, Institute for Higher Studies on Childhood, Ain Shams University, Egypt (in Arabic).

El-Saati, S. H. (1969). *Marriage choice and social change.* Unpublished doctoral thesis, Faculty of Arts, Ain Shams University, Egypt (in Arabic).

El-Sayed, A. M. (1980). *Self-image of Egyptian women in the light of some psychological dimensions.* Unpublished doctoral thesis, College of Girls, Ain Shams University, Egypt (in Arabic).

Esposito, J. L. (Ed.). (1995). *The Oxford encyclopedia of the modern Islamic World,* Vol. 1. New York: Oxford University Press.

Farag, T. S. M., & Abdalla, M. H. (1999). Assertiveness and marital adjustment. *Arab Journal for the Humanities,* Kuwait, *17*(67), 178–213 (in Arabic).

Gold Schmidt, A., Jr. (1994). *Historical dictionary of Egypt.* Metuchen, NJ: Scarecrow.

Hashem, S. M. M. (1999). A study for some variables determining marital adjustment. *Proceedings of the 7th Annual Convention of the Counseling, Center Ain Shams University, Egypt. Counseling in the 21st Century,* December 2–4, 1999 (pp. 57–103) (in Arabic).

Jacoup, N. S. (1974). *Family planning in Egyptian society: A comparative field study in urban and rural settings.* Unpublished doctoral thesis, Faculty of Arts, Ain Shams University, Egypt (in Arabic).

Kandeel, B. A. (1964). *A comparative study of personality traits in samples of children of working and non-working mothers.* Unpublished doctoral thesis, Faculty of Education, Ain Shams University, Egypt (in Arabic).

Kasem, N. H. (1988). *Basics of mate selection among female university students.* Unpublished master's thesis, Faculty of Arts, Ain Shams University, Egypt (in Arabic).

Khalil, N. S. (1989). *The relationship between psychological adjustment, role conflict, and some personality traits in working student mothers.* Unpublished master's thesis, Faculty of Humanities, Al-Azhar University, Egypt (in Arabic).

Mahmoud, M. H. (1989). A study of some personality traits among unemployed university graduates. *Journal of Sciences and Arts, Helwan University,* Egypt, *1*(4), 25–52 (in Arabic).

Mahmoud, M. A. (1997). *A study on the relationship between job satisfaction and psychological adjustment among working children.* Unpublished master's thesis, Institute for Higher Studies on Childhood, Ain Shams University, Egypt (in Arabic).

Minai, N. (1981). *Women in Islam: Tradition and transition in the Middle East.* London: John Murray.

Mohammed, M. R. (1986). The influence of gender differences on students' attitudes toward some social issues. *Journal of Psychology,* Egypt, *2*(8), 20–40 (in Arabic).

Mohammedian, H. M. M. (1996). *Father absence and its relation to the psychosocial adjustment of wives/mothers and children at the age of adolescence.* Unpublished master's thesis, Institute for Higher Studies on Childhood, Ain Shams University, Egypt (in Arabic).

Mourad, W. F. (1997). *Manifestations of frustration as a result of unemployment among well educated youth.* Unpublished master's thesis, Faculty of Arts, Ain Shams University, Egypt (in Arabic).

Muharram, I. I. (1973). *Women and work: A field study of some well educated working women in Cairo.* Unpublished master's thesis, College of Girls, Ain Shams University, Egypt (in Arabic).

Musalem, A. S. A. (1997). *Parental behavior and its relation to achievement motivation in male and female children.* Unpublished master's thesis, Institute for Higher Studies on Childhood, Ain Shams University, Egypt (in Arabic).

Mustapha, M. M. (1986). *The impact of unemployment among heads of the family (husbands/fathers): A comparative and sociological study of a group of families.* Unpublished master's thesis, Faculty of Arts, Ain Shams University, Egypt (in Arabic).

Mustapha, S. A. (1993). *Unemployment and its relation to alienation among university graduates.* Unpublished doctoral thesis, Faculty of Arts, Assiut University, Egypt (in Arabic).

Radwan, N. (1997). *The role of televised drama in forming women's conscience.* Cairo: General Egyptian Book Organization (in Arabic).

Rizk, K. (1989). Attitudes of female university students toward choosing their mates. *Journal of the Faculty of Education, Demiat, Mansoura University,* Egypt, *12,* 50–75 (in Arabic).

Sadek, Y. A. (1979). *The relationship between family size and some personality traits in children.* Unpublished master's thesis, College of Girls, Ain Shams University, Egypt (in Arabic).

Sanders, J. L. (1986). Egyptian and American university students' attitudes toward parents and family. *Journal of Social Psychology, 126*(4), 459–463.

Serrey, E. M. (1982). *Psychological adjustment among married and divorced female teachers and its relation with some personality variables.* Unpublished doctoral thesis, Faculty of Education, Ain Shams University, Egypt (in Arabic).

Shehetta, A. M. (1992). Characteristics of the preferred future husband among university students. *Journal of the Faculty of Arts, Menoufia University,* Egypt, *8,* 1–25 (in Arabic).

Shehatta, A. M. (1999). Mate selection among female academic workers and female university students. *Journal of the Social Sciences,* Kuwait, *27*(4), 101–119 (in Arabic).

Shend, S. M. (2000). *Psychological disturbances in working woman.* Cairo: Zehara el-Sharak Bookshop (in Arabic).

Shoukry, A. (1985). *Recent trends in studying the family* (3rd ed.). Alexandria: Dar el-Maarefa el-Gamaiaa (in Arabic).

Shoukry, M. M. (1998). The relationship between Type A behavior, job related variables, and marital relations in a sample of working women. *Proceedings of the 5th International Conference of the Counseling Center, Aim Shams University, Egypt, Counseling and Human Development, December 1–3, 1998* (pp. 113–148) (in Arabic).

Simmons, C., & Simmons, C. (1994). Personal and moral adolescent values in England and Saudi Arabia. *Journal of Moral Education, 23*(1), 3–16.

Sobhey, S. M. S. (1975). *The influence of parental attitudes and cultural levels on the development of creativity in children.* Unpublished doctoral thesis, Faculty of Education, Ain Shams University, Egypt (in Arabic).

Strong, B., & Devault, C. (1989). *The marriage and family experience* (4th ed.). St. Paul, MN: West.

CHAPTER 10

CONTEMPORARY TURKISH FAMILIES

DIANE SUNAR
İstanbul Bilgi University

GÜLER OKMAN FIZŞEK
Boğaziçi University

To describe "the Turkish family" in a few pages is a demanding task, given the population heterogeneity, multiplicity of cultural influences, geographic and ecological variation, and rapid, ongoing social and economic transformations that characterize present-day Turkey. In order to reduce this complexity, our strategy will be to focus to a large extent on salient features of the traditional, rural Turkish family and its cultural setting, and use these as a basis for comparison with emerging characteristics of modern urban families. Before introducing the families, however, a brief sketch of Turkish society and culture will be helpful.

BASIC HISTORICAL AND DEMOGRAPHIC INFORMATION

Geography and History

Turkey is a unique country in many respects. Geographically, it spans two continents (Europe and Asia), and its 800,000 square kilometers encompass a wide variety of ecologies (mountain, plateau, plain, and seacoast; rainy, moderate, and arid; cold, hot, and temperate). Historically the land has been host to a multitude of cultures (e.g., Hittite, Greek, Roman, Byzantine, Seljuk, and Ottoman), which have blended to produce today's sociocultural mix.

With the overthrow of the Ottoman Sultan and the Islamic Caliphate, the Republic of Turkey was established in 1923 as a secular state with a parliamentary government, and it continues to be the only predominantly Muslim country with a fully secular system of government and administration. Despite some economic and political turmoil at various points, the republican reforms have proved durable, and Turkey has entered the twenty-first century as an active candidate for admission to the European Union.

Ethnic Composition and Language

Since ancient times, Turkey has been a crossroads and a bridge between the East and the West, and its social and cultural mosaic still reflects this characteristic. The population of Turkey is heavily dominated by ethnic Turks, but a number of other groups are represented, notably Kurds, Armenians, Greeks, Sephardic Jews, Circassians, Gypsies (Roma), Laz, Syriacs, and others. Except for Kurds, who are estimated to constitute up to about 20 percent of the population, these minority groups are quite small. Other than the Jews and the Christian groups (Greeks, Armenians, and Syriacs), which altogether account for about 2 percent of the population, all other groups are Muslim. Two major divisions of Islam, Sunni and Alevi, are represented, with the Sunni being more numerous. The official language of the nation is Turkish, but various languages such as Kurdish, Ladino, Armenian, Greek, and the Laz language are spoken within minority communities.

Social Change

Turkish society is being rapidly transformed from a traditional, rural, agricultural, patriarchal society to an increasingly modern, urban, industrial, egalitarian one. Until recently, much of the variation has been masked by the prevailing ethos of a traditional, rural, agricultural society as well as by a highly nationalistic state ideology. However, the figures on urbanization tell a dramatic story of change. From the founding of the Republic in 1923 to 1950, the proportion of the population living in urban areas grew only slightly, from 13 to 19 percent; but by the year 2000, not only had the population grown to over 65 million, but nearly 70 percent had become urban (State Institute of Statistics, 1991, 2001). A very large proportion of the "urban" population consists, of course, of recent migrants from rural areas, who tend to be concentrated in poor-quality housing on the periphery of the city. This huge demographic shift has taken place in concert with industrialization, the mechanization of agriculture, and the construction of highways and railways linking all parts of the country, as well as electrification of even remote rural areas and the introduction of mass media and telecommunication systems.

In terms of political and social change, the constitution mandates secular, egalitarian democracy. Women have had the right to vote in national elections since 1934. Eight years of elementary education are legally required, and further education is encouraged by the state.

However, not all areas of social functioning have changed equally rapidly; cultural values, norms, and attitudes lag behind economics and even actual practices. Nowhere is this more evident than in the case of interpersonal relations in general, and gender and family relations in particular. In this context the culture can still be characterized as traditional, authoritarian, and patriarchal.

Age Distribution

The Turkish population is very young, with about two-thirds under the age of 35 and about half under 25. This age structure has resulted from a time lag between the introduction of public health measures and a lowering of birth rates. Improvements in hygiene, nutrition, and medical care have greatly lowered infant mortality, to about 35 per 1,000 live births, and raised average life expectancy to about 69 years. The estimated fertility rate for the year 2000 was about 2.3 (State Institute of Statistics, 2001). With such a youthful population, growth is expected to continue at a high rate for another 20 years or so, despite falling birth rates.

Marriage and Divorce

Over 95 percent of both men and women marry, with a very large proportion of marriages taking place near the mean age of first marriage (about 22 for women, 25 for men) (State Institute of Statistics, 1995). It should be noted that these figures for age of marriage are based on registered civil marriages, which tend to be concentrated in urban areas; ages are likely to be lower for those who marry in unregistered religious ceremonies, particularly for females.

Although figures regarding divorce are problematic, census figures from Istanbul, where divorce could be expected to be more common than elsewhere in Turkey, indicate that less than 2 percent of the population is divorced. Levine (1982) has shown that the sectors with the highest rates of divorce are the barely literate, semiskilled, urban poor, and that increases in the divorce rate are linked with periods of expansion of the economy, increased availability of housing, and decreases in the inflation rate. Thus, the prevalence of divorce (or lack of it) probably depends more on opportunities for economic independence, especially for women, than on marital happiness or unhappiness. It should be pointed out that remarriage is not viewed in the same light for men and women. While a divorced woman is stigmatized, this is not the case for men; and remarriage is an accepted and common practice for divorced men (Özbay, 1989). This is reflected in the fact that more than twice as many women as men are shown as "divorced" in the most recent census report. Acceptance of divorced women appears to be greater among the educated urban elites, who constitute too small a segment of the population to have much effect on overall patterns.

Most households are nuclear in structure, consisting of parents and their dependent children. However, the extended (three-generation) family household represents a cultural ideal, and many families experience a "transitional extended family" phase in the first few years following the marriage of a son (Timur, 1972). Regardless of household composition, however, the Turkish family is often "functionally extended," with a great deal of mutual support and contact among close relatives, who also tend to live as near as possible to one another (Kağitçibaşi, 1982; Kandiyoti, 1974).

Maternal Employment

According to the census figures, just over a quarter of Turkish married women are gainfully employed. However, this should be seen in the context of women's unpaid family work: according to the United Nations Human Development Report of 2001, fully 65 percent of rural Turkish women (married and unmarried) work in agriculture. Taken together, these figures indicate that only a minority of women are full-time housewives, whether or not they are paid for their labor outside the home.

Depending on the social class of the woman and her family, employment can mean very different things in terms of its impact on the woman's status within the family. While highly educated urban women who work in the professions garner high status both inside the family and in the society at large (Kağitçibaşi, 1986; Kağitçibaşi & Sunar, 1992), the situation is more mixed for women of lower social status. Citing a 1973 countrywide survey, which found that the majority of employed married women of childbearing age were not happy about working outside the home, Özbay (1982) states that for the woman, whether or not she works is a sign of her husband's level of affluence, and being able to stay at home is a reflection of higher status. Kuyaş (1982) and Bolak (1997, 2002) have shown that lower-class women's economic contributions to their households may not result in higher power or status for them in the family. This is not surprising, considering that most low-socioeconomic-status women are undereducated, work at menial and poorly paid jobs, and gain no prestige by working, while their husbands lose prestige by not being the sole support of their families. Unpaid family farm labor, of course, makes even less of a contribution to a woman's status within her family.

These negative aspects of employment are compounded by the general unavailability of childcare. While workplaces employing 200 or more women are required by law to provide facilities for the care of workers' infant and preschool children, most working women must rely on the help of relatives, neighbors, or older children in the family for care of their children while they are at work (Bekman, 1993).

A final drawback seems to be in the area of role conflict. There is no decrease in the traditional domestic expectations of women because of employment, regardless of the status of the job (Erkut, 1982; Özkalp, 1989). Consequently, the attempt to balance home and workplace responsibilities may lead to reduced standards of professional performance (Acar, 1989). The fact that fully 48.9 percent of academic women, and 29.8 percent of women in high-level academic administrative posts, are single, compared to 38.15 and 3 percent, respectively for men, is an index of this conflict.

Attitudes regarding maternal employment appear to be changing along with increases in women's education and expanding employment opportunities for women. A nationwide survey (Ergüder, Kalaycioğlu, & Esmer, 1991) revealed more ambivalence on this topic than the earlier studies cited above. While a large majority of respondents saw the woman's primary responsibilities as her home and children, both women and men endorsed the claims that the road to emancipation for a woman is through employment, and that a working mother can be as nurturing as a nonworking mother. Furthermore, the idea that women should contribute to family income was also endorsed.

RELIGIOUS AND OTHER SOCIOCULTURAL BELIEFS THAT MAY INFLUENCE FAMILY PRACTICES

Islam

As noted above, the overwhelming majority of Turks are Muslim, so the main religious influence is that of Islam. The primacy of the husband and father in the family (to be discussed below) is supported by Islamic teaching. Although Turkish law forbids multiple marriages, Islam has traditionally looked favorably on men taking more than one wife if they can afford to support them, as a means of ensuring that

all women benefit from the safeguards of marriage; many Turkish men in rural sectors of the population carry on this religiously permitted tradition, generally marrying one wife legally or at least through formal religious ceremonies, and later acquiring one or more other wives either through religious ceremonies or by informal agreement. The second wife may join the first household, or in some cases she may live in a separate household. Children from these unions are regarded by traditional communities as legitimate, whether or not the marriage is legally registered.

Islamic teaching specifically appoints the husband/father as the family disciplinarian. Despite other interpretations by urban religious scholars, at the level of folk religion these teachings are often interpreted as approval for physical punishment meted out to "disobedient" wives (and children). There is currently a very active movement among intellectuals and in the media to expose the problem of domestic violence and to call into question the idea that it is justified by religious teaching.

Honor

The dominant value of the traditional social system is *namus,* or honor, which is maintained in large part by the men in the family being responsible for the sexual behavior (chastity) of the women (Fişek, 1993; Kağitçibaşi & Sunar, 1992; Meeker, 1976; Sunar & Aral, 1999). Kandiyoti (1987) has suggested that this is partly based on the Muslim view of women as highly sexual creatures who would lead men astray if they were not kept separate. However, as Peristiany (1965), Ortaylı (2001), Baştuğ (2002), and others have pointed out, honor—far from being a feature unique to Muslim societies—is a value common to most southern European and Mediterranean cultures. While the power of honor as a value has declined with industrialization and urbanization, throughout the region it maintains a strong hold on family relationships and relationships between the sexes, particularly in rural areas (Baştuğ, 2002).

Under the honor code, women are assumed to be under the surveillance and protection of their husbands or male kin; any suggestion of illegitimate sexual contact with any man other than a woman's husband leads to loss of the protectors' honor. The maintenance or loss of honor is a social affair more than a matter of personal sin or virtue (Meeker, 1976). This communal nature of honor reinforces the close ties binding the individual, family, kin, and community, and lost honor can only be restored through actions (sometimes violent) that are recognized by the community (Meeker, 1976; Özgür & Sunar, 1982). It is clear that the honor system is one that is profoundly subordinating of women, albeit in the name of their protection, and maintenance of family honor requires considerable restriction of female behavior. Underlying the honor system is a broader understanding that tradition, family, and authority are more important than individual happiness.

Urban, educated middle-class and elite groups constitute an important exception to the foregoing description of the honor system. Among educated urban youth, male–female encounters are much less closely controlled than in other sectors of the population, and Western-style dating is common. Relative autonomy is recognized by young people in the management of their affairs, including their marriage decisions. The importance of virginity is openly questioned in the media, and cohabitation without marriage is occasionally seen. Many educated women pursue careers and achieve economic independence, reducing the importance of marriage and easing the stigma of divorce. In other words, although traditional values have not disappeared in the urban setting they have been heavily moderated by a new emphasis on love, personal fulfillment, independence, and happiness. These values in turn may be expected to exert considerable influence on urban marriage and family.

Macho Ideology and Sex-Role Stereotypes

Traditional Turkish culture idealizes masculinity, equating it with activity, power, courage, and competence; likewise it denigrates femininity, equating it with passivity, weakness, cowardice, and inadequacy (Gürbüz, 1985; Yalvaç, 1986). Men prize their manliness and guard themselves against showing any

sign of feminine weakness; a man must be strong, sexually potent, vigilant, quick and brave in response to threat or danger. In such a cultural setting, sex-role stereotypes take on special importance.

However, sex-role stereotypes in Turkish culture differ in some important and surprising respects from those found in Western societies. Generally, Western investigators have suggested that "masculine" and "feminine" differ primarily with regard to the concepts of "instrumental" and "expressive," with the male sex-role calling for instrumental orientation and behavior, and the female sex role calling for expressive orientation and behavior (see, among others, Bem, 1974; Best, Williams, & Briggs, 1980). Only weak evidence for the instrumental-versus-expressive dimension has been found in studies of sex-role stereotypes in Turkey. Following the suggestion of Bem (1974) and others on the concept of androgyny, that instrumentality and expressiveness may be independent dimensions, Gürbüz (1985) showed that the instrumentality dimension, including concepts such as active/passive and dominant/subordinate, accounts for most of the content of sex-role characteristics endorsed by Turkish respondents, a result that was partially supported by an earlier investigation by Sunar (1982).

The most striking findings of the Gürbüz study were that both male and female Turkish respondents regarded a number of expressive characteristics as being equally descriptive of and equally desirable for the two sexes, while some instrumental characteristics were seen as undesirable for both sexes although dependency was likewise seen as desirable for both sexes. Thus, the Turkish child is socialized into a view of sex typing that is rather different from that to which the Western child is exposed.

Individualism–Collectivism

Not only does the honor tradition underwrite male dominance, it also contributes to the closely knit relationships of the traditional family: honor belongs to individuals, not as individuals but as members of families. Thus each person is dependent on the behavior of all the rest of the family for his or her status as an honorable member of the community.

This mutual interdependence within the traditional Turkish family suggests that Turkish culture should be classified as "collectivistic" (as defined by, e.g., Hofstede, 1980; Triandis, Bontempo, Villareal, Asai, & Lucca, 1988). Collectivistic cultures, as compared to individualistic cultures, are marked by subordination of the interests of the individual to the interests of the group (usually the family). Group loyalty is strong, and concern for intragroup harmony is paramount. Individual behavior tends to be controlled more by group surveillance than by private conscience, and the individual conceptualizes the self more in terms of relationships than of personal characteristics. (For a fuller description of characteristics of collectivistic societies, see Markus & Kitayama, 1991; Triandis, 1990.) Hofstede's (1980) study rated Turkey as a collectivistic culture, and Kağitçibaşi (1985, 1996) has repeatedly described Turkish culture as a "culture of relatedness." On the other hand, a number of recent studies (Anamur, 1998; Göregenli, 1995; Haskuka, 2001) have found urban Turkish respondents to be neither strongly collectivistic nor individualistic. Once again, the traditional rural culture must be contrasted with the modern urban culture.

Kağitçibaşi (1990, 1996) has proposed a model of the changes seen in this transition. She portrays the modern urban Turkish family as emotionally (but not economically) interdependent, and predicts "a *combination,* or *coexistence,* of individual and group (family) loyalties" (Kağitçibaşi, 1996, p. 89), suggesting that the new childrearing practices will produce an "autonomous-relational" rather than an independent or interdependent self in the child.

MARITAL, CHILDCARE, AND HOUSEHOLD ROLES

Marriage and Property

Marriage in Turkey has traditionally been very much a matter of property exchange and conservation. In effect, it is an economic transaction between two families more than an individual decision by two autonomous persons, a pattern that leads to a preference for arranged marriages, and marriages among

relatives (Fişek, 1982, 1993; Kağitçibaşi, 1982). Practices differ from one part of the country to another, but the most prevalent customs involve a bride price paid to the bride's family, or alternatively the provision to the young couple of the necessities of an independent household by the groom's family. It is interesting that religious law stipulates that an amount of money or other goods (*mehr* or *mihir*) must be given by the groom's family for the exclusive use of the bride, to protect her in case of need (Duben & Behar, 1991), but this requirement is very often overlooked because it does not fit with patriarchal, familial custom. The tradition of marriage between children of brothers, found in some parts of the country, clearly has its roots in the desire to keep property within the family.

In urban sectors the trend is very much toward "romantic" marriages based on mutual attraction and consent, especially as the level of education of the potential spouses increases (Hortaçsu, 1995; İmamoğlu, 1991). However, families remain highly influential in most marriage decisions. Because of the property exchanges involved, families typically attempt to optimize their outcomes, with the result that—although exceptions are fairly common—most marriages are essentially homogeneous with regard to social class (cf. Hortaçsu, 1995).

Family Hierarchies and Boundaries

Relationships in the family are marked not only by the closeness discussed above, but also by a clear hierarchical organization. Along with the generational hierarchy that can be observed almost universally, there is also a strong gender hierarchy: male superiority is the norm, and women are regarded as lower in value, prestige, and power than men (Fişek, 1982, 1993; Kağitçibaşi, 1982; Kandiyoti, 1988; Kiray, 1976; Sunar, 2002). It is fair to say that, along with generational hierarchy, patriarchy or gender hierarchy is a basic structural feature of the Turkish family, and by extension, Turkish society (Fişek, 1991, 1993, 1995).

The patterns depicted above are illustrated in Fişek's (1991) observational study of family interaction. She found that family hierarchy over generations, expressed in the strength of control and nurturance on the part of the parents, was pronounced regardless of the educational or clinical status of the family, maternal employment, or family size. In Fişek's study, gender hierarchy effects between the parents were subtle, indicating that while the mother's interactions with her children were characterized by control more than the father's, the father maintained his superiority by interacting more with her than with the children (Fişek, 1995).

Status or power relations between spouses have consequences for other aspects of family life, notably fertility. Studies of urban families show that male dominance and traditional female roles are associated with higher levels of fertility, whereas egalitarian intrafamily relations, with increased communication and role sharing between spouses and decreased male decision making, are related to lower levels (Ataca, Sunar, & Kağitçibaşi, 1996; Kağitçibaşi, 1982). Ataca and Sunar (1999) showed that urban couples who had larger numbers of children tended to be characterized by husband domination in decision making, relatively less marital communication and role sharing, and higher feminine identification of the wife.

In Fişek's (1991) study, proximity or interpersonal interconnectedness, expressed in the level of sharing and permeability of personal boundaries, was relatively high but varied depending on demographic variables. The finding of greatest closeness in high-socioeconomic-status, mother-working families is consistent with other findings indicating that modern, educated Turkish couples enjoy a more egalitarian, companionable relationship than their more traditional counterparts (Çanakçi, 1992; Fişek, 1993, 1995; Kağitçibaşi, 1986). However, more equality in decision making is beginning to be reported among the working classes (Fişek, 2000).

Other studies have produced congruent results. Many fathers are affectionate and playful with their infants and small children, but as the children grow, themes of authority and respect begin to dominate the relationship. Open displays of anger, toward either the father or other authority figures such as teachers, are not tolerated (Sever, 1985; Sunar, 1994, 2002). By the time a child reaches adolescence, there

is usually considerable distance from the father in terms of communication. Recent research shows that, at least among urban youth, adolescents are much more likely to report feeling emotionally close to their mothers than to their fathers (Sever, 1985; Sunar, 2002), and that they are more likely to communicate with their mothers than with their fathers (Hortaçsu, 1989).

Fişek's (1991) study suggests that differences in closeness to mother and father are more complicated than a simple preference for one parent over the other. In her study, information about self and decisions were shared to a larger extent in father–child pairs, while mother–child pairs had more emotional sharing and touching, suggesting that proximity tends to be instrumental for fathers and expressive for mothers.

These and other studies may indicate that, compared with Western family patterns, Turkish families are less articulated in terms of the personal boundaries of each individual family member (Fişek, 1982; Levi, 1994). These studies suggest that a level of intimacy and interdependence that would be perceived in some other societies as "enmeshment," to use the terminology of family-systems theory (Minuchin, 1974), is the norm among Turkish families (as may be the case in many other collectivistic cultures). The important point here is that relatively high proximity is offset by strong hierarchy, thus providing differentiation while still allowing for interconnectedness (Fişek & Schepker, 1997; Sunar, 2002).

Family Conflict

The pattern of strong gender hierarchy and high interpersonal interconnectedness fits well within a traditional social structure, but the weakening of hierarchy due to social change can be accompanied by increased uncertainty and potential for marital conflict (Fişek's, 1982). Modern couples share an idealized notion of equality and a wish for a kind of intimacy and companionship for which they do not have role models or prescriptions. Modern parents are similarly desirous of a less hierarchical relationship with their children, but without a similar lessening of proximity or interconnectedness. Thus they are likely to run into difficulty with the negotiation of autonomy, connection, nurturance, and control, with the final result being couple and family conflict (Fişek & Scherler, 1996). This state of affairs holds for families who have migrated to urban centers, in Turkey or in Europe. The pressures to adapt to a changed context inevitably exert stress on the traditional family structure, and conflict is a frequent outcome (Fişek & Schepker, 1997). It is interesting that a recent study of physical and psychological well-being among the urban working classes indicated that the ability to mix traditional features such as control with concern for the emotional welfare of the family augurs well for both parents and children (Fişek, 2000).

Sex Segregation

Concerns about morality and honor lead to strict sex segregation of unmarried young people, except for the relatively few who continue their education in coeducational institutions. In traditional sectors of the population, sex segregation continues nearly full force even after marriage (Kandiyoti, 1982). Olson (1982) has described a "duofocal" family structure in Turkey, in which wives and husbands live in virtually separate worlds—the wife in a world of female relatives, neighbors, and children, and the husband in a world of male relatives, friends, and workmates. This separation is reinforced by the clear sex typing of traditional male and female work roles. In the traditional context, sex-role differentiation includes a relatively strict division of labor between men and women, based on what is defined as domestic labor versus what is not (Fişek, 1993). This pattern is moderated in families in which the wife is employed, and in better-educated urban families, but a sharp distinction between male and female roles may be considered the norm throughout Turkish society, and the status value of a particular task depends strongly on whether it is "men's work" or "women's work" (Fişek, 1993; Kağıtçibaşi & Sunar, 1992). This pattern of distinctiveness of sex roles and lack of sharing between spouses, coupled with sup-

portive same-sex kinship and friendship networks, extends into the towns and is also common among recent rural migrants to the large cities (Kağıtçibaşi, 1982; Kandiyoti, 1977, 1982).

PARENTING AND SOCIALIZATION

Value of Children

In a nationwide study of the values attributed to children as reasons for having a child (or another child), Kağıtçibaşi (1982, 1990) showed striking rural–urban differences. Rural families valued children in large part for their potential material contributions to the family's welfare, either for their labor potential while still children, or more important, as support for their parents in their old age.

Rural respondents overwhelmingly preferred boys, who were expected to stay with or near the family, as opposed to girls, who were expected to marry out into other villages. In contrast to this material or economic value of children, urban respondents endorsed "psychological" values such as the loving relationship between parent and child, disregarded the issue of old-age security, and showed less boy preference. Later partial replications have shown that urban parents, even those with limited education, consistently stress the psychological value of children and show no clear preference for one sex over the other (Ataca, 1992), and that this trend has increased over three generations (Sunar, 1994, 2002). This shift has been accompanied by many other changes, including more equal treatment of sons and daughters and greater autonomy for children in the family (see, e.g., Ataca, 1992; Ataca & Sunar, 1999; Ataca, Sunar, & Kağıtçibaşi, 1996; Kağıtçibaşi, 1982; Sunar, 1994, 2002). Thus, the way children are perceived and the values attributed to them by parents appear to be functions of social circumstances and social change (cf. Kağıtçibaşi, 1985).

Socialization Goals

As in any culture, the ultimate goal of socialization in Turkish culture is to produce a person who can function effectively in the institutional, normative, and relational structure of the society. In traditional rural Turkish culture, these structures are centered to a large extent in the family. Traditional family relationships, as noted above, are characterized by both material and emotional interdependence within and between generations; strong emphasis on the authority of the parents, especially the father, and obedience by the children; and a clear pattern of male dominance. For this structure to function smoothly, children must feel their gratitude, loyalty, and responsibilities to the family keenly, accepting the parents' authority and subordinating their own interests and ambitions to the needs of others in the family group; they must identify with and accept their sex roles; and they must cultivate a sensitivity to the needs of others in the family. Conflict within the family is minimized, feelings of closeness, gratitude, and loyalty are stressed, and individualistic achievement is not a particular goal.

In contrast to this pattern, educated urban families are oriented toward a rather different set of socialization goals. As material interdependency and with it the instrumental value of the child decrease, the importance of the child's individual success and achievement increases (Kağitçibaşi, 1996; Sunar, 2002). Nevertheless, the traditional emotional intimacy and expectations of closeness and sensitivity to the needs of others persist or are even enhanced in the urban middle class (Kağitçibaşi, 1996; Sunar, 2002).

Let us now examine some of the parent practices that result in effective functioning in the family.

Practices Promoting Interdependence

In the traditional rural family, children are reared in an atmosphere of mutual emotional attachment and loyalty among family members, but with considerable emphasis on control as well. Kağitçibaşi (1972) has argued that control in this arena does not connote lack of love, as might be the case in Western cultures. Rather, control of children is only one aspect of the overall surveillance and control of all members of the family (Kağitçibaşi & Sunar, 1992). Both sons and daughters are brought up with an em-

phasis on obedience, dependency, conformity, and quietness, with autonomy, initiative, activity, and curiosity being discouraged (Fişek, 1993; Kağitçibaşi & Sunar, 1992; Öztürk, 1969). While indulgence prevails over discipline for infants and very young children, the general attitude is one of protectiveness and restriction of autonomous activity (Fişek, 1982). Mothers frequently express their affection openly, either through physical means such as hugging and kissing the child, or verbally, and they encourage the child to reciprocate (Kağitçibaşi, Sunar, & Bekman, 1988). Although children are not encouraged to express anger toward their mothers, such expression is not as rigidly forbidden as in the case of fathers.

Summarizing findings from a study of childrearing practices in three generations of urban middle-class Turkish families, Sunar (2002) points out several areas of continuity between traditional and modern families. All three generations report parental behaviors that support the importance of the family over the individual. Likewise, all three generations report considerable emotional closeness in the family, especially between mothers and children, and also to some extent between fathers and daughters. This atmosphere of closeness is accompanied by low levels of parent–child conflict, flexibility, avoidance of hard-and-fast rules, and avoidance of physical and other coercive punishment.

While there are important areas of continuity, the same study shows that there are important differences from traditional family practices as well. There is a trend toward increased encouragement of emotional expression across generations, although with continued suppression of negative emotions within the family. Also, greater encouragement of independence in the child is observed. While these trends do not appear to have reduced the level of emotional closeness within the family, they do constitute a potential individualizing trend which could influence family relations in future generations.

Parental Disciplinary Practices

In a sample of mostly rural-origin, traditional Turkish mothers, Kağitçibaşi, Sunar, and Bekman (1988,

2001) found that the single characteristic that they most wanted to see in their children was obedience. To this end these mothers reported using primarily "power-assertive" disciplinary techniques (Hoffman, 1994), including physical punishment, scolding, and threats. Other observers concur, reporting that the most commonly used methods are forms of power assertion such as threats of bodily harm, beating, scaring with supernatural agencies, and shaming, with reasoning seldom being used (Öztürk, 1969; Yörükoğlu, 1978).

On the other hand, Sunar (2002) has found that middle-class urban parents rarely use physical punishment and other forms of authoritarian control, but rather rely on a combination of rewards, reasoning, and shaming to shape their children's behavior. LeCompte, Özer, and Özer (1978) and Fişek (1982) have also reported avoidance of corporal punishment and more democratic attitudes toward childrearing among the urban middle and upper classes.

Studies by Helling (1966) and Olson (1982) have pointed out that discipline can be inconsistent in traditional families, and Sunar (1994, 2002) found that clear, well-established rules are rarely found in urban middle-class families. It may be conjectured that this flexible, personalistic approach to discipline fosters the emotional interdependence and sensitivity to other family members' states that distinguish both rural and urban Turkish families.

Gender Role Training

Turkish kinship terminology and linguistic practice combine to make a child's gender, and the gender of others, almost continuously salient. A child is less likely to be addressed by name than as "my son" or "my daughter" by a parent (or indeed by any close adult). A younger child typically addresses an older sibling, not by name, but as "older brother" or "older sister." Other family members (grandparents, aunts, uncles, and relatives by marriage) are all addressed by titles that are specific not only to position but to gender. (It may be noted that these linguistic conventions reflect and maintain the age hierarchy along with the gender hierarchy.)

Education of Male and Female Children

As pointed out above, male and female children are attributed different values by parents. In rural families, boy preference is exceedingly strong, and a number of practices flow from the greater valuation of male offspring. For example, families often attempt, even at considerable sacrifice, to educate their sons, while low expectations regarding the economic utility of female offspring are reflected in reluctance to educate daughters. Official statistics show higher literacy rates and higher levels of educational attainment for males than females at all ages. Even among young people, ages 20–24, whose general educational level is higher than that of the population as a whole, 28 percent of males, but only 19 percent of females, have attained at least a high-school education (Shorter & Angin, 1996). This is not surprising, because education does not have much impact on the life or labor force participation of rural women (Özbay, 1982). Also, because they are expected to marry out, there is no benefit to the family in educating them (Gök, 1995). In effect, most rural youth are directed toward activities that will provide the basis of their adult roles, in a sex-stereotyped fashion.

In comparison to rural sectors, the urban elite groups place very great emphasis on education for both sons and daughters. Children of both sexes are strongly and similarly encouraged to pursue a professional education, even in traditionally male-dominated areas such as engineering (Acar, 1989; Erkut, 1982). Interestingly, comparing the educational attainment of those who continue in regular academic training, women tend to be more persistent and successful than their male peers (Erkut, 1982).

Kağitçibaşi (personal communication) has argued that female university students come from a more privileged background on average than male students, because if economic constraints necessitate making a choice, priority will be given to sons rather than daughters. Other observers have offered a number of explanations for the encouragement of superior educational attainment and professional achievement of elite urban women. Erkut (1982) and Öncü (1981) suggested that the power of elite men is less threatened by female success than that of lower-class males would be; Öncü (1981) and Kağitçibaşi (1986) pointed out that elite women benefit from the supportive domestic services of lower-class uneducated women, which obviates the necessity of sharing the domestic load with their spouses, thereby reducing potential conflict; and Öncü (1981) argued that, because the early days of female professionalism coincided with other democratic reforms, the professions were opened up to women before they could be sex-typed.

Sex-Typed Socialization Practices

Apart from differences in formal education, children of the two sexes are socialized quite differently in preparation for their sex-typed roles (Ataca, 1992), as is found throughout the literature on sex-role socialization in Western countries. Turkish parents permit more independence and aggressiveness in their sons and expect more dependence and obedience in their daughters, with restrictions on girls becoming steadily more marked with increasing age of the child (Ataca, Sunar, & Kağitçibaşi, 1996; Başaran, 1974). Thus boys are allowed more freedom of movement and are expected to be more rambunctious and combative, while girls are expected to be less assertive and more subservient, especially in the rural areas (Fişek, 1993; Yörükoğlu, 1978). These expectations start early (Kağitçibaşi & Sunar, 1992), and empirical findings are consistent with these expectations as early as the preschool years (Kozcu, 1987). From an early age, girls are encouraged to engage in activities and games that can lay the groundwork for their eventual domestic roles, and boys are encouraged to practice male skills (Öztürk, 1969).

The extent to which urban families differ from rural tradition in terms of gender socialization depends to a large extent on social class. Studies of the value of children consistently show that, compared to rural and rural-origin groups, female children are attributed higher value by urban middle-class parents (Ataca, 1992; Kağitçibaşi, 1982; Sunar, 2002). Başaran (1974) also reported a higher proportion of girl preference in her urban group compared to other groups. An interesting finding (Ataca, 1992) is that

old-age security was mentioned by urban respondents as a reason for preferring girls over boys. This unexpected finding indicated that mothers in this urban middle-class sample perceived *daughters,* more than sons, as a prospective help in old age, and when the women did prefer a son it was often to please their husbands.

While socialization differences influence boys' and girls' behaviors and perceptions, socioeconomic status seems to be an important mediator of final outcomes. Differential treatment of sons and daughters is greater in urban lower-class groups as compared with middle-class groups (Pehlivanoğlu, 1999). Tunali (1983) found that a sample of urban, lower middle-class adolescent girls indicated a high degree of affiliative concern, but did not display a similar degree of initiative, and instead focused on external blocks to their needs. Similarly, female adolescents have been found to score lower on ego-strength, to be more anxious and pessimistic, and to be more helpless and nervous (Fişek, 1982; Yanbasti, 1990). Silay (1987) explored urban children's pictorial depictions of interaction in same-sex and mixed-sex dyads. Boys tended to depict more aggression, skill orientation, and competition, indicating a power and dominance emphasis, compared to girls, who were more interpersonally oriented. However, high-socioeconomic-status (SES) children of both sexes were more interpersonally oriented, while lower-SES children were more skill-oriented. Gender and SES interacted in many areas, indicating that the higher the social class level, the less rigid the sex-role stereotypes of children of both sexes. Looking at three generations, Sunar (2002) concluded that, despite continued relative restriction of daughters, a general trend toward increased egalitarian treatment of sons and daughters can be observed in urban families.

FAMILY POLICIES

Family law and policy have traditionally been conservative and patriarchal. The family is legally considered to be the foundation of the society and is under the protection of the law. Until recently, the husband was considered the head of the household and was responsible for being the provider. He also had certain rights over his wife and children, including the right to decide whether his wife could work. Thus gender inequality was structured into the law, albeit along with statements regarding equal rights for all citizens.

People from many sectors of the society, especially women, certain nongovernmental organizations, and the decade-old directorate established under the auspices of the prime ministry to further the interests of women, have been working to change many such policies, with final success in the last year or so. Among the most important changes affecting women's family status are new laws stipulating that the husband is no longer the head of the household and that the wife can use her maiden name upon marriage. In addition, there is a new law that recognizes intrafamily violence as a problem and specifies sanctions against it. Turkey is a signatory to the 1995 Beijing Declaration on the Rights of Women and has set up a number of projects to improve the lot of women and, by implication, families. The National Action Plan of 1996, which covers areas as diverse as health, education, economics, and decision-making power as they involve women and girl children, is starting to have radical impact on the way family life is construed by the state.

The latest development is a thoroughly updated civil code that went into effect at the beginning of 2002. The new code brings new provisions regarding property division in the event of divorce and recognizes the value of housewives' unpaid labor as well as protecting the rights of working women. Ear- lier laws guaranteeing that males and females have equal rights of inheritance, and protecting the right of a spouse to continue to use the family home in case of death of the other spouse, have been preserved. While legal innovation does not bring about rapid social change, taken together these developments promise to bring about significant changes in the politics of family life over time.

SYNOPSIS

Just as it is a bridge connecting East and West geographically, Turkey harbors elements of Eastern and Western cultural features in its social fabric. The Turkish family is a microcosm of the heterogeneity that characterizes this society, so that there are a number of Turkish family prototypes. While it may be safely stated that overall its features are still largely traditional, at the same time highly modern or Western features coexist with the traditional. It seems that a gradually emerging synthesis will combine those traditional practices to which the populace is strongly wedded (e.g., high interconnectedness) with new patterns that fulfill the demands of a changing world (e.g., more individual autonomy). Thus the complexity and heterogeneity we see today are likely to continue. The social-structural parameters that seem to underlie this complexity have to do with urban–rural differences and differences in social class, especially as determined by education. A thorough exploration of the impact of these parameters will help significantly in understanding the varieties of Turkish family life.

REFERENCES

Acar, F. (1989). *Women's participation in academic science careers: Turkey in 1989.* Paper presented at the meeting of the UNESCO-Vienna Center joint project "Women's Participation in Positions of Responsibility in Careers of Science and Technology," Lisbon, Portugal.

Anamur, Z. (1998). *Individualism-collectivism, self-concept and sources of self-esteem.* Unpublished master's thesis, Boğaziçi University, Istanbul.

Ataca, B. (1992). *An investigation of variance infertility due to sex-related differentiation in child rearing practices.* Unpublished master's thesis, Boğaziçi University, Istanbul, Turkey.

Ataca, B., & Sunar, D. (1999). Continuity and change in Turkish urban family life. *Psychology and Developing Societies, 11,* 77–90.

Ataca, B., Sunar, D., & Kağitçibaşi, Ç. (1996). Variance in fertility due to sex-related differentiation in childrearing practices. In H. Grad, A. Blanco, & J. Georgas (Eds.), *Key issues in cross-cultural psychology* (pp. 331–343). Lisse: Swets & Zeitlinger.

Başaran, F. (1974). *Psychosocial development: A study on 7–11 year old children.* Ankara: Ankara University Press (in Turkish).

Baştuğ, S. (2002). Household and family in Turkey: An historical perspective. In E. Özdalga & R. Liljestrom (Eds.), *Autonomy and dependence in family: Turkey and Sweden in critical perspective* (pp. 99–115). Istanbul: Swedish Research Institute.

Bekman, S. (1993). The preschool education system in Turkey revisited. *OMEP International Journal of Early Childhood, 25,* 13–19.

Bem, S. L. (1974). The measurement of psychological androgyny. *Journal of Consulting and Clinical Psychology, 42,* 155–162.

Best, D. L., Williams, J. E., & Briggs, S. R. (1980). A further analysis of the affective meanings associated with male and female sex-trait stereotypes. *Sex Roles, 6,* 735–746.

Bolak, H. C. (1997). When wives are major providers: Culture, gender, and family work. *Gender and Society, 11*(4), 409–433.

Bolak, H. C. (2002). Family work in working class households in Turkey. In E. Özdalga & R. Liljestrom (Eds.), *Autonomy and dependence in family: Turkey and Sweden in critical perspective* (pp. 239–262). Istanbul: Swedish Research Institute.

Çanakçi, Ö. (1992). *The psychological well being and marital satisfaction of involuntarily childless women in Turkey.* Unpublished master's thesis, Boğaziçi University, Istanbul.

Duben, A., & Behar, C. (1991). *Istanbul households: Marriage, family and fertility, 1880–1940.* Cambridge, UK: Cambridge University Press.

Ergüder, Ü., Kağitçibaşi, E., & Esmer, Y. (1991). *The values of Turkish society.* Istanbul: TUSIAD Publications.

Erkut, S. (1982). Dualism in values toward education of Turkish women. In Ç. Kağitçibaşi, (Ed.), *Sex roles, family and community in Turkey* (pp. 121–132). Bloomington: Indiana University Press.

Fişek, G. O. (1982). Psychopathology and the Turkish family: A family systems theory analysis. In Ç. Kağitçibaşi, (Ed.), *Sex roles, family and community in Turkey* (pp. 295–322). Bloomington: Indiana University Press.

Fişek, G. O. (1991). A cross-cultural examination of proximity and hierarchy as dimensions of family structure. *Family Process, 30,* 121–133.

Fişek, G. O. (1993). Turkey. In L. L. Adler (Ed.), *International handbook of gender roles* (pp. 438–451). Westport, CT: Greenwood.

Fişek, G. O. (1995). Gender hierarchy: Is it a useful concept in describing family structure? In J. van Lawick & M. Sanders (Eds.), *Family, gender and beyond* (pp. 63–72). Heemstede, The Netherlands: LS Books.

Fişek, G. O. (2000). *Child health and family process in the Turkish urban context: Final project report.* Istanbul: Boğaziçi University.

Fişek, G. O., & Schepker, R. (1997). Kontext-Bewusstsein in der transkulturellen Psychotherapie [Contextual awareness in transcultural psychotherapy]. *Familiendynamik, 22*(4), 396–413.

Fişek, G. O., & Scherler, H. R. (1996). Social change and married couples: A therapy approach to extend the limits of gender scripts. *Türk Psikoloji Dergisi, 11*(36), 1–11 (in Turkish).

Gök, F. (1995). Women and education in Turkey. In S. Tekeli (Ed.), *Women in modern Turkish society: A reader* (pp. 131–140). London: Zed Books.

Gürbüz, E. (1985). *A measurement of sex-trait stereotypes.* Unpublished master's thesis, Boğaziçi University, Istanbul.

Göregenli, M. (1995). Individualism-collectivism orientations in the Turkish culture: A preliminary study. *Türk Psikoloji Dergisi, 10,* 1–14 (in Turkish).

Haskuka, M. (2001). *Effects of war and attachment representations on moral reasoning.* Unpublished MA thesis, Istanbul: Boğaziçi University.

Helling, G. A. (1966). *The Turkish village as a social system.* Unpublished monograph. Los Angeles: Occidental College.

Hoffman, M. L. (1994). Discipline and internalization. *Developmental Psychology, 30*(1), 26–28.

Hofstede, G. (1980). *Culture's consequences: International differences in work-related values.* Beverly Hills, CA: Sage.

Hortaçsu, N. (1989). Targets of communication during adolescence. *Journal of Adolescence, 12,* 253–263.

Hortaçsu, N. (1995). Prelude to marriage in Ankara: Educational level, reasons for marriage, feelings for spouse and families. *Bogaziçi Journal, 9,* 185–205.

İmamoğlu, O. (1991). *Changing intra-family roles in a changing world.* Paper presented at the Seminar on the Individual, the Family and the Society in a Changing World, Istanbul.

Kağitçibaşi, Ç. (1972). *The psychological dimensions of social change.* Ankara: Turkish Social Science Association.

Kağitçibaşi, Ç. (1982). *The changing value of children in Turkey* (Publ. No. 60-E). Honolulu: East-West Center.

Kağitçibaşi, Ç. (1985). Culture of separateness-culture of relatedness. In C. Klopp (Ed.), *1984: Vision and reality. Papers in comparative studies* (Vol. 4, pp. 91–99). Columbus: Ohio State University.

Kağitçibaşi, Ç. (1986). Status of women in Turkey: Cross-cultural perspectives. *International Journal of Middle East Studies, 18,* 485–499.

Kağitçibaşi, Ç. (1990). Family and socialization in cross-cultural perspective: A model of change. In F. Berman (Ed.), *Nebraska symposium on motivation, 1989* (pp. 135–200). Lincoln: Nebraska University Press.

Kağitçibaşi, Ç. (1996). *Family and human development across cultures: A view from the other side.* Mahwah, NJ: Erlbaum.

Kağitçibaşi, Ç. & Sunar, D. (1992). Family and socialization in Turkey. In J. P. Roopnarine & D. B. Carter (Eds.), *Parent–child relations in diverse cultural settings: Socialization for instrumental competency.* Annual Advances in Applied Developmental Psychology, (Vol. 5, pp. 75–88). Norwood, NJ: Ablex.

Kağitçibaşi, Ç., Sunar, D., & Bekman, S. (1988). *Comprehensive preschool education project: Final report.* Ottawa: International Development Research Centre.

Kağitçibaşi, Ç., Sunar, D., & Bekman, S. (2001). Long-term effects of early intervention. *Applied Developmental Psychology, 22,* 333–361.

Kandiyoti, D. (1974). Some social psychological dimensions of social change in a Turkish village. *British Journal of Sociology, 15*(1), 47–62.

Kandiyoti, D. (1977). Sex roles and social change: A comparative appraisal of Turkey's women. *Signs: Journal of Women in Culture and Society, 3,* 57–73.

Kandiyoti, D. (1982). Urban change and women's roles in Turkey: An overview and evaluation. In Ç. Kağitçibaşi (Ed.), *Sex roles, family and community in Turkey* (pp. 101–120). Bloomington: Indiana University Press.

Kandiyoti, D. (1987). Emancipated but unliberated? Reflections on the Turkish case. *Feminist Studies, 43*(2), 317–339.

Kandiyoti, D. (1988). Bargaining with patriarchy. *Gender and Society, 2*(3), 274–290.

Kiray, M. (1976). Changing roles of mothers: Changing intra-family relations in a Turkish town. In J. G. Peristiany (Ed.), *Mediterranean family structures* (pp. 261–271). London, UK: Cambridge University Press.

Kozcu, S. (1987). An investigation of aggressive behaviors in preschool children and their mothers' reactions. *Psikoloji Dergisi* [Journal of Psychology], Special issue of the 3rd National Congress of Psychology, *6*(21), 19–22 (in Turkish).

Kuyaş, N. (1982). Female labor and power relations in the urban Turkish family. In Ç. Kağitçibaşi (Ed.), *Sex roles, family and community in Turkey* (pp. 181–206). Bloomington: Indiana University Press.

LeCompte, G., Özer, A., & Özer, S. (1978). Child rearing attitudes of mothers from three socioeconomic levels in Ankara: Adaptation of an instrument. *Psikoloji Dergisi* [Journal of Psychology], *1,* 5–8 (in Turkish).

Levi, H. R. (1994). *The relationship between self and self-objects: A demonstration of Kohut's self psychology outside the clinical setting.* Unpublished doctoral dissertation, Fielding Institute, Santa Barbara, CA.

Levine, N. (1982). Social change and family crisis: The nature of Turkish divorce. In Ç. Kağitçibaşi (Ed.), *Sex roles, family and community in Turkey* (pp. 323–348). Bloomington: Indiana University Press.

Markus, H., & Kitayama, S. (1991). Culture and the self: Implications for cognition, emotion, and motivation. *Psychological Review, 98,* 224–253.

Meeker, M. (1976). Meaning and society in the Near East: Examples from the Black Sea Turks and the Levantine Arabs, Parts I and II. *International Journal of Middle East Studies, 7*(2–3), 243–270, 383–423.

Minuchin, S. (1974). *Families and family therapy.* Cambridge, MA: Harvard University Press.

Olson, E. A. (1982). Duofocal family structure and an alternative model of husband-wife relationship. In Ç. Kağitçibaşi (Ed.), *Sex roles, family and community in Turkey* (pp. 33–72). Bloomington: Indiana University Press.

Öncü, A. (1981). Turkish women in the professions: Why so many? In N. Abadan-Unat (Ed.), *Women in Turkish society* (pp. 271–286). Leiden, The Netherlands: E. J. Brill.

Ortaylı, I. (2001). *The family in Ottoman Society.* Istanbul: Pan Press. (in Turkish)

Özbay, F. (1982). Women's education in rural Turkey. In Ç. Kağitçibaşi (Ed.), *Sex roles, family and community in Turkey* (pp. 133–150). Bloomington: Indiana University Press.

Özbay, F. (1989). *Family and household structure in Turkey: Past, present, and future.* Paper presented at the conference on "The Changing Family in the Middle East," Amman, Jordan.

Özgür, S., & Sunar, D. (1982). Social psychological patterns of homicide in Turkey: A comparison of male and female convicted murderers. In Ç. Kağıtçıbaşı (Ed.), *Sex roles, family and community in Turkey* (pp. 349–382). Bloomington: Indiana University Press.

Özkalp, E. (1989). *Employment reasons and problems of female public sector employees.* Paper presented at the 2nd National Congress of the Social Sciences, Ankara, Turkey.

Öztürk, M. O. (1969). *Inhibition of autonomy and initiative in the Anatolian personality.* Paper presented at the 5th National Congress of Neuropsychiatry, Ankara (in Turkish).

Peristiany, J. G. (Ed.). (1965). *Honour and shame: The values of Mediterranean society.* London: Weidenfeld & Nicolson.

Pehlivanoğlu, P. (1998). *Differences in Turkish parenting practices due to socioeconomic status and sex of the child.* Unpublished MA thesis, Istanbul: Boğaziçi University.

Sever, L. (1985). *Change in women's perceptions of parental child rearing practices, attitudes and beliefs in the context of social change in Turkey: A three generation comparison.* Unpublished master's thesis, Boğaziçi University, Istanbul.

Shorter, F. C., & Angin, Z. (1996). *Negotiating reproduction, gender and love during the fertility decline in Turkey.* Cairo: Population Council.

Silay, S. (1987). *Nature of boys' and girls' perceptions of interactions in same, opposite and mixed sex dyads.* Unpublished master's thesis, Boğaziçi University, Istanbul.

State Institute of Statistics (1991). *Statistical Indicators, 1923–90.* Ankara: SIS.

State Institute of Statistics (2001). *Women's indicators and statistics.* www.die.gov.tr.

Sunar, D. (1982). Female stereotypes in the U.S. and Turkey: An application of functional theory to perceptions in power relations. *Journal of Cross-Cultural Psychology, 13*(4), 445–460.

Sunar, D. (1994). *Changes in child rearing practices and their effect on self-esteem in three generations of Turkish families.* Poster presented at American Psychological Association Annual Convention, August 12–16, Los Angeles, California.

Sunar, D. (2002). Change and continuity in the Turkish middle class family. In E. Özdalga & R. Liljestrom (Eds.), *Autonomy and dependence in family: Turkey and Sweden in critical perspective* (pp. 217–238). Istanbul: Swedish Research Institute.

Sunar, D., & Aral, S. O. (1999). Social psychological factors affecting the spread and prevention of AIDS and other STDs in Turkey. *Bogaziçi Journal: Review of Social, Economic and Administrative Studies,* Special Issue: Symposium on Social, Economic and Cultural Aspects of AIDS in Turkey, *13*(1), 63–80.

Timur, S. (1972). *Family structure in Turkey.* Ankara: Hacettepe University Press.

Triandis, H. C. (1990). Cross-cultural studies of individualism and collectivism. In F. Berman (Ed.), *Nebraska symposium on motivation, 1989* (pp. 41–133). Lincoln: Nebraska University Press.

Triandis, H. C., Bontempo, R., Villareal, M. J., Asai, M., & Lucca, N. (1988). Individualism and collectivism: Cross-cultural perspectives on self-ingroup relationships. *Journal of Personality and Social Psychology, 54,* 323–338.

Tunali, B. (1983). *An investigation on need affiliation and its relation to family cohesion in Turkish adolescents.* Unpublished master's thesis, Boğaziçi University, Istanbul.

Yalvaç, F. (1986). *Some cultural correlates of aggression as a response to frustration.* Unpublished master's thesis, Boğaziçi University, Istanbul.

Yanbasti, G. (1990). Self evaluation of mental health by male and female students: A comparison. *Psikoloji Dergisi,* Special issue of the 5th National Congress of Psychology, *8,* 57–63 (in Turkish).

Yörükoğlu, A. (1978). *Child mental health.* Ankara: Türkiye İşBankasi Press (in Turkish).

CHAPTER 11

FAMILISM, POSTMODERNITY, AND THE STATE
THE CASE OF ISRAEL

SYLVIE FOGIEL-BIJAOUI
Academic College of Management and Beit-Berl Academic College

In Israel, as in other postindustrial societies, social institutions, including the family, are undergoing a process of individualization. The family is becoming a private concern, and state involvement in matters of marriage, divorce, and fertility is being reduced to mediating between the individual and the society and to giving a legal seal to the individual's preferences and decisions. The perception is that adults, both men and women, are autonomous individuals, entitled to shape their own biography in the private and public spheres. As a result, the rate of marriage is declining, the divorce rate rising, total fertility rates are decreasing, while the percentage of out-of-wedlock births is growing.

These developments have enabled various and sundry family structures to come into being, including "two-career families," "second families" (following divorce or separation), "single-parent families," and "single-sex families." Members of these families live together under the same roof or separately; they are married or cohabit without marriage; they married in accord with religious law and/or signed a civil contract. The number of children in these families is generally small, and parent–child relations tend to be democratic. These are "the new families" or "postmodern families" (Beck & Beck-Gernsheim, 1995; Chafetz & Hagan, 1996; de Singly, 2000; Dumon, 1995; Illouz, 1997; Stacey, 1990; Thorne & Yalom, 1992; Trost, 1996).

In Israel today, the same postindustrial processes are taking place. Yet along with them, one sees the amazing continuation of familism: familism continues to characterize Israeli society, and for the Israelis, "the family" continues to play a crucial role, at the individual as well as at the collective level (Fogiel-Bijaoui, 1999; Izraeli, 1999; Kulik, 2000; Peres & Katz, 1980; Shemgar-Handelman & Bar-Yossef, 1991).

As a cultural code, familism takes for granted an unequal gender division of labor. The woman is constructed as a mother and wife, whose primary obligations are to bear children and take care of her home and family. Her paid work is accepted, if at all, as a secondary contribution to the family livelihood. Familism also entails the construction of marriage as the only framework for the birth of legitimate children and the construction of divorce as an aberration of the norm. As a cultural code, it thus dictates to the individual his or her proper way of life: the duty of heterosexual marriage, rejection of divorce, bringing (many) legitimate children into the world, prohibition of out-of-wedlock births, and, as stated above, an unequal and gendered division of labor. This code is exemplified both by the modern nuclear family that characterizes industrial society (with a father, who supports the family, a mother, who is a housewife, and children all in a single household) and by the traditional family (a multigenerational structure, consisting of the father, his children and their wives, and unwed daughters living together under the same roof and managing a joint household). The aim of this chapter is to explain the paradoxical continuation of the centrality of familism in Israeli society, despite the processes of individualization the society is undergoing and despite its affinity for Western culture.

To this end, the first section presents data that point to the continued existence of familism in Israeli society in comparison to other postindustrial societies. The second section argues that familism is a marker of Israeli society, because it rests on the institutionalization of religious laws as far as marital status is concerned. Actually, among each ethnoreligious group,[1] religious laws are generally conceived of as "national assets," functioning as borderlines between the different ethnoreligious groups and as a basis for their "normative collective memory" and their "normative collective identity." The third section contends that class stratifications and ecological differentiations, which not infrequently overlap with the ethnoreligious dimensions, are also structural mechanisms that strengthen and perpetuate familism, both among the Israeli Jews and among the Israeli Palestinians (Adva Center, 2000; Al-Hadj, 1996; Ram, 1999; Saadi, 1995; Smooha, 1999; Yiftachel, 1999). In other words, I claim that the various dimensions of familism in Israel and its continued cultural dominance in Israeli society are the products of the meeting between the country's institutionalized religious laws and its stratified postindustrial reality.[2] In the conclusion, I deal with the future of "the family" in Israel.

FAMILISM IN ISRAEL: INDIVIDUALIZATION AND ITS LIMITS

According to economic and technological criteria, Israel belongs to the industrial nations. In fact, since 1994 Israel has been a member of the exclusive club of the industrialized nations with the highest revenues (World Bank Report, 1996, pp. 238–239).

One of the features of these countries since the 1960s has been the consistent and significant rise in the level of high education of women and their massive participation in the workforce, especially of married, middle-class women with small children: the constitution of the postindustrial society required a huge, varied, available, and cheap labor force, and women definitely formed the major reservoir of such labor. More and more women became "working mothers," and this dramatic process became the lever for family change in postindustrial societies (Beck

& Beck-Gernsheim, 1995; Chafetz & Hagan, 1996; de Singly, 2000; Dumon, 1995; Illouz, 1997; Stacey, 1990; Thorne & Yalom, 1992; Trost, 1996).

A similar process took place in Israel, especially after the 1967 Six Day War. Over the years women came to constitute an increasingly marked proportion of those who received academic degrees. For example, in the 1997–1998 academic year, women constituted 57 percent of those who received academic degrees, as opposed to 48 percent in 1987–1988 (Central Bureau of Statistics [C.B.S.], 2000b, p. 5).

In parallel, the rate of women in the labor force (percentage of women in the labor force among women aged 15 and over), which had not exceeded 30 percent until the 1970s, reached 47.3 percent in 1998, so that in that year, women constituted 45 percent of the Israeli labor force. In that year also, 55 percent of all the married women in Israel—that is, more than 70 percent of all the married mothers of children under 15 years old—were in the job market (C.B.S., 2000a, Tables 12.4, 12.5; Izraeli, 1999; Maor, 1997).

As a result of the massive entry of married women/mothers into the labor market, the normative model of the family in Israel—the father provider, mother housewife, living under the same roof with their biological/adopted children—steadily declined (Shemgar-Handelman & Bar-Yossef, 1991). The two-provider family became the prevalent model of the family in Israel (Izraeli, 1999).

Processes of liberalization accompanied these structural changes, on both the institutional and cultural levels. Israel became a more pluralistic society, and it created social mechanisms and institutional arrangements that freed various groups in the civil society from the supervision and control of the parties and the machinery of the state. The individual, his or her rights and wishes, became more central in the public discourse, and greater emphasis was placed on individuals' ability to determine their own destiny. These developments were reflected in legislation, in court rulings, and in what has been termed the Supreme Court's "Constitutional Revolution" (Association for the Citizen's Rights in Israel, 1996; Harel, 2001; Radai, 1999; Shapira, 1977).

It is thus no wonder that between 1985 and the end of the 1990s, the marriage rate declined from 6.9 to 6.7 (1998). The divorce rates rose from 1.2 to 1.7 (1999), and the total fertility rates declined from 3.12 to 2.98, while the percentage of live births to never-married women rose from 1.3 to 2.5 percent (1998) (C.B.S., 1986, Tables C/1, C/2; C.B.S., 2000a, Tables 3.1, 3.12, 3.16). During these same years, the percentage of single-parent families also rose, from 5 percent of all households with children below 17 years old in the middle of the 1980s to 10 percent in 1998 (Geist, 2000, p. 26).

Moreover, beginning in the 1970s, the social construction of childhood in Israel also went through a process of individualization, with children being considered more and more as individuals and as autonomous subjects, with legitimate needs and legitimate wills (Tsionit & Ben Aryeh, 1999).

Consistent with the 1989 United Nations Convention on the Rights of the Children (ratified by Israel in 1991), many laws were (and are) amended or adopted to promote children's human rights, well-being, and protection. One of these laws is the 1989 Law for the Prevention of Child Abuse and for the Protection of Vulnerable People in the Family; this law invites state and welfare interventions in case of physical, mental, or sexual violence; injury or abuse; neglect or negligent treatment; maltreatment or exploitation (Kadman, 1999). In the same vein, in matters of divorce and child custody, the child's human rights, his or her will and needs, have become determinant in Israeli society, instead of the more traditional/religious ways of thought, which constructed the child as his father's property (Layish, 1995; Shamai, 1999).

The educational system itself both reflects and reinforces these trends. More and more children complete high school, and gender gaps are narrowing—though there is still a significant difference in the choice of scholastic tracks between the sexes and serious problems of dropout, especially among Israeli Palestinian boys, with far-reaching implications for future employment and earning potential (Abu-Assbah, 1999; Ayalon, 2000; London-Sapir, 2000, pp. 6–8).

Actually, there is no education gap between Jewish men and women as measured by years of schooling. In 1998, the median number of schooling years was 12.4 for both sexes. The rate of those aged 15 and more who studied 13 years or more was 38 percent for both sexes. Among the Palestinians there is not yet parity, but women's level of education is rising faster than men's and the gaps are closing. In this community, women's median education is 10.4 years, while men's is 11.0 (London-Sapir, 2000, pp. 6–8).

One of the results of this trend is that in Israel's public education system, as far as the (Jewish) secular junior high school is concerned, the "gender play"—the social process through which children as active agents of their world construct gender (Thorne, 1993)—is becoming based more on androgyny and individual qualities than on gendered stereotypes and segregation. In other words, it seems that gender as an organizing principle is becoming less salient in school life, at least at the junior high school level (Klein, 2000).

In addition, it appears that attitudes about family life are also undergoing a process of individualization. For instance, Kulik (2000) has found that (Jewish) adolescents maintain more liberal attitudes than their fathers—but less liberal ones than their mothers—with respect to gender roles in family and society. This reflects a certain shift away from traditional family norms and values.

Nonetheless, and despite the processes of individualization that have been described, a quick glance at Table 11.1 confirms the claim that Israeli society is the most familistic of the postindustrial societies: Israelis "marry a lot," "divorce little," "give birth to many (legitimate) children" and to relatively few children out of wedlock. Even in Japan, which, much like Israel, is considered a postindustrial society with a clear familistic tradition, total fertility rates are 50 percent lower than in Israel.

Also, even a cursory look at Table 11.2, which provides data on three indicators of familism among the ethnoreligious groups in Israeli society, shows that different forms of familism exist among these groups.

Table 11.1   Demographic Indicators in 1996: Comparison between Israel and Other Postindustrial Societies

COUNTRY	DEMOGRAPHIC INDICATORS			
	Marriage Rate[a]	Divorce Rate[b]	Total Fertility Rate[c]	Live Births to Never-Married Women (%)[d]
Israel	6.6	1.6	2.9	2.3 (Jews only)
European Union[e]	5.1	1.8	1.4	24
United States	8.8	4.4	2.04	32
Canada	5.2	2.6	1.62	31
Japan	6.4	1.6	1.44	1 (1994)

[a]Number of marriage certificates issued per 1,000 persons by a recognized official licensing authority.

[b]Number of legal divorce certificates issued per 1,000 persons.

[c]Number of children a woman is expected to bear in her lifetime.

[d]Births to never-married women per 100 live births.

[e]The fifteen countries of the European Union are Austria, Belgium, Britain, Denmark, Finland, France, Germany, Greece, Holland, Ireland, Italy, Luxemburg, Portugal, Spain, and Sweden.

Source: Central Bureau of Statistics, 2000a, Tables 3.1, 3.12, 3.16; *Eurostat Yearbook,* 1998–1999, pp. 84, 86, 88.

Table 11.2 Familism in Israel's Ethoreligious Groups: Demographic Indicators, 1985–1999

	POPULATION	1985[a]	1999
Marriage rate	Total—Israeli	6.9	6.7 (1998)
	Jews	6.7	6.1
	Muslims	8.6	7.9
	Christians	6.2	5.7 (1998)
	Druze	9.5	9.3
Divorce rate	Total—Israeli	1.2	1.7
	Jews	1.3	1.9
	Muslims	0.8	1.1
	Christians	0.2	0.2
	Druze	0.7	0.8
Fertility	Total—Israeli	3.12	2.98 (1998)
	Jews	2.85	2.67 (1998)
	Muslims	5.54	4.76 (1998)
	Christians	2.41	2.62 (1998)
	Druze	5.40	3.10 (1998)

[a]1985: In this year, the first National Union Government instituted the neoliberal economic policy that still characterizes the Israeli economy.

Source: Central Bureau of Statistics, 1986, Tables C.1, C.3; Central Bureau of Statistics, 2000a, Tables 3.1, 3.12.

Among the Jews, there has been a moderate process of individualization of the family institution, and the dimensions of familism have shrunk somewhat in the last 15 years. The situation is quite different among the Palestinian Arabs, citizens of Israel, whether Muslims, Christians, or Druze. Despite slight fluctuations in the various dimensions, Arab society in Israel retains a strong emphasis on familism.

The percentage of births to never-married women is not included in Table 11.2. It appears only in Table 11.1, and only for the Jewish population. This fact is not accidental: among the Muslim, Christian, and Druze citizens of Israel, giving birth out of wedlock is viewed as a violation of family honor, which may be punished by the murder of "the deviant woman" by her father, brother, or, in recent years, husband (Hassan, 1999). As a result, births to never-married women are not reported.

It is also evident from Table 11.2 that familism has different forms and different dimensions among the Palestinian Arabs, citizens of Israel: the Muslims have particularly high marriage and birth rates, the Christians (most of them Catholic) have very low divorce rates, and the Druze have high rates of marriage and low rates of divorce, accompanied, however, by a consistent decline in fertility since the 1970s. They are the only ethnoreligious group in Israel to have seen such a decline (C.B.S., 2000a; Table 3.12).

In addition, the average age at first marriage among Arab women has remained more or less stable since the 1970s, while among the Jews there has been a gradual, moderate rise. In 1998, the average age at first marriage among Christian women was 23.7; among Muslim women, 21.6; among Druze women, 21.2; and among Jewish women, 25.5. Among men, the average age at first marriage in that year was 29.3 for Christians, 26.3 for Muslims, 25.9 for Druze, and 28.5 for Jews. Moreover, the average difference between the mean age of the bride and groom among the Israeli Palestinians has remained more or less stable, while the average difference among the Jews has somewhat decreased over the years (C.B.S., 2000a, Table 3.5).[3]

How can one explain the strength of familism in Israel in comparison to other postindustrial societies? How can one account for the different dimensions of familism among the different ethnoreligious communities?

FAMILISM AS A NATIONAL ASSET

In order to explain the familism that characterizes Israeli society, we must investigate first and foremost the institutional arrangements that govern the society, that is, Israel's family laws. The laws that regulate marriage and divorce in Israel, namely, the Rabbinical Court Law–1953 (Marriage and Divorce) and the Druze Religious Courts Law–1962, take the place of civil law and bestow exclusive authority over personal status (marriage and divorce) on the religious courts of Israel's four ethnoreligious communities. In other words, familism is institutionalized and reproduced by the country's laws (Shalev, 1995a; Radai, 1999).

As Carmel Shalev writes: "The most salient feature of the marriage and divorce laws in the Israeli legal system is the almost total application of religious law to matters of personal status. This means that, excluding certain exceptions, Israeli law does not contain civil mechanisms for marriage and divorce" (Shalev, 1995a, p. 460).[4]

In the next part of this chapter, I analyze the implications these religious laws have for both men and women. Following that, I explain why these laws are conceived of as "national assets" by most of the Israeli Jews and most of the Israeli Palestinians—even though they violate basic human rights.

Religious Laws and Familism[5]

In the world view underlying all the recognized religions in Israel, the man, the husband, is regarded as the pillar of the family and is given authority over his wife and children. The man's power is based on an unequal gender division of labor in the family: the wife belongs to her husband and must obey him. In exchange, the husband is responsible for the physical and economic security of the home, including his wife. The main aim of marriage is to bring legitimate children into the world. Hence, while men are allowed a certain amount of sexual freedom, women are allowed to have sexual relations only with their husband. In this way, religious laws legitimize a double standard, characterized by strictness toward women and leniency toward men, as far as family life is concerned. In addition, there are many restrictions on the right to marry and divorce.

Among Jews, the following categories of people are not allowed to marry.

1. *Illegitimate children (Mamzerim):* These are children born of a relationship between a married woman and a man not her husband. These children are not permitted to marry with a "kosher daughter of Israel," but only with another *Mamzer* or a convert. The status of illegitimacy (*mamzerut*) lasts for ten generations, and is passed on from one generation to the next until the tenth. (When a nonmarried woman

gives birth to a child, the child is not a *Mamzer,* and is legitimate.)

2. *Cohens:* As descendants of the priests of the ancient Temple, they are not allowed to marry a divorcee.

3. *Adulteresses:* These are women who had a relationship with a man other than their husbands while they were married. Such women are sexually forbidden both to their husbands and to the men with whom they had intercourse.

4. *"Agunot":* These are women whose husbands have disappeared, whether through unproven death or otherwise, or whose husbands refuse to grant them a writ of divorce. These women are prohibited from remarrying for fear of adultery and *Mamzerut* (illegitimate children). Men, however, whose wives have disappeared or refuse to grant them a writ of divorce may obtain permission to marry from the rabbinate, though the process is long and cumbersome.

Religious law thus strengthens marriage and prevents divorce, at least for women whose husbands do not agree to it.

The situation is not different in the other religions, and in some cases is even more problematic. Catholics cannot divorce at all. In Islam and in the Druze religion, a woman cannot divorce her husband, though in certain cases she may ask the Qadi (the religious authority) to permit her to do so. In Islam, which is polygamous, a man can easily divorce his wife: in most cases, it is enough for him to tell her "You are divorced" before witnesses, with no need for judicial proceedings, since the Sharyia Court (Muslim Court) will authorize the divorce retroactively. In many cases, the woman is divorced without appropriate compensation; and if she has children, they remain in the custody of her husband's family and she loses them. In the Druze religion, although it is monogamous, the situation is similar: a wife cannot divorce her husband, though a man can divorce his wife with relative ease. Moreover, Druze women may not remarry after being divorced (or after being widowed). In addition, among Muslims in Israel, there are polygamous marriages, cemented in religious ceremonies, which are not reported to the Ministry of Interior. Among Muslim, Druze, and Christian Arabs, girls are sometimes married as children. In many cases, such marriages are arranged by the girl's relatives, without the girl's participation in the decision and without her consent or agreement. Most of these practices, it should be noted, occur in circumvention of Israeli civil laws prohibiting polygamy, child marriage, and one-sided nonjudicial divorce.

Israeli law also discriminates between Jews, Druze, and Christians, on the one hand, and Muslims, on the other. In the event of divorce, Jews, Druze, and to a fair extent also Christians may turn to a civil court with regard to alimony, child support, and the division of assets. That is, they can choose between the religious and civil courts. Women generally hurry to the civil courts, which generally pay more attention to their civil rights and human rights. Men usually prefer the religious courts, which, in accord with religious law, usually give them preferential treatment.

For the Muslims in Israel, however, the only legal authority, even with respect to the practical matters involved in the end of the marriage, is the Shariya Court. Thus Muslim women, citizens of Israel, do not have the freedom of choice that is available to the country's other women, whether Jews, Druze, or Christians (Hassan, 1999; Layish, 1995; N.G.O. Report, 1997; Shifman, 1995b).

Women as a Threat to the Social Order

The religious laws of all the religions institutionalize, to one degree or another, a single central value, modesty (*tzniut*), which consigns women to a lower status by virtue of their being women. Modesty is a value that constructs women as a danger to men and to the social order because of their sexuality. Women must thus suppress all expression of their sexuality and conceal it in the public sphere. Modesty is also a value that applies to men. However, it does not have the same far-reaching implications in the public and private spheres for men as for women.

Modesty as a value is differently interpreted in the various religions, and sometimes in the different streams within each religion. This value is nourished by customs and traditions, most of which are ancient and from different origins. However, whatever the variations, basic similarities exist in the way modesty is socially constructed: *modesty excludes women from the public sphere and institutionalizes the wife's subordination to her husband's authority within her home, where she is obliged to channel her sexuality to the highest aim of helping her husband fulfill the commandment "be fruitful and multiply."*

1. Among Jews, Muslims, and Druze, though not among Christians, modesty entails the separation between men and women not only in the public sphere, but also in the private sphere. In the latter, there are various degrees of separation between "outsider" (meaning unrelated) men and women and even between husband and wife.

For example, Jewish law constructs the menstruating woman as "unclean" and forbids sexual contact and even touch between her and her husband (Niddah, according to Leviticus). These restrictions come on top of the fact that her perceived "uncleanliness" bars her from any participation in the public sphere in synagogue, cemetery, and so on.

2. In all the religions, the ultimate meaning of marriage is the bringing of legitimate children into the world to ensure the biological and cultural continuity of the collective. In this context, virginity constitutes the highest value. Under the best of circumstances, the loss of virginity means the loss of the opportunity to marry—the opportunity to be introduced to a prospective mate, since among a substantial portion of Muslims and Druze and a not insignificant portion of Jews marriages are made through matchmaking. Under less propitious circumstances, her loss of virginity leads the "deviant woman" to be killed by the men in her family, usually her father and brothers, with the cooperation of her mother. We will return to this subject below.

3. Modesty also means that girls and women must cover and conceal their body and head, to one degree or another, by a veil, wig, and/or long dress, so as not to arouse the "evil instinct" in men. Although there is little consensus about the age at which the body must be covered, the means by which it must be covered, or how thoroughly it must be covered, this moral code is found among Jews, Muslims, and Druze, as well as among Christians to a more limited extent. Covering the body and head is important to women as well, because the cover serves as a kind of passport that gives them a certain, though sometimes most limited, "freedom of movement." When her body is covered, a woman may leave her home and move about in the public sphere, to one degree or other.

4. Modesty also means that the woman's sexuality does not exist in and of itself, but only in connection with childbearing. As a result, decisions about contraception, abortion, and so on, are not permitted to the individual (the woman), but are instead precisely coded by religious norms and laws. Among Catholics, contraceptives and abortions, the voluntary cessation of pregnancy, are totally forbidden. Muslims and Druze take a similar approach, though they sometimes apply more liberal interpretations or permit "exceptions," mainly when the pregnancy endangers the mother. Contraceptives are also forbidden among Jews, though different streams of Judaism, even some of the Orthodox streams, allow women to use them under certain circumstances. Jewish women are permitted abortions when the fetus endangers their life.

5. Violation of modesty norms leads to different responses in accord with the context, the persons, and the type of violation. The strongest and most extreme reactions are found among some Muslim, Druze, and Christian groups and refer to the "violation of the family honor." Such a violation can occur as a result of the woman's dress, contact of any sort with "an outsider," loss of virginity, and so on. In such instances, the men of the family are expected to restore the family honor, to show the society that they can enforce proper social order in their household, and to punish—that is, to kill—the "deviant woman/girl."

Every year, between twenty and thirty women—Muslim, Druze, and Christian citizens of Israel—are murdered in Israel for "violating the family honor." Police files (and media reports, when the information reaches the media) refer to these women as "missing," "accident victims," or "suicides." The police and courts in Israel treat such murders with understanding and clemency. Their "liberalism" is prompted by their reluctance to upset the delicate balance between the Arab citizens of Israel and the State's governing bodies, since many—not all—Palestinian Arabs, citizens of Israel, accept and even support "family honor" killings (Hassan, 1991, 1999).

Naturally, the question arises of how such laws and customs exist in a state that is committed to democracy and human rights. These laws infringe upon the human and individual rights of both men and women, though not to the same extent. As Carmel Shalev (1995a, p. 462) reminds us:

> *The right to marry and establish a family is recognized as one of the basic Human Rights in International Law, in several agreed upon treaties. Complementing this recognition is the obligation of the state to protect the family as "the basic unit of society." Every adult—regardless of race, citizenship, or religion—has the right to equality in all that relates to marriage, married life, and divorce.*

Part of the answer is undoubtedly anchored in the delicate balance in Israel between religious laws and the various means of circumventing it. Alongside the Religious Courts, which have exclusive jurisdiction over marriage and divorce as such, Israel has a system of Family Courts that rule in accord with civil law and have jurisdiction in matters relating to property, alimony, custody, and visiting rights. With the exception of Muslims, Israeli citizens can choose between the two courts. Moreover, marriages abroad (e.g., "Cyprus marriages") are recognized. In addition, many laws lend legitimacy to cohabiting couples, both heterosexual and homosexual, and are well anchored in the legal and social system of Israel. This situation makes possible a kind of *modus vivendi* that enables Israel's citizens to live in this legal-institutional framework. Nonetheless, it is still necessary to explain the hegemony of religious laws—the same hegemony that serves as the major mechanism for the institutionalization of familism.

Familism as a Jewish National Asset

Many researchers have analyzed the relation between Jewish religion and Jewish nationhood in the State of Israel (Ben-Rafael, 2001; Kimmerling, 1994; Peled, 1993; Smooha, 2000). According to Kimmerling (1994), one of the most taken-for-granted assumptions among Jews in Israel is the non-separation of religion and nationhood as far as Jewish Israeli identity is concerned: the collective identity, the collective values, the collective symbols, as well as the collective memory, are anchored in the Jewish religion.[6]

As Hervieu-Leger notes, religion plays a major role in the formation of the "normative collective memory" and its transmission and perpetuation over generations: "Religion is an ideological, practical, and symbolic instrument through which the individual and the collective consciousness of belonging to a specific believers descendency is formed, maintained, developed, and controlled" (Hervieu-Leger, 1993, p. 129).

Moreover, according to Shifman (1995a), more than anything else, family laws symbolize for many Israeli Jews the symbiosis religion/nation. For them, whether religious or not, marriage carried out in accord with Jewish law (*Halakha*), is an essential component of the integrity of the Jewish people and of its historical continuity in Israel and the Diaspora. It is also an essential component of the connection between Israel and the Diaspora. This is one of the most taken-for-granted and difficult-to-challenge assumptions among Israeli Jews (see also Ben-Rafael, 2001, pp. 23–95). Moreover, as Durkheim (1995) argues, religion plays a major role in all that relates to the social integration and cohesion of the community. In the eyes of many Jews in Israel, the religious laws play an integrative and unifying role in at least three areas.

1. Religious laws are needed to prevent mixed marriages between Jews and non-Jews both in and outside of Israel. In other words, family laws in Israel delineate the boundaries of the Jewish collective and serve as a dividing line between the Jewish and Arab citizens. For all practical purposes, this demarcation is the desired situation, not only in the eyes of religious Jews but also in those of most Jews who are not religious. In other words, religious laws are instrumentalized on behalf of a national project, which can be defined as preserving the boundaries of the national collective.

2. Out of similar motives, many of the Jewish Israelis accept (Orthodox) religious laws as a means of facilitating the identification of the religious people with the State. Their readiness to do so is accompanied by ambivalence toward the Conservative and Reform streams of Judaism and their family laws (marriage and divorce), which are not recognized in Israel. Although an important proportion of Israeli Jews declare that they support Jewish pluralism, many of them, (self-defined) secular as well as religious, feel that non-Orthodox marriages will lead to a split in the nation (not to a split in the religion!)—and oppose these marriages.

3. The religious and family laws, the core of which is the commandment to "be fruitful and multiply and fill the land," make a substantial normative contribution to the "demographic competition" that exists both overtly and covertly between the Jewish and Palestinian Arabs, citizens of Israel. "The demographic problem," that is, the need to ensure a Jewish majority for the future of Zionism, is raised in many and varied occasions: in the discussion about the Palestinian–Jewish conflict, in the discussion on the civil status of the Arab citizens of Israel; in the discussion on abortion, and so on (Berkovitch, 1999; Shalev, 1995b). As a normative discourse, religious laws create attitudes, values, and behaviors that construct childbirth as a national commandment for the reproduction and numerical bolstering of the nation. It constitutes a major component of what Anson and Meiri (1996) term the "strategy of group survival" (see also Yuval-Davis, 1980, 1997).

It is thus clear that religious laws, and the institutionalization of familism in marriage, divorce, and childbirth, constitute a central component in the crystallization of the Jewish collective at both the symbolic and the demographic levels.

Aside from its religious aspects, familism is a "national asset" in another way as well. In the perpetual state of war in Israel, it reinforces and justifies as self-evident a clear and rigid unequal gender division between the "fighting man" in the public-national sphere and the "protected woman and her children" in the private-personal sphere. This gendered division acts as an organizing principle that is interwoven, both overtly and covertly, in all areas of life: in the language, in images and myths, in norms and customs, and in the legal system. As a result, the "fighting" (Jewish) man is situated at the center of the society, while the (Jewish) woman, who participates only partially in the defense of the nation, is located at the margins of the society and at the margins of "the family," in her view as well as that of the society (Bar-Yossef & Padan-Eisenstark, 1977; Berkovitch, 1999; Herzog, 1998; Izraeli, 1997; Naveh, 2001).

Familism among Jews, though "dressed in religious garb," constitutes a central component of the social and cultural weave, in that it is one of the pillars of the national identity. A similar situation exists among the other national community that lives in the State of Israel: the Palestinian Arab community.

Familism as a Palestinian National Asset

Among the Palestinian citizens of Israel, religion and family religious laws also constitute a basis for "normative collective memory," as well as a basis for "normative collective identity" against the Jewish majority. For Arabs, as for Jews, religious laws provide a "boundary marker," both between Arabs and Jews and among themselves: as Muslims, Christians, and Druze. Moreover, religious laws, particularly among Muslims and Druze, are viewed as reinforcing Arabs' historical identity as a fortress against Westernization—increasingly perceived as a danger in today's age of globalization. In addition, religion and religious laws serve as a bridge to the world out-side: to the Christian and Muslim worlds, with which the Israeli Palestinian Arab communities have ramified connections on both the personal and collective levels.

As among the Jews, demography is regarded as a major issue and is seen as a "strategy of survival" of a minority against a majority (Anson & Meiri, 1996), a strategy that Jews define as a "demographic threat." In other words, demography is also a major component of the national strategy of the Palestinian Arab collective (Al-Hadj, 1996), and, as among the Jews, the religious discourse contributes to this strategy. It is thus no wonder that Shifman (1995a, p. 5) found that "among non-Jewish ethnic groups, there is nearly no opposition to that legal-religious domination. On the contrary, this situation is interpreted as an important part of the legal-religious autonomy which these religions enjoy."

The importance of religious laws and family laws as a basis for national (not only religious) identity for both the Jews and the Palestinians, citizens of Israel, is precisely the reason that religious family laws are institutionalized in Israel, despite Israel's commitment to democracy. Thus, the religious family laws are seen as promoting the "common good," even at the price of infringing upon basic human rights, especially basic women's human rights. This approach explains the findings in Table 11.1, which compares the dimensions of familism in Israel with those in other postindustrial societies.

I will now discuss the various dimensions of familism among the different ethnoreligious groups composing the Israeli Society.

FAMILISM AND CLASS AMONG ISRAELI CITIZENS

For this discussion, we must take into account the positioning of the different ethnoreligious groups in the Israeli economy and their exposure to the patterns, values, and norms that have been created by capitalism in Israel. The positioning of each group in the Israeli economy in the age of globalization refers, above all, to the access that the group and its members have to the structures of educational and occupational opportunities created by postindustrial capitalism (Adva Center, 2000; Al-Hadj, 1996; Ram, 1999; Saadi, 1995; Smooha, 1999; Yiftachel, 1999). This access is what enables the mass participation of women in the labor market, which, as may be recalled, has been the major lever in changing the institution of the family. In addition, access to educational and occupational opportunities exposes women to the ethos of individualism, which is based on competition and achievement and emphasizes the individual's abilities, wishes, and responsibility for his or her fate. Clearly, not every person who is exposed to and lives in an individualistic environment will support this ethos in the family. The opposite is quite often the case. On the other hand, the absence of an environment that enables people to live on their own, economically and normatively, will make it difficult for persons to think in individualistic terms and even more difficult for them to realize their individualism in practice.

In Israeli society, exposure to individualism as a norm and access to educational and occupational opportunities correspond almost completely with the division of the population into ethnoreligious groups. Here too there is a clear distinction between the Jewish and Arab citizens of Israel, and within the Jewish and Arab citizens as well. Israeli society is characterized by ethnoreligious and class stratification in addition to gender stratification. As a result, familism takes on different forms in the various groups, in keeping with the group's encounter with postindustrial capitalism and globalization. Among those groups that, as a result of the country's ethnoreligious and class stratification, were not exposed, or only minimally exposed, to the processes of globalization, the level of familism is high: married women do not join the work force *en masse,* and family patterns have changed only slightly. In contrast, among those groups who were maximally exposed to postindustrial capitalism or who have led the postindustrial processes, the dimensions of familism are much lower: many women/mothers have joined the labor market and have become

working women/mothers—the very experience defined as the lever for family changes in postindustrial societies.

Familism Among Palestinian Arabs, Citizens of Israel

About 22 percent of Arab women, in contrast to 51.1 percent of Jewish women, are in the labor force (Geist, 2000, p. 59). This means that about 78 percent of the Arab women in Israel do not work outside their homes. Moreover, most of those who do work are employed in simple, ill-paid, and low-status jobs, mostly without social benefits—in agriculture, industry (textiles, food), personal services, and low-level clerical work. At the same time, about 20 percent of Israeli Arab women hold semiprofessional jobs, in education, social work, and nursing, and about 4 percent are in the liberal professions (N.G.O. Report, 1997, p. 33).

This situation stems from the geographic and occupational stratification between Arabs and Jews in Israel: about 85 percent of the Arabs in Israel live in separate communities and about 15 percent live in mixed cities, but in separate neighborhoods (Al-Hadj, 1996). The "Arab sector" lacks a developed economic infrastructure, and its business activity is most limited. Unemployment, especially for skilled and educated workers, is chronic in their areas of residence. Moreover, the "Jewish sector" and the public sector are reluctant to include Arab citizens, with the exception of some spheres, such as the government services, local authorities, institutions of higher learning, the arts, the electronic and printed media, finances, and the law, in which Israel's Palestinian Arab citizens are somewhat more integrated. In other words, most Arab citizens of Israel have hardly any access to the postindustrial society—and if they do have access, it is generally in low-status and low-paid occupations.

It is no wonder that under these conditions the structural economic changes that would permit the massive entrance of Arab women into the paid labor force have not taken place, and that there has been no significant change in the social construction of women in the private and public spheres.

This is the state of affairs nowadays, so that the power of the *hamula,* the extended family, is still significant, even though it has somewhat declined. (The individual's economic dependency on the *hamula* has declined, mainly because of the entrance of the young men into the paid labor force. Besides, the *hamula* tends to interfere less in the lives of its members than it had previously and it tends to impose rigid norms less often). Nonetheless, the *hamula* still plays a major role in promoting, not obstructing, its members' adjustment to the processes of social change that the Palestinian Arab population in Israel is undergoing. It serves as a basis of identity and belonging, as an economic security net, and as a source of instrumental support given the limited state services in the Arab sector, as well as a base for political organization and activity at the local and national levels. For women, however, this centrality of the *hamula* in the community's life generally means control and domination by the men and women of the *hamula,* that is, the enforcement of familistic patterns of behavior (Al-Hadj, 1989, 1995; N.G.O. Report, 1997). Given all these factors, one can understand the continued existence of the most traditional family patterns among the Arabs in Israel, though there are also other family patterns.

Familism Among the Christian Arabs, Citizens of Israel

In general, the Christian Arabs, citizens of Israel, are a familistic population (see Table 11.2); however, since a not-insignificant portion of the population is urban, it has been somewhat exposed to the educational and occupational opportunities of Israel's postindustrial society. It is thus not surprising that of all the Palestinian women citizens of Israel, Christians make up a relatively large group in the labor force. About 33 percent of Christian women of working age are in the paid labor force (C.B.S., 1998, p. 8). Similarly, women's working is increasingly perceived as a norm (N.G.O Report, 1997, pp. 40–42). It is thus not surprising that among the Christians in Israel, modern and postmodern family patterns are found alongside traditional ones.

Familism Among the Muslim Arabs, Citizens of Israel

In general, the Muslim Arab, citizen of Israel, population has the most familistic family patterns (see Table 11.2). It has high rates of marriage along with the highest birth rates (more or less stable since the 1980s) of all the ethnoreligious groups in Israel, whether Jewish or Palestinian (Sabatello, Adler, Starkschal, & Peretz, 1996).

It is true that the divorce rate has risen somewhat in recent years (Table 11.2), but one must ask about the significance of this rising divorce rate in a society in which only 13 percent of women work for wages (C.B.S., 1998, p. 8), and in which it is unacceptable for a woman to live alone. On the whole, though there are slight fluctuations here and there, it seems that the power of familism is stable and strong among the Muslim citizens of Israel, even if sometimes it has taken a new face. I contend that the main cause of this state of affairs is the lack of civil equality, which entails a lack of equality of opportunities as far as access to educational and occupational opportunities are concerned. With structured economic inequality and underdevelopment, only a small number of Muslim women in villages as well as cities can join the paid labor force, even if they studied for many years (cf. above). As a consequence, the necessary condition for changing the family structure— access to paid employment—exists for only a small proportion of this population. Among most of the Muslim Arabs, citizens of Israel, many traditional family patterns are still preserved, with all that this implies for the roles of women and mothers in the family and society. It seems that this process is occurring along with the strengthening of the religious and fundamentalistic movements or as an expression of them.

Familism Among the Druze, Citizens of Israel

As far as the Druze, citizens of Israel, are concerned, the most salient fact is their significant and constant fall in birthrates (Table 11.2), even though these rates are still high in comparison to those of the Christians and the Jews. Druze birthrates have not yet stabilized and continue in a steady annual decline: the fertility rates among Druze women was 7.21 in the mid-1950s, 4.19 in the mid-1980s, and 3.10 in 1998 (C.B.S., 2000a, Table 2.12). It may be that the status of Druze as the "preferred minority," who do compulsory military service in the Israel Defense Forces, has given them somewhat more access to the various resources of the Israeli society. Indeed, in recent years, the rate of Druze women in the paid labor force has steadily increased, and in 1996 it reached 29 percent (C.B.S., 1998, p. 8). However, in-depth and comprehensive research is needed to enable us to better understand this process.

Familism Among the Jewish Citizens of Israel

A different reality, in terms of both structures and values, exists among Israeli Jews. In general, Jewish society has entered the postindustrial world, though there are substantial differences between different groups of Jews, between the "center" and the "periphery." The Jewish families in Israel are constituted by the "meeting" between Israel's institutionalized family laws and the class stratification that postindustrialism reinforces/creates. Three types of family are so constituted.

*Ultraorthodox Families (*Haredi *Families).*

Ultraorthodox families are not a single bloc: there are different trends among the *Haredi*. They have different geographic and ethnic origins. They are very much stratified by class. Nonetheless, these families have some similar basic features.

The marital age is low: girls generally marry at 18; the purpose of marriage is to perpetuate the Jewish People according to the Law (*Halakha*), and to enable the man to fulfill the commandment, "Be fruitful and multiply." Most marriages are made through arranged matches, though today there are more personal ways to meet a future spouse.

At home, there is a clear, hierarchical gendered role division: between husband and wife, parents and children, boys and girls. The number of births is very high, sometimes over ten. From a young age, the girl covers her body with a long dress and long stockings

(the length differs in different streams). When the young bride marries, she covers her head with a wig, handkerchief, or hat (here too there is little agreement, and the issue is highly disputed among the *Haredi*).

However, many changes are also occurring in the ultraorthodox world. As a result of the Compulsory Education Law (1949), all the girls go to school, most of them until age 18, though in a school system that does not enable high school matriculation. More and more women, including mothers of young children, join the job market so as to realize the ideal of the ultraorthodox society: to have paid work as part of "household" chores performed by women/mothers so as to enable their husbands to devote themselves to the study of the Bible (Torah) without having paid work (Elior, 2001; El-Or, 1993; Friedman, 1995). As a consequence, more and more ultraorthodox women work in places that respect the rules of modesty: in education, small businesses, clerical jobs; in ultraorthodox institutions; in the arts and crafts: graphics, drawing, music; and recently in computers, literature, journalism, and radio. There are even ultraorthodox women who work as "rabbinic pleaders" (*Toanot Rabbaniot*)—women who represent women in the Rabbinic Courts (Shamir, Shatrai, & Elias, 1997).

These processes—which clearly explain part of the high poverty rates among the *Haredim*—are beginning to affect the normative role division in the ultraorthodox families, as the man takes upon himself some of the household chores—his wife being sometimes the main or the sole provider (El-Or, 1993; Friedman, 1995; see also Levy, 1989). As Friedman (1995, p. 289) summarizes: "The Ultra-Orthodox woman is today a dynamic factor who is certainly changing the patterns of Ultra-Orthodox life." In other words, the more ultraorthodox women assume the role of "working mothers," the more changes one can expect in ultraorthodox communities and their families.

Neomodern Families.

The normative, typical family in Israel is the nuclear family headed by a heterosexual couple who have an average of three children. The couple is married according to the

Jewish law, and both spouses have paid work: the man as the " main provider," the woman as the "second wage earner"—a distinction that perpetuates the dependency of wives on their husbands.

In 1998, the rate of women in the workforce was about 51 percent; in 1999, it rose to 52.5 percent. In the 25–34-year-old-cohort, 76.1 percent of the women were in the paid labor force; and in the 35–44-year-old cohort, 78.5 percent were. Women's participation in the workforce varies somewhat according to whether the father was born in Israel, Asia–Africa (Eastern origin), or Europe–America (Western origin). In both cohorts and regardless of the ethnic origin, over 70 percent of the women were in the labor force (C.B.S., 2000a; Table 12.3).

Yet, although women of "Eastern" and "Western" origin do not differ in the fact of working for wages, they do differ in the type of work they can obtain. In general, the "Westerners" work in more prestigious and better-paid "feminine jobs"; the "Easterners" in lower-paid and lower-status "feminine jobs." This is a class difference that reflects the still existing inequality of educational and occupational opportunities among Eastern and Western Israeli Jews (Bernstein, 1983; Dahan-Calev, 1999; Fogiel-Bijaoui, 1997; Izraeli, 1999).

In addition to both spouses having paid jobs, there are other postmodern parameters in the "Israeli normative family": increased involvement of the fathers in taking care of and bringing up their children ("the New Fathers"), democratization of intrafamily relationships; and more participatory and more egalitarian decision-making processes, especially with regard to children and their needs.

In fact, these are all modifications that alter central aspects of "the family" in Israel without changing its essence, that is, the superiority of the man and the dependency of the woman. In other words, these are all changes that enable preserving "the normative Israeli family" in the age of postmodernity.

Postmodern Families. As defined at the beginning, postmodern families are families in which the individual, his or her wants, his or her needs, are the center and the purpose of the institution. These include two-career families, single-parent families, homo-

sexual and lesbian families, second families, families established through marriages (whether between Jews or between persons of different religions) that circumvent the religious establishment, common-law marriages, cohabiting couples, and couples in which the spouses live separately. The members of these families are characterized by the fact that they are not religious in the sense accepted in Israel but are religious in accord with their own definition—or they are fully atheist. These families generally live in urban centers, because, sociologically, cities not only enable access to the developed capitalist economy and to varied services, but also make it possible to live far from the social control of the family and community, in an atmosphere in which individualism is both legitimate and approved. The vast majority of postmodern families live in Tel-Aviv and other cities in the center of Israel, as well as in the cities of Haifa, Beer Sheba, Eilat, and Jerusalem (on Tel-Aviv as the "City of Freedom," see Bar-On, 1997, pp. 221–234). Postmodern families are also found in rural areas, such as on *kibbutzim.*

From the above analysis, we can learn that there are not very many postmodern families in Israel. The members of these families are mostly "Western Jews" (from European–American origins). But there are also a fair number of "Easterners" (from Asian–African origins) as well as a small number of Palestinian Arabs, who by their education and income belong to the middle class or above.

Welfare Policy and the Establishment of the Normative Family

As many studies have shown, welfare policies can either support or not support the constitution of different family forms by fostering—or hindering—the economic autonomy of the man and of the woman. Where wage policies, social services, and welfare allowances do not permit women to live on their own, welfare policies perpetuate women's dependency on men. Thus it can be said that prevailing welfare policies contribute substantially to the "stability of the family," by preventing women from being economically autonomous (Esping-Andersen, 1999; Haas, 1996; Orloff, 1993; O'Connor, 1996).

One of the salient features of Israel's wage policies, social services, and transfer payments is that they are based on the "obvious" distinction between "the man, the provider" and "the woman, the second wage earner" (Eisenstadt & Gal, 2001; Fogiel-Bijaoui, 1997; Gal, 1997; Izraeli, 1997; Swirski, 1998).

One of the outcomes of this distinction is the economic deprivation of single-parent families, especially those headed by women. As may be recalled, single-parent families with a child up to 17 years old constitute 10 percent of the households in Israel: 11 percent among Jews, 5 percent among the Palestinian citizens (Geist, 2000, p. 26). Approximately 90 percent of single-parent families in Israel are headed by a woman (data for the year 1998; C.B.S., 2000b, p. 3). About 30 percent of single-parent households are poor, in contrast to 16.7 percent of the households in the population as a whole (Geist, 2000, p. 96). This means that among children who live in poverty—the percentage of which is very high compared to other postindustrial societies, for it amounts to 22 percent of all Israeli children (Gal & Aryeh, 1999, p. 83)—children of women-headed families (together with Arab and *Haredi* children) are clearly overrepresented. As Gal (1997, p. 8) explains:

This should not be surprising. It is not only that these families do not have a second provider; often the need to take care of the children prevents the head of the family from finding a full-time job with reasonable wages. That is, the single parent may not earn a living at all or only a partial living, and the family is dependent on social welfare payments. As a result, many children from single-parent families belong to the category: "poor children."

These facts clearly show the negative effects of wage and welfare policies on women and children, in a country in which children represent more than 33 percent of the population—as compared to 25 percent in other postindustrial societies (Gal & Aryeh, 1999, p. 88). The very fact that poverty and single parenthood are associated in the public discourse creates an ideological mechanism that supports "normative families," since it implies that women will find it difficult to live and raise children at a reasonable standard of living outside marriage.

Today, when the issue of wife beating is on the national agenda, these points must be kept in mind. My claim is that Israel's legal system, social norms, unequal wages (in 1998 the average hourly gross income for women was 83 percent of the average hourly gross income for men for similar or identical work [C.B.S., 2000b, p. 8]), and welfare policies make the vast majority of women in Israel dependent on their husbands.

Against this background, we can understand why only a small portion of women who are beaten by their husbands, whose total number in Israel stands at around 200,000 (London-Sapir, 2000), report the abuse to the authorities. We can also understand why, after their stay in shelters, about two-thirds of abused women return to their homes. Their home becomes a death trap for about twenty women every year. This was already pointed out 30 years ago by radical feminists who raised the issue in Israel and abroad (Swirski, 1993).

No fundamental change in this situation is to be expected without changes in the factors that create and perpetuate this dependency in all of its psychological, legal, social, and economic aspects (Bilski, 1997; London-Sapir, 2000, pp. 12–16; Shadmi, 1997; Swirski, 1993).

SUMMARY AND CONCLUSIONS

Despite the "mutations" of the family institution in postmodern societies, as Dumon (1995) termed it, familism clearly remains a marker of Israeli society. The main reason for this is that familism in Israel rests on the institutionalization of religious family laws for the different ethnoreligious groups. As this chapter has argued, for all the ethnoreligious groups in Israel, religious law serves as a "national asset": as a boundary marker between the different groups and as a foundation for the "normative collective memory" and the "normative collective identity" of each and every group. In addition, religious laws and the familism they foster are a major normative mechanism in the process of biological and cultural reproduction of the different ethnoreligious groups, and thereby also contribute to the covert and overt "demographic competition" that exists between Israeli Jews and Israeli Palestinians.

Capitalist development works in the opposite direction: it fosters individualism in both practices and discourses. So it promotes and accelerates the individualization of Israeli institutions, among them, the family.

Capitalist development is also the main lever for the integration of women/mothers into the paid labor market, while the massive entrance of women/mothers into the labor market is a major factor in family changes in postindustrial societies.

The conclusion to be drawn from these two trends is that *the different dimensions of familism in the Israeli population are the product of the meeting between Israel's postindustrial ethnoreligious stratification and its institutionalized religious laws.*

1. The educated, urban stratum of the middle- and upper-middle classes (also found to a certain extent in *kibbutzim*) is the smallest stratum and the stratum most exposed to postindustrial processes and, in part, at the forefront of these processes. This stratum has the lowest levels of familism and the bulk of the postmodern families (with the exception of a certain portion of poor single-parent families). In these families, women/mothers are in the labor market. The vast majority, though not all, of these families are Jewish. A small number are Palestinian Arabs, citizens of Israel.

2. In keeping with the class–religious–national and gender stratification that characterizes Israel, the social strata with the highest level of familism are those with low access to educational and occupational opportunities. In these strata, the proportion of women/mothers in the labor market is relatively low. These strata are generally located on the "periphery" of Jewish society (that is, in development towns, poor neighborhoods, and ultraorthodox neighborhoods), and they include a substantial portion of the Arab population in Israel.

3. Between these two poles are neomodern families that combine religious elements with "postmodern" features. In these families, the man and woman are married in orthodox religious ceremonies, but are also exposed to postmodern processes. Both work for wages, the man as the "main provider," the woman as the "second wage earner." Sometimes the man "helps" the woman at home. These families have an average of three children among the Jews, and four children among the Arabs. In general, the family atmosphere is not authoritarian. The neomodern family is the most prevalent family model in Jewish society and is beginning to become stronger in Palestinian Arab society in Israel.

No significant change is expected in the near future in the institution of the family in Israel or in the familistic character of Israeli society. One of the main reasons for this is that no improvements are expected in welfare policy or in the status of women in the labor market, which would promote the (economic) autonomy of "working women." On the contrary: as these lines are being written, with the El-Aqsa Intifada in process, the economy in deep recession, and unemployment high, women are being turned out of the labor market.

However, the main reason that no significant changes are expected in the family institution in Israel is the institutionalization of religious laws and the norms that this institutionalism creates. Today more than ever, when we hear the trumpets of war, religion and religious law serve as major devices in the crystalization of the collective identity and belonging of all the ethnoreligious groups in Israel, "the Civil Revolution" about which Prime Minister Ehud Barak spoke in the summer of 2000 seems farther away than ever before.

ACKNOWLEDGMENTS

This is an extended version of a paper which appeared in 2002 in the *Journal of Israeli History* (special double issue on Women's Time: New Studies from Israel, Vol. 21, Nos. 1–2, Tel-Aviv University).

I would like to thank wholeheartedly Professor Hannah Naveh, from Tel-Aviv University, and Professor Anita Shapira, Head of the Institute for Research in the History of Zionism at Tel-Aviv University, for helping me to complete this research. I am thankful to Professor Jaipaul Roop-narine, from Syracuse University, for his insightful suggestions and for his friendly and nonetheless highly professional support. Last but not least, I would like to thank Philippa Shimrat, Assistant Editor of the *Journal of Israeli History,* for her highly helpful comments.

NOTES

1. Israel had about 6 million inhabitants in 1999: about 80 percent Jewish, about 15 percent Muslim Arabs, about 2 percent Christian Arabs, about 1.5 percent Druze Arabs and only about 1.5 percent without any religious classification (Central Bureau of Statistics [C.B.S.] 2000a, Table 2.1). The term *ethnonational groups* refers to the Jewish community (with no distinction between the religious and national dimensions of Judaism), and to the three religious groups that comprise the Arab Palestinian community in Israel.

2. In this chapter, *family* is defined as the legitimate framework adults create to raise their children. This legitimacy is necessary because the family is still the major framework for the biological and cultural reproduction of society, notwithstanding the achievements of medical technology.

3. These ages are lower than the normative ages in the postindustrial countries, including the ages in the fifteen countries of the European Union (as defined in Table 11.1). See *Statistiques Demographiques* (1999), p. 134.

4. As Shalev points out, the State of Israel recognizes civil marriages only if they are made outside of Israel. It also recognizes marriages carried out by an emissary when the couple does not leave the country, as in "Mexican" marriages. A "Mexican marriage," for example, is conducted by a person in Mexico who has been given power of attorney before a public notary in Israel to marry the couple in their absence. The marriage certificate is then sent to Israel. Marriages conducted by non-Orthodox rabbis (Reform, Conservative, etc.) and "mixed marriages" (between persons of different religions) are not recognized in Israel. For their marriages to be recognized, mixed couples, and those who marry outside the accepted legal/religious norms, must have civil marriages abroad (e.g., in Cyprus, the Russian Federation) and then register as married in the Population Register. As for guest workers, they can marry at their country's consulate.

5. This section is based on comprehensive bibliographic material (in Hebrew): Amir, 1995; Elior, 2001; El-Or, 1993; Fogiel-Bijaoui, 1999; Harel, 2001; Hassan, 1999; Layish, 1995; Naveh, 2001; Radai, 1999; Shamir et al., 1997; Shifman, 1995a, b; Yanai & Rapaport, 2001; (in English and French): Abu-Lughod, 1988; Al-Krenawi & Graham, 1998; El-Saadawi, 1982; Fogiel-Bijaoui, 1997; Foucault, 1976, 1984; Hassan, 1991; Minces, 1990; Mernisssi, 1996; Moghadam, 2000; Moghissi, 1999; N.G.O. Report, 1997; Shaloufeh-Khazan, 1991; Shaloub-Kervokian, 1999; Tzoreff, 2000.

6. In the Israeli (Jewish) collective memory, the Shoah is mainly constructed in terms of nationhood as conveyed in the Hebrew expression, "Shoah VeTkuma" (Shoah and National Resurrection), cf. Gorny (1998).

REFERENCES

Abu-Assbah, H. (1999). Dropouts of high school among Arab adolescents in Israel. In A. Ben Arieh & Y. Tsionit (Eds.), *Children in Israel and the new millennium* (pp. 105–123). Jerusalem: National Council for the Child and Ashalim (in Hebrew).

Abu-Lughod, L. (1988). *Veiled sentiments.* Berkeley: University of California Press.

Adva Center. (2000). *Israeli society in 2000—An overview.* Report by Swirski Shlomo, Konor Ethy, Tel-Aviv (in Hebrew).

Al-Hadj, M. (1989). Social research on family life styles among Arabs in Israel. *Journal of Comparative Family Studies, 20*(2), 175–195.

Al-Hadj, M. (1995). Kinship and modernization in developing societies: The emergence of instrumentalized kinship. *Journal of Comparative Family Studies, 26*(3), 311–328.

Al-Hadj, M. (1996). *Education among Arabs in Israel: Control and social change.* Jerusalem: Jerusalem University Press (in Hebrew).

Al-Krenawi, A., & Graham, J. R. (1998). Divorce among Muslim Arab women in Israel. *Journal of Divorce and Remarriage, 29*(¾), 103–119.

Amir, D. (1995). Responsible, committed, intelligent: Abortion and the constitution of the Israeli woman. In *Theory and criticism* (Theororia Ve Bikoret), *7,* 247–254. Jerusalem: The Jerusalem Van Leer Institute (in Hebrew).

Anson, J., & Meiri, A. (1996). Religiosity, nationalism and biological reproduction. *Bitakhon Sociali, 46,* 43–63 (in Hebrew).

Association for the Citizen's Rights in Israel. (1996). *Human rights in Israel—An overview.* Jerusalem (in Hebrew).

Ayalon, H. (2000). Course taking of mathematics and the sciences among Arab students in Israel: A case of unexpected gender equality. In S. Shlasky (Ed.), *Sexuality and gender in education* (pp. 85–110). Tel-Aviv University: Ramot Publishing House (in Hebrew).

Bar-On, B.-A. (1997). Sexuality, the family and nationalism. In H. Lindemann Nelson (Ed.), *Feminism and families* (pp. 221–223). New York and London: Routledge.

Bar-Yossef, R., & Padan-Eisenstark, D. (1977). Role system under stress: Sex roles in war. *Social Problems, 20,* 135–145.

Ben-Rafael, E. (2001). *Qu'est-ce qu'être Juif? Cinquante intellectuels répondent à Ben-Gurion.* Paris: Balland.

Beck, U., & Beck-Gernsheim, E. (1995). *The normal chaos of love.* Cambridge, UK: Polity Press.

Berkovitch, N. (1999). Women of valor: Women and citizenship in Israel. *Sotzologiah Yisraelit, 2*(1), 277–318 (in Hebrew).

Bernstein, D. (1983). Economic growth and female labor: The case of Israel. *Sociological Review, 31*(2), 264–292.

Bilski, L. (1997). Beaten wives: From self-defense to defense of selfhood. *Plilim, 4,* 65–88 (in Hebrew).

Central Bureau of Statistics (C.B.S.) (1986). *Statistical abstract of Israel,* No. 37. Jerusalem: Bureau of the Prime Minister (in Hebrew).

Central Bureau of Statistics (C.B.S.) (1998). *Women in statistics.* Jerusalem/Tel-Aviv: Central Bureau of Statistics (C.B.S.), (in English).

Central Bureau of Statistics (C.B.S.) (2000a). *Statistical abstract of Israel,* No. 51. Jerusalem: Bureau of the Prime Minister (in Hebrew).

Central Bureau of Statistics (C.B.S.). (2000b). *Israeli women in statistics.* Jerusalem: Bureau of the Prime Minister (in Hebrew).

Chafetz, J. S., & Hagan, J. (1996). The gender division of labor and family change in industrial societies: A theoretical accounting. *Journal of Comparative Family Studies, 27*(2), 187–210.

Dahan-Calev, H. (1999). Israeli feminism between East and West. In D. Izraeli, A. Friedman, S. Fogiel-Bijaoui, M. Hasan, H. Herzog, & H. Naveh (Eds.), *Sex, gender, and politics: Women in Israel* (pp. 217–266). Tel-Aviv: Hakibbutz HaMeuchad. (in Hebrew).

de Singly, F. (2000), *Libres ensembles, L'individualisme dans la vie commune* [Free together: Individualism and family life]. Paris: Editions Nathan.

Dumon, W. (1995). The Western European families: An overview. *Bitakhon Sotziali, 44,* 5–23 (in Hebrew).

Durkheim, E. (1995). *The elementary forms of religious life: The totemic system in Australia.* New York: Free Press.

Eisenstadt, M., & Gal, J. (2001). *Gendering the welfare state in Israel.* Jerusalem: The Welfare Research Institute, The Hebrew University of Jerusalem, mimeo (in Hebrew).

El-Or, T. (1993). *Educated and ignorant: From the world of ultra-Orthodox women,* Tel-Aviv: Am Oved (in Hebrew).

El-Saadawi, N. (1982). *La face cachée d'Eve* [The hidden face of Eve]. Paris: Editions des Femmes.

Elior, R. (2001). Missing presence, silent nature and a pretty maiden without eyes: On the question of the presence and the absence of women in the Jewish religion and Israeli reality. In Y. Azmon (Ed.), *Will you listen to my voice? Representations of women in Israeli culture* (pp. 41–82). Jerusalem: Van Leer Institute; Tel-Aviv: HaKibbutz HaMeuchad (in Hebrew).

Esping-Andersen, G. (1999). *Social foundations of postindustrial economics.* Oxford, UK: Oxford University Press.

Eurostat Yearbook (1998–1999). The European Commission.

Fogiel-Bijaoui, S. (1997). Women in Israel: The social construction of citizenship as a non-issue. *Israel Social Science Research, 12*(1), 1–30.

Fogiel-Bijaoui, S. (1999). Families and familism in Israel. In D. Izraeli, A. Friedman, H. Dahan-Kalev, S. Fogiel-Bijaoui, H. Herzog, M. Hasan, & H. Naveh. (Eds.), *Sex, gender and politics* (pp. 107–167). Tel-Aviv: Kav Adom (in Hebrew).

Foucault, M. (1976). *Histoire de la sexualité, I* [History of Sexuality, Vol. 1]. Paris: Gallimard.

Foucault, M. (1984). *Histoire de la sexualité, II, III* [History of Sexuality, Vols. 2–3]. Paris: Gallimard.

Friedman, M. (1995). The ultra-Orthodox woman. In Y. Azmon (Ed.), *A view into the lives of women in Jewish societies* (pp. 273–290). Jerusalem: Zalman Shazar Center for Jewish History (in Hebrew).

Gal, J. (Ed.). (1997). *Poor children in Israel.* Jerusalem: National Council for the Child and the League against Poverty (in Hebrew).

Gal, J., & Aryeh, A. B. (1999). Children and poverty in Israel: New directions for change. In A. B. Aryeh & Y. Tsionit (Eds.), *Children in Israel in the new millennium* (pp. 81–96). Jerusalem: National Council for the Child and Ashalim (in Hebrew).

Geist, I. (2000). *Israel 2000: Social report, No. 3.* Jerusalem: Central Bureau of Statistics (in Hebrew).

Gorny, Y. (1998). *Between Auschwitz and Jerusalem.* Tel-Aviv: Am-Oved (in Hebrew).

Haas, L. (1996). Family policy in Sweden. *Journal of Family and Economic Issues, 17*(1), 47–93.

Harel, A. (July, 2001). The rise and fall of the homosexual revolution in Israeli law. *Ha-Mishpat, 12,* 10–20 (in Hebrew).

Hassan, M. (1991). Growing up female and Palestinian in Israel. In B. Swirski & M. P. Safir (Eds.), *Calling the equality bluff: Women in Israel* (pp. 66–74). New York: Pergamon.

Hassan, M. (1999). The politics of honour: Patriarchy, the state and the killing of women for family honor. In D. Izraeli, A. Friedman, H. Dahan-Kalev, S. Fogiel-Bijaoui, H. Herzog, M. Hasan, & H. Naveh (Eds.), *Sex, gender and politics* (pp. 267–307). Tel-Aviv: Kav Adom (in Hebrew).

Hervieu-Leger, D. (1993). *La religion pour memoire* [The religion for memory]. Paris: du Cerf.

Herzog, H. (1998). Homefront and battlefront and the status of Jewish and Palestinian women in Israel. *Israeli Studies, 3,* 61–84.

Illouz, E. (1997). *Consuming the romantic utopia: Love and the contradictions of capitalism.* Berkeley: University of California Press.

Izraeli, D. N. (1997). Gendering military service in the Israel defense forces. *Israel Social Science Research, 12*(1), 129–166.

Izraeli, D. N. (1999). Gendering the labor market in Israel. In D. Izraeli, A. Friedman, H. Dahan-Kalev, S. Fogiel-Bijaoui, H. Herzog, M. Hasan, & H. Naveh (Eds.), *Sex, gender and politics* (pp. 167–217). Tel-Aviv: Kav Adom (in Hebrew).

Kadman, Y. (1999). Child abuse in Israel. In A. B. Aryeh & Y. Tsionit (Eds.), *Children in Israel and the New Millennium* (pp. 151–162). Jerusalem: National Council for the Child and Ashalim (in Hebrew).

Kimmerling, B. (1994). Religion, nationalism and democracy in Israel. *Zmanim, 50,* 116–131 (in Hebrew).

Klein, E. (2000). The process of gender construction in junior high schools. In S. Shlasky (Ed.), *Sexuality and gender in education* (pp. 113–134). Tel-Aviv University: Ramot Publishing House (in Hebrew).

Kulik, L. (2000). Intrafamiliar congruence in gender-role ideology: Husband–wife versus parents–offspring. *Journal of Comparative Family Studies, 31*(1), 91–106.

Layish, A. (1995). The Muslim women and the Muslim court in Israel. In F. Raday, C. Shalev, & M. Liban-Kooby (Eds.), *Women's status in Israeli law and society* (pp. 364–379). Tel-Aviv: Schocken (in Hebrew).

Levy, A. (1989). *HaHaredim* [The Ultra-Orthodox]. Jerusalem: Keter (in Hebrew).

London-Sapir, S. (2000). *Progress in the status of women in Israel since the 1995 Beijing conference: A feminist perspective.* Submitted to the Beijing + 5 Conference, New York, The Israel Women's Network Report.

Mernissi, F. (1996). *Women's rebellion and Islamic memory.* London, UK: Zed Books.

Minces, J. (1990). *La femme voilée, L'Islam au feminin* [The veiled dream: Feminine Islam]. Paris: Calman-Levy.

Moghadam, V. M. (2000). Gender, national identity and citizenship: Reflections on the Middle-East and North Africa. *Hagar, International Social Science Review, 1*(1), 41–69.

Moghissi, H. (1999), *Feminism and Islamic fundamentalism: The limits of postmodern analysis.* London/New York: Zed Books.

Naveh, H. (2001). The Israeli experience and the experience of the Israeli woman in the military cemetery or: Where is Shula Mellet? In Y. Azmon (Ed.), *Will you listen to my voice? Representation of women in Israeli culture* (pp. 305–325). Jerusalem: Van Leer Institute; Tel-Aviv: Hakibbutz Hameuchad (in Hebrew).

N.G.O. Report. (1997). *The working group on the status of Palestinian women citizens of Israel.* Submitted to Convention on the Elimination of all Forms of Discrimination Against Women, United Nations.

O'Connor, J. (1996). From women in the welfare state to gendering welfare state regimes. *Current Sociology, 44*(2).

Orloff, S. A. (1993). Gender and social rights of citizenship: The comparative analysis of gender relations and welfare states. *American Sociological Review, 58*(2), 303–328.

Peled, Y. (1993). Ethnic democracy and the legal construction of citizenship: Arab citizens of the Jewish state. *American Political Science Review, 86*(2), 432–443.

Peres, Y., & Katz, R. (1980). Stability and centrality: The nuclear family in modern Israel. *Megamot, 26,* 37–56 (in Hebrew).

Radai, F. (1999). Woman's voice in Israeli democracy. In R. Cohen-Almagor (Ed.), *Basic issues in Israeli democracy* (pp. 143–166). Tel-Aviv: Sifriat Poalim (in Hebrew).

Ram, U. (1999). Between nation and corporations: Liberal post-Zionism in the global age. *Sotziologia Ysraelit, 2*(1), 99–145 (in Hebrew).

Saadi, A. (1995). Incorporation without integration: Palestinian citizens in Israel's labour market. *Sociology, 29*(3), 429–451.

Sabatello, A., Adler, I., Starkschal, R., & Peretz, A. (1996). Fertility rates among Muslim women in Israel in the last decade. *Bitakhon Sotziali, 48,* 64–86 (in Hebrew).

Shadmi, E. (1997). Policy handling in wife beating in Israel: Radical feminist critique and public policy. *Israel Social Science Research, 12*(2), 55–74.

Shalev, C. (1995a). The freedom to choose? Marriage in Israel. In F. Radai, C. Shalev, & M. Liban-Koobi (Eds.), *Women's status in Israeli law and society* (pp. 459–502). Tel-Aviv: Schocken (in Hebrew).

Shalev, C. (1995b). Fertility law and the right of parenthood. In F. Radai, C. Shalev, & M. Liban-Koobi (Eds.), *Women's status in Israeli law and society* (pp. 508–533). Tel-Aviv: Schocken (in Hebrew).

Shaloufeh-Khazan, F. (1991). Change and mate selection among Palestinian women in Israel. In B. Swirski & M. P. Safir (Eds.), *Calling the equality bluff: Women in Israel* (pp. 82–89). New York/London: Pergamon.

Shaloub-Kervokian, N. (1999). Law, politics and violence against women: A case study of Palestinians in Israel. *Law, 21*(2), 189–211.

Shamir, R., Shitrai, M., & Elias, N. (1997). Faith, feminism and professionalism: Rabbinic pleaders in the Orthodox religious community. *Megamot, 35*(3), 313–348 (in Hebrew).

Shapira, J. (1977). *Israeli democracy.* Massada: Ramat-Gan.

Shamai, M. (1999). Children and divorce: The child's point of view. In A. B. Aryeh & Y. Tsionit (Eds.), *Children in Israel and the new millennium* (pp. 53–74). Jerusalem: National Council for the Child and Ashalim (in Hebrew).

Shemgar-Handelman, L., & Bar-Yossef, R. (Eds.). (1991). *Families in Israel.* Jerusalem: Akademon (in Hebrew).

Shifman, P. (1995a). *Civil marriage in Israel: The case for reform.* Jerusalem: Institute for Israel Studies, Research Series No. 62 (in Hebrew).

Shifman, P. (1995b). Custody and child support. In F. Radai, C. Shalev, & M. Liban-Kooby (Eds.), *Women's status in Israeli law and society* (pp. 534–545). Tel-Aviv: Schocken (in Hebrew).

Smooha, S. (1999). Changes in Israeli society after fifty years. *Alpa'im, 17,* 239–398 (in Hebrew).

Smooha, S. (2000). The regime of the state of Israel: Civil democracy, lack of democracy or ethnic democracy? *Sotziologiyah Ysraelit, 2*(2), 565–630 (in Hebrew).

Stacey, J. (1990). *Brave new families.* New York: Basic Books.

Statistiques Demographiques (1999). Thème 3: Population et Conditions Sociales, Commission Européenne [Theme 3: Population and social conditions, European Commission].

Swirski, B. (1993). Control and violence: Women battering in Israel. In U. Ram (Ed.), *Israeli society: Critical perspectives* (pp. 222–244). Tel-Aviv: Breirot (in Hebrew).

Swirski, B. (1998). *A short exercise on sameness and difference in the Israeli welfare state.* Paper presented at the Founding Meeting of the Israeli Association for Feminist and Gender Studies, Bar-Ilan University, Israel.

Thorne, B., & Yalom, M. (Eds.). (1992). *Rethinking the family: Some feminist questions.* Boston: Northeastern University Press.

Thorne, B. (1993). *Gender play.* New Brunswick, NJ: Rutgers University Press.

Trost, J. (1996). Family structure and relationships: The dyadic approach. *Journal of Comparative Family Studies, 27*(2), 395–408.

Tsionit, Y., & Ben Aryeh, A. (1999). Children in Israel and the New Millennium: An overview. In: A. Ben Aryeh & Y. Tsionit (Eds.), *Children in Israel and the new millennium* (pp. 1–36). (in Hebrew).

Tzoreff, M. (2000). Fadwa Tuqan's Autobiography: Restructuring a personal history into the Palestinian discourse. In B. Shoshan (Ed.), *Discourse on gender—Gendered discourse in the Middle East.* Westport, CT: Praeger.

Yanai, N., & Rapoport, T. (2001). Ritual impurity and religious discourse on women and nationalism. In Y. Azmon (Ed.), *Will you listen to my voice? Representation of Women in Israeli culture* (pp. 213–224). Jerusalem: Van Leer Institute and Tel Aviv: Hakibbutz Hameuchad (in Hebrew).

Yiftachel, O. (1999). Ethnocracy: The politics of Judaizing Israel/Palestine. *Constellations, 6*(3), 364–390.

Yuval-Davis, N. (1980). The bearers of the collective: Women and religious legislation in Israel. *Feminist Review, 11*(4), 1–27.

Yuval-Davis, N. (1997). *Gender and nation.* London: Sage.

World Bank Report. (1996).

PART FOUR

EUROPE

CHAPTER 12

FAMILIES IN GREECE

JAMES GEORGAS, TSABIKA BAFITI, KOSTAS MYLONAS, AND LITSA PAPADEMOU
University of Athens

Our analysis of the Greek family elucidates the issue of changes in the structure and function of the traditional Greek family as a result of economic and other social changes in Greek society stemming from modernization and urbanization. The chapter is based on an ecocultural framework that analyzes elements of the Greek culture and relates them to the family. The chapter begins with an outline of the history of the Greek state. The next section describes the ecology of Greece, relevant to its means of economic subsistence and to the development of the types of communities and to the extended family system, the organization, and the institutions of Greek society—diachronically and in terms of

changes in the family system in today's Greece. These institutions include economic, political, and legal institutions, the educational system, religion, and bonds with groups in the community. This is followed by an analysis of the traditional Greek family and the roles of the family members. The question of the degree of transition of the Greek traditional extended family system to the nuclear family system in modern Greek society is then discussed based on demographic statistics and current research on family values and social networks. Employing Parsons' theory of the nuclear family and modernization theory, the definitions of the nuclear family are examined. These changes in kin networks are compared with changes in other cultures to provide an indication of the degree of changes in Greece. The last section discusses conclusions regarding the Greek family system.

A HISTORICAL OUTLINE OF GREECE

The Byzantine Empire was established in the fifth century on a peninsula on the Bosphorus by Constantine, a Roman, and the capital of "New Rome" was Constantinopolis—today's Istanbul. The "Hellenes," or as they called themselves, the "Romioi" or Hellenophone Romans, with their distinct language, culture, and Orthodox religion, resided in an area that spread across North Africa, the middle East, what is today Turkey, around the shores of the Black Sea, what are currently the Balkans, southern Italy and Sicily, and of course the land mass and islands of modern Greece. One thousand years later, in 1453, after centuries of debilitating aggressions by the Romans, the Crusaders, the Venetians, and others from Western Europe, Constantinople fell to the Ottomans. After the demise of the Byzantine Empire the Romioi were one of many ethnic groups, with a distinct language, religion, and culture within the Ottoman Empire, and despite the lack of a nation-state of "Hellas" or Greece, the continuity of Hellenic identity was maintained.

Greeks rebelled against the Ottoman Empire in 1821, and aided by England, Russia, and France, the nation-state Greece or Hellas was established at the end of the 1820s, with borders that included only the Peloponnese, a few islands, and a small section of mainland Greece. King Otto of Bavaria was imposed on by the three powers to become its monarch in 1834, in order to play a mediating role among the quarreling factions of those who fought for independence. However, within 30 years Otto was deposed, and King George of Denmark became the new head of a constitutional monarchy. Athens became the country's principal city, its population growing exponentially from 10,000 in 1834, to 31,500 in 1848, to 179,700 in 1896 (Cassia & Bada, 1992). This urbanization was due not so much to industrialization as to the migration of farmers, fishermen, herders, and others from the provinces desiring a better life in the new and growing capital. These migrants sought employment in the new, highly centralized state administration, sent their sons for the opportunity of education at the newly established University of Athens, sought the opportunity to establish themselves as tradesmen or in other economically viable jobs as water carriers, servants, stevedores, builders, and so on.

During the late 1800s and early 1900s, with the further weakening of the Ottoman Empire and the revolution that established modern Turkey, the geographic borders of Greece expanded to include what is currently northern Greece and the city of Thessalonike, Thrace, the island of Crete, the Ionian islands, and after World War II, the Dodecanese Islands. The monarchy in Greece had a turbulent history in the twentieth century: it was overthrown by coups, brought back, rejected, brought back by plebiscite after World War II, and rejected by plebiscite in 1974, when Greece became a republic.

Until the 1930s, industrial development in Greece was meager and primarily met domestic needs. At the end of World War II a civil war erupted in Greece, which did not end until 1950. However, during the 1950s Greece began to industrialize, albeit tardily in relation to other European nations also devastated by war. The rapid industrialization led to another wave of internal migration, primarily toward Athens, but also to Thessalonike, which was the second largest city in the Ottoman Empire. Greece became a member of the European Union (EU) in 1981.

The population of Greece is approximately 10,500,000. The population of Athens in 1928 was 802,600; in 1951 the population was 1,378,500, it was 3,000,000 in 1976, and approximately 4,500,000 in 2001.

AN ECOCULTURAL FRAMEWORK

The traditional Greek family and changes in its nature in today's society will be discussed within the context of cultural and ecological theory: the effects of history and environment on maintenance systems

(Whiting, 1963); a probabilistic model of the relationships of variables within an ecological context (Brunswik, 1955); achievement motivation, cultural and ecological variables (McClelland, 1961); effects of the ecology on social systems and feedback effects on the normative environment (LeVine, 1973); an ecological model influenced by general systems theory (Bronfenbrenner, 1979); and the developmental niche (Super & Harkness, 1980).

The analysis of the Greek family will be based on Berry's ecocultural framework (1976, 1994). The framework hypothesizes that human psychological diversity (both individual and group similarities and differences) can be understood by taking into account two fundamental sources of influences (ecological and sociopolitical), and a set of variables that link these influences to psychological characteristics (cultural and biological adaptation at the population level, and various "transmission variables" to individuals such as enculturation, socialization, genetics, and acculturation). Elements of the sociopolitical context of Berry's ecocultural framework were further elaborated by Georgas (1993). The first element is the *institutions of society,* such as the subsistence or economic system, the political and judicial systems, the educational system, religion, and means of mass communication. The second element, derived from social psychology, is *bonds with groups in the immediate community,* and refers to the degree and quality of contact with significant groups within the community, such as students, co-workers, neighbors, judges, and so on. Distinctions between the institutions of society and the bonds with representatives of these institutions, in regard to the degree of influence in shaping values, attitudes, cognitions, behavior, and so on, refer to Toennies' (1961) concepts of *Gemeinschaft* and *Gesellschaft.* The third element is *family,* which is placed in a separate category from groups in the immediate community because of its critical role in the socialization of the child.

Ecological Features of Greece

The characteristic geographic features of Greece are its many mountains, the hundreds of islands scattered throughout the Ionian, Aegean, and Cretan Seas, and a few fertile plains. Small, isolated communities were founded in the mountains and on the many islands, and relatively large cities were founded on the plains, on natural ports on the mainland, and on some islands. During the Ottoman rule, many Hellenes fled the exposed communities in the plains and the coastal areas because of punitive military expeditions and in order to protect themselves from brigands, thereby establishing small communities in the mountains, which, because of their isolation, offered natural protection. Historians have ascribed different personality traits to inhabitants of the plains and those of the mountains. In the austere and harsh conditions of the mountains, ". . . survival required hard work, which had as a result the development of physical and mental traits, and the creation of different types of personality traits. Under these harsh conditions, the families returned to a more primitive type of life, to herding and small crop agriculture. The mountain people adapted by developing the personality traits of the insurgent, the indomitable, who refused to compromise with authority, and who became a brigand in order to survive" (Sfyroeras, 1975). Communication or travel between isolated communities in the mountains was very difficult. This resulted in these small isolated communities becoming autonomous and self-sufficient. Even in present-day Greece, ships travel to some islands only once a week or less. Although small communities still exist in Greece, many are populated mainly by the elderly, and are no longer autonomous as in the past.

Organization and Institutions of Greek Society

Economic Organization.   The ecological features of Greece shaped specific types of subsistence patterns, which remained unchanged for hundreds of years. The plains, essentially the broad valleys between mountains, permitted crop cultivation. Cities in the plains and ports on the mainland or on the islands became trading and mercantile centers. In the mountains, the ecology was amenable to herding of goats and sheep, and vine and olive oil cultivation.

Fishing was the standard mode of subsistence in communities by the sea, together with merchant shipping. During the past 20 years, the traditional forms of subsistence patterns have given way to decreased agriculture, increased industrialization, and services related to tourism.

Political Institutions and the Legal System.

Because of the many small, isolated, and economically self-sufficient communities, effective political control of such communities by a central government was almost impossible (Zakynthinos, 1976). For example, the Ottoman rulers must have realized that effective political control of each of the thousands of small communities would have required a military presence well beyond their manpower capacities. The situation in the cities on the accessible plains and by the sea was different, and the Ottomans concentrated their forces in controlling these larger centers.

Thus, the Ottomans were most likely forced by ecological conditions to permit partial self-government of these isolated communities, with the provision that the communities pay their taxes. The system of taxation, as old as the Byzantine Empire, was adopted by the Ottomans, consisting of taxation of the community as a whole, and not individuals. The political organization of the communities consisted of a president and a board of councilors, elected by the community members, responsible for the administration of the community and for assigning to each family its share of the community tax burden. This relative autonomy and self-government in each community, which essentially set its own traditions, customs, and right to judge its own members according to local customs and "laws," was a critical factor that affected the Greeks' social perception of law, fairness, government, and suspicion of central government, which has continued until the present time.

Legal issues related to the family, on the basis of both local customs and Greek law, gave the rights of property ownership (with exceptions on islands, primarily) to the father. Marriages were usually arranged on the basis of contracts, in which the father's dowry of a house to the groom represented legal transfer of property (Cassia & Bada, 1992). The patriarchal rights of the head of the family were codified to favor control by the father; in case of divorce the father retained the property, became custodian of the children, maintained control of all family finances, and so on.

Since the 1980s, institutional changes regarding women's rights have been codified by new laws. They include, for example, sharing of property and becoming custodian of children after divorce, the right of the woman at marriage to retain her patriarchal name, children having the names of both mother and father, and at maturity, to maintain on reaching adulthood both names or to choose the mother's or father's.

The Education System.

After the establishment of the Greek state in the early 1800s, educational opportunities were limited to very few young people. The University of Athens was established in 1837, and one of the highest values of the traditional agricultural family was to educate at least one of the sons, even if this required selling land to finance his education. At the present time, the Greek educational system is an integral part of the EU educational system. Approximately 90 percent of the population is considered literate.

Religion.

Perhaps the most important single influence in maintaining the language and the identity of the Hellenes during Ottoman rule was the Orthodox Church. The clergy taught children to read and write the Greek language, maintained the rites of the Orthodox religion, were arbitrators in small communities, were sometimes elected to the board of councilors, and were often the only literate members of the community. In addition, the church and the clergy were often the leaders of insurgencies against the Turks, and thus martyrs and symbols of opposition. The church played a major role in the revolution against the Ottomans.

At the present time, 95 percent of the population is Greek Orthodox. Although the proportion of people attending church regularly in the urban areas is probably around 10 percent at the present time, recent polls indicate that the great majority of the population considers itself a believer in the Orthodox religion.

Bonds with Groups in the Immediate Community. Greek historians argue that the characteristic political organization of the small Greek community, together with its traditions and behaviors, have a basic continuity extending backward to ancient Greece. These small, isolated, autonomous communities were characterized by suspicion of outsiders and tight social control of families or clans. Violations of ethical standards or religious customs provoked reaction and sanctions from the entire community. The members of the community were judge, jury, and punishers of those who violated their customs, whatever the law of the central government. The collective responsibility of the community members, respect for life, respect for one's honor and one's property, institutions collectively supported by the community, were carefully protected. The fair distribution of the tax burden among the community members, the right to elect their own leaders, the right to choose their teachers, and the right to reject their priest, were rights carefully nurtured and guarded (Giannopoulos, 1975).

On the other hand, intragroup relationships, the factions composed of different extended families within the community, were often characterized by hostility and contention. As Giannopoulos (1975, p. 141) describes, "The same community system which nurtured collective responsibility as a protection against outside intervention by the Ottomans, enclosed within itself the causes of complaints, disputes, and the division of the community into factions. The assignment of the amount of taxes by the elected councilors was often unfair, which led to complaints and disputes. Thus, self interest, ambition and animosity divided the leaders and many of the family into factions." According to Triandis and Vassiliou (1972), the concept of "fairness," in the Anglo-Saxon sense, does not exist in Greece. Concepts such as "justice" referred to vindication of rights and demands of the family.

HISTORY OF THE TRADITIONAL GREEK FAMILY

Definitions of Family

Before describing the Greek family system, it is important to clarify the definitions to be employed, since there are multiple definitions of family, dependent on different theoretical perspectives (Doherty et al., 1993). Indeed, Aerts (1993) maintains that there is no current consensus of what makes up families, with disagreements as to the number of people involved in a family, who they are, what determines the creation of a family, and its boundaries. A traditional definition of the family from the anthropological perspective was that of Murdock (1949): "The family is a social group characterized by common residence, economic cooperation, and reproduction. It includes adults of both sexes, at least two of whom maintain a socially approved sexual relationship, and one or more children, own or adopted, of the sexually cohabiting adults" (p. 1). The functions of family were sexual, reproduction, socialization, and economic. A more recent minimal definition of the family, which takes into consideration the one-parent family and the changes in the social and economic position of women in postindustrial societies, according to Popenoe (1988), is "A relatively small domestic group of kin (or people in a kin-like relationship) consisting of at least one adult and one dependent person, the adult . . . being charged by society with carrying out . . . the social function of procreation and socialization of children, provision of care, affection and companionship, sexual regulation, and economic cooperation" (p. 6). There are three significant differences between the two definitions: Popenoe specified one adult as compared to two, elimination of the criterion of adults of both sexes, and the elimination of "a *socially approved* sexual relationship."

On the other hand, Murdock (1949, p. 2) made an important contribution to the clarification of the relationship of the nuclear family to other forms of the extended family: "The nuclear family is a universal human social grouping. Either as the sole prevailing form of the family or as the basic unit from which more complex familial forms are compounded, it exists as a distinct and strongly functional group in every known society." This is an important distinction, which will be referred to below in discussing the structure and function of the Greek family.

Structure and Functions of the Traditional Greek Family

The extended family is the type most closely characteristic of the Greek family during its history. Stanton (1995) defined the extended family as ". . . a corporate economic and political unit, as well as a kinship-based group. The extended family is an ongoing body with a geographical base and it transcends the lifetime of its members. The composition of the extended family with its nuclear families and independent single adults changes constantly, but the extended family itself continues with new leaders and new members as individuals depart or as the generations pass away" (p. 100). The traditional Greek extended family could be described as *patrilineal* in terms of lineal descent, *patriarchal* in terms of authority structure, and *patrilocal* in terms of residence of married sons. The lineal kin are *cognatic,* and the *collateral* kin are *affinal* relatives as well as *koumbari,* collateral kin through baptism of the children or "best man/maid of honor" at marriage of offspring.

A graphic description of the dynamics of the Greek family in relation to the ecocultural context was written by the sojourner Thiersch in 1833:

> Because there never was a central government able to control or protect the people, one had to search elsewhere for protection and support. The most natural and secure support was found in the family, whose members, including second cousins, are nowhere so united and so willing to help each other than in Greece. The isolated individual has to ally himself with some group. He becomes a follower, or a leader of a group. In this case, a prominent person has a group of followers dependent on him, who call on him, who ask his advice, who execute his wishes, who protect their common interests, always being careful to be worthy of his esteem and his trust. This

> is the nature of the many groups in Greece. . . . Rather than being astonished regarding this, one must recognize in this system, the course and the natural and necessary organization of a political society which was left to its own devices for survival.

Triandis and Vassiliou (1972) described the Greek ingroup as composed of more than the extended family, including, for example, best man at the wedding, the godfather, in-laws, and friends, with the criterion that they showed concern and support during times of need. The appropriate behaviors toward members of the ingroup were cooperation, protection, and help, while appropriate behaviors toward members of the outgroup were competition and hostility. Also, a key central value of the ingroup, which encompasses many other values, was *philotimo* (Vassiliou, 1966; Triandis & Vassiliou, 1972; Vassiliou & Vassiliou, 1973). *Philotimo* can be loosely translated as "honor," but Vassiliou (1966) suggested that it has a special meaning for the Greek ingroup, that is, "to give to others," "to be correct in fulfilling your obligations," "to sacrifice yourself for others," "to respect others."

One should not conclude, however, that the extended family was homogeneous throughout Greece. For example, Cassia and Bada (1992) studied matrimonial patterns and property transmissions and reported regional variation in property transmission. Pastoralists with extended families and neolocal island farmers gave a trousseau to daughters at marriage; continental farmers with nuclear families presented land and trousseaux to daughters. However, women from the islands had a comparably freer status. In nineteenth-century Lesbos, seventeenth-century Naxos, and Nisyros, fishermen gave houses to daughters and practiced unigeniture, with the eldest daughter receiving the bulk of the family estate; on the island of Naxos, daughters were endowed from the patrimony and sons from the matrimony; on Karpathos, bilinearity was the practice, with the eldest daughter inheriting from the mother and the eldest son from the father. Mainlanders in Eripus, Peloponnese, Mani, Crete, Cyprus, and Corfu were agnatically oriented, with sons receiving the bulk of family property and daughters receiving goods at marriage. In Athens and elsewhere on the mainland, most couples at marriage lived with the groom's kin in his parental household, with the main condition of house transfer to the son-in-law being an expectation of care for the elderly parents until their deaths.

Traditional Roles of Family Members

What are the traditional roles of the family members? These can be described based on a series of studies of traditional Greek family values. Traditional values of family members were delineated in studies of 417 university students, 227 from small communities from throughout Greece and 190 students either born or raised in Athens (Georgas, 1989), and 678 subjects, members of 226 three-person families, consisting of the father, the mother, and a son or daughter from Athens and from small communities (Georgas, 1991). These traditional values related to family roles were determined by the Greek literature on the family, and by eliciting family roles through group discussions with students. Values regarding roles were retained only if at least 90 percent of a group of students agreed they were traditional. Following are examples of the roles and values of the traditional Greek family, based on these studies.

> *Father* should be the head of the family . . . handle the money in the house . . . punish the children when they are disobedient . . . give a dowry to his daughter . . . the breadwinner . . . closer to his sons . . . the critic in the family . . . concerned only with the serious matters in the family.
>
> *Mother* should be the go-between the father and the children . . . place is in the home . . . should live for her children . . . always know where her children are . . . tell the father the problems of the children . . . help her children with their homework . . . agree with the father's opinion in matters which concern the children . . . accept the decisions of the father, yield and be compromising . . . be always there for everyday matters . . . give way when father becomes upset . . . vote the same party as the father . . . wom-

an's first goal in life should be to be a good mother.

> *Parents* should teach their children to behave properly . . . know their children's friends . . . help their children financially . . . be involved in the private lives of their married children . . . shouldn't argue in front of the children.
>
> *Women* shouldn't have children if they are not married. Girls shouldn't have premarital sexual relationships. Find a wife who is good like your mother? A separated woman should return to her family home. A clever woman knows how to find the weak point of her "macho" man.
>
> In order to have a happy *marriage,* one should select a spouse from one's village. A bad marriage should be maintained for the sake of the children. Marriages should take place in a church. Children should have their parents' approval when they decide to marry. One should avoid the divorced as potential spouses.
>
> One should maintain good relationships with one's *relatives.*
>
> The oldest *son* should take over the father's business or work. When the father dies, the son should be responsible for making certain his sister marries.
>
> *Children* shouldn't talk back to their parents . . . be seen and not heard . . . shouldn't have secrets from their parents . . . should eat with their parents on Sundays . . . the obligation to care for their parents when they become old . . . obey their parents . . . help with the chores of the house . . . ask their parents' permission before going out with their friends . . . respect their grandparents.
>
> The problems of the *family* should be solved within the family. We should be honorable (*philotimoi*). We should honor and protect our family's reputation.

The close bonds, the interdependence, the mutual obligations, the unity of the Greek extended family have been described by anthropologists, sociologists, and psychologists, and a list of references is presented for the interested reader: Besevegis & Pavlopoulos

(1998); du Boulay (1974); Campbell (1964); Campbell & Sherrard (1968); Doumanis (1983); Friedl (1963); Dragonas (1983); Hatzichristou (1993); Katakis (1984); Lee (1966); Mousourou (1976, 1981, 1985, 1999); Peristiany (1965); Pipinelli-Potamianou (1965); Polemi-Todoulou (1981); Safilios-Rothschild (1967).

In concluding this section on the traditional Greek family, it is clear that Greece was a homogeneous country in terms of ethnic composition. The extended family system was characteristic in Greece, although there were variations in different areas of Greece. The roles of mother and father, sons and daughters, grandparents, aunts and uncles, and other relatives were institutionalized primarily by local communities and secondarily by the larger society—the local priest, the village council, the state, the Orthodox Church. This overall homogeneity of Greeks as an ethnic group and of its institutions facilitates the analysis of the Greek family, in comparison with countries in which there may be two or three ethnic groups, or in polyethnic countries such as the United States or Canada.

CHANGES IN THE FAMILY

This section describes the changes in the modern Greek family. These changes will be discussed in terms of demographic statistics, family values, social support and interaction with kin, the role of women, parent–child relations, and the nuclear and extended family.

Demographic Statistics

Demographic statistics can provide a snapshot of changes in the Greek family in comparison with the picture of other member states of the European Union.

According to Mousourou's (1999) analysis of figures from *Eurostat 1996,* the number of marriages per thousand persons has been declining in Greece, from 9.4 in 1965 to 5.4 in 1994. The same trend was

found in the fifteen EU nations, but the number of marriages in Greece was higher than the average of EU nations—7.8 in 1965 and 5.2 in 1994.

A second demographic statistic is the increasing divorce rate. According to Mousourou (1999), the frequency of divorce per thousand persons in Greece, while increasing, is increasing at a slower rate in comparison to other EU nations. Greece had a rate of 0.4 in 1965, as compared to a 0.6 average in the fifteen EU countries, and a 0.7 rate in 1993 as compared to a 1.7 average in the EU, with the highest rate being 3.5 in Belgium.

Greece also has the lowest rate of one-parent families in the EU, with a rate of 5.6 for nonadult children per total number of households, as compared to a high of 19 in the United Kingdom (Eurostat, 1989; European Observatory on National Family Policies, 1995). However, as Maratou-Alibranti (1998) has pointed out, in order to obtain a true picture of what is meant by one-parent families, one has to analyze the proportions of never-married one-parent families; that is, the highest numbers of one-parent families in EU countries are the separated, divorced, and widows.

The number of births per thousand women of childbirth age in Greece has been declining, from a rate of 2.39 in 1970 to 1.35 in 1994, which is somewhat higher than the average for EU countries. Regarding births of unmarried women, Greece has the lowest rate of 3.0, as compared to the highest rate of 53.0 per 100 births in Sweden (*Eurostat,* 1995a).

Another demographic measure is attitudes toward importance of the family. According to *Eurobarometer* (no. 39.0/1993), 95.7 percent of EU and 99.4 percent of Greeks believe that the family is the most important thing in their lives.

On the basis of these demographic figures, the clear indication that the rate of divorce, the number of one-parent families, and the number of children born to unmarried women in Greece are the lowest in the EU. This suggests that changes in the family system in Greece, from a demographic perspective, are fewer than in the other EU countries. Let us now look at the psychological level, to investigate which changes have occurred within the Greek extended family system.

Family Values

Values related to family roles and functions are a psychological measure of changes in the family system. As indicated above, a series of studies investigated changes in traditional family values (Georgas, 1986, 1989, 1991). The values were measured on a 5-point scale. Factor analysis of the 64-item questionnaire resulted in three dimensions. The same three factors were obtained in a number of other studies with different populations and with different age levels—e.g., Papademou (1999), Bafiti (2000)—indicating a very stable structure.

The results of Papademou (1999), based on a representative nationwide sample of $N = 1,300$, ages 18 to 80, and from an unpublished study by the first author with 500 children ages 10–15, will be presented below.

The strongest factor that emerged from these studies was termed *Hierarchical Roles of Father and Mother,* based on value statements such as: The father should be the head of the family . . . handle the money in the household . . . the breadwinner . . . provide a dowry for the daughter. The mother should live for her children . . . accept the decisions of the father . . . agree with the opinions of the father . . . place is in the home. This factor contained values related to the traditional roles of the patriarchal extended family, in which the father was the head of the family, acted in an authoritarian manner, controlled the finances, while the mother was submissive, conciliatory, a housewife, who cared for the children.

The second factor that emerged consistently was *Responsibilities of the Parents toward the Children,* based on value statements such as: Parents should not argue in front of the children . . . should teach their children to behave properly. The problems of the family should be solved within the family.

The third factor was *Responsibilities of the Children toward the Family and the Relatives,* based on value statements such as: The children have the

obligation to take care of their parents when they become old . . . should obey their parents . . . help with the chores of the house . . . respect their grandparents. One should maintain good relationships with one's relatives.

The next step was to compare the means of the values on each factor for different age levels. Figure 12.1 presents the mean scores from Papademou (1999) for ages 10 to 85. The means on Hierarchical Roles of Father and Mother showed the greatest variability across ages. Children 10–15 years old were "not certain," 18–25-year-olds "disagreed" most among the age groups, followed by slightly less disagreement of 26–35- and 36–45-year-olds, and approximately the same level of "not certain" of 46–85-year-olds as with 10–15-year-olds. These scores also varied on the basis of urban–rural residence: Athenians rejected these traditional roles more than residents from small communities. They also varied according to gender, with females rejecting these roles more than males. Gender and residence interacted, in that there was a greater discrepancy in mean values of the Hierarchical Roles between young males and young females from small communities, and less discrepancy in disagreement between genders in Athens (Georgas, 1989). Also, correlations of hierarchical mother–father roles between the offspring and the mother and father indicated that male adolescents correlated higher with fathers than daughters, suggesting that sons identified with the father's position regarding these hierarchical mother–father roles, while there was little correlation between fathers' and daughters' values (Georgas, 1991).

An interpretation of these results might be that family values associated with the patriarchal authority of the father were rejected by people of all ages in Greece, or at least, they did not agree with them. This interpretation might appear to extend also to the conclusion that the extended family type is disappearing in today's Greece. However, let us look at the mean scores of the other two factors in Figure 12.1.

In contrast with the rejection of *Hierarchical Roles of Father and Mother,* young people did not reject values associated with *Responsibilities of the*

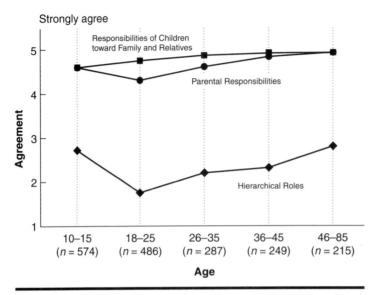

FIGURE 12.1   Mean Agreement Ratings for Hierarchical Roles of Mother and Father, Parental Responsibilities toward Children, and Responsibilities of Children toward Family and Relatives According to Age Groups 10–15, 18–25, 26–35, 36–45, 46–85

Parents toward the Children and *Responsibilities of the Children toward the Family and the Relatives.* These latter values are related to responsibilities of children to the family and also to the importance of maintaining ties with members of the extended family—that is, traditional values of the Greek extended family system.

We can come to the conclusion that children, adolescents, and young people in Greece do not reject all values of the traditional extended family, but only those associated with the traditional hierarchical roles of father and mother, son and daughter, male and female. These are roles related to father having the economic and social power, the strict obedience of children, the dutiful and acquiescent mother, and so on—roles consistent with the agricultural extended family in many cultures. Safilios-Rothschild (1967) found over 30 years ago that in Athenian nuclear families, with fathers employed in the professions, the father's social power was diminished in

relation to the mother's. Our findings suggested that the father's power within the family has lessened and the mother's has increased, due to the increased entry of women into the workforce beginning in the 1980s, the equal proportion of women attending universities, and other developments. These trends have also been widely observed in Europe and the United States (Aerts, 1993). On the other hand, young people in Greece agreed with values of the traditional extended family with regard to the importance of maintaining relations with relatives, of respect for grandparents, of offering help to parents, of obligations toward the family, and so on. These are values related to maintaining close emotional relationships and ties with kin. In a recent study of attitudes of EU 12-year-olds (*Eurobarometer,* no. 39.0/1993) in response to the question, "If in the future working people should care more for their elderly parents," Greek children had the highest level of agreement, 80 percent, as compared to less than 40 percent in Belgium.

Thus, there is evidence that many values of the traditional Greek extended family are still functional within the present family unit. What about other aspects of the Greek extended family? We shall have more to say about this in the next section.

DEFINITIONS AND DEMOGRAPHIC MEASURES OF THE NUCLEAR FAMILY

Parsons (1943, 1965) was perhaps the most influential theoretician who shaped thinking about the nuclear family in the postwar United States. Parsons argued that the adaptation of the family to the industrial revolution resulted in a nuclear family fragmented from its kinship network, with psychological isolation from its kin. Transition of the extended family type to the nuclear family type has also been linked to the process of modernization (Lerner, 1958; Inkeles, 1998). Historians of the family, sociologists, and anthropologists have criticized Parsons' ideas of isolation of the nuclear family from kin, based on historical analysis and evidence from social support and other studies (Kessler, Price, & Wortman, 1985; Segalen, 1986). Uzoka (1979, p. 1,096) referred to the "myth of the nuclear family . . . as structurally nuclear but functionally atomistic." It might be fair to say that most family studies, particularly in the United States and northern Europe, focus solely on the nuclear family as the basic unit of study. On the other hand, those interested in social support from kin employ the nuclear family as the basis for examining the social networks of members of nuclear families with kin (Marks & McLanahan, 1993).

How is the nuclear family defined and how is it measured in demographic studies? Parsons' definition of the nuclear family included gender and occupation—that is, a working father, a homemaker mother, and their children. Bernardes (1997) reported that this classic model of the nuclear family was found in only 14.6 percent of households in 1991 UK statistics, and that Ricketts and Achtenberg (1989) found only 7 percent of such households in the United States. Most would agree that the commonly accepted structural definition of the

nuclear family is two generations: parents and their children.

In addition to "parents and children," the term *household* is an essential part of the definition of family. Household means "common residence," in Murdock's (1949) definition of family. The terms *common residence* and *household* imply, respectively, an "independent" or "separate" residence, and a specific group composed of two generations with specific ties—in the case of the nuclear family— either socially sanctioned or by consensual union. However, an "independent" residence may be hundreds of miles from the grandparents, or may be, as occurs in many countries, the apartment next door or in the neighborhood. If one's in-laws reside next door, the question—not entirely rhetorical—arises of how "independent" this household is in relation to the grandparents. Murdock also employed the concept of *economic cooperation* as a functional criterion of family. It is possible to interpret economic cooperation in different ways in different cultures. It might imply economic cooperation among three generations necessary for planting or harvesting crops in an agricultural society. It might also imply mother and father working in different jobs and sharing the expenses of the household in New York City. However, a young married couple with a newborn child, even in New York, may be helped either economically or in terms of services by grandparents. In other words, independent or separate residence does not necessarily imply geographically distant residence from the grandparents. Nor does economic independence necessarily imply economic autonomy of the nuclear family.

One method of determining the degree of transition of family types from extended to nuclear is to count the number of households with two adults with dependent children. In a recent *Eurostat* European Community Household Panel (1995b), the average of these nuclear family households in the fifteen EU nations was 36 percent, and ranged from 30 percent in Austria to 43 percent in Belgium and France. The percentage in Greece was 35 percent; that is, at the average of EU nations and, surprisingly, slightly higher than Germany, with 33 percent. And yet, as will be discussed below, Greece cannot be described as a nation with more nuclear families than Germany from a functional point of view. So much for the analysis of demographics without looking at the functional aspects of family.

For our purposes, we will define family more broadly, as the constellation of nuclear families in which the individual is embedded: the individual's nuclear family and the nuclear families of significant kin. It is clear that the second part of the definition, "nuclear families of significant kin," refers to the extended family without, however, employing the term "extended family" as a value-laden family system. Thus, it can be used as a working definition for the study of functional relationships of the members of the nuclear family within the context of relationships with their kin in high-affluent societies as well as in low-affluent "traditional cultures."

IS TODAY'S GREEK FAMILY EXTENDED OR NUCLEAR?

One of the probes employed in our research to attempt to answer the question of the degree of transition of the Greek traditional extended family system to the nuclear family system was based on methods of social support theory (Adler, 1994). We studied the patterns of residence of kin in relation to the nuclear family, and in addition, functional aspects such as emotional distance, social interaction, and communication with kin (Georgas, 2000; Georgas et al., 2001). Kin were defined as grandparents, aunts/uncles, and cousins. Data (Papademou, 1999) were collected from a nationwide representative sample of $N = 1,300$, ages 16–80, $n = 522$ from Greater Athens, which includes Piraeus and suburban areas; $n = 307$ from Cities, defined as population more than 10,000; and $n = 432$ from Towns, defined as population less than 10,000.

Patterns of Residence of Kin

One way of determining degree of contact with members of the extended family was through residence patterns of the nuclear family in relation to

kin. Geographic distance was defined as residence of kin (grandparents, uncles/aunts, cousins) in: *same house, same building, nearby building, same neighborhood, same community, same city, far away.* This was also separated into Greater Athens, Cities, and Towns. *Nearby residence* was defined on the scale as ranging from residence *in same house* to *in same community*. The subtotals of percent of responses (Table 12.1, italics) to the above categories provided a measure of *nearby residence* according to kin and in Athens, Cities, and Towns. The percentage of grandparents who resided near the nuclear family in Athens (29.9 percent) was, as would be expected in a country with a high level of urbanization in the past 40 years, less than in Towns (39.3 percent) and Cities (39.7 percent). However, grandparents who resided either in the same house (8.5 percent), the same building (10.1 percent), or a nearby building (1.6 percent) summed to 20.2 percent. That is, one in five grandparents in Athens resided either in the same building or in a building near the nuclear family. And more interesting was the pattern of residence of grandparents in these same categories was virtually identical (21.0 percent) in Towns.

Maratou-Alibrante (1999) found even higher percentages of parents or in-laws (27.9 percent) who resided in the same apartment or a separate apartment in the same building in Piraeus. She also found that 38 percent resided in a nearby neighborhood of Piraeus. Piraeus is the port of Athens, and the sense of community and neighborhood there has been more stable than in Athens.

The residence patterns of aunts and uncles and cousins in the same house, the same building, and nearby building were also very similar in Athens (8.8 percent), Cities (10.1 percent), and Towns (9.3 percent).

Meetings with Kin

Degree of contact with members of the extended family was determined through frequency of meetings with kin, a measure of interaction. Frequency of meetings were on a scale: *daily, once or twice a week,*

Table 12.1 Geographic Distance of Residents of Athens, Cities, and Towns to Grandparents, Uncles/Aunts, and Cousins[a] (in percent)

	GRANDPARENTS			UNCLES/AUNTS			COUSINS		
	Athens (%)	Cities (%)	Towns (%)	Athens (%)	Cities (%)	Towns (%)	Athens (%)	Cities (%)	Towns (%)
Same house	8.5	9.3	10.1	1.5	0.5	0.6	1.4	0.8	1.1
Same building	10.1	9.9	7.7	6.3	5.5	6.1	6.3	5.0	6.0
Nearby building	1.6	6.0	3.2	1.0	4.1	2.6	1.4	4.5	1.4
Same neighborhood	3.6	9.9	13.0	2.7	5.5	9.9	3.8	7.0	9.2
Same community	6.1	4.6	5.3	9.0	6.0	7.3	9.5	6.6	7.6
Subtotals/nearby residence	*29.9*	*39.7*	*39.3*	*20.5*	*21.6*	*25.5*	*22.4*	*23.9*	*25.3*
Same city	21.5	23.8	19.4	43.8	39.9	32.3	43.8	40.1	30.9
Far away	48.6	36.4	41.3	35.8	38.5	41.3	33.9	36.0	43.9

[a]Athens: Greater Athens, including Piraeus and suburban areas (N = 522).

Cities: Population more than 10,000 (N = 307).

Towns: Population less than 10,000 (N = 432).

Source: Papademou, 1999.

every two weeks, once a month, every six months, holidays, rarely. The kin were once again grandparents, uncles/aunts, and cousins. *Frequent* meetings were defined on the scale ranging from *daily* to *every two weeks.* The percentages of frequent meetings, suggesting close interaction with grandparents, were 40.4 percent in Athens, 59.9 percent in Cities, and 53.8 percent in Towns; as expected, they were more frequent interaction with grandparents in cities near their towns, and also in towns. However, frequent meetings with aunts and uncles showed a different pattern, with an expected highest frequency, 38.3 percent in Towns, but with an unexpected 30.1 percent in Athens as compared to 23.3 percent in Cities. That meetings with kin in Athens were relatively more frequent than in Cities was an indication of the maintenance of contact with kin even in Athens.

Telephone Contacts with Kin

Telephone calls with kin are a measure of contact at a distance. The same scale employed for meetings

with kin was employed for frequency of telephone contacts. The percentage of *frequent telephone calls* with grandparents was 47.8 percent in Athens, 57.8 percent in Cities, and 47.5 percent in Towns, an equal level of interaction in Athens and Towns. Significantly, frequent telephone calls with aunts and uncles were higher in Athens (38.3 percent) than in Cities (33.5 percent) and Towns (29.5 percent). This same pattern emerged with cousins: Athens (42.2 percent), Cities (38.5 percent), Towns (35.1 percent). This was another indication of the maintenance of contact with kin at a distance in Athens.

Conclusions

What is the answer to the question, "Is today's Greek family extended or nuclear?" The above findings suggest that the types of residence patterns and interactions with kin in Athens are very similar to those of the traditional towns. Grandparents, aunts, uncles, and cousins reside very near the nuclear family, either in the same apartment building, in the neighborhood, or in the community. Kin visit each other frequently and telephone each other more frequently. In addition, it appears that they also telephone each other frequently even when the kin live outside of Athens.

The family values of the extended family, as discussed above, particularly those related to relationships with kin, are still accepted, even by young people. Thus, one can conclude, at least on the basis of the evidence presented, that aspects of the extended family are still active in Greece and in Athens. It appears that the form of the rural extended family in Greece has been transplanted to Athens. Thus, one can characterize the Athenian family type as an *urban extended family*.

These conclusions also provide a partial answer to why the percentage of nuclear families in Greece was at the average of EU nations and slightly higher than in Germany based on the 1995 *Eurostat* European Community Household Panel. We first have to add that the same panel also found that the percentage of three-generation households in Greece, over 20 percent, was the highest in the EU. However, just comparing demographic statistics is not enough. One has to look at the interactions between the members of the constellation of nuclear families that constitute the extended family, and not just the nuclear family itself, in order to understand the degree of maintenance of ties between the nuclear family and kin.

Further, historical and ethnographic information is also vital in interpreting data. Common residence of two or three generations is one way of differentiating between the nuclear and the extended family. Nuclear family households have been found (Georgas et al., 2001) to be more prevalent in affluent countries. For example, an adult son or daughter can afford, because of the high level of gross national product (GNP) in New York, to rent or buy an apartment and live separately from his or her parents. This is more difficult in a less affluent society such as Greece. However, one of the values in modern Greek society, stemming from older traditions of property transmission (Cassia & Bada, 1992), is that the father/

potential grandfather plans for a separate residence for the daughter, even before adolescence, for *when* she marries. The economics of Greece are an imperative here. A typical process of many fathers/ potential grandfathers with a piece of property or an old house in Athens or cities would be to make an arrangement with a building contractor. The arrangement was that the father would provide the property and the contractor would finance the construction of the apartment building, with the provision that the father would retain two or three apartments, e.g., one for himself and his wife, and two for the daughters, and the contractor would sell the other apartments. This explains why such a large proportion of Athenian families live in the same apartment building. According to the definition of the nuclear family—two generations in a household—each of these families is structurally nuclear, but functionally their ties are that of an extended family or joint family.

A CROSS-CULTURAL COMPARISON

A case has been made in this chapter that the Greek family is phenomenologically nuclear but functionally extended. Can we compare these changes in the Greek family with other countries? Demographic statistics indicated that the rate of divorce, the number of one-parent families, and the number of children born to unmarried women in Greece are the lowest in the EU. The social support data described above were used (Georgas et al., 2001) in a cross-cultural study of sixteen countries: Canada, the United States, Mexico, the United Kingdom, the Netherlands, Germany, the Czech Republic, Ukraine, Bulgaria, Yugoslavia, Greece, Cyprus, Turkey, Hong Kong, China, and India. In terms of means of geographic proximity, Greece was fourth after Cyprus, India, and China. Cyprus and Greece had the highest means of meetings with siblings, aunts/uncles, and cousins. Greece also had the second highest means, after Greek-speaking Cyprus, in telephone contacts with grandparents, aunts/uncles, and cousins. These are indications that residence patterns, interaction, and communication with kin are relatively close in comparison with other countries that also have an extended family system.

Modernization Theory and the Nuclear Family

As discussed above, family change has been associated by Parsons with the process of industrialization. *Modernization theory* (Inkeles, 1998) assumes that with increasing economic level and industrialization, countries reject traditional values and traditional culture, and all countries inevitably converge toward a system of "modern" values and increasing individualization. One of the consequences of modernization is the transition of the extended family system found in former agricultural societies to the nuclear family characteristic of industrial societies. European demographic statistics show that there have been changes in the Greek family. Divorce rates, one-parent families, and so on, may be the lowest in the EU, but they are increasing from 20 or 30 years ago. Greece, particularly Athens, may be characterized by an urban extended family system today, but what about tomorrow? Modernization theory predicts that traditional societies such as Greece may be presently "underdeveloped" but that economic well-being will inevitably result in changes in its family system to predominately nuclear, with fewer close relationships, more one-parent families, more divorces, and so on.

Huntington (1996) has recently challenged modernization theory, arguing that cultural values have replaced ideological distinctions, and play a major role in the shifting of national identities and loyalties to long-standing "civilizations." Inglehart and Baker (2000) explored the relationships between modernization theory and religion, employing the dimensions Traditional versus Secular-Rational values and Survival versus Self-Expression values. They concluded that although their data supported the type of cultural change predicted by modernization theory, they also acknowledged the influence of long-standing cultural zones described by Huntington's theory, in which religion plays a major role. Furthermore, they concluded that the results were consonant with Weber's (1904) theory that traditional religious values exercise an enduring influence on the institutions of a society.

The question is, as globalization and modernization theory would predict, is there only one road leading toward the nuclear and one-parent family structure and function as found in North America and Western Europe, bulldozed by an economic engine? Or are there many paths leading to different forms of family structure and function, influenced by economic growth but also influenced by long-standing cultural traditions? The answer is not yet in to these questions. But there are many who are asking them. Smith (1995) has cautioned, ". . . we have not yet understood variations in family structure, function, and interaction because we have viewed all families in comparison with a white middle-class nuclear family model, rather than on their own terms and in a particular sociohistorical context" (p. 5). However, Huntington's theory, as applied to family change, predicts that although increasing affluence in a culture will lead to certain changes, for example, more nuclear family households, cultural values will also be strong enough to maintain ties with members of the extended family.

CONCLUSIONS

How much has the family changed in Greece? Values are learned from parents and from society. Changes in values are a good indication of family change. Findings from studies in Greece indicate that some family values have changed, but primarily those related to the roles of the father and mother. The father has lost the autocratic power over the mother and the children, and as "nature abhors a vacuum," this power has been absorbed by the mother, and to a lesser degree, by the children. However, this does not mean that the extended family system has decomposed into isolated nuclear units. In fact, family values associated with maintaining close contact with relatives, children respecting grandparents, and children's obligations toward parents are still accepted by young people in Athens and in Greece as a whole.

Values also are an important factor in the prediction of behavior. Findings indicate that nuclear family members in Greece maintain close contacts with relatives: they visit them regularly, or if living at some distance, telephone them very regularly. Indeed, in comparing the frequency of these contacts with those in other cultures, Greece has one of the highest rates of visits and telephone contacts with relatives.

Another change has been the increase of nuclear family units in Athens, and in other cities. However, this does not necessarily imply a decrease of importance of extended family networks. Nuclear family units have increased in Greece because increasing affluence in Greece during the past 30 years has permitted the acquisition of a separate home for the married children. This is clearly a change from 100-year-old family traditions in Greece, when the groom would receive a home as a dowry from the father-in-law, but the bride would live in the home of the father-in-law. One has to differentiate between the concept of geographic proximity and the concept of psychological distance. A separate domicile for the nuclear family members, either next door or far away, is technically geographic separation, but does not necessarily imply psychological separation. Thus, although the percentage of nuclear family units is actually higher in Greece than in Germany, research findings suggest that an urban extended family system is the functional norm in Greece because the nuclear family members in Greece, in contrast to Germany, maintain closer physical and emotional contacts with the members of their extended family.

Thus, it suggests that, at least in Greece, although affluence has been increasing in recent years, the traditional agrarian extended family has not decomposed into isolated nuclear families, but it has changed its configuration, and its morphological equivalent is the extended family system in the urban setting with a continuation of its contacts with its network of kin.

Whether the Greek form of the family, and that of other similar cultures, will inevitably follow the models of the families of the affluent nations of Western Europe and North America is a question that cannot be answered at this point in history. It is related to the issue of whether "globalization" refers to total convergence of all cultures in a modern world, or primarily to economic and information convergence, and cultural patterns play a significant role in determining directions of cultural change. It is also a question of whether the centrifugal forces of economic and institutional changes, which tend to weaken emotional ties among family members, are more powerful than the centripetal psychological forces that establish emotional bonds between people and particularly among family members. The authors have to bet on the second outcome.

REFERENCES

Adler, N. (1994). Health psychology. *Annual Review of Psychology, 45,* 229–259.

Aerts, E. (1993). Bringing the institution back in. In P. A. Cowan, D. Field, D. A. Hansen, A. Skonick, & G. E. Swanson (Eds.), *Family, self, and society* (pp. 3–41). Hillsdale, NJ: Erlbaum.

Bafiti, T. (2000). *Diaprosopikes scheseis stin oikogeneia kai psychosomatike hygeia* [Interpersonal relations in the family and psychosomatic health]. Unpublished doctoral dissertation, University of Athens, Athens, Greece.

Bernardes, J. (1997). *Family studies.* London: Routledge.

Berry, J. W. (1976). *Human ecology and cognitive style: Comparative studies in cultural and psychological adaptation.* New York: Wiley.

Berry, J. W. (1994). Ecology of individualism and collectivism. In U. Kim, H. C. Triandis, Ç. Kagitçibasi, S.-C. Choi, & G. Yoon (Eds.), *Individualism and collectivism* (pp. 77–84). Thousand Oaks, CA: Sage.

Besevegis, E., & Pavlopoulos, V. (1998). Personality components in parental ratings of 12-year-olds: Mothers vs. fathers, boys vs. girls. In I. Mervielde, I. Deary,

F. De Fruyt, & F. Ostendorf (Eds.), *Personality Psychology in Europe, 7,* 129–140.

Bronfenbrenner, U. (1979). *The ecology of human development: Experiments by nature and design.* Cambridge, MA: Harvard University Press.

Brunswik, E. (1955). Representative design and probabilistic theory. *Psychological Review, 62,* 192–217.

Campbell, J. K. (1964). *Honour, family and patronage: A study of institutions and moral values in a Greek mountain community.* Oxford, UK: Clarendon.

Campbell, J. K., & Sherrard, P. (1968). *Modern Greece.* London: Ernest Bern.

Cassia, P. S., & Bada, C. (1992). *The making of the modern Greek family.* Cambridge, UK: Cambridge University Press.

Doherty, W. J., Boss, P. G., LaRossa, R., Schumm, W. R., & Steinmetz, S. K. (1993). Family theories and methods: A contextual approach. In P. G. Boss, W. J. Doherty, R. LaRossa, W. R. Schumm, & S. K. Steinmetz (Eds.), *Sourcebook of family theories and methods* (pp. 3–10). New York: Plenum.

Doumanis, M. (1983). *Mothering in Greece: From collectivism to individualism.* New York: Academic Press.

Dragonas, T. (1983). *The self-concept of preadolescents in the Hellenic context.* Unpublished doctoral dissertation, University of Aston, Birmingham, UK.

du Boulay, J. (1974). *Portrait of a Greek mountain village.* Oxford, UK: Clarendon.

European Observatory on National Family Policies (1995). *A synthesis of national family policies.*

Eurostat (1989). *Labour Force Survey.* Luxembourg.

Eurostat (1995a). *Demographic statistics.* Luxembourg.

Eurostat (1995b). *European Community Household Panel.* Luxembourg.

Eurostat (1996). *Demographic statistics.* Luxembourg.

Friedl, E. (1963). *Vassilika: A village in modern Greece.* New York: Holt, Rinehart & Winston.

Georgas, J. (1986). Oikogeneiakes axies foititon. [Family values of students]. *Greek Social Science Review, 61,* 3–29.

Georgas, J. (1989). Changing family values in Greece: From collectivist to individualist. *Journal of Cross-Cultural Psychology, 20,* 80–91.

Georgas, J. (1991). Intra-family acculturation of values. *Journal of Cross-Cultural Psychology, 22,* 445–457.

Georgas, J. (1993). An ecological-social model for indigenous psychology: The example of Greece. In U. Kim & J. W. Berry (Eds.), *Indigenous psychologies:*

Theory, method & experience in cultural context (pp. 56–78). Beverly Hills, CA: Sage.

Georgas, J. (2000). H psychodynamiki tis oikogeneias stin Ellada: Omoiotites kai diafores me alles hores [The psychodynamics of the family in Greece: Similarities and differences with other countries]. In A. Kalantzi-Azizi & E. Besevegis (Eds.), *Themata epimorphosis evaisthetopoisis stelehon psychikis hygeias paidion kai efevon* [Issues of education and sensitization of child and adolescent mental health personnel] (pp. 231–251). Athens: Hellenika Grammata.

Georgas, J., Mylonas, K., Bafiti, T., Christakopoulou, S., Poortinga, Y. H., Kagitçibasi, Ç., Orung, S., Sunar, D., Kwak, K., Ataca, B., Berry, J. W., Charalambous, N., Goodwin, R., Wang, W.-Z., Angleitner, A., Stepanikova, I., Pick, S., Givaudan, M., Zhuravliova-Gionis, I., Konantambigi, R., Gelfand, M. J., Velislava, M., McBride-Chang, M., & Kodiç, Y. (2001). Functional relationships in the nuclear and extended family: A 16 culture study. *International Journal of Psychology, 36,* 289–300.

Giannopoulos, I. (1975). Koinotites [Communities]. *History of the Greek nation* (Vol. 11, pp. 134–143). Athens: Ekdotiki Athenon.

Hatzichristou, C. (1993). Children's adjustment after parental separation: A teacher, peer and self-report in a Greek sample. *Journal of Child Psychology and Psychiatry, 34,* 1469–1478.

Huntington, S. P. (1996). *The clash of civilizations and the remaking of world order.* New York: Simon & Schuster.

Inglehart, R., & Baker, W. E. (2000). Modernization, cultural change, and the persistence of traditional values. *American Sociological Review, 65,* 19–51.

Inkeles, A. (1998). *One world emerging?: Convergence and divergence in industrial societies.* Boulder, CO: Westview.

Katakis, C. (1984). *Oi tris tautotites tis ellenikis oikogeneias* [The three faces of the Greek family]. Athens: Kedros.

Kessler, R. C., Price, R. H., & Wortman, C. B. (1985). Social factors in psychopathology. *Annual Review of Psychology, 36,* 531–572.

Lee, D. (1966). *Rural Greece.* Athens: Institute of Child Health.

Lerner, D. (1958). *The passing of traditional society: Modernizing the Middle East.* New York: Free Press.

LeVine, R. A. (1973). *Culture, behavior and personality.* London: Hutchinson.

Maratou-Alibrante, L. (1998). Monogoneikes oikogeneies [One-parent families]. *Greek Review of Social Research, 95,* 185–208.

Maratou-Alibrante, L. (1999). Diageneakes sxeseis sti synchrone epoche. [Intergenerational relationships in modern epoch]. *Greek Review of Social Research,* 49–76, 98–99.

Marks, N. F., & McLanahan, S. S. (1993). Gender, family structure, and social support among parents. *Journal of Marriage and the Family, 55,* 481–493.

McClelland, D. C. (1961). *The achieving society.* Princeton, NJ: Van Nostrand.

Mousourou, L. M. (1976). *E synchrone Hellenida* [The modern Greek woman]. Athens.

Mousourou, L. M. (1981). *Vasika stoicheia gia tin Hellenike oikogeneia* [Basic elements of the Greek family]. Athens: Gutenberg.

Mousourou, L. M. (1985). *Oikogeneia kai paidi stin Athena* [Family and child in Athens]. Athens: Estia.

Mousourou, L. M. (1999). Crise tis oikogeneias kai crise axion [Crisis of the family and crisis of values]. *Greek Review of Social Research,* 5–19, 98–99.

Murdock, P. M. (1949). *Social structure.* New York: Free Press.

Papademou, L. (1999). Koinonike kai psychologike analyse tis oikogeneias [Social and psychological analysis of the family]. *Psychologia, 6,* 165–173.

Parsons, T. (1943). The kinship system of the contemporary United States. *American Anthropologist, 45,* 22–38.

Parsons, T. (1965). The normal American family. In S. M. Farber (Ed.), *Man and civilization: The family's search for survival* (pp. 34–36). New York: McGraw-Hill.

Peristiany, J. G. (1965). *Honour and shame: The values of Mediterranean society.* London: Weidenfels & Nicolson.

Pipinelli-Potamianou, A. (1965). *Personality and group particpation in Greece.* Athens: Center for Mental Health and Research.

Polemi-Todoulou, M. (1981). *Cooperation in family and peer group: A study of interdependence in a Greek island community.* Unpublished doctoral dissertation, Bryn Mawr College, Bryn Mawr, PA.

Popenoe, D. (1988). *Disturbing the next: Family changes and decline in modern societies.* New York: Aldine De Gruyter.

Rickets, W., & Achtenberg, R. (1989). Adoption and foster parenting for lesbians and gay men: Creating new traditions in family. *Marriage and Family Review, 14,* 83–118.

Safilios-Rothschild, K. (1967). A comparison of power structure and marital satisfaction in urban Greek and French families. *Journal of Marriage and the Family, 29,* 345–349.

Segalen, M. (1986). *Historical anthropology of the family.* Cambridge, UK: Cambridge University Press.

Sfyroeras, B. (1975). Somata antistaseos tou ellenismou [Resistance groups in Hellenism]. *History of the Greek nation* (Vol. 11, pp. 144–151). Athens: Ekdotiki Athenon.

Smith, S. (1995). Family theory and multicultural family studies. In B. Ingoldsby & S. Smith (Eds.), *Families in multicultural perspective* (pp. 5–35). New York: Guilford.

Stanton, M. E. (1995). Patterns of kinship and residence. In B. Ingoldsby & S. Smith (Eds.), *Families in multicultural perspective* (pp. 97–116). New York: Guilford.

Super, C., & Harkness, S. (1980). Anthropological perspectives on child development. *New Directions for Child Development, 8,* 7–13.

Thiersch, F. (1833). *De l'état actuel de la Grece* [On the contemporary situation of Greece]. Leipzig.

Toennies, F. (1961). Gemeinschaft and Gesellschaft. In T. Parsons, E. Shils, K. Naegele, & J. Pitts (Eds.), *Theories of society* (Vol. 1, pp. 191–201). Glencoe, IL: Free Press.

Triandis, H. C., & Vassiliou, V. (1972). An analysis of subjective culture. In H. C. Triandis (Ed.), *The analysis of subjective culture* (pp. 299–335). New York: Wiley.

Uzoka, A. F. (1979). The myth of the nuclear family. *American Psychologist, 34,* 1095–1106.

Vassiliou, G. (1966). *Diereunesis metavleton ypeiserhomenon eis tin psychodynamikin tis hellenikis oikogeneias* [Exploration of factors related to the psychodynamics of the Greek family]. Athens: Athenian Institute of Anthropos.

Vassiliou, V., & Vassiliou, G. (1973). The implicative meaning of the Greek concept of philotimo. *Journal of Cross-Cultural Psychology, 4,* 326–341.

Weber, M. (1904/1958). *The Protestant ethic and spirit of capitalism.* Translated by T. Parsons. New York: Charles Scribner's Sons.

Whiting, B. (Ed.). (1963). *Six cultures: Studies in child rearing.* New York: Wiley.

Zakynthinos, D. (1976). *The making of modern Greece from Byzantium to independence.* Oxford, UK: Oxford University Press.

CHAPTER 13

THE ITALIAN FAMILY
PAST AND PRESENT

ANNA LAURA COMUNIAN
University of Padua

Live with full conviction of the fundamental values of the family and the community. Authentic human progress cannot fail to consider these values.
(Pope John Paul II, *L'Osservatore Romano*, 22–29 December 1986, p. 12)

Italy is a national state with a relatively recent history that dips her roots in an inheritance of antique civilizations and rich historical events. Its name derives from the population of *Italici*. One century before Christ, the Romans extended the name to all populations of the peninsula as part of their attempt to assimilate them into their own culture. In more recent years, the modernization of Italian society began slowly and only in the early twentieth century. However, poor balances between industry and agriculture, and above all, between the north and the south of the country, persist today.

On June 2, 1946, an institutional referendum in which all male and female citizens of full age participated, ratified the birth of the Republic. The Italian Constitution came into force on January 1, 1948. It was born as a compromise in which we can notice the respective influences of the Communist Party (protection of workers and the recognition of social rights), the Catholic Party (emphasis on family life and the relationship between Church and State), and various minor parties and liberal democratic groups.

Between the time of Italian unification in 1861 and 1990, the population more than doubled, from 25 million to 57 million inhabitants. The demographic growth was particularly rapid between the end of the nineteenth and the first decades of the twentieth century, but has slowed down considerably in recent decades. One of the more significant phenomena of the last twenty years has been the increasing percentage of those over the age of 60 years. It was about 6 percent at the time of national unity, but increased to 10 percent around 1900, to 13 percent after World War II, and to 20 percent during the last decade. Furthermore, the percentage of young people (below 20 years), which in the last century was more than 40 percent, decreased to less than 25 percent in the 1990s. At the same time, Italy changed from being a historical land of emigration—about 30 million emigrants left Italy between 1861 and 1985—to being an immigration country.

During the last forty years Italy entered into a developmental process that led to deep-rooted changes in the lifestyles of its citizens as well as

fundamental changes in the country's economic situation. Beginning in the 1990s, the process of international economic integration with other European and many non-European countries (in particular with the United States) accelerated, and exports now total about 5 percent of the gross national product. While these economic developments have led to many positive changes in society, they also resulted in many unresolved economic problems, especially in the latter half of the 1990s. Not unexpectedly, these economic changes have gone hand in hand with changing forms of family life, gender roles, and socialization practices.

This chapter discusses various aspects of Italian family life. The emphasis is on the family structures of the past century, the historical instability of family structures, major contemporary family structures, and the diversity of contemporary family structures. Cultural changes are described in terms of parental and children's attitudes, new forms of family life, changing relationships between family life and working conditions, and how Italian legislation views the family.

Over the last three decades, there have been striking changes in the family structure of all European countries, including Italy. In particular, there has been a notable trend away from a "standard family model" to a plurality of models. The ongoing demographic revolution reflects major socioeconomic and cultural transformations, although these transformations have occurred with different intensities and rhythms in the various countries. Marriage rates have declined and, to various degrees, a variety of family models have been adopted in the industrialized countries. Beginning in the 1960s, the traditional family system founded on marriage has gradually become less attractive to many Europeans.

The institutional crisis of the family and its recent changes are reflected in the following demographic phenomena in Italy:

- The average marriage age has increased.
- The percentage of unmarried couples living together has increased.
- Rates of separation and divorce have increased.

- The percentage of one-parent families has increased.
- The percentage of reconstituted families has increased.
- Birth rates have declined dramatically.
- The rate of illegitimate births has increased.

Likewise, the nature of marriage and the family has changed: today, marriage is no longer a symbol of one's passage from adolescence to adulthood, nor is it necessarily the legal base of the family and of procreation, as had been the case until the early 1960s. It is difficult to define which of the above factors are most important, but according to Italian family sociologists (e.g., Barbagli, 1990; Saraceno, 1988, 1996; Zanatta, 1997), the most influential factors causing the contemporary family to change are cultural in nature. One important change has been the increased "liberation" of women in society since the 1960s.

The laws have been influenced by these sociocultural changes, and in many European countries—Italy included—divorce on the basis of mutual consensus was introduced. Increasingly, family laws recognized equality between husband and wife as well as providing greater protection for minors.

Although marriage remains the family model favored by laws, nevertheless in all the European countries two apparently contradictory trends have appeared. On the one hand, the family has become more "private," meaning that the law promotes the protection of women and minors as individuals rather than protecting the family as an institution. This means that the role of the state in validating the making or breaking of bonds between couples has decreased. On the other hand, paradoxically, the family has become more "public," that is, the state has increasingly regulated the social and economic consequences of individual familial choices by trying to protect the children as well as the less financially secure partner in case of divorce.

At present, Italian family life presents contradictory images. While marriage crises are widely discussed, the lifestyles of married couples often remain different from those of couples in many other European countries. Simultaneously, recent national and international opinion polls have found that adults and young people continue to value the institution of the family. In a period of tremendous social changes and increasing fragmentation, the family remains an important point of reference for the majority of people in that it conveys lasting emotional and existential meaning to their lives.

What is Italy's place within the context of well-entrenched European demographic and familial changes within the last forty years? To answer this question is difficult because the Italian situation is rather unusual in comparison to many other European countries due to the following: In Italy, as in other Mediterranean countries, both traditional and modern family patterns coexist, although changes have occurred within the traditional family model. Married couples with children are still the familial nucleus in most cases; fewer young people marry, and if they do, at a later age. However, rather than remaining single or cohabiting, single people live for a longer period as part of their families of origin. The birth rate has recently increased slightly, but it remains at a very low level even when compared to those of many other European countries; fertility has decreased, but the majority of couples have a child. Rates of separation and divorce have increased and new forms of the family unit are being established, although these trends lag behind similar trends in other European countries.

In the 1990s in Italy, there were 8 (or 12.5 percent) divorces and 16 (or 25 percent) separations for every one hundred marriages. The Italian divorce rates can be compared to the 44 percent rate of Sweden and England, the 34 percent–35 percent rates of France and Austria, and the 29 percent–31 percent rates of the Netherlands and Hungary. At present, one can observe a delayed but very significant increase in Italian divorce rates, comparable to what happened in the other European countries from the end of the 1960s to the beginning of the 1980s (Barbagli & Saraceno, 1997).

The uniqueness of the Italian situation reflects the country's strong emphasis on religious and cultural traditions, which have portrayed family attachment as central to life's purposes. Further, it is influenced by economic constraints that induce couples to marry later and to have fewer children, in order to accomplish individual goals. Although these factors are important, it must be noted that the delay of Italian industrialization and modernization has led to a prolonged survival of the extended family when compared to most other European countries. Additionally, the economic and social imbalance between northern and southern Italy, and the relatively late and limited entry of women into the workforce, have been of importance. Nevertheless, Italian changes have followed a similar course as elsewhere in Europe, although with a different intensity and at different times.

More recent investigations confirm that in Italy, while marriage remains the preferred form of family life, other family styles are spreading, as is the case in other European countries. However, within Italy, deep-seated regional differences persist. They have their roots in the history of the traditional family and are the result of historical, social, and political upheavals that occurred in the various regions.

FAMILY STRUCTURES IN THE PAST

Barbagli (1990) has described the family structure of the central and northern provinces together with the changes that occurred there over the centuries. The author shows that in the nineteenth and twentieth centuries, industrialization and urbanization favored the existence of nuclear families. Nevertheless, even before industrialization, the Italian traditional family was frequently not a three-generation family. In the south, the nuclear family structure had already existed prior to industrialization. For many centuries, because of high population densities and division of property, many Italians lived in villages but not on their own land. An example is provided by the numerous sharecroppers of Emilia, Toscana, and Lombardy. In contrast, in the central and northern towns and already from the fourteenth century on, the majority of the population adopted neolocal residence and lived in nuclear families (Barbagli, 1984).

Between the fourteenth and twentieth centuries, the urban Italian family structure passed through four major changes:

1. Gradual reduction of high mortality rates after 1660, as a result of the decrease of famines and contagious diseases
2. A decrease in single-parent families as a result of declining mortality rates
3. A decrease in the complexity of family structures based on social status among urbanites, where the nobility changed the patrilineal transmission and inheritance system
4. A decrease in the number of domestic staff present in urban homes beginning in the seventeenth century, which resulted in children residing for a longer period with the family unit

According to Barbagli (1984), who confirms Ruggero Romano's (1971) thesis, between the sixteenth and twentieth centuries in the central South of Italy, the urban-versus-rural division existed not only at the political/cultural level but was also a part of domestic organization. As a result of control by urban families of the countryside, plots of land were unified into exclusive holdings. This meant that a significant number of men and women—both adults and minors—were needed to work the land, and dwellings were needed in which they could live. This led to complex family systems such as the family farm productive organization, with an important part of the population adopting this system.

The nuclear family was established between the second half of the eighteenth century and the first half of the nineteenth century in towns among all social groups, while in the countryside the extended family, where family units of parents, children, and relatives lived together, prevailed until about World War II.

Developments in agriculture together with the expansion of the proletariat supported the development of the nuclear family and an increase of contract workers. In this context, Barbagli (1984) gave the example of contract workers on cattle farms who were dispersed to various provinces because of prevailing economic conditions. Compared to sharecroppers, their contracts were annual rather than seasonal. When a cowherd accepted his contract, he knew he had security for himself and his family: the owner was very interested in the composition of his cowherd family, the number of its members, and the quality of his resources.

Italy's history has shown that economic activities strongly influence family structures. Over time, the Italian family displayed not only a variety of family structures, but also no linear transformations, even if, in the long run, the nuclear family has prevailed.

UNSTABLE FAMILY STRUCTURES OF THE PAST

The individuals and families of the past frequently encountered catastrophic and unexpected events, which affected the individual, the composition of the family, and the survival of the family units. Although epidemics and famines had decreased in frequency by the middle of the nineteenth century, mortality rates remained nevertheless very high for all age groups. Many people died before reaching old age. For example, Saraceno (1988) documented that only 30.9 percent of the men who at age 40 had fathered their last son, could expect to witness this son's marriage.

Large families changed their composition over time when different relatives adopted orphans, members migrated, and new families came into existence because of remarriage. Sex and age were crucial variables affecting the fortunes not only of the individual but also of the family. The women, different from today, were more likely to die earlier than the men because of complications during childbirth. For this reason, newborn and younger children frequently became orphans, and stepmothers were more common than stepfathers. On the other hand, as the availability of rural and artisan work increased for both sexes, having a fragmented family proved inefficient for agricultural production.

The presence of children could be an obstacle to the remarriage of a widow (or to hereditary succession), in part because this might prove an economic hindrance for the potential husband (D'Amelia, 1986). A man, on the contrary, because he had direct access to property and the means of subsistence,

found it easier to remarry, and did so sometimes by marrying a sister of his deceased wife. This meant that the widow's, rather than the widower's children, were more likely to remain in a broken family or to be scattered among relatives. The family of the past was indeed more unstable than today's family. Given that, the presence of widows, orphans, remarriages, and/or new parents led to many complicated family situations.

In the past, migration was another source of family instability. Migration was attractive to all but the richest landholding families. For economic reasons, some of the (mostly rural) family members migrated to other areas of Italy, especially the younger sons, and worked as servants for other landowning families, while some of the daughters became servants for urban families. Even at the beginning of this century, in the mountainous regions where agriculture proved difficult, the adults, generally males, migrated across the Alps to find work in the French mines (Revelli, 1977). These migrations involved mainly the "excess" sons and daughters—that is, those not destined to become heirs because of primogeniture. Other cases involved sharecropping or lease contracts when a person's relationships with the community and with relatives were abandoned or became weaker.

Finally, there was the seasonal migration of the shepherds, the day laborers, and the traveling shoemakers, tinsmiths, pitchmen, and so on. These "journeymen," who invariably belonged to an impoverished class, traveled from one village to another and from house to house, causing considerable instability in the family.

The instability of the family, caused by poverty, high mortality rates at all stages of life, and high geographic mobility especially among the rural populations, has led researchers to abandon the stereotypic image of a "motionless" past, characterized by supposedly stable family structures and relationships. Frequently, just the opposite was true (Laslett, 1975). The present high levels of divorce and separation are occurring only after a long historical stabilization process of family structures starting from the second half of the 1800s up until World War II (Saraceno, 1988).

In the period between the two world wars, the tendency toward increased family nuclearization was interrupted: while the rate of increase of the urban population rate had been high and constant for sixty years, around 1920 it slowed down. In 1921, there were 3,916,000 agriculture-based families; in 1931 this number had decreased by a mere 7,000 units. The data collected show that as late as 1931, most farmers, tenants, and sharecroppers lived in multiple families, because this type of family reinforced their economic and social position.

During the days of World War II, the family was shaken only on the surface. In those days of ordeal, during bombardment, persecution, flight, exile, and concentration camps, the full importance of family ties came to the fore. People frequently relied almost exclusively on the help of parents, husbands, wives, brothers, and children. The closest relations, and only they, never gave up the struggle for endangered family members and showed enough persistence to plan their rescue. In this period, too, the love of children for their parents, which was thought to have weakened, showed itself clearly.

When the people had recovered physically after the liberation, the desire for marriage intensified. Once married, people took a renewed interest in their surroundings and their future. Many sons pursued traditional occupational interests, planning to become farmers, teachers, and administrators. Parents of other adolescents were unhappy about the diminution of their traditional authority, especially so when their children opted for some of the more "outlandish" new and modern occupations.

After World War II, Italy underwent great economic and social transformations, although important social inequalities remained between the different classes. Furthermore, the process of industrialization led to the establishment of more nuclear families, at first slowly but then much more rapidly as industrialization began to spread throughout the whole society. These changes were stronger in the northern and central areas than in the South. These differences occurred not only because in the South the industrialization process was less important, but also because many Southerners in the countryside had already

lived for centuries in nuclear families. Research agrees on the fact that urbanization and industrialization have generated a strong incentive toward neolocal residence and the nuclear family (Barbagli, 1984).

CONTEMPORARY FAMILY STRUCTURES

At first glance, it appears that the family boundaries in the form of cohabitation are more definite in today's society than was true in the past. Two of today's more general family characteristics, cohabitation and a common family budget, remain the same as before, but without the previous economic exchanges between the traditional family production unit and various relatives as well as the community at large. However, even today internal family budgets may include exchanges and forms of integration with the "external world." The Italian National Institute of Statistics (ISTAT) took note of this fact beginning with the 1991 census, when the definition of the family as having a common budget was abandoned.

Today, more ample and systematic statistical data on the family are available than was true in the past. They are based on periodic census figures, on special investigations employing national samples, and on many more limited investigations. Although all these are useful for historical and cross-cultural comparisons, they do not always provide the same information about family structures and the vicissitudes of "soul states" as those compiled by the parishes of the past that performed both fiscal and moral "bookkeeping."

According to Saraceno (1988), the distinctive characteristics of the family are: (1) the nature of the relationship that joins one person with other persons, (2) cohabitation by all the family members in the same house, and (3) income and expenses take care of all or most of the family's primary needs, such as food and living quarters. Although this seems to be a broad and apparently flexible definition, it nevertheless interprets cohabitation merely in terms of a common legal residence.

The simplification of family structures in the census survey is well exemplified by the four family categories introduced by ISTAT beginning in 1981: (1) one-person households, (2) couples without children, (3) couples or single parents with children, (4) extended families.

Because the family definitions used by the census were homogeneous only between 1951 and 1981, it is difficult to make historical comparisons (Cortese, 1986). It also leads to difficulties in delineating clearly what the real boundaries of the Italian family are and finding clear criteria for its definition. The criteria include residential but also social and relational considerations together with resource-sharing criteria. For instance, the cohabiting unmarried child is considered from the point of view of the registry office (but not always from the fiscal point of view) as part of the family of origin regardless of his or her age. In contrast, children 25 years and older are considered to be independent of the family in other European countries. Of course, these are not only questions of bookkeeping or terminology, but also of the prevailing cultural models of the family, of family relationships of dependency and autonomy, of political considerations, and so on.

DIVERSITY OF CONTEMPORARY FAMILY STRUCTURES

After World War II, the number of families increased more rapidly than the overall population. This reflected an increase of nuclear conjugal and one-parent families. For instance, during the period from 1961 to 1991, the number of families increased by 30 percent, from 13,747,000 to 19,909,000, in comparison to a population increase of only 5 percent, from 50,623,600 to 56,778,000. Figure 13.1 depicts the distribution of five family types in 2000.

The recent increase in the number of marriages confirms on the one hand the people's inclination toward the nuclear family, and on the other hand the need to consider the effects of increased life expectancies. The decrease in the number of births and declining family sizes points to an imbalance between the population and the family. Separations and divorces are also giving rise to new forms of cohabitation that are reflected in the statistical sources. Ac-

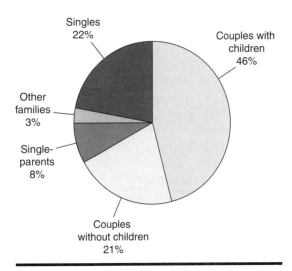

FIGURE 13.1 Distribution of Five Family Types in 2000

Census figures as of December 31, 2000, for five categories of families: couples with children, couples without children, single parents, other families, and singles.

cording to the 1991 census, half of the 25–29-year-olds and more than a sixth of 30–34-year-old persons still live with their family of origin. This phenomenon reflects both the delay of marriage and the persistent tendency to leave one's family of origin only when one is married. It is a tendency that distinguishes Italian family life from that of many other European countries.

More than 30 percent of the aged live either in an extended family or they live alone. It should be noted that most of the aging persons living alone are women, generally widows, while most of the young people living alone are male. A higher percentage of persons live alone in the North, whereas a higher percentage of extended families can be found in the South. As was mentioned before, this phenomenon is due to a modest increase of births and to the growing number of aged persons in the population. Both phenomena started first in the North and particularly in the big towns and have led not only to different family composition but also to different individual and familial experiences.

The combined incidence of legal separations, divorces, and factual separations is lower in Italy than in the other European countries, and is currently about 25 percent. Particularly in the North, one can find so-called "new" families. These include one-parent families as a result of the aging population, the breakup of marriages, procreation outside of marriage, and the presence of unmarried couples. Among one-parent families, 83 percent are headed by women; and among those not due to the death of one of the parents (that is, 25 percent of these families), 90.5 percent are headed by women. In general, families headed by single mothers are increasing (Cinciari Rodano, 1986).

Another type of family structure is the "reconstituted family" (Spanier & Furstenberg, 1987). Here, two persons, both or one coming from another marriage, live together with children originating from a previous marriage and sometimes also with the children stemming from the new marriage. Although this type of family is still fairly uncommon because of the relatively low number of divorces, its numbers are steadily increasing. It indicates new varieties of the family cycle for both adults and children. Because of the availability of more varied individual choices, family structures are likely to change over time. There are grandparents who give up being an independent family when they join the family of one of their children. There are husbands and wives, fathers and mothers, who do not live together anymore and enter into new relationships and forms of living together. There are children who pass from one family structure to the next, for example, from a nuclear structure family with two parents to a one-parent family and perhaps on to a reconstituted family.

Another nontraditional family type is based on uxorial cohabitation. This phenomenon is not so popular in Italy, as may be seen in the last census figures and in investigations by the Register's Office. In 1991, 1.4 percent of cohabiting couples were not married to each other. This percentage included both adults living together without being married because they were awaiting the divorce of one or both of the partners as well as those who considered marriage "inconvenient." Among the latter are widows who do not want to lose their pension as well as widowers/widows who wish to guard the inheritance rights of their children (Barbagli, 1990). From the point of view of traditional family conventions, those homosexual couples that claim the right to adopt a child represent an extreme case. They may wish to warrant the "continuity of generations" that constitutes one of the fundamental characteristics of the family.

The 1960s seemed to prefigure the new model of future family relationships. Some utopian communes appeared that represented a type of cohabitation in which neither the sex of the persons involved nor relationships between generations prove decisive. This type is also distinguishable from the simple sharing of a living space by a group of friends who pursue a common life project, often founded on the socialist ideology of total sharing of resources. Other communes are inspired by religious ideals. Many communes are unstable and evolve and devolve over time.

From the structural point of view, this multiplicity of family typologies has provided problems not only for researchers but also for lawgivers and policy makers who wish to establish definite criteria for various family forms, but encounter problems when trying to do so.

PARENTS AND CHILDREN: NEW FORMS OF FAMILY LIFE

Common sense dictates that there is a family when there are children. The expression "making up" a family, which refers to marriage, means in fact that the marriage is a necessary but not sufficient passage to form a family that will continue the chain of generations. Among those interviewed as part of an investigation by the Instituto di Ricerche sulla Popolazione (IRP) in 1983, 35.8 percent declared that the aim of marriage is the procreation of children (even if this might mean no more than one or two children). A second and more recent investigation by IRP showed that the majority of respondents considered having a child a very important experience, and only a minority said they might not have children, or more definitely, did not want children altogether (Palomba, 1991). According to an influential Catholic doctrine, marriage should above all be instrumental to procreation. By contrast, the Second Vatican Council in the 1970s declared that well-being and mutual relations between the couple possess the same dignity as having children (*Encilica Gaudium et Spes,* 1965). However, more recent Church documents (such as *Humanae Vitae,* 1968; *Familiaris Consortio,* 1981; *Orientameni Educativi sull'Amore Umano,* 1983) state that the main aim of conjugal sexuality continues to be procreation.   .

Ariès' (1968) historical studies of Western European families and children have shown that the modern family image as a private emotional relationship became popular first, before emphasis began to be placed on the loving conjugal couple. The modern family as a center of positive emotional relationships first redefined the children's place in the family, before the couple relationship was defined. One important consequence of this development has been a decrease in the number of children per family.

If the steady decline of fertility for more than a century followed a different course in the various European countries according to their specific eco-nomic and social situation (Festy, 1979), the changes in the years following 1950 have shown an increasingly similar course. In particular, Santini (1986) observed that in Italy more than anywhere else, the decline in fertility rates after 1965 took place in two phases: first a phase of consistent decline prior to 1981 (see Figure 13.2), followed by a gradual leveling out in more recent years (see Figures 13.2 and 13.3).

Until the 1960s the average number of children hovered around 2.3, but subsequently this number decreased to 1.8 at the beginning of the 1980s and finally to a very low 1.3 in the 1990s. This decline places Italy among the world's countries with the lowest fertility rates (Figure 13.3). Just in the last few years, a very lively and critical discussion has developed among researchers about the traditional explanations for the dramatic fertility decline. They discuss the relative influences of effective methods of contraception, the decline in infant mortality, and the importance of economic changes (because they have led to a reduction in the number and the importance of family businesses and the importance of family economies) (Coale & Watkins, 1986; De Sandre, 1987; Gillis, Tilly, & Levine, 1993; Kertzer, 1987). Currently, the reason why the various social groups

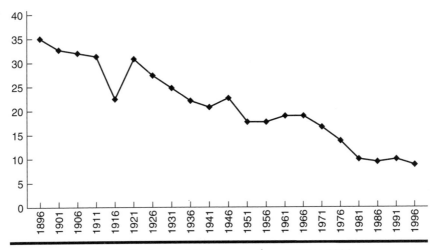

FIGURE 13.2   Italian Birthrates per 1,000 Persons from 1896 to 1996

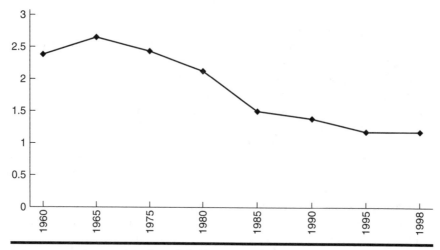

FIGURE 13.3   Average Number of Children per Italian Woman from 1960 to 1998

have reduced their fertility to today's minimum levels appears much more complex, less linear, and less irreversible than was believed true even a few years ago.

The new family is less authoritarian than in the past, and the trend to favor the independence and higher status of women has become widely accepted. However, the responsibility for childrearing still falls primarily on the mother, since the father's role is considered collaborative in helping the wife, and sometimes also that of a distant or feared disciplinarian.

Violence in families has become an important problem in Italy, and it must be considered as a multiform phenomenon without clear boundaries. Different forms of violence exist, such as physical violence, sexual violence, and psychological abuse including injury and humiliation. Hidden behind family walls, family violence can be discovered only with difficulty. As various studies (e.g., Barbagli & Saraceno, 1997) have confirmed, abuse involving minors and women can continue for a very long time. Only a small proportion of these offences become public, if one compares known incidences with the data derived from other sources such as Telefono Azzurro and Telefono Rosa e Case di Accoglienza— hotlines that deal with cases of abuses and physical or psychological violence against children, women,

and young people. The increasing incidence of sexual child abuse points to numerous traumatic events for the victims and their families. The victims and their families, the family risk factors, the importance of timely psychological treatment, and the possible preventive interventions are all taken into consideration by the psychologists, sociologists, and social workers studying the phenomenon.

In particular, Telefono Azzurro has filled a gap in the net of services for families and children at risk, offering an informal and friendly but nonetheless professional form of help. The experience acquired through listening to children, and to the adults working and caring for them, has underlined the necessity for society-wide engagement. This has meant a direct involvement in the "political" activity of promoting children's rights at the local, regional, national, and international levels.

FAMILY LIFE AND WORKING CONDITIONS

In analyzing the 1970s labor market, Del Boca and Turvani (1979) utilized the expression of a "happy meeting" between the labor market and the family. Since then, the most important changes concern women's participation in the labor market, which in turn have led to changed family structures. There were changes in consumerism, the development of domestic technology, and the transformation of daily family activities: a shift occurred from incessant involvement in domestic work to the availability of much more leisure time. Beginning with these factors, for the person and for the family, the spread of unemployment, changes in consumption patterns, improvements in household machines, and changes in daily family activities have all led to more leisure time for the family members. The wives tend to organize their priorities so they can more easily meet family needs in the case of conflicts, whereas the husbands tend to give priority to their work. Because of the double workload created by the family and paid work, wives cook less, invite friends and relatives less often to dinner, and dedicate less time to housework.

The different presence of men and women in the labor market has had a pervasive impact on who does the homework. Originally, very young men entered full-time positions in the labor market, whereas very young women became full-time housewives. In this context, Del Boca and Turvani (1979) and Paci (1978) arrived at similar conclusions in their respective analyses of the Italian labor market. The "fullness" of male presence in the labor market required an analogous "fullness" of the female presence in the family, especially when the family includes school-age and pre-school-age children. Lack of day care centers, Italian eating habits (lunch at home), and an absence of school and farm canteens reinforced this necessity.

According to official data, the housewife emerged as the mirror of the worker in the 1960s, but in the 1970s, the figure of "mother-worker" began to become popular. ISTAT investigations have shown that in the late 1980s and early 1990s, the percentage of working mothers with children under 18 years old had grown to more than 40 percent. The incompatibility—or poor compatibility—between paid work and domestic work emerges in a comparison between the work conditions and familial responsibilities of housewives and workers in various professions: those wives holding a full-time position have fewer children (Bielli, Pinnelli, & Russo,

1973; Bielli, Maffioli, Pinnelli, & Russo, 1975). Saraceno (1981) has documented this fact in research conducted in Lombardy, and the researchers Barile and Zanuso (1980) have done so in Trentino.

Many women prefer positions requiring fewer working hours, such as positions in the service industry and in teaching, because these provide conditions more compatible with domestic work. Autonomous work is possible only under certain conditions, for example, when it is conducted in a family business.

Many families continue the tradition of the family as a production unit, in spite of industrialization. However, it emerges that the male adults are typically placed in the official and guaranteed positions. While some family members work in positions guaranteeing a sure income as well as social security benefits, others participate in unofficial work that has been called "black" or "gray" work.

Some of the young and others may work "off the books." A study coordinated by Gallino (1982) about persons holding more than one position showed that highly qualified workers living in areas offering many job opportunities are also those who have better access to the more or less unofficial, but in any case more qualified and better-remunerated, secondary work positions. Vice versa, Becchi Collidà (1979) indicated how in southern Italy, official incomes for families frequently do not exist at all. For this reason many families "offer" to the informal economy—ranging from the building industry, to retail commerce, to domestic work, to handicrafts—the work capacity of their members, including both adults and minors (Perna, 1978; Petrillo & Serino, 1978).

Research about the family (Ceres, 1986) indicates how gender differences within the family are reinforced by the possibility of gaining access to the better-remunerated positions that also guarantee greater job security. This is true both for the informal and the formal sectors. Utilizing a variety of data, researchers have drawn a map of the different family strategies in response to different socioeconomic conditions, in terms of the labor market, the relationship between the formal and informal economies, the country's infrastructures, and the available services (see Martinotti, 1982, about

Torino; Ingrosso, 1984, and Balbo, May, & Micheli, 1990, about Emilia and South Italy). These different conditions not only favor different family strategies, they also lead to different relationships between the sexes and the generations within the family. In fact, in the past, sexual equality was applied more in a negative way, when it was needed to defend the woman against the man, supporting gender separation rather than new collaborative relationships between genders. Whereas men and women in the past enjoyed reciprocal but different rights and tasks, today gender roles are more similar and more shared. The man gives more attention to the woman's needs, but in practice most women continue to be involved in traditional family roles. New alternative styles, intended to realize a major "sharing of gender" between the couple, depend, apart from personal variables (such as higher levels of education and knowledge) on: (1) the material resources possessed by the family; (2) legislation that allows more flexibility in professional work and forms of family life that couples can pursue without losing their jobs (e.g., parental leave) for both men and women; and (3) the possibility of receiving help from other persons (relatives or domestic collaborators) and from the primary and secondary networks in which the couple is involved.

Changing family relationships can lead to changes in work involvement (for young people who wish to be economically independent, for example, or for women who look for economic independence and/or a professional identity). Changes in work demands can in turn produce changes in family organization. The increase of service jobs for females in the 1970s and 1980s, for example, led to various changes in female behaviors. The amount of time married women spend on domestic work (an average of 6–8 hours a day) has remained constant even though household technology and material conditions have changed greatly in the past decades. This is so because technological developments, though making work easier, also seem to favor the emergence of new demands in domestic work, of new needs and new standards. Each domestic task now requires different competencies, so that the var-

ious generations of women can no longer pass them from mother to daughter. With reference to this, there are interesting replies to a questionnaire presented to a Southern Italian sample of 900 women (two-thirds of whom enjoyed stable job positions). The better-educated women argued for their right to work as well as the husband's obligation to participate in domestic work. As Accornero and Carmignani (1986) point out, in the South, where gender differences are pronounced, people are now confronted with an "anthropological disaster" because the slow change in attitudes about gender roles does not match the faster change in economic and personal opportunities.

Regarding relations between the generations, in Italy, older people tend to be better integrated into society and family life than in many other European countries (Kahana, Biegel, & Wykle, 1994). The demographic data show that they enjoy strong emotional relationships with their sons, daughters, and nephews. Few are the aging persons who do not have children or whose children live far away. ISTAT data indicate that there are few isolated old people and that instead, they tend to be well integrated in a social context of primary relationships. The family is the main reference context within which the elderly lead emotionally satisfactory and interpersonally connected lives. In contrast, "external" relations with neighbors, friends, and volunteers tend to be more limited, whether the old people are living alone or with their family. Within the family, the flow of help goes in two directions: the old person is not only the "addressee" but also the "supplier" of care. Especially below an age of about 75 years, the aging person is the one who "gives" in the form of rearing grandchildren, shopping for the family, and other domestic activities in their child's home. The elderly are a strong resource for the family and facilitate the professional activities of the younger wives.

Positive relationships between grandparents and grandchildren are important for children's psychological development, and not only for material reasons. They are also occasions for an active and satisfactory societal role for the elderly.

Socialization in the family provides the individual with the idiom for behaving in the wider community. Modern Italian families emphasize respect and love more than obedience toward those who are older, together with care for the younger. Avoiding negative aspects such as aggressiveness, dependency, laziness, and so on, is also stressed by many. However, in the rural areas, nuclear families are more concerned with conformity and less with independence.

The child's relations with his or her parents improve over time. During the middle years of childhood the parents still provide children with positive instruction in how they should behave, and their discipline becomes somewhat more consistent. A very common socialization practice for children in Italy consists of involving them in family dinner discussions and arguments: parents and children interact, mothers evaluate and respond to the younger child, fathers evaluate and respond to the older child, and family members who are being evaluated or challenged turn for support to some family member who is not participating in the evaluation process. The research on this topic suggests that in most families, relations are based more on reciprocal interaction than on opposition and contrast (Menghini, Gnisci, & Pontecorvo, 2000). Findings indicate a gradual process of democratization across generations and between the sexes. Discipline is no longer authoritarian, all of the members contribute to family decision making, and parental roles are less rigid than they were in the past. However, the presence of the mother remains strong during the process of socialization. In addition, Bianchi's research (1983) shows that differences in socialization practices between different social classes and between urban and rural environments are steadily diminishing.

HOW ITALIAN LEGISLATION VIEWS THE FAMILY

Changes in Italian legislation after World War II with respect to family relations are instructive. The Italian Constitution defines the general basis for family norms in two articles. Article 29 underlines that the Republic recognizes the rights of the family as a natural group based on marriage. Marriage, in turn, is based on the moral and legal equality of the couple, with some limits established by the law to guarantee family unity. Article 30 reads as follows: "Parents have the right and the duty to maintain, instruct, and educate their children even if they are born out-of-wedlock." The law assures that such children enjoy similar legal and social rights as legitimate children. The law also stipulates the conditions for a person's inquiries about who his or her father is.

The family appears as a natural social group that is simultaneously expected to follow institutional norms regulating questions of legitimacy, relationships between the couple, and relationships between the generations. It is mostly a society of equals, but one in which equality can be limited in favor of unity, both with regard to the relationship between husband and wife and that between parents and children, whether legitimate or not. These contradictory indications not only testify to the hard work necessary to arrive at a compromise between the different political parties within the Constituent Assembly (Rodotà & Rodotà, 1981), they also express the coexistence of different family models held by individuals and by various cultural groups.

Many living persons have, over time, experienced dramatic societal changes that in turn influenced their conjugal and familial situations. Some legal and political changes are very old, such as the introduction of the Concordat marriage in 1929 as administered by the Catholic Church. (This institution is based on the distinction between two official types of marriage, the civil and the religious ones.)

The Fascist Civil Code in 1942 had reinforced the husband's authority with the institution of property separation and other laws that put the wife at a disadvantage. Subsequently, Articles 29 and 30 of the Italian Constitution were introduced, which created the basis for more equality between husband and wife. The articles were effectively included in the law only in 1975, but they had been anticipated by the introduction of legal divorce proceedings in

1970 and by the discussion that had followed before the referendum in 1974. Important new legislation about adoption, in turn, had already been introduced in 1967.

The new rights of the family ensure that they can adopt a form of living close to their culture and their values. However, not all families and individuals enjoy the necessary resources to realize their preferred values. In connection with the juridical changes, there have been other changes that have concerned the family relationships, in particular between the two sexes. It took quite some time before various articles of the Fascist Law of 1942, which strongly favored asymmetrical relationships between men and women for various sexual offenses and crimes, were abolished. About these crimes and the ensuing minor punishments, a literary and movie tradition sprang into existence as may be seen in the film *Divorzio all'Italiana* [Divorce Italian Style]. These articles were changed in different years: the differential treatment of women and men in cases of adultery in 1968, the laws punishing abortion in 1978, and the laws regulating punishment for crimes of honor later on. These gradual changes point to the difficulties Italian society (or at least some of its parts) had in establishing new models of equality and of freedom in individual decision making. In addition, it should be kept in mind that family rights are not reducible to civil legislation only, but must also include the right to economic and social security (Rodotà & Rodotà, 1981).

CONCLUSION

The new opportunities that Italians are enjoying are the threads that connect the different and changing forms of family life. One concerns the emotional freedom of the individual, which in the past was crushed by family authority. Others include the evolving conditions for true equality between men and women, including the liberation of women from the subaltern conditions on which traditional marriage was based. The new networks of relationships and solidarity that can be developed through social policies and social communication offer still another opportunity. Influential studies and research into the sociology and psychology of the family confirm that the concern with aid for families has accentuated the private and individualistic dimensions of the family, thereby weakening forms of solidarity that maintain the community (Garelli, 1994; Scabini, 2000; Scabini & Cigoli, 2000). This phenomenon is revealed in the multiplication of social intervention services that has left the family subject to a variety of services, up to the point of creating the phenomenon of the "assisted family."

However, individual autonomy and freedom of choice often entail costs and risks, such as greater conjugal instability, conflicts between parents especially about the children, and the decline in financial support for the former partner after the breakup of the family that frequently leads to economic impoverishment and even social degradation. To these risks one may add a certain lack of adult responsibility and the difficulty people may experience when they attempt to develop a coherent "life project." These are typical phenomena to be found in the culture of today's young people. They are also among the reasons why young adults may remain in the parental family for such long periods of time.

In a society distinguished by a multiplicity of ideas and lifestyles, a balance between potentially conflicting values must be reestablished for everybody to promote and to guard. These values include personal self-realization and gender equality, but also family stability. While these observations are valid for other European countries as well, they have a particular meaning for Italy. Here, the development of "the" new family occurred later than elsewhere, but today separation and divorce are increasingly common. Consequently, the number of one-parent families, reconstituted families, new forms of cohabitation, and persons living alone are all steadily increasing. Because these changes have been occurring later than in other countries, Italian society should make use of the opportunity for examining its experiences, in order to prepare itself better for the impending family changes.

The little scientific knowledge we have acquired so far allows us to provide some partial indications about how to raise private and public awareness about these difficult matters. On the private responsibility plane, for example, family stability could be increased by greater sharing of family tasks between men and women, by more solidarity and mutuality between couples, and by an increased awareness of the negative psychological, social, and economic effects that family breakups have for all members, and in particular for children. If breakup has taken place, the new partners should know that the degree of parental conflict influences the psychological well-being of the children and that positive relationships between both parents and the children have to be maintained.

Public policies, though proclaiming the high value of the family, have often failed to support it in practice while delegating to it almost completely the responsibility for the well-being of the individuals. Today, some positive policy-related changes have been accomplished, but much remains to be done.

Public policies have frequently been unable to guide family changes for the better. The experience of other countries shows that public policies cannot prevent family instabilities, because these are more connected to private responsibilities. Indirectly, however, it is possible to promote family functioning and well-being. For example, more and better social services need to be offered for children and adolescents. Policies need to encourage the participation of fathers in the raising of their children by ensuring more flexible ways of organizing work that are also more attentive to the requirements of family life. New public policies need to be introduced for the amelioration of the negative consequences of family instability. For example, family mediation services must be supported to help ensure more positive solutions for the psychological and material problems connected to the dissolution of marriages. They can help guard the interests and welfare of the children and of the weaker partners, while preparing unemployed single mothers to reenter the world of work. The entry of a growing number of women in the world of work demands improved public policies ensuring the coordination of working conditions with the requirements of family life as well as new kinds of social services.

As societal change accelerates, work is the field in which new opportunities arise together with new contradictions. New forms of economic and social cooperation, professional training, and protective laws must be developed so that weaker families can avoid the precariousness of living on the margins of society.

Harmonization of the interests of the individual and of society could make Italy not only richer but also more aware and more satisfied with prevailing customs, more trusting in herself, and more capable of contributing to the civil, economic, and social development of Europe.

REFERENCES

Accornero, A., & Carmignani, F. (1986). *I paradossi della disoccupazione* [The paradox of unemployment]. Bologna: Il Mulino.

Arìes, P. (1968). *Padri e figli nell'Europa medievale e moderna* [Fathers and children in Medieval and Modern Europe]. Bari: Laterza.

Balbo, L., May, P., & Micheli, G. (1990). *Vincoli e strategie della vita quotidiana* [Bonds and strategies of daily life]. Milano: FrancoAngeli.

Barbagli, M. (1984). *Sotto lo stesso tetto* [Under the same roof]. Bologna: Il Mulino.

Barbagli, M. (1990). *Provando e riprovando. Matrimonio e famiglia in Italia e in altri paesi occidentali* [Trying and retrying. Marriage and family in Italy and in other western countries]. Bologna: Il Mulino.

Barbagli, M., & Saraceno, C. (1997). *Lo stato delle famiglie in Italia* [The family situation in Italy]. Bologna: Il Mulino.

Becchi Collidà, A. (1979). *Politiche sociali e garanzie del reddito* [Social politics and income guarantees]. Bologna: Il Mulino.

Bianchi, L. (1983). Giovani, famiglia e classe sociale [Youth, family and social class]. *Rassegna Italiana di Sociologia, 24*(2), 169–210.

Bielli, C., Maffioli, D., Pinnelli, A., & Russo, A. (1975). *Fecondità e lavoro della donna in ambiente urbano*

[Woman's fertility and work in the urban environment]. Roma: Istituto di Demografia.

Bielli, C., Pinnelli, A., & Russo, A. (1973). *Fecondità e lavoro della donna in quattro zone tipiche italiane* [Women's fertility and work in four typical Italian areas]. Roma: Istituto di Demografia.

Ceres (1986). Famiglia ed economia sommersa[Family and the hidden economy]. *Economia del Lavoro, 1,* 3–85.

Cinciari Rodano, M. (1986). *Relazione presentata a nome della commissione per i diritti della donna sulle famiglie monoparentali* [Report presented to the Women's Rights Commission on Single-Parent Families]. European Community-European Parliament, Session documents, March 12th.

Coale, A. J., & Watkins, S. C. (1986). *The decline of fertility in Europe: The revised proceedings of a conference on the Princeton European Fertility Project.* Princeton, NJ: Princeton University Press.

Cortese, A. (1986). Le modificazioni della famiglia attraverso i censimenti [Family changes according to the census]. In ISTAT, *Rapporto sull'Italia* (pp. 145–166). Bologna: Il Mulino.

D'Amelia, M.(1986). Scatole cinesi. Vedove e donne sole in una società d'ancien regime [Chinese boxes. Widowers and lonely women in an ancient regime society]. *Memoria, 18*(3), 465–524.

Del Boca, D., & Turvani, M.(1979). *Famiglia e mercato del lavoro* [Family and the labor market]. Bologna: Il Mulino.

De Sandre, P.(1987). Ricambio tra generazioni: regole nuove verso equilibri incerti [Change between generations: New rules toward uncertain balances]. *Polis, 1,* 161–172.

Festy, P.(1979). *La fécondité dans les pays occidentaux de 1870 à 1970* [Fertility in western countries from 1870 to 1970]. Paris: Ined.

Gallino, L.(1982). *Occupati e bi-occupati* [Being employed and being employed in two positions]. Bologna: Il Mulino.

Garelli, G. (1994). Genitori e figli verso il Duemila [Parents and children to the year 2000]. In G. Chiosso (Ed.), *Nascere figlio. Le Famiglie Italiane verso il Duemila* (pp. 13–28). Torino: UTET

Gillis, J. R., Tilly, L. A., & Levine, D. (Eds.). (1993). *The European experience of declining fertility. A quiet revolution, 1850–1970.* Cambridge, UK: Blackwell.

Ingrosso, M.(1984). *Strategie familiari e servizi sociali* [Family strategies and social services]. Milano: FrancoAngeli.

Kahana, E., Biegel, D. E., & Wykle, M. L. (Eds.). (1994). *Family care-giving across the life span.* Thousand Oaks, CA: Sage.

Kertzer, D. (1987). Verso una nuova teoria del declino della fecondità [Toward a new theory on the fertility decline]. *Polis, 1,* 176–188.

Laslett, P. (Ed.).(1975). *Il mondo che abbiamo perduto* [The world we have lost]. Milan: Jaca Book.

Martinotti, G. (Ed.). (1982). *La città difficile* [The difficult city]. Milan: FrancoAngeli.

Menghini, D., Gnisci, A., & Pontecorvo, C. (2000). Chi problematizza chi nelle cene in famiglia. Regole condivise e convenzioni familiari. [The assessment and challenging of discourse during family dinners: Shared rules and family conventions]. *Giornale Italiano di Psicologia 27*(2), 347–375.

Paci, M.(1978). *Capitalismo e classi sociali in Italia* [Capitalism and social classes in Italy]. Bologna: Il Mulino.

Palomba, R.(1991). Gli italiani e le opinioni sulla natalità e le politiche demografiche [Italians' opinions about the birth rate and demographic politics]. In A. Golini (Ed.), *Famiglia, figli, e società in Europa* (pp. 301–332). Turin: Edizioni Fondazione Agnelli.

Perna, T. (1978). Un caso di lavoro nero. Il lavoro minorile a Reggio Calabria [A case of "black" (unofficial) work. The work of minors in Reggio Calabria]. *Quaderni di fabbrica e stato, 1,* 187–209.

Petrillo, G., & Serino, C.(1978). Scuola e lavoro minorile in un'indagine nel centro storico di Napoli [School and minor work: An inquiry in Naples' historical center]. *Inchiesta, 35–36,* 94–98.

Pope John Paul II. (1986, 22–29 December). *L'Osservatore Romano, 51–52,*12, 20.

Revelli, N. (1977). *Il mondo dei vinti* [The world of the vanquished]. Turin: Einaudi.

Rodotà, C., & Rodotà, S.(1981). Il diritto di famiglia [Family law]. In S. Acquaviva (Ed.), *Ritratti della famiglia negli anni ottanta* (pp. 161–206). Bari: Laterza.

Romano, R. (1971). *Tra due crisi: l'Italia del Rinascimento* [Between two crises: Rinascimento Italy]. Turin: Einaudi.

Santini, A.(1986). Recenti trasformazioni nella formazione della famiglia e della discendenza in Italia e in Europa [Recent changes in the formation of family and family descent in Italy and Europe]. In ISTAT, *Rapporto sull'Italia* (pp. 121–144). Bologna: Il Mulino.

Saraceno, C.(1981). Modelli di famiglia [Family models]. In S. Acquaviva (Ed.), *Ritratti della famiglia negli anni ottanta* (pp. 45–114). Bari: Laterza.

Saraceno, C. (1988). Il genere della cittadinanza [The gender of citizenship]. *Democrazia e diritto, 1,* 273–298.

Saraceno, C. (1996). *Sociologia della famiglia* [Sociology of the family]. Bologna: Il Mulino.

Scabini, E. (2000). Parent-child relationships in Italian families: Connectedness and autonomy in the transition to adulthood. *Psicologia Teoria e Pesquisa, 16*(1), 23–30.

Scabini, E. & Cigoli, V. (2000). Il famiglire. Legami, simboli e tradizioni [Familial ties: Symbols and traditions]. Milano: Raffaello Cortina.

Spanier, G. B., & Furstenberg, F. F., Jr. (1987). Remarriage and reconstituted families. In M. B. Sussman & S. K. Steinmetz (Eds.), *Handbook of marriage and the family* (pp. 419–434). New York: Plenum.

Zanatta A. L. (1997). *Le nuove famiglie* [The new families]. Bologna: Il Mulino.

CHAPTER 14

THE GERMAN FAMILY
FAMILIES IN GERMANY

HEIDI KELLER, ULRIKE ZACH, & MONIKA ABELS
University of Osnabrück

The acceptance of the primary role of the family for both shaping individuals' developmental pathways and constituting the basic cells of society is shared across cultures with differing value orientations. Yet the definition of family is far more complex than a first glance would suggest. Defining family and family relationships is a particularly challenging task both across and within cultures. In this vein, it is difficult to arrive at a concise and a coherent picture of "the" German family. In this chapter, we therefore try to portray different family systems in present-day Germany. Before we take a closer look at families in Germany, we briefly introduce the broader German context.

FAMILIES IN CONTEXT: A SNAPSHOT OF GERMANY

Germany's 357,022 square kilometers cover a geographic variety of alpine regions, mountains and highlands, plains and seashores. Germany has approximately 80 million inhabitants. The average yearly income per person is US$ 28,550; 11.7 percent of the working population are unemployed, with distinct regional differences between the old and the new German states. About 30.8 percent of the population are employed in industry, 67.9 percent work in the service area, and 1.3 percent in the agrarian area.

Germany is one of the global information societies, with 948 radios, 580 TV sets (including VCRs), 588 telephones, 286 cellular phones, 73 fax machines, 270 PCs, and 20 Internet accesses per 1,000 inhabitants. There are 355 daily newspapers with a total of 24 million copies. Urbanization covers 87 percent of the population.

The birth rate per 1,000 inhabitants is 9.4 (world average: 25.5), reflecting a total fertility rate of 1.3 and a death rate of 10.8 per 1,000 inhabitants (world average: 9.3). The infant mortality rate is 0.5 percent. In 1999 life expectancy at birth in Germany was 73.7 years for men and 81.1 years for women. The main cause of death in 1998 was diseases of the cardiovascular system. The yearly population increase is 0.5 percent. A medical doctor provides 298 people with care on the average. Due to increasing life expectancy, high unemployment rates and slowly increasing public income, the social system is at the borderline of operating successfully. To hold the rate of contribution to retirement insurance (20.3 percent), in 1998 the value-added tax (VAT) was raised from 15 percent to 16 percent. Presently, 17.5 million retired people receive money from the public old age pension. In the face of the explosion of costs in public health, the government is preparing a health reform, which, on the one side, is aimed at reducing the income of physicians, hospitals, and the pharmaceutical industry and, on the other side, calls for a greater private contribution, for example, for medication.

Education underlies the federally constituted freedom of the individual states (*Bundesländer*), which is supervised by the conference of ministers of culture. In Germany, school attendance is obligatory from age 6 to 14–18 years, depending on the mode of education. However, 10 years of schooling are mandatory. The school system consists of four years of primary school and differentiates thereafter into vocational school (*Hauptschule,* 5 years) with a

consecutive work-oriented education (apprenticeship), graduation after 10 years of schooling (*mittlere Reife*), or high school with baccalaureate (*Abitur*) after 12 to 13 years of schooling, depending on the state. Moreover, an integration of these types of schooling is also possible (integration school, *Gesamtschule*).

In 1998, 558,000 apprenticeship contracts were signed. With governmental support, the 635,000 applicants successfully secured apprenticeship positions, although the unions have complained about a gap that exists between the number of applicants and the number of apprenticeships available. The different evaluations are due mainly to regional differences between the number of applicants and the number of available positions. *Abitur* is the general entrance qualification for the German university system. The most attractive disciplines (e.g., medicine, jurisprudence, psychology, and eight others), however, have additional entrance requirements (*numerus clausus*), with admissions to university programs being distributed centrally. Germany has 84 universities and 243 other institutions of higher education (147 universities of applied sciences, 7 integrated schools [*Gesamthochschulen*], 46 academies of fine arts, and 16 universities of theology). For the winter term 1997/1998, 1.83 million students were enrolled at the universities, with 226,744 of them beginning their first semester.

Roman Catholics represent 2.9 percent of the German population, 41.6 percent are reformed and traditional Lutherans (Protestants), 2.7 percent are Muslims, 0.1 percent are Jews, and 12.7 percent belong to other religions.

CONCEPTIONS OF FAMILY IN GERMANY

Historical shifts and the stratification of a modern society complicate a unitary conception of the German family. A recent political survey emphasizes that different conceptions of families and family relationships exist in pluralistic Germany (6th Family Survey, 2000).

A historical review reveals that in the German language, the term "family" first appeared around the seventeenth century, replacing concepts such as "kin" (*Sippe*), "wife and child" (*Weib und Kind*), or "house" (*Haus;* cf. Zach, 1997). A house was a genealogically comprised household, in which unrelated individuals as well as servants or apprentices resided. Houses constituted basic economic units. Permission to marry and hence to found a house (and a household) was regulated on the basis of the social and thus socioeconomic affiliations of the individuals. Above all, economic constraints were faced by the poorer classes and there were strict prescriptions of the guilds (*Stände*). Moreover, aristocracy followed their own cultural codes. The result was a variety of household and family types reflecting different economic propensities and an absence of psychologically close relationships.

With increasing industrialization during the nineteenth century, households lost their independent economic basis. Paralleling the economic changes, family relationships became more and more centered on emotional relationships, resulting in the concept of the "modern nuclear family" (Peuckert, 1999).

In the present era, the German state has created a body of law that regulates what it means to be a family as well as the relationships among the family members. Family politics are designed by the mammoth Ministry of Family, Senior Citizens, Women and Youth, and special protection of the family is guaranteed by the constitution ("Die Familie steht unter besonderem Schutz der staatlichen Ordnung," Article 6 of the German *Grundgesetz*). A closer look reveals that the special emphasis on the protection of the family is rooted in its role as the main socialization agency of children and, thus, of the future generations of citizens (Zach, 1997). Today, however, Germany's postmodern society, with its multiple living arrangements and its multicultural composition of citizens, which identifies Germany more and more as an immigration country, allows a multiplicity of contexts in which children are raised and socialized. Especially since the 1970s, the package "family" has been undergoing a process of decomposition: love, marriage, parenthood, and households appear to represent independent components that individuals can utilize according to their particular life circumstances (Vaskovics, Garhammer, Schneider, & Job, 1994), but that can also be seen as inextricably intertwined because of cultural norms. Furthermore, the special political situation of two German states with two different sociopolitical ideologies between 1945 and reunification in 1989 has created a special arena for understanding how political agendas shape cultural traditions with respect to different socialization scenarios (Ahnert, 1998).

At the dawn of the new century, magazines are often declaring the death of the nuclear family. Increasingly, couples decide to live together outside the context of marriage, a first pregnancy precedes rather than follows marriage, dual-career families are in evidence, women decide to be single mothers by choice, and gay or lesbian parents claim the same rights as "traditional" families (cf. also Blossfeld, 1995). In addition, the family cannot be described as a static unit that, once founded, exists until its members die. Instead, families undergo complex changes over time, signified by a perpetuation of different stages (Martinson & Wu, 1992). Changes in the family structure often precipitate changes in social environments, peer groups, and institutions, with a specific impact on individuals' development. In this context, developmentally oriented family research focuses on the transient developmental periods of living in a family and on cycles of family development (Zach, 1997).

The manifold images of families in Germany may be contrasted with a predominant cultural family stereotype: a married couple with one to two children, living together according to the widely shared values of family life (see below) is said to constitute a typical "complete" German family. Germans usually marry at the end of their twenties and expect the husband to be two to three years older than the wife. The marriage contract is signed at the civil registry office. The majority of couples marry additionally in their churches. The mean age of primiparous mothers is about 28 years and that of first-time fathers approximately 30 years. The stereotypical German family has 1.3 children (Keller & Zach, 2002).

This normative family model is based on positive attitudes toward marriage and family. In a survey completed in the late 1980s, 72 percent of East German male and female blue-collar workers under 35 years of age confirmed their intention to marry. In the group of 16–18-year-old adolescents, the rate was 80 percent. The proportions of West Germans who would advise young people to marry is a comparable 71 percent (Vaskovics et al., 1994). In 1995, 90 percent of newly married Germans in the East as well as the West reported that love constitutes the main motivation to marry. For East Germans, besides love, the following reasons play major roles in their decision making: having a real family life (women 58 percent, men 56 percent), security and intimacy (women 50 percent, men 37 percent), children (women 25 percent, men 26 percent), and the fact that married people can cope better with the present changes in society (women 19 percent, men 29 percent). For West Germans, besides love, it is important to marry in order to have children (women 47 percent, men 41 percent), a real family life (women 38 percent, men 41 percent), and security and intimacy (women 34 percent, men 28 percent). For all Germans, religious reasons were mentioned by about 10 percent (Peuckert, 1999; Vaskovics et al., 1994). However, the actual reason for marriage is reinforced mainly through an existing pregnancy or the wish to have children now (Sander, 1999).

Thus, for Germans, the conception of the family rests on the institution of marriage as specifying emotional bonds between husband and wife with the clear perspective of raising children. Accordingly, German mothers and fathers view children as fulfilling their life purposes (Gauda & Keller, 1987; Jagenow & Mittag, 1984). The 6th Family Report of the Federal Ministry for Family, Senior Citizens, Women and Youth (2000) reveals that 76 percent of Germans share this perspective with the majority of their foreign compatriots (55 percent of Greek, 59 percent of Italian, 88 percent of Turkish, 70 percent of Vietnamese, and 66 percent of Eastern immigrant parents). Furthermore, 84 percent of the German parents confirmed that having children in the house is fun (66 percent of Greek, 55 percent of Italian, 97 percent of Turkish, 79 percent of Vietnamese, and 67 percent of Eastern immigrant parents).

In the following section, the roots of the conception of the family in Germany, as we see it, will be briefly traced.

FAMILY IDEOLOGY IN GERMANY: PAST AND PRESENT

The main characteristic of the German family can be traced back to the historic epochs of *Biedermeier* (an epoch mainly in Germany and Austria lasting approximately from 1815 to 1848) and *Romantik* (Romanticism; an epoch starting at the beginning of the nineteenth century). During these historical epochs, the rediscovery of "emotionality" laid the ground for the glorification of the child "as the ideal state of being" and resulted in a "child cult" that influenced education within and outside the family (Schmidt, 1998). The new concept of childhood altered the everyday reality of children (Weber-Kellermann, 1987), when, for the first time, they were assigned their own rooms (*Kinderstube*) in the household and when children's fashion, children's toys, and children's literature appeared. All this culminated in a festivity of giving gifts to children, the center of the still-ongoing Christmas tradition.

The cultural foundation of the German family and its typical analysis are certainly based on the norms and values that characterized the Prussian state during the nineteenth century. Until the beginning of the nineteenth century, Germany was characterized by territorial fragmentation and cultural heterogeneity. The economically motivated unification process confirmed Prussia as the politically, economically, and culturally most influential power in Germany. The political testimony of King Friedrich II stressed the dominance of military principles for all life spheres. As a result, values that characterized army life, such as discipline, obedience, and authority, penetrated public life and exerted a major influence on the educational values and practices of German families (Ahnert, Meischner, & Schmidt, 1995). The second major impact on the value systems of the German family arose from Protestantism, which dominated the religious force in Prussia and the whole of Northern Germany. The famous

German novelist Thomas Mann emphasized that Protestantism and Germany form a cultural unit ("Solange es überhaupt ein Deutschland gebe, . . . sei seine Aufgabe das Protestantentum gewesen" ["as long as there has been a Germany at all, . . . its task has been Protestantism"]; Mann, 1983, p. 197; cited by Ahnert, 1998, p. 68). Protestantism, especially in its pietistic branches, stressed individual responsibility, freedom, and inwardness (Ahnert, Krätzig, Meischner, & Schmidt, 1994), thus laying the ground for individualism as a major cultural value. Combined with Prussian authority and obedience, Protestant individualism and its achievement ethics shaped the characteristics of "Germanness." These values became ingrained in the families' socialization practices as well as in the public educational programs (e.g., Fröbel, 1926; Herbart, 1976).

As a direct consequence of World War II, two German states were created with substantial differences in the sociopolitical orientations impinging on those common cultural traditions. The official doctrine in the former German Democratic Republic (GDR) espoused the socialist value system within the collectivistic framework of the Soviet sphere of influence. The developmental pathway of an individual was defined by plasticity and the immediate social surroundings. One's identification with group values was expected to guide one's adaptation to the collective life (Ministerrat der DDR, 1986).

The establishment of state-wide day care institutions as the first crucial socialization context mirrored the state's interest in directing the development of individuals into approved channels from early on. State organizations for children, such as the Young Pioneers (*Junge Pioniere*), took over the children from the day care centers and reinforced the socialistic doctrine. The *Jugendweihe* (youth consecration) initiated 14-year-olds at the end of their eighth school year into adult society. Based on the Soviet theory of Trofin Lysenko (Ahnert et al., 1994), the socialistic personality was the developmental goal within the context of an assumed unlimited potential for biopsychological changes. After reunification in 1989, the socialistic ideology and the Western individualistic values of family life collided and thus cre-

ated multiple transition problems that persist until this day.

The pluralistic society of the West German Federal Republic promotes the individualistic personality as an ideal. Education stresses the recognition and acceptance of the basic normative and value structure of the society together with its social roles and expected behavior patterns (Kienbaum, 1995). A person's acceptance of these norms should, however, reflect a critical and emancipatory process instead of mere obedience to the governmental authorities. Originality, competitiveness, creativity, and uniqueness are the developmental goals that most traditional as well as nontraditional families share. Equal rights for women and men in the job market and developing individuals' potentials up to their limits represent the governmental doctrine.

Yet the perspectives of young couples who start a family and their longitudinal development are frequently not in line with cultural stereotypes and expectations. Therefore, the following images of the family can only be regarded as snapshots of momentary stages of the family life cycle. In the next section, we characterize family structures in present-day Germany in terms of momentary snapshots of life phases.

A SNAPSHOT OF THE TRADITIONAL "MODERN NUCLEAR FAMILY"

At the turn of the twenty-first century, the "modern nuclear family" of two generations, that is, parents and their children, that emerged as a result of the increasing economic prosperity of the nineteenth and twentieth centuries, represents the "old traditional German family," which nevertheless remains in vogue. Furthermore, households of three or more generations were never as popular in Germany as in many Eastern European countries. Low life expectancy and relatively old age at procreation are reported by family sociologists as reasons for the prevalence of the two-generation model. With the *Wirtschaftswunder* (economic miracle) after World War II, the economy of the society improved during the 1950s together with a concurrent boom in marriages. Still, in 1996, the greater proportion of all households—about 57 percent—still were two-generation households with married couples and their unmarried children. Another 23 percent of households consisted of married couples that were either childless or had children who no longer lived with the parents.

In the traditional sense, family is defined through the emotional relationships between two individuals and their genetically related offspring. The role distribution in the traditional family was "classical," with the husband playing the instrumental part when interacting with the outside world, earning the living, and representing the family outside, and the wife embracing the expressive part of the family, educating the children and regulating the socioemotional needs of the family. The three K's that governed women's life (*Kinder* [children], *Küche* [kitchen], and *Kirche* [church]), however, came under serious sociopolitical criticism, particularly during the time of the student revolts starting in 1968 and the resulting feminist movement.

Nevertheless, despite changing public attitudes and the increasing presence of women in the labor force, the role distribution in the majority of German families remains more or less traditional in the described sense (Vaskovics, 1999), at least during the so-called family phase from the time when children are small until they enter school at 6 years. Only 1.6 percent of fathers take a paternity leave. However, the persistence of traditional family values appears to bolster a special German problem when it comes to combining parenthood and career for women. This the majority of women finds extremely difficult to handle. A major consequence is that the participation of German women in the labor force remains comparatively low (for every 36,000 employees there are 15,000 women), and their fertility rate is among the lowest in the world.

As has been outlined earlier, children were and still are absolutely crucial for the definition of German family life. The fertility rates over the last decades have continuously declined, from 812,000 births in 1997 to 770,000 births in 1999. In the former GDR, the fertility rate dropped dramatically

after reunification, but has stabilized today. Almost 93 percent of GDR women gave birth to at least one or, more often, two children (Ahnert, 1998). Barrenness was considered a crucial deficit in the life perspective of a GDR woman (Ahnert, 1998). In addition, 90 percent of West Germans report an ideal of two children per family, and only 7 percent of West German adolescents do not want to become a mother or a father.

The decreasing number of children per family is often explained by a negative or even hostile societal attitude toward children (*Kinderfeindlichkeit*) plus increasing urges for self-realization and independence of individuals, especially that of women. Besides that, the government is criticized for not providing enough financial support for young families. In 1998, there were approximately 40,000 extrafamilial caretaking places for children between the ages of 3 and 5, with 25 percent of the places providing lunch. Although surveys report that people believe the economic recovery would lead to an increasing fertility rate, empirical data prove that there is no such long-term effect (Gauda & Keller, 1987).

Women enjoy a completely paid 14-week maternity leave. Two years of parental childrearing leave are compensated with an income-corrected flat rate, but the leave is unpaid for the third year. Families who want a second child often prefer close spacing between the children. Accordingly, the prolonged maternity leave often makes it difficult for women to remain competitive in the labor market, even though their jobs are guaranteed for the time of their leave. For East Germans, the adaptation to the new societal circumstances was especially difficult. Before reunification, 91 percent of women under 60 years were working or continuing their education and returned to the labor force soon after delivery. The 100 percent provision of day care was one of the governmental flagships of the GDR. All children had the right to visit year-long full-day day care institutions for the modest rate of 1.40 GDR Mark per day (Ahnert, 1998). With reunification, many of the day care centers were closed and the unemployment rate increased substantially.

The traditional family seems to have constituted a protective factor for child development at least in Western Germany. Whereas the mortality rate of children born outside a marriage was twice as high as that for children born within the legal framework of a family, in the former GDR the discrepancy was lower because of the different living environment (Höhn, 1998). During the 1990s, illegitimately born boys died significantly more often than legitimately born boys (1990, 7.6 vs. 11.7; 1995, 5.6 vs. 8). For girls, the difference was less pronounced (1990, 5.8 vs. 8.2; 1995, 4.5 vs. 5.4).

In conclusion, although the collapse of the traditional family is celebrated in the media, it is obviously still very much alive and forms the major framework for the lives of most German citizens. However, due to many societal factors, such as financial independence of women, divorce rates have been increasing progressively. The traditional family is becoming more of a transitory life phase rather than a fundamental framework for conducting one's life.

A SNAPSHOT OF NONTRADITIONAL FAMILIES IN GERMANY

The Patchwork Family

The modern label of "patchwork family" refers especially to the fact that biological and social parenthoods are not necessarily identical. Families are composed, decomposed, and recomposed again with new members. However, foster parents raise only about 1 percent of children in Germany (0–18 years). A larger group of children is affected by the divorce of their biological parents: 70 percent of divorces in East Germany and 50 percent in the West affect minors (Vaskovics et al., 1999). Since 1992 there has been a continuous increase in the percentage of children of divorced parents. The majority of these children lives with their mothers, although most of the parents share custody. A considerable number of divorced parents remarry divorced partners with children. Family structures become binuclear, with a substantial increase in the complexity and dynamics of family relationships. However, genetic relation-

ships obviously matter more than the modern zeitgeist would suggest. With advanced gene technology, it has become easy to test paternity. Gene laboratories that specialize in paternity tests are rapidly expanding as more and more men want to know whether they are the genetic parent of the offspring they raise. The majority of clients wants to settle monetary disputes as related to divorce or alimony payment. About 25 percent of the men who asked a laboratory for a genetic analysis learned that they were not the biological father of the child they raised (e.g., Genedia laboratory, Munich).

Families with In-Vitro-Fertilized Children

Since Louise, the first "test tube" baby, was born in England in 1978, about 80,000 in-vitro-fertilized infants have been born in the world. In fact, 120 *Kinderwunsch-Kliniken* (child-wish hospitals) in Germany offer this technique. Of approximately 50,000 artificial inseminations each year, 10,000 are successful. Since 1990, the procedure is regulated by law (Embryonic Protection Law or *Embryonenschutzgesetz*). Whereas prenatal diagnosis is allowed in Germany, reimplantive diagnosis (PID) is not. However, information about the impact of in-vitro fertilization on family relationships and family life is not yet available.

The Single-Parent Family

Today, 14.6 percent of minors live with single parents, mainly their mothers (Bauerreiss, Bayer, & Bien, 1997). Some 12.8 percent of single mothers (West, 10.9 percent; East, 19.8 percent) are divorced (West, 4.9 percent; East, 9 percent) or never married (West, 2.8 percent; East, 7.8 percent). In the West, the proportion of children of single parents increases with age as opposed to the East. For example, in the state of Mecklenburg-Vorpommern, 45 percent of children under 3 years of age live with single parents. Some of these women will marry later on, after the child's birth.

Temporary poverty is a special challenge for single parents (Krause, 1994; Walper, 2002), and it is becoming more and more prevalent in Germany. According to the Socioeconomic Panel, between 1984 and 1992, 45 percent of the total population in West Germany was affected at least once in their lives by income poverty (ethnic Germans, 30 percent; foreigners, 58 percent). In 2001 (Wagner, 1984ff), the federal government published the first poverty report in Germany, according to which only 7.3 percent of the population lived for at least eight years in relative income poverty (ARB Bericht, 2001). Since poor families often live in residential areas with insufficient infrastructures, family poverty and neighborhood poverty go hand in hand (Spiekermann & Schubert, 1998; Walper, 2002). If one takes the minimum wage guaranteed by the state (social support quota, *Sozialhilfequote*) as an indicator for poverty, this figure increased, in West Germany, from 1971 to 1988 for single parents with one child from 4.4 percent to 20 percent. In comparison, this index increased for two-parent families with one child from a mere 0.2 percent to 1.9 percent (Walper, 2002). Furthermore, in families with three or more children, the index more than doubled. Finally, migrating families run a substantially higher poverty risk than families with an ethnic German household head (in West Germany, 26.1 percent vs. 10 percent).

Poverty is a well-documented risk factor for psychological development. Children in poverty often complete only a few years of schooling, are exposed to higher health risks and suffer from higher infant mortality and exhibit lesser general well-being and experience, social integration, and self-confidence (Walper, 2002). Poverty produces multiple forms of stress, especially in those contexts that may mediate moderate developmental risks and problems.

Recently, a new law acknowledging children's traumatic experiences (*Kindschaftsrecht*) has been introduced in Germany. The Federal Cabinet has approved a comprehensive reform of the *Kindschaftsrecht* law governing custody. According to the bill, custody may be granted in the future to unmarried but de-facto couples. After a divorce, the shared responsibility for the children will usually remain in effect as long as both partners agree. The

bill also makes the *Umgangsrecht* (law of conduct) more liberal, guaranteeing children the right to see the relatives of that parent who was not awarded custody. The implementation of the privilege, however, seems to be less successful than planned. As a result, many grandparents have formed an association to increase their contact with their grandchildren. This association includes predominantly paternal rather than maternal grandparents (about 90 percent).

Homosexual Couples

As of August 1, 2001, gay and lesbian couples are allowed to register their partnerships and attain more rights that are equivalent in nature to those of traditional families. The registered partnership is available for partners of the same gender, who are not married or have another registered partnership, and is terminated either through the court or the death of one of the partners. If the partners decide to separate and one of the partners cannot earn a living, the other partner is expected to support him or her. If one partner dies, the other inherits part of his or her property and keeps the shared apartment. The partners can choose a common name as their last name, or keep their respective names. If one of the partners has a child or children, the other partner may get partial custody, if he or she wishes to become involved in the child's life. The registered partners do not have the right to obtain full custody with respect to adopting a child and sharing the responsibilities of raising children as married couples usually do. If the partners separate, the partner may be allowed to meet the children (*Umgangsrecht*). A registered partner does not have to bear witness against his or her partner, and the registered partners are treated the way married couples are treated in terms of health insurance. A foreign partner in a registered partnership is allowed to move to Germany.

While many politicians (e.g., Volker Beck, of the Green Party) and organizations (e.g., the organization of lesbians and gays in Germany) welcomed the new law as a necessary step toward more equality for homosexual partnerships, others criticized the law for different reasons. One lesbian organization (*Lesben-ring*), for example, claims that marriage is an invention of the patriarchy and, as a result, rejects any form of marriage or similar organization or legalization of couples. The Furien & Companjeras, an organization of lesbian mothers, seeks more protection for families (defined as adults living with and caring for children), outside marriage or registered partnership. On the other hand, some conservative politicians reject the new law because it undermines the special position of marriage. Cardinal Alfonso Trumillo (Gesellschaft im Wanken, Berlin: *Die Welt,* 6 August 2001; www.welt.de/daten/2001/08/05/0805pg272555htx), a Catholic priest, also criticizes the law and argues that giving rights to homosexual couples is against God's will, common sense, and order. He claims that allowing homosexual couples to adopt children is a risk, and that not giving rights equal to those of married couples to homosexual couples is not discrimination.

FEMINISM AND FAMILY IN GERMANY

In Germany, the first women's movement came into existence after the revolution of 1848 (Nave-Herz, 1993; Sommerhoff, 1995). The first women's movement was bourgeois and rather apolitical because it did not aim at changing the perception of women or their role within the family (Nave-Herz, 1993). Instead, the goal of the movement was to get more education for women (Nave-Herz, 1993; Sommerhoff, 1995) and to be able to secure their living, that is, to participate in the labor force (Sommerhoff, 1995). One of the arguments used by women was that education was necessary because they had to bring up children, which society had begun to see as a responsible task (Müller, 1989). One of the outcomes of the women's movement was that their journal was outlawed (Nave-Herz, 1993). Others reacted by pointing out the dangers of education for the woman's offspring (Nave-Herz, 1993). Even within the women's movement, motherhood and working outside the house were seen as mutually exclusive by the majority (Nave-Herz, 1993). For working-class women, who were also represented by a women's movement, the situation was very different. Their

ideas were more socialistic and they did not see the proletarian men as their opponents, but saw the factory owners as their common enemy (Nave-Herz, 1993). Their struggle aimed at protection for women and mothers and for wages equal to men (Nave-Herz, 1993). In addition, they were more interested in acquiring the right to vote than the middle-class women (Nave-Herz, 1993). Although both groups focused on housewives, the proletarian women's movement aimed at organizing them, whereas the middle-class women aimed at stressing the value of housework in society (Nave-Herz, 1993). In a way, this strengthened the traditional conception of women as mothers and housewives.

After World War I, many of the women's requests were heard, but women's rights were drastically reduced under the rule of Hitler. In turn, the end of World War II marked the reorganization of women's associations. The equality of men and women was acknowledged in both German constitutions.

The East German government tried increasing the number of women in traditionally male-dominated occupational fields, developed a multitude of regulations, and established institutions to support women with children. Women did not see much necessity to complain about these "mother's politics," even though the family structures continue to resemble the traditional ones to a large extent (Nave-Herz, 1993; Vaskovics, 1999). If protest was articulated by women, the government-controlled women's organization calmed it down (Nave-Herz, 1993). Only after women formed groups to promote peace in the 1980s did a new women's movement question the woman's position in church, society, representation in school books, and so on (Nave-Herz, 1993). In West Germany, the women's movement formed in 1968 when female university students found that their voices were not heard in the students' movement. The new women's movement started questioning the hierarchy in families, authority, and the definition of a woman presented by society. They created houses for women and began discussing violence in relationships, abortion, and other pivotal issues in public (Nave-Herz, 1993).

Whereas the first German women's movement recognized men and women as responsible for different chores, guided by intrinsically and naturally determined roles, the second women's movement of the 1970s placed greater emphasis on socialization processes (Nave-Herz, 1993). "We are not born as girls, we are made girls" (Scheu, 1977, as cited in Leyrer, 1988, p. 8). With regard to the latter statement, Leyrer (1988) describes how the second women's movement stressed the importance of treating boys and girls equally, so that girls would get a chance to become something else rather than housewives. Such equal treatment usually meant treating both boys and girls the way boys had been treated earlier. Girls were told to be more assertive and to fight back. Katja Leyrer (1988) argues that this is not the intended "neutral" treatment, but that this treatment maintains the patriarchal ideas that the male way is more valuable than that of the female. She accepts this as a fact in present-day society, but argues that for real emancipation it is necessary not only to give privileges to girls, but also to take away certain privileges from boys. She shows that in many situations men as well as women counteract real gender equality in their everyday lives. Boys are still told that they should not "behave like girls," that they should not cry, and so on; and girls are praised for being "nice girls" and punished for being aggressive.

Though the laws have been changed, women remain the main caretakers of children and responsible for most of the household work (Beck-Gernsheim, 1998; Höhn, 1998; Nave-Herz, 1993; Peuckert, 1999; Sommerhoff, 1995). Women who have children and want to work outside the house still find it difficult to justify their decision. Part of the women's movement idealizes the experiences of motherhood, for example, breastfeeding (Nave-Herz, 1993). Similar to the people supporting the traditional role of women, they oppose women's decision to work (Ortmann, 1981). Therefore, working mothers find it extremely difficult to find positive, feminist role models for themselves (Müller, 1989). The traditional models are not an option as more and more women find personal satisfaction in outside work

and the traditional models do not fit their day-to-day reality (Müller, 1989; Ortmann, 1981; Oubaid, 1981).

AGING IN GERMANY

In line with other highly industrialized societies, Germany is being seriously affected by demographic aging (Bundesinstitut für Bevölkerungsforschung, 1999). Today, the German population consists of 21 percent children and adolescents, 56 percent adults between 20 and 60 years of age, and 23 percent persons beyond their sixties. A brief historical review highlights the phenomenon of increased aging: at the beginning of the twentieth century, 44 percent of German citizens were below the age of 24 years, and only 8 percent were older than 60 years. Although it is expected that in the year 2050 more than 30 percent of the population will be 60 years and older, only 16 percent are expected to be younger than 20 years of age. Reasons for the so-called overaging of the society are the declining birthrate and improved medical care. For example, for the newborn cohort 1996/1998, life expectancy is 73 years of age for boys and 80 years for girls.

Differential analyses for the German states (*Bundesländer*) reveal that the aging effect is far more pronounced in the Eastern part of Germany than in the Western part. This effect is related to the birthrate decline in East Germany, accompanied by an increase of migration into the Western part of Germany after reunification. German citizens with foreign origin also seem to be affected by overaging, but in a different way. Because of higher birthrates and decreased mortality rates, the process of overaging is expected to be slower for these groups when compared to ethnic German inhabitants.

A snapshot of actual living conditions of the elderly in Germany (based on 12,4451,773 Germans older than 65 years of age in 1994 as identified by the Statistisches Bundesamt, 1999) revealed that the overwhelming majority of the elderly (93 percent) continued living in their familiar surroundings, such as owned or rented houses, flats, or apartments. Only approximately 9 percent lived in nursing homes. Analyses of co-residence of elderly people with relatives, however, reveals a slightly different picture. Among 70–85-year-old Germans who have at least one living child, only 9 percent live together with the child in the same household (Kohli, 1999; Kohli, Künemund, Motel, & Szydlik, 1997). If those who are not members of the same household but who live in the same house are considered, the proportion rises to 27 percent. When the elderly who live in the same neighborhood as children are taken into account, the proportion is 45 percent. According to these data, nine-tenths of the elderly have a child living within a two-hour driving distance.

Overaging: Challenges for the Welfare State

In Germany, senior citizens (men 65 years +; women 60 years +) who have worked for at least 25 years and paid their share into a retirement fund receive a retirement pay of 70 percent of their latest income. This arrangement is based on a generation contract, implying that the actual retirement payments are provided by the employed generation, who are actually contributing to the fund. One first step to match the new challenges of the evident process of overaging is to lower the percentage paid by the retirement fund. Furthermore, German citizens are encouraged to contract private retirement assurances, which are supported only minimally by the government. Women who have been working in their households, and thus have not contributed to the state-supported retirement fund, are disadvantaged by this law. Attempts to improve this situation, for example, by honoring the years spent as caretakers to a certain degree, are still controversial.

The higher life expectancy presents challenges for different domains. With the goal of maintaining life quality, new professions for the care of elderly people are emerging. For example, private care services provide a whole array of services that can prevent elderly people from being institutionalized. The need for care is defined within three levels of seriousness by the health insurers who cover the expenses if neediness is confirmed by them. However, epidemiological findings have revealed that more than half of the suicides are committed by persons

over 65 years of age (Schmitz-Scherzer, 1999), with the main reasons being physical or mental illness but also because of the fear of radical changes in life circumstances. Yet middle-aged persons have a more positive expectation for their old age than persons who have already entered this period of life (Stoerzbach, 1992). A central challenge for German society is obviously to activate the unused potential of the graying population to master the developmental tasks of the postretirement period.

FAMILIES OF FOREIGN ORIGIN IN GERMANY

Families of foreign origin contribute substantially to the multiple realities of families in Germany. More than 7 million immigrants live in Germany and thus represent 9 percent of the population. Ninety-one percent of these immigrants are naturalized Germans, their origins being 2.5 percent Turkish (1990), 0.5 percent Kurds, 1.0 percent Yugoslavian, 0.7 percent Italian, 0.4 percent Greek, 0.4 percent Bosnian, 0.3 percent Polish, 0.2 percent Austrian, 0.2 percent Croatian, 0.2 percent Spanish, and 2.9 percent others. The 6th Family Report (2000) states that the overwhelming majority of migrants has become successfully integrated into the German society, especially with the help of special sociopolitical programs. Fifty-eight percent of the immigrants live in cities with more than 500,000 inhabitants and 21 percent in cities with 100,000–500,000 inhabitants, thus providing existing networks of social support for newly arriving co-patriots. However, there are pronounced differences between the immigrating nationalities, because of ethnic and cultural diversity, with respect to relationships between the generations, gender-specific role expectations, and overall personal autonomy. Different value systems often form unbridgeable gaps between members of different nationalities.

On the other hand, integration is expressed in an increasing consensus of foreign parents that their children may marry German spouses. In 1985, 31–44 percent of Turkish, Italian, and Greek parents agreed to this, versus 50–88 percent in 1995. The children of these Greek, Italian, and Turkish parents even reported a considerably higher inclination to marry a German partner than their parents have estimated. This is not true for the Eastern immigrants, who came to Germany later than the former ethnic groups. The reported probabilities for bi-national marriages were also very low.

The majority of immigrants still comprise the first-generation group. The second generation have reached the age of their parents at the time they came to Germany, and the third generation consists mainly of the children of the second generation. Meanwhile, migration is considered to be an integral part of German citizenship, which has led to various legislative adaptations. Foreign people, for instance, can acquire German citizenship, including the right to vote, thus replacing the *ius nascendi* (birthright).

A crucial difference between family conceptions of ethnic Germans and other ethnic groups concerns the obligations between the generations. Whereas explicit contracts between the generations (*Generationenvertrag*), such as the provision of financial support beyond the legal age of employment, are regulated by the government in Germany, safeguarding against threatening life events and social-emotional support in families of foreign origin are relegated among family members. In this context, approximately 10 percent of German parents believe that in old age they will be supported by their children, but far more foreign parents hold this belief. Yet there are also remarkable differences among immigrants; for example, 21 percent of Italian fathers and 73 percent of Turkish fathers expect support from their children in old age.

In contrast to earlier decades, the social structure of the immigrant population has recently become more heterogeneous and diversified. The social status of immigrants changes, depending on family resources, socioeconomic development in Germany, and successful integration. Upward social mobility is dependent on education, job security, and economic safety. However, there are still significant differences between ethnic Germans and immigrants: for instance, 36 percent of ethnic German married men are blue-collar workers, whereas the respective rate in the group of immigrants comprises

78 percent. The same pattern emerges with respect to married women (22 percent versus 68 percent).

The 6th Family Report (2000) recognizes the need to improve the employment situation for immigrants. A special program focuses on the development of young people in social foci where a particularly large number consists of foreign youth. Moreover, special programs aimed at mastering the German language are regarded as crucial for successful integration. However, as Family Minister Bergmann stated when she introduced the 6th Family Report to the public: "Integration is a continuous task and its success is dependent on whether the ethnic German population helps the foreigners to identify with the country and find a new home." This, in turn, constitutes a crucial problem, especially in the new German states. A recent Survey of the European Office for the Observation of Racism (2001) reports that 26 percent of young people in the new states regard minorities as disturbing. In the old states, the comparable number is still too high, 13 percent. On the other hand, recent linguistic research programs, for example, at the University of Hamburg, revealed the surprising result that among youth, immigrant languages have become popular and are also spoken by ethnic German youngsters. The Turkish language has acquired cult status among certain youth scenes, in line with similar developments in other European countries such as France and England.

SOCIALIZATION BELIEFS AND PRACTICES IN GERMANY

The "Germanness" in terms of Protestant and Prussian values that defined socialization practices at the beginning of the last century has acquired a pejorative connotation as a consequence of the crimes of the Nazi regime. To be German and to develop a cultural identity as a German therefore presents a major developmental task for the present young generation. Moreover, to feel proud to be a German is politically incorrect, as a recent statement of the German government (*Bundestag*) indicated ("it is not desirable that Germans feel proud to be Germans"). This attitude is obviously motivated by the disgust that many

Germans feel about ongoing neo-Nazi activities, especially in the new states, which are directed mainly against immigrants and minorities of foreign origin. On the other hand, adolescents are often confronted in European exchange programs by Italian or French youth who are extremely proud of their cultures and their countries. A result is often a confused state of mind with respect to one's national identity.

What has not been contaminated by the Nazi terror, however, is the firm belief in individuality that Germans hold and that they want to instill in their children. The selection of the first name of their unborn child already expresses that endeavor. Germans prefer original names, and traditional family names such as grandparents' names come into play only as a second or third name.

During the earliest stages of development, sleeping independently and often in a separate room through the night is an example of how parents support the autonomous self-regulation of their infants. According to various parental guides and magazines, this developmental milestone is expected to be achieved as soon as the child turns 3 months of age. Not surprisingly, problems such as not sleeping, crying too much, and refusing feeding are the major reasons parents seek professional help with their infants. Parents consider eye contact, face-to-face communication, and object play as the crucial contexts for early socialization (Keller, Chasiotis, & Runde, 1992), thus further supporting the early development of an independent agency (Keller & Eckensberger, 1998; Keller, Völker, & Yovsi, in press). It is interesting that although the parents claim that gender does not matter, it obviously makes a difference in their attention and interaction preferences with boys and girls. In an extended observational study of infants' daily experiences, we reported that first-born boys receive significantly more attention in terms of the joint presence of their mothers and fathers than later-born boys and first- and later-born girls (Keller & Zach, 2002). The striving for independence is also obviously involved in regulating the attachment–exploration balance in 1-year-old children. In a comparative study between U.S. and Northern German 1-year-old children, we confirmed the attachment theoretical prediction that infants regulate uncertainty (novel situation) with close proximity to their mothers only for the U.S. children (Zach & Keller, 1999). The German infants regulated distress without their mothers' assistance (significant negative correlation with visual references).

Since communal provision of day care does not cover the parents' need, mothers who know each other from birth preparation classes or other child- and family-related clinics create their private day care centers. Parents explain the need for day care in terms of getting their youngsters in touch with peers, since many remain only children. Although social skills are expected to develop within this peer context, parents still have an eye on their children's ability to be assertive. However, a second motivation for these day care activities, mainly for first-time parents, is to get some personal time. Specifically, young mothers are often frustrated by their social isolation with the baby. They miss the social environment of their workplace and general freedom and independence for personal growth and development.

The core of independence is education. Accordingly, parents start early to send their youngsters to special extracurricular programs such as sports, arts, and music. In view of the fact that mothers tend to drive their children from class to class on a frequent basis, environmental psychologists suggest that this practice puts the development of place identity in children at risk because they are transported from island to island without a concrete opportunity to develop a spatial map of their environment (Keller & Leyendecker, 1989; Keller, 1998). Children attend kindergarten between the ages of 3 and 6 at least for a half-day, with socializing instruction to become independent from their parents' presence and to adapt to peers and teachers. School children's leisure activities are highly gender-segregated. Boy groups meet at the same places several times a week, whereas girls, especially those from higher socioeconomic backgrounds, visit several places of different sociocultural contexts during the week (Nissen, 1992, as cited in Peuckert, 1999, pp. 135–136;

Wilk & Bacher, 1994, as cited in Peuckert, 1999, p. 135; Zach & Künsemüller, 2001)

Later on, education is still the major tenet of parents' efforts to prepare their children for adult life. Females as well as males are expected to complete a certain educational level and to settle in a career before they marry. Economic goals such as a car, an apartment, or a house are expected to be achieved before having children of their own. Children leave the parental home soon after they have finished their education and earn their own money. Despite this fact, most of them stay in close emotional relationship with their family of origin and communicate regularly with their parents (Georgas, 2000).

CONCLUSION: STAGES OF FAMILY LIFE

Although the media proclaim changes in the very conceptions of family and family relationships, an ontogenetic view of family development identifies stages rather than qualitative changes. For example, statistics indicate that the number of one-person households has increased tremendously over previous decades, from about 8 percent in 1900 to about 36 percent in 2001 (Statistisches Bundesamt), with a plateau since 1987. Yet this increase in number masks the fact that single-person households constitute mainly transitory phenomena. Individuals live alone before they marry, after divorce, or in old age, when their spouse has died. The vast majority of single mothers has not deliberately chosen this situation, but rather single-parent families arise from broken relationships. Only very few individuals deliberately and intentionally decide to live a single life.

In the 2000 World Values Survey, Germans rank only number 33 in happiness. Only 16 percent of Germans report that they are "very happy," 14 percent report that they are "unhappy," and a majority of

70 percent say they are "quite happy." It should be thought-provoking that countries with a comparatively low gross national product, such as Venezuela and Nigeria, rank number 1 and 2, with the majority of people being very happy. These figures raise questions about relational qualities in general. Based on attachment theory, Zach (1997, 2001) presented first results on how Germans view themselves with respect to relational styles that have been proposed for adults (for an overview, see Simpson & Rholes, 1998). In general, secure self-views (comprising a basic trust in the availability of others, the ability to relate to them, and also to feel comfortable with others depending on oneself) dominated; prevalence data were comparable to those reported for U.S. inhabitants. However, younger adults (mean age 24 years) and older adults (mean age 41 years) differed significantly with respect to the prevalence rates of a secure attachment style, with older adults seeing themselves more often as securely attached than younger ones. Gender differences also became evident, but predominantly for younger adults. Young German women view themselves more often as secure with respect to intimate relationships than young German men. Content analyses about adults' childhood narratives indicate that German women report a substantial amount of nonsupportive attachment relationships with their parents (53 percent of all attachment-relevant statements; 47 percent reported supporting relational experiences). Although these data are cross-sectional and do not indicate the longitudinal complexities, differences between generations and genders are substantial. Further research on families across cultures has to consider an ontogenetic perspective that incorporates phases of family development and the individual's family relationships into a more integrated understanding of their impact on developmental trajectories.

ACKNOWLEDGMENT

We are grateful to Marita Bojang for her help in collecting information for this chapter.

REFERENCES

6th Family Report of the Federal Ministry for Family, Senior Citizens, Women and Youth. (2000). Bonn, Germany.

Ahnert, L. (Ed.). (1998). *Tagesbetreuung für Kinder unter drei Jahren: Theorien und Tatsachen* [Day care for children younger than three years: Theories and facts]. Göttingen: Huber Verlag.

Ahnert, L., Krätzig, S., Meischner, T., & Schmidt, A. (1994). Sozialisationskonzepte für Kleinkinder: Wirkungen tradierter Erziehungsvorstellungen und staatssozialistischer Erziehungsdoktirinen im intra- und interkulturellen Ost-West-Vergleich [Socialization concepts of infants: Effects of traditional pedagogic concepts and governmental socialist pedagogic doctrines in an intra- and intercultural East–West comparison]. In G. Trommdsdorff (Ed.), *Psychologische Aspekte des sozio-politischen Wandels in Ostdeutschland* [Psychological aspects of the socio-political change in East Germany] (pp. 94–110). Berlin, New York: Walter de Gruyter.

Ahnert, L., Meischner, T., & Schmidt, A. (1995). Äquivalenzen in frühkindlichen Interaktionsmustern. Ein Vergleich von russischen und deutschen Mutter-Kind-Dyaden [Similarities in early interactional patterns. A comparison of Russian and German mother-child dyads]. In G. Trommsdorff (Ed.), *Kindheit und Jugend in verschiedenen Kulturen* [Childhood and adolescence in different cultures] (pp. 65–81). Weinheim/München: Juventa Verlag.

ARB Bericht (2001). Lebenslagen in Deutschland. Der erste Armuts- und Reichtumsbericht der Bundesregierung [Life situations in Germany. The first report about poverty and wealth in the Federal Republic]. www.bmgs.bund.de/de/sichenrung/armutsbericht/ARBBericht01.pdf

Bauerreiss, R., Bayer, J., & Bein, W. (1997). *Familienatlas II—Lebenslagen und Regionen in Deutschland. Karten und Zahlen* [Family atlas No. 2: Life situations and regions in Germany. Maps and figures]. Opladen, Germany: Leske & Budrich.

Beck-Gernsheim, E. (1998). *Was kommt nach der Familie? Einblicke in neue Lebensformen* [What comes after the family? Views on new lifestyles]. München: Beck.

Blossfeld, H. P. (Ed.). (1995). *The new role of women.* Boulder, CO: Westview.

Bundesinstitut für Bevölkerungsforschung. (1999). Das Altern der Bevölkerung [The aging of the population]. In Bundesinstitut für Bevölkerungsforschung [Federal Institute for Population Research] (Ed.), *Bevölkerung: Fakten, Trends, Erwartungen* [Population: Facts, trends, expectations] (pp. 11–12). Wiesbaden: Brochure of the Federal Institue for Population Research.

Fröbel, F. (1926). *Die Menschenerziehung* [The people's education]. Leipzig: Verlag Philipp Reclam jun.

Gauda, G., & Keller, H. (1987). Das subjektive Familienkonzept schwangerer Frauen [The subjective family concept of pregnant women]. *Zeitschrift für Entwicklungspsychologie und Pädagogische Psychologie, 19*(1), 32–45.

Georgas, J. (2000). *Families in Europe.* Paper read at the 2000 Socrates Conference, Osnabrück, Germany.

Herbart, J. F. (1976). *Ausgewählte Schriften zur Pädagogik* [Selected essays on pedagogy]. Berlin: Verlag Volk und Wissen.

Höhn, C. (1998). *Demographische Trends, Bevölkerungswissenschaft und Politikberatung. Aus der Arbeit des Bundesinstituts für Bevölkerungsforschung* [Demographic trends, population science, and political counseling. From the work of the Federal Institute of Population Research]. (BiB9), 1973–1998. Schriftenreihe des Bundesinstitutes für Bevölkerungsforschung: Opladen: Leske & Budrich.

Jagenow, A., & Mittag, J. (1984). Weiblicher Kinderwunsch und Sexualität [The female wish to have children and sexuality]. *Psychosozial, 21,* 7–26.

Keller, H. (1998). Exploratory behavior, place attachment, genius loci, and childhood concepts: Elements of understanding children's interactions with their environments. In D. Görlitz, H. J. Harloff, G. Mey, & J. Valsiner (Eds.), *Children, cities, and psychological theories: Developing relationships* (pp. 455–468). Berlin/New York: de Gruyter.

Keller, H., Chasiotis, A., & Runde, B. (1992). Intuitive parenting programs in German, American, and Greek parents of 3-month-old infants. *Journal of Cross-Cultural Psychology, 23*(4), 510–520.

Keller, H., & Eckensberger, L. H. (1998). Kultur und Entwicklung [Culture and development]. In H. Keller (Ed.), *Lehrbuch Entwicklungspsychologie* [Textbook of developmental psychology] (pp. 57–96). Bern: Huber Verlag.

Keller, H., & Leyendecker, B. (1989). Ortsidentität und Genius Loci als Konzepte der Mensch-Umwelt-Interaktion. Das Verständnis von Regionalität des

Osnabrücker Kulturzentrums Kind (OKKI) [Place identity and genius loci as concepts of human-environment interaction. The understanding of regionality of the Osnabrücker Kulturzentrum Kind (OKKI)]. In C. Salzmann & W. D. Kohlberg (Eds.), *Modelle des regionalen Lernens in der Umwelterziehung in Europa* [Models of regional learning in environmental education in Europe] (pp. 453–469). Heinsberg: Agentur Dieck.

Keller, H., Voelker, S., & Yovsi, R. D. (in press). Conceptions of good parenting in West Africa and Germany. *Social Development*.

Keller, H., & Zach, U. (2002). Gender and birth order as determinants of paternal behavior. *International Journal of Behavioral Development, 26*(2), 177–184.

Kienbaum, J. (1995). Sozialisation von Mitgefühl und prosozialem Verhalten. Ein Vergleich deutscher und sowjetischer Kindergartenkinder [Socialization of compassion and prosocial behavior. A comparison of German and Soviet kindergarden children]. In G. Trommsdorff (Ed.), *Kindheit und Jugend in verschiedenen Kulturen* [Childhood and adolescence in different cultures] (pp. 65–81). Weinheim/München: Juventa Verlag.

Kohli, M. (1998). Private and public transfers between generations: Linking the family and the states. *European Societies, 1*(1), 81–104.

Kohli, M., Künemund, H., Motel, A., & Szydlik, M. (1997). Generationenkonstellationen, Haushaltsstrukturen und Wohnentfernungen in der zweiten Lebenshälfte. Erste Befunde des Alterssurveys [Generation constellations, houshold structures, and residential distances in the second half of life. First results of an aging survey]. In R. Becker (Ed.), *Generationen und sozialer Wandel* [Generations and social change] (pp. 157–175). Opladen: Leske & Budrich.

Krause, P. (1994). Zur zeitlichen Dimension von Einkommensarmut [About the temporal dimension of income poverty]. In W. Hanesch (Ed.), *Armut in Deutschland. Der Armutsbericht des DFG und des Paritätischen Wohlfahrtsverbands* [Poverty in Germany. The poverty report of the German Research Council and the Parity Charity] (pp. 189–206). Reinbek bei Hamburg: Rowohlt.

Leyrer, K. (1988). *Hilfe! Mein Sohn wird ein Macker* [Help! My son is becoming a macho]. Frankfurt am Main: Fischer Taschenbuch Verlag.

Mann, T. (1983). Aufsätze, Reden, Essays [Compositions, monologues, essays] (2 vols.). Berlin: Aufbau Publikationen.

Martinson, B. C., & Wu, L. L. (1992). Parent histories: Patterns of change in early life. *Journal of Family Issues, 13*(3), 351–377.

Ministerrat der DDR. (Ed.). (1986). *Programm für die Erziehungsarbeit in den Kinderkrippen* [Program for the educational work in daycare centers]. Berlin: Verlag Volk und Gesundheit.

Müller, U. (1989) Warum gibt es keine emanzipatorische Utopie des Mutterseins [Why is there no feminist utopia of motherhood?]. In B. Schön (Ed.), *Emanzipation und Mutterschaft. Erfahrungen und Untersuchungen über Lebensentwürfe und mütterliche Praxis* [Emancipation and motherhood. Experiences and studies of life plans and practical motherhood] (pp. 55–79). Weinheim/Munich: Juventa.

Nave-Herz, R. (1993). *Die Geschichte der Frauenbewegung in Deutschland* [The history of the women's movement in Germany]. Bonn: Bundeszentrale für politische Bildung.

Ortmann, H. (1981). *Intellektualität und Mutterschaft* [Intellectualism and motherhood]. In *Sozialwissenschaftliche Forschung und Praxis für Frauen, Beiträge 7 zur feministischen Theorie und Praxis. Dokumentation der Tagung weibliche Biographien in Bielefeld, Oktober 1981. Geschäftsstelle Frauenforschung* [Socialscientific research and practice for women, contributions 7 on feminist theory and practice. Documentation of the conference on female biographies in Bielefeld, October 1981. Office for women's research] (pp. 102–104). München: Frauenoffensive.

Oubaid, M. (1981). *Mutterschaft und Beruf* [Motherhood and occupation]. In *Sozialwissenschaftliche Forschung und Praxis für Frauen, Beiträge 7 zur feministischen Theorie und Praxis. Dokumentation der Tagung weibliche Biographien in Bielefeld, Oktober 1981. Geschäftsstelle Frauenforschung* [Socialscientific research and practice for women, contributions 7 on feminist theory and practice. Documentation of the conference on female biographies in Bielefeld, October 1981. Office for women's research] (pp. 105–106). München: Frauenoffensive.

Peuckert, R. (1999). *Familienformen im sozialen Wandel* [Family forms in the process of social change] (2nd revised and extended edition). Opladen: Leske, & Budrich.

Sander, D. M. (1999). Soziologische Erkenntnisse zum Eheschließungsverhalten [Sociological aspects of marriage]. *Deutsches und Europäisches Familienrecht, 1,* 16–24.

Schmidt, A. (1998). Mütterliche Rollenerwartungen und Nachwuchsbetreuung in Deutschland: Enge und Weite unterschiedlicher Konzepte im historischen Kontext [Expectancies about maternal role and care of offspring in Germany: Narrowness and width of different concepts in historical context]. In L. Ahnert (Ed.), *Tagesbetreuung für Kinder unter drei Jahren: Theorien und Tatsachen* [Day care for children under three years: Theories and facts] (pp. 58–68). Bern: Huber.

Schmitz-Scherzer, R. (1999). Reflections on cultural influences on aging and old-age suicide in Germany. In J. L. Person, & Y. Conwell (Eds.), *Suicide and aging: International perspectives* (pp. 99–106). New York: Springer-Verlag.

Simpson, J. A., & Rholes, W. S. (1998). *Attachment theory and close relationships.* New York: Guilford.

Sommerhoff, B. (1995). *Special: Frauenbewegung* [Special: Women's movement]. Reinbek: Rowohlt.

Spiekermann, H. & Schubert, H. (1998). Verkehrssicherheit von Kindern in Abhängigkeit vom sozialen Umfeld [Traffic security of children depending on the social environment]. In J. Mansel & G. Neubauer (Eds.), *Armut und soziale Ungleichheit bei Kindern* [Poverty and social inequality in children]. Reihe Kindheitsforschung (Vol. 9, pp. 164–172). Opladen: Leske & Budrich.

Statistisches Bundesamt. (1999). *Kinder in der Sozialhilfe-Statistik* [Children in the social welfare statistics]. Wiesbaden: Statistisches Bundesamt.

Stoerzbach, B. (1992). Transition to a new life phase: Expectations about life in old age. *Zeitschrift für Bevölkerungswissenschaft, 18,* 291–311.

Survey of the European Office for the Observation of Racism (April, 2001). Vienna: European Monitoring Center on Racism and Xenophobia (www.eumc.at).

Vaskovics, L. A., Garhammer, M., Schneider, N. F., & Job, O. (1994). Familien- und Haushaltsstrukturen in der ehemaligen DDR und in der Bundesrepublik Deutschland von 1980–1989—ein Vergleich [Family and household structures in the former GDR and the Federal Republic of Germany from 1980–1989—a comparison]. *Materialien zur Bevölkerungswissenschaft. Sonderheft 24* [Materials on demography. Spezial 24]. Wiesbaden, Bundesinstitut für Bevölkerungsforschung.

Vaskovics, L. A. (Ed.).(1999). *Gewalt in der Familie und gesellschaftlicher Handlungsbedarf* [Violence in the family and the necessity for societal intervention]. Bamberg Universität, Staatsinstitut für Familienforschung.

Wagner, G. G. (1984ff). Sozio-ökonomisches Panel. Repräsentative Längsschnittstudien privater Haushalte in der Bundesrepublik Deutschland [socioeconomic panel: Representative longitudinal studies of private households in the Federal Republic of Germany—yearly reports.] www.diw.de/deutsch/sop/

Walper, S. (2002). Armut und ihre Auswirkungen auf die Entwicklung von Kindern. [Poverty and its consequences on the development of children]. In A. V. Schlippe, G. Lösche, & C. Hawellek (Eds.), *Kontexte früher Kindheit. Lebenswelten kleiner Kinder in Beratung und Therapie* [Contexts of early childhood. Living environments of small children as a topic of counseling and therapy] (pp. 151–177). Münster: Votum Verlag.

Weber-Kellermann, I. (1987). *Die deutsche Familie. Versuch einer Sozialgeschichte* [The German family. An attempt of a social history]. Frankfurt am Main: Suhrkamp.

Zach, U. (1997). Familie und Kindheit. Beiträge aus der psychologischen Familienforschung und moderner Evolutionsbiologie [Family and childhood. Contributions from psychological family research and modern evolutionary biology]. In H. Keller (Ed.), *Handbuch der Kleinkindforschung* [Textbook of early infancy research] (2nd ed., pp. 287–314). Berlin: Springer-Verlag.

Zach, U. (2001). *Attachment in adolescence.* Paper presented at the 10th European Conference on Developmental Psychology, Uppsala, Sweden, 1st–5th September.

Zach, U., & Keller, H. (1999). Patterns of the attachment-exploration balance of one-year-old infants from Northern U.S. American and Northern Germany. *Journal of Cross-Cultural Psychology, 30*(3), 381–389.

Zach, U., & Künsemüller, P. (2001). Die Entwicklung von Kindern zwischen dem 6. und 10. Lebensjahr: Theorien und Forschungsbefunde [The development of children between 6 and 10 years of life: Theories and research results]. In W. Fathenakis & M. Textor (Eds.), *Familienhandbuch* [Family handbook]. www.familienhandbuch.de/index.html/f_Fachbeitrag/a_Kindheitsforschung/s_280.

CHAPTER 15

NORWEGIAN FAMILIES FROM A PSYCHOCULTURAL PERSPECTIVE
A CHALLENGE TO THERAPEUTIC THEORY AND PRACTICE

WENCKE J. SELTZER
University of Bergen

HOW DO WE DEFINE THE NORWEGIAN FAMILY?

The family in Norway, historically and today, can be viewed from a variety of positions, depending on whether it is seen from the perspective of the rich and powerful, or the less influential, the poor and suffering. Likewise, life in a Norwegian family is influenced by the *Zeitgeist* of cultural and societal con-

ditions in general. These may include political issues, economic conditions, the impact of historical events (periods) on present and future developments, global influences, educational trends, and predictions of future evolvement.

Furthermore, many people find it difficult to relate to historical and present understandings of "the" Norwegian family. I have asked some of my colleagues and a great number of students of higher education how we could define the Norwegian family, and I am now convinced that a great number of ideas and characteristics may be attributed to the "common" definition of the "Norwegian family." The generation older than 50 years tends to define the family mostly in terms of the traditional extended family concept, the ones immediately below 50 tend to define the family as a nuclear unit separated from the extended family, and the young college and university students tend to define the family more as associations of a variety of persons choosing to live together. I will return to a further elaboration of these family forms and definitions later in this chapter.

GEOGRAPHIC AND CLIMATIC CONDITIONS AS DETERMINANTS OF FAMILY LIFE

Influences on Norwegian lifeways have to do with the harsh climatic, geographic, and topological conditions of this country. These conditions are permanent and unavoidable, and as such are "imprinted" upon Norwegian culture as well. Some of these imprints may be specific, in the sense that they possibly imply survival traits not to be found in societies subject to milder climates. Geographic and climatic conditions *are* survival issues in this country. These vary according to what the sea, land, forests, wildlife, natural goods, educational institutions, health and social service institutions, and industrial endeavors may have to offer in the context of the local environment. Norway, with a coastline of more than 21,000 kilometers, and a length of more than 1,700 kilometers, shows great variability in terms of rural or urban communities, and between the eastern and western and the southern and northern parts of the country. There were periods in history when small communities along the shoreline were populated mostly by women and children. A great portion of the male population lost their lives while fishing in the fierce North Sea (Seltzer, 1989). Thus, weather and climatic conditions are not trivial matters; in fact, they often represent life-and-death issues. Many of the small communities were isolated, since mountainous topology and severe climatic conditions made travel and social exchange difficult.

Thus, with limited communication between family settlements for hundreds of years, combined with severe climatic and mountainous conditions, local communities continue to exhibit cultural practices and belief patterns that vary from one community to the next.

POINT OF DEPARTURE FOR THIS CHAPTER

Professionally, I am primarily a psychologist and family therapist, not a historian. In view of this, I will refer to partial knowledge of the family in Norway, with no intention of portraying an "objective" and complete history of this very complex topic. My main points of reference as a "reporter" on the Norwegian family are as follows.

I am approaching the topic from the position of a native who has lived through many changes in Norwegian society since the World War II years. Furthermore, my extended family of origin is historically known to me for many generations, and much of my knowledge of Norwegian history stems from oral narrations, told by the "old and wise" in my own and other extended families in a rural district of Norway. In addition, I have been influenced by the officially narrated history, as this was taught in the public Norwegian school system from grammar school through the final years of a university education.

In the district I am writing about (a small industrial community in the vicinity of Oslo), there were two major socioeconomic classes: those who were farm workers and/or industrial workers at the town's paper mill and affiliated industrial sites on the one hand, and those who owned farms and tillable land, held leadership positions at the mill, or owned businesses affiliated with the paper industry on the other hand. Thus, as a child with friends from all layers of this small society, I learned about "the world" as seen through a great variety of local and inside perspectives of family beliefs and practices.

Furthermore, I am writing from the perspective of someone who as a young person left Norway for some years to study psychology and work in the United States and who also started a family in that "foreign country." Upon my return to Norway, I viewed the society I grew up in from a more varied and hopefully slightly less egocentric perspective. Yet I continue to believe that it is impossible to avoid an egocentric portrayal of any story, official or private.

From my ethnographic training in the United States with the cultural anthropologist Jules Henry in the late 1960s and early 1970s, I learned that one must be "culturally transplanted" for some time in order to be able to observe the otherwise obvious in one's own culture. Thus, the "obvious" in one's own culture is frequently that which is overlooked in any experienced and retold accounts. Through cultural transplantation, one gains a perspective from which one is able to see that which is otherwise taken for granted in one's culture of origin. The taken-for-granted may be tacit, and consequently not available for shared community discussions. Thus, upon our return, we may be better equipped as observers in and reporters of the affairs of our own societies. An observer in this situation resembles a "sleeping beauty" who awakens from her long sleep, begins to observe, asks questions, and makes comments on a new and fresh world, which she had not "seen" before. She also listens and hears the "silenced" voices of her culture in ways she had not perceived them before.

Since I am not a newly awakened sleeping beauty, this chapter is not meant as a neutral presentation, viewed from a totally "fresh" observer's stance. On the contrary, in addition to the points mentioned above, I see the situation from the perspective of a professional psychologist, with many decades of experience working with troubled people in my country of origin, but also in other countries. This cross-cultural professional experience has included sites of involvement in the courtroom (e.g., expert evaluations), the therapy room (as a therapist or supervisor), the child welfare office (as an evaluator), the institution for the mentally ill (as a clinician), family therapy offices (as a therapist and supervisor), child guidance clinics (as a child clinical psychologist), hospitals treating somatic and severe psychosomatic disorders (as a clinical psychologist), university sites as a lecturer, supervisor, writer, and researcher, and as an international participant in all these areas.

My thinking is also influenced by the Russian philosopher Michail Bahktin, his use of the term "chronotope," and his application of the terms Epic (the established and dominant discourse) and Novel (stories that may be untold so far and that diverge from the official line), and are created through dialogue, in new contexts (see Dentith, 1995, on Bachtinian thought, and Mandelker and Emerson, 1995).

From the above points of departure, I focus on a variety of intertwined societal, cultural, family, and individual human experiences. These experiences may manifest themselves in the "problems" that families and their individual members bring to the therapy room. Toward the end of the chapter, I bring in excerpts from current dialogues with clients. These dialogues may provide the reader with a first-hand glimpse of how Norwegian society and family life is "lived" by some young people today. I am writing this chapter at a time when our country appears to be in the midst of rapid, major changes.

POVERTY AND CLASS ISSUES IN NORWEGIAN SOCIETY

An Almost Erased Part of History: "Housemen" and Their Families

Let us now look back at a historical period that shows how some families, situated in a rural part of the Norwegian farmland, worked and lived their lives. The form of family life as described here is only vaguely recognized by young Norwegians today, yet it is a very real part of our history. This is a part of our history that is not comfortably recognized officially. Thus, family living in the *husmanns'* home (houseman's home) is rarely written about, and the "houseman's place" is scarcely known abroad.

One way a great many families in Norway survived for many centuries until well into the late 1940s was to work and live as *husmenn* (translated directly as *housemen*). The term *housemen* should be understood as a collective concept, since it refers to a whole group of related family members, who provided comprehensive labor services for a farm/landowner, and who were allowed to have a small dwelling on the farmer's land, framed by a small piece of land.

Viewed from the perspective of today's welfare state, the word *husmann* was, mostly, a euphemism for a kind of serf or even slave. One criterion for the term *serf* is that she or he does not receive monetary wages that he or she can control, but is allocated food and shelter in order to survive for the purpose of delivering services for his or her "provider." Housemen and their families worked for hundreds of years in a feudal farming system in those parts of the country where land was tillable. Up to the end of World War II, most work on the farms had to be done by hand.

Tillable land is scarce in Norway, and consequently, it was very valuable.[1] The housemen and their families lived and worked for the owners of the land. In return, the workers were entitled to food and lodging. The houseman's family and the farmer's family made up a mutually dependent unit for the sake of survival. A few of the farmers were well off. Yet in some parts of the country the farms were small, and the farmers themselves were barely able to feed their families. In some instances, poverty was so severe that people died from hunger, and some contracted illnesses related to extreme suffering in the cold. Others lived on the farm from cradle to grave, in families composed of several generations. In the severe winter climate, family members, children included, went to bed many a night cold and hungry. As late as the immediate post–World War II years, I recall from my own childhood that some children were absent from school for many days, because their only pair of shoes was at the shoemaker for repairs.

Structurally, in terms of family composition, the farmers' families and the housemen's families differed from one another in some ways. When the children reached the age of 14, the State Church demanded that they be confirmed. This religious ceremony served to reaffirm the young people's religious belonging in the Church. For most of the participants, however, the ceremony served first of all as a rite of passage, marking a status transition of

the 14-year-old boys and girls from child to adult. From this time on the houseman's son or daughter was on his or her way to becoming economically independent from the family. The houseman's family could no longer provide for them, and this frequently meant dramatic separations between the young and their families as part of the family life cycle. The young ended up as temporary helping hands on the farms, or had to leave the community to find work somewhere else. Many of these young men and women found no other way out than to leave their country and to emigrate to other lands, such as the United States. From this time on in their lives, quite a few of the young ones helped provide for the elders. The young immigrants often sent money back home, to aid the survival of the families left back in the "old country."

The farmers' children, on the other hand, did not have to leave home at such an early age. The farm houses were mostly built around a yard, and consisted of many dwellings. The elderly moved into their own dwelling because the main farm house was inhabited by the oldest son and his family, who by law (*Odelsrett*) had first right to take over all parts of the farm and its activities (primogeniture). The younger sons were paid with some portion of the value of the farm. The girls most often stayed on the farm and helped out until they were married. The girls were typically sent to household schools, to learn the arts of cooking, keeping a house, and caring for babies. In some instances they were taken in by one of the well-off farm owners to learn through apprenticeship. It was common to marry within the farming community. Unmarried girls often kept on living as part of the extended family on the farm.

Housemen in rural areas may have enjoyed better living conditions than the poor people in the urban areas, in part because in the cities, there were few opportunities for natural *husholdning* (natural food production at home). In other parts of the country, people made a living by fishing, hunting, and selling home-made products. The majority of the population lived in poverty. This, of course, was also what instigated the massive migration of Norwegians to the United States in the past two centuries, including the pre– and post–World War II years.

Class Differences and Some Common Attitudes toward Poverty

Deeply rooted class differences existed in Norwegian society. Even though it was recognized that the workers and owners of work-producing properties were mutually dependent on one another for survival, segregation practices existed. Higher degrees of human worth were magically attributed to those who owned land, while lower degrees of human worth were attributed to those who worked for the owners. Workers who were strong and healthy achieved high appraisals as housemen. In the houseman families, the extended family assumed responsibility for the care of the old and the sick, but because of the extreme poverty, and the demands made on those who were healthy enough to work on the farm, the weak, ill, and aged had few ways out. Given that no governmental social and health services existed at that time,[2] many families had to see their dear close ones suffer until death took them away.

Thus, it is not by chance that the people in the farming districts were politically divided and frequently adopted extreme political positions. One of the most commonly debated ideological and political issues in the post–World War II years centered around efforts to equalize societal conditions in such ways that work, pay, housing, education, and social and medical care became available to all citizens. Despite the fact that a large portion of the population suffered from poverty, the idea that the poor were themselves to blame still persisted. It was their "own fault," due to laziness, stupidity, or a failure to assume responsibility when taking care of their own affairs. Many popular proverbs continue to reflect such attitudes, such as "You are the smith who forges your own luck," and "As you make your bed, so you sleep."

Today, the official silencing of poverty is still found in various forms of social/welfare and child protection work. An example of this might be the child welfare worker who expresses her concern for the child's behavior and relates this to the fact that the mother engages in frequent moves with her child. On closer examination, it turns out that the mother's frequent moves occur because her landlord threw her out because of her inability to pay the rent. In this case, a poverty problem is evident. This, however, does not agree with the official ideology, namely, that we are all well taken care of by official social policies. If that is true, the ones who do not make it are themselves to blame, or they exhibit an inner individual psychological "defect." We are then dealing with what could be called a "societal silent story." This and similar silent stories implicitly place the blame on the victim, and there is an inclination on the part of the social and health workers to "psychologize" the problem. The workers gain respect in their jobs if they can detect and identify psychological problems in the mother–child relation and effectuate "treatment" for this, rather than helping the mother with her daily survival issues.

I have found that many people in therapy today are still ridden by feelings of shame associated with poverty. The shame prevents them from talking about their problems in making ends meet. This accords with the dominant ideology, which tells us that we live in a wealthy society in which everyone is properly cared for, and no one who likes to work suffers from poverty. Many single mothers tell me in the therapy room that their child was unable to join his or her class on the school's yearly skiing trip, because she (the mother) could not afford to buy the sports equipment required for participation. Instead of saying to her or his teachers and comrades that he or she could not afford to take part in the outing, the child would often report illness or another fictitious reason for not joining.

Foreign Families, Poverty, and Marginalization

Norwegian individuals often declare themselves free of racist attitudes. Norwegians refer to their reluctance to mingle with people from "culturally distant" ethnic origins as caused by language problems and a "fear of the unfamiliar" called *fremmedfrykt*. This term serves as an agreeable "explanation" of segregation between ethnic groups as well. A frequently heard argument states that it is "natural that they, the foreigners, who within their own groups are alike in terms of physical traits or cultural specificity, keep to themselves, and that 'we' do the same." After all, Norwegian society in the post–World War II years cherished sameness and unification to "standard" ways of looking, believing (as exemplified by the State Church), and acting. These are deeply rooted values in Norwegian society, and as such they do not fare well in a world about to be transformed into an arena where human biology, ethnicity, ideologies, material cultures, and so on, intermingle in countless ways. This may be seen in Oslo, the capital of Norway, which is segregated into east and west sections. Most of the nonwhite foreign families and poor people live in the eastern section. In recent years, parts of this section have been rehabilitated, and wealthier groups are moving in. This, in effect, pushes some of the foreign families further into the Old City of Oslo.

Studies carried out by the State Statistical Bureau and incorporated in The Parliamentary Report No. 14 (1994–1995) discuss the marginalization of foreign and other groups in Oslo affected by poverty and other "disadvantaged life conditions." They show that over one-quarter of the population at the core of this area (Old Oslo) came from a "distant cultural background." In parts of inner Oslo, as many as 38 percent of the native-born residents came from "distant cultural origins." There is massive evidence that their difficult living conditions cause health problems for immigrants and native-born Norwegians alike. The report states that there is a greater accumulation of life quality problems in this area of Oslo than in any other part of the country.

A study of native-born residents of this part of the city showed that they suffered from at least four major life quality problems. Among these are fear of violence, poor housing, poor milieu (noise and air pollution), and low income. In addition, 42 percent of this population experienced serious health problems. Asthma and other respiratory problems in children were among the serious problems. The most baffling finding, however, indicates that the population on the east side of the city had a much lower life

expectancy than those residing on the west side of the city.

Today, children of Norwegian origin hear about poverty in school, but appear to believe that this concerns people of other ethnic backgrounds, not "native" Norwegians. Norwegian children are seldom told about poverty in their own country—only about poverty, war, and violence in "exotic places" far away from Norway. A due concern in this portrayal of the world situation is that "these people," far away from us, are also viewed as disadvantaged. Some of these concerns are of course also related to open or covert racist ideology. This and similar concerns may have a direct yet mostly subconscious impact on our children's attitudes toward refugee and foreign families who have come here to live and work. Similarly, this kind of camouflage pushes those persons who themselves are in need of help to the outer margins of our society. If a person is a foreign worker, it is viewed as "natural" if he or she is poor, but if you are "one of us," poverty is associated with shame and calls for due skepticism about a person's "character."

Norway's Current Material Situation

In the past three decades, Norway has become a wealthy society because of the discovery of oil in the North Sea, and it is now one of the major oil producers in the world. From being considered a society without natural resources, as my generation had learned in school, to a nation full of "black gold," major changes have taken place at all societal levels. Still, our society has unemployment and poverty problems.

A recent report from the State Statistical Bureau (reported in *Aftenposten,* March 5, 2002), shows that single parents are hit hard in periods of rising unemployment. Within this group, the portion of unemployed single fathers is significantly higher than among married or cohabiting fathers, and the portion of unemployed mothers is extremely high. Researchers explain this last finding in terms of employers' reluctance to hire single mothers. Yet no research is quoted that would support the idea that single mothers are more unreliable workers than others.

THE NORWEGIAN FAMILY
IN HISTORICAL PERSPECTIVE

As I mentioned earlier, one of the tasks I view as important in grasping an understanding of the current Norwegian family is to view it from societal, cultural, and historical perspectives. One way to do this is to follow the Norwegian family through its movements in the last century. In doing so, we find dominant forms of family life for periods of time, appearing in accordance with other general changes in our society. These periods may be categorized as premodern, modern, and late modern/postmodern. The periods tend to coincide with changes in family forms and family life. In the following, I describe how family life evolved from identifiable traditional/ extended patterns, to nuclear patterns, to a variety of less predictable current postmodern family life ways. Today, all these forms of family constellations exist side by side, yet there is less evidence that any one of these forms is more "dominant" than the others. Societal discourse, however, mostly views the "real" or "correct" family as that which conforms to extended or nuclear patterns.

The Extended (Traditional) Family

Up to the period before World War II, the dominant family pattern in Norway followed that which had been established and consolidated over many centuries, most often referred to as the extended or traditional family (Seltzer, 1992a, 1992b, 1999). This family unit was first and foremost characterized by strong, collective identity ties within the extended group. The family clan was a tight and often somewhat closed unit, bound together by blood relationships, and as working teams responsible for the survival of the collective unit. Many lived on farms, or in small fishing and/or other working communities. The extended family unit was composed of many generations, and in addition to vertical relations (from grandparents to parents to offspring), it could as well include horizontal relations such as uncles, aunts, cousins, and so on. Important transitions in life were often marked by old beliefs and manifested themselves in the form of acted rituals. Some

of these were/are of pre-Christian origin. Norway was officially christianized approximately 1,000 years ago. Still, in rural areas, practicing clinicians and therapists are confronted with persons who bear within them deeply rooted and collectively shared superstitious beliefs, and who participate in heathen practices (Seltzer et al., 2000).

Childraising was a collective duty in the extended family. Thus, the child represented "new" life, and was viewed as a gift to the collective family. Similarly, many family members participated in raising the child, and assuming responsibility for its care. In those cases where the family was well established as an extended and collective unit, in the period after World War II when many farming units were dissolved, we witnessed how the child's grandparents or aunts/uncles functioned as primary caretakers for the child, while his or her mother and father were sent off to participate in industrial work. To the child and the collective family, such arrangements were perceived as "natural," and they did not, as far as we know, impose suffering on the child. The child was accustomed to having members of the collective family unit care for her or him.[3] The child was viewed as an "investment" in the family's future survival, and this called for good care of the child, although such care depended also on material conditions. The close relations between the child and many family members also reinforced feelings of kinship, togetherness, belonging, and dependency within the family unit. This also promoted the child's ability to develop skills in relating to many people, from all phases of the life cycle, and also learn to be compassionate, and to trust others as well. In my view, Helm Stierlin's term "related individuation" (Stierlin, 1978) is very well illustrated in these extended family compositions. The child develops flexibility in understanding, interpreting, and acting in response to a group of significant others, and she or he also learns how to instigate and draw differential attention to her or his own needs and interests. The child learns to attend to a variety of perspectives, yet all the time she or he is "safely grounded and framed" by a familiar and somewhat predictable environment.

Because many family units were somewhat isolated, social relations took place within the family boundaries, for better and for worse.

The Nuclear Family, a Creation of an Industrial and Unified Society on Its Way to Modernity

The years after 1945 led Norwegian society into a period of modernity. The Labor Party was powerful and kept its position as the leading political party for many decades. The most pronounced mission of the Labor Party was to create a unified society, built on equality and solidarity for all. With much destruction from the years of war, the country had to be restored, at all levels. Industry was built and rebuilt, jobs were created, severe poverty was reduced, and children and young people were provided equal financial opportunities for an education through free schooling and various forms of financial support from the government. Social and health programs were created, and families moved into housing provided by the government at the new industrial sites. The welfare state evolved, and previously established class differences in our society became less visible, in material terms. With the building of industry and the emergence of modern society, the Norwegian family was headed for new living patterns, away from the extended family group. During this period, the houseman family faded away as most workers were offered paid jobs and subsidized housing at the new industrial sites.

The massive material changes involved new childraising practices, new ways of socializing, regular employment for at least one adult in each family, and engagement of the young in public childcare and educational programs. As masses of young workers with their spouses and children migrated to the big industrial sites where new and modern housing waited for them, the nuclear family became a self-contained unit, separate from the traditional family.

Official health and social programs took over some of the care functions provided by the extended family during earlier times. Childraising became the job of one couple or one adult, mostly the women. In the course of a few decades, ties were weakened between the extended relatives and the nuclear family, and friends from outside the family clan entered into social relations in the homes of nuclear families. Life cycle and other rituals, which had been established as transitional practices in traditional families for hundred of years, were frequently left behind.

Education and "rationally based knowledge" replaced old ways of reasoning. The latter had included folk tales, superstition, and mythology, which in some instances varied from one local community to another. Modernity led to standardized and unified patterns of family life and care, as well as "rational" explanations and solutions to any problem. In this context, beliefs not based in "scientific" and "educated" knowledge were no longer respected. An almost baffling confidence in science and technology swept across our unprepared and formerly somewhat uneducated and partly isolated Norwegian population.

The modern state ideology transferred its confidence in standardized patterns for machinery and technical plans onto human relations and categorizations.[4] Machines and household technology made life easier in the new Norwegian society. This may have led our society into an almost "blind" belief in standardized technical means, official rules, and conformity. The modern state welcomed and reinforced regularity, order, conformity, and uniformity. The state wanted sameness in an educated, standardized, and conforming population. I recall a study performed by Stanley Milgram from the early 1960s that measured and compared conformity in various countries. Norway was selected to participate, and came out in the top portion on the conformity scale (Milgram, 1961). This was surprising to some of us who thought of ourselves as bright and independent social science students at the University of Oslo.

Retrospectively, and in lieu of our role as the new force of young Norwegian academicians whose task it was to bring the country forward into an educated and advanced world, I think we unknowingly conformed to the dominant voices of the welfare state which impressed upon us that uniformity and conformity were desired. After all, we owed our country obedience, for bringing us alive out of the war, for supporting our education, and for promising us a modern and prosperous future.

As their ties to the extended family weakened, nuclear family members transferred their family identity to this much smaller and less powerful familial group, a weaker unit in society at large. Despite the public services that were developed by the new welfare state, the family remained vulnerable in terms of what would happen to the old, weak, and unproductive family members left behind as the younger generation moved (in groups of nuclear families) to the industrial sites where jobs were available. Old patterns of multigenerational family care were no longer feasible. Yet many old belief patterns remained, although they were not much discussed in public. Rationalism did not always fit well with some of those deeper and culturally based beliefs and old practices of care. Society developed selective hearing, so that only happy and "rationally based solutions" were promoted in our quickly modernized and official society.

The Modernistic Welfare State and Its Helping Systems in Practice

As the family became nuclear and gradually weakened its ties with the extended family, the government filled in the gaps with various public health and social care institutions. These provided for those who did not fare well in the modern arena, and undoubtedly reduced the suffering of many people in need of help. Yet for many of those who needed help, official services evolved, in practice, into unfeeling systems dominated by rigid hierarchies of people in official positions of power. In the following, I have focused on some of the less desirable aspects of the practice of the new Norwegian welfare state.

Caring practices changed hands, from emotionally bound and often blood-related family hands to the extended bureaucracy of "official services" for "cases" who needed help. With the assistance provided by the official apparatus, another side of the complex new structure appeared. If you went to the "officials" for help, you also had to conform to

the "educated" professional helpers, who dictated and effectuated "rational and knowledge-based help," often portioned out in accordance with a "professionally qualified" judgment of what you deserved and needed, in that order of priority. Values in the social and health system were dominated by Lutheran puritanical and religiously influenced ideology, as represented by the Norwegian State Church. The word "deserve" was also heard frequently in the service camps of the social and health care systems. Welfare workers often took on self-imposed roles as judges, who in guise of "educated reasoning" decided what a client deserved and should be allocated in terms of help.

In practice, the officially idealized service sector of modernized society showed itself from another angle: it exercised power, and this in many instances was perceived by recipients as cold, heartless, and unfair. In a Norway where an ideology of self-sufficiency had existed for hundreds of years, the users of public social care and health systems often felt displaced and estranged in their own society. I remember from my student years in Oslo, when I visited my rural home, that the women would be whispering about the poor old people who were now placed in old people's "homes." The word "home" was voiced with great sarcasm. They said: "No wonder the old people stopped talking." The women attributed the old people's lack of talking to estrangement from their "own flesh and blood." The old had been separated from their close family, and soon they would die from sorrow and anxiety as a result of the separation, or so the women feared. As people gathered some experience with the new institutions, and the first "honeymoon period" began to fade, the "modern" placements of the old were also viewed as examples of deep betrayals by one's own kin. Some felt that such "treatment" of the old might bring punishment from God upon the family, who should have protected their old and weak family members against such "placements."

I am tempted to speculate that the old people's muteness, as reported and interpreted by the local women in whispering voices, was related to the official (dominant) policy of the new state, proclaiming that the elderly enjoyed the material comfort offered by the modern institutions. Thus, in view of official policy, complaints were viewed as betrayals. Complaints were not rational in the new and modern society. In other words, it was not "normal" to long for the old life and the old house with its primitive facilities, when the government had built the most modern institutions to serve the needs of the weak and old. Thus, the whispering and critical voices of the women at their old home sites gave way to a new, dominant, and officially accepted ideology. Gradually, the whispering and slightly critical voices were silenced and no longer heard.

The Postmodern Family: Variations of Family Living and Family Composition

Today, with the appearance of postmodern living, family relations take ever new directions. Because coherent overviews and discussions of the web of issues involved in these recent and still ongoing life changes in our society are premature, I do not claim to offer a complete or "correct" picture of the postmodern situation in our country today. The extended family, the nuclear family, and the postmodern family clearly are not separate and distinct forms existing apart from one another. On the contrary, we see a mixture of all these forms, existing side by side. We see mixtures of family forms operating under the same roof and alongside the dominant family practices, and we may see changes from one form to another as different phases of family life continue to evolve.

In current Norwegian society, many people live alone, and many mothers are raising children without much family support. In addition, many people migrate to Norway from other countries in order to survive the evils of war, poverty, and unemployment in their former homelands.

One identifiable trend of the postmodern society is that many people are separated from their families, many define themselves as existing without a family, and many appear to value transient relationships as the closest they can come to meaningful relations with others. In an unpublished study, I asked persons attending various educational courses to in-

dicate their definition of the family and their ages. Many of the respondents under the age of 45–50 (as many as 40 percent out of approximately 600 answers), defined the family as consisting of one adult and child(ren) as the permanent group, plus "significant others" or friends. These were viewed as transient relations, who may come and go. When I ask my students to answer the question, "What is a family?" they come up with as many definitions as they are in numbers. Many in the group between 20 and 30 years of age construct a great variety of family definitions, of which a great portion fails to include reference to biological relations.

In line with other Western societies of today, Norwegian society, with its variety of family living patterns, is often referred to as "postmodern." Postmodern life is marked primarily by data communication, globalization, serial relationships between men and women, and social, ethnic, cultural, and geographic border crossings. Stacey (1998), an American sociologist, characterizes postmodernity as that which is not identifiable by patterns of permanency. On the contrary, postmodern living is found in many variations, one said to be as good or bad as the other. This is also the case with the family.

Today Norway is the homeland of many constellations of family-like groups, many of which last only for short periods of time. Members of today's postmodern Norwegian families are likewise recognized as living in temporary human constellations, and in some instances also as crossing many geographic zones within short periods of time. Children may change schools and neighborhoods many times during their growing years, and they may have the same friends for only brief periods of time. Furthermore, the State Statistical Bureau reports for the year 2000 that 21 percent of the total Oslo population come from foreign ethnic backgrounds (*Statistical Yearbook for Oslo,* 2000). Thus, we see a movement here that includes transient relations in the "native" Norwegian population, and at the same time we see groups of people coming from many parts of the world to settle and work in Norway. While people in the Norwegian society were steadfast (mostly living their lives from cradle to grave in one place) only a few decades ago, people today move frequently in the course of a lifetime. With the immigrants, who are also transient as they may have to move numerous times before they find satisfactory work and housing for their families, Norway has become a "mobile" and consequently a changing society in process.

We know very little about what this means in people's lives. We also know very little about how these frequent changes actually "imprint" upon individuals and groups of people, families, and the like. Also, we know little about how established institutional practices and other societal structures absorb the quick and somewhat "silent" changes taking place, and how they are actually meeting the challenges which are here. However, we do know that many children experience frequent losses of close relations, adults, siblings, and peers, and are often subjected to major changes in their lives. These facts call for some reflection in the clinical/therapy arena.

Challenges Confronting Clinicians and Therapists

Some of the greatest challenges to family therapy in Norway today have to do with the changes that have taken place in our society since the World War II years, and how these have affected the family as a source of primary care. Overwhelmingly complex challenges have entered our practices, and these appear to be related to the "new" lives of the young in our society. We need to meet these challenges from the perspective of our clients in their current situation, including attempts at understanding their particular belonging in their actual family lives, or their lack of such.

The therapy room has the potential for being turned into a place where that which is not easily discussed in other situations can be expressed, heard, and shared through dialogue. When something is shared, it is moved from being isolated within the individual as a "silent" and in some instances shameful and unarticulated burden, to something recognized by someone else, and thereby processed into shared psychocultural understanding. In order to do this, it is important that the therapist learn about the client's "history of significance" and view this through heard and spoken dialogues with the client. In therapy, it often turns out that issues embedded in clients' "history of significance" (borne by individuals and family groups) are also found in general culture, frequently in a tabooed form, which means it is not spoken of. One issue central to the challenges faced by therapists is the great variety in family life, the lack of "therapy models" and/or theory available encompassing all the changes that take place, and the meaning these may have to the persons who experience them. As students of "science," we tend to be trained in the area of "modernistic" thinking, most often based on the idea that one can find ways to conduct therapy that are generalizable from one case to another. This is no longer true. Most likely, we are facing several paradigm shifts, which eventually will demand new ways of developing therapeutic work in accordance with the complex variety of family and individual lifeways. In an edited book entitled *Stabilitet og forandring* (Stability and Change), by Berit Brandt and Kari Moxnes, we can find this central theme in today's Norway discussed from a wider societal perspective (Brandt & Moxnes, 1996).

Silenced Stories and Their Many Expressions

In the early 1980s, I carried out a study at the National Hospital of Norway (*Rikshospitalet*) of fifteen families with children who suffered from severe conversion disorder. The children were hospitalized with what was believed to be a serious, organically based, and treatment-resistant chronic disorder, yet no evidence of organic disease was found (Seltzer, 1985a, 1985b). The families presented themselves as a conforming, obedient, and orderly group. They could offer no explanations as to what might have happened to the child. They were eager, however, to explain to the therapists that the family was "normal," with no problems, except for the afflicted child. In the course of working with these families, the term "silent story" became a prominent concept in my own understanding of what had happened in the family, how and in what context the child's symptoms were frozen into a chronic state, and how to conduct therapy with the highly "sensitive" family and child. I developed a story-telling method, in which the term *imaginary narrative* became a key concept in the therapeutic construction of coherence and anchorage of the child in her family history (Seltzer, 1985b).

This narrative approach (possibly the first described application of a narrative approach in family therapy practice) served as a nonimposing and nonthreatening therapy process. This in turn helped to defrost the otherwise isolated encapsulation of the "problem" in the child alone. As family members began to share themes related to otherwise taboo, forbidden, and consequently silenced family themes, thirteen of the fifteen "chronic cases" regained normal function after approximately five or six therapy sessions. The children's conversion disorders were related to subactive and silenced themes of severe shame, class issues, poverty in the parental generation, violence, and other humiliating issues, borne by the whole family system. At that time, I found Sennet and Cobb's book, *Hidden Injuries of Class,* where they masterfully demonstrate the subconscious imprints of class, extremely helpful (Sennet & Cobb, 1972).

In my own writing on the "conversion families" and their physical ailments, I introduced the terms "silent story" and "silent depression." In these families, the child's body seemed very wisely, and in a silent and "diplomatic language," to express the otherwise tabooed and painful humiliation and shame borne by the family through several generations. The concepts related to silence became important tools in understanding dissociated disorders (in these cases the conversion of psychological and psychocultural pain into physical manifestations), and provided as well indicators for the direction of therapeutic practice in treating such conditions (Seltzer, 1985a, 1985b).

Since that time, I have developed a "third ear" for listening to the many versions of silent themes (Seltzer, 2003) and as I encounter many individuals with dissociated disorders today, I am often working at the edge of what would be "normally accepted" in the established family culture.

That which is not spoken of is often just as devastating to the child as that which is brought into the open for discussion. If such issues are taken to the table for discussion, it is important that the nondominant voices are encouraged to speak and be heard. Unfortunately, there is much evidence to indicate that the voices of these nonpowerful others are all too often silenced.

Encounters with Postmodern Norwegian Families in the Therapy Room

Recent statistics from the official annual reports (*årsmeldinger*) of a number of randomly chosen child guidance clinics in urban and rural Norway for the year 2000 show that eight of ten referrals to the clinics are related to problems in adult couple relationships. Problems in multiple transient couple relationships often have undesirable consequences for the children who live with the couples. Most often the couples consist of the child's biological mother and her adult companions. The adult relationships may last only for short periods of time, yet these periods may be crucial to the child's development. Consequently, we face challenges in the therapy room relating to a great range of family compositions and family living, as was discussed before. In the following, I attempt to provide a glimpse into some of the dilemmas I have encountered and of some of the difficulties I have experienced in trying to grasp what is going on at the ideational and material levels of familial groups encountered in the therapy room. These are not meant as in-depth discussions, but rather as glimpses into the everyday problems of child and adolescent clients of state-sponsored clinics.

I see children who have experienced numerous parental compositions, and in the course of frequent changes, they have also experienced numerous losses. In Oslo, the capital of Norway, 50 percent of newborn babies are born outside of wedlock (reported by the State Statistical Bureau, 2001). This does not mean that all the babies included in this group are without officially stated fathers, although many are. This is so because many young parents prefer cohabitation without juridical or religious marital bonds being placed on them.

We know very little about what this practice *means* in the lives of the participants, though there are strong indications that relationships between cohabiting couples dissolve more frequently than those among married couples. Official statistics from the State Statistical Bureau (2001) show that 40 percent of the Norwegian population live in single-person households and 28 percent live in households made up of two persons. In this latter group, many single parents, mostly women, are likely to be included. Thirty-one percent of the population are made up of households composed of three to five persons.

In a recently reported study carried out by NOVA (Norwegian Social Research Institute, 2001), it is stated that one-third of all girls in their early teens are forced to have sex with boys in the same age group or older. The forced-sex situations most often take place at private parties, and are associated with a heavy consumption of alcohol among the young. These findings certainly raise numerous questions about how the young view themselves, and how they (girls and boys) view themselves in relation to one another. One also wonders whether this "forced acceptance" reflects in any way models of cohabiting relations among adult women and men.

Traumatization by Observation in the Context of Intimate Relations

Many young people, who themselves are the children of divorce or of parents who have broken up, view relationships bound by religion or law as undesirable. Disappointments related to the divorce or breakup of their parents seem to signal to many young people that it is better to practice "trial family living" than to enter marriage. Although marriages may still be viewed as more "real," they are also viewed as riskier emotionally.

A haunting association here involves young couples from well-to-do families who celebrate glamorous wedding ceremonies, set up "perfect" homes, and "play house" in an idyllic world, much as our great author Henrik Ibsen portrayed in *A Doll's House,* more than a hundred years ago.[5] When everyday tasks make demands on the young in their idyllic existence, and less pleasant issues come their way, a common "solution" is a flight reaction, resulting in disrupted relationships.

In therapy, clinicians have seen these somewhat puzzling problems numerous times. In some in-

stances it appears that the young meet with a panic reaction to what to others might appear as undramatic events. They respond as if they have already been abandoned by their mate. In my "clinical language," I have thought of some of these young people's reactions as dissociative. In the course of therapy, many end up talking about vague or "foggy" memories of shameful and consequently "silenced" episodes of conflict, involving verbal and/or physical abuse between their parents.

I have called these scenes and their impact on observing children "traumatization by observation in the context of intimate relations."[6] What characterizes these situations is that they are inescapable for the observing child. The helplessness of a child in such a situation, and the loss of actual mastery in handling the situation, places the child in a position of pure victimization. In addition, the idea that the child loves both mother and father, and depends on both, puts the child in a position where she or he cannot condemn one or the other. The child is consequently placed in a double-bind situation, where he or she is physically, cognitively, and emotionally trapped. A splitting off of the one while feeling sympathy with the other is therefore the only chance the child has in "dealing with" the traumatic event. This may create a psychological preparedness to split off and to dissociate, reactions opposite to processes of integration and association. Thus, the preparedness for dissociation is already present in the child, and she or he may be somewhat prone to react with fear to situations that "normally" would not cause a fight-or-flight reaction. Many young people report having developed special skills in effectuating physical and/or psychological flight reactions in response to "unpleasant" situations. Thus, flight reactions in their own adult couple relationships may represent a subconscious elicitation of retraumatization (by proxy), which effectively route them into previously engraved neural-emotional escape channels.

Feelings of vulnerability and unpredictability, as well as deep fears of abandonment, are shared by many young people. One young woman told me that most people her age are "allergic" to promises. To them, life may bring unpleasant surprises. Another adolescent girl said: "You never know if the person you meet really means that he loves you, so I am never going to marry. He might suddenly like another woman better." What if one should feel unsatisfied in the relationship? Will she or he walk away? Thus, a serious doubt about the permanency of relationships, and a fear of being abandoned without warning and with helpless feelings of loss, are prominent in the stories told by many children and young people in the therapy room today. Feelings of vulnerability and unpredictability appear overwhelming to many, and emotional and cognitive skills to cope with these seem poorly developed.

Positive Thinking

Based on conversations with some young people in therapy, it appears that they, in contrast to their parental generation, have grown up in a period of societal ideology which in the past 10–15 years has emphasized "positive thinking" and quick solutions to problems. "Positive thinking" in our culture often means that one should be obedient. One should look away from the problem, and thereby prevent conflict from being exposed. Thus, obedience promotes silence. This is particularly the case when the problem, such as domestic violence, is associated with shame and loss of control.

Some young people, especially those from the middle and upper-middle social strata, seem to have grown up believing that if you think positively and learn to look away from human conflict, things will turn out well. Thus, when some men are left by their spouses without having been able to pick up some prior warnings, they express feelings of devastation and abandonment. One young man expressed the feeling that he was being "locked in a container," isolated and trapped.

Another therapist told me about a client who ended his own life. The client had left a suicide note in which he said the therapist was "a good therapist, . . . but . . . he himself . . . [the client] was hopeless." He [the client] excused himself for having been such a "bag of dirt" (translated from the word *drittsekk*) in therapy. He had not been able to learn to "think in positive terms," so he continued to carry

the dirt (*dritt*) with him. And so, feeling helpless, and not worthy of the good therapist's time, the young man ended his life.

Many men seen by therapists today express desperate feelings of a lack of shared community. A story typically expressed by a man is that he thought everything was going fine, until one terrible morning, at the breakfast table, he was informed by his wife that she was leaving him and, sure enough, the same day she was gone. Or he gets an unexpected phone call from his wife who tells him she has moved back to her mother's house, as she can no longer withstand the pressure of the relationship. Many of the women, in turn, report that they have tried to engage their men in conversations regarding their growing sense of loneliness within the relationship, but that they have had no luck in catching their husband's attention.

Past Chronotype and New Living Patterns

The above examples could be framed and understood in a contextual-cultural perspective. They could be understood as patterns that were transferred from previous family cohabitation and work practices, but that are maladaptive in current and future contexts. Thus, living patterns from past "chronotopes" may prove maladaptive in current and future contexts. Bakhtin viewed the chronotope as a value laden ideological focus, which was marked and framed by its societal/cultural context (Mandelker & Emerson, 1995). In such cases, we have to deal with a cultural lag, a term indicating that technical developments in a society are absorbed much more quickly than changes in culturally evolving forms of life. The historical separation of members from their extended family, followed by sudden isolation in the nuclear family, and then the rapid moves into postmodern life patterns, may have created disjointed ideological and behavioral patterns, and placed some people outside their "chronotope."

In the extended family, close, trusting, though sometimes also conflictual, relations were taken for granted. Participants were joined together as a tightly bound group through good and bad days.

Women worked side by side in the family community, and their practicing of discourse also prepared them for the "handling" of conflicts. These women had much experience in the endurance and patience needed to remain in the situations in which they were put. The men also worked together in the fields or on small fishing vessels. They carried out prescribed tasks at a distance from one another, often without much verbal exchange. They had developed a tacit understanding of expectations and shared efforts. These work-related understandings and practices, developed over many generations, were also practiced in their personal relationships. In the "old days," there was little distinction between free time and work time. Social relations were taken care of within the family group, and centered very often around work activities.

In the nuclear family, most women remained at the home site, with the children, while their men went to the industrial site to work. The women's socializing took place in the small daytime community where they lived and raised their families. Thus, while the tradition of verbal sharing of their daily experiences continued among the women, the men continued their somewhat mute way of operating together at the production line of industrial sites. Thus, if this interpretation is approximately correct, two cultures evolved, one female and one male. One led to the practice of sharing thoughts and feelings with others, while the other led to tacit work practices in which little verbal exchange evolved.

In today's society, most women are employed outside the family. During a portion of her pregnancy, a woman is entitled to partial financial support from her employer, while remaining at home. After the child is born, the father and the mother may divide their parental leave, and be paid full time by their respective employers, for 9 months. Single mothers are allocated a few more weeks of partial pay while staying home with their babies. Since the extended family is a family form of the past, and members of the parental generation are often involved in building new relations, many single mothers raise their children in far from optimal conditions.

Many of the mothers have little or no contact with the father of the child. In the therapy room, however, we often meet children who are searching for their fathers, and who know very little about their biological paternal family. Yet, in therapy, modern and postmodern families often tell previously silenced stories related to the biological origin of the child (Seltzer, 1994). A talk with Anne, 6 years old, illustrates this child's conception of "father." When the therapist asks Anne about her father, she becomes physically uneasy, shifting around in her chair. The therapist makes the question more specific, and asks who her father is. She says she is not sure, but maybe Ole, because he lives with her mother, her, and her brother (= half-brother). She obviously thinks about it for a while, then she adds: "But, he is mostly my brother's father, but a little bit my father too." Here, Anne categorizes the term "father" as someone who may be *more or less* a father. When the therapist asks Anne who might be mostly her father, she says: "Well, Knut was my father before . . . but not any more." Therapist: "He is not your father any more?" Anne: "No, because he used to live with us . . . before . . . but not now." Here Anne clearly categorizes the term father as a temporary concept, a "father" can be a father as long as he stays with the child and the mother in their household, but when contact between the mother–child unit and the father is severed, the man is no longer categorized as "a father." The therapist asks if she thought about "who feels like a father inside her, what might be the answer then?" She says: "Maybe Svein, because he lived with us when I was in my mother's tummy." Then she carefully wipes tears from her eyes, and adds: "And his eyes look like mine." Here the 6-year-old alludes to biological connections, and perhaps some feeling of "likeness of the soul." She does, after all, have a deep feeling that only one person is *her* special father, and that she and he are somehow connected, even though she has no more contact with him. This, it appears, is important for the child's own view of herself as a unique person, and may serve, in postmodern context, as an "identity icon."

Many children in postmodern Norway grow up in blended families composed of siblings from different adult unions and combinations of reunions. Many of them are confused about family nomenclature, such as father, aunt, uncle, sister, brother, grandparents, and the family relations indicated by such terms. This, however, is not only a Norwegian problem. In a recent report from Great Britain, similar problems were found among children whose names were frequently being changed, as different men entered and departed their mothers' households (*The Independent,* October 25, 2001, p. 5). In school, teachers have trouble identifying sibling relations between their pupils, as the pupils may have different family names, yet live at the same address or at different addresses.

Such frequent changes of a child's name, which serves as an identity label, and the lack of protection of a child's family name, are in fact violations of Articles 7 and 8 of the United Nations Convention on the Rights of the Child. The latter emphasizes the protection of the child's identity, which includes name, nationality, and family ties. Such issues point to a broader problem complex involving the feelings of children who have been emotionally injured when the ties they have established to adults are severed time and time again.

Another article from a British newspaper (*The Observer,* June 10, 2001, p. 23) reports how the child's right to a father is often overlooked by official societal institutions, and describes how this serves as a hindrance for these children striving to know their father as a parent. The article states that societal institutions treat men as economic providers, and seem to overlook the value a father represents to a child as a permanently caring parent, and as a mature and responsible adult male model.

Clinical records describe many children in Norway today who are confused about identity matters. They report major difficulties related to existential questions such as "who am I," "who are my relatives," and "with whom do I belong." They express feelings of insecurity as to who they will be with today, next week, or in the foreseeable future. In contrast to earlier periods of Norwegian history, when family members lived out their lives and died in the same place, many children's lives today include frequent changes of home sites and schools. Many, too, live with the constant fear of mentioning her or his "lost" parent, since mother and father are declared enemies. In a recent

count of children referred to the Child and Adolescent Psychological Clinic at the University of Trondheim (NTNU), 22 of 25 of the children lived in family constellations with only one biological parent present— usually their biological mother, with or without other household cohabitants. For more discussion on the many faces of divorce, see Moxnes et al. (2001).

It is not uncommon for children experiencing adult cohabitation problems to develop emotional, behavioral, psychosomatic, and somatic problems for which they are brought into clinical practices for treatment. Most often they are referred by the schools, and brought to the clinic by their mothers. Many exhibit variations of trauma-related disorders, concentration problems, conversion disorders, eating disorders, speech problems such as extreme stuttering or selective mutism, self-inflicted injury, Munchhausen proper, Munchhausen by proxy, and other psychological disorders. The above-mentioned disorders, often understood as individual psychological disorders, are indeed relationally, reactively, and contextually aroused and maintained.

Although one may argue that many of these disorders were known in child psychiatry and psychology long before postmodern family variations appeared, the severity and frequency of such problems seen in children and young people today may indicate a violation of some basic needs among the young. These needs may involve feelings of belonging, being appreciated in a group of primary caretakers, some degree of predictability, knowledge of one's own origin and history, acceptance by peers, being in a school situation long enough to be recognized by teachers and peers as belonging in "the class," and being convinced that somewhere there is someone who loves them "for always" (as a 6-year-old girl who had been placed in a foster home told me), and unconditionally. Moreover, children need to be in milieus where they are spared from observing and/or directly experiencing violence and abuse.

CONCLUDING COMMENTS

In this chapter I have attempted to bind together family forms and lifeways through various periods and chronotopes in Norwegian culture, history, and society. In an otherwise fragmented world, reductionism is still the simplest way of selecting a small slice of a view, and discussing it from that limited scope. I believe it is imperative to look at the family as an institution embedded in a web of contexts. The complexity here is very well illustrated by clients who seek help with their daily living problems in social offices, clinics, and other helping institutions.

I have connected micro and macro societal/cultural/psychological issues with that which is presented to us as clinicians and therapists, in the secluded therapy room. In this room, a safer frame can be created, for voicing not only the already established and dominant discourses, but also those themes that are often kept silenced, in society, in culture and history, in institutions, by families and individuals, and their helpers as well. Most of all, I hope that this chapter succeeds in bringing attention to the "new world of close relations," or a lack of these, faced by some less privileged children and youth in Norway today.

Last but not least, I hope our newly prosperous country does not forget that we still have poor people, and that a majority of the poor today are single mothers and their small children, and people from other continents and ethnic backgrounds, who are desperately trying to settle and find work here. Today, single mothers are often left in a lonely situation, where support from official sources, and from extended family relations, is insufficient. Therapists, social workers, and others representing "official" power need to learn to "see" these situations, and listen to the voices of their clients, more than to the "official" voices, which tend to portray idyllic stories and images. The distances between these officially narrated tales and the clients' lived lives push our clients far into the margins of our society.

In the area of social and clinical work, I feel what we need more than anything is to be trained in *compassionate listening,* learning to focus on the clients' tales, and engage in evolving dialogues with our clients' *own tales* as a point of departure. It is important to be reminded that as clinicians and therapists, we are not judges, and that we in most cases do not need to evaluate what our clients *deserve, but rather what they need.*

Too many people feel lonely, unworthy, and marginalized in our otherwise successful society today. When I, in my postmodern life, was being transported from a hotel to a clinic in a small town in a rural area, I asked the foreign taxi driver (from Eastern Europe) how it was for him to be in a small place here in Norway. He said he was O.K., because he has a job, but his wife and children felt unwelcome and lonesome. And he continued, as I walked out of the taxi into a fierce snowstorm: "For human beings, Norway is a cold place to be in."

ACKNOWLEDGMENTS

Gratitude is extended to Uwe P. Gielen and to Michael R. Seltzer for their encouragement and assistance during the writing of this chapter.

NOTES

1. Today, this is somewhat changed, as much of our food is imported from large farming communities in Southern Europe and elsewhere in the world.
2. In the pre–World War II years, there were few governmental welfare institutions. However, church and other voluntary and religious welfare organizations provided some help to those who suffered.
3. If this happened today, society, represented by child welfare institutions, would have raised doubts about the child's well-being during the parents' absence. This may be a good example of how childraising practices must be evaluated relative to time, place, and ideological contexts.
4. In the social and health sciences, research funding was and is in most cases rewarded to projects based on standardized quantitative and biological methodologies, often following very restrictive rules regarding design, procedure, etc. Modernistic ideology still prevails, even though our current society calls for new ways of practicing and conceptualizing clinical work and research.

5. Henrik Ibsen (1828–1906) was an excellent critical reporter of Norwegian society. Many of his dramatic plays from the period 1877–1899 dealt with shameful and silenced themes, often emerging inside closed family relations, yet always in contrast to the dominant and official voices of nineteenth-century society.

6. Because in the 1970s a law was introduced against corporal punishment of children, we have fewer direct reports of physical abuse of children today. However, there is no law against the beating of women within the frame of intimate couple relationships, often referred to as "within-house disorder" (*husbråk*). Within this context of privacy, many women are repeatedly beaten by their husbands/men. We know that many children witness such beatings, and react with helpless fear in their roles as observers of these "private" events. The police may look into *Husbråk*, yet these episodes are rarely followed up in terms of court trials and sentencing of the perpetrators.

REFERENCES

Brandt, B., & Moxnes, K. (1996). *Stabilitet og forandring* [Stability and change]. Oslo: Tano Aschehoug.

Dentith, S. (1995). *Bahktinian thought: An introductory reader.* New York: Routledge.

Mandelker, A., & Emerson, C. (1995). *Bahktin in contexts: Across the disciplines.* Evanston, IL: Northwestern University Press.

Milgram, S. (1961). Nationality and conformity. *Scientific American, 205,* 45–51.

Moxnes, K., et al. (Eds.). (2001). *Skilsmissens mange ansikter* [The many faces of divorce]. Kristiansand: Høgskoleforlaget.

Nova (2001). Reports by Norwegian Institute on Conditions for Growth, Welfare and Aging. Oslo, Norway.

Seltzer, W. J. (1985a). Conversion disorder in childhood and adolescence: A familial/cultural approach. Part I. *Family Systems Medicine, 3*(3), 261–280.

Seltzer, W. J. (1985b). Conversion disorder in childhood and adolescence, Part II: Therapeutic issues. *Family Systems Medicine, 3*(4), 397–416.

Seltzer, W. J. (1989). Myths of destruction: A cultural approach to families in therapy. *Journal of Psychotherapy and the Family, 4,* 17–34.

Seltzer, W. J. (1992a). En narrativ fremstilling av familieterapiens utviklijng i Norge: En kritisk analyse av grunnleggende teoretiske og metodiske problemstillinger. Deil [A narrative account of the evolvement of family therapy in Norway: A critical analysis of basic theoretical and methodological issues]. *Tidsskrift for Norsk Psykologforening, 29,* 689–698.

Seltzer, W. J. (1992b). Det narrative perspektiv innen rammen av familiekulturell tilnærming til terapi: Teoretiske og metodiske problemstillinger. Del II [The narrative perspective within the frame of a cultural approach to family therapy: Theoretical and methodological issues]. *Tidsskrift for Norsk Psykologforening, 29,* 669–709.

Seltzer, W. J. (1994). Therapeutic application of universal mythology in the construction of the 10-year-old selectively mute Peter Petersen's saga, and his mother. Translated into Hungarian and published as: Mi a csalad? Univerzalis mitoszok es terapias vonatkozasaik. *Csalad, Gyermak, Ifjusag (3–4),* 16–22.

Seltzer, W. J. (1999). The family and family therapy in Norway. In U. P. Gielen & A. L. Comunian (Eds.), *International approaches to the family and family therapy* (pp. 195–223). Padua, Italy: Unipress.

Seltzer, W. J. (2003). *Familiehemmeligheten. Tause fortellinger fra terapirommet* [Family secrets. Silent stories from the therapy room]. Oslo: Gyldendal.

Seltzer, M., Kullberg, C., Olesen, S. P., & Rostila, I. (2001). *Listening to the welfare state.* Burlington, VT: Ashgate.

Seltzer, M., Seltzer, W. J., Homb, N., Midtstigen, P., & Vik, G. (2000). Tales full of sound and fury: A cultural approach to family therapeutic work and research in rural Scandinavia. *Family Process, 39*(3), 285–306.

Sennett, R., & Cobb, J. (1972). *The hidden injuries of class.* New York: Random House.

Stacey, J. (1998). *Brave new families.* Berkeley: University of California Press.

State Statistical Bureau. (1994–1995). The Parliamentary Report No. 14. Oslo: State Statistical Bureau.

State Statistical Bureau. (2001).

Statistical Yearbook for Oslo, 2000.

Stierlin, H. (1978). *Delegation und Familie* [Delegation and family]. Frankfurt am Main: Suhrkamp.

CHAPTER 16

THE RUSSIAN FAMILY

ERIC SHIRAEV
George Washington University

JULIA GRADSKOVA
Moscow State University

RUSSIA AND ITS PEOPLE: SOME STATISTICS

The Russian Federation, the world's largest country, stretches over 6.5 million square miles (17 million square kilometers) and eight time zones. The country's population is 145 million, which makes Russia the sixth most populous country in the world, following China, India, the United States, Indonesia, and Brazil. The great majority of the country's people, nearly 80 percent, are ethnic Russians, who share Slavic ancestral roots with many peoples of Eastern Europe. In addition to ethnic Russians, there are also over 30 million people of about 70 smaller ethnic groups, which are officially called *nationali-* *ties* in the Russian language—which is quite confusing to the Western observer. Some ethnic groups are concentrated mainly in thirty-one administrative ethnic units, while others live all over Russia. Among the largest groups are Tatars, Ukrainians, Belarusians, Chuvash, Bashkir, and Mordovans. There are substantial contingents of Russian citizens of German and Jewish decent, but their numbers declined in the 1990s due to massive emigration from Russia to Israel, Germany, and some other developed countries. Most Russians, Ukrainians, and Belarusians are Orthodox Christian. Most Turkic groups are Muslim. However, religious affiliation does not entirely correspond to linguistic groupings. It should also be mentioned that the overwhelming majority of ethnic groups speaks Russian, and for many individuals, especially in interethnic marriages, this is their first language. According to estimates, there are from 700,000 to 1.5 million residents in Russia from many countries, such as former republics of the Soviet Union, as well as China, Afghanistan, North Korea, Somalia, and Ethiopia. Most of them left their homelands for marriage-related or economic reasons, whereas others were trying to avoid political persecution in their home countries (Lambroschini, 2000).

At the beginning of the millennium, there were approximately 52 million households in Russia. Of these families, 24 million had nonadult children. Almost 4 million family units in Russia are single-parent families, with more than 5 million children being raised there. The vast majority of single parents—94 percent—are women. Almost 75 percent of Russian families live in towns and cities; the rest of the population resides in villages in rural communities (Rimashevskaya & Vannoi, 1996; VTUZ, 1999).

THE IMPORTANCE OF DEFINITIONS

In the English language, the word *Russian* refers to anything or anybody associated with Russia. In the Russian language, however, an important distinction is made between two particular adjectives, a distinction that is not always obvious to non-Russian speakers. One adjective (*Roosski*) refers to "Russian" as an ethnic category; the other (*Rossiyski*) refers to something or somebody belonging to or associated with the Russian Federation as a sovereign state. For example, when an English-speaking person says, "Russian family," he or she ought to provide follow-up clarification, because this family, in theory, could live in Moscow, Riga, or New York; the members of this family could be Jewish, Christian, practice no religion, and so on. A Russian-speaking individual, on the other hand, will use more unambiguous adjectives. If the speaker wants to describe a family, the members of which are ethnically Russian, this family will be called *Rooskaya semya*. If the speaker talks about a family of

any ethnic background, whose members are Russian citizens living on Russian territory, then the other term (*Rossiyskaya semya*) will be used. Many non-Russian ethnic groups living in the Russian Federation are very sensitive about the incorrect use of the linguistic labels.

To simplify our descriptions, we should understand by "Russian family" any family unit whose members live within the confines of the contemporary Russian Federation, regardless of their particular or mixed ethnic background.

A BRIEF HISTORIC OVERVIEW

Over time, the Russian family has been changing together with Russian society, which underwent dramatic and rapid transformations, especially in the twentieth century. Pervasive economic, technological, and large-scale political transitions have affected Russia as a country, its social infrastructure, and its people. Nevertheless, during almost all years of its existence, the social order in Russia was exclusively authoritarian. Overall, the Russian people have had very little exposure to democratic institutions, democratic traditions, and basic individual liberties over the course of the country's history. Whereas some democratic elements of self-government existed in various forms and elements of collectivism have become major attributes of Russian culture, authoritarianism was and continues to be the backbone of the Russian civilization.

Unified first by Kiev dukes and then by Moscow rulers, Russian Slavic tribes scattered among the forests, swamps, and valleys of Eastern Europe formed a centralized state sometime in the sixteenth century. Suffering immensely after numerous invasions on its territory during the earlier stages of the country's history, Russia as a state and empire was expanding tremendously during the second half of the past millennium, relentlessly conquering new territories and peoples in Europe and Asia. It remained an authoritarian empire ruled by Czars up to World War I. The Communist revolution of 1917 put an end to the old empire and started a new one, which was renamed the Soviet Union seven years later.

After 1917, ideological, political, and social changes throughout a period of more than seventy years significantly transformed the role of the Russian family. On the one hand, the role of the family in the socialization process diminished due to an ideological doctrine that emphasized the importance of primary work units, or "collectives" in the individual's life and development. Therefore, one of the prime goals of socialization in the Soviet Union was the promotion of collectivist values and norms. Official ideology and propaganda contrasted the assumed advantages of socialist collectivism with the pitfalls of bourgeois individualism with its attention to individual achievement and material success. The cult of collectivism was favored not only for ideological but also for pragmatic reasons, because "the socialist collective" (a primary work unit) in factories, offices, schools, or research institutions was a powerful instrument of governmental control over the individual. Furthermore, for many individuals, this *collective* was a major source of informational, financial, and even emotional support. Work units were often essential for getting access to scarce products and services, gaining legal protection, securing a place in a prestigious university for children, and for many other purposes directly linked to the people's well-being (Shlapentokh, 1984, 2002).

On the other hand, the Soviet government initiated policies aimed at the strengthening of the family. Over the years, special family-related benefits, including monetary payments, were established for individuals with children. According to the law, women would get a paid vacation from work (typically up to twelve months) before childbirth and after it. Every working mother could get a paid leave of absence from work if her child was sick. The government established a nationwide and affordable system of daycare centers and kindergartens for preschoolers. Affordable twenty-four- and forty-eight-day summer camps for children of all ages were very popular among Soviet families. Although college education was not available for many, because of the highly competitive selection process, millions of Soviet families did not have to pay college tuition for their children because the government subsidized higher education. Overall, throughout the years, the Soviet educational system, despite major inner problems and limitations imposed on it by the state, was relatively successful in providing basic knowledge and skills to young Soviet individuals (Shiraev, 1988).

Despite a wide range of benefits available to the average Soviet family, the general scarcity of products and services coupled with the ideological pressure from an intrusive totalitarian regime were two significant factors shaping the lives of the vast majority of families. The changes came in the late 1980s, after Soviet leader Mikhail Gorbachev had started the process leading to the breakdown of the Soviet Union, and the collapse of the entire communist system of government.

Since 1992, Russian families have been living in a country that is quite different from the one just a decade earlier. From a historical viewpoint, the period from 1992 to the time when you read this chapter is incredibly short. At the same time, these years have few parallels in Russian history because they have been filled with a remarkable set of dramatic events. These were years of rapid change, turbulence, both growing and diminishing hopes marked by most people's tremendous anxieties about their future. The aftershock resulting from the breakup of the Soviet Empire was soon followed by the new country's economic collapse. Inflation in the early 1990s was rampant and drained the meager resources of the vast majority of Russian families. Government had severely limited resources to support millions of state employees. Thousands of state enterprises were sold into private hands. Many individuals started looking for and changing their jobs, while others started their own businesses. Some individuals began to work for others' private enterprises. While millions were simply looking for an occupation that would guarantee regular wages, the economic revival of the mid-1990s was interrupted by the devastating financial crisis of 1998, which had an unprecedented and profoundly sobering effect on the overall socioeconomic situation of the Russian family. The aftershocks of that crisis have been and will be felt in Russian society for years to come.

THE RUSSIAN FAMILY DURING THE SOCIETAL TRANSFORMATION

The establishment of major democratic freedoms, considerable economic difficulties, and the economic polarization of society are among the most significant factors that affect Russian families at the beginning of the new millennium. In the 1990s, the gross domestic product (GDP) per capita in Russia was approximately $5,000, which was twice as much as in China, about the same as in Brazil, but four times as low as in most developed countries (*The Economist,* July 12, 1997, pp. 3–18). From 1992 to 1995, the earliest period in Russia's post-Communist history, GDP declined by 49 percent while real income diminished by 29 percent. The most difficult process for the families to cope with was inflation, especially in the early 1990s, which further drained most families' scarce resources (*Argumenty I Facty,* July 1996, p. 2). In 2000, the average individual income was $70 per month, not much above the U.N. per-capita poverty line of $60 per month (Vlasova, 2001). More than half of all Russians in the mid-1990s reported that they did not have any savings in a bank (*CISS Index to International Public Opinion,* 1995–1996).

The August 1998 financial crisis worsened the situation in virtually every Russian home, and almost everyone lost approximately three-fourths of the monthly wage. Millions of people saw their savings disappear from their bank accounts for the second time since 1992. In just a matter of a few days, money that could have been converted into dollars was frozen, turned into nonexchangeable rubles, and then gone. According to an All-Russian Center of Public Opinion study, the number of Russians who kept savings in banks in 1999 had dropped to 11 percent. More than half of all families with children could be qualified as poor, that is, making less than $16 per month per person (Ovcharova & Prokofieva, 1999). Between 1991 and 1993, the gap between the richest and poorest 10 percent of the Russian population tripled (*Izvestia,* September 16, 1994, p. 1). By 1999, according to the Russian Federation's State Committee for Statistics, the richest 10 percent reported making 14 times more money than the poorest 10 percent—an unprecedented departure from the social stratification of the Soviet Union. Under these conditions, many symbols of the "Russian dream"—a high-quality city apartment, a decent country house, a new foreign-made car, a top-of-the-line video system, and trips to top-of-the-line Mediterranean resorts, again became out of reach for most people.

These economic disparities are most evident between urban and rural populations. People in the "bigger" Russian cities enjoyed, in general, better economic opportunities than individuals living in smaller communities and rural areas. For instance, Moscow residents spend two to three times more per capita than those in Russia in general. In 1996, the average employee's salary in Moscow was $145 a month, which was about five times higher than in some other Russian regions. At the same time, poverty was not confined only to the provincial zones. Based on the Moscow City Statistics Committee, in 1999, city residents with incomes lower than the subsistence level numbered 29 percent. In the second largest city, St. Petersburg, according to a survey, 24 percent of households could not even afford meat or fish once a week (Ovcharova & Prokofieva, 1999). People's access to computers and the Internet is also limited by mostly economic reasons: a vast majority of public schools and millions of households do not have enough money to buy computers and purchase access to the World Wide Web. Surveys suggest that in 2000, more than 74 percent of Russians had never used a computer. Only 16 percent of respondents had computers at home (ROMIR, 2000). To compare, according to a U.S. survey taken at approximately the same time as the Russian poll, among the poorest Americans—those who made less than $15,000 per year—28 percent owned computers (Gallup/*USA Today,* December 1999, telephone, *N* = 1,011).

Fortunately, unemployment has not become a devastating problem threatening Russian families. Due to the government's attempts to support employees of most bankrupt state enterprises, millions of Russians continued to earn their wages although their plants and factories did not generate a profit. Among the most vulnerable categories were the young: people under 30 represented almost 40 percent of all the unemployed in the country (Artyukhov, 1998). Nevertheless, it is important to mention that many people in Russia try to find additional sources of income, so that in many families working adults can bring home additional earnings. Many find additional resources by working several jobs, doing part-time work, working unofficially, getting nonmonetary payments and benefits from employers, and harvesting from private household plots.

The lack of social protection and low income are two major problems that most Russian families are facing in the second decade of the period of post-Communist transition. Among many specific problems, two of them—violence and alcoholism—stand out as the most profound. Official statistics indicate that some 15,000 Russian citizens die from domestic violence every year. More than 12,000 of these victims are women. In addition, official reports suggest that 54,000 women suffer severe injuries because of domestic abuse every year. Experts argue that these numbers do not represent a real picture of domestic violence because in seven out of ten cases, women—because their husbands or boyfriends are involved—prefer not to tell anyone, including the police, about attacks against them (Tselms, 2000). A government report (Soviet Federatsii, 1999) suggests that more than 50,000 children run away from their homes each year. Family violence is the major reason for this.

Alcohol abuse has been a serious societal problem in Russia for many years. There are different assessments of how much alcohol Russians consume; estimates published in newspapers and other sources in 2001 ranged from 30 to 80 liters of vodka per person per year. Despite this disagreement in assessments, there is a concurrence of opinions that alcohol is a major contributor to health problems, low life expectancy, family violence, and a wide range of behavioral problems that affect the Russian family's life. For instance, in 1996, more than 35,000 people in Russia died from accidental alcohol poisoning (Francis, 2000). Russian women are twice as likely to die from alcohol poisoning or alcohol-related injury as American men. Similar to what happens in many other countries, alcohol addiction is both stigmatized by many Russian people and viewed as a character flaw by others. This results in many individuals' reluctance to seek help for their substance-related problems.

HOUSING AND LIVING ARRANGEMENTS

To understand living conditions of the Russian family, one should keep in mind that local governments are still responsible for the construction, renovation, and distribution of a substantial proportion of housing in the country. Although the vast majority of houses and apartments are in private hands—so people can buy and sell their property—a substantial proportion of the Russian population is still not able to purchase permanent accommodations: the cost is too high. Therefore, as a matter of social policy, local authorities keep official waiting lists of those families who need improvement of their living conditions. After a substantial waiting period, which may last three, five, or even ten years, the family receives its new accommodations from the government free of charge or for an affordable fee. Sometimes factories and other institutions become sponsors of their employees, who, as a result, may get a place to live from their employer. Later on, for a small fee, which is significantly lower than the actual cost of the house or apartment, the family can privatize its new property.

To be included on this waiting list a family should be qualified. Although the qualification standards vary from region to region (they may include, for example, the family's income), the family typically should prove that its members occupy less than 80 square feet per person. There were more than 6 million Russian families, which is more than 11 percent of all households, on the housing waiting list in 1999 (Interfax, 1999). Although thousands of families are receiving new housing every year, new families are also added to the list. In 2001, for example, more than 300,000 families of retiring or retired military officers were placed on the official federal government's waiting list (*Vremya*, 2001).

Compared to Western standards, and taking into consideration the size of Russia, most observers would find that Russian citizens, as a group, have modest accommodations and live in relatively crowded conditions. In the middle of the 1990s, some nine out of ten Russians had accommodations covering less than 25 square meters (roughly 15 × 15 feet) per person. Every fifth Russian family has people of three generations living under one roof. The proportion of young adults aged 20–24 who still live with their parents is close to two-thirds (Zimmerman, 2001). This is happening not because of collectivist cultural traditions or the goodwill of family members, but chiefly because of the housing shortage (Rimashevskaya & Vannoi, 1996).

The housing problem was one of the most difficult problems in the Soviet Union and Russia for many years. There is little financial assistance available to the average family that wants to purchase housing on the market. Loans and mortgages were uncommon in Russia at the beginning of the millennium. In view of these facts, it is no wonder that it is very difficult for many young people in Russia to lead a more independent life or to start their own family: the lack of accommodations is a major obstacle.

BIRTH- AND DEATH RATES

Today, women in Russia give birth to fewer children than they did ten or twenty years ago. Throughout the 1990s, Russia's birthrate continued dropping, falling from 13.4 per 1,000 people in 1990 to 8.6 per 1,000 in 1997 (Bohlen, 1999). In the early 2000s, a slight in-

crease in birthrate has been observed. In 1993, for every 100,000 births in Russia, 70 women died during pregnancy or childbirth, while for each 1,000 children under 1 year of age, 19 died. In both categories, the rates were roughly three times those in Western European countries. In 1998, the maternal mortality rate had fallen to 50 per 100,000 births and the infant mortality rate to 17 per 1,000 infants. Despite some improvements, both infant and maternal mortality rates are still much higher than those of Western Europe, the United States, Japan, or Australia.

In 1999, fewer than 1 million children were born and about 1.6 million people died (*Economica i Zhizn,* 1999, p. 50). In 2000, deaths exceeded births even more, and the population loss reached 700,000. In 2000, the State Statistics Committee reported an increase in the birthrate in 66 Russian regions. Just 14 regions posted a natural population growth. However, the death rate grew in 81 regions. Natural population decline, calculated as a difference between births and deaths, continues in a steady trend in the country. If this trend continues, the Russian population will drop by 2.8 million by 2005, by 10 million by 2016—to an 80-million level by 2050 (Karush, 2001).

The average size of the Russian family was 3.2 in 1989. It dropped to 2.6 in 1995 and kept declining thereafter. There were about 7 million infertile women in Russia by the end of the 1990s. Most of them could not afford the expensive medical treatment for their problem related to infertility. Contemporary fertilization procedures are simply unavailable in many Russian regions. At the same time, during the 1990s, people expressed less interest in having many children (Bohlen, 1999). For instance, according to one poll, the "ideal" number of children a person was willing to have had dropped from 2.0 in 1989 to 1.5 in 1995 (Glad & Shiraev, 1999). According to a November 2000 poll conducted by the National Center for Public Opinion Research (VTsIOM), more than one-half of the middle-class Russian respondents preferred to have no more than one child, and only 20 percent of respondents said they would like to have two or more children.

The life expectancy for women dropped from 74 in 1989 to 72 years in 1996. The average life expectancy in 1999 for Russian men has dropped to 60 years. Overall, Russia's average life expectancy ranked 125th among 188 nations (Francis, 2000). The number of deaths among the population in 2001 has risen to 15 per every 1,000 people, which is 10 percent higher than in 1998 (ITAR-TASS, 2001). Among European countries, Russia has the highest rate of injuries leading to death, seven times higher, for instance, than in the Netherlands (Zimmerman, 2001). Many families lose their children and adolescents prematurely. About half a million children and young people of this generation died between 1989 and 1999. In 1998, the danger of a young person dying was around three times greater in Russia than in Slovakia, the Czech Republic, or Hungary—the countries that defeated their communist governments at the same time as Russia did.

There are many causes contributing to the high death rates and the population decline. The economic hardship that most people in Russia endured after the fall of the Soviet Union caused a significant change in many people's lifestyle, habits, and diet. Although most food products are generally available year-round and store shelves around the country are stuffed with groceries, many items are simply unaffordable for the average family because of the cost of high-quality products.

Overall, health-related problems and treatment of illness were and will continue to be a central concern for most Russian families. Heavy drinking, drug abuse, as well as diseases such as tuberculosis and AIDS, have soared in the 1990s and early 2000s. Many kinds of effective medications are not available or too expensive for families of average income to purchase. Psychologists show evidence that persistent frustration based on an inability for people to provide normal living conditions for themselves and for their families often contributes to serious psychological and other health problems. Environmental pollution plagues virtually every Russian region. Social uncertainties contribute to continuous stress and burnout among

a very large proportion of Russian people (Shlapentokh & Shiraev, 2002).

STAGES OF FAMILY LIFE: CUSTOMS AND PRACTICES

The former totalitarian system guaranteed the Russian family a certain level of economic and social stability. Capitalism brought the Russians family freedom and vast new opportunities, but at the same time, a great deal of insecurity. Meanwhile, with many socioeconomic aspects of family life changing and declining after the late 1980s, many behavioral patterns and norms remain relatively unaffected by economic and political changes.

Courtship today remains an extremely important part of interpersonal relationships. Arranged marriages, with extremely rare exceptions, are not practiced in Russia. Having no legal rights to affect the actions of their adult children, parents, nevertheless, often give their advice about their son or daughter's marital choices. In some ethnic groups, especially Muslims, and those living in rural areas, parents can play a greater, even crucial, role in the process of matchmaking.

With the exception of rural regions, premarital sex is as commonly practiced in Russia as in most countries in Western and Eastern Europe. Most Russians pay relatively little attention to the important elements of courtship, such as engagement. While this is a very important stage of courtship for most Americans, it does not have a special symbolic significance to most Russians. Of course, the question "Will you marry me?" is asked, but typically, there is no engagement ring given to the future bride. The couple simply announces that they are getting married and the wedding follows relatively soon—within a few months—after the decision is made.

In the Soviet Union, the local government registered all marriages, and wedding ceremonies were often held in special municipal facilities. Religious wedding ceremonies were not officially prohibited by the Communist government, but were not practiced by the vast majority of people. These days, although the couple should register their marriage with the government, men and women have freedom of choice regarding how to conduct their wedding. In a national survey, 46 percent of those polled believed that a wedding ceremony should be held in church. However, another 40 percent of those polled said a church wedding is not important to them (ROMIR/ ITAR-TASS, 2000, February 9; the sample included 2,000 respondents from 41 regions). Overall, the "typical" wedding celebration in Russia may resemble one in Europe, North America, or Asia: relatives and guests eat, drink, dance, take pictures, and give presents—including cash—to the newlyweds. However, the contemporary U.S. practice of gift registration is foreign to most Russians.

The average age of first marriage has declined since the 1980s and is now relatively low: almost one-half of all Russians are married or have been married by the age of 24 (Guboglo, 1998). At age 17, the majority of boys and girls are already thinking about their future family. According to a survey, 79 percent of boys and 86 percent of girls are planning to be married before they are 31 years old (Guboglo, 1998).

Russians get divorced about as frequently as people in some other Western countries. Both governmental and independent sources suggest that there are approximately 60 divorces for every 100 marriages registered (VTUZ, 1999). UNICEF, in 2000, estimated 70 divorces per 100 marriages. Whereas the marriage rate dropped from 9.7 per 1,000 in 1985 to 6.7 in 1995, the divorce rate rose from 4.0 to 4.7 per 1,000 people (Zhuravlev, Kuchmaeva, Melnikov, & Orlova, 1996, p. 61). Consequently, the number of divorces grew faster than the number of registered marriages (*Economica i Zhizn,* 1999, no. 50). According to sociological studies (Golod, 1998), the overall attitude of Russian people toward marriage changed during the 1990s and after: most young people nowadays believe that marriage is not a once-in-a-lifetime event, but rather an important happening, which can be reexperienced again, if necessary.

According to the federal law known as the Russian Family Code, monogamy is the only lawful form of marriage in Russia. Some politicians, however, have attempted to amend the existing law. For example, the leader of the Ingush Republic in the south of Russia, with a predominantly Muslim population, issued a decree in 1999 allowing every male to take up to four wives. He asked the State Duma—the Lower House of the Russian Parliament—to make relevant amendments to the law. This bill was defeated, but it found a few supporters, who argued that people of certain ethnic groups have a right to follow their religious traditions. In addition, the country needs to do something about its poor demographic situation and allow men to marry several wives. Some argued that thousands of men in Russia's south were already practicing de facto polygamy (ITAR-TASS, July 23, 1999).

The vast majority of women in Russia gives birth in special maternity hospitals and wards. The procedure is free of charge, unless the mother chooses and can pay for a private hospital, which is beyond reach for most people. Unlike in the United States, Russian men are not allowed in the delivery room in state-run hospitals. Moreover, they are generally prohibited from entering maternity wards, so they cannot communicate with their wives directly until they and their babies are discharged from the facility. In private hospitals, however, the requirements are more liberal and include more options for the mother and her family.

The state subsidizes families with newly born children. Each woman, working or nonworking, receives a one-time payment of 15 national minimal daily wages for the birth of the child. The working mother is also given a monetary benefit during 70 days before and 70 days after giving birth. The size of the benefit should be equal to the size of the mother's wage. Women can choose not to work for 18 months after giving birth. The compensation they will receive is 2 minimal salaries a month, the size of which is standard and established by the government (Temicheva, 2000). According to a 1996 law, either parent can get a short-term leave of absence to take care of a sick child (Rimashevskaya & Vannoi, 1996).

One of the emerging trends in Russia is an increase of out-of-wedlock births, which by 1999 was at a 27 percent level, almost twice as much as in 1989 (VTUZ, 1999). Even though their fathers later adopt approximately 40 percent of those born out-of-wedlock, many children grow up apart from their biological parents, and even without having a family at all. As an illustration, about 10 percent of Russian newborns in one year were given up for adoption (Ballaeva, 1999, p. 7). Almost 500,000 children have living parents but are raised in state facilities: neither parents nor relatives are capable of taking care of these children (Babasyan, 1999). In the early 1990s, another devastating problem—child homelessness—began to expand in Russian cities. As a result of social cataclysms and natural calamities, acute economic problems, ethnic conflicts, substance abuse, lack of funding at the federal and local levels, and the neglect and indifference of too many adults, there are now hundreds of thousands of children and adolescents who live on the streets, without a permanent home (Pavlova, 2001).

On a more positive note, Russia still can boast a solid system of state-sponsored preschool, middle school, elementary, and high school education. Most preschool-age children in Russia, especially those who have both parents working, attend day nurseries and kindergartens. Unless the family qualifies for a waiver, parents normally pay a relatively small fee for sending their children to preschool. However, the number of preschool facilities dropped from more than 8,000 in 1980 to 5,000 by the late 1990s (Artyukhov, 1998, p. 29). According to the State Statistics Committee of the Russian Federation, the number of children in Russian preschools has also dropped sharply, from 9 million in 1990 to 5.1 million in 1996 (*Argumenty I Facty,* March 1997, p. 1). These changes occurred partly because of the lack of funding available for care providers and partly because of the declining number of children in Russia.

The Russian school system is presently undergoing reforms, so some facts related to education must be omitted. Free compulsory schooling begins at age 6 and lasts for at least seven or eight years. After the completion of middle school, approximately one-third of students continue their education in vocational schools, whereas others move to high schools. Public schools in Russia are managed by federal and local agencies. Their curricula are typically developed and approved in Moscow. Most local governments, although they can influence what is taught in public schools, tend to follow the required national curriculum. After 1992, the system of public schooling was deregulated. This sparked the development of a growing number of private schools and schools for academically advanced children. (Russians may call these private schools *gymnasia.* However, there is no special emphasis on fitness or physical training in these schools; the word was borrowed from the old prerevolutionary Russian vocabulary, when it typically referred to private schools.) Non-Russian schoolchildren in their regions are typically taught in two languages: Russian and their native language. Russian becomes a compulsory subject at the secondary level. Private schools may offer advanced curricula to their students and have better facilities than public schools; however, only a fraction of Russian families can afford tuition to these schools. Educational loans are uncommon. Admission to higher education is selective and highly competitive: most colleges and universities set four admission exams—both written and oral tests—to select the best candidates. Colleges and universities in Russia conduct their instruction almost entirely in Russian, although there are a few institutions, mainly in the minority republics, in which the local language is also used.

Every Russian family is entitled to receive free medical care. The government runs most health care facilities in the country, so doctors, nurses, and other medical personnel are on a government payroll. Medical treatment that most Russian people receive is limited by several circumstances. Among them is the unavailability of qualified specialists, medical equipment, and medication. In addition to standard mandatory medical coverage, some Russians can purchase supplementary plans in private clinics. One of the biggest problems for the public system is the deteriorating medical services, especially in small towns and in the countryside. In the mid-1990s, 50 percent of Russian medical facilities did not have hot water, 25 percent lacked a sewage system, and up to

20 percent had no tap water at all (Feshbach, 1995). Although the situation has been slowly improving since the early 2000s, the overall picture has not changed dramatically.

Because of the lack of available housing, especially in urban areas, poor economic conditions, and other social factors, people in most Russian families stay in much closer contact with each other and to a greater extent than most of their counterparts in many European countries and the United States. It is common for couples to rely every day on grandparents to take care of the young, such as meeting after school, walking, playing, and feeding; it is not uncommon for grandparents to live with or close to their children and grandchildren. Some specialists suggest that with the increase of work-related activities of most adults in contemporary Russia, compared to the Communist years, the role of grandparents in bringing up the young is increasing (Semionova, 1996).

Many families in the Soviet Union kept their religious traditions by passing knowledge from one generation to the next. Although the Soviet Constitution officially guaranteed freedom of religion, there were severe restrictions imposed on most religious practices and even beliefs. For example, it was prohibited to publish any favorable information about religion or clergy. Religious beliefs were exclusively a private matter, about which people preferred not to talk in order to avoid likely sanctions from authorities. Ten years after Russia became an independent state, about 60 percent of residents said in a national opinion poll that they believed in God, whereas 30 percent stated they did not. To compare, in the United States, in the same period, more than 90 percent of individuals say they believe in God (Shiraev & Sobel, 2004). Some 42 percent of the polled Russians said they would turn to God if they needed to solve family problems. Responding to a question on whether or not a baby born to Christian parents should be baptized soon after birth (an old Orthodox tradition), 67 percent of those polled answered in the affirmative and 22 percent disagreed. However, most people do not think that religion can be a source of societal improvements. Overall, only 18 percent think that religion can provide answers

for the problems that Russia faces (ROMIR/ITAR-TASS, 2000, February 9; the sample included 2,000 persons from 41 regions).

In general, the more religious the family is, the more traditional values its members follow. This tendency was revealed, for example, in several books and articles describing the life of contemporary Muslim families, mostly from the Northern Caucasus and Volga regions (Babich, 2001; Magomedov, 1996). In historically Muslim regions, many families today face many difficult choices related to their national identity, civil rights and responsibilities, and local customs. If a family adopts more traditional values and lifestyles, the distribution of gender roles becomes more traditional, with men responsible for finding resources and women responsible for the households and children. Traditional values also pose serious restrictions on premarital and extramarital sex. Muslim families have typically two to three times higher fertility rates compared to other families in Russia, and religious tradition is perhaps one of several factors contributing to the gap.

FAMILY PLANNING

How do people in Russia learn about family planning? Since the late 1970s, high school students in the former Soviet Union have been offered special "mandatory" classes designed to develop and advance the adolescents' knowledge about family, relationships, marriage, sex, and birth control. However, the lack of qualified specialists, the absence of educational materials, and sometimes the resistance of the school bureaucracy have generally prevented these courses from making a substantial contribution to the educational process.

From the late 1980s on, with the collapse of state-sponsored censorship, there has been practically no limit to the distribution of sex-related information. An avalanche of easily available yet unofficial pornography and pop-sex "educational" materials has inundated the market. Sex education has not only been abandoned by the school system, but several powerful conservative groups, including the Orthodox Church, want to make sure that any "family planning" courses are expelled from school curricula. These restrictions, however, did not add decency to society. As was true 20 or 30 years ago, young people obtain knowledge about sex, safe sex, and contraceptives primarily through peers and other easily available sources, often of questionable quality. In short, although Russia has achieved sexual liberation, it still lacks decent sex education.

Women in Russia have the right to abortion, which was reestablished in the USSR in 1955. National surveys show that the vast majority of Russians supports this right (Glad & Shiraev, 1999). There are no substantial legal obstacles to a woman's obtaining an abortion in contemporary Russia, and overall, it was and remains the leading means of birth control used by Russian women (Ballaeva, 1999; Fong, 1993). Abortions, available in Russia without restriction through the first 12 weeks, and for medical and social reasons up to 22 weeks, occur at a higher rate than anywhere in Europe except Romania. Overall, based on numerous sources, it is possible to suggest that in Russia, during the 1990s and the first years of the new millennium, from five to eight pregnancies out of every ten have been interrupted by an abortion. One of the main difficulties in such estimations is caused by the fact that hundreds of thousands of abortions were and are performed illegally. Nevertheless, it is generally agreed among specialists that the number of legal abortions continued to drop throughout the 1990s, from approximately 4.6 million in 1988 to 2.5 million in 1997. During the same period, it is believed that the number of illegal abortions also dropped 50 percent (Babasyan, 1999). The number of maternal deaths caused by abortion has also fallen dramatically, from 349 in 1989 to 154 in 1997 (Bohlen, 1999).

Such a decrease in abortion rates is caused by several factors, one of which is that many Russian women have finally begun to explore various means of birth control, although with a great delay compared to Western Europe. For years, relative availability of abortions, immature attitudes toward sex, lack of knowledge, and reliable contraceptives all contributed to most unwanted pregnancies. Still, some women hold a prejudice against contraceptives, especially hormonal birth-control pills. Another factor that makes the pills unavailable to many women is their cost. For instance, a 1-month supply of contraceptive pills may cost $5 or $10, which is the equivalent of the weekly wage of the average person. Even though these contraceptives were used by 2.5 million Russian women in 1999, this constitutes only about 6 percent of all the women of fertile age (Ballaeva, 1999; Bohlen, 1999).

In the 1990s, the Russian government began to sponsor special programs and local consulting centers on contraception and reproductive rights. The Russian Health Ministry began a family-planning program, opening more than 200 clinics around the country, retraining specialists, and providing ordinary people with advice on sex and pregnancy (Ballaeva, 1999). However, because of criticism from religious organizations and some lawmakers, the funding for these programs was later withdrawn.

GENDER ROLES

In the Soviet Union, the commitment of the communist rulers to the Marxist idea of equality between the genders resulted in the implementation of governmental policies directed against gender discrimination. Laws guaranteed equal political rights and opportunities with men to all women in Soviet Russia. Socialism provided for a high level of literacy for women, and many new occupations opened up for women in Soviet society. Soviet policies, however, only marginally changed the underlying distribution of social roles between men and women. In the family, men continued their role as traditional breadwinners and women remained housekeepers. Russian women were certainly considered the "second sex." Though new occupations were opened to women under the Soviet regime, the individuals at the top were still predominantly male (Shlapentokh, 2002; Smith, 1976).

Social transformations taking place in Russia from the late 1980s affected gender roles in the country. One of the biggest disappointments of the reform process was that political declarations about economic freedom and freedom of choice were not supported by corresponding economic and social measures. Russian men are overall in a better economic position than are women. As the Moscow Center for Gender Studies reported, Russian women at the beginning of the 1990s earned on average 75 percent of what men earned. By the mid-1990s, when free-market realities began to yield social results, the figure had fallen to 40 percent (Young, 1996). By this time, men owned more than 80 percent of Russian private business. Even though Russian women are on the average better educated than men, among the unemployed with college degrees, 67 percent were women, twice as many as men (Aivazova, 1999).

One of the distinctive gender-related features is the division of responsibilities in the Russian family. Courtship is often said to be a man's "struggle" to "conquer" his partner's affection. The verb *to marry* has two gender-based versions in the Russian language. The first is used to describe men's behavior, and the other one is saved for women's. In the former, the meaning is "active": Men marry women—they "take" them. The other version, reserved to describe women's behavior, is "passive": The woman is "being taken" by her man. It would be grammatically incorrect to use the stronger and active version of the verb while describing the woman's marriage.

Even when working outside the home, women take care of the routine problems and chores such as shopping, cooking, cleaning, and taking care of children. In the early 1990s, the average Russian woman worked 40 hours a week more than a man as a result of her duties at home and for the family, including shopping, childcare, and housework (Juliver, 1991). This traditional division of labor and responsibilities in the family seems to be acceptable to many individuals. According to surveys, most Russian women are ready to give men more power and responsibility in the family. However, most men were satisfied with the status quo and are not ready to accept more responsibilities at home (Arutyunian, 1997).

Moreover, in the late 1990s and early 2000s, as revealed by polls, there were signs of the emergence of a new "neoconservative" thinking among a growing number of Russian adults. According to this view, gender roles are distributed according to "natural" predispositions of men and women, so that work and career should be the male's preoccupation, whereas the female's role is to take care of the family and the children. Many women seem to be accepting inequality as a "natural" process, thus sheltering themselves inside the walls of traditionalism.

CONCLUSION

While summarizing information about Russian families' practices, it is important to mention the changing patterns of socialization. In the Russian mainstream media, it is frequently discussed that "old" collectivist values, relentlessly promoted during the Communist years at all levels of society, are increasingly being replaced by values and beliefs associated with free-market individualism. The major socialization task of previous decades, which aimed at the formation of the loyal member of society, has been transformed in many cases into the task of training family members for basic survival skills. Most family-based ad-hoc strategies of socialization promote today the learning of the most essential coping mechanisms in the still unpredictable social environment of modern Russia. In light of the difficulties many Russian families face today, including poverty, lawlessness, and the lack of essential services including medical care, many parents look for ways to promote stable cultural values and traditions. As a result, some families turn to more conservative traditions of rearing, which focus on discipline, accept physical punishment, and emphasize the child's obedience. On the other hand, there is hope that democratic changes and societal transitions will soon offer Russian families new and sustained educational and economic opportunities. Improved socioeconomic conditions together with the cultural elements of traditional Russian authoritarianism and collectivism are changing the edifice of the Russian family at the beginning of the twenty-first century.

REFERENCES

Aivazova, S. (1999). *Russkiye zhenshiny v labirinte ravno-pravia* [Russian women in the labyrinth of equality]. Moscow: Rusanova.

Artyukhov, A. V. (1998). Rossiyskaya semia v period reform [The Russian family in the period of reforms]. *Semia v Rossii, 3–4,* 21–33.

Arutyunian, M. (1997). *Gender relations in the family. Materials of the First Russian Summer School on Women's and Gender Studies* (pp. 131–136). Moscow: Moscow Center for Gender Studies.

Babasyan, N. (1999). Secular and Russian Orthodox organizations unite in a struggle against reproductive freedom for women. *Izvestia,* February 26, p. 5.

Babich, I. (2001). Islam v sovremennoi Kabardono-Balkarii: Pravoviye aspekti [Islam in modern Kabardino-Balkaria: Legal aspects]. *Etnograficheskoye Obozreniye, 3,* 131–144.

Ballaeva, E. (1999). Reproduktivniye prava rossiskikh zhenszhin [Reproductive rights of Russian women]. *Zakonodatelstvo i praktika, 8,* 3–11.

Bohlen, C. (1999). Russian women turning to abortion less often. *The New York Times,* March 29, p. A3.

CISS Index to International Public Opinion. (1995–1996). Greenwood Publishing Group. *Economica I Zhizn.* 1999, no. 50, p. 2.

Feshbach, M. (1995). An interview. *Blue and Gray* (Georgetown University), October 10.

Fong, M. (1993). *The role of women in rebuilding the Russian economy: Studies of economies in transformation.* Paper Number 10. Washington, DC: World Bank.

Francis, D. (2000). Russia's growing health crisis. *Christian Science Monitor,* January 5.

Glad, B., & Shiraev, E. (Eds.). (1999). *The Russian transformation.* New York: St. Martin's.

Golod, S. (1998). *Semia i brak: Istoriko-sotsiologicheskiy analiz* [Family and marriage: Historical and sociological analysis]. St. Petersburg: Petropolis.

Guboglo, M. N. (1998). Formirovaniye gendernoi identichnosti: Empiricheskiy opyt molodezhi Rossii. [Gender identity formation: An empirical study of Russian youth]. *Genderniye problemi v ethnografii* (pp. 14–46). Moscow: Russian Academy of Sciences.

Juliver, P. (1991). Human rights after perestroika. *Harriman Institute Forum, 4* (June), 1–10.

Interfax. (1999). Vladimir Putin's opening remarks during a Cabinet session, October 10.

ITAR-TASS (2001). *Deaths outstrip births in Russia.* (A report submitted to the Russian Health Ministry), August 7, 2001.

Karush, S. (2001). Russia looks to halt population drop. ITAR-TASS/Associated Press, February 15.

Lambroschini, S. (2000). Illegal immigrants see little hope of gaining official status. *RFE/RL,* January 24.

Magomedov, F. (1996). *Dagestan na poroge XXI veka* [Dagestan on the threshold of the 21st century]. Makhachkala: Academy of Sciences.

Moscow City Statistics Committee. *1999 annual report.* Moscow.

Ovcharova, L., & Prokofieva, L. (1999). Bednost i mezhsemeinaya solidarnost v Rossii v perekhodniy period [Poverty and cross-family solidarity in Russia during the transitional period]. *The Russian Public Opinion Monitor, 4,* 23–31.

Pavlova, N. (2001). Problemi domov rebionka [The problems of orphanages]. *Sotsialnoie Obespechenie, 1,* 32–35.

Rimashevskaya, N., & Vannoi, D. (1996). *Okno v russkuyu chastnuyu zhizn: Supruzheskiye pari v 1996* [The window on Russia's private life: Married couples in 1996]. Moscow: Academia ROMIR/ITAR-TASS (2000). Wireless News. Transmitted via Johnson's Russia List, Washington, DC, February 9.

ROMIR. (2000). January. *Recent survey results.* Disseminated via Johnson's Russia List. Washington, DC.

Russian Federations' State Committee for Statistics. *1999 annual report.* Moscow.

Semionova, V. (1996). *Babushki: Semeiniye i sotsialniye funksii praroditelskogo pokolenia.* [Grandmothers: Family and social functions of the grandparents' generation]. Moscow: Institute of Sociology of the Russian Academy of Sciences.

Shiraev, E. (1988). I semya v otvete [The family is responsible too]. In A. Sventsitsky (Ed.), *The authoritative power of discipline* (pp. 83–97). Leningrad: Lenizdat.

Shiraev, E., & Sobel, R. (2004). *People and their opinions: Introduction to public opinion.* New York: Longman.

Shlapentokh, V. (1984). *Love, marriage and friendship in the Soviet Union.* New York: Praeger.

Shlapentokh, V. (2002). *A normal totalitarian society.* New York: Sharpe.

Shlapentokh, V., & Shiraev, E. (Eds.). (2002). *Fears in post-communist societies.* New York: Palgrave.

Smith, H. (1976). *The Russians.* New York: Quadrangle/ The New York Times Book Co.

Sovet Federatsii. (1999) Analiticheskaya zapiska po problemam rosta nasilia vc semie [Analytical report on the growth of family violence]. *Vestnik Komiteta Federatsii po Voprosam Sotsialnoi Politiki, 2–3,* 10–15.

Temicheva, E. (2000). Zhenskiy trud: Prava i lgoty [Women's work: Rights and benefits]. *Zhenszhina, 2,* 16–18.

Tselms, G. (2000). War on women. *Noviye Izvestia,* November 14, p. 5.

Vlasova, E. (2001). Russian society becoming less stratified. *Nezavisimaya Gazeta,* No. 2, January.

Vremya. (2001). Daily information TV program, ORT, February 22, 9:10 P.M. Moscow time.

VTUZ (Vserossiskiy Tsentr Urovnia Zhizni) [All-Russian Center of Well-being]. (1999). *Analiticheskaya za-piska o sotsialno-economicheskom polozhenii nepol-nikh semei.* [Analytical report on the socioeconomic situation of the incomplete families]. Vol. 4. Moscow.

Young, K. (1996). Loyal wives, virtuous mothers: Women's Day and Russian women of the 90s. *Russian Life,* March.

Zhuravlev, G., Kuchmaeva, O., Melnikov, B., & Orlova, I. (1996). The socio-demographic situation. In C. Williams, V. Chuprov, & V. Staroverov (Eds.), *Russian society in transition* (pp. 57–74). Aldershot, England: Dartmouth.

Zimmerman, E. (2001). *UNICEF report highlights situation of children in Eastern Europe and the former Soviet Union: The terrible price of capitalist restoration.* Retrieved January 6, 2001 from World Socialist Web Site, www.wsws.org.

PART FIVE

THE AMERICAS

CHAPTER 17

MARRIAGES AND FAMILIES IN THE UNITED STATES

BRENT C. MILLER, SPENCER C. LEAVITT, JUNIUS K. MERRILL, AND KYUNG-EUN PARK
Utah State University

Diverse marriage and family patterns existed among Native Americans long before the first visit of Christopher Columbus to the Americas in 1492. However, Native American marriage and family practices were neither understood nor respected by white colonists, who soon displaced and sought to Christianize native peoples. A vast tide of emigration from Europe, which started in the early 1600s, swept over North America, propelled by powerful religious, political, and economic forces. White/ Anglo Americans quickly became the dominant majority group in North America, having asserted their independence from British and European monarchies. As Native American populations declined, African Americans soon became the largest minority group in North America. Between 1650 and the 1800s, historians estimate that over 28 million Africans were forcibly removed from Central and Western Africa and brought to America as slaves (Becker, 1999). Mexican Americans also established a presence early in the history of what is now the United States. In the early seventeenth century, frontier settlements of Mexicans were present throughout what was then northern Mexico. Descendants of these early Mexican residents in the present-day southwestern United States are now vastly outnumbered by more recent Latino immigrants from Mexico and many Central and South American countries (Cherlin, 1996). After the U.S. Immigration Act in 1965, the number of Asian families in the United States increased rapidly (Cherlin, 1996). The melting-pot metaphor, which remains somewhat descriptive in the United States today, is tremendously important for understanding the variety and complexity of American marriages and families.

DEMOGRAPHIC RATES AND TRENDS

Population Characteristics of the United States

In the year 2000, there were approximately 275 million people living in the United States. As shown in Figure 17.1, since 1970 the portion of the population under age 17 has decreased substantially, while the proportions of working-age and older adults has increased (AmeriStat, 2000a).

The population pyramid of the United States resembles a squat bowling pin, with a slight bulge in the middle (see Figure 17.2), composed of the baby-boom cohort (persons born between 1946 and 1964). As the generation of the baby boomers gets older, the bulge in the population pyramid will move upward. Its relatively narrow base is made up of the baby-bust cohorts born since the late 1960s (AmeriStat, 2000d).

The majority of the U.S. population (about 72 percent) is white, but the population is racially and ethnically diverse and rapidly becoming more so. African Americans were until recently the largest minority (12.1 percent) in the United States, but Hispanics, or Latinos, have been the fastest-growing racial/ethnic group since 1980 (see Figure 17.3). About 11.5 percent of persons classify themselves as Hispanic; 3.8 percent are Asian or Pacific Islander; and less than 1 percent are American Indian or Alaska Native. According to projections, Hispanics will account for 18 percent of the U.S. population by 2025, when 13 percent of the population will be

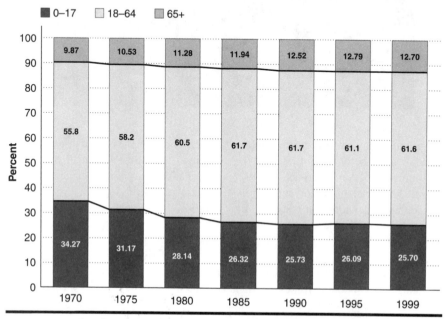

FIGURE 17.1   Population Distribution of the United States by Age, 1970–1999
Source: AmeriStat, 2000a.

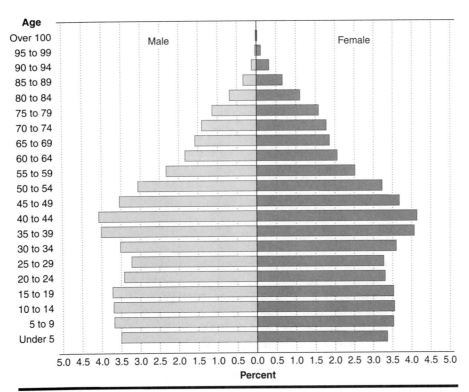

FIGURE 17.2 Population Pyramid of the United States as of July 1, 2000

Source: National Projections Program, Population Division, U.S. Census Bureau, Washington, DC (www.census.gov/population/www/projections/np_p2.pdf)

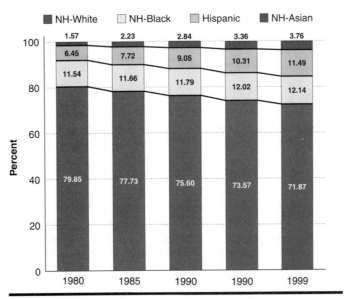

FIGURE 17.3 Population Distribution of the United States by Race/Ethnicity

Source: AmeriStat, 2000f.

African American. Over the same period, the percentage of whites will decline by 10 percentage points, to 62 percent (Ameristat, 2000b).

Couple Relationships

Historically, young adults in the United States began couple relationships through engagement and marriage, but cohabitation increased dramatically after 1970 (Cherlin, 1996). Between 1970 and 1994, the number of unmarried couples living together increased sevenfold, from about 500,000 to almost 3.7 million. For many, cohabitation is a prelude to marriage. Whereas just 11 percent of marriages between 1965 and 1974 were preceded by cohabitation, by 1994, 44 percent of all marriages involved at least one spouse who had cohabited. It is estimated that half of all couples who married after 1985 began their relationship as cohabitors (Rodriguez, 1998). In the 1990s many families with children that are officially defined as "single parent" actually contain two unmarried partners (Rodriquez, 1998).

Declining marriage rates and increasing divorce rates have characterized formal relationships among U.S. couples in recent decades (Teachman, Tedrow, & Crowder, 2000). In 1920 there were seven times as many marriages as divorces; in 1998 there were just twice as many marriages as divorces (Riche, 2000; see Figure 17.4). Over the past 30 years, the percentage of persons who never have been married has increased from about 22 to 28 percent. The largest increases in the never-married population have occurred among African Americans. Between 1975 and 1999, the percentage of African Americans who never have been married increased from 32 to 44 percent, and the percentage of African Americans who were married declined from more than 42 percent in 1975 to 32 percent in 1999 (Ameristat, 2000c)

Divorce rates increased for many decades (see Figure 17.4), but the increase during the 1960s and 1970s was by far the most dramatic. Divorce rates per 1,000 population increased from 2.0 in 1940 to 5.3 in 1980, but declined to 4.2 in 1998. In 1972,

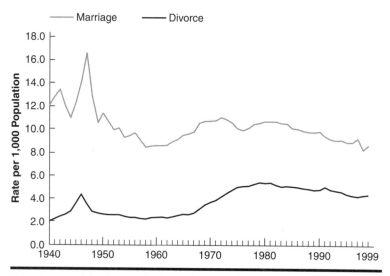

FIGURE 17.4   Marriage and Divorce Rates in the United States, 1940–1999

Sources: Clarke, 1995; Singh et al., 1995; Births, marriages, divorces, and deaths for 1997; *Monthly Vital Statistics Report, 46,* No. 12 (1998); Births, marriages, divorces, and deaths for November 1999, *National Vital Statistics Reports, 48,* No. 17 (2000).

nearly 15 percent of American adults age 18 and older had been divorced, regardless of whether they had remarried (Riche, 2000). Since the 1970s, the annual divorce rate has averaged just more than 20 per 1,000 married women, more than twice the rate of the 1950s and early 1960s. The incidence of divorce in the United States is still high by historical (and international) standards. Because of the cumulative increase in divorce experience, in 1996 there were 167 divorced adults for every 1,000 married adults, compared with only 100 per 1,000 in 1980 (Bianchi & Spain, 1996). However, the long-term upward trend in U.S. divorce rates has leveled off, and the 1980s and 1990s saw a slow but steady decline in the divorce rate.

Birth, Fertility, and Infant Mortality

The crude birthrate fell steadily during the 1920s and 1930s, bottoming out during the Great Depression. It began to rise again during the 1940s war years, and then reached a high point of over 25 births per 1,000 population during the postwar baby boom. Since then the crude birth rate has fallen to its current

(1999) level of 14.5 births per 1,000 population (Ameristat, 2000e). (See Figure 17.5.)

In 1999, the total fertility rate was 2.1, which means that contemporary American women bear an average of just more than two children during their lifetimes. After reaching 3.6 children per woman toward the end of the baby boom (1956 to 1961), the total fertility rate fell during the 1960s and 1970s, dipping to 1.7 in 1976. Since then, the total fertility rate has remained fairly stable and its fluctuations have been moderate, ranging between 1.8 and 2.0 for most of the past 20 years.

One of the most dramatic family-related trends in recent decades is the increase in nonmarital childbearing (see Figure 17.6). In the 1950s, childbirth outside of marriage was more stigmatized (it was called illegitimacy), and it was rare (less than 5 percent), but in 1999 about one-third of all births in the United States were to unmarried women.

Infant mortality has declined sharply in recent decades around the world and in the United States. In 1950 infant mortality in the United States was about 29 deaths per 1,000 births, although infant mortality of African Americans (43 per 1,000), was

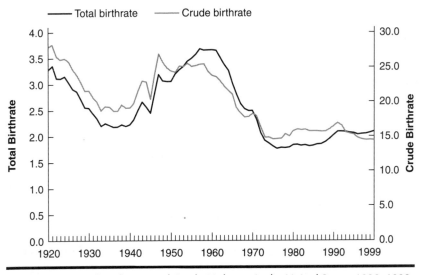

FIGURE 17.5   Total Birthrates and Crude Birthrates in the United States, 1920–1999
Source: Mathew, Salle, Curtin, & MacCorman, 2000.

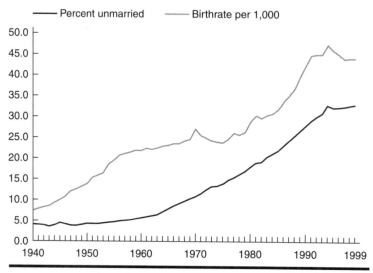

FIGURE 17.6   Birthrate for Unmarried Women in the United States, 1940–1999

Source: Ventura & Bachrach, 2000.

much higher than that of white infants (26 per 1,000). (See Figure 17.7.) Infant mortality rates have fallen considerably, but the mortality of African American infants still is much higher than that for white infants.

CULTURAL AND RELIGIOUS INFLUENCES

Cultural Dimensions of Marriage and Family Life

Marriage in the United States is inextricably tied to the national culture. While traditional marriage has and continues to go through transformation, there remains an underlying connection to the nuclear family form. The majority of Americans continues to define their family according to its conformity to or departure from a heterosexual couple and their biological children. Terms such as "step-families," "same-sex couples," and "single-parent families" define family forms according to their relationship to a biological, nuclear family. This central cultural form transcends racial barriers. Father, mother, and children are still the cultural family "norm" in the United States.

The United States has not lost its identity as a melting pot. This society represents a collection of ethnic groups from a myriad of backgrounds. Despite this celebrated ethnic diversity, family culture in the United States seems to be on what Aponte, Beal, and Jiles (1999, p. 111) call "the elusive trend toward convergence." While many studies have identified differences between ethnic groups, to a large degree these can be explained by differences in socioeconomic status or class as well as by differing cultures. The differences between these groups are not nearly as pronounced as the variation that is found within groups in any particular area (Aponte et al., 1999). Radical family change in the United States over the past several decades can be seen as a trend toward unification of family forms across various cultural or ethnic groups. This trend is not toward one particular family form, but toward greater similarity in the diverse forms found from one cultural group to another. Aponte et al. (1999) found this trend toward convergence to be true in varying degrees among every minority group except the Amish, whose divergence from the norm is maintained through a deliberate and concerted effort. In

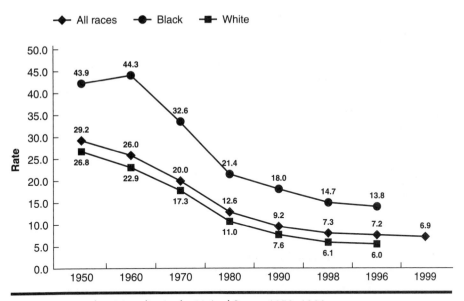

FIGURE 17.7   Infant Mortality in the United States, 1950–1999

Sources: Mathew, Salle, Curtin, & MacDorman, 2000; Births, marriages, divorces, and deaths for June 1999, *Monthly Vital Statistics Report, 48,* No. 8 (2000).

other words, the United States truly is a melting pot, especially where family is concerned.

Religious Affiliation, Beliefs, and Practices

About nine out of ten people in the United States acknowledge having a religious affiliation. Trends indicate that the total population of people reporting religious affiliation has not changed more than 4 percent in the past two decades. From 1980 to 1998, the total population reporting Protestant, Catholic, Jewish, or other religious affiliation fluctuated from 89 percent to 93 percent. Between 7 and 11 percent reported no religious preference over the same time period (U.S. Bureau of the Census, 1999).

Compared to other industrialized countries, religious affiliation and participation are relatively high in the United States (Sherkat & Ellison, 1999). According to a 1993 survey, 90 percent of Americans believe in God or a higher power, 80 percent pray regularly, and 70 percent identify with a religious group (Strupp, 1999). Other surveys of Americans and their religious beliefs report that 81 percent believe they will live in heaven with God after they die, 88 percent believe they will meet friends and family members there, 87 percent of Americans believe God answers prayers, and 82 percent believe God doesn't have favorites in answering prayers. However, only 25 percent of Americans report praying at least once a day ("Polls show Americans are still deeply spiritual," 1997).

Connection between Religion and Family Patterns

Marriage and family patterns in the United States are based on a heritage of Judeo-Christian beliefs. For example, Biblical teachings against divorce were apparent in restrictive state laws until the no-fault divorce revolution of the 1970s and 1980s. Other traditional American beliefs with a biblical basis are that sexual relationships should be confined to marriage, and that children need parental discipline: "Train up a child in the way he should go: and when he is old, he will not depart from it" (Proverbs 22:6, King James Version).

The Judeo-Christian religious cultural context of the United States affects various aspects of marriage, everyday family life, and child socialization. In marriage, religious beliefs influence sex roles, marriage quality and satisfaction, and likelihood of divorce. Members of more conservative religious groups tend to prescribe more traditional sex roles for their adherents; women are more likely to remain in the home and rear children, while men work to provide for their families (Ammerman & Roof, 1995; Heaton & Goodman, 1985; Hertel & Hughes, 1987). A review of studies through 1989 found that religiosity is related to higher levels of marital satisfaction (Bahr & Chadwick, 1988). In addition, couples who report higher levels of religious beliefs and behavior are less likely to divorce (Colasanto & Shriver, 1989; Glenn & Supancic, 1984), especially when spouses share the same religion (Lehrer & Chiswick, 1993; Wineberg, 1994). Interfaith marriages have a higher divorce rate than same-faith marriages (Bumpass & Sweet, 1972; Chan & Heaton, 1989).

Religion also has pervasive effects on family-related issues such as sexuality, cohabitation, fertility, and childrearing practices. Teens with a religious affiliation are less likely to engage in premarital sex (Heaton, 1988; Wilcox, Roltosky, Randall, & Wright, 2000), and religiosity is inversely related to extramarital sex. Young adults who reported frequent church attendance and strong religious beliefs are less likely to cohabit before marriage (Thornton, Axinn, & Hill, 1992).

Historically, members of Catholic and conservative Protestant religious groups tended to have larger families (Ammerman & Roof, 1995; Goodson, 1996; Heaton, 1988) than Jews and those reporting no religion (Dashefsky & Levine, 1983). This was partially due to these religious groups' teachings against the use of artificial methods of birth control. In more recent studies, however, the family size of Catholics is close to the national average (Althaus, 1992; Bahr & Chadwick, 1988). Members of a rapidly growing U.S. religion, Mormons (the Church of Jesus Christ of Latter-Day Saints), remain distinctive in their high rates of marriage and childbearing (Heaton, 1988, 2000; Spicer & Gustavus, 1974; Thornton, 1988). A more extreme example of religious effects on childbearing is evident among the Hutterites; in that group there is virtually universal marriage, no attempt to limit fertility, and an average of 10–11 children are born per family.

MARRIAGE AND COUPLE RELATIONSHIPS

U.S. Marriage Patterns

A higher proportion (over 90 percent) of people in the United States marry than in any other industrialized nation (Defrain & Olson, 1999). Even among those who divorce, a large majority (about 70 percent) will marry again (Faust & McKibben, 1999), over 60 percent within two years of their divorce (Ahrons & Rodgers, 1987). Despite the popularity of marriage in the United States, divorce rates remain at near historically high levels. Marriage in the United States appears to have taken on a new meaning over the past several decades, shifting away from marriage as a social obligation or family duty, toward the view of marriage as a source of personal fulfillment (Thornton et al., 1992). Despite continuous changes in the meaning of marriage in the United States, it remains extremely important to individuals and to society (Waite & Gallagher, 2000).

Americans are delaying first marriage to a later age than any time in history, and are marrying partners closer to their own age. Figure 17.8 shows the average age of first marriage for men and women, and average differences in age at first marriage. While contemporary men are first marrying at more than 26 years of age (nearly the same as 100 years ago), women today are marrying at considerably older ages (age 25 now, versus age 20 in the 1950s). Thus, the average first-marriage age difference between husbands and wives today is less than two years, compared to four years or more at the turn of the twentieth century (U.S. Bureau of the Census, 1999).

Americans are also leaving marriage more quickly and more often than at any time in the past.

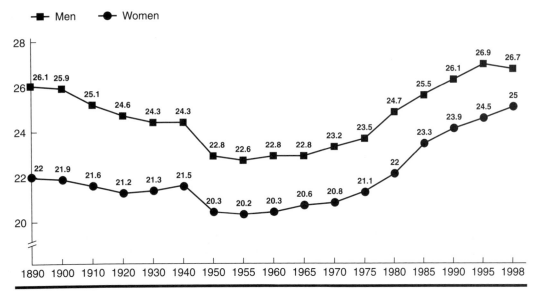

FIGURE 17.8   Age at First Marriage in the United States, 1890–1998
Source: U.S. Bureau of the Census, 1998.

The restructuring of divorce laws in the 1970s, away from adversarial to no-fault systems, has both reflected and created new norms about divorce (Coontz, 1997). Historically a stigmatized rarity, divorce is now a common part of life that most of the population experience in their immediate or extended family.

In the United States, marriage traditionally has been expected to be a relatively permanent heterosexual union of a man and a woman. Culturally, however, the definition of marriage is undergoing considerable debate in the United States. Movements to recognize same-sex unions on equal footing with heterosexual marriage recently have gained momentum. While initiatives and legal battles for recognition of same-sex unions failed in Hawaii and California just before the turn of the century, the movement gained a victory of sorts in Vermont, where the legislature granted "civil unions" benefits equal to marriage in most arenas.

Despite continuing high marriage rates, a smaller proportion of Americans are marrying today than in the recent past. One possible explanation for this slight downward trend in marriage is the increased acceptance and practice of cohabitation. Because much of the social stigma against nonmarital sexual relationships is gone from U.S. society, about half of American couples now choose to live together prior to marriage. There is evidence to suggest that Americans are still forming sexual unions at nearly the same rate as before, and most of the delay in marriage is offset by the dramatic increase in cohabitation (Bumpass & Sweet, 1989). Cohabitation has, however, proven to be much less enduring than marriage (DeMaris & Rao, 1992; Hall & Zhao, 1995; Lillard, Brien, & Waite, 1995; Schoen, 1992; Teachman & Polonko, 1990).

New Marriage: Shifts in Roles and Relationships

Marital roles are another aspect of traditional marriage in the United States that has undergone dramatic recent changes. Marriages consisting of a breadwinner husband and a homemaker wife have become the exception, representing only 33 percent of families (Defrain & Olson, 1999). The new ideal of egalitarian marriage, where work inside and outside the home is shared between spouses, is still not fully realized. More married women than ever are employed outside the home, but most still have a "second shift" of housework (Hochschild, 1989). Men have not increased their share of the domestic workload at home, although some studies have found that women and men are putting in almost equal time when hours at home and hours at work are combined (Kluwer, Heesink, & Van De Vliert, 1996; Rossi, 1996). Rossi (1996) found that, including things like commuting time, men and women worked an almost identical number of hours per week (128 for women and 127 for men). Wilkie and Ferree (1998) found that husbands averaged 73 hours of labor per week (49 paid and 24 domestic), while wives averaged 78 (39 of each), with most wives still doing most of the housework. Women also tend to be responsible for the largest proportion of childcare responsibilities, despite recent increases in father involvement.

Marital Satisfaction and Happiness

Conflict in marriage increased, and satisfaction declined, over the same period of time that divorce was on the rise (Gottman & Krokoff, 1989; Bush, 1996; Rogers & Amato, 1997; Tschann, 1999). From 1973 to 1988 the percentage of spouses reporting that their marriages were very happy declined steadily (Rogers & Amato, 1997). This decline might be caused by several factors, including growing individualism, increased premarital cohabitation, conflict over changes in gender roles, increase in the employment demands of working mothers, the drop in men's real wages, and easy access to divorce. Each of the factors mentioned above was found to account for part of the decline in marital quality (Rogers & Amato, 1997). In their comparison of two marriage cohorts, the younger cohort had lower interaction, higher conflict, and increased marital problems (Rogers & Amato, 1997). The cohorts involved in that study were only 12 years apart

in age and were measured at the same age, yet the difference in marital quality was significant. The findings of Rogers and Amato are consistent with other recent studies showing a general decline in marriage satisfaction and a corresponding increase in marital conflict (Booth & Johnson, 1988; Glenn, 1991; Amato & Booth, 1995).

Marital Stability after the Divorce Revolution

Although marriage is still very popular in the United States, the stability of marriage unions is much lower than it has been historically. Americans remain committed to the concept of marriage in general, but are less committed to staying with a particular spouse. The reasons for these changes are difficult to explain. Some believe that a shift away from community values and toward increased individualism is to blame (Baumeister, 1992). According to Faust and McKibben (1999), the improved economy, changing cultural attitudes, increased life expectancy, improved health status, and a changed legal climate are all part of what Weitzman (1985) called the "Divorce Revolution."

In the current economy, women are more likely to attend college and to be employed outside the home, for higher wages, than ever before. Because of their relatively greater economic independence, women may be more likely to leave unsatisfying marriages (Bachu, 1993; Waldrup, 1994).

Attitudes toward divorce have changed to the degree that the stigma against divorce is greatly reduced. While some blame the increase in divorce on these changing attitudes, Cherlin (1981) noted that the beginning of the divorce revolution predated this attitudinal shift. Americans also are living longer and in better health than at any time in history. Weeks (1994) pointed out that those 85 and older are increasing faster than any other age group. Couples have much more time together before a marriage ends with the death of one partner.

A social legal change that is often blamed for the increase in divorce is the no-fault movement (Weitzman, 1985). No-fault divorce allows one spouse to seek a divorce without the consent of the

other, and without showing fault. While no-fault divorce certainly opened the floodgates in the divorce
courts, it is not entirely clear that it was a *cause* of
the divorce revolution. Guttman (1993) suggested
that the no-fault movement was simply a symptom
of larger societal changes that included the wom-
en's movement, the sexual revolution, and growing
individualism.

Risk factors for divorce are better established
than the causes of increasing divorce rates over time.
In a recent review of divorce literature, Faust and
McKibben (1999) found that younger age at marriage, especially teen marriages (Kurdeck, 1993;
Martin & Bumpass, 1989), premarital pregnancy or
birth (Martin & Bumpass, 1989; Morgan & Rindfuss,
1985; Norton & Miller, 1992; Waite & Lillard, 1991),
being African American (Sweet & Bumpass, 1987),
having few or no children (Heaton & Pratt, 1990), cohabiting before marriage (Lillard et al., 1995), having divorced parents (Amato, 1993), having been
divorced, and having a lower socioeconomic status
(Martin & Bumpass, 1989) increase the likelihood of
divorce among U.S. couples.

PARENTING AND CHILDCARE

Throughout history, different views about children
and conceptions of childhood have affected parent–
child relationships. Inherent in conceptions of children is the degree to which nature (biological effects)
and nurture (environmental effects) are thought to influence child development and behavior.

Historical Perspective

The view that children are "born evil" developed
primarily from a theological view of children as
being bad from birth because of their evil nature.
Based on the biblical story of Adam and Eve and
their original sin, John Calvin believed that the nature of man is depraved. Feeling guilty for his "depraved" nature, man's purpose in life was to learn
to overcome "evil" desires. John Wesley felt that
children must be conquered, and that indulging

children was bad. He reasoned that denying children was good because the child's will had to be
overcome. This view extended to the Puritans, who
felt that because children were inclined to evil, parents should vigilantly watch for and punish misbehavior. Freud also believed that humans have a base
nature (the id), and that life is a constant conflict
dominated by impulses of and strivings for hunger,
sex, and aggression. As a result of these views,
many, perhaps most, American parents punished
their children in order to subdue and conquer their
evil and disobedient natures, and so that the children would be better socialized. Complete submission to the parents' (and God's) will was the
optimal child outcome.

A contrasting Anglo-Saxon perspective posits
that children are blank slates who need to be
molded by "nurture," particularly by kindness and
punishment. According to this view, children are
born completely void of inherent characteristics
and therefore must be "molded" by their environment (especially parents) into responsible humans.
For instance, John Locke believed that a child's
mind is like wax, and that nine of ten things children learn come by education (Synnott, 1983). On
the other hand, Watson dismissed motivations or inclinations, teaching instead that parents shouldn't
love their children too much (Watson, 1928). According to Watson's view, parents are completely
responsible to "mold," or "nurture" their children
into caring human beings.

Contemporary American beliefs are that children are basically good from birth, but that they
come with genetic inclinations and predispositions.
For example, Maslow (1954, pp. 118, 122) believed
that children are without hatred or malice for the
first two years of life. Scarr (1992) argued that parents don't have to be "super" parents, just "good
enough" parents, because children will "become
themselves." According to this view, parents should
guide their children to help them develop what they
are genetically inclined to do. In addition, children
need a positive environment in which to develop
positive characteristics and learn to control potentially negative characteristics. In other words, inborn

characteristics developed in a positive environment will produce "optimal" child outcomes.

Parent Effects Perspective

According to Peterson and Hann (1999), the parent effects perspective is "the extent to which parental styles, behaviors, and characteristics contribute to various social and psychological qualities in children" (Maccoby & Martin, 1983; Peterson & Rollins, 1987; Rollins and Thomas, 1979). This perspective presupposes a one-way flow of influence and information from parent to child. Based on the parent effects assumption, that a change in parent behavior should produce a change in children's behavior, "parent training" teaches parents to better socialize their children to become socially competent (Peterson & Hann, 1999).

Within the parent effects perspective, much work has been done to identify parenting styles and connect them with children's behavior patterns. Baumrind (1971, 1989, 1991) identified three types of parenting styles: authoritarian, authoritative, and permissive (Baumrind, 1989, 1991), which are characterized by varying levels of control (firmness, reasonable demands, and monitoring) and support (warmth, acceptance, responsiveness, and nurturing).

Authoritarian parents provide low support, but high levels of control without verbal give and take, emphasizing obedience to parents. Generally, authoritarian parents are more detached or controlling and less warm; children of such parents are influenced to become more discontented, withdrawn, and distrustful (Baumrind, 1989, 1991).

Authoritative parents use high levels of support and control. Authoritative parents generally have high expectations and direct children's activities, but are also warm, rational, and receptive to children's communication (Baumrind, 1989, 1991). In the preschool years, children with authoritative parents are likely to be self-reliant, self-controlled, explorative, and content. During middle childhood, they are socially assertive and socially responsible. High parental support, and moderate to high parental control (monitoring), decreases the likelihood of at-risk behavior

in adolescents (Barber, 1997; Baumrind, 1991; Miller, 1998; Dumka, Roosa, Michaels, & Suh, 1995).

Permissive parents provide low control and relatively high support and have been characterized as either neglectful or indulgent (Maccoby & Martin, 1983). These parents make few demands and attempt to act as resources for their children, not as parents responsible for socializing their children, but rather allowing children to socialize themselves. Their children are generally the least self-reliant, explorative, and self-controlled.

Changes in culture, work demands, and social pursuits influence parent's choices about how much they interact with their children. Parents interested solely in their own pursuits, careers, and activities tend to be more neglectful of children's needs, less responsive, and less likely to monitor their children's behavior. On the other hand, child-focused parents "seek to make their children happy and foster their development" by playing, spending time with, and teaching their children (Peterson & Hann, 1999).

Child Effects

In contrast to the predominant parent effects perspective just presented, some researchers have proposed a child effects perspective that "examines how children influence the attitudes, values, behaviors, experiences, and circumstances of parents" (Bell & Harper, 1977; Maccoby & Martin, 1983; Miller, 1993; Peterson & Hann, 1999; Peterson & Rollins, 1987). For example, it is well documented that children's severe disabilities have a dramatic effect on parents' lifestyles, especially affecting marriage and increasing the risk of divorce (Ambert, 1992). It also has been demonstrated experimentally that children with difficult, oppositional temperaments provoke more negative reactions from care-giving adults (Lytton, 1990). There is substantial evidence that children's characteristics and behavior can influence their parents (Ambert, 1992, 1997; Lytton, 1990).

Reciprocal Socialization

A reciprocal conceptual perspective emphasizes that children and parents influence each other. However, this does not imply that the strength of influence is equal (Maccoby, 1992), or that parents or children influence each other in similar ways. Current trends in research on parent–child relationships in the United States suggest that greater attention needs to be given to parents' sensitivity to their child's changing needs. Optimally, parent behavior would be sensitive to how each child feels at a given time (Goddard, 1999). Rothbaum and Weisz (1994, p. 69) suggested that "the quality of the parents' responsiveness to children's needs, more than specific behaviors or characteristics of parents, fosters children's responsiveness to the expectations and desires of their parents." For example, a tired child has different needs than a belligerent one. Consequently, sensitive parents would adjust their parenting behavior to best fit the changing needs of their children. Gottman's (1997) studies of parent–child interaction also suggest that effective parents become "emotion coaches" to their children.

Childcare Roles

Traditionally, childcare has been home-based in the United States, with the mother taking primary responsibility. However, childcare arrangements have undergone great changes in recent decades (Hofferth, 1998). With most mothers in the United States now employed, and an increase in the number of single-parent families, a growing majority of young children receive some type of nonparental childcare (Moen & Forest, 1999). With so much of the responsibility for the socialization of children provided by childcare workers, some are concerned about the quality of substitute care. Evidence suggests that young children receiving high-quality daycare do not suffer adverse effects, although some have pointed out that much childcare is of lower quality and that negative effects are most likely for infants (Belsky, 1990). Most of the childcare within the home is still performed by mothers (about two-thirds), although fathers show increasing involvement (Bianchi, 2000; Walker, 1999).

About 90 percent of single-parent households are headed by mothers, and most single-parent households are the result of divorce or separation, with a growing number resulting from nonmarital childbearing (U.S. Bureau of the Census, 1998). In either case, about 85 percent of children residing in single-parent homes reside with their mothers, with most of these arrangements resulting from divorce (Lin, 2000). Among children living with mothers, about 40 percent are mothers who never married (U.S. Bureau of the Census, 1998). About 45 percent of children living with single parents also live with a nonrelative adult, so in many cases childcare in the home is shared with nonparents (U.S. Bureau of the Census, 1998).

Single-parent families are of particular interest in the United States for several reasons. Households headed by single women have lower income, on average, and are much more likely to live in poverty, than two-parent families. Thus, single-parent families are disproportionately of concern in the need to provide public policy support for disadvantaged populations. Another reason for policy attention to single parents has to do with concern for the well-being of children. For some time it was debated whether or not having single parents adversely affected children, but during the 1990s the evidence became clear and convincing that children born to single parents, as well as children whose parents divorce, are at greater risk on many social, psychological, and health indicators (Acock & Demo, 1994; Amato, 1993; Rodgers & Pryor, 1998).

No-fault divorce laws appear to be associated with a decrease in the financial involvement of fathers. Even when the courts order child support, less than half of fathers pay the full amount. This lack of support is associated with results in decreased academic achievement and increased behavioral problems for children (Amato & Gilbreth, 1999). In two-parent families, fathers are much more likely to be involved in the care of older children and of sons than with younger children or daughters. The involvement of noncustodial fathers has been on the rise over the past decade (Pleck, 1997). In the early 1980s about 50 percent of noncustodial fathers had seen their children at least once in the past year, but less than 20 percent saw them weekly. By the end of that decade about 25 percent saw their children weekly and less than 20 percent had not seen them in the past year. While many absent fathers still lag behind in child support payments, the number paying is also on the increase (Coontz, 1992).

SUMMARY AND CONCLUSIONS

Marriage and family patterns in the United States can be characterized as diverse, complex, and changing. To some extent this has always been so. From earliest history it is clear that Native American marriage and family customs differed by tribe and clan. Anglo or Euro American immigrants brought with them variations in marriage and family life from dozens of different homelands, principally from the British Isles and Western Europe, but also from Scandinavia, the Mediterranean, and other regions. African Americans deserve specific mention because their immigration was involuntary, persistent prejudice and discrimination affect their marriage and family experiences, and they became the largest and most visible minority group. In the latter half of the twentieth century the United States experienced particularly large influxes of populations from Asian and Latin American countries. Partly because of the diverse cultural and religious backgrounds of the population, marriage and family patterns in the United States remain very heterogeneous.

Rapid social change is another reason for the great diversity of marriage and family patterns in the contemporary United States. The post–World War II era, especially the 1950s, has come to be regarded as a time of unusual conformity and belief in the "traditional" American family. Many of the funda-

mental elements in marriage and family values and relationships were changing before that period, but beginning in the 1960s the pace of change in marriage and family patterns accelerated. Less traditional gender roles, increasing rates of cohabitation and declining rates of marriage, declining fertility, and increasing divorce and single parenthood are some of the marriage and family trends that have been highlighted. The extent and speed of social change in recent decades contribute to diversity, because it has become very difficult for young people to imitate the marriage and family patterns of their parents and grandparents.

While there are large cultural, religious, and race-ethnic differences, the population of the United States is unusually marriage-oriented when compared to many European populations. About 90 percent of Americans still marry, but contemporary marriages differ from those of earlier generations. Young people marrying for the first time tend to be older, more likely to have cohabited, to have nontraditional gender roles, and plan to have fewer children, when compared with previous generations. Because of postponing marriage, never marrying, and continuing high divorce rates, contemporary young Americans will spend less of their lives in marriage and parenthood than ever before. Still, by comparison with more traditional cultures and countries, Americans remain relatively marriage-oriented. In traditional cultures extended family blood relationships predominate, whereas in the United States the conjugal relationships between marital partners are emphasized.

REFERENCES

Acock, A. C., & Demo, D. H. (1994). *Family diversity and well-being.* Thousand Oaks, CA: Sage.

Ahrons, C. R., & Rodgers, R. C. (1987). *Divorced families.* New York: Norton.

Althaus, F. (1992). Differences in fertility of Catholics and Protestants are related to timing and prevalence of marriage. *Family Planning Perspectives, 24,* 234–235.

Amato, P. R. (1993). Children's adjustment to divorce: Theories, hypotheses, and empirical support. *Journal of Marriage and the Family, 55,* 23–38.

Amato, P. R., & Booth, A. (1995). Changes in gender role attitudes and perceived marital quality. *American Sociological Review, 60,* 58–66.

Amato, P. A., & Gilbreth, J. G. (1999). Non-resident fathers and children's well-being: A meta-analysis. *Journal of Marriage and the Family, 61,* 557–573.

Ambert, A. M. (1992). *The effects of children on parents.* Binghamton, NY: Haworth.

Ambert, A. M. (1997). *Parents, children, and adolescents: Interactive relationships and development in context.* Binghamton, NY: Haworth.

AmeriStat. (2000a). American resident population of the United States, 1970 to 1999, by age. Available: www.ameristat.org/estproj/estage.xls.

AmeriStat. (2000b). Changing American pie, 1999 and 2025. Available: www.ameristat.org/estproj/pie.htm.

AmeriStat. (2000c). The never married: Single, stable, and satisfied? Available: www.ameristat.org/marfam/nevermar.htm.

AmeriStat. (2000d). The aging of the United States, 1999 and 2025. Available: www.ameristat.org/estproj/aging.htm.

AmeriStat. (2000e). U.S. fertility trends: Boom and burst and leveling off. Available: www.ameristat.org/fertility/FertilityTrendsBoomBustLevelingOff.html.

Ameristat. (2000f). Resident population of the United States, 1970 to 1999, by race/Hispanic origin. Available: www.ameristat.org/estproj/estrace.xls.

Ammerman, N. T., & Roof, W. C. (1995). Old patterns, new trends, fragile experiments. In N. T. Ammerman & W. C. Roof (Eds.), *Work, family, and religion in contemporary society* (pp. 1–20). New York: Routledge.

Aponte, R., Beal, B. A., & Jiles, M. E. (1999). Ethnic variation in the family: The elusive trend toward convergence. In M. B. Sussman, S. K. Steinmetz, & G. W. Peterson (Eds.), *Handbook of marriage and the family* (2nd ed., pp. 111–141). New York: Plenum.

Bachu, A. (1993). Fertility of American women: June 1992. U.S. Bureau of the Census, *Current Population Reports,* pp. 20–470). Washington, DC: U.S. Government Printing Office.

Bahr, H. M., & Chadwick, B. A. (1988). Religion and family in Middletown, U.S.A. In D. L. Thomas (Ed.), *The religion and family connection: Social science perspectives* (Religious Studies Center Specialized Monograph Series, Vol. 3, pp. 51–65). Provo, UT: Brigham Young University.

Barber, B. K. (1997). Adolescent socialization in context: The role of connection, regulation, and autonomy in the family. *Journal of Adolescent Research, 12,* 5–11.

Baumeister, R. F. (1992). *Meanings of life.* New York: Guilford.

Baumrind, D. (1971). Current patterns of parental authority. *Developmental Psychology, Monograph, 4*(1, Pt. 2), 1–103.

Baumrind, D. (1989). Rearing competent children. In W. Damon (Ed.), *Child development today and tomorrow* (pp. 349–378). San Francisco: Jossey-Bass.

Baumrind, D. (1991). The influence of parenting style on adolescent competence and substance use. *Journal of Early Adolescence, 11,* 56–95.

Becker, E. (1999). Chronology on the history of slavery and racism. Available: www.innercity.org/holt/slavechron.html.

Bell, R. Q., & Harper, L. V. (1977). *Child effects on adults.* Hillsdale, NJ: Erlbaum.

Belsky, J. (1990). Child care and children's socioemotional development. *Journal of Marriage and the Family, 52,* 856–884.

Bianchi, S. M. (2000). Maternal employment and time with children: Dramatic change or surprising continuity. *Demography, 37,* 401–414.

Bianchi, S. M. & Spain, D. (1996). Women, work, and family in America. *Population Bulletin, 51.* Available: www.prb.org/pubs/population_bulletin/bu51_3/family.htm.

Booth, A. & Johnson, D. (1988). Premarital cohabitation and marital success. *Journal of Family Issues, 9,* 255–272.

Bumpass, L., & Sweet, J. (1972). Differentials in marital stability: 1970. *American Sociological Review, 37,* 756–766.

Bumpass, L., & Sweet, J. (1989). National estimates of cohabitation. *Demography, 26,* 615–625.

Bush, T. (1996). Happily married with children. *Christian Century, 113,* 109–113.

Chan, L., & Heaton, T. B. (1989). Demographic determinants of delayed divorce. *Journal of Divorce, 13,* 97–112.

Cherlin, A. J. (1981). *Marriage, divorce, and remarriage.* Cambridge, MA: Harvard University Press.

Cherlin, A. J. (1996). *Public and private families: An introduction.* New York: McGraw-Hill.

Clarke, S. C. (1995). Advance report of final divorce statistics, 1989 and 1990. *Monthly Vital Statistics Report, 43,* 9.

Colasanto, D., & Shriver, J. (1989). Middle-aged face marital crisis. *Gallup Report, 284,* 34–38.

Coontz, S. (1992). *The way we never were: American families and the nostalgia trap.* New York: Basic Books.

Coontz, S. (1997). Divorcing reality. *Nation, 265,* 21–24.

Dashefsky, A., & Levine, I. M. (1983). The Jewish family: Continuing challenges. In W. V. D'Antonio & J. Aldous (Eds.), *Families and religions: Conflict and change in modern society* (pp. 163–190). Beverly Hills, CA: Sage.

Defrain, J., & Olsen, D. (1999). Contemporary family patterns and relationships. In M. B. Sussman, S. K. Steinmetz, & G. W. Peterson (Eds.), *Handbook of marriage and the family* (2nd ed., pp. 309–326). New York: Plenum.

DeMaris, A., & Rao, K. V. (1992). Premarital cohabitation and marital stability. *Journal of Marriage and the Family, 54,* 178–190.

Dumka, L. E., Roosa, M. W., Michaels, M. L., & Suh, K. W. (1995). Using research and theory to develop prevention programs for high risk families. *Family Relations, 44,* 78–86.

Faust, K. A., & McKibben, J. N. (1999). Marital dissolution: Divorce, separation, annulment, and widowhood. In M. B. Sussman, S. K. Steinmetz, & G. W. Peterson (Eds.), *Handbook of marriage and the family* (2nd ed., pp. 475–499). New York: Plenum.

Glenn, N. D. (1991). The recent trend in marital success in the United States. *Journal of Marriage and the Family, 53,* 261–270.

Glenn, N. D., & Supancic, M. (1984). The social and demographic correlates of divorce and separation in the United States: An update and reconsideration. *Journal of Marriage and the Family, 46,* 563–575.

Goddard, H. W. (1999). Control strategies. In C. A. Smith (Ed.), *The encyclopedia of parenting theory and research* (pp. 91–92). Westport, CT: Greenwood.

Goodson, P. (1996). *Protestant seminary students' views of family planning and intention to promote family planning through education.* Unpublished doctoral dissertation, University of Texas at Austin.

Gottman, J. M. (1997). *Raising an emotionally intelligent child.* New York: Fireside.

Gottman J. M., & Krokoff, L. J. (1989). Marital interaction and satisfaction: A longitudinal view. *Journal of Consulting and Clinical Psychology, 57,* 47–52.

Guttman, J. (1993). *Divorce in psychosocial perspective: Theory and research.* Hillsdale, NJ: Erlbaum.

Hall, D. R., & Zhao, J. Z. (1995). Cohabitation and divorce in Canada: Testing the selectivity hypothesis. *Journal of Marriage and the Family, 57,* 421–427.

Heaton, T. B. (1988). The four C's of the Mormon family: Chastity, conjugality, children, and chauvinism. In D. L. Thomas (Ed.), *The religion and family connection: Social science perspectives* (Religious Studies Center Specialized Monograph Series, Vol. 3, pp. 51–65). Provo, UT: Brigham Young University.

Heaton, T. B. (2000, October 19). *Mormon families over the life course.* Paper presented at the Virginia Cutler Lecture series, Brigham Young University, Provo, UT.

Heaton, T. B., & Goodman, K. L. (1985). Religion and family formation. *Review of Religious Research, 26,* 343–359.

Heaton, T. B., & Pratt, E. L. (1990). The effects of religious homogamy on marital satisfaction and stability. *Journal of Family Issues, 11,* 191–207.

Hertel, B. R., & Hughes, M. (1987). Religious affiliation, attendance, and support for "pro-family" issues in the U.S. *Social Forces, 65,* 858–882.

Hochschild, A. (1989). *The second shift.* New York: Viking.

Hofferth, S. L. (1998). Children in families: A report on the 1997 Panel Study of Income Dynamics. Washington, DC: Institute for Social Research, University of Michigan.

Kluwer, E. S., Heesink, J. A., & Van De Vliert, E. (1996). Marital conflict about the division of household labor and paid work. *Journal of Marriage and the Family, 58,* 958–969.

Kurdek, L. A. (1991). Predictors of increases in marital disinterests in newlywed couples: A 3-year prospective longitudinal study. *Developmental Psychology, 27,* 627–636.

Lehrer, E. L., & Chiswick, C. U. (1993). Religion as a determinant of marital stability. *Demography, 30,* 385–404.

Lillard, L. A., Brien, M. J., & Waite, L. J. (1995). Premarital cohabitation and subsequent marital dissolution: A matter of self-selection. *Demography, 32,* 437–458.

Lin, I-F. (2000). Perceived fairness and compliance with child support obligations. *Journal of Marriage and the Family, 62,* 388–398.

Lytton, H. (1990). Child and parent effects in boys' conduct disorder: A reinterpretation. *Developmental Psychology, 26,* 683–697.

Maccoby, E. E. (1992). The role of parents in the socialization of children: A historical overview. *Developmental Psychology, 28,* 1006–1017.

Maccoby, E. E., & Martin, J. A. (1983). Socialization in the context of the family: Parent–child interaction. In E. M. Hetherington (Ed.), *Handbook of child psychology. Vol. 4: Socialization, personality, and social development* (pp. 1–101). New York: Wiley.

Martin, T. C., & Bumpass, L. (1989). Recent trends in marital disruption. *Demography, 26,* 37–52.

Maslow, A. H. (1954/1970). *Motivation and personality.* New York: Harper & Row.

Miller, B. C. (1993). Families, science, and values: Alternative views of parenting effects and adolescent pregnancy. *Journal of Marriage and the Family, 55,* 7–21.

Miller, B. C. (1998). *Families matter. A research synthesis of family influences on adolescent pregnancy.* Washington, DC: National Campaign to Prevent Teen Pregnancy.

Moen, P., & Forest, K. B. (1999). Strengthening families: Policy issues for the twenty-first century. In M. B. Sussman, S. K. Steinmetz, & G. W. Peterson (Eds.), *Handbook of marriage and the family* (2nd ed., pp. 309–326). New York: Plenum.

Morgan, S., & Rindfuss, R. R. (1985). Marital disruption: Structural and temporal dimensions. *American Journal of Sociology, 90,* 1055–1057.

Norton, A. J., & Miller, I. F. (1992). *Marriage, divorce, and remarriage in the 1990s* (U.S. Bureau of the Census, Current Population Reports Series, pp. 23–180). Washington, DC: U.S. Government Printing Office.

Peterson, G. W., & Hann, D. (1999). Socializing children and parents in families. In M. B. Sussman, S. K. Steinmetz, & G. W. Peterson (Eds.), *Handbook of marriage and the family* (2nd ed., pp. 327–370). New York: Plenum.

Peterson, G. W., & Rollins, B. C. (1987). Parent-child socialization. In M. B. Sussman & S. K. Steinmetz (Eds.), *Handbook of marriage and the family* (pp. 471–507). New York: Plenum.

Pleck, J. H. (1997). Paternal involvement: Levels, sources, and consequences. In M. E. Lamb (Ed.), *The role of the father in child development* (3rd ed., pp. 66–103). New York: Wiley.

Polls show Americans are still deeply spiritual. (1997). *Skeptic, 5,* 12.

Riche, M. F. (2000). America's diversity and growth: Signposts for the 21st century. *Population Bulletin, 55.* Available: www.prb.org/pubs/population_bulletin/bu55_2/55_2_intor.htm.

Rodgers, B., & Pryor, J. (1998). *Divorce and separation: The outcomes for children.* New York: Joseph Rowntree Foundation.

Rodriguez, H. (1998). Cohabitation: A snapshot. Available: www.clasp.org/pugs/familyformation/cohab.html.

Rogers, S. J., & Amato, P. R. (1997). Is marital quality declining? The evidence from two generations. *Social Forces, 75,* 1089–1100.

Rollins, B. C., & Thomas, D. L. (1979). Parental support, power, and control techniques in the socialization of children. In W. R. Burr, R. Hill, F. I. Nye, I. R. Reiss (Eds.), *Contemporary theories about the family* (Vol. 1, pp. 317–364). New York: Free Press.

Rossi, A. S. (1996). *How Americans spend their time: Time allocation to job, family, home, and community.* Paper presented at National Council of Family Relations, Kansas City, MO.

Rothbaum, F., & Weisz, J. R. (1994). Parental caregiving and child externalizing behavior in nonclinical samples: A meta-analysis. *Psychological Bulletin, 116,* 55–74.

Scarr, S. (1992). Developmental theories for the 1990s: Development and individual differences. *Child Development, 63,* 1–19.

Schoen, R. (1992). First unions and the stability of first marriages. *Journal of Marriage and the Family, 54,* 281–284.

Sherkat, D. E., & Ellison, C. G. (1999). Recent developments and current controversies in the sociology of religion. *Annual Review of Sociology, 25,* 363–394.

Singh, G. K., Mathews, M. S., Clarke, S. C., Yannicos, T., & Smith, B. L. (1995). Annual summary of births, marriage, divorce, and deaths: United States, 1994. *Monthly Vital Statistics Report, 43,* 13.

Spicer, J. C., & Gustavus, S. O. (1974). Mormon fertility through half a century: Another test of the Americanization process. *Social Biology, 21,* 70–76.

Strupp, J. (1999, May 15). *Editor & Publisher, 132,* 28–31.

Sweet, J., & Bumpass, L. (1987). *American families and households.* New York: Russell Sage Foundation.

Synnott, A. (1983). Little angels, little devils: A sociology of children. *Canadian Review of Sociology and Anthropology, 20,* 79–95.

Teachman, J. D., & Polonko, K. A. (1990). Cohabitation and marital stability in the United States. *Social Forces, 69,* 201–220.

Teachman, J. D., Tedrow, L. M., & Crowder, K. D. (2000). The changing demography of America's families. *Journal of Marriage and the Family, 62,* 1234–1246.

Thornton, A. (1988). Reciprocal influences of family and religion in a changing world. In D. L. Thomas (Ed.), *The religion and family connection: Social science perspectives* (Religious Studies Center Specialized Monograph Series, Vol. III, pp. 27–50). Provo, UT: Brigham Young University.

Thornton, A., Axinn, W. G., & Hill, D. H. (1992). Reciprocal effects of religiosity, cohabitation, and marriage. *American Journal of Sociology, 98,* 628–651.

Tschann, J. M. (1999). Assessing interparental conflict: Reports of parents and adolescents in European American and Mexican American families. *Journal of Marriage and the Family, 61,* 269–284.

U.S. Bureau of the Census. (1998). Estimated median age at first marriage, by sex: 1890 to the present. Available: www.census.gov/population/socdemo/ms-la/tabms-2.txt.

U.S. Bureau of the Census. (1999). *Statistical abstract of the United States, 1999* (119th ed.). Washington DC: U.S. Government Printing Office.

Ventura, S. J., & Bachrach, C. A. (2000). Nonmarital childbearing in the United States, 1940–99. *National Vital Statistics Reports, 48,* 16.

Waite, L. J., & Gallagher, M. (2000). *The case for marriage: Why married people are happier, healthier, and better off financially.* New York: Doubleday.

Waite, L. J., & Lillard, L. A. (1991). Children and marital disruption. *American Journal of Sociology, 96,* 930–953.

Waldrup, J. (1994, September). Change is good unless it happens. *American Demographics,* 12–13.

Walker, A. J. (1999). Gender and family relationships. In M. B. Sussman, S. K. Steinmetz, & G. W. Peterson (Eds.), *Handbook of marriage and the family* (2nd ed., pp. 309–326). New York: Plenum.

Watson, J. B. (1928). *Psychological care of infant and child.* New York: Norton.

Weeks, J. R. (1994). *Population* (5th ed.). Belmont, CA: Wadsworth.

Weitzman, L. J. (1985). *The divorce revolution: The unexpected social and economic consequences for women and their children in America.* New York: Free Press.

Wilcox, B. L., Rostosky, S. S., Randall, B., & Wright, M. L. C. (2000). *Adolescent religiosity and sexual behavior: A research review.* Washington, DC: The National Campaign to Prevent Teen Pregnancy.

Wilkie, J. R., & Ferree, M. M. (1998). Gender and fairness: Marital satisfaction in two-earner couples. *Journal of Marriage and the Family, 60,* 577–594.

Wineberg, H. (1994). Marital reconciliation in the United States: Which couples are successful? *Journal of Marriage and the Family, 56,* 80–88.

CHAPTER 18

CARIBBEAN FAMILIES IN ENGLISH-SPEAKING COUNTRIES
A RATHER COMPLEX MOSAIC

JAIPAUL L. ROOPNARINE
Syracuse University

RONALD SINGH
Hunter College, The City University of New York

PAULINE BYNOE
Brooklyn College, The City University of New York

ROMMEL SIMON
Brooklyn College, The City University of New York

As the title of this chapter suggests, Caribbean families comprise a diverse group of individuals whose family structures and functions vary tremendously (Roopnarine & Brown, 1997). Sharing common histories of conquest and colonization, Caribbean families represent different ethnic groups who speak different languages (e.g., Chinese, Dutch, English, French, Haitian Creole, Hindi, Patois, and Spanish). To avoid making global statements that would mask the richness cloistered in the diverse ethnic groups in the Caribbean, this chapter focuses primarily on English-speaking families from Guyana, Jamaica, Barbados, St. Kitts, Nevis, Trinidad and Tobago, Grenada, and the other smaller islands of the eastern Caribbean. Along these lines, our discussions pertain to two ethnic groups: African Caribbean and

Indo Caribbean families. By limiting our focus to these two groups, we were in a better position to look at within as well as between ethnic group variability in family life. This overview is organized around five major issues: geography and sociohistorical considerations, family organization patterns and the division of household roles, parental beliefs and practices as they relate to childhood socialization, parent–child relations and developmental outcomes, and family policies. In the preparation of this chapter, we relied heavily on material presented in previous manuscripts on the topic (e.g., Roopnarine, 2002; Roopnarine & Brown, 1997; Roopnarine, Clawson, Benetti, & Lewis, 2000; Roopnarine & Shin, 2003).

GEOGRAPHY AND SOCIOHISTORICAL CONSIDERATIONS

The Anglophone Caribbean stretches from the Bahamas to Trinidad and Tobago and includes the continental countries of Belize and Guyana. This geographic definition emerges out of the collective colonial histories of the countries. Following the voyages of Christopher Columbus, the region was claimed on behalf of Spain. In the 1620s, the British colonized St. Kitts, Barbados, Nevis, and Barbuda, and in 1655 seized Jamaica from Spain. By way of the Seven Years War, Britain was able to settle the former French possessions of Dominica, St. Vincent, and Grenada. It acquired Trinidad from Spain in 1797, and after alternate possessions with France, St. Lucia was under British control in 1814. British Guyana emerged out of the former Dutch colonies of Berbice, Demerara, and Essequibo in 1815, and Belize was obtained in 1840.

Soon after the Spanish conquest of the so-called New World, family life among the native people of the region—the Caribs and Arawak-speaking Tainos— would changed dramatically. Enslavement, diseases introduced to the region during conquest, and Christianity all took an inexorable toll on patterns of family life and the very survival of the native people. Needless to say, they were decimated. Currently, small numbers of native people live in scattered areas across some countries of the region (e.g., Amerindians in Guyana). The exploitation of human beings would continue with the importation of Africans as slaves (between 9.42 and 11.77 million) (Curtin, 1975; Deerr, 1949–1950), and after slavery was abolished in 1834, with the introduction of East Indians (Ramdin, 2000; Mansingh & Mansingh, 1999) and Chinese as indentured servants (see Lai, 1993; Samaroo, 2000) (see Table 18.1). Harsh British rule continued beyond the postemancipation period until the 1960s, when many of the English-speaking Caribbean countries achieved independence (e.g., Guyana in 1966) (Williams, 1966, 1970).

Between emancipation and this writing, there have been active population movements within countries, between countries, and to North America and Europe (Foner, 2001; Grosfoguel, 1997; Marshall, 1982; Roopnarine & Shin, 2003). A few scholars (Marshall, 1982) have outlined four major phases of population movements within and external to the Caribbean. The first occurred after emancipation around 1835 and continued to about 1870. People moved away from the plantations to other regions within and across countries in pursuit of other forms of labor and stable employment (e.g., from Barbados to British Guyana and Trinidad) and to set up in-

Table 18.1 Indentured Servants Brought to the British Colonies between 1838 and 1917

COUNTRY	EAST INDIANS[a]	CHINESE[b]
British Guiana (Guyana)	238,909	13,533
Jamaica	36,412	1,152
Trinidad and Tobago	143,939	2,645
Grenada	3,200	—
St. Vincent	2,472	—
St. Lucia	4,354	—

[a]From Ramdin (2000), includes Hindus and Muslims.
[b]From Lai (1993); the Chinese presence in the Caribbean predated the abolition of slavery.

dependent villages. The second phase was marked by movement to regions outside of the Caribbean. With the building of the railroad across the Isthmus of Panama and the excavation of the Panama Canal, it is estimated that between 1853 and 1914 over 130,000 people, mainly from Barbados and Jamaica, may have moved to Central America (Hall, 1971). The period between 1889 and 1915 also witnessed the movement of 43,698 Caribbean people to the United States (Reid, 1970). Following these two periods of active population movement, the Great Depression in the United States, discriminatory immigration practices, social change in labor practices, the completion of the Panama Canal, and differential wage structures for Caribbean immigrants all contributed to return migration and a cessation to outmigration (Marshall, 1982). Finally, the current phase, which began after World War II and continues to this day, saw population movement from the English-speaking Caribbean to the United Kingdom, Canada, and the United States. Between 1953 and 1962 more than 175,000 Jamaicans moved to Great Britain (Patterson, 1978). By 2000, more favorable immigration policies in the United States and Canada (e.g., the Postimmigration Act of 1965 in the United States) and poor economic and political conditions all helped to accelerate the rate of movement of people out of the Caribbean. There is documentation of the impact of outward migration on family life in the Caribbean and on how transmigration—from the Caribbean to the postindustrialized societies and back to the Caribbean—influenced family organization, socialization patterns, and economic activities (Foner, 1997; Singh, 2000; Thompson & Bauer, 2000). A profile of recent population movement from the English-speaking Caribbean to the United States is presented in Table 18.2.

Today, the Caribbean has a population of over 30 million people. In the English-speaking Caribbean, Belize has a population of around 239,000 people (44 percent Mestizo, 30 percent Creole, 11 percent Mayan, 7 percent Garifuna; 8,803 square miles); Guyana has a population of around 849,000 people (51 percent Indo Caribbean, 38 percent African Caribbean, 11 percent mixed race and Amerindians; 83,000 square miles);

Table 18.2   English-Speaking Caribbean Immigrants to the United States between 1988 and 1998

COUNTRY	1988–1992	1993–1998
Barbados	6,276	5,413
Belize	10,987	4,397
Grenada	5,009	4,202
Guyana	51,628	60,163
Jamaica	113,245	100,063
St. Vincent and Grenadines	3,994	3,131
Trinidad and Tobago	31,496	36,898

Source: Statistical Yearbook of the Immigration and Naturalization Service, U.S. Department of Justice, 1998.

Jamaica, 2,576,000 people (90 percent African Caribbean, 10 percent mixed and other ethnic groups; 4,441 square miles); Barbados, 270,000 people (166 square miles); Trinidad and Tobago, 1,385,000 people (40 percent African Caribbean, 40 percent Indo Caribbean, and 14 percent mixed race; 1,980 square miles); Grenada, 93,065 people (133 square miles); and St. Kitts and Nevis, 41,000 people (104 square miles) (UN, 2001 and *World Bank Atlas,* 2000). A majority of the people in the English-speaking Caribbean are of African ancestry, with sizable numbers of East Indians in Guyana and Trinidad and Tobago, and smaller concentrations of people of mixed ethnic backgrounds (e.g., black Caribs), people from European, Middle Eastern, and Chinese backgrounds, and Amerindians (native people).

As a result of the sustained periods of British colonization and rule, vestiges of the English system of education, government, and commerce are still present in various countries of the Caribbean. This is not surprising given the systematic attempts by the British to impart their cultural, educational, and political values to their subjects. Because of exposure to other cultural values and practices (see Chevannes, 1994, for a discussion of Rastafari life), internal and external migration during the post-emancipation period, harsh social and economic conditions, and exposure to different cycles of sociopolitical ideologies (e.g., socialism and other economic ideologies tied to cooperative socialism), the degree to which African and Indo Caribbean people have maintained different aspects of their cultural heritage is a matter of debate. By most analyses, what exists currently is an admixture of institutional practices that are tied to the legacy of British domination and an emphasis on ethnic identity formation based on social and cultural customs that have their roots in African and Indian traditions but that have been transformed significantly over time (Vervotec, 1991). All of this is further being modified by access and exposure, through direct and indirect means, to the political, social, and economic systems of North American and European societies.

FERTILITY, INFANT MORTALITY RATES, AND LIFE EXPECTANCY

Table 18.3 displays the infant mortality, fertility, and average life expectancy rates for select countries in the English-speaking Caribbean. As can be gleaned from this table, data gathered by the United Nations indicate that the average life expectancy ranged from 64 years in Guyana to an impressive 85 years in Grenada. Because of poorer economic, health, and social conditions, Guyana has an infant mortality rate of 57, second only to Haiti, which has a rate of 71. Barbados—a country that enjoys one of the best standards of living in the Caribbean as a whole—has an infant mortality rate of 14, a figure that is comparable to those in the postindustrialized world. Although population growth has been a constant concern for the economically unstable countries of the Caribbean, fertility rates have been declining over the last five decades.

FAMILY STRUCTURES AND FUNCTIONAL ORGANIZATIONS

Unlike most other societies, there is a preponderance of nonmarital unions in the English-speaking Caribbean. It is well documented that mating and childrearing in the English-speaking Caribbean occur in diverse family structural-functional arrangements: marital, common-law, visiting, and single heads of households. Men/fathers may not be physically or psychologically present in children's lives, and pair bond stability between mating partners can be ephemeral (see Table 18.4 for fathers present in the household in various Caribbean countries). As a result, Caribbean women commonly assume a large share of the economic and childrearing responsibilities for their children. Because a number of scholarly pieces have addressed the diverse structural arrangements of African Caribbean (Leo-Rhynie, 1997; Roopnarine, 2002; Senior, 1991; Smith, 1996) and Indo Caribbean families (Jayawardena, 1963; Mansingh & Mansingh, 1999; Ramdin, 2000; Roop-

Table 18.3   Infant Mortality, Fertility, and Life Expectancy Rates in Selected Caribbean Countries

COUNTRY	INFANT MORTALITY[a]	FERTILITY	LIFE EXPECTANCY
Bahamas	17	2.6	74
Barbados	14	1.5	76
Guyana	57	2.3	64
Jamaica	21	2.5	75
Trinidad and Tobago	16	1.6	73

[a]Infant mortality rates reflect per thousand live births during the first year of life.
Source: World Bank Atlas, 2000.

Table 18.4   Percentage of Mothers and Fathers Present in the Home in Selected Caribbean Countries

COUNTRY	MOTHERS	FATHERS
Antigua	94.7%	35.5%
Barbados	96.8%	49.2%
Jamaica	90.2%	54.5%
St. Kitts	91.7%	29.2%
St. Lucia	85%	45%
St. Vincent	87.1%	37.9%

Numbers refer to percentage of parents who were present, regardless of marital status.

Source: Leo-Rhynie, 1997.

narine et al., 1997), only the bare outlines of their morphology and functions are provided here.

AFRICAN CARIBBEAN FAMILIES

Structural and Social Organization

Despite the existence of nonmarital unions for more than 150 years in the Caribbean, we are only now beginning to understand their adaptive significance, internal dynamics, and impact on childhood development (Crawford-Brown, 1999; Ramkissoon, 2002; Roopnarine & Brown, 1997). Among low-income African Caribbean people under age 25, most sexual relationships and childbearing begin in visiting relationships. Men and women do not live together; they meet at a prearranged location for sexual and social relations. In cases in which the man does not provide economic support to his partner and offspring, hegemony may still be on his side. This notwithstanding, his legal and financial obligations to the mating partner and offspring are not well defined in most Caribbean countries. Women see visiting relationships in a temporary light, as they do not believe that such family arrangements are a barrier to their personal desires or prospects for marriage later on (Powell, 1986). In a sample of four different communities in Jamaica, between 19 and 34 percent of relationships were described as visiting unions

(Brown, Anderson, & Chevannes, 1993; see also Ramkissoon, 2002).

Having borne children in visiting relationships, women tend to enter common-law relationships (roughly 20.8 percent, Smith, 1996). In these unions, men and women share a dwelling and economic resources, though the man often has the upper hand in dictating his wishes and desires regarding household and couple roles. The division of household labor mimics a traditional pattern, as women are expected to assume primary responsibility for domestic and childrearing tasks, whereas men are expected to assume the instrumental breadwinner role. With the exception of Barbados, there is little legal protection accorded women in common-law relationships. But some countries (e.g., Guyana, Jamaica, St. Vincent) do have legislation in place that requires the support of children after paternity is established (Senior, 1991). Nonetheless, for the most part, the legal rights of women and children in common-law unions are ambiguous.

The other two family forms—marital unions and single-headed households—usually occur later after progressive mating (between 35 and 54 years of age) (Powell, 1986; Senior, 1991). Marriage rates are generally low among African Caribbean people, but they increase with better economic conditions and educational attainment (for Jamaican men under 30 years it was 9.35 percent) and after progressive mating (for Jamaican men over 50 years it was 54.3 percent) (Brown, Newland, Anderson, & Chevannes, 1997). As with common-law unions, husband–wife roles within marital unions tend to follow a traditional dichotomy. Despite the inclination toward later marriages among African Caribbean couples, most women view marriage as a positive step for them (Powell, 1986). However, they do not necessarily see marriage as a way to salvation and personal happiness. Caribbean women endorse the notion of "partnership" regardless of the type of union (see Clarke, 1957). This spirit pervades a significant number of Caribbean women who are heads or *de facto* heads of their households. A majority of single women have been in prior relationships with multiple male partners. They may have abandoned or are not presently in a relationship. Data from over a decade ago suggest that 22.4 percent of women in Guyana, 27 percent in Trinidad and Tobago, 33.8 percent in Jamaica, 42.9 percent in Barbados, and 45.3 percent in Grenada are the heads of their households (Massiah, 1982; Powell, 1986). Newer statistics gathered in the 1990s substantiate some of these trends, at least in Guyana and Jamaica (Brown et al., 1997). About half of all female household heads have never been married, have low educational attainment, and are less likely to be employed.

It has been suggested that the proclivity toward nonmarital unions among African Caribbean families is tied to sociohistorical experiences such as slavery (Frazier, 1951; Herskovits, 1941), socioeconomic and educational opportunities (Brown et al., 1997), and ideological beliefs about manhood and fatherhood (Roopnarine, 2004). What is clear is that African Caribbean women strongly accept motherhood as a symbol of womanhood and devote a good deal of energy toward meeting the economic and social needs of their children and those of others. Remarkably, they have historically done this in the absence of male partners or financial support from them.

Religious Beliefs

African Caribbean families embrace the precepts of Christianity (e.g., Anglican, Baptist, Methodist, Presbyterian, Roman Catholic, Moravian, Pentecostal, Seventh-Day Adventist, African Methodist Episcopalian [AME] Zion), Revivalism, Rastafari, and Orisha practices. Religious practices have been a centerpiece in African Caribbean family life from slavery onward. Their maxims have provided diverse psychological and social mechanisms for organizing family life and coping with degradation, oppression, and challenging economic conditions. Baptisms, marriages, and burial rites are performed under the aegis of the principles laid out in the different branches of Christianity and other religions. Furthermore, Christian doctrines are central to parent–child relationships as they are used in childrearing practices, particularly

in guiding and disciplining children. Because Christian doctrines are widely known, we turn, albeit briefly, to two sets of religious beliefs that are "more indigenous" to the Caribbean: Rastafari and Orisha (Chevannes, 1994; Houk, 1999).

Although commonly associated with the popular Reggae musician Bob Marley and Jamaicans, Rastafari (*Ras,* Ethiopian for Prince, and *Tafari,* the Ethiopian Emperor's personal name) beliefs have become more appealing to people in other parts of the Caribbean and to a lesser extent the world (Chevannes, 1998b; Yawney, 1999). Of interest in this chapter is the relative role of religious beliefs and practices in the differentiation and structuring of family life—what Turner (1969) termed *communitas* (see Houk, 1999, for a discussion). In various communities, religious practices form the basis of social relationships. From the early days of the Rastafari movement to identify God as black and living (Jah or Jah-Jah), through various political struggles against racism, to the dread hairstyles and musical lyrics of the 1990s, there has always been a strong push toward racial identity (Chevannes, 1998a) and an understanding of oppression and economic exploitation. Through music, food, hair, the lion, and color symbolism, Rastafarians have galvanized support among the downtrodden in Jamaica and the youth culture in North America and Europe (see Pulis, 1999). Rastafari practices (e.g., Bhingi; ritualization in private life), void of many religious rituals *per se,* emphasize getting along with others and using natural elements in everyday life. In the original rhythms of Rastafarian beliefs, members should not use sharp instruments to disfigure the body, strive to be vegetarians, worship only the God Rastafari, love and respect humankind while abhorring hate, deceit, jealousy, and so on, disapprove of the pleasures of modern-day society, extend charity to others, and stick to the laws of Ethiopia (see Pulis, 1999). Rasta life focuses on African concepts and artifacts (Chevannes, 1998a). Communalism is valued but women (*dawtas,* or sisters) are excluded from basic Rasta functions. Power, gender, and economic conditions continue to define Rastafari beliefs as they are becoming modified and are spreading in the

Caribbean and elsewhere in the early twenty-first century (Yawney, 1999).

Staying with the concept of religion and community ties, the Orisha practices of Trinidad and Tobago combine African, European, Hindu, and Kabbalistic traditions (Houk, 1999). Owing to its multicultural base, the Orisha religion continues to evolve as it incorporates input from its worshippers. During the Ebo (feast of offering and celebration), people participate in a feast, drumming and dancing, and animal sacrifices. Communities of worshippers gather at shrines (which consist of *palais,* where dancing and singing are conducted for the Orisha; the *chapelle,* where religious artifacts are housed; the *perogun,* where the shrines are kept; and spiritual objects from other religions) "for Orisha rites and ceremonies and Spiritual Baptist services and rituals" (Houk, 1999, p. 300). These services meld Christian, ancient Yoruba, Hindu, and other religious traditions and draw people from different walks of life. In addition to praying and singing in the Spiritual Baptist tradition, there is a notable ritual that involves a lengthy period of mourning that may last up to a week or more. "Pilgrims" embark upon a journey of "spiritual travels" during which they are in touch with spirits from other parts of the world (e.g., Africa, India, the United States), who grant advice on different aspects of spirituality. Accounts of the journey are then divulged by the mourning pilgrim (Houk, 1995, 1999). These rituals and practices serve to cement cultural pride among the African Caribbean people of Trinidad and Tobago and begin to map the interrelationships between human beings and spiritual powers and pull together religious traditions in a seemingly nonhierarchical manner (the validity of the spiritual journeys goes unabated). The Opa Orisha (*Shango*) organization of Trinidad and Tobago has won recognition from the government as it celebrates its polytheistic foundations while struggling with the Africanization of key practices (Houk, 1999).

Beliefs and Practices about Childrearing

Until quite recently, considerations of childrearing practices in the Caribbean have mostly focused on

the pathological tendencies of parents to beat their children and/or abandon them (Roopnarine & Brown, 1997). This emphasis is not only stereotyped but quite misguided, because recent work has pointed to the extreme variations in parenting beliefs and practices within cultures (Roopnarine, Shin, Jung, & Hossain, 2003; Super & Harkness, 1997), and some have begun to speculate about the cross-cultural meaning of different parenting styles for child development outcomes (e.g., Baumrind's parenting typologies; Chao, 1994). Not unlike families in other societies around the world (see Value of Children Study described by Kagitiçibasi, 1996), Caribbean families place a high value on children.

In laying out childrearing practices in any culture, it is important to consider childrearing beliefs because they may be important for the structuring of everyday cognitive and social experiences for children (Sigel & McGillicuddy-DeLisi, 2002; Super & Harkness, 1997). Their implications for childhood development have been delineated (Roopnarine et al., 2003; Super & Harkness, 1997). What, then, are some parental beliefs and practices about childhood socialization that are germane to African Caribbean families? What follows appears fairly typical across the Caribbean.

Parental Beliefs

1. Parenting involves authoritarian/punitive control mixed with indulgence and protectiveness (Leo-Rhynie, 1997), with families in the higher socioeconomic groups showing more indulgence (Ricketts, 1982) and those with better educational attainment placing more emphasis on the development of autonomy (Morrison, Ispa, & Milner, 1998). However, authoritative parenting styles have been observed among middle- and upper-class Jamaicans with school-aged children (Ramkissoon, 2002).

2. As in many other societies (e.g., many Asian societies), there is the expectation that children should be obedient, compliant, and show unilateral respect for parents and other adult members of society. This sentiment is echoed in the views of low-income parents across the Caribbean: 100 percent of parents in Antigua, 96 percent in St. Kitts, 85 percent in St. Lucia, 94 percent in St. Vincent, 82 percent in Barbados, and 95 percent in Jamaica believe that children should obey their parents (Grant, Leo-Rhynie, & Alexander, 1983).

3. Parents believe in the biblical admonition, "Spare the rod and spoil the child." They generally favor harsher and stricter forms of discipline throughout childhood (Arnold, 1982). A survey by Anderson and Payne (1994) of 10–11-year-old children in Barbados on "how often" they were flogged showed that 82.4 percent of boys and 85.4 percent of girls reported from "very often" to "a few times." As can be deduced, only a small number had never been flogged.

4. Parents recognize the utilitarian value of children. It is believed that children, and especially boys, should provide economic support and care for their aging parents, but often do not. In many low-income African Caribbean families, mothers prefer girls over boys because they believe that daughters will care for them in their old age and perceive that boys may be too difficult to raise in the absence of fathers (Leo-Rhynie, 1997).

5. Parents believe that religious indoctrination is a central force in raising children. They rely on Christian (at Revivalist gatherings, families may practice healing [*obeah*] to win over a lover, avenge someone; the *Table* feast is held to give thanks, observe an anniversary, for petitions, destructions, and memorials) (Chevannes, 1998b), Rastafari, and Orisha principles to guide family practices (births, baptisms, discipline, weddings, spiritual journeys of the Orish, the Ebo feast of offering) and rituals (from dread hairstyles and death ceremonies to food habits and sociopolitical organizations) (Chevannes, 1998a; Houk, 1999).

6. A majority of men and women (96 percent of men and 94 percent of women in single-earner and 74 percent of men and 72 percent of women in dual-earner families in a Jamaican sample) believe that the primary role of fathers is that of economic provider and protector, and the primary role of mothers is that of caregiver and nurturer to children (Brown et al., 1997; Roopnarine et al., 1995).

Parental Practices

1. Because of multigeneration family units, fosterage, and child-shifting practices, grandparents, aunts, uncles, and other relatives are important socialization agents in children's lives. In a study of Trinidadian families, multiple individuals were observed to care for very young children (e.g., 16.3 percent of caring interactions by siblings and 17.6 percent by grandparents) (Flinn, 1992). Other studies (Powell, 1986; Rodman, 1971) too have reported that sizable numbers of children are cared for by relatives—as many as 50 percent in the Eastern Caribbean.

2. Discipline/physical punishment techniques employed by parents are often harsh and in the form of denigration, such as verbal putdowns about the child's inadequacies and/or beating with a belt or stick (Anderson & Payne, 1994; Payne, 1989). These forms of punishments are sanctioned at home and in school by parents and pupils alike.

3. Child shifting, which involves "giving" children (informal adoption) to be raised by others, is done when adults enter a new relationship, move in search of better economic conditions, or are unable to meet the child's economic and social needs. The underlying goal is to provide a better life for the child (Russell-Brown, Norville, & Griffith, 1997). Between 15 and 33 percent of children in the Caribbean are shifted and sometimes raised by neither a mother nor a father (Dann, 1987; Roberts & Sinclair, 1978; Russell-Brown et al., 1997).

4. Parents dispense praise or reward to children sporadically, and public displays of affection are rather rare. In one survey, only 23.6 percent of parents used praise after children did something that pleased them, and a meager 3.7 percent used affection (Leo-Rhynie, 1997).

5. Low-income parents in particular appear unresponsive to children's social overtures and make feeble attempts to furnish children with play objects or engage them in play activities (Leo-Rhynie, 1997).

At this point it may be appropriate to warn the reader that there are relatively few psychological studies of parental beliefs and practices regarding childrearing in the English-speaking Caribbean. Undergirding various beliefs and practices about childrearing are the daily struggles most African Caribbean parents engage in to meet the basic needs of their families. Quite possibly, with greater economic and educational opportunities and exposure to North American society, the vicissitudes of parenting laid out above are in the process of changing. Indeed, in the Caribbean Gender Socialization Project (GSP) (Brown et al., 1997), men in Guyana and Jamaica reported greater involvement in childrearing and household tasks, perhaps suggesting a shift in beliefs about manhood and fatherhood.

Parent–Child Relationships

The predominance of nonmarital unions among African Caribbean families has raised several concerns about their adequacy for calibrating positive developmental outcomes in children. Note that family structure and instability are not isomorphic. Although some researchers point to the increased psychological and educational risks associated with mate shifting and child shifting (Crawford-Brown, 1999; Sharpe, 1997), results from large-scale projects do suggest that throughout the Caribbean mothers and fathers display keen interest in their children's welfare and well-being (Brown et al., 1997). Yet far too many (Indo Caribbean families included) do not understand basic developmental processes in children or provide cognitive and social experiences for children that would optimize their growth. In this segment, we present the little we know about parent–child relationships in African Caribbean families.

It is worth repeating that motherhood is the province of African Caribbean women. It is the signature of their womanhood. These women have always found room in their lives for their own children and those of others—a phenomenon that Brodber (1986) terms "emotional expansiveness." Often in the absence of financial support from men

and with assistance from other kinship and nonkinship members, African Caribbean women tackle parenthood with stern determination. They appear fiercely maternal, engaging in formal infant handling routines that include massage, stretching, and motor exercises (Hopkins & Westra, 1988), and value propinquity to children in order to respond to their fretfulness, crying, and interrupted sleep patterns in a very relaxed manner (Landman, Grantham-McGregor, & Desai, 1983). If necessary, they draw on the support of other women in the immediate neighborhood (in the yard) to provide support for childcare, "child watching," and general companionship (Brodber, 1975).

From the early childhood years onward, mothers continue to assume overwhelming responsibility for children, so much so that they have been personified as "fathering children" (Clarke, 1957). Mothers are protective of daughters, confining them to the yard and surrounding neighborhood, while at the same time boys are given greater latitude to roam about, engaging in sports, gambling, and the "street economy." Boys are the recipients of more severe punishment from mothers and fathers than girls (Brown et al., 1997). The punishment is seen as necessary to toughen boys up, to prepare them to meet the challenges of the "rough outside world." Despite such harsh treatment, mother–son bonds appear close, and as they grow older sons may be called on to protect the family. Boys are repeatedly urged to prove their masculinity through sexuality soon after pubescence, to demonstrate "manhood." Daughters are relegated to assisting with domestic tasks and are nurtured to be supportive to male partners later on (from the Caribbean Gender Socialization Project; Brown et al., 1997). Overt demonstrations of affection are more likely to be directed at girls than boys and to be discouraged between fathers/stepfathers and daughters as they mature into young women (Brown et al., 1997).

Turning to father–child relationships, the once-immutable portrait of the irresponsible Caribbean father is under severe scrutiny. An examination of a patchwork of studies from the last five decades reveals a more encouraging profile of Caribbean men as fathers (see review by Roopnarine, 2004). Across a broad range of investigations that include observations, surveys, and interviews and focus on black Carib, Jamaican, Trinidadian, Barbadian, and Guyanese men, levels of father involvement seem inconsistent and qualitatively different depending on whether the offspring is biologically related to the male present in the household. More specifically, black Carib men in Belize showed negligible levels of involvement with young children and rarely, if ever, cared for them (Munroe & Munroe, 1992), and similar tendencies have been noted for black Carib men in Dominica (Layang, 1983). By contrast, men in Guyana, Trinidad, and Jamaica showed levels of involvement that were comparable to those of men in other societies (Ramkissoon, 2002; Roopnarine, 2004). For instance, low-income Jamaican men in common-law unions spent 0.94 of an hour feeding, 0.52 of an hour bathing, and 2.75 hours a day playing with infants (Roopnarine et al., 1995), more than two-thirds of Guyanese fathers reported changing infants' diapers and bathing them (Wilson, 1989), and in a Trinidadian sample, 10.3 percent of care interactions dispensed to children were by fathers (Flinn, 1992). There is some indication that men in Trinidad engage in more harmonious interactions with biological than nonbiological children (Flinn, 1992), raising further questions about the commitment of nonbiological fathers to children (Brown et al., 1997).

Beyond the information provided above, the focus has been on father absence, mate shifting, and child shifting and their impact on parent–child relationships and childhood development. Next we attempt to address the question posed earlier about the possible outcomes of being raised in nonmarital unions where men and women have multiple mating partners and children experience child shifting. Also covered is the impact of harsh discipline on childhood development.

Parent–Child Relationships and Developmental Outcomes

Broadly speaking, Caribbean mental health specialists have warned against the impact of being raised in "unstable" marital and nonmarital unions (Sharpe, 1997). In exploring the impact of being raised in unstable family unions or circumstances, studies are far from determining how economic factors and demographic variables destabilize Caribbean men's and women's roles in the family. As a result, research on the impact of father absence on children's intellectual and social functioning is equivocal. On the one hand, it has been argued that, given normative patterns of female-headed households, father absence does not have the same deleterious effects on educational and social outcomes for children in the Caribbean as it does for children in, say, the United States (Crawford-Brown, 1997, 1999; Miller, 1991). On the other hand, some suggest associations between father absence and increased risk for poor nutrition, abuse, developmental delays, running away from home, and early sexual activity (Sharpe, 1997), and passive dependency (Allen, 1985). Boys are prone to higher psychological and educational risks than girls, but the reasons are complex (Miller, 1991; Roopnarine, 2004) and include interrelated factors such as a lack of good male models, poor parenting skills on the part of mothers and their partner(s), unstable living arrangements (multiple residences), and so on. It has been reported that with better incomes and educational attainment, father presence increases; this has the potential of reducing psychological and educational risks to children (Brown et al., 1997). Further, the role of "father figures" and sensitive surrogate female caregivers in attenuating the impact of father absence should not be ignored (Roopnarine, 2004).

The relative consequences of child shifting on the psychosocial functioning of children are even more undefined than those for father absence. When not in the confines of sensitive caregivers, the practice of child shifting can impinge on children's general well-being and welfare (Crawford-Brown, 1997, 1999), and even short separations can cause children to become distressed as measured by elevated cortisol levels in their saliva (Flinn, 1995). A critical issue to mental health specialists is the nature of the child's attachment bond to adult caregivers. Children who are shifted during their parents' migration to another region or country and those who have experienced multiple shifts in a short period of time are at heightened risk for the development of impaired attachment relationships with adults (Sharpe, 1997) and conduct problems (Crawford-Brown, 1997). It is unlikely that the act of child shifting alone compromises children's psychological functioning. Consider for a moment that few, if any, of these children receive counseling and often mourn the absence of their parents silently, some experience extreme instability in living arrangements, yet others may be in the care of aging family members who may be incapacitated or are simply unable to devote energy and resources to the care of young children. Remember though, that grandparents, aunts, and other caregivers are centrally involved in raising children. Under conditions where there are adequate economic and social supports, child shifting may not have discernible negative consequences on children's mental health (Russell-Brown et al., 1997).

Another topic of relevance that has implications for childhood outcomes is physical punishment. While there is ample evidence that physical punishments are administered in the home and at school across ethnic groups and around the Caribbean, discussions about their deleterious effects on childhood development have increased (Rohner, Kean, & Cornoyer, 1991). An impressive body of work from the postindustrialized societies (e.g., Rohner, Bourque, & Elordi, 1996; Turner & Finkelhor, 1996) suggests that physical punishment is associated with poor psychosocial adjustment, aggressive tendencies, delinquency, low self-esteem, and emotional problems in children. Of course, the severity of the physical punishments and the contexts in which they occur must be considered. Recent research findings (Baumrind, 1996; Baumrind, Larzelere, & Cowan, 2002) have alluded to the affection and reassurance children receive in a family as mitigating the harmful effects of physical punishment, and a threshold phenomenon has been proposed that recognizes a point of severity beyond which children's mental health might be compromised (Rohner et al., 1996). A problem with physical punishments in the Caribbean is that

they can be so brutal that they would constitute abuse elsewhere. Parents are rather clueless about the possible physical and psychological harm they inflict on children. From her clinical practice, Sharpe (1997) intimated that children who were maltreated showed an enhanced susceptibility to being depressed, having conduct disorders, and running away from home.

INDO CARIBBEAN FAMILIES

As noted already, Indo Caribbean families, both Hindus and Muslims, are the descendants of indentured servants who were brought to the Caribbean (mainly to Jamaica, Guyana, and Trinidad and Tobago between 1837 and 1917) after slavery was abolished, to supplant the labor shortages in the former British colonies. Under British domination, they struggled to maintain seminal aspects of their cultural heritage. Attempts to define a tapestry of "Indianness" in the Caribbean have been contradictory. It has been argued that an "Englishification" or a "creolized" version of Indianness exists (Skinner, 1955) that is a product of exposure to other cultural influences and to political and socioeconomic changes over the last 150 years. Others (e.g., Vervotec, 1991, 1995) disagree and propose instead that ethnic traditions are the foundations of relationships among Indo Caribbean people. Even though there is documentation of Indian family life in the Caribbean (Mansingh & Mansingh, 1999; Ramdin, 2000), it is rather difficult to speak authoritatively about cultural continuity between India and the Caribbean without strong data. Thus we eschew any discussion of cultural continuity. It is our contention that, like families in other parts of the world, the Indo Caribbean family is in a state of flux. The enumeration that comes next straddles the traditional and some aspects of contemporary Indo Caribbean family organization patterns and parent–child relationships.

Structural and Social Organization

The structural organization of Indo Caribbean families reflects a mixture of nuclear and extended households that are based largely on legal marriages. Consequently, Indo Caribbean families are more likely to have a resident father in the household than African Caribbean families. There are lavish ceremonies to celebrate marriages, but this is waning as a result of economic and social factors (for Hindu weddings, see Kanhai, 1999, for a description of *Matikor,* initiation of the marriage ceremony by a religious blessing and subsequently by women singing traditional songs and dancing in lewd and sexually suggestive ways in an attempt to educate the bride about sexual and other relations; Mohammed, 1997, and Prasad, 1999, for a discussion of *Kanyadan,* gift of the virgin girl; for Muslims the *Nikkah,* wedding and the processes involved). Marriages are still arranged by parents and other adults, but increasingly young people prefer to choose their own marital partners or covertly elope. Marriage partners are usually within religious preferences. Upon marriage the wife typically resides with her husband's parents. Major sources of marital instability may stem from infidelity on the wife's part or her scandalous behavior, alcoholism (the husband drinking too much rum; or "he de all about"—meaning he loafs), husband's immaturity and patriarchal orientation, and interference from in-laws (viz., mothers-in-law) (Jayawardena, 1963; see also Roopnarine et al., 1997). If couples establish a household separate from the ancestral dwelling, they continue to maintain emotional ties to and share economic resources with cognate (functional relatedness).

Steeped in ancient Hindu and Muslim patriarchal traditions (e.g., *Laws of Manu*) and edicts in religious texts (e.g., *Upanishads, Ramayana, Mahabharata,* and *Qu'ran*), husband–wife roles and responsibilities remain bifurcated (Jayawardena, 1963; Mansingh & Mansingh, 1999; Mohammed, 1997; Rauf, 1974; Roopnarine et al., 1997; Schimmel, 1992). Husband–wife relationships, being authoritarian and androcentric, permit men the freedom to exercise control over financial and family affairs and to establish outside liaisons or have multiple wives in Muslim families (Deputy Imam Mohamed Nasar Hack, personal communication, October 2001). The father/husband is seen as the head of the household and is often the main economic provider. Men have strong ties to their father and brothers, though these relationships can be contentious and divisive. In Hindu families, the eldest son (*Shravan Kumar,* devoted son) is responsible for sacraments and is expected to care for his aging parents (Kakar, 1991; Mansingh & Mansingh, 1999; Rauf, 1974; Roopnarine et al., 1997). Even in the face of sociopolitical changes, wives in both Hindu and Muslim marriages are expected to be loyal to their husbands, and to be chiefly responsible for household chores and childrearing. This is tempered a bit by education and the socioeconomic status of families, but may become intensified in multigeneration households, in which the daughter-in-law may be required to show deference to her husband's parents. In the latter, younger women may openly refuse to obey the dictates of the mother-in-law. As one mother-in-law remarked to one of us, "You can't tell them young gals anything today."

Family boundaries are permeable, and fosterage and informal adoptions are not uncommon. Social relationships are hierarchically defined, and there are specific kinship terms that denote affinal ties (e.g., *aaji,* paternal grandmother; *aaja,* paternal grandfather). Relationships between family members, neighbors, and other social partners revolve around a good deal of conflict and solidarity (Jayawardena, 1963). Disagreements are usually resolved by achieving consensus around the notion that there are common threads that weave Indo Caribbean people together (e.g., *Jahagi-Bhai*—brotherhood of the boat—referring to the friendship cemented on the trip to become indentured servants; *matee,* we are one).

At the moment, the Indo Caribbean family is undergoing unprecedented changes. Higher rates of divorce, common-law unions, alcoholism, suicides, poverty, unemployment, movement away from core Hindu and Muslim values and beliefs, coupled with outward migration and an appetite for North American lifestyles, all conspire to undermine traditional modes of Indo Caribbean family life. Additionally, to the consternation of men, women are less tolerant of male dominance and irresponsibility (Kanhai,

1999). These challenges to patriarchal tendencies do not go unheeded. Women often pay a heavy psychological and economic price.

Religious Beliefs

After decades of steady decline in the ability to speak Hindi or Urdu, there has been a resurgence of interest on the part of religious leaders and a few educational organizations to resurrect these languages in the Hindu and Muslim communities, respectively. Insufficient background in these languages could make it difficult to convey and reinforce the tenets of religious beliefs and practices to younger generations. This aside, in both groups, religious practices have offered varying degrees of cohesion to family organization and the socialization of children. To be sure, within the two dominant branches of Hinduism in the Caribbean, *Arya Samaj* (reformists) and *Sanatan Dharma* (orthodox), there is adherence to religious observances (*Deepavali, Janam Ashtami, Holi, Ram Nouni, Shewratri*), and Hindu rituals are incorporated into births, marriages, and burials. Similarly, among Muslims there are observances such as *Ramadan* (fasting during the entire ninth months of the Islamic lunar year), *id al-fitr* (feast at the end of fasting) (Schimmel, 1992), *Eid-ul-Adha* (prayers, sacrifice, and philanthropy), some men make the *hajj* (the pilgrimage to Mecca), and religious beliefs set the stage for prayers at the birth of children, circumcision, marriage, and death (*Kalimah* prayers and *Kaba*—at death the face is turned to the right in the direction of Mecca; Deputy Imam Mohamed Nasar Hack, personal communication, October 2001).

Beliefs and Practices about Childrearing

Perhaps because Indo and African Caribbean families have lived adjacently in the Caribbean for so long, there is some overlap in their beliefs and practices about childrearing. For example, as in African Caribbean families, Indo Caribbean families engage in fosterage and raise children in extended kinship households with multiple caregivers. In addition, Indo Caribbean parents employ harsh discipline in childrearing. Having said this, there are beliefs and practices that do distinguish the two ethnic groups. Listed below are beliefs and practices, some of which may have had their origins in India but were transformed over time. Unless otherwise stated, they generally apply to both Hindu and Muslim families.

Parental Beliefs

1. Parents believe that older members of society should be accorded unilateral respect by children and younger adults. Politeness and manners are always expected and demanded, especially in the presence of elders.

2. In conjunction with physical punishment, parents believe in shaming the child, using threats (e.g., "The policeman will come for you") and negative comments (e.g., "You are a wicked or bad boy") to thwart behaviors deemed undesirable.

3. Largely unaware and void of childhood development information, parents believe that children should learn certain skills/practices without formal instruction. This should occur by watching others, as parents rarely engage in play or parent–child stimulation activities. Children are expected to get in line with adult routines.

4. Parents believe in and expect a strong allegiance to the family regardless of the circumstance and behavioral and social transgressions by individual members. Interdependence is stressed.

5. As in African Caribbean families, there are strong beliefs about men as the head of the family and the primary economic provider and women as nurturer and caregiver.

Parental Practices

1. Parents co-sleep with children and there are no formal feeding or sleeping routines; in Hindu families, children are massaged with oil starting on the sixth day after birth and regularly thereafter in the morning before a bath and again before bedtime;

social rules and expectations are relaxed during the early childhood years. In this vein, mothers generally follow the child's inclinations. To them, young children can do no wrong because they are *Bhagwan ke den* (a gift from God).

2. There are several rituals and practices that are performed during the child's life: in Hindu families, naming ceremony (*namakaran sanskar*), where, on the day of the birth, parents consult a Hindu priest, who after determining the astrological configurations of the child's birth, selects a letter that begins the child's name; head shaving (*mhool sanskar*) about 3 months after birth but usually before the first birthday and among older children when a parent dies; *nine-day* birth ceremony; and *Janew,* during which a child takes a spiritual leader and is under his tutelage (Pundit Artideo Sharma, personal communication, September 28, 2001). Parents may invite the help of a Pundit to *Jharee* (passing objects over the child seven times, while reciting a sacred mantra) the child if it is not feeling well or if someone casts an "evil eye" on it (Kahn, 1999); the mother and other caregivers may *Ouchee* the child with an elixir, usually made by sautéing pepper, garlic, and onion peels, that is then passed in a clockwise manner five times over the child's body (Pundit Artideo Sharma, personal communication, September 28, 2001). Among Muslim families, parents/adults recite *Azaam* (religious prayers) in the child's ears at birth and place a sweet substance, usually honey, in the child's mouth to symbolize the sweetness of the verses and life, shave the heads of both boys and girls on or before the seventh day after birth, and boys are circumcised on or before the seventh day if they are healthy (Deputy Imam Mohamed Nasar Hack, personal communication, October 2001).

3. Indo Caribbean parenting style is a mixture of extreme permissiveness and indulgence intertwined with harsh discipline and denigration. In this context, praise and rewards are rare; admonitions occur frequently. By the early school years there is a sudden shift from indulgence toward the expectation of academic independence and school success.

4. When they occur, public displays of affection may manifest themselves in the form of kissing, pinching, and grabbing the young child. This plummets as children get older, to the point where there are few if any attempts to hug or kiss them. Fathers maintain considerable physical and emotional distance from daughters.

5. Parents make tremendous sacrifices for their children, and they monitor and provide input into children's lives up to the time of marriage and beyond.

6. As indicated earlier, men's and women's roles are quite differentiated, and boys and girls are treated differently during socialization. Girls receive far more protection from parents than do boys.

Parent–Child Relationships—Strict and Distant Father, Responsible Mother

Drawing on a handful of ethnographic studies, parent–child relationships in Indo Caribbean families can be summarily described as situated within a patriarchal structure where mothers are indulgent and permissive and fathers are largely distant and strict. Starting in infancy through middle childhood, the East Indian mother and other women are primarily involved in caring for children and meeting their emotional needs. Indian mothers serve as a social bridge between children and fathers and other adult members of the society. The mother–son relationship may be characterized as a blend of subservience on the child's part and parental authority, while the mother-daughter relationship is governed by greater parental control and scrutiny (Jayawardena, 1963). Generally, boys and girls are raised under a tight system of gender differentiation.

Admittedly in the process of changing (Roopnarine et al., 1997; Wilson & Kposowa, 1994), fathers are minimally involved in caring (bathing, feeding, cleaning) for young children. Revered as an authority figure, fathers command respect (Jayawardena, 1963). They are the disciplinarians. As children get older, sons are expected to show deference to the father and avoid expressions of familiarity; girls are expected to remain subservient to the wishes of the father. A striking aspect of Indo Caribbean father–child relationship is the emotional distance that most fathers maintain toward children; familiarity is discouraged (Jayawardena, 1963).

Parent–Child Relationships and Child Development Outcomes

There is a paucity of data on parent–child relationships in Indo Caribbean families and on cognitive and social development in children. We can intuit from studies conducted in other cultures (Hetherington & Stanley-Hagan, 1997; McLoskey, Figueredo, & Koss, 1995; Sternberg, Lamb, & Dawud-Noursi, 1996) that family instability due to marital discord and dissolution, increased alcoholism, domestic violence, and harsh socioeconomic conditions would place Indo Caribbean children at significant risk for the development of mental health and academic problems (Wilson, Williams, & Williams, 1992). In Trinidad, alcoholism and suicides are more prevalent in the Indo than the African Caribbean population (Sharpe, 1997), and in Guyana far too many adolescents and young parents commit suicide. Adolescent suicides are often provoked by interpersonal conflicts with parents or spouses. To speculate, intergenerational conflicts are bound to escalate as Indo Caribbean children insist on less austere methods of treatment from parents or show open defiance of absolute parental authority over their lives. A more complete analysis of the etiology of mental health problems and academic performance in Indo Caribbean children must await research data, however.

POLICIES AND CARIBBEAN FAMILIES

In focusing on policies and Caribbean families we concentrate on three that we deemed the most important for the welfare of the family: domestic violence, paternity and child support, and physical punishment. Beginning with domestic violence, several Caribbean countries have passed laws (see Jamaica's Domestic Violence Act, passed in 1995; Trinidad's Domestic Violence Act, passed in 1992), to protect women against domestic violence. These laws, however, are often ignored. Women are at the mercy of a male-dominated legal system, and there are few shelters and counseling services available to them. Sadly, in the absence of these services and given conditions of poverty, women and children in abusive relationships have few alternatives, and most experience persistent violence from men. The situation is not better when it comes to child abuse. Although most countries have some legal standard for child endangerment, there needs to be better attention paid to the welfare of children through a well-developed social service system that stands up for the legal rights of children. Simultaneously, parenting and counseling programs would help to attenuate harsh treatment of children. Lastly, as indicated earlier, in common-law relationships women are offered little legal protection. Laws that hold men accountable for the economic support of wives/partners and children and parenting programs for men such as Fatherhood Incorporated in Kingston, Jamaica (Brown et al., 1997), would have far-reaching implications for the overall welfare of the Caribbean family.

SUMMARY

English-speaking Caribbean families assume diverse structural configurations. Among African Caribbean families, there is the tendency to establish common-law unions before marriage. Within both ethnic groups, gender roles follow a traditional pattern and boys and girls are treated accordingly. Multiple caregivers who adopt parenting styles that range from authoritarian, punitive control to permissiveness raise children. There are symmetries in parental beliefs and practices between the two ethnic groups in the areas of multiple caregiving, respect for older members of society, roles of mothers and fathers, discipline/punishment, and display of affection. As might be expected, because of their different histories of cultural traditions and religious beliefs, there are childhood and adult socialization rituals that differentiate the two groups. With the exception of Jamaica, historically intermarriages between the two groups considered here have been discouraged but are increasing (see Kempadoo,

1999, for a discussion of *Dogla,* offspring of mixed parenting). Unfortunately, we could not find reliable statistics on these families ("mixed race" is an amorphous term used to designate children born to different ethnic groups) and there is little research on them.

What is clear from our consideration of family life in the English-speaking Caribbean is that socioeconomic conditions, population movements, intermarriage, and cultural contacts with people and customs in the postindustrialized world all play an essential role in the continuing evolution of the way families meet the needs of individual members. Cataloging these changes and their meaning for childhood development outcomes in the Caribbean must be a strong priority of researchers.

REFERENCES

Allen, A. (1985). Psychological dependency among students in a "cross-roads" culture. *West Indian Medical Journal, 34,* 123–127.

Anderson, S., & Payne, M. (1994). Corporal punishment in elementary education: Views of Barbadian school children. *Child Abuse and Neglect, 18,* 377–386.

Arnold, E. (1982). The use of corporal punishment in childrearing in the West Indies. *Child Abuse and Neglect, 6,* 141–145.

Baumrind, D. (1996). The discipline controversy revisited. *Family Relations, 45,* 405–414.

Baumrind, D., Larzelere, R. E., & Cowan, P. A. (2002). Ordinary physical punishment: Is it harmful? *Psychological Bulletin, 128,* 580–589.

Brodber, E. (1975). *A study of yards in the city of Kingston.* Mona, Jamaica: Institute for Social and Economic Research, University of the West Indies.

Brodber, E. (1986). Afro-Jamaican women at the turn of the century. *Social and Economic Studies,* (Special Issue: Women in the Caribbean Project, Pt. 2), *35,* 3.

Brown, J., Anderson, P., & Chevannes, B. (1993). *The contribution of Caribbean men to the family.* Report for the International Development Centre, Canada, Caribbean Child Development Centre, Mona: University of the West Indies.

Brown, J., Newland, A., Anderson, P., & Chevannes, B. (1997). In J. L. Roopnarine & J. Brown (Eds.), *Caribbean families: Diversity among ethnic groups* (pp. 85–113). Norwood, NJ: Ablex.

Chao, R. (1994). Beyond parental control and authoritarian parenting style: Understanding Chinese parenting through the cultural notion of training. *Child Development, 65,* 1111–1119.

Chevannes, B. (1994). *Rastafari: Roots and ideology.* Syracuse, NY: Syracuse University Press.

Chevannes, B. (1998a). A new approach to Rastafari. In B. Chevannes (Ed.), *Rastafari and other African-Caribbean worldviews* (pp. 20–42). New Brunswick, NJ: Rutgers University Press.

Chevannes, B. (1998b). Introducing the native religions of Jamaica. In B. Chevannes (Ed.), *Rastafari and other African-Caribbean worldviews* (pp. 1–19). New Brunswick, NJ: Rutgers University Press.

Clarke, E. (1957). *My mother who fathered me: A study of family in three selected communities in Jamaica.* London: George Allen & Unwin.

Crawford-Brown, C. (1997). The impact of parent–child socialization on the development of conduct disorder in Jamaican male adolescents. In J. L. Roopnarine & J. Brown (Eds.), *Caribbean families: Diversity among ethnic groups* (pp. 205–222). Norwood, NJ: Ablex.

Crawford-Brown, C. (1999). *Who will survive our children? The plight of the Jamaican child in the 1990s.* Kingston, Jamaica: Canoe Press, University of the West Indies.

Curtin, P. (1975). Measuring the Atlantic Slave Trade. In S. L. Engerman & E. D. Genevose (Eds.), *Race and slavery in the western hemisphere: Quantitative studies* (pp. 107–128). Princeton, NJ: Princeton University Press.

Dann, G. (1987). *The Barbadian male: Sexual beliefs and attitudes.* London and Bassingstoke: Macmillan.

Deerr, N. (1949–1950). *The history of sugar.* 2 vols. London: Chapman & Hall.

Flinn, M. (1992). Paternal care in a Caribbean village. In B. Hewlett (Ed.), *Father–child relations: Cultural and biosocial contexts* (pp. 57–84). New York: Aldine de Gruyter.

Flinn, M. (1995). Childhood stress and family environment. *Current Anthropology, 36,* 854–866.

Foner, N. (Ed.). (2001). *Islands in the City: West Indian migration to New York.* Berkeley: University of California Press.

lies: Diversity among ethnic groups (pp. 223–242). Norwood, NJ: Ablex.

Samaroo, B. (2000). "Chinese and Indian Coolie" voyages to the Caribbean. *Journal of Caribbean Studies, 14,* 3–24.

Schimmel, A. (1992). *Islam: An introduction.* Albany, NY: SUNY Press.

Senior, O. (1991). *Working miracles: Women's lives in the English-speaking Caribbean.* Institute for Social and Economic Research (ISER), University of the West Indies, Barbados. London, James Curry, and Bloomington, Indiana University Press.

Sharpe, J. (1997). Mental health issues and family socialization in the Caribbean. In J. L. Roopnarine & J. Brown (Eds.), *Caribbean families: Diversity among ethnic groups* (pp. 259–273). Norwood, NJ: Ablex.

Skinner, E. P. (1955). *Ethnic interaction in a British Guiana rural community: A study.* Unpublished doctoral dissertation. Columbia University, New York.

Sigel, I., & McGillicuddy-DeLisis (2002). Parental beliefs are cognitions: The dynamic belief systems model. In M. H. Bornstein (Ed.), *Handbook of parenting* (Vol. 3, 2nd ed.). Mahwah, NJ: Erlbaum.

Singh, S. (2000). Ethnic associations and the development of political consciousness in Indian diaspora communities: The Indo-Caribbean experience in Canada. *Wadabagei, 2,* 38–75.

Smith, R. T. (1996). *The matrifocal family: Power, pluralism, and politics.* London: Routledge.

Sternberg, K. J., Lamb, M. E., & Dawud-Noursi, S. (1996). *Understanding domestic violence and its effects: Making sense of divergent reports and perspectives.* Bethesda, MD: National Institute of Child Health and Human Development.

Super, C., & Harkness, S. (1997). The cultural structuring of child development. In J. Berry, P. Dasen, T. Saraswathi (Eds.), *Handbook of cross-cultural psychology. Vol. 2: Basic processes and human development* (pp. 1–39). Boston: Allyn & Bacon.

Thompson, P., & Bauer, E. (2000). Jamaican transnational families: Points of pain and sources of resilience. *Wadabagei, 2,* 1–36.

Turner, V. (1969). *The ritual process: Structure and anti-structure.* Chicago: Aldine.

Turner, H. A., & Finkelhor, D. (1996). Corporal punishment as a stressor among youth. *Journal of Marriage and the Family, 58,* 155–156.

United Nations (2001). *World population prospects: 2000 revision, Volume 2: Sex and Age.* New York.

Vervotec, S. (1991). East Indians and anthropologists: A critical review. *Social and Economic Studies, 40,* 133–169.

Vervotec, S. (1995). Hindus in Trinidad and Britain: Ethnic religion, reification, and the politics of public space. In P. van der Veer (Ed.), *Nation and migration: The politics of space in the south Indian diaspora* (pp. 132–156). Philadelphia: University of Pennsylvania Press.

Williams, E. (1966). *British historians and the West Indies.* New York: Africana.

Williams, E. (1970). *From Columbus to Castro: The history of the Caribbean 1492–1969.* New York: Vintage Books.

Wilson, L. C. (1989). *Family and structure and dynamics in the Caribbean: An examination of residential and relational matritocality in Guyana.* Unpublished doctoral dissertation, University of Michigan, Ann Arbor.

Wilson, L. C., & Kposowa, A. J. (1994). Paternal involvement with children: Evidence from Guyana. *International Journal of the Sociology of the Family, 24,* 23–42.

Wilson, L. C., Williams, D., & Williams, K. (1992). Family stucture and mental health in Guyana. *Anthropology, 10,* 117–126.

World Bank Atlas (2000). The World Bank, Washington, D.C.

Yawney, C. (1999). Only visitors here: Representing Rastafari into the 21st century. In J. W. Pulis (Ed.), *Religion, diaspora and cultural identity: A reader in the Anglophone Caribbean* (pp. 153–181). Amsterdam, The Netherlands: Gordon & Breach.

CHAPTER 19

FAMILIES IN BRAZIL

L.-A. REBHUN
Yale University

Brazil's international image, shaped by tourist advertising and journalists' accounts, includes the sexy icons of Rio de Janeiro's *Carnaval* and beach scenes, the misery of urban slum dwellers and landless rural workers, the tragedy of children living and working on the streets, and the environmental impact of forest burning and gold mining in the Amazon. Brazil also has been described as hosting a "cult of the family" (Wagley, 1971, p. 167), a nation in which family groups dominate social life and politics. Recent scholarly work on the history, sociology, and anthropology of the family in Brazil has shown both breakdowns and resilience as massive social and economic change transforms family structures.

In this chapter, I review some of the major issues involving the family in Brazil, including extended families, changes in forms of marriage, transformation in gender roles, adoption and abandonment of children, and developments in reproductive and child health issues. My information comes partly from established social science literature, and also from my own research on family issues in Northeast Brazil, where I have studied child survival (Nations & Rebhun, 1988a, 1988b, 1996) and couple formation (Rebhun, 1994, 1995, 1999a, 1999b). At the time of my research (1988–1990), shifts in gender roles galvanized the country as a whole, the result not only of an organized feminist movement, but also of political and economic changes following World War I and the consequent impact on both legal and popular concepts of marriage, the family, and the role of women (Besse, 1996). The contemporary situation of families in Brazil reflects this ongoing transformation.

Sociologist Jeni Vaitsman describes the contemporary Brazilian family as "flexible and plural" (1994). To understand contemporary families in Brazil requires comprehension of their historical development, their demographic situation with particular attention to both social and regional inequality and rapid social change, and important cultural complexes around gender roles, especially concepts of male honor and female respectability. And finally, phenomena such as the burgeoning urban population of impoverished single mothers and children separated from families, and increasing diversity in gender roles and sexual identities, need to be understood in the context of major changes in the family in the last hundred years. In this chapter, I attempt to give the reader a basic introduction to these topics.

GEOGRAPHIC AND DEMOGRAPHIC ASPECTS OF BRAZIL

Contemporary anthropologists, sociologists, and historians take the enormous regional, ethnic, and economic diversity of Brazil into account when characterizing aspects of the family. Comprising 3.3 million square miles, Portuguese-speaking Brazil constitutes 48 percent of the landmass of South America and could almost contain all of Europe (Schneider, 1996, p. 1). Its twenty-six states can be divided into several regions (most commonly South, Southeast, Center-West, Northeast, and North), each with its own history, dialect, and local customs. In addition, Brazil is one of the most sharply divided countries in the world by class, and calculations show that social inequality has increased in the last twenty years (Nations & Rebhun, 1996; Pastoré, 1979).

Sources of diversity in family forms include geographic, economic, ethnic, religious, and demographic factors. Southern Brazil, home to famous cities such as Rio de Janeiro and São Paulo, has predominated politically and economically since 1889. The state of São Paulo alone has some 34 million inhabitants—as much as the entire population of Argentina (Schneider, 1996, p. 4). Brasília may be the capital of the country, but São Paulo boasts the nation's stock exchange, primary port, and commercial and industrial centers (Schneider, 1996, pp. 5–7), while Rio de Janeiro State, with a population of 13.2 million (more than Denmark and Switzerland combined) boasts of the country's primary cultural resources: museums, universities, and a natural setting that draws tourists from around the world (Schneider, 1996, p. 10).

The South has a higher percentage of persons of European descent than other regions; in addition, the bulk of Japanese Brazilians live in São Paulo, constituting the largest population of Japanese descent outside of Japan. Brazil's middle class is concentrated in the capital cities of Rio de Janeiro and São Paulo and neighboring cities, and to a lesser extent, other state capitals, especially in the South. Northeast Brazil, in contrast, until 1888 an area of plantation slavery, remains sharply divided by class, and is home to the bulk of the population of African descent. Instability in the Brazilian national economy complicates the process of bringing this region into the market-driven global economy. The past thirty years have seen the largest rural to urban migration in Brazil's history; one in five Brazilians migrated to cities between 1960 and 1970 (Perlman, 1976, p. 5), and by 1980 the Northeast had shifted from majority rural to majority urban (de Araujo 1987, p. 167), with a major impact on family forms as detailed below. In addition, Northeasterners, especially men, have streamed to Southern cities seeking employment. Some 3,000,000 live in shantytowns in Rio de Janeiro, and a further 3,600,000 live in slums alongside São Paulo's glittering highrises (Schneider, 1996, pp. 4–12). The emigration of men from the Northeast has had an impact on family forms there, skewing the sex ratio and creating greater competition among women for mates; family forms of impoverished Northeasterners in the South reflect the influences of urban poverty including nucleation of families, matrifocality, and circulation of children among loosely related households (as described below).

Brazil has large populations of native descent, including both people of mixed Native, European, and/or African descent, and indigenous people still living in hunting, gathering, and horticultural tribal groups. Although the government restricts access to protected tribal reserves, a 1996 law allowing land claims in Native territories has opened reserves to economic development, often against the wishes of tribal leaders (Rocha, 1997). The sometimes-violent conflicts among Natives, gold miners, forest-clearing farmers, and rubber tappers have increased. Lawyers and politicians continue to battle over the place of Native Brazilians in Brazilian societies; however, academically the study of Natives constitutes a separate specialty. Tribal kinship systems do not form part of how scholars conceptualize the Brazilian family in general.

Religiously, Brazilians have displayed an open and enthusiastic embrace of spirituality of many types, a country as catholic in the sense of diversity as Catholic in terms of the Roman church. As in the Caribbean, forms of African religious practice, including veneration of *orixas* or African deities, and practices of spirit mediumship and magico-religious rituals have coexisted with the folk Catholic cult of the saints since the early days of settlement. Forms of the religion including Umbanda, Candomblé, and Macumba vary in their practice and their relative degree of formal organization. Large-scale immigration from Asia has brought Shinto, Taoist, Hindu, and Buddhist practitioners to Brazil, along with Muslims from the Middle East and Jews from Europe. Religious practices from these groups mix and match freely with Christian ideas and a great variety of types of mystical practices ranging from Kardecism to New Age spirituality.

In addition, such European Protestant sects as Lutherans and Anglicans have historically had small numbers of adherents in a mostly Roman Catholic country. Evangelical Protestant groups of U.S. provenance, such as the Jehovah's Witnesses, Assemblies of God, and Seventh-Day Adventists, as well as the Latter Day Saints (LDS) church (Mormons) have enjoyed great success in proselytizing, especially among the poor. The homegrown evangelical Universal Church of the Kingdom of God is the fastest growing of these sects in Brazil. From 1990 to 1992, 710 new Evangelical churches opened doors in Rio de Janeiro alone, compared to one new Catholic Church (Rocha, 1997, p. 29), and an estimated 35 million Brazilians have converted to Evangelical Protestantism starting in the 1970s (Schneider, 1996, p. 189).

Pentecostal and Evangelical sects and the LDS church, despite their considerable theological differences, share an explicit emphasis on what they call "clean living" and "family values," including not only prohibition of intoxicant use but also a focus on premarital chastity, monogamous love marriage, and child education. In many ways, such sects serve as a corrective to some of the excesses of machismo: women may join in the hopes of getting their men to stop drinking alcohol and chasing other women, men join hoping the churches will give them the structure they need to control their own behavior (cf. Brusco, 1995). Although these churches are associated with the political right in the United States and may be considered antifeminist, in many ways they respond to women's concerns about male behavior, and can serve as a form of empowerment for women (Brusco, 1995; Griffith, 1997). There is some anecdotal evidence that infant mortality rates may be slightly lower among impoverished evangelical families in Brazil than among Catholics, but more research needs to be done to see how conversion affects family well-being, as well as whether it makes a difference if women convert, if men convert, or if both members of the couple adhere to these churches' strictures.

Brazil's economic situation also strongly affects families. We may think of the family primarily as a social and emotional unit, but production, consumption, and distribution also form a basic part of family function. Transition to an urban, industrial, cash economy changes the nature of the economic equation that underlies family units. Wage labor can fragment family units into groups of individual earners, although low wages and high un- and underemployment in the lower classes keep extended family units interdependent. In the upper classes, issues of property inheritance also bolster generational connection. Brazil's transition from a largely agrarian, export-oriented economy to a major world economic power has buffeted families of all classes with a series of sharp economic shifts.

From 1967 through 1974, economists described what they called an "economic miracle" of high growth (Skidmore & Smith, 1997, p. 185) that modernized Brazil's economy while increasing its international debt, sparking cycles of currency instability, and exacerbating the differences among the regions. In the Northeast, migration has brought thousands to swollen cities, transforming the kinship-based small-town rural life of the recent past to adjust to life among urban strangers. The North, including much of the Amazon, has seen increased deforestation, an influx of peasants seeking land, gold, or both, and an increasingly visible and active Native Brazilian movement. All of these changes have influenced the way people think about the nature of the family, of marriage, of sexuality, and cohabitation, and of childrearing, as well as their abilities to live out their ideas of proper family life.

The 2000 national census estimates Brazil's total population at 169.5 million, showing an annual growth rate of 1.63 percent, a drop from the 2.48 percent of the 1970s (Reuters, December 21, 2000). UNICEF estimates that 59,861,000 Brazilians have not yet seen their 18th birthday. About 4 in 100 children nationwide do not reach their fifth birthday, a total of about 134,000 child deaths a year (UNICEF, 2001), although this represents a 30 percent drop in infant mortality over the last thirty years (Reuters, December 12, 2000). Brazil also shows a marked rate of rural to urban migration, with 81.2 percent of the population now residing in cities, as compared to 75.6 percent in 1991 (a figure more comparable to urbanization percentages in most of Europe) (Reuters, December 21, 2000).

Brazil's bottom-heavy population pyramid means that issues involving children and youth take a higher national priority than geriatric concerns, which affect a much smaller proportion of the population. Brazil did not experience the baby boom of countries more directly involved in World War II, so children and teens constitute the largest single demographic group, unlike the United States, where people in their forties and fifties predominate, and where those entering their eighties are the fastest-growing demographic group. During my fieldwork in a small city in the Northeastern interior, I found that many women began their reproductive lives in their early to mid-teens and that people's ideas about youth and old age were pushed forward in the life course earlier than I was accustomed to, having grown up in the U.S. middle class. For example, if a woman had a daughter at age 15 or 16, and that daughter also had a child before age 17, the woman would be a grandmother in her mid- to late thirties. The combination of early childbearing and the wear and tear of hard physical labor, frequent illness, short life expectancies, and the many sorrows of deprivation made women in their forties old before their time.

SCHOLARLY APPROACHES TO THE FAMILY IN BRAZIL

Although most empirical studies of the Brazilian family focus on the poor and working classes (Bilac, 1995, p. 46), the field remains dominated by ideas derived from historical study of elites. A small but growing literature focuses on the middle classes (see especially Albuquerque, 1977; Boschi, 1986; O'Dougherty, 2002; Saes, 1977, 1985). Middle-class members also increasingly buy and read self-help and personal-confessional literature to help them understand their own family lives and their attempts to attain happiness. Until the 1970s most historians of the family in Brazil, following the seminal work of Gilberto Freyre (1933), characterized the Brazilian family as universally patriarchal. Freyre's analysis, based on considerations of slave-owning plantation families, painted a portrait of a male-dominated system in which a single legitimate wife provided inheriting, white offspring, while one or more enslaved women provided illegitimate children. Freyre also emphasized the absolute power that patriarchs held over family members. However, by the late 1960s, both historical and contemporary studies began to show diversity in family forms in Brazil (Samara, 1983; Samara & Costa, 1997).

In addition, scholars began to reconsider the nature and impact of the type of family group described by Freyre, seeing it as more loosely constructed than he had, and examining in detail how it varied historically among social classes, and how it changed over the course of Brazilian history. Although it is now clear that Brazilian families are not now and never were rigidly patriarchal, still Freyre's model and more recent modifications of it remain important to understanding Brazilian families from colonial times through the present. In addition, the image of the patriarchal family remains an important part of how many Brazilians understand their own history, and evaluate the nature of the contemporary family.

THE CLASSIC PATRIARCHAL FAMILY MODEL

The historical enslavement first of Native Brazilians and then of Africans, and the creation of a racially stratified society following slavery (Schwartz, 1985, p. 245), strongly affected patterns of marriage, love affairs, and family structure in Brazil. From the beginning, Portuguese colonist men practiced male authoritarianism, had sexual access to low-status women, and confined high-status females to the nuclear family dwelling (Bruschini, 1990, pp. 61–62). They also showed a preference for forming families with native and enslaved women, especially given the small numbers of Portuguese women who immigrated to the colony (Figueiredo, 1993; Russell-Wood, 1978; Soeiro, 1978). Ideally, upper-class women were supposed to leave home only three times: for baptism, for marriage, and for burial (Russell-Wood, 1978, p. 66). Although this ideal was rarely achieved in practice, it was then, and remains today, an important image of how high-status women ought to behave.

In the upper classes, practices such as arranged cousin marriage helped keep property within the same extended family over generations (Schwartz, 1985, pp. 289–291). Historically, wealthy families took the form of a *parentela* or large, loosely defined bilateral kindred uniting people related by blood, by marriage, and by social fiction, as when household servants, adopted and fostered children, and tenant farmers blended into the family group (Wagley, 1971, pp. 167–169). The Portuguese word *agregado,* defined in most dictionaries as "tenant farmer," can also be used to describe an adopted or fostered child. This etymology reflects the common historical situation of landowners having biological ties to servants and tenants, as men of the household fathered children with subordinate women. Such children were fostered into the main household or, in rural areas, given some portion of the land to farm on the periphery of the main holdings. Nonrelated children of the lower classes were also fostered in better-off households (Candido, 1951; Wagley, 1971).

CONTEMPORARY FORMS OF EXTENDED FAMILY

Although many writers place this *parentela* system in the past, I found during fieldwork in 1988–1990 that it remained an important aspect of family formation in the rural interior Northeast in my research, and not only among the wealthy but also among small landholders as well. Various forms of extended family were very important, even among the urban poor in this region. Extended family affected patterns of couple formation, as the area began a transition from semiarranged cousin marriage to love marriage.

People I spoke with in the small, interior city of Caruaru described the idea of young people marrying or cohabiting with nonrelatives of their own choosing, on the basis of personal attraction, as very new and very urban. Young people exclaimed about how their parents and grandparents had married strangers (*desconhecidos*), by which they meant that brides and grooms had little chance to get to know one another privately under the old regime of chaperoned courtship. Older people complained to me that young people nowadays marry strangers, by which they meant persons unknown to their families. The very recent shift from *parentela*-based rural society to an urban society of friends and neighbors had changed the meaning of the word "stranger" from an emphasis on people unknown to the family group to one on people unknown to the individual.

Most couples older than about 40 years of age, as well as younger couples I interviewed in rural villages, had married cousins and maintained social relationships mainly within the *parentela*. In addition, most young men spent the majority of their time with a *turma* (social group) composed of their brothers, brothers-in-law, and cousins, and most women socialized mainly with mothers, sisters, cousins, and female in-laws. In the urban working class, many women tended to have children by more than one man. In an extension of the *parentela*, their social networks included the female relatives of several baby-fathers as well as those of their current boyfriend.

Many poor and working-class households contain children who were not born to the women of the house. These include grandchildren, godchildren, cousins, nieces, nephews, and other relatives, as well as children adopted from unrelated families, and children fostered for purposes of servitude. Lower-class and rural children commonly shift among more than one household during their minority (Candido, 1951; Fonseca 1995; Hecht, 1998). Just as cohabiting women may call their live-in boyfriends "husband" (*marido*), people call foster mothers and children the Brazilian words for mother (*mãe*), son (*filho*), and daughter (*filha*).

In addition, godparentage constitutes a common way to extend or enhance family relationships in Catholic families. Godparents, who formally declare their relationship with a child during baptism and occasionally other important events, have a responsibility to support and guide their godchildren, and take on their custody should the parents not be able to raise them. The relationship between parents and their *compadres* and *comadres* (children's godparents) is a major kinship category. *Compadres* and *comadres* have incest prohibitions between them, must treat one another with respect, and in general enjoy a sibling-like relationship. People can use godparenthood to intensify an existing kinship relationship or to create a new one with an unrelated person, such as a neighbor or patron.

It is also not uncommon for poor women to foster children, including not only their nieces and nephews or grandchildren, but also the children of boyfriends or former boyfriends with other women, and even the children of neighbors. Here we see a looser, more flexible, and less patriarchially defined form of extended family developing out of the *parentela*.

In the state capital Recife, nonrelative friendships were common, and the rural extended family struck people as comically old-fashioned, part of the backward way their rural ancestors lived. Urban people regarded cousin marriage in particular as embarrassingly hillbilly-ish. And in southern cities such as Rio de Janeiro and São Paulo, the classic *parentela* seems even farther back in time, and cousin marriage quite foreign. However, the matrifocal extended family remains strong, especially in the lower classes, reflected in women's strong social networks, and in practices such as informal fosterage of children. Like the *parentela*, this family form reflects the consequences of male sexual liberty with its production of extramarital children and division of women into separate categories of legitimate, respectable, and illegitimate, nonrespectable.

HOUSE AND STREET

Scholars have written a portrait of Latin American cultures divided by gender into complementary but conflicting segments. In particular, theorists have noted far-reaching consequences of the shift from agrarian to urban economies on gender roles, because of the impact of agrarian transformation on the gendered basis of economic cooperation in the household (Bustos, 1980; Kelly & Sassen, 1995; Pearlman, 1984; Roldan, 1988; Rothstein, 1983; Stevens, 1973).

Roberto da Matta first formalized the discussion of house and street as complementary gendered spheres in Brazil, with "house" (*casa*) being the domain of women and "street" (*rua*) that of men (1985). Of course men live in houses together with women, and women move about towns and cities on streets, so the two spheres overlap. But conceptual differences partly contiguous with the physical architecture of buildings and roads intertwine with ideas of how to be a proper man or woman. Here, the house, characterized by familiarity, hospitality, love, and honorable dealing, becomes the realm of women, children, and domestic servants (da Matta, 1985, pp. 41–42); the street, where individuals fight for dominance, the realm of men, violence, and exploitation. The relationships of individual couples form a microcosm of the dynamic complementarity of house and street in the broader society, and the family, located in the house, becomes a refuge from the impersonality of the street (da Matta, 1985, p. 47).

House and street, of course, are urban categories; in rural areas architecture and land-use patterns differ, and women's and men's work patterns include more cooperation, less division, and less direct competition than in the urban wage economy. Concepts of the division between house and street are also influenced by the 1880s hygiene movement, which promoted the love-based, monogamous nuclear family as conducive to social order and political progress (Parker, 1991, pp. 78–83). People redefined marriage as a relationship of love licensed by the state, and the formation and maintenance of a loving, hygienic nuclear family became an act of patriotism within that state (Costa, 1989, p. 63). However, legal and religious marriage (legally separate in Brazil) remained uncommon in rural areas, where both clergy and civil registrars rarely appeared, and the urban lower classes practiced cohabitation more commonly than marriage.

By the middle of the nineteenth century, upper-class Brazilians were contracting what Muriel Nazzari has called a "new marriage bargain" (Nazzari, 1991, p. 131). As families shifted from units of production to units of consumption, men, as the major public producers and managers of family consumption, gained in economic power over women, especially in the middle and upper classes (Nazzari, 1991, p. 148). In the emerging Brazilian urban society of the time, deep racial and class stratifications kept darker-skinned lower-class women from access to legitimate marriage, continuing to highlight the importance of European appearance, premarital virginity, and legitimate marriage to respectability. Despite periods of accelerated economic mobility (Pastoré, 1979), Brazil retains a deeply felt division between respectable and nonrespectable women, defined by color, class, and sexual history, and many people still associate legal marriage with modernity, urban living, the middle class, progress, patriotism, and female respectability.

Confinement of women to the home and dominance of men over the streets have never been absolute, especially among the poor, where women frequently head households and work as major breadwinners. Brazilian anthropologist Klass Woortman usefully describes the *favelados* (shantytown dwellers) of his research as holding simultaneously an ideal model of the proper family in which a male breadwinner supports a wife and children at home, and what he calls a *modelo da praxis* (practice model) adapted to the exigencies of poverty (Woortman, 1987, p. 59).

In the practice model adopted by poor families, the boundaries between house and street blur, and some women adroitly manipulate concepts of domestic virtue to justify and lend moral weight to their political and economic activities outside the family home. Issues around confinement of women to the house are strongest in the working classes. Here, where tension between men's actual and expected economic power is greatest, shutting the women away in the home in imitation of popular images of the white plantation wife of old becomes symbolically important.

MIDDLE-CLASS FAMILIES IN BRAZIL

The Brazilian middle class has three main origins: some descend from immigrants who came to the country with education and/or resources that kept them economically above the laboring classes but could not equal the very wealthy; others descend from small farmers whose entrepreneurial acumen prompted them to buy up properties, arrange carefully chosen marriages for their children, and thereby achieve an economic status higher than their origins; and a third group reflects downward mobility of descendants of large land- or business owners who lost land or failed at business. This last group constitutes a higher percentage of the Brazilian middle class than of the middle class in the United States, for example, reflecting the impact of downward mobility in economically unstable Brazil in contrast to the economic opportunity that is such a hallmark of the United States' international image (Hansen, 1977).

Middle classes can be distinguished from the poor and working classes not only by economic accumulation, but also by educational attainment, professional rather than manual labor, and an orientation toward ostentatious consumption of goods (O'Dougherty, 2002; Owensby, 1994). They have fewer material resources than the wealthy classes, often also have not been prosperous as long, and live more off earned income than those whose ancestors retained large landed estates and noble surnames. Middle classes in Brazil demonstrate their status through education, manners, house size and decoration, clothing quality and style, leisure activities such as vacation travel, and enjoyment of expensive sports such as tennis, golf, or skiing, as well as employment of servants. People often see the difference between middle and working classes in color terms: people of greater means are more likely to consider themselves white than people of similar appearance but more modest assets (O'Dougherty, 2002).

Families and gender roles in the Brazilian middle classes have been profoundly affected by influences from the United States and Western and Southern Europe, as well as by a national feminist movement, itself taking inspiration from both U.S. and international feminism. Of necessity, poor and working-class women have always worked outside

the home, but as mentioned above, Brazilians have long seen keeping women secluded in chaperoned isolation within the home as an important marker of status. However, feminists have promulgated the idea that working outside the home can be a source of personal satisfaction as well as economic independence for women, and larger numbers of middle- and upper-class women participate in the extradomestic world through both volunteer and remunerated work. In addition, greater numbers of middle- and upper-class parents insist on university and professional training for their daughters than in the past, and opportunities for women to rise to positions of power in both business and political circles have increased. Political activism has led to legal changes bringing greater awareness of issues of rape, sexual harassment, and sexual emancipation for women (Besse, 1996; Westfried, 1997).

Middle-class women in Brazil increasingly hold university degrees and expect professional attainment, have enjoyed international travel, especially to the United States,[1] speak more than one language, and insist on equality with men not only in the public arena but in the intimacy of the family as well. These attainments and expectations are in direct conflict with conservative, patriarchal attitudes, and achievement of the aims of equality remain uneven (Westfried, 1997, p. 27). Alex Huxley Westfried, in a comparison of U.S. and Brazilian middle-class families (1997), finds that what he calls "family democracy" is a newer idea in Brazil than in the United States, and conflicts more strongly with the deep-seated patriarchal ideal. In addition, the Brazilian family is less nucleated than that of the United States, and the interests and opinions of extended family members affect the aspirations of younger women, who may face opposition not only from conservative husbands but also from fathers, uncles, and in-laws, including especially mothers-in-law looking out for the interests of their married sons. On the other hand, the availability of household servants makes issues of who will do housework and how to provide childcare when the mother works outside the home less contentious (Westfried, 1997). Middle- and upper-class women can rely on the labor of working-class women rather than demanding domestic labor from their husbands as in the United States. Many of these domestic servants must leave their own children at home to work in middle-class homes, and return from their labors only to clean their own homes and cook for their own families.

Brazilians are more likely than families in the United States to have three generations living at home, and to retain even sick or disabled elderly in the family home rather than institutionalize them (Westfried, 1997, pp. 35–36). Young adults are less likely than those in the United States to leave the family home to attend college, and more likely to live in their parents' home until marriage. Contemporary women in both the middle and lower classes increasingly reject multiple childbearing in favor of having one or two children (Dalsgard, 2000; Westfried, 1997). Middle-class women also increasingly both marry and bear children at older ages than in the past, and engage in more sexual experimentation before marriage than their mothers (Westfried, 1997), whereas lower-class women continue to bear children young, even as young as the early preteens.

Female sterilization is among the most popular forms of birth control in Brazil: just over 40 percent of married women in Brazil were sterilized in 1996, according to a national survey. Although sterilizations were not authorized by the national Public Health Service before 1997, they were often performed at the same time as caesarian sections (also very common in Brazil) for poor women and became popular as an alternative to birth control pills and clandestine, illegal abortion. The practice remains controversial, with some critics seeing racist motives and others concerned about the use of sterilization in women as young as their early twenties. In addition, it is not clear how sterilization intersects with lingering high infant mortality rates in some areas, how many poor women who undergo sterilization realize that the procedure is irreversible, and to what extent women may be coerced into having tubal ligations by their doctors (Dalsgard, 2000, pp. 3–9). Sterilization has contributed to a drop in birthrates, and a shift from the

traditional large Catholic family of the past to an ideal family with two to three children per couple. High infant mortality lingers in focal areas such as urban shantytowns. The extent to which maternal behavior both responds to and possibly contributes to it remains controversial (Scheper-Hughes, 1984, 1985, 1992). The recent drop in infant mortality, however, suggests the primacy of economic and hygienic reasons for the mortality over the maternal neglect thesis (Nations & Rebhun, 1988b).

Another major change that has strongly affected marital relations in middle-class Brazil is the legalization of divorce in 1977, which allowed women to escape unhappy or abusive marriages (an earlier law in 1962 allowed women greater freedom to own property and manage money without needing spousal permission). The impact of liberalization of marital law was less in the lower classes, because they less frequently marry legally. However, Brazilian women contend to a greater extent than U.S. women with open infidelity by their husbands, and the "other woman" remains a well-established institution despite erosions of patriarchal privilege in other domains. Although middle-class women can threaten to divorce errant husbands and claim half of marital property (Westfried, 1997, p. 42), as well as to claim any property given directly to the husband's mistress (Rocha, 1980, p. 101), many men continue to claim their historical license in sexual matters.

FUNCTIONAL POLYGYNY

Once, when I was interviewing a woman about Brazilian marital practices, she joked; "The North Americans only have one woman, and the Brazilians also have one—one on every street!" Her jocular comment referred to common male infidelity. Some married or cohabiting men engage in short-term relationships with other women, either in the form of brief, extramarital courtships, of picking up women for occasional one-night stands in bars, or of frequenting prostitutes. But sometimes men support more than one woman with children, with one being considered *a legitima* (the legitimate woman) and the others referred to legally as *concubinas* (mistresses) and commonly as *as outras* (the others).

Sometimes concubinage results from a breakdown in an earlier liaison. Historically, in the absence of divorce, men sometimes used to move in with a new woman, legalizing neither the split from the earlier family nor their new status. Today, some men continue this practice, not wishing to deal with the economic and social difficulties of a legal divorce. A responsible man continues to support and visit his legitimate wife and children even after starting a new relationship. Here concubinage is more a form of serial semimonogamy than informal polygyny. There also exist men who maintain more than one concubine at a time, although the expense makes it prohibitive, and rare.

In the lower classes, women pursue relationships with men, including married men, for a variety of motives. Some do not know the man is married until they are already involved, or do not care whether he is married, or derive a sense of status from stealing other women's men. Since association with a man is important for a woman who wants a house and children, women may seek out relations regardless of whether the man is married: as long as they like the man and can get the economic support they need, they do not feel any necessity to marry legally or to worry about previous or current relationships. Other women have personal and ideological aversions to marriage. For such women, a married man is the perfect partner: there is no danger that he will want the relationship to turn more serious.

Keeping concubines or pursuing prostitutes also responds to popular ideas about proper and illicit sexual acts. A man might pursue a girlfriend in order to spare his wife the demands of his appetite for sexual diversity and frequency. Transgressive sexual acts (especially anal sodomy) dishonor a decent wife. Here, infidelity reflects an expected male lack of sexual refinement in comparison to women. Functional polygyny interacts both with feminist ideas of sexual emancipation and contemporary hopes of true love in complex ways.

Historically, practices of arranged or semi-arranged marriage, combined with greater sexual liberty for upper-class men, allowed men to pursue romance in extramarital liaisons rather than within marriage itself. Today's greater emphasis on romance within marriage makes this historical bifurcation of men's affections more problematic than ever (Rebhun, 1999b).

The concept of *a outra* (the other woman) has deep resonance among Brazilians, many of whom come from families in which the relationship between the wife and *a outra* and among half-siblings dominates sources of tension. The *novellas* (soap operas) that constitute prime-time programming in this fourth largest world television market frequently center on struggles among the various women of one man, or tragedies when young lovers discover that their previously secret half-sibling relationship prevents the culmination of their love. In 1990, an anthropology dissertation on concubinage became a best-seller (Goldenberg, 1990), reflecting the allure of this topic among Brazilians.

It would be an error to regard such relationships as simply the result of powerful men preying on vulnerable women, for poor women have their own sentiments, aspirations, and desires, and their own uses for such alliances. The complexity of the interplay of desire, affection, and power in a society as marked by legal, economic, and social inequality as Brazil (both historic and contemporary) confounds even more the already multiple intricacies of sexual relationships.

Functional polygyny also means that extended families include not only spouses and children but also half-siblings divided by legitimate and illegitimate status and often of different social classes as well. In the lower classes, some women may adopt children in the custody of their boyfriends, as well as taking in the children of other relatives, or even children of former girlfriends of their current boyfriend by former boyfriends of the former girlfriends—creating very tangled family networks indeed.

STREET CHILDREN

On July 25, 1993, eight street children were killed by a group of adult men, including several police officers, as the children lay sleeping on the steps of the Candelária Cathedral in Rio de Janeiro in an incident publicized around the world. This was not the first international attention paid to the often violent world of Brazilian street children, which had previously been publicized in Hector Babenco's 1980 film *Pixote,* as well as in several social science publications (Hecht, 1998, pp. 118–120). But it became the most enduring symbol of the tragic victimization of these children.

Estimated numbers vary, but at least tens of thousands of children, subsisting on a combination of odd jobs, prostitution, and petty crime, sleeping, urinating, and defecating in public, sniffing glue, drinking alcohol, and begging, throng the downtowns of many urban areas in Brazil.[2] Although often called "abandoned children," they actually present a more complex family situation. A study in Rio found that most street children had moved to Rio from rural areas, that 50 percent came from families with five or more children, and that 80 percent had no father in the household at the time they left, with a majority of the rest reporting an abusive, heavy-drinking father. Most had left abusive situations at home, only to find more violence from other street children, youth gangs, and the police (Logie, 1990).

Tobias Hecht, in an ethnographic study of street children in Recife, posits that, rather than making a sharp distinction between impoverished children who live in families and those who live on the street as distinct types, theorists should consider a continuum model. He points out that childhood in poor and working-class families does not constitute a protected status; that poor children often engage in both household and remunerative labor, that they may have major responsibility for younger children in the household, and that they frequently shift among different households. Many work regularly outside the home, and come from loosely constituted households, with weak conjugal bonds, changing couple membership, and circulating children. Some street children have no contact with any household in which they have grown up, but many have continuing ties with households, attend school in the morning and beg in the afternoon, and sometimes sleep at

home and other times sleep in the street (Hecht, 1998, pp. 100–105).

Children living in shantytowns may come from houses located in areas distant from schools, businesses, and so on, and constituting such flimsy physical structures that they offer little contrast to the streets themselves, which Hecht describes as a resource used by members of households rather than an opposite to the home. Many street children contribute a portion of their earnings to their mothers or foster mothers, retain ties to siblings and other children of their mothers' households, and spend varying amounts of time engaged both in the streets and in their mother's residences. Rather than evidence of the breakdown of the family, they represent a type of dispersed, fluctuating family life among people whose economic resources permit neither the construction of comfortable houses nor the sustenance of children in a stable, nonproductive capacity (Hecht, 1998, pp. 188–214).

Claudia Fonseca's (1995, 2000) work on family life, adoption, and fosterage in impoverished families in Southern Brazil similarly demonstrates how the informal circulation of children in lower-class urban families reflects a number of Brazilian cultural values. First, she examines the primary role of women as mothers, including the possibility of mothering by a variety of women including older sisters, aunts, grandmothers, stepmothers, and neighbors, who may take on a mother-like role with any and all children. Because people believe that children have an immutable tie to their birth mothers, they can create residential and emotional ties to other kinds of mothers without strongly threatening the birth mother's ideological primacy. Second, an emphasis on the child's immediate well-being motivates some women to give up primary custody to better-off relatives, and such relatives to accept the responsibility of raising a child.

Fonseca found that middle-class mothers spoke of their children as long-term projects, worrying about education toward future economic and professional opportunities. Lower-class families, in contrast, tended to have a present-time orientation with children, looking at the most basic requirements to keep them alive, and emphasizing enjoying their company and exploiting their labor in the short term (Fonseca, 1995, pp. 134–135). These differences reflect contrasts in the role of children within families in different classes: the middle class has the luxury of indulging children in a protected, nurtured status, whereas lower-class children themselves are forced into responsible, nurturant roles way too young, taking care of siblings, and working to support themselves and other family members (Hecht,1998, pp. 70–92).

CONCLUSIONS

The contemporary Brazilian family reflects both historical and contemporary influences. The legacy of colonial families with their multiple levels of legitimate and illegitimate women, inclusion of servants, slaves, and tenants, practices of arranged cousin marriage, and male dominance mixes uneasily with today's emphasis on romantic conjugality between nonrelated partners. Although economic pressures fracture family ties, the ideal of a loving mother nurturing many children and a strong father protecting and supporting his women and children continues to guide how people speak about the family and what it ought to be in contemporary Brazil. Such phenomena as large numbers of street children reflect as much the strength as the breakdown of family values and family forms in Brazil, since many such children retain ties, however tenuous, to their natal families. And despite liberalization in women's roles, the increased participation of middle-class women in public and economic life, and greater public debate on women's sexual emancipation, patriarchal customs such as functional polygyny continue to affect relationships within the family. Marked economic and social inequality combine with massive social change—especially agrarian and economic transformation—to make the Brazilian family an evolving and diverse social form.

NOTES

1. Travel to the United States, especially to Miami, is often less expensive for Brazilians than travel within Brazil or to Spanish America or the Caribbean, because higher passenger traffic encourages airlines to offer package deals that profit more from volume than price.

2. Tobias Hecht disputes estimates, commonly ranging from about 7 to about 10 million; based on his research he estimates that the numbers of children regularly sleeping in the streets in Brazil is closer to 39,000, still a tragically high figure (1998, pp. 100–102).

REFERENCES

Albuquerque, J. A. G. (1977). *Classes médias e política no Brasil* [Middle classes and politics in Brazil]. Rio de Janeiro: Paz e Terra.

Besse, S. K. (1996). *Restructuring patriarchy: The modernization of gender inequality in Brazil, 1914–1940*. Chapel Hill: University of North Carolina Press.

Bilac, E. D. (1995). Sobre as transformações nos estructuras familiars no Brasil. Notas muito preliminaries [About transformations in family structures in Brazil. Very preliminary notes]. In I. Ribeiro & A. C. T. Ribeiro (Eds.), *Familia em processos contempâneos: Inovações culturais na sociedade Brasileira [The family in contemporary processes: Cultural innovations in Brazilian society]* (pp. 43–65). São Paulo: Edições Loyola.

Boschi, R. (1986). A abertura e a nova classe média na política brasileira: 1977–1982 [The opening and the new middle class in Brazilian politics: 1977–1982]. *Dados, 29*(1), 5–24.

Bruschini, M. C. A. (1990). *Mulher, casa e família cotidiano nas camadas médias paulistanas* [Women, house and daily family life in the Paulista middle class]. São Paulo: Editora Revista dos Tribunais Ltda. Edições Vértice.

Brusco, E. E. (1995). *The reformation of machismo: Evangelical conversion and gender in Colombia.* Austin: University of Texas Press.

Bustos, J. G. (1980). Mythology about women, with special reference to Chile. In J. Nash & H. Safa (Eds.), *Sex and class in Latin America: Women's perspectives on politics, economics, and the family in the third world* (pp. 30–45). New York: J. F. Bergin.

Candido, A. (1951). The Brazilian family. In T. L. Smith & A. Marchant (Eds.), *Brazil: Portrait of half a continent* (pp. 291–312). Westport, CT: Greenwood.

Costa, J. F. (1989). *Ordem médica e norma familiar* (3rd ed.). Rio de Janeiro: Edições Graal.

Dalsgard, A. L. (2000). *Matters of life and longing: Female sterilization in Northeast Brazil.* Unpublished doctoral dissertation, University of Copenhagen, Denmark.

Da Matta, R. (1985). *A Casa e a Rua* [In the house and on the shelf]. São Paulo: Editora Brasilense.

de Araujo, T. B. (1987). Nordeste: Diferenciais demográficas regionais e seus determinantes [Northeast: Regional demographic differences and their causes]. *Cadernos de Estudos Sociais Recife, 3*(3), 167–192.

Figueiredo, L. (1993). *O avesso da memória: Cotidiano e trabalho da mulher em Minas Gerais no século XVIII* [The wrong side of memory: Daily life and women's work in Minas Gerais in the Eighteenth Century]. Rio de Janeiro: José Olympio.

Fonseca, C. (1995). *Caminhos da adoção* [Paths of adoption]. São Paulo: Cortez Editora.

Fonseca, C. (2000). *Família, fofoca e honra: Etnografia de relações de gênero e violência em grupos populares* [Family, gossip, and honor: Ethnography of gender relations and violence in popular groups]. Porto Alegre: Editora da Universidade Federal do Rio Grande do Sul.

Freyre, G. (1933). *Casa grande e senzala: Formação da família brasileira sob o regime de economia patriarchal* [Mansions and shanties: Formation of the Brazilian family under the patriarchal economic regime] (3rd ed.). Rio de Janeiro: Maia & Schmidt.

Goldenberg, M. (1990). *A Outra: Um estudo sobre a identidade da amante do homem casado* [The other woman: A study about the identity of the married man's lover]. Rio de Janeiro: Editora Revan.

Griffith, R. M. (1997). *God's daughters: Evangelical women and the power of submission.* Berkeley: University of California Press.

Hansen, E. R. (1977). *Santana: Middle class families in São Paulo, Brazil.* Unpublished doctoral dissertation, City University of New York.

Hecht, T. (1998). *At home in the street: Street children of Northeast Brazil.* New York: Cambridge University Press.

Kelly, M. P. F., & Sassen, S. (1995). Recasting women in the global economy: Internationalization and changing definitions of gender. In C. E. Bose & E. Acosta-Belen (Eds.), *Women in the Latin American development process* (pp. 99–124). Philadelphia: Temple University Press.

Logie, D. E. (1990). Brazil: Neither angels nor devils. *The Lancet,* June 2, p. 1332.

Nations, M., & Rebhun, L. A. (1988a). Mystification of a simple solution: Oral rehydration therapy in Northeast Brazil. *Social Science and Medicine, 27*(1), 25–38.

Nations, M., & Rebhun, L. A. (1988b). Angels with wet wings won't fly: Maternal sentiment and the image of neglect in Northeast Brazil. *Culture, Medicine, and Psychiatry, 12,* 141–160.

Nations, M., & Rebhun, L. A. (1996). Development and disease: Lessons from Brazil. In R. Guerrant, M. A. de Sousa, & M. K. Nations (Eds.), *At the edge of development: Health crises in a transitional society* (pp. 3–28). Durham, NC: Carolina Academic Press.

Nazzari, M. (1991). *Disappearance of the dowry: Women, families, and social change in São Paulo, Brazil, 1600–1900.* Stanford, CA: Stanford University Press.

O'Dougherty, M. (2002). *Consumption intensified: The politics of middle-class daily life in Brazil.* Durham, NC: Duke University Press.

Owensby, B. (1994). *Stuck in the middle: Middle class and class society in modern Brazil, 1850–1950.* Unpublished doctoral dissertation, Yale University, New Haven, CT.

Parker, R. G. (1991). *Bodies, pleasures and passions: Sexual culture in contemporary Brazil.* Boston: Beacon.

Pastoré, J. (1979). *Desigualdade e mobilidade social no Brasil* [Inequality and social mobility in Brazil]. São Paulo: T. A. Queiroz.

Pearlman, C. (1984). Machismo, marianismo, and change from indigenous Mexico: A case study from Oaxaca. *Quarterly Journal of Ideology, 8*(4), 53–59.

Perlman, J. (1976). *The myth of marginality.* Berkeley: University of California Press.

Rebhun, L. A. (1994). A heart too full: The weight of love in Northeast Brazil. *Journal of American Folklore, 107*(423), 167–180

Rebhun, L. A. (1995). The language of love in Northeast Brazil. In W. A. Jankowiak (Ed.), *Romantic passion: The universal experience?* (pp. 239–261). New York: Columbia University Press.

Rebhun, L. A. (1999a). For love and for money: Romance in urbanizing northeast Brazil. *City and Society, 11*, 1–2.

Rebhun, L. A. (1999b). *The heart is unknown country: Love in the changing economy of Northeast Brazil.* Stanford University Press.

Reuters (2000). Website: www.reuters.com.

Rocha, H. de M. L. (1980). *Os direitos da mulher casada* [The rights of the married woman]. Rio de Janeiro: Editora Technoprint.

Rocha, J. (1997). *Brazil: A guide to the people, politics, and culture.* New York: Interlink Books.

Roldan, M. (1988). Renegotiating the marital contract: Intrahousehold patterns of money allocation and women's subordination among domestic outworkers in Mexico City. In D. Dwyer & J. Bruce (Eds.), *A home divided: Women and income in the third world* (pp. 229–247). Stanford, CA: Stanford University Press.

Rothstein, F. (1983). Women and men in the family economy: An analysis of relations between the sexes in three peasant communities. *Anthropological Quarterly, 56*(1), 10–23.

Russell-Wood, A. J. R. (1978). Female and family in the economy and society of colonial Brazil. In A. Lavrin (Ed.), *Latin American women: Historical perspectives* (pp. 60–100). Westport, CT: Greenwood.

Saes, D. (1977). Classe média e política de classe [Middle class and class politics]. *Contraponto, 2,* 96–102.

Saes, D. (1985). *Classes média e sistema política no Brasil* [Middle classes and the political system in Brazil]. São Paulo: T. A. Queiroz.

Samara, E. de M. (1983). *A familia brasileira* [The Brazilian family]. São Paulo: Brasiliense.

Samara, E. de M., & Costa, D. I. P. (1997). Family, patriarchalism, and social change in Brazil. *Latin American Research Review, 32*(1), 212–226.

Scheper-Hughes, N. (1984). Infant mortality and infant care: Cultural and economic constraints on nurturing in Northeast Brazil. *Social Science and Medicine, 19*(5), 535–546.

Scheper-Hughes, N. (1985). Culture, scarcity, and maternal thinking: Maternal detachment and infant survival in a Brazilian shantytown. *Ethos, 13*(4), 291–317.

Scheper-Hughes, N. (1992). *Death without weeping: The violence of everyday life in Brazil.* Berkeley: University of California Press.

Schneider, R. M. (1996). *Brazil: Culture and politics in a new industrial powerhouse.* Boulder, CO: Westview.

Schwartz, S. B. (1985). *Sugar plantations in the formation of Brazilian society: Bahia, 1550–1835.* Cambridge, UK: Cambridge University Press.

Skidmore, T. E., & Smith, P. H. (1997). *Modern Latin America* (4th ed.). New York: Oxford University Press.

Smith, T. L. (1972). *Brazil: People and institutions.* Baton Rouge: Louisiana State University.

Soeiro, S. A. (1978). The feminine orders in colonial Bahia, Brazil: Economic, social, and demographic implications. In A. Lavrin (Ed.), *Latin American women: Historical perspectives* (pp. 173–197). Westport, CT: Greenwood.

Stevens, E. P. (1973). Machismo and marianismo. *Society, 10*(6), 57–63.

UNICEF (2001). Website: www.unicef.org.

Vaitsman, J. (1994). *Flexíveis e plurais: identidade, casamento e família em circunstâncias pós-modernas* [Flexible and plural: Identity, marriage, and family in post-modern circumstances]. Rio de Janeiro: Rocco.

Wagley, C. (1971). *Introduction to Brazil* (rev. ed.). New York: Columbia University Press.

Westfried, A. H. (1997). The emergence of the democratic Brazilian middle-class family: A mosaic of contrasts with the American family (1960–1994). *Journal of Comparative Family Studies, 28*(1), 25–54.

Woortman, K. (1987). *A família das mulheres* [Family of women]. Rio de Janeiro: Edições Tempo Brasileiro.

PART SIX

AFRICA

CHAPTER 20

FAMILIES IN CENTRAL AFRICA
A COMPARISON OF BOFI FARMER AND FORAGER FAMILIES

HILLARY N. FOUTS
National Institute of Child Health and Human Development

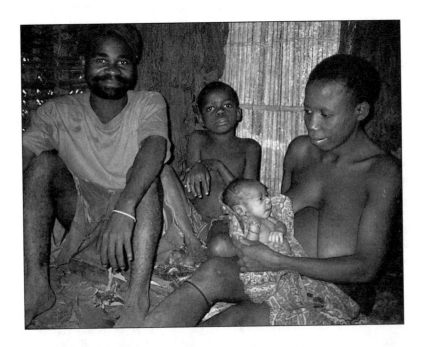

The purpose of this chapter is to provide descriptions and comparisons of families among two cultures in Central Africa, the Bofi foragers and the Bofi farmers. The Bofi foragers and farmers have long lived in social and economic association, speak the same language, but remain very distinct culturally. These distinctions are seen vividly in their family patterns, including distinct patterns of marriage and divorce practices, spousal roles, childcare techniques, and cultural values.

Bofi is an Oubanguain language, closely related to the Gbaya language. In the Bofi language there are names referring to "pygmies," all of which are derogatory. While the Bofi foragers are considered "pygmies," I choose to refer to them as the Bofi foragers because of the derogatory nature of the word "pygmy" as well as its indigenous equivalents and also to distinguish them from the other Bofi, the Bofi farmers. These two groups have not been studied prior to the research project on which this chapter is based.

The Bofi foragers and farmers live in the tropical regions of the northern Congo Basin rainforest in the southwest of the Central African Republic (CAR). These two groups are the northern neighbors of the better-known Aka foragers (Bahuchet, 1985; Hewlett, 1991), as well as the southern neighbors of the Gbaya farmers (Burnham, 1996). Like other forager and farmer groups in the area, the Bofi foragers and farmers have lived in complex and many-stranded relations with each other for some time.

The Bofi foragers and farmers in this study are associated with the villages of Grima and Poutem. There are approximately 190 Bofi foragers associated with Grima and 180 associated with Poutem, while 250 Bofi farmers reside in Grima and 500 reside in Poutem.

METHODS

The data presented in this chapter are the result of thirteen months of fieldwork among the Bofi farmers and foragers. The purpose of this fieldwork was to: (1) collect basic ethnographic data on both groups; (2) observe and examine differences in the social and emotional development of children between 18 and 59 months of age, especially during the transition from nursing to cessation; and (3) collect data on Bofi forager and farmer parental practices and beliefs. Three methods were used to accomplish these aims: (1) participant observation of daily life among both groups, (2) verbal questionnaires, and (3) ethnological observations of child and parent behaviors. Participant observation was a continual and imperative element in collecting the ethnographic data, as well as contextualizing the quantitative data. Questionnaires were verbally administered to parents on a variety of subjects, including fertility, childbirth, alloparenting, weaning methods, and children's emotional development. Pseudonyms are used in all of the examples and vignettes throughout the chapter.

Quantitative behavioral observations were taken using a focal child sampling technique (Altmann, 1974). This technique involves observing one child at a time, and recording a specific set of child and caregiver behaviors and child–caregiver interactions.

The behaviors were recorded on-the-mark, as indicated by a tape recording with a verbal message of "observe" to begin 20 seconds of observation, followed by "record" to mark down the current behaviors on a detailed checklist in 10 seconds. Signaling of the observe/record regimen took place through a small earphone worn by the observer. The behaviors recorded included child visual orientation, child states (e.g., sleeping and drowsiness), child emotional states (e.g., fussing, smiling, and aggressiveness), child attachment behaviors, child nursing and feeding behaviors, caregiver responses to child emotional states (e.g., soothing), caregiver affection, caregiver–child physical proximity and touching, and mother's work/leisure status. Observational sessions spanned 45 minutes and were followed by a 15-minute rest.

Behavioral data were collected with 22 Bofi forager children and 21 Bofi farmer children. Twenty of the forager children and 21 of the farmer children were observed for a total of 9 hours spanning 12 daylight hours. Two of the forager children were observed for 8 and 6 hours due to the health status of one child and scheduling conflicts. The forager children, therefore, were observed for a total of 194 hours and the farmer children for 189 hours.

ETHNOGRAPHIC BACKGROUND

Cultural History

Little is known about the cultural history of the Bofi farmers and foragers. As previously mentioned, the Bofi language is closely related to the Gbaya language. Bofi farmer oral history exemplifies clearly that the Gbaya and Bofi farmers have a history of tribal warfare, with the Gbaya being the Bofi farmers' longtime enemy. The Bofi farmers attribute their largest victories against the Gbaya to the bravery of their legendary hero, Samba Ngotto.

Bofi farmer oral history also indicates that they originally lived in a savanna area, but eventually moved south toward the forest. Likewise, Vansina (1990) reports that after the vast settlements of Bantu peoples near the rainforest, groups speaking Oubanguain languages (including Gbaya and Bofi) moved in north of the Bantu people. Vansina remarks that the Oubanguian speakers had previously lived in savanna regions and that "These people were not well equipped for life in the forest . . ." (1990, p. 65). Vansina also notes that the Oubanguian speakers were influenced by the Bantu speakers, and that "Culturally, . . . the western Bantu assimilated them (Oubanguian speakers) to a large extent" (1990, p. 66). Consequently, the Bofi farmers have very similar cultural characteristics (e.g., material culture, core values, social organization) as many of the other farming groups in this region.

After 1870 rubber became a major trade between Africa and Europe, and correspondingly farmer populations moved farther into the forest to exploit this resource. It seems that sometime during this period of the rubber trade some Bofi farmers and Aka foragers became closely associated and for unknown reasons, groups of these Aka adopted the Bofi language and ceased to speak the Aka language; these foragers are now known as the Bofi foragers. In accordance, elderly Bofi farmers indicated in interviews that their deceased grandparents and parents spoke Aka as a third or fourth language in order to trade with the foragers living near them.

The Bofi foragers are ethnically and culturally very similar to the better-known Aka foragers. The Bofi foragers and the Aka have very similar material culture, subsistence methods, social organization, and core values. The Aka tend to farm more often than the Bofi foragers, and the Bofi foragers do not have several of the Aka social positions, such as *dzengi* (great forest spirit), *tuma* (great hunters), or *kombeti* (clan leaders) (Hewlett, 1996b).

Subsistence

The Bofi foragers subsist principally through hunting and gathering in the rainforest, while a minority of the foragers also has small gardens in which they grow manioc and maize. The Bofi foragers primarily hunt using large nets. Like other net-hunting foragers, such as the Aka and Mbuti (Bahuchet, 1985; Hewlett, 1996a), Bofi men, women, and children participate in the net hunt. The most common type

of net hunt is one in which the men beat the brush to scare up animals and women guard the nets and trap the animals. Spears are also widely utilized by men during net hunts. The Bofi foragers also hunt using crossbows, small net traps, and wire traps. The Bofi foragers hunt mostly duikers with nets and spears, wild pigs with spears, monkeys with crossbows, and porcupine and rats with small traps.

Both men and women gather in the forest, although women do the majority of the day-to-day gathering. Men exclusively collect honey. Both men and women collect many species of caterpillars, termites, grubs, snails, wild yams, mushrooms, nuts, and leaves (especially *koko, Gnetum* spp.).

Although there is some sexual division of labor, with men having a few exclusive hunting techniques, men and women do much of the same work. Furthermore, spouses and family units often cooperate on a daily basis in subsistence activities. Thus, immediate family members spend much time together, interacting and cooperating daily.

The Bofi foragers gain a large portion of their carbohydrates through trade with the Bofi farmers. Every evening Bofi forager camps are inundated by Bofi farmer women and children, arriving to exchange manioc for forest products, especially *koko* leaves, *payo* nuts (*Irvingia* spp.), and meat, and more seasonal foods such as caterpillars, snails, and mushrooms.

The Bofi farmers subsist primarily through "slash and burn" horticulture, their main crop being manioc; they also grow coffee, maize, peanuts, yams, taro, okra, and a variety of fruits. Farmer men hunt periodically in the forest using shotguns and snares, and women gather leaves, insects, and mushrooms. However, the Bofi farmers acquire most of these forest products through trade with the Bofi foragers.

Bofi farmers have sexual division of labor. Men are exclusively responsible for burning fields and for much of the clearing of fields. Women do the majority of the labor involved in farming, including planting, weeding, harvesting, processing the food grown, as well as some of the clearing of the fields. Men spend the majority of their time involved in intervillage trade, hunting, and politicking within the village.

Bofi farmer men and women spend most days apart, with women and older children mostly in the fields or processing manioc near the fields and men in the village politicking.

SOCIAL ORGANIZATION

Both the Bofi farmers and foragers are organized into patriclans called *zim,* and live patrilocally. They are both exogamous, not marrying within one's own clan. Although these general patterns are similar, both the inter- and intracultural differences in social organization are described below.

Bofi Foragers

The Bofi foragers are loosely organized into patriclans, and live patrilocally after matrilocal bride service, which usually includes the first 3 to 5 years of marriage. A minority of the Bofi foragers does, however, continue to live matrilocally after bride service, and furthermore, some foragers also associate themselves with their mother's rather than their father's clan.

The Bofi foragers are highly egalitarian, deemphasizing any kind of rank and emphasizing leveling mechanisms, and therefore do not have chiefs or age deference. However, individuals with particular skill specialties sometimes receive limited deference. These individuals are usually the traditional healers (*ngangas*) and midwives (*wanbakoi*).

The Bofi foragers, like other Central African foragers such as the Aka, practice prestige avoidance, which helps to maintain their egalitarianism (Hewlett, 1991). For example, on one occasion I observed a European biologist passing through Grima looking for Bofi who knew the fauna well. The biologist asked all of the foragers camped near Grima, "Who here is a good hunter?" The responses from the foragers ranged from walking away to "I do not know." No one claimed being an especially good hunter, avoiding prestige attention. Along with prestige avoidance, Hewlett (1991) lists two other cultural practices that help the Aka to maintain egalitarianism: rough joking and demand sharing.

The Bofi foragers also commonly use rough joking to level rank differences. For example, during my fieldwork in Grima the farmer chief designated a forager to be the chief of the local foragers. Thereafter, Grima foragers teased the candidate about being their "chief" by mocking him and often calling him chief and laughing. Demand sharing, which according to Hewlett "means that whatever one has will be given up if requested" (1991, p. 26), is also common among the Bofi foragers and reinforced through stories about supernatural afflictions that happened to people who do not share appropriately.

Related to their egalitarianism, independence and personal autonomy are highly valued and respected among the Bofi foragers. As individuals are not given particular rank and power, people also do not sanction the actions of other individuals. The value of personal autonomy is exhibited in many ways, from the decisions of a child to misbehave, to adults going to hunt by themselves for few days, to individuals taking their mother's clan name rather than their father's, as well as to the general reluctance to verbally judge the actions of other individuals.

The egalitarianism of Bofi foragers extends to gender relations as well. As mentioned previously, there is much cooperation between spouses during subsistence activities. Spouses eat together with their children and share in childcare to varying degrees. I have not observed any instance of physical abuse between spouses. Spousal arguments are common, and women seem to take the more aggressive role in these arguments, yelling loudly and sometimes attempting to destroy their own house. Husbands most commonly walk away during arguments or take spontaneous trips to the forest in response to these conflicts.

Bofi Farmers

The Bofi farmers are strictly patrilocal, and every adult Bofi farmer in Grima and Poutem identified with a patrilineal clan. There are several official and unofficial status positions in the village: the chief, the chief's secretary, the village announcer (distributes information from the chief to the village by loudly shouting while walking through the village), clan chiefs, Christian pastors, elderly men, midwives, *ngangas,* school teachers, and pharmacy technicians.

Age deference and respect are core values among the Bofi farmers and are prime designators of hierarchy. For example, during meetings people quiet down when an elderly village man stands up to speak. Furthermore, at these meetings elderly men are given the biggest and nicest-quality chairs to sit in, while most other people sit on the ground.

Status in the village is also designated by skill specializations; for example, in Grima the Protestant pastor, school teacher, and pharmacy technician are often called on during meetings to offer their opinions in matters. These individuals also tend to bring up new topics of discussion at meetings and make proposals to better the village.

Except for the midwife, men occupy all of the prestige positions described above. These prestige positions are all very public positions and reflect the importance of politicking to Bofi farmer men. Bofi farmer young men publicly flaunt and seek prestige; often they wear new clothes and hang out at the wealthiest households or where the largest amount of bush meat is being sold.

Bofi farmer women are never chiefs; their influence is exerted in more informal ways. Elderly women are distinguished by being called grandmother (*Ka'a,* a general term for male and female grandparents). Midwives are also known to have special healing knowledge, similar to a *nganga.* At village meetings, women often speak up and are listened to.

Women sell manioc, *koko,* and maize whisky and often set up temporary restaurants to sell pastries, hot coffee, and meat stews. All of these sales are important sources of revenue in the village. The money that a woman makes is her own money, and is often used to buy herself and her children clothes and medicine; rarely do women share their income with their husbands.

The income that men make is from selling hunted game meat and goods from larger villages such as clothing, soap, utensils, and from working for logging companies and conservation groups. The money that men make is also theirs to keep; they are not obligated to give any to their wife. However, not providing money to buy clothing and medicine for one's children is grounds for divorce.

Generally men and women do not eat together, and children usually eat with their mother, though young boys are often invited to eat with their fathers. Women have told me several times that it would be impossible to eat with men, because "men would eat everything and leave us with nothing to eat," therefore, "women must separate a portion of food for themselves."

I have observed cases of physical abuse between spouses on several occasions. The most common forms are mild physical fights between spouses in which neither party is harmed. These fights may begin by husband or wife, hitting the spouse or throwing an object (such as a hard piece of fruit) at the spouse. Over the course of twelve months in Grima, there were three severe cases of spousal abuse, in which jealous husbands initiated physical violence toward their wives. These events were brought to an end by the intervention of numerous people living near the couple. The chief and village elders verbally condemn these severe cases of domestic violence, but no punishment is given to these abusive husbands. People generally comment that it is the responsibility of one's clan to deal with marital problems. Both physical and verbal disputes between husband and wife occur outside of the house in view of their children, extended family, and the entire village.

FERTILITY, MORTALITY, MARRIAGE, AND DIVORCE

The demographic data presented in this section are based on 182 Bofi foragers associated with the village of Grima, 136 Bofi foragers associated with the village of Poutem, 236 Bofi farmers living in the village of Grima, and 426 Bofi farmers living in the village of Poutem.

Fertility

Table 20.1 compares the age and sex distributions of Bofi foragers and Bofi farmers. The two distributions

Table 20.1   Age Distribution

AGES IN YEARS	PERCENTAGES OF PEOPLE	
	Bofi Foragers, n = 318	Bofi Farmers, n = 662
0–14	43.7	47.7
15–34	32.4	25.8
35–54	17	18.3
>55	6.9	8

are very similar, both with fairly high numbers of individuals in the juvenile category. Table 20.2 contrasts the total fertility rate (TFR) differences of men and women among both groups. Not unlike other groups, the TFR variance is higher for men than for women (Hewlett, 1991), although note the much larger discrepancy between the farmer men and women's TFR variance. All of the farmer men with more than 12 infant births had a polygynous marriage for some portion of their life.

The Bofi foragers and farmers have similar TFRs. Interestingly, though, they have different interbirth intervals (IBI): the Bofi foragers' IBI is 4–5 years, whereas the Bofi farmers' IBI is 2–3 years. Considering the shorter IBI of Bofi farmer women, one might predict that they would have a higher TFR than do Bofi forager women. Bofi farmer women have much variance in their TFR, in contrast to the forager women. Among Bofi forager women, infertility is infrequent: of 25 postmenopausal forager women, only 1 had never given birth, and only 1 woman had given birth less than three times. In contrast, of 58 Bofi farmer postmenopausal women, 4 women had never

given birth, 15 others gave birth less than three times and reported having difficulties conceiving thereafter, while 14 women gave birth nine to twelve times.

Bofi farmer women often comment on how Bofi forager women have many children, while many farmer women have only one or two children. In a questionnaire conducted with 20 Bofi farmer women and 19 Bofi forager women in Grima, Grima farmer women confirmed that many of them experience fertility problems. The most common explanation offered by Grima farmer women was that both Bofi farmer and forager women contract illnesses in their wombs, but that forager women have more knowledge of medicines found in the forest than they do. Therefore forager women are able to treat their illnesses quickly, while farmer women's wombs become damaged. Several farmer women also believed that illnesses of the womb occurred when women slept with many men besides their husband.

Bofi forager women also confirmed that they have fewer fertility problems than do Bofi farmer women. The most common explanation given by Grima forager women for these differences was that farmer women sleep with many men besides their husbands and wear cords to prevent becoming pregnant from these extramarital relationships. The second most common explanation was again that farmer women sleep with many men and that this causes them to contract illnesses in their wombs.

Infant and Child Mortality

The Bofi foragers and farmers have similar infant (up to 12 months) mortality rates: 18.8 percent for

Table 20.2   Comparison of Total Fertility Rates

	BOFI FORAGER MEN OVER AGE 45, n = 20	BOFI FORAGER POST-MENOPAUSAL WOMEN, n = 24	BOFI FARMER MEN OVER AGE 45, n = 47	BOFI FARMER POST-MENOPAUSAL WOMEN, n = 58
TFR[a]	6.15	5.54	5.68	5.32
Variance of TFR[a]	9.18	4.34	24.46	12.38
SD of TFR[a]	3.03	2.08	4.95	3.52

[a]TFR = total fertility rate.

the Bofi foragers and 20.3 percent for the Bofi farmers. However, they differ considerably in their overall child (birth to 15 years) mortality rates: 40.6 percent for the Bofi foragers and 30.6 percent for the Bofi farmers. Contributing to this discrepancy in child mortality is that the Bofi farmers frequently utilize pharmacies and hospitals with Western medicines. Most Bofi foragers do not accumulate money with which to pay for medicine or services at pharmacies and hospitals.

The health of infants and children is of great concern for all Bofi forager and farmer parents. Among the Bofi foragers, infants and children are adorned with magical waist cords, necklaces, bracelets, and charms to protect them from food taboos, sorcery, and dangerous animals. The Bofi farmers also adorn their children with waist cords, bracelets, necklaces, charms, lotions, perfumes, and clothing to protect their children from food taboos, sorcery, and cold temperature.

Marriage

Bofi Farmers. Bofi farmer women first marry between the ages of 15 and 17 years, while men are usually in their early to mid-twenties. Farmer young men and women may have premarital relationships, but if the family of the woman suspects that there is a sexual relationship, then they will demand a bride price. There is no marriage ceremony, but once a bride price (*kopay*) has been agreed on, the couple is considered married. Typically one's *kopay* consists of money, goods such as palm wine, domesticated animals, clothing, and services such as clearing fields. *Kopay* can be met entirely with money and goods—this is the preferred pattern—although many men are unable to meet the price that their in-laws demand and thereafter must provide work in lieu of the payment. *Kopay* is not always definitive, and when a specified amount is completed, the bride's family often continues to ask for more *kopay.* During the *kopay* period brides continue living with their family or sometimes near their family in their husband's house. Once *kopay* is finished, the newlyweds move to the clan or village of the husband to live pa-

trilocally. Men who marry women from the same village often complain that *kopay* goes on and on, even after they have had one or two children. On the other hand, men who move back to their natal village with their wife face a different problem: if their in-laws deem that more *kopay* is in order, the wife may move back home until it is met.

Bofi Foragers. Bofi forager women also marry between the ages of 15 and 17 years, while Bofi forager men are usually in their early twenties. There is also no formal marriage ceremony among the Bofi foragers; essentially, once the couple is sleeping in the same house they are considered married. The Bofi foragers also have *kopay,* but it is in the form of bride service. The length of service is much less defined than among the Bofi farmers. *Kopay* usually ranges from 2 to 7 years. While conducting *kopay* the bride and groom live matrilocally. After the service is finished, they usually move and live patrilocally. However, I know of several instances in which after *kopay* was finished the couple chose to continue to live matrilocally. The reasons for this were various—for example, in one case much of the husband's family was deceased and his wife's family was part of a large clan. In another case, a husband explained to me that his wife simply refused to move and wanted to stay with her family, and he had no choice if he wanted to maintain his marriage.

Table 20.3 compares the marital histories of Bofi forager and Bofi farmer men. There is very little difference between the current number of polygynous marriages, although Bofi farmer men are more likely than Bofi forager men to have more than two wives.

Divorce

Bofi Foragers. As shown in Table 20.3, Bofi forager men are more likely to have been through a divorce than are Bofi farmer men, and are also more likely to have had more than one marriage previous to their current marriage. From my own observations and discussions with individuals, I found Bofi forager marriages to be more flexible in initiation and in

Table 20.3   Marital Status and History

		CURRENT MARITAL STATUS			MARITAL HISTORY		
	Total No. of Married Men	One Wife	Two Wives	Three Wives	Has Been Divorced	One Previous Marriage	Two Previous Marriages
Bofi farmer men, n = 121	103	77.7%	6.6%	0.8%	33.1%	19%	5%
Bofi forager men, n = 50	44	80%	8%	0	48%	42%	10%

divorce. Following is a vignette describing the first marriage of a young Bofi forager woman:

> *Yerro had been married to her first and only husband, Morri, for less than a year. Morri was, in fact, still performing bride service, and they had recently been away together on a voyage. Yerro returned to her parents' camp without Morri; word was passed around that their marriage was over. From time to time people in the camp would casually ask about Yerro and Morri, with Yerro's response being a shrug of her shoulders or a shake of her head. One day when discussing the upcoming snail season with Yerro's parents, I asked them, "Are Yerro and Morri still married?" Yerro's mother responded, "I don't know, ask Yerro," and Yerro's father laughed. So I asked him, "What do think?" He responded, "I don't know, maybe they will continue with their marriage, only Yerro knows." I then further asked, "Do you want them to stay together?" Yerro's father laughed again, shrugged his shoulders, and said, "It is good if they are together <pause> he can do bride service (kopay) for me <laughs> only Yerro knows, ask her."*

Here we see Yerro's parents' reluctance to give their opinion on their daughter's marriage. Personal autonomy is highly valued among the Bofi foragers; within the family and outside the family, individuals, both adults and children are given the flexibility to act in their own way without verbal or physical sanctions. This cultural value affects the marriage system by making marriage and divorce flexible to the intentions of individuals. Because of the high instances of divorce and remarriage, many Bofi forager families are blended families. Generally after a

divorce, young children (3-, 4-, and 5-year-olds) and infants will live with their mother, whereas older children are allowed to decide for themselves with whom they will live and may circulate at their discretion between parents and extended family.

Bofi Farmers.   Divorce among Bofi farmers is also very common, as seen in Table 20.3, but couples wishing to divorce often face pressure from their families to stay together. Following is a vignette about a Bofi farmer woman named Bodako, who is over 40 years old and has been married three times:

> *I sat with Pari, conducting my demography questionnaire. "Who lives in your house?" He responded, listing off his two wives and his four young children, and "my older sister Bodako lives here now." I had greeted Bodako when I arrived; she had been pounding manioc. I had assumed she was just visiting her brother's house today. After I finished my demography questionnaire with Pari, I sat down with Bodako, asking if I could ask her some demography questions as well. She agreed, smiling, and continued to pound her manioc and monitor the 1-year-old clinging to her leg. When I asked her about her current marriage, she informed me that she was divorced, stating that her husband had taken a third wife and that she "refused them both." No sooner than her response began, her elderly uncle began shouting over her, "The marriage continues! There is no divorce, she will go home soon. The marriage continues!" Bodako shook her head and continued to pound manioc. We continued with the questionnaire. Bodako listed off all of her children, after which she stated, "I have*

many children; I will not have any more children. Never, I am finished." Then Pari walked toward us and loudly said to her: "You are still young and strong; you will have more children." He then looked at me: "She will go back to her husband's house soon." Bodako laughed, and proceeded to explain to me how she will put a charm on her waist cord, and how then there will be no child. In response to this Pari shook his head, muttering, "Look at her, she is still strong and young," and walked away.

Here we witness Bodako's brother and uncle pressure her to return to her husband. In order for Bodako to leave her husband she must deal not only with pressure from her husband, but with pressures from her family as well. I commonly hear Bofi farmer men and women using social pressure on couples, through gossip, direct statements as illustrated above, and even formal political pressure. Marriage represents more than the union of two individuals; to the Bofi farmers there are always political issues between clans underlying marriages. Therefore, the pressure exerted by Bodako's uncle and brother are also reminders to her of her communal responsibility, or her responsibility to put the interests of her clan above her own interests. Communal responsibility is a core value among the Bofi farmers and greatly affects the process of marriage and divorce.

Blended families are also common among the Bofi farmers. Generally, infants and young children (2-, 3-, and 4-year-olds) stay with their mother and older children live with their father's clan.

Family Roles

Bofi Foragers.   Forager families spend a great deal of time in close contact, they sit close together, and they frequently work together and eat together. Oftentimes mothers cook meals for the family; however, fathers, sons, and daughters also cook meals intermittently. Forager parents are physically affectionate with their children and do not discipline them. Forager mothers and fathers play similar roles within the family. Mothers and fathers cooperate in work and childcare, usually collecting food and hunting together as well as taking turns holding infants and young children. Although mothers and fathers cooperate in childcare, mothers are the primary caregivers.

Daughters and sons also play similar roles within the family. Infant daughters and sons are carried around all of the day and sleep with their entire family. In early childhood, daughters and sons begin to be left at home when their parents go to the forest. These children spend their days interacting and playing with other children and adults. Daughters and sons begin accompanying their parents to the forest around the age of 7 or 8 years. Adolescent sons and daughters spend much of their time with same-sex peer groups. On net hunts, adolescent boys tend to travel together during the hunt. Adolescent daughters typically build a small house beside their parents' house, while adolescent sons continue to live in their parents' house. Adolescents often contribute to family work by collecting water and food during the day.

Bofi Farmers.   Mother and father roles are much more differentiated among the Bofi farmers. Mothers cook most meals, provide the majority of work in the fields, discipline the children, and provide caregiving tasks such as cleaning, dressing, and grooming infants and young children. Fathers are relatively uninvolved in childcare, and focus their attention toward village politics and economic endeavors. Women always cook the manioc for each meal, men very rarely cook manioc, and even bachelors usually have a female relative cook manioc for them. Cooking manioc is a strictly female task. Farmer males often joke about how the amount of manioc their wives serve them is indicative of how happy the wives are with them. Fathers eat with their brothers and sometimes their sons, while mothers and children of both sexes eat together.

Infant sons and daughters are carried by their mothers to the fields during the day. Infants and nursing children are rarely scolded; it is not until after weaning that children begin to receive discipline. Infants usually sleep with their mothers, whereas children sleep in a bed with all their other siblings. Around the age of 7 years, daughters begin to accompany their mothers to the fields and are expected to work throughout the day helping to process manioc and transport water. Adolescent daughters are expected to work as much as their mother and often are responsible for cooking the manioc for the family; they also discipline younger siblings with the same authority as their mother. Sons are not expected to go the fields with their mothers; instead they usually stay around the village all day and play with other children or go to school. Adolescent sons spend most of their day with other adolescent boys, fishing in the river or building small bachelor houses.

PARENT–CHILD RELATIONS

This section will examine parent–child relations by focusing on early childhood among both groups. Super and Harkness (1986) provide a useful framework by which to examine child development. Their framework, the developmental niche, consists of: (1) physical and social settings, (2) childcare customs, and (3) the psychology of caregivers. In the following sections, data and examples from early childhood (1½–4 years of age) will be used to examine parent–child relations. Children described below, unless otherwise indicated, are between the ages of 18 and 59 months.

Physical and Social Setting

The general framework of the physical and social setting of life among the Bofi foragers and Bofi farmers has been described above, including locality, marriage, subsistence, and demographic patterns that affect with whom children live, where their parents go during the day, and how many siblings they have. Described below are social settings that involve specific caregivers who interact with children.

Juvenile/Juvenile Interactions.   Konner (1976) posits that play relations are favored by selection because they allow children to practice adult behaviors such as parental, sexual, and agonistic behaviors that may be beneficial in finding future mates. Both Bofi forager and Bofi farmer children between ages 1½

and 4 years spend nearly half of their time involved in play, including solitary and social play. Bofi farmer children spend large amounts of their time with other juveniles, participating in multiaged playgroups. Bofi farmer children were observed in close proximity (within a forearm's length) with other juveniles 49.6 percent of all intervals, whereas Bofi forager children of the same age range spent only 30.2 percent of intervals in close proximity to other juveniles. In contrast to the farmer children, Bofi forager children are still spending large amounts of time with their parents (68 percent of intervals in close proximity to parents); play groups and juvenile interactions become more pronounced among Bofi forager children 5 years of age and older.

Part of the differences in time spent with juveniles and parents, between Bofi forager and farmer young children, is due to the fact that juveniles are the most common alloparents (nonparental caregivers) among the farmers. In contrast, Bofi forager young children continue to receive high amounts of parental care; alloparental care becomes more important after weaning and is usually provided by aunts, uncles, and grandparents.

Parental Context.   Not only are Bofi forager parents and children around each other more often, they also have more physically intimate relationships with each other than do Bofi farmer parents and children. The Bofi forager parent–child relationship in early childhood contains high amounts of physical contact and holding. For instance, of the intervals spent in close proximity with parents, 81.1 percent of those intervals Bofi forager parents and children were also in physical contact with each other; in contrast, Bofi farmer parents and children were in physical contact with each other significantly less (66.1 percent of close proximity intervals).

Breastfeeding is another important factor to consider in understanding these proximity differences. Bofi farmer children are weaned between 1½ and 2 years of age, while Bofi forager children often continue to breastfeed through age 3 and sometimes 4 years. Therefore, more of the forager children observed were still breastfeeding. Breastfeeding, however, does not account for all of the variation. Bofi forager weaned children were held by their parents (17.2 percent of intervals) significantly more than were Bofi farmer weaned children (1 percent of all intervals).

Customs of Childcare

Super and Harkness define customs of childcare as "sequences of behavior so commonly used by members of the community, and so thoroughly integrated into larger culture, that they do not need individual rationalization and are not necessarily given conscious thought" (1986, p. 555).

Use of Language.   The Bofi forager and Bofi farmer kinship terminology pattern is Hawaiian, in that brothers and sisters and all cousins are called by the same name (*Yanam,* my sibling). However, there are some variations in gender terminology. Bofi farmers distinguish in their kin terms between an older sister (*Danam*) and an older brother (*Ngaweenam*). On the other hand, the Bofi foragers do not always distinguish in terminology the difference between an older or younger sibling or cousin, calling them all *Yanam.* Occasionally, Bofi foragers do utilize the word *Ngaweenam* to refer to older siblings and cousins. Here we see how, among the farmers, social gender-role differences are reflected in their kin terminology. In comparison, the Bofi forager kinship terms are consistent with their gender egalitarianism.

Age deference is also reflected in the kinship terminology of the Bofi farmers. Bofi farmer children call their mother and all adult women *Nana* (mother) and their father and all adult men *Bafa* (father), whereas Bofi forager children call their parents by their given names rather than *Nana* and *Bafa.*

Negation terms such as *Yori, Wiya, Soona* (wait/ stop, stop, finish) are common words used around young Bofi farmer children. For example, a child may be scolded "*Wiya!*" as he reaches a hand into the manioc his mother is pounding. These negation terms are used to modify the behavior of children. A swat, administered by a parent or older sibling, is often paired with these words to increase the intensity of the command. Bofi farmer parents and siblings also use negation terms to protect infants and children from potential dangers such as sharp objects, campfires, and hot cooking pots.

The Bofi foragers use these words as well, but rarely to discipline children. Instead these words are used to tell someone that their "illness is finished" (*Zelay Soona*) or to "wait here" (*Yor'day*). Interestingly, negation words are not often used even to prevent children from potential harm. For instance, an infant may crawl dangerously close to a campfire without a caregiver intervening; however, if she begins to cry she is immediately picked up. Infants and young children are allowed to play with sharp knives and machetes, as well as to pull burning sticks from fires.

Bofi farmer mothers normally use a very melodic, singsong-type voice (a form of "motherese") when speaking to infants and small children. I have never heard motherese-type speech being used among the Bofi foragers. Bofi farmer parents tend to express their affection to children verbally, whereas forager parents tend to rely on physical affection.

Methods of Holding.   Bofi farmer infants and children (up to the age of 3 years) are typically held on their caregiver's back and secured with a shawl tied around them. Therefore, when infants want to nurse, mothers must untie them and bring them around to their breast. Also, there is little chance for mother–child face-to-face interactions with this style of carrying. However, infants and children become used to this carrying style and are comforted by it. For example, when a child is inconsolable, a mother or alloparent will often tie the child onto her back, resulting in the child calming down and usually falling asleep.

Bofi forager infants and children (up to the age of 3–4 years) are carried in a sling on the side of their caregiver. Hewlett (1991) has suggested that caregiver–child face-to-face interaction is facilitated by the side-sling carrying style. Furthermore, Bofi forager infants and nursing children have easy access to their mother's breasts from this position and can see where their caregiver is going and what she or he is doing.

Breastfeeding and Weaning.   For Bofi farmer children, breastfeeding ends abruptly, with their mother normally placing a bandage on their nipple to simulate a wound. Thereafter, children being weaned are told that their mother's nipple is wounded and bleeding, to frighten the children and stop them from wanting to nurse. Weaning among the farmers is also characterized by increased amounts of fussing and crying. Bofi farmer parents respond to this by giving their children rice gruels.

Bofi forager children gradually stop breastfeeding. There is no abrupt weaning method administered by mothers; instead mothers wait for the child to decide to quit nursing. Therefore, many children continue to breastfeed through the first and second trimester of their mother's subsequent pregnancy. In cases when mothers do not become pregnant, children generally continue to nurse and occasionally do not stop until they are 5 or 6 years old. Ivey (1993) also noted that Efe forager mothers commonly said that their children decided to quit nursing on their own. Bofi forager children around the time of self-weaning do not fuss and cry more than younger or older children.

Because of the close physical contact involved in breastfeeding, resistance to cessation is not simply about health but also about retaining social and emotional affection. Fouts, Hewlett, and Lamb (2001) suggest that the presence of caregiving by fathers and grandparents also contributes to the emotionally calm pattern of weaning among the Bofi foragers.

Discipline.   Corporal punishment is common among the Bofi farmers, whose children are often swatted and spanked for misbehaving. Fear is used as an important tool used by Bofi farmer parents to modify their children's behavior. Farmer parents and alloparents often purposely evoke fear in their children about strangers and places (such as the forest) perceived as dangerous. For example, I have often heard parents teasing their children about the risk of the *moonju* (white person, i.e., me) taking them back to the United States, which frightens the children.

Respect for personal autonomy between parents and children is exemplified in the absence of corporal punishment and relative lack of verbal negations among the Bofi forager parents. For example, if children refuse to do something, there are no sanctions against them; no one punishes them or even persists in the request.

Psychology of Caregivers

Super and Harkness posit that the psychology of caregivers is made up of ethnotheories, which "are beliefs concerning the nature and needs of children, parental and community goals for rearing, and caretaker beliefs about effective rearing techniques" (1986, p. 556).

Productivity.   Two work-related themes occurred in interviews with Bofi farmer parents. The first theme illustrates how Bofi farmer parents value strong, active children who work well. Many Bofi farmer parents criticized Bofi forager parents and children, commenting on how they allowed their children to do anything and how Bofi forager children were consequently lazy and weak. Furthermore, several parents noted how their own children were "stronger" and more "active" than were Bofi forager children.

The second theme expresses how important adult work is to Bofi farmers and the trade-offs between adult work and childcare. Bofi farmer mothers generally leave young children (2- and 3-year-olds) at their house with older siblings, while they leave to work in the fields. Bofi farmer mothers feel that this is problematic, because sibling alloparents have high instances of negligent behavior, for example, not watching the child carefully because of social distractions. However, Bofi farmer mothers feel that there are no other available caregivers to help out, because all of the adults are occupied with work. Therefore, 2-year-olds are often looked after by 4- and 5-year-olds, not because they provide the best care, but because there is no one else available. Although Bofi farmer fathers frequently spend their days in the village, they rarely perform caregiving tasks for their children and instead spend the majority of their time politicking with other farmer men.

Once Bofi farmer children are walking, they are encouraged by their parents to fetch items and help individuals who are working. There is a great deal of direct training of children in work activities. Furthermore, Bofi farmer children spend more time in play imitation of parental work (subsistence play) than do Bofi forager children.

Bofi forager children are also occasionally asked to fetch items for adults, but if the child does not respond to the task, adults do not persist in their request. Instead, it is left up to each child to decide how much he or she will or will not help with work activities. Children begin to go on hunts with their parents once they are old enough to keep up with their parents (usually around 7 or 8 years of age). I asked the parents of some of these children why their child did not go on the hunt a particular day. The responses were consistently: "He/she did not want to," and "Only he/she (their child) knows why." Here again, the value of personal autonomy among the Bofi foragers strongly influences the interactions within the family.

Despite these differences in guidance toward learning subsistence skills, prior to adolescence both the Bofi forager and farmer children exhibit many specialized adult skills and often help their parents in various work situations.

Spirits, Sorcery, Trust, and Sharing.   The Bofi foragers and farmers both have a belief in ancestor spirits as well as more generalized spirits. Both groups believe in helpful and harmful spirits. Illnesses are commonly associated with bad ancestor spirits hanging around a person. Ill individuals often seek out *ngangas* to cleanse them of these menacing spirits. Spiritual cleansing usually consists of a series of treatments, including medicines rubbed on the skin, bloodletting, and ritual cleansing. These treatments also include the *nganga* conducting long conversations with the spirit, trying to convince the spirit that it must leave the individual alone. As mentioned previously, both forager and farmer parents adorn their children with protective cords and charms to ward off bad spirits.

The Bofi foragers and farmers also both believe in sorcery or witchcraft (they make no distinction be-

tween male and female powers; both are thought of as sorcery). Bofi farmers are generally more mistrustful of other people than are the foragers. For example, sorcery and theft accusations are a daily occurrence among the farmers. Fear of sorcery attacks is expressed through Bofi farmer childcare in the form of stories told to children as well as warnings given to children about potential sorcerers and places where evil spirits reside. On one occasion, a 7-year-old, named Giya, stopped me on a path and said to me, "I saw you pass this way yesterday to go into the forest. Why are you not scared? *Mbong'go* (generalized evil spirit[s]) lives in the forest; if you see *Mbong'go* you will die!"

Bofi farmer parents give their children many warnings about spirit and sorcery dangers from other individuals and from exploring dangerous areas, such as the forest. The Bofi foragers, on the other hand, reflect their general trust in their environment by allowing children exploration and independence.

Sharing is also a theme that permeates Bofi forager social patterns and is related to trust. In order to share extensively, one must believe that others will share with you as well. This theme of sharing influences the forager alloparenting pattern. As described above, Bofi farmer parents feel that sibling alloparents are far less than ideal. Bofi forager parents also share this belief; they, however, have solved this dilemma differently. Bofi forager parents generally leave 3-, 4-, and 5-year-olds under the protection of an elderly camp member, oftentimes a grandparent of the child. These grandparents are still capable of going to the forest to hunt and gather, and frequently do. The grandparents are able to stay in camp because when the parents of the children return, they receive a portion of the food hunted and gathered that day. Thus, this pattern of grandparent alloparenting is made possible by the high degrees of sharing among the Bofi foragers.

Sharing is less extensive among Bofi farmers as compared to Bofi foragers. Bofi farmer families do share with other households, but not on a daily basis like the foragers. Sharing patterns among the Bofi farmers are regulated through sorcery accusations.

For example, households accumulating more than others are often accused of using sorcery.

Autonomy and Communalism. The Bofi foragers' value of autonomy is a prominent schema used in their parenting. Respect for autonomy is most vividly seen in the parental roles during significant childhood events. Two of the most significant events are male circumcision and teeth filing. Bofi forager boys are generally circumcised in early adolescence (between the ages of 10 and 13). Usually several boys go through the procedure together. Parents report that they do not decide when their sons will be circumcised, but that it is their sons who decide. Likewise with teeth filing; adolescent girls and boys decide on their own when they are ready.

Male circumcision among the Bofi farmers is a clan event; it is proposed and arranged by an adult male clan member, oftentimes unbeknownst to the boys. Boys are usually between the ages of 5 and 7 years when they are circumcised. In one case, the mother of one of the children was not told about the plans for the circumcision of her son. She only found out when she returned from the fields to her upset son. Communalism is prevalent in much of Bofi farmer life, and the intentions of the clan influence parent–child relations as well as spousal relations as discussed previously.

CONCLUSIONS AND SUMMARY

Even though the Bofi farmers and foragers live in close contact with each other and share a language, they have very different family patterns. The Bofi farmers and Bofi foragers have distinct systems of social organization, cultural values relating to productivity, hierarchy, autonomy and sharing, and childcare practices. Table 20.4 contrasts the differences in social organization and cultural values.

Daily subsistence activities provide the setting for children to relate to their parents. The differences between the Bofi farmer and forager in the sexual division of labor have one of the greatest impacts on

Table 20.4 Differences in Subsistence, Social Organization, and Core Cultural Values

	BOFI FORAGER	**BOFI FARMER**
Subsistence	Hunting and gathering, infrequent farming	Farming, some hunting and gathering
Sexual division of labor	Cooperation between sexes on net hunt and gathering	Men burn and clear fields, women plant, weed, harvest, process, and sometimes clear fields
Social organization and cultural values	Egalitarianism, respect for personal autonomy, extensive sharing	Age and gender hierarchy, emphasis on productivity, communalism, responsibility

family nuances. The Bofi farmer pattern yields a situation in which spouses spend lots of time apart during the day and in which children are more often with their mothers and siblings. In contrast, the Bofi forager pattern entails much spousal and family cooperation on a daily basis and ample time for family members to work alone as well as together, depending on one's personal interest.

The social organization and cultural values of the two groups vary in many ways, but most especially in the presence of gender and age hierarchy and communalism among the farmers and egalitarianism and autonomy among the foragers. These Bofi forager social patterns yield an absence of corporal punishment of children, a presence of gender egalitarianism between spouses, extensive intra- and interfamilial sharing and cooperation, and much intracultural variation in locality and divorce patterns. The Bofi farmer patterns of hierarchy and communalism yield patterns of age deference, corporal punishment of children, juvenile allocare, and strict rules of locality and marriage.

Productivity is a prevalent theme among the Bofi farmers, contributing to the activities of children (e.g., subsistence play) and to the interactions between parent and child (e.g., direct teaching of skills). Finally, the threat of sorcery controls much of Bofi farmer behavior and contributes to mistrustful attitudes toward neighbors, extended family, and the environment. This mistrustfulness is reflected in parents warning their children of dangerous forces in the forest and evoking fear of strangers.

In many ways the Bofi foragers and farmers are also very much alike. Among both groups, divorce, stepparenting, nonmaternal care of children, breastfeeding beyond 12 months, and death of siblings within the family are very common, and families always live with relatives. Compared to U.S. families the Bofi foragers and farmers seem quite similar. First of all, the physical and social settings of U.S. families are much different, living as they do in a highly stratified society, with much physical separation between households and extended families. Furthermore, among U.S. families, living with relatives, death within the family, breastfeeding beyond 12 months, and nonmaternal care of children are all much less frequent compared to the Bofi forager and farmer patterns.

Bofi foragers and farmers have very different parenting techniques. Bofi farmer parents tend to express their affection verbally rather than physically, discipline their children, evoke fear in their children, wean their children abruptly, and direct them in subsistence types of activities. In contrast, the Bofi forager parent–child relationship is characterized by close physical contact including large amounts of holding; forager parents do not discipline their children, and they allow their children to make their own choices about activities as well as important events such as weaning and teeth filing. One might predict that such different caregiving patterns would have a striking impact on the emotional development of Bofi farmer and forager children. However, despite these differences, there is no significant difference in the overall frequencies of crying between Bofi for-

ager and farmer children in the age range of 1½ through 4 years.

Hewlett (1992) found that the Aka parenting styles did not fit with predicted developmental psychology outcomes proposed by Baumrind (1971). According to Baumrind (1971) and to Maccoby and Martin's (1983) categorizations of parenting styles, Bofi forager parents are "indulgent" or "permissive," rarely using punishment and not exerting power over their children, but instead responding to the desires of their children. However, Bofi forager children, like the Aka, do not fit the behavioral outcome pattern associated with the indulgent/permissive parenting pattern. This child behavior outcome includes aggressiveness, dependence, and low control of impulses. Bofi forager children are not aggressive, exhibit much independence in exploration, and interact in very culturally acceptable ways. The Bofi farmers fall into the "authoritarian" parenting style, which includes parents deliberately trying to control and modify their children's behavior and valuing obedience and respect. Bofi farmer children do not fit into the predicted child behavior outcomes, which include the following features: often socially withdrawn, lack of empathy, aggressiveness, and little initiative. Bofi farmer children are very active, show much initiative, are rarely withdrawn, and exhibit empathy in many contexts. Although this particular developmental model works very well in evaluating parenting and child development among Americans, it has very little explanatory power among the Bofi foragers and farmers. This raises the question of how much of our development theories are based on Western standards and how much on human universals. For example, much of what Bofi farmer parents do (e.g., evoking fear in children) may be considered pathological by Western standards. Similarly, aspects of the Bofi forager's permissive (e.g., lack of negation in even potentially dangerous situations) parenting style may be considered negligent by Western standards. However, children in both groups grow up to be productive members of their cultures; all adults work, get married, and participate socially within their cultures.

ACKNOWLEDGMENTS

I would like to thank the Bofi farmer and forager families for welcoming me into their lives so graciously and for tolerating my long observations and frequent questions. I acknowledge and thank the government of the Central African Republic for authorizing this research. I also offer my thanks to the forest and water ministry in the CAR and ECOFAC-RCA project, especially George Ngasse and Alain Pènelon, for logistical support and authorization to work in the Ngotto forest. Thank you to Barry Hewlett for comments on earlier drafts. This research was supported by the National Institute of Child Health and Human Development.

REFERENCES

Altmann, J. (1974). Observational study of behavior: Sampling methods. *Behaviour, 49,* 227–267.

Bahuchet, S. (1985). *Pygmées Aka et la forêt centrafricaine: Ethnologie écologique* [Aka pygmies and the Central African forest: An ecological ethnography]. Paris: Selaf.

Baumrind, D. (1971). Current patterns of parental authority. *Developmental Psychology Monographs, 4*(no. 1, part 2), 1–103.

Burnham, P. (1996). *The politics and cultural differences in northern Cameroon.* Edinburgh, UK: Edinburgh University.

Fouts, H. N., Hewlett, B. S., & Lamb, M. E. (2001). Weaning and the nature of early childhood interactions among Bofi foragers in Central Africa. *Human Nature, 12*(1), 27–46.

Hewlett, B. S. (1991). *Intimate fathers.* Ann Arbor: University of Michigan Press.

Hewlett, B. S. (1992). The parent–infant relationship and social-emotional development among Aka pygmies. In J. L. Roopnarine & D. B. Carter (Eds.), *Parent–child socialization in diverse cultures* (pp. 223–243). Norwood, NJ: Ablex.

Hewlett, B. S. (1996a). Cultural diversity among African pygmies. In S. Kent (Ed.), *Cultural diversity among twentieth-century foragers* (pp. 215–244). Cambridge, UK: Cambridge University Press.

Hewlett, B. S. (1996b). *Foragers and rural development.* Unpublished manuscript, Washington State University, Pullman, WA.

Ivey, P. K. (1993). *Life-history theory perspectives on allocaretaking strategies among Efe foragers of the Ituri Forest of Zaire.* Unpublished doctoral dissertation, University of New Mexico, Albuquerque, NM.

Maccoby, E. E., & Martin, J. A. (1983). Socialization in the context of the family: Parent-child interaction. In E. M. Hetherington (Ed.), *Handbook of child psychology: Vol. 4. Socialization, personality and social development* (pp. 1–101). New York: Wiley.

Super, C., & Harkness, S. (1986). The developmental niche: A conceptualization of the interface of child and culture. *International Journal of Behavioral Development, 9,* 545–569.

Vansina, J. (1990). *Paths in the rainforests.* Madison: University of Wisconsin Press.

CHAPTER 21

FAMILY LIFE IN SOUTH AFRICA

ENGELA PRETORIUS
University of the Orange Free State

The current and varied state of family life in South Africa has its roots in the ramifications of a not uneventful history that has brought its influences to bear on the family. In order fully to comprehend family life in this country, one has to take cognizance of these rich and varied influences.

Although identifiable signs of human settlement 25,000 years ago have been found, and the first pastoral people occupied the area some 2,000 years ago, the first European settlers—mainly Dutch, French, and German—only reached this country around the middle of the seventeenth century. The descendants of these European settlers collectively came to be called *Afrikaners.* South Africa was governed by the Netherlands from 1672 to 1810 and then by the British as two British colonies plus several independent republics until 1901. It then became a self-governing member of the British Commonwealth (1910–1961), and finally, in 1961, South Africa became an independent republic. During the first 300 years, the white minority dominated governance. Since 1994, South Africa has been a democracy with a nonracial franchise (Byrnes, 1996; Preston, 1989).

Of particular significance in the twentieth century was the coming into power of the National Party in 1948, marking the onset of the era of Apartheid in this country. In the next forty years, massive social engineering took place in the country. At first marriages between whites and people of color were prohibited (The Prohibition of Mixed Marriages Act 1949), even though since 1946 there had been only 75 mixed marriages compared to 28,000 white marriages. In 1950, the Population Registration Act was introduced. In terms of this act, a national register was compiled in which every individual was classified according to race. The Group Areas Act, passed in 1950, was the instrument by which the government implemented the process of physical separation between the various races. Sometimes communities were forcefully removed—as was the case with Coloreds from Cape Town and Asians from Durban. One of the most contentious laws was the Separate Amenities Act (1953), which made provision for a color bar in all public buildings, amenities, and public transport by means of "Europeans Only" or "Non-Europeans Only" signs (Coetzer, 1992, p. 278).

When the National Party came into power in 1948, dissatisfaction among blacks already existed regarding the discriminatory measures of the white government. The acceptance of a militant Program of Action by the African National Congress in 1949 marked the first step in the black political struggle. Over the years, dissatisfaction with the education system, an escalation in the forced removals of black people from certain areas, and the continued denial of rights to the majority of the population led to confrontations, violent racial unrest, and eventually to a state of emergency in 1985. An economy under siege, foreign commitment to peace in the region, and the advent of a new state president (F. W. de Klerk) led to unprecedented reform in 1990 to 1991 (Cameron & Spies, 1992).

POPULATION PROFILE

South Africans represent a rich array of ethnic backgrounds, but the idea of ethnicity became highly explosive during the Apartheid era, when the government used it for political and racial purposes. Whites in South Africa had often attributed the centuries of warfare in the region to the varied origins of its peoples, rather than to the increasing economic pressures they faced. In the Apartheid era, government officials, accordingly, imposed fairly rigid ethnic or tribal categories on a fluid social reality, giving each black African a tribal label, or identity, within a single racial classification.

Apartheid doctrines taught that each black population would eventually achieve maturity as a nation, just as the Afrikaner people, in their own view, had done. During the 1950s and 1960s, the government established language areas for each of these ethnic groups and assigned them separate residential areas according to perceived ethnic identity. Over the next decade, portions of these language areas became Bantustans, and then self-governing homelands; finally, in the 1970s and 1980s, four of the homelands—Transkei, Bophuthatswana, Venda, and Ciskei—were granted nominal "independence." Although the independent homelands were not recognized as separate nations by any country other than

South Africa, people assigned to live there were officially "noncitizens" of South Africa.

Apartheid policies further empowered the government to remove Africans from cities (Group Areas Act 36/1966). These actions disturbed family support networks, while migrant labor and influx control measures led to problems of illegitimacy, family breakdown, and an increase in single-parent families. The stated aim of these measures was to preserve the "ethnic character" of neighborhoods in the African townships that were created, legally and illegally, around the cities. Many township neighborhoods were given specific "tribal" designations. Township residents generally ignored these labels, however, and reacted to the divisiveness of the government's racial policies by either minimizing the importance of their ethnic heritage, or by disavowing it entirely. Many Africans embraced the notion that ethnicity was an outdated concept, a creation of governments and anthropologists, invoked primarily to create divisions among people of a particular class or region. The word "tribe" assumed especially pejorative connotations during the Apartheid era, in part because of the distortions that were introduced by applying this concept to society.

The entirely new dispensation, which was officially introduced by the first democratic elections in 1994, heralded the so-called African Renaissance, and many South Africans today reclaim their ethnic heritage and acknowledge pride in their ancestry. The new constitution also reaffirms the importance of ethnicity by elevating nine African languages to the status of official languages of the nation, along with English and Afrikaans. The most widely spoken of South Africa's eleven official languages in the mid-1990s are isiZulu, isiXhosa, Afrikaans, and English. Most Colored people (81 percent) and most whites (58 percent) use Afrikaans as their home language. Some 93 percent of Indians/Asians use English as their first language. Among Africans, the single largest proportion (29 percent) use Zulu as their home language (Forgey et al., 1999). The other official languages are all African languages, namely, isiNdebele, Sepedi, Sesotho, Setswana, SiSwati, Tshivenda, and Xitsonga. Despite the variety of African languages, simplistically speaking it is possible to divide all the African-speaking peoples into two broad groupings: the Nguni and the Sotho.[1] The Nguni, including the Zulu, Xhosa, Swazi, Pondo, and Ndebele, account for nearly 45 percent of the population, while the Sotho, who are divided into the South, West (Tswana), and North Sotho, comprise about 25 percent of the South African population (Forgey et al., 1999; Van Warmelo, 1974).

All the Nguni peoples share a similar language and culture. Traditionally, they were primarily pastoralists, while agriculture—mainly the preserve of women—was of secondary importance. Men have made cattle their exclusive preserve to the extent that women are prohibited from milking the cows, touching the milking utensils, or going near the cattle *kraal,* especially during menstruation, when their "unclean state" poses a threat to the herd.

Unlike the Nguni, who are structured in terms of clans, the Sotho are structured around totem groups, each with its own totems, usually an animal such as a crocodile (*Kwena*) or a baboon (*Khatla*). The myths and rituals once associated with these totemic animals, such as restrictions on eating or touching them, have to a large extent died out due to Westernization and detribalization (Morris & Levitas, 1984). Although about 54 percent of the South African population was urbanized in 1996, in five of the nine provinces most people (mainly Africans) were not urbanized (Forgey et al., 1999). The highest rate of urbanization occurs among Indians (97.3 percent), whites (90.6 percent), and Coloreds (83.4 percent), while the rate for Africans is only 43.3 percent. In these nonurban areas, many Africans continue to live in a traditional tribal manner. They practice certain traditions and customs that have shown remarkable resilience to change and an ability to survive and adapt to new circumstances. However, it is equally true that in urban and semiurban contexts these traditional social groupings have lost much of their relevance and have ceased to be major determinants of social behavior (Morris & Levitas, 1984).

Many of the changes in family life are the result of underlying demographic trends such as population, age, and gender composition, geographical location, and so on. Some of these will be discussed briefly.

By mid-1999 the South African population had grown to 43.1 million, with roughly 50 percent living in urban areas and 50 percent in rural areas, and was estimated to be increasing at an average annual rate of 2 percent (excluding net migration). The growth rate is the result of a decline in infant mortality rates and a relatively high fertility rate—calculated at 3.8 in 1997 by the World Health Organization (Forgey et al., 1999). Figure 21.1 depicts a breakdown of the population composition by race according to the 1996 census statistics.

In 1996, 34 percent of the population was under the age of 15. Some 5 percent were over the age of 65. More boys (35 percent) than girls (33 percent) were under 15, while fewer men (4 percent) than women (6 percent) were over 65. Some 36 percent of Africans were under the age of 15, compared with 21 percent of whites (Forgey et al., 1999). Figure 21.2 shows age profiles of the population by race in 1996.

Figure 21.3 provides a racial breakdown of infant mortality rates in South Africa from 1984 to 1994 (the latest year for which information was available). In the period 1991–1995, infant mortality in South Africa dropped by some 26 points. The 1998 *South Africa Demographic and Health Survey* showed disparities among races in terms of infant mortality. Africans had the highest infant mortality (47), followed by Colored people (18.8) and whites (11.4).

In 1998, the maternal mortality rate in South Africa was 150 deaths per 100,000 live births. Reports of maternal deaths were mandated in 1997, to enable the Department of Health to investigate every maternal death. A 1998 report on maternal deaths found that delay in seeking help was a prominent feature of such deaths occurring from septic and related complications (Department of Health, 1999). The report also found that 15 percent of maternal deaths were due to non-pregnancy-related infections, the most common being AIDS. One of the aims of the Choice on Termination of Pregnancy Act[2] was to reduce the number of deaths from unsafe abortions. According to the Department of Health, during 1998 more than 46,000 safe abortions were performed countrywide (Forgey et al., 1999).

In 1998, the U.S. Census Bureau revised its estimate of average life expectancy in South Africa from

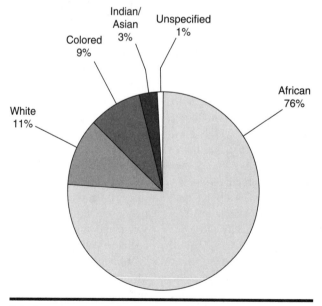

FIGURE 21.1   Population by Race, 1996
Source: Forgey et al., 1999.

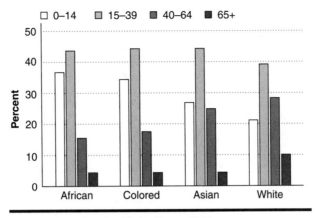

FIGURE 21.2   Age Profile by Race, 1996
Source: Forgey et al., 1999.

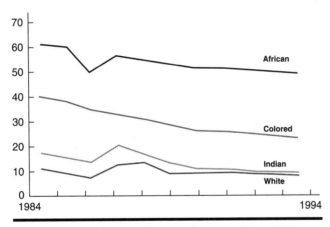

FIGURE 21.3   Infant Mortality Rate by Race, 1984–1994
Source: Forgey et al., 1999.

65 to 56 because of AIDS. According to UN AIDS estimates, by 2010 life expectancy will fall to 48 years because of AIDS. The population growth rate estimate was also revised, from 1.9 to 1.4 percent a year. The crude death rate (number of deaths per 1,000 people) was 12.3, whereas without AIDS it would have been 7.8 (Forgey et al., 1999).

FAMILY LIFE IN SOUTH AFRICA

The rich ethnic diversity in this country means that there is also much diversity in terms of family life.

This diversity is apparent not only with respect to family structures, support networks, normative behavioral patterns and values, but also with respect to socioeconomic circumstances, and the influences of industrialization, urbanization, and geographic location. In spite of this diversity, for the past fifty years data about the South African population have always been made available in terms of the quadripartite division institutionalized by the Apartheid regime, that is, in terms of the black (Africans),[3] Colored, Indian, and white population groups. This reality also informs the framework of this discussion, which will of necessity distinguish among the four population groups.

FAMILY DIVERSITY

An overview of research on family life in South Africa brings one to the inevitable conclusion that the existing research, both on family structures and on family relationships, is deficient in many ways. Not only has research been inadequate and fragmentary—especially in the case of the African family—it is also in many cases outdated. In addition, this research often displays methodological inadequacies, and it is often selective in that only some aspects or some groups are studied. Bearing these shortcomings in mind, I will attempt to provide an overview of the diversity of family life in South Africa.

The African Family

During the precolonial period, traditional kinship structures and the extended family were basic family norms. These essential societal structures were changed fundamentally during the periods of colonialism and neocolonialism. The discovery of gold and diamonds around 1870 was accompanied by mining and commercialized agriculture, which increased the necessity for (cheap) labor in order to increase the surpluses of the capitalist economy. The introduction of the hut tax[4] forced people from their subsistence economy into a capitalist economy, where they sold their labor in order to pay the tax. This also affected the family in that a migrant labor system was established in this country: young, strong men were recruited for the mines and farms, while women and children were expected to remain in the rural areas. In the cities, men were housed in singles quarters, and neither industry nor the state took responsibility for family housing and services. This absence of the father led to the disruption of family life, as well as to poverty and dependence.

In a later period, Apartheid policies—such as influx control and relocation—directly attacked family cohesion and the ability to provide for family members, thereby reinforcing the already destructive influences on the family of urbanization and industrialization. The African family in South Africa in particular suffered much greater disintegration than was experienced in most of the rest of the continent (Burman, 1996; Viljoen, 1994).

The Colored Family

There are numerous similarities between the evolution of the Colored family in South Africa and African Americans. Both were subject to circumstances that led to relatively unstable family life and also to a very high rate of births out of wedlock. The most significant of these circumstances is the fact that a large section of the present-day Colored population is of slave extraction.[5] The slave system in the seventeenth and eighteenth centuries discouraged the institution of marriage—for some 200 years after settlement, these people were not allowed to marry. Dispersion and the difficulty of maintaining contact among slaves further hampered the formation of slave-family groupings.

Although the divorce rate among Coloreds is low compared with that of whites—10.3 as opposed to 14.8 in 1994—this is a result of a high rate of cohabitation and desertion (Cunningham, Boult, & Popenoe, 1998; Steyn, 1993).

The Indian Family

Originally, settlers from the Indian subcontinent came to the subcontinent of Africa in 1860 as indentured laborers and later as groups with commercial and business interests. They brought with them a very long history and background of religion, philosophy, values, and culture—much of which still colors their lifestyles several generations later (Ramasar, 1997).

The Indian community is not homogeneous as far as cultural traits are concerned. For instance, nearly two-thirds of the population are followers of the Hindu religion and less than 20 percent endorse the Islamic faith, while the rest follow various Christian denominations. The community of the Indian population is also made up of a number of different language groups. Within the complex South African society, it is also in contact with a number of other cultures so that some degree of acculturation is inevitable. Despite the diversity within the South African Indian community, both of the major religious groupings, Hinduism and Islam, have in the past tended to be strongly conservative regarding the retention of traditional family forms and processes such as arranged marriages and a strong emphasis on family solidarity (Mantzaris, 1988).

The White Family

Historically, the white family differs markedly from the family in other population groups. The white component of the South African population comprises the descendants of Europeans who came from the Netherlands, Germany, and France during the seventeenth century, a sizable community of English speakers who came here in 1820, and also other immigrants from the Western world. The white family consequently displays characteristics of Western European family life. Although no detailed historical information is available about this kind of family, it appears that near the end of the nineteenth century, whites lived in extended-type families, strongly embedded in a wider kinship group, the community, and the church. They were subject to strong social control and experienced virtually no family disorganization (Steyn, 1993). It was the discovery of gold and diamonds and the resulting processes of industrialization and urbanization, together with events such as the South African War (1899–1902), that caused the nuclear family to become an autonomous unit. However, this nuclear family has become quite vulnerable, as is evident from the divorce rate, which at 14.8 is the highest of all the population groups (Cunningham et al., 1998).

The following section will describe in more detail the structure and dynamics of family life in South Africa.

FAMILY STRUCTURES

In a comprehensive study conducted among the different population groups, Steyn (1993) found that the nuclear family is the family structure with the highest frequency among all the groups. However, its incidence varies from population group to population group: whereas 70.2 percent of white households are nuclear families, this is true for only 60.5 percent of the Asian households, 45.8 percent of the Colored households, and only 39.8 percent of the urban black households. Thus, apart from the nuclear family, a range of other family structures can also be found among the population groups.

The original Indian family system was that of the "joint family." Only some of the 150,000 indentured laborers who came to South Africa between 1860 and 1911 brought their wives, with the result that family life had to be reconstructed, with new extended families emerging among the poor and the workers (Freund, 1991). Several researchers have indicated that this family system is gradually being replaced by a nuclear family system as a result of the influence of Westernization. This conclusion of Steyn (1993) is supported by Jithoo (1975), who wrote on the splintering of the Hindu family, and by Schoombee and Mantzaris (1984), who tentatively concluded that only people over 40 years of age favored the extended family.

Contrary to these research findings, Mason et al. (1987) found that in the families in their study, the extended family system predominated, providing a wide range of support for family members. This preference for the extended family applied in spite of the overcrowding prevalent in the low-income housing area in which the study was conducted. In this study of Indian preschool children, it was found that of the forty-two families, 61 percent lived in an extended family system.

The Indian population group also displays a rising divorce rate from 4.8 in 1984 to 7.8 in 1996 (Cunningham et al., 1998; Forgey et al., 1999). However, while the divorce rate is still low compared with that prevailing among the other population groups, one could expect an increase in single parenthood.

Because of historical developments, two distinct classes developed among the Colored population group:[6] a higher social class characterized by a more frequent occurrence of the nuclear family with a male-dominated or syncratic authority pattern, and a lower social class in which the single-parent family and a woman-headed multigenerational family became more prominent (De Kock, 1980; Steyn, 1993).

Among the urban African elite, which forms a minority of the population, the nuclear family predominates, while rural blacks tend to live in extended families. The destructive influences that have affected African family life have resulted in the development of family structures other than these among the majority of the urban lower social classes, notably the single-parent family and the multigeneration family. Altogether, 28.8 percent of the households among urban blacks have a multigeneration structure. The latter comprises the single mother, her children, and parents, but often only her mother, resulting in matrifocal multigeneration families. The incidence of multigeneration families is illustrated in Figure 21.4.

According to Steyn (1993), the one-parent family with the highest incidence is the mother–child family. The population groups with the highest incidence of mother–child families include the urban blacks with 9.3 percent and the Coloreds with 9.6 percent of the household structures. The incidence is much lower among whites (4.7 percent) and Indians (5.8 percent).

MARRIAGE CUSTOMS

The marital institution in South Africa will be considered more fully under the section on family policy. In view, however, of the particular nature of the marital institution among both Indian and African families, some salient aspects will be addressed here.

The Role of Customary Marriage[7] among Africans

According to Dlamini (1997), some of the prominent features of the customary marriage include a number of ceremonies that mark the beginning of the marriage, the demand and delivery of *ilobolo* for marriage, polygamy, patrilocal residence, and an emphasis on procreation.

Ilobolo (*Bridewealth*).   Among the Xhosa, the parents of either the bride or the groom take the initiative in the negotiations that precede marriage—often without the knowledge of their offspring. They send a matchmaker to the other family, who leaves an assegai or beads as a token of the marriage proposal. If the idea is accepted, the groom's house appoints a master of ceremonies who negotiates betrothal be-

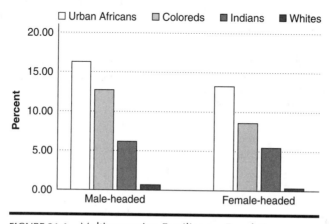

FIGURE 21.4   Multigeneration Families per Population Group
Source: Steyn, 1993.

tween the groom and the bride. This is sealed by a gift of an assegai or cattle. This gift forms part of the price paid as *ilobolo* (Gray & Ferris, 1984). In traditional societies, *ilobolo* is an imperative for a valid customary marriage. It constitutes evidence of the beginning of the new marital relationship and attests to the transfer of the husband's marital power over his wife and also over the children of the marriage.

Although *ilobolo* still continues in some way to serve the traditional functions, it has in the process of Westernization and acculturation acquired new functions, of which some are of a socioeconomic nature. It is in this regard that *ilobolo,* besides its beneficial functions, causes some problems in modern marriages, such as delaying it and thereby encouraging elopements, premarital pregnancy, and illegitimacy. This is often caused by the tendency in the African community to make excessive economic demands (Dlamini, 1997).

Polygamy.   Another important aspect of customary marriage is polygamy. At present the incidence of polygamy is declining, mainly as a result of economic considerations and an urban lifestyle. In rural areas it continues, though on a limited scale, because it is incompatible with the monogamous nature of civil marriage and because it conflicts with modern ideas regarding the status of women that have come about because of education, Christianity, and Westernization (Dlamini, 1997).

According to Motshologane (1997) polygamy has partly been replaced by concubinage. The prevalence of extramarital sex and cohabitation in African urban areas can be explained in terms of sociopolitical and economic factors. It is a response to the pressures and the frustration caused by the circumstances that the African migrant worker must face. In the urban setup, concubinage meets the needs of both the isolated migrant men and single women.

Pauw (cited by Motshologane, 1997) points out that the most notable feature of family growth among urban blacks is the large proportion of children born of illicit unions. Although often deplored, illegitimate birth has become a regular and accepted feature of the social structure, and illegitimate chil-

dren are usually integrated into the domestic families to which their mothers belong.

Procreation of Children.   Another traditional feature of a customary marriage is the emphasis on the procreation of children. Traditionally, a child ratifies the bridewealth contract between a woman's family and that of her husband and completes her status as an adult woman; thus sterility can have unpleasant consequences. Although Africans still regard children as important in a marriage, these customs are mostly on the wane, as the traditional emphasis on procreation is incompatible with modern trends of limiting the number of children and improving the quality of family life because of limited resources.

Customary marriages were recognized for the first time under the Recognition of Customary Marriages Act of 1998. The act also recognized polygamy in customary marriages. Provisions regulating customary marriages were spelled out in the act. Previously, African women were regarded as minors before the law. They could not buy or sell property without the permission of a male head of a household, regardless of age or marital status. Traditional laws, originally aimed at granting some protection to the African woman, lost their inherent flexibility when institutionalized by white legislators, to the detriment of the interests of African women (Wilson, as cited in Lemmer, 1989; Dlamini, 1997).

Arranged Marriages among the Indian Population

Among the Indians, conduct was traditionally regulated by a variety of social and religious sanctions. Premarital sex was totally denounced, as female chastity has always been very highly valued. This is reflected in many of the rituals in the Hindu marriage ceremony that are symbolic of chastity and loyalty. The moral development of children and youth was closely tied to ideas of prosperity and progress of one's country. Violation of socially sanctioned codes or socially prohibited behavior signified degeneration, poverty, and unhappiness. In both the Hindu and Islamic religions, adultery is prohibited. Having more than one wife among the followers of Islam does not violate rules of extramarital sex, provided that each woman is given equal treatment in all respects. It therefore embraces the concept of the protection of women.

One of the basic elements in mate selection and marriage was the absence of any prior commitment on the part of either the young man or woman—hence the belief that marriage comes first and love develops from the marriage. What is today called a "love marriage" was referred to in the *Vedas*[8] as *gandharva* marriage, which means the reciprocal sexual union of a man and a woman with a mutual desire proceeding from lust in which all social laws were utterly disregarded and violated (Ramasar, 1997).

Although the concept of arranged marriages is foreign to modern Western culture, it is still practiced in Indian society (Schoombee & Mantzaris, 1985). However, several variables, such as industrialization, Western education, upward social and economic mobility, and the continuous disintegration of the traditional Indian way of life, seem to have resulted in a decline of the custom. In 1985, Schoombee and Mantzaris conducted a pilot study to examine the attitudes of Indian South Africans regarding arranged and interreligious marriages. They found that the attitudes of younger and better-educated members of the community tend to be similar to those of the white "Western" community in this regard. This may be regarded as a significant indication of the extent of sociocultural change taking place within the Indian community. In urban areas, a modification in mate selection is increasingly in evidence. Partner selection or marriage is no longer a mysterious or blind event.

However, Indian society is still conservative in its views on what constitutes a situation in which sexual union is fully appropriate. Its strong religious ties have a great deal of influence on such matters. Indian parents do not as a rule openly embrace an "existential view of sex," and the stigma attached to illegitimacy is still very much alive.

Today, there is a ferment of conflicting views about how men and women ought to relate to each other. Traditional marriage has been attacked as being unsuited to the times and as being inconsistent with contemporary Indian life in South Africa (Ramasar, 1997).

MARITAL AND HOUSEHOLD ROLES AND RELATIONSHIPS

South African society is generally regarded as being largely patriarchal. Lemmer (1989) has posited that the patriarchal nature of the society is intensified by the presence of strong authoritarian norms that are linked to a more rigid sex-role differentiation. Intercultural studies within South Africa have revealed some variation in the depth and extent of authoritarian attitudes held by the various population groups. Orpen (cited in Lemmer, 1989) found that authoritarian attitudes among Afrikaans-speaking whites were among the highest recorded in the relevant literature, probably caused by the strictly disciplined socialization of Afrikaans-speaking children in school and at home. Africans also showed highly authoritarian attitudes as a result of a firm patriarchal upbringing (Heaven & Niewoudt, cited in Lemmer, 1989). Patriarchy manifests itself in the African family in that traditionally these women were subordinate to men within a wider kinship system, with the chief as the controlling male. An unequal division of labor according to sex and age prevailed, and this system was exacerbated by the absence of men from the home because of migrant labor. Despite the far-reaching changes in African family life, Smuts (1987, cited in Lemmer, 1989) contends that patriarchy remains the dominant ideology with regard to gender relationships.

Although English-speaking South Africans also revealed fairly authoritarian attitudes, this appeared to result from exposure to and accommodation of the prevailing norms of the ruling Afrikaans groups, and they were not incorporated into deeper levels of personality (Orpen, cited in Lemmer, 1989).

Research indicates that overall there has been a movement away from the traditional male-dominated pattern of authority, although such a trend varies among the different population groups (Steyn, 1997).

The most significant factor that has contributed to the profound changes in family relationships is the fact that women have increasingly entered the labor market.

In South Africa the participation of women in the workforce has increased considerably, from 36.3 percent in 1985 to 50.7 percent in 2002 (ILO, 2003). This trend applies to all population groups, although different patterns of participation are found among them. White women usually enter the workforce upon completion of their schooling or training, although a small percentage temporarily become full-time homemakers between the ages of 20 and 30, these being the most important childbearing years. The majority, notably the more educated, have a continuous employment pattern. Increasingly, those who may have left the workforce for longer periods reenter it again at a later stage. African women tend to enter the labor force somewhat later. Many are single parents who need extensive support from an extended family. Colored and Asian women tend to work until marriage or the birth of their first child and then leave the workforce (Erwee, cited in Gerdes, 1997a).

The greater participation by women in the workforce, notably the increase in the number of married women working, has raised many questions about the work distribution in the home in terms of both household activities and parenting. This has been the focus of an extensive body of research during the past decade.

Le Roux (1997) concluded that the possibility that a woman regards her work as a career, or that she defines herself as a co-breadwinner, has not been institutionalized. Expectations regarding the husband's role in the marriage are also based mainly on the fact that he is supposedly the head of the family. It seems that these values are still being transmitted through the socialization of youth. This view is borne out by research done by Viljoen (1994) among African families, where the traditional view of the "man as undisputed head of the household" was preferred during discussions on the role of the male/father. This was frequently linked to Christian dogma and the Bible. The respondents in this research upheld a rigid division of tasks, in which the woman was responsible for household tasks and the man was seen as the breadwinner and disciplinarian.

In 1992, Maconachie undertook a postal survey of a national South African white sample and found considerable diversity in household labor task and childcare arrangements. Few tasks were shared; most were performed by either husbands or wives. Wives were responsible for 25 tasks (58 percent of all tasks), which included 13 daily tasks, 10 weekly tasks, and 2 occasional tasks. Husbands carried out 16 tasks (37.8 percent of all tasks). Of these only 1 was performed daily, 5 weekly, and 10 occasionally. Among dual-earner couples there was a more flexible task allocation and men shared more tasks for which, however, wives usually took the greater responsibility (Gerdes, 1997a).

As with the division of household tasks, the increased employment of women led to the expectation that her sharing of the provider role would result in greater participation by fathers in their parental role. Research findings overwhelmingly support the idea that the wife's economic participation has not had a substantial effect on the husband's involvement in childcare. The findings have not changed noticeably in the course of the last decade. In both single- and dual-earner families, mothers still perform far more parenting tasks than fathers (Gerdes, 1997a).

Gerdes, Cronje, and Coetzee (cited in Gerdes, 1997a) examined parental task division as perceived by husbands and wives—their own and each other's. The sample in their study included Africans, Coloreds, Indians, and whites. Task performance was related to three stages of childhood development: babyhood, the preschool stage, and the primary school (grades 1–7) stage. Several areas of childcare and development were examined. No substantial differences in the husband's participation were found between single-earner and dual-earner couples. The reported perceptions also revealed that men thought they were doing more than their wives gave them credit for. The greatest discrepancy in men's and women's parental task performance related to physical care, the least to discipline and control.

In general, husband–wife relationships have been neglected in South African research. In studies that focus on the role fulfillment of women, the relationship is sometimes mentioned, but the main emphasis has been on the experience of the woman. One such study, by du Toit (1993), focused on the professional orientation and family life of the white working women. She found that the stronger the woman's career ambition, the more likely she would be committed to growth in her marriage, and receive support from her husband, and the less likely she would be to experience role conflict.

PARENTAL ROLES AND SOCIALIZATION PRACTICES

Because of a lack of relevant research on Colored, Indian, and white socialization practices, this discussion will of necessity focus on the African family.

The relationship between an African mother and her infant child is generally very close, both physically and emotionally. The child is carried on her back and goes wherever the mother goes. The infant's first major physical separation occurs when she or he is weaned at the age of about 3. After the first few months, the father too will play with the children and sing to them when they need consoling (Van der Vliet, 1974). According to Morris and Levitas (1984), it has been observed among certain Swazi groups that parents treat their very young infants rather coldly—they do not name them and refrain from much physical contact during the first 3 months of the child's life. This may be the result of the very high infant mortality rates endemic in tribal people. Traditionally, very young children are cared for by older girls. This teaches them the responsibility of childcare from an early age.

Many Africans have rites marking the first physical signs of puberty. Among the Venda, Tsonga, Zulu, and Ndebele, the boy's first nocturnal emission signals physical maturity. The Zulu have an extensive ritual in which the boy is secluded in a hut. He must observe certain food taboos and avoid contact with women. He is also given a certain amount of instruction concerning sexual behavior.

The Ndebele father may give the boy an animal as a token of manhood. The boy is instructed about the duties of a father and how to settle disputes in a polygamous situation. Puberty ceremonies for girls usually occur at the time of first menstruation. As in the case of boys, girls are also secluded for the duration of this menstrual period. Pedi and Tsonga give a certain amount of instruction during the seclusion period, including warnings on how to behave during menstruation, but there is no mention of instruction given among the Nguni or Zulu (Bozongwana, 1990; Gray & Mertens, 1984; Van der Vliet, 1974).

The most dramatic examples of puberty rites in the process of socialization occur in the initiation schools. Among the Xhosa a child is not regarded as a person. This status is achieved only through initiation ceremonies that mark the end of a carefree childhood and the acceptance of adult responsibilities (Gray & Mertens, 1984). Among the Ndebele it is the boy who has not been circumcised who in particular is regarded as "not being united with his soul" and therefore not really human. He is relatively free to do as he pleases, and any form of misbehavior is expected and condoned. Once the circumcision ceremony and accompanying rites have been completed in his mid-teens, however, he is expected to adopt a responsible attitude (Elliot, 1989).

Today, African childrearing practices have changed dramatically. According to Van der Vliet (1974), missionary influence led to the curtailment of many traditional beliefs and customs about the socialization of youth, for instance, initiation at puberty. Although the popularity and importance of initiation rite have gone through periods of decline and resurgence in African society, these persist as viable customs. However, problems associated with this custom in modern-day South Africa are frequently reported in the media, indicating that the way initiation is now practiced is very different from its traditional intention. The main problem seems to be the deaths that occur among initiates. These deaths are the result of either unhygienic circumcisions, or assaults, or loss of blood. Even the spread of HIV is enhanced because the same dirty blade is used to circumcise all the boys attending the initiation school (*Beeld*, 2000; *Die Burger,* 1996). Another problem, especially in rural areas, is that initiates are kept from school for up to three months, which is not beneficial for their academic progress. Some students become so demoralized because of the backlog that they become dropouts from school. After initiation, others regard themselves as "adults" who do not need any further education (Joubert, 2000). Yet another problem in this regard is that initiation has become a money-making enterprise. Boys are abducted from cities to initiation schools and circumcised against their wills. The parents of those who survive the ordeal are then forced to pay large amounts (*Beeld,* 1999).

As has been indicated already, the white family in South Africa closely resembles its Western European counterpart, and this also holds true with respect to socialization practices.

INTERGENERATIONAL FAMILY RELATIONSHIPS

Very little research has been done with regard to the internal functioning of the different family types among the various population groups (Steyn, 1997). However, the research on this topic is in agreement about the changing nature of intergenerational relationships. Both Viljoen (1994) and Campbell (1992) identified the decline of parental authority to be one of the most serious problems in the family life of Africans in South Africa. On the one hand, the decline manifests itself in disobedience and the fact that parents cannot fulfill their roles as socialization agents. On the other hand, it manifests itself in the children's loss of respect for parents. To parents this is evident in, among other things, the fact that children no longer stand up for parents (e.g., in buses), that they are loud, and that they participate in inappropriate discussions in the presence of elderly people. Furthermore, their dress, demonstrations of affection in public, and smoking and drinking reveal disrespect.

In Viljoen's study, there was an appeal from children to address the absence of the father, since his lack of involvement as "head of the family" was seen as a factor contributing to the decline of parental authority. These children also appealed for more communication between parents and children, for an awareness of their own political consciousness, and for greater sensitivity about the inability of parents and grandparents to understand the heightened political awareness among their children. The younger respondents frequently referred to the bad example set by parents who abused alcohol and were guilty of marital infidelity. This was again related to respect and authority: children lost their respect for their parents and consequently parents no longer had authority over their children. Parental responses varied from bewilderment to anger to fear. This problem has multifaceted causes. It can be attributed to the youth revolutions of the 1960s, in which many youth turned against traditional values, which they associated with weakness and acquiescence to domination (Morris & Levitas, 1984). Other factors are poverty and migratory labor, which in turn contribute to the formation of single-parent families. The absence of a large percentage of men from the rural areas for long periods of time has caused a marked increase in unruly, even delinquent behavior in the youth, who openly flout the authority of the women and the elderly who remain the main source of discipline in the rural areas (Van der Vliet, 1974). Because of the inferiority of the so-called "black education" of the Apartheid era, or the total lack of parents' education, the youth in Campbell's study questioned their parents' qualifications to act as social guides in the context of modern township life.

The process of Westernization has also affected the parent–child relationship in the Indian family and reportedly has often led to major friction between the generations, with the youth aspiring to be like white-culture role models and parents clinging to the traditional Indian culture (Bhana, 1984).

Apart from the parent–child relationship, the role of grandparents has become a significant feature of family life in South Africa. Demographic trends in South Africa reveal an increasing proportion of older persons in the population because of declining birthrates and increasing life expectancy, especially among whites. The role of grandparents has varied greatly across cultures and time. In the African community, they are regarded as one of the strengths of these families. They provide support for their families in various ways. In the first instance, they often provide housing for the extended family. Second, their pension is incorporated into the family income—sometimes even forcibly (Burman, 1996). Another way in which the elderly provide support for their families is in terms of looking after the children. The high number of single-parent families has already been mentioned. These result largely from pregnancy outside marriage and divorce. Statistics are not collected for customary-law divorces, and both divorce and illegitimacy figures are far from reliable for most groups. However, fieldwork indicates that in Cape Town the probability is that among Africans over 50 percent of all marriages (by either Roman-Dutch or customary law) will end in permanent separation or divorce (Burman, 1996). This fact, coupled with a high illegitimacy rate, which could be around 60 percent–70 percent, means that among lower-income groups in South Africa, single-parent families take the children to live with relatives, most commonly the children's grandparents. This is a result both of childcare problems, given the dearth of crèches, and also the reluctance of many employers to have the children of their "live-in" domestics on the premises. These patterns of nonparental care were also reinforced under Apartheid by a law preventing employees who were not classified as white from having their children with them in areas set aside for whites. Research in Xhosa-speaking areas has shown that schooling and employment opportunities, migrant labor, and urban school riots have also increased the number of African children living for part of their lives with relatives, frequently grandparents. Medical sources have pointed out that malnutrition among African pensioners is compounded by the number of dependents they often have. It also seems likely that there could be an increase in family care by grandparents because of the AIDS epidemic. In August 1999 the Minister of Health stated that by 2005 there would be 1 million AIDS orphans in South Africa (Forgey et al., 1999).

Among white families, grandparents appear to be assuming more supportive roles. Several reasons may account for this, such as the high divorce rate, the increase in single parents, the number of mothers going out to work, and economic constraints that make the sharing of households necessary. Moreover, today's grandparents may, in general, be enjoying better health than in the past, when the rather passive role ascribed to them may have been the result of poor health (Gerdes, 1997a).

In research done by Mason et al. (1987), it was established that 68 percent of Indian families had daily involvement with the extended family. In 24 percent of the families, the extended family spent more time with the children than the parents, because both parents were employed and the children were cared for by their grandparents. The extended family was included when major decisions were made, even when the family lived as a nuclear unit. In 55 percent of the sample, the extended family contributed to the family income.

FAMILY POLICY

As part of the change to a democracy, South Africa acquired a new constitution (Act 108/1996). This Constitution aims at entrenching important democratic values, such as human dignity, equality, and freedom. The rights that protect these values are contained in the Bill of Rights in Chapter 2 of the Constitution. Apart from the Constitution, South Africa is bound by certain international conventions (e.g., CEDAW and other United Nations conventions on human rights).

Fundamental Rights

The Bill of Fundamental Rights has a pervasive influence on family policy. Statutory provisions concerning the relationship between spouses, between spouses and their children, or between them and outsiders, must, however, be interpreted in terms of the spirit and purport of the Bill of Rights. This is an important aspect, especially when dealing with some African customary laws and certain religious practices. For instance, a woman who has entered into a customary marriage, may, in the event of divorce, claim a fair share of the property, even though customary law dictates otherwise.

One of the Constitution's most important aims is to protect the fundamental right to equality. The Preamble to the Constitution contains a commitment to equality between men and women. Sections 119 and 120 of the Constitution make provision for the establishment of a Commission on Gender Equality. Its purpose is to promote gender equality and to advise and make recommendations to Parliament or any other legislature about any laws or proposed legislation that affects gender equality and the status of women. This Commission was established according to Act No. 39 of 1996. The Commission has thus far played a major role in, among others, the recognition of customary marriages (Act 120/98).

The Constitution recognizes and respects the right to marry and to have a family; the right not to marry without full and free consent; and equal rights to, in, and after marriage (Sections 9, 10, 12, 14, 34). In the last couple of years, various laws have been passed to create equality between spouses (Bosman, 1997). Previously the husband's marital power was virtually the cornerstone of a marital relationship. If the parties married by antenuptial contract, the husband's marital power was normally excluded, but in marriages based on community of property, the husband controlled the person and property of his wife. In terms of the General Law Fourth Amendment, Act 132 of 1993, all marital power was abolished and spouses married in community of property now enjoy the same powers to administer and control the joint estate.

A married woman's domicile is no longer determined by that of her husband. In terms of Section 11(1) of the Domicile Act 3 of 1992, a married woman may acquire a domicile of her own choice. This, among other things, places the parties in divorce proceedings on an equal footing in determining the jurisdiction of the court.

Under the new Constitution, both spouses have the right to end a marriage. Previously women were generally at a disadvantage with regard to marital property. More often than not, husbands accumulate more wealth than their wives, for obvious reasons. Upon dissolution of the marriage by divorce, the wife was often left penniless, or almost so, except for a dubious claim for maintenance. Various measures have been introduced to alleviate the situation of women. Parties may, for instance, marry by antenuptial contract with inclusion of the accrual system. At the dissolution of the marriage by death or divorce, the accrual of the assets is equally divided. If the husband's estate has shown an accrual, the former spouse is entitled to half. Pension benefits and annuities now also form part of the estate to be divided upon divorce. To make courts accessible to all, the Divorce Courts Amendment Act (65/1997) was promulgated. The act provides for people of all races to obtain a divorce either in the High Court or in the Central Divorce Court. Previously, obtaining a divorce in the Central Divorce Court was limited to Africans. Litigants do not require legal representation in the Central Divorce Court, so the process is less costly (Forgey et al., 1999). In addition, family courts have been introduced with the purpose of being more family-friendly, less expensive, and more inclined to use mediation to resolve conflicts (Bosman, 1997).

The Constitution also contains the right to decide about having children. This has resulted in the Choice of Termination of Pregnancy Act (92/1996). Previously, the father of a child born of a marriage was the child's only guardian. In terms of the Guardianship Act 192 of 1993, both parents now have equal powers of guardianship regarding such children. Legislation was also passed to make provision for the possibility of access to and custody and guardianship of children born out of wedlock by their natural fathers (Act 86/1997). Under Section 30 of the Constitution, children are guaranteed the right to a name and nationality, parental care, and security, basic nutrition, health, and social services. A child also has a right not to be subjected to neglect, abuse, or exploitative labor practices or to be required or permitted to work in harmful or hazardous circumstances. These basic rights have also been entrenched in specific acts, such as the Child Care Amendment Act (13/1999). The Employment Equity Act (55/1998) and the Basic Conditions of

Employment Act (75/1997) stipulate spouses' rights with respect to maternity leave and family responsibility leave. Thus, a woman is entitled to four consecutive months' leave in the case of pregnancy, and any employee is entitled to three days' leave when a child is born.

Finally, the Constitution gives one the right to be free from violence and abuse in the home. This was entrenched in the Domestic Violence Act No. 116 of 1998.

In the last six to seven years, profound changes have occurred in the field of family policy. Most of the changes were necessary to improve the lot of married women, who previously were more or less the inferior or minor partners in marriage relationships. As a consequence of the legislation that has been discussed, women are at present in a far better legal position *vis-à-vis* men than they were ten years ago. However, a justifiable bill of rights alone does not guarantee the achievement of real social and economic benefits. It merely constitutes a framework within which real transformation can be effected. The law therefore has its limits, as is evident, for example, in the case of divorce. According to Bosman (1997), divorces are still as traumatic, acrimonious, and expensive as ever. In addition, maintenance for women and children still seems to be a gamble, since only some of them manage to obtain it.

SUMMARY

The current and varied state of family life in South Africa has its roots in the ramifications of a not uneventful history that has brought its influences to bear on the family. In order fully to comprehend family life in this country, one has to take cognizance of these rich and varied influences. Apart from the various indigenous pastoral peoples who had occupied the area 2,000 years ago, European settlers came here during the seventeenth to nineteenth centuries.

Governance was also of particular significance in the recent history of the country. Apartheid rule of fifty years from the middle of the twentieth century played a major role in shaping the sociocultural fabric of the country. The massive social engineering that accompanied it impacted negatively on family life in the country in various ways. Legislation

such as the Prohibition of Mixed Marriages Act, the Population Registration Act, and the Group Areas Act served to separate people and disrupt lives. An entirely new dispensation dawned at the beginning of the 1990s, heralding an era of democracy and freedom for all South Africans.

The South African population of 43.1 million represents a rich array of ethnic backgrounds, resulting in much diversity in family structures, support networks, normative behavioral patterns and values, and also with respect to socioeconomic circumstances, the respective influences of urbanization, industrialization, and geographic location. In spite of this diversity, for the past fifty years data about the South African population have always been made available in terms of the quadripartite division institutionalized by the Apartheid regime, that is, in terms of the black (Africans), Colored, Indian, and white population groups. This reality also informs the framework of this discussion, which of necessity distinguishes among the four population groups.

The indigenous African family was fundamentally influenced by colonialism and neocolonialism and also by the discovery of diamonds and gold at the end of the nineteenth century. However, it was Apartheid policies that made the African family suffer considerable disintegration. Family life among the Colored peoples—mostly of slave extraction—suffered because of being denied marriage for the first 200 years after settlement. The Indian population arrived during the nineteenth century, mostly as indentured laborers. Its main religions—Hinduism and Islam—have been instrumental in the retention of traditional family forms, processes, values, and norms. The white family comprises the descendants of Europeans who came to South Africa between the seventeenth and nineteenth centuries, and consequently it displays characteristics of Western European family life.

In accordance with the diversity among the different population groups, a range of family structures and marriage customs can be found. Particularly interesting are customary marriage among Africans and arranged marriages among Indians. According to research, a common feature among all groups is patriarchy. It has also been indicated that the greater participation by married women in the workforce has affected marital and household roles. A serious problem that was identified in the African family was the decline of parental authority and the absence and/or lack of involvement of the father in the family. Another salient feature of family life is the very important role of grandparents in families. The latter has especially benefited the role and status of women in the family in South Africa.

As part of the change to a real democracy, South Africa has acquired a new constitution containing a Bill of Fundamental Rights that has had a pervasive influence on family policy.

NOTES

1. There are two other important tribal groups, the Venda (2.2 percent of the population) and the Tsonga (4.3 percent of the population), which are, for historical reasons, not included in either the Nguni or Sotho group.
2. See section on family law.
3. "African" is preferred to "blacks."
4. The hut tax was introduced in 1870 to ensure industrial labor. Differential amounts were levied—blacks and whites who were employed paid less tax than those who were unemployed (Cameron & Spies, 1992).

5. The so-called Cape Coloreds evolved from four main groups: slaves, Khoi-San, whites, and Africans.
6. Slaves who were able to buy their freedom—before the general emancipation of slaves—experienced better socioeconomic circumstances than those who were freed later.
7. Marriages concluded in accordance with customary law, i.e., the customs traditionally observed among indigenous Africans of South Africa.
8. Ancient sacred writings on which Hinduism is based.

REFERENCES

Beeld. (1999, September 22). *Inisiasie word geld-maakbedryf* [Initiation is becoming a money-making enterprise]; p. 10.

Beeld. (2000, December 27). *Een sterf, 10 erg beseer in inisiasie* [One die, 10 seriously injured in initiation]; p. 4.

Bhana, K. (1984). Indian parents and their youth: Some perceived and actual differences. *South African Journal of Sociology, 15*(3), 124–128.

Bosman, F. J. (1997). Preface. In Human Sciences Research Council, *Marriage and family life in South Africa: Research priorities. Theme 6—The family and family law: Research in the social sciences and legal development* (pp. 1–11). Pretoria: Human Sciences Research Council Publishers.

Bozongwana, W. (1990). *Ndebele religion.* Gweru, Zimbabwe: Mambo Press.

Burman, S. (1996). Intergenerational family care: Legacy of the past, implications for the future. *Journal of Southern African Studies, 22*(4), 585–599.

Byrnes, R. M. (Ed.). (1996). *South Africa—A country study.* Washington, DC: Library of Congress.

Cameron, T., & Spies, S. B. (Eds.). (1992). *A new illustrated history of South Africa.* Johannesburg: Southern Book Publishers and Human & Rousseau.

Campbell, C. (1992). *Identity and gender in a changing society: The social identity of South African township youth.* Unpublished doctoral dissertation, Department of Psychology, University of Bristol, UK.

Coetzer, P. W. (1992). The era of Apartheid, 1948–1961. In T. Cameron & S. B. Spies (Eds.), *A new illustrated history of South Africa* (pp. 271–289). Johannesburg: Southern Book Publishers and Human & Rousseau.

Cunningham, P., Boult, B., & Popenoe, D. (1998). *Sociology.* Cape Town: Prentice Hall.

De Kock, C. P. (1980). *Buite-egtelikheid by Kleurlinge in die Kaapse Skiereiland* [Illegitimacy among Coloreds in the Cape Peninsula]. Pretoria: Human Sciences Research Council Publishers.

Department of Health. (1999). *Annual report.* Pretoria, South Africa.

Die Burger. (1996, July 22). *Witskrif kom na inisiasie lewe van 4 jong mans eis* [White Paper expected after initiation claims lives of 4 young men], p. 3.

Dlamini, C. R. M. (1997). The need for research in the social sciences for family law in respect of blacks. In Human Sciences Research Council, *Marriage and family life in South Africa: Research priorities. Theme 6—The family and family law: Research in the social sciences and legal development* (pp. 59–78). Pretoria: Human Sciences Research Council Publishers.

du Toit, D. (1993). *Die professionele oriëntasie en gesinslewe van die werkende getroude vrou* [The professional orientation and family life of working married women]. Pretoria: Human Sciences Research Council Publishers.

Elliot, A. (1989). *The Ndebele art and culture.* Cape Town: Struik.

Forgey, H., Jeffery, A., Sidiropoulos, E., Smith, C., Corrigan, T., Mophuthing, T., Helman, A., Redpath, J., & Dimant, T. (1999). *South Africa Survey 1999/2000— Millennium edition.* Johannesburg: South African Institute of Race Relations.

Freund, B. (1991). Indian women and the changing character of the working class Indian household in Natal 1860–1990. *Journal of Southern African Studies, 17*(3), 414–422.

Gerdes, L. C. (1997a). Preface. In Human Sciences Research Council. *Marriage and family life in South Africa: Research priorities. Theme 3—Family relationships* (pp. 1–17). Pretoria: Human Sciences Research Council Publishers.

Gerdes, L. C. (1997b). General perspective. In Human Sciences Research Council, *Marriage and family life in South Africa: Research priorities. Theme 3—Family relationships* (pp. 19–42). Pretoria: Human Sciences Research Council Publishers.

Gray, F., & Mertens, A. (1984). *The Xhosa.* Johannesburg: Centaur.

ILO, Geneva. (2003). 2003–2004 key indicators of the labour market. www.ilo.org/kilm.

Jithoo, S. (1975). Fission of the Hindu joint family in Durban. *Journal of the University of Durban-Westville, 2*(3), 55–62.

Joubert, J.-J. (2000). *Inisiasie knou leerders se vordering op skool* [Initiation curtails learners' progress in school]. 6 *Rapport,* September 24, p. 12.

Lemmer, E. (1989). Invisible barriers: Attitudes toward women in South Africa. *South African Journal of Sociology, 20*(1), 30–37.

Le Roux, T. (1997). The economically active married woman and dual-income couples. In Human Sciences Research Council, *Marriage and family life in South Africa: Research priorities. Theme 3—Family relationships* (pp. 43–64). Pretoria: Human Sciences Research Council Publishers.

Maconachie, M. (1992). The allocation of domestic tasks by white married couples. *South African Journal of Sociology, 23*(4), 112–118.

Mantzaris, E. A. (1988). Religion as a factor affecting the attitudes of South African Indians towards family solidarity and older persons. *South African Journal of Sociology, 19*(3), 111–116.

Mason, J. B., Moodley, T., Fourie, M. C., Candotti, S., & Lamprecht, E. A. M. (1987). An analysis of family variables and intellectual functioning of a group of pre-school Indian children. *South African Journal of Sociology, 18*(3), 110–117.

Morris, J., & Levitas, B. (1984). *South African tribal life today.* Cape Town: College Press.

Motshologane. (1997). Attitudes and practices pertaining to extramarital sex and cohabitation. In Human Sciences Research Council, *Marriage and family life in South Africa: Research priorities. Theme 2—Premarital and extramarital sex and cohabitation.* (pp. 47–60). Pretoria: Human Sciences Research Council Publishers.

Preston, A. (1989). *Pictorial history of South Africa.* London: Bison Books.

Ramasar, P. (1997). Attitudes and practices relating to premarital and extramarital sex and cohabitation among Indians. In Human Sciences Research Council, *Marriage and family life in South Africa: Research priorities. Theme 2—Premarital and extramarital sex and cohabitation* (pp. 115–140). Pretoria: Human Sciences Research Council Publishers.

Schoombee, G. F., & Mantzaris, E. A. (1984). Attitudes of South African Indians towards extended and nuclear family groups in South Africa. *The Journal of the University of Durban-Westville, New Series, 1,* 75–89.

Schoombee, G. F., & Mantzaris, E. A. (1985). Attitudes of South African Indians towards interreligious and arranged marriages: A preliminary study. *South African Journal of Sociology, 16*(2), 59–64.

Schoombee, G. F., & Mantzaris, E. A. (1986). Attitudes of South African Indians towards Westernization and its effects on their family life: A pilot study. *South African Journal of Sociology, 17*(1), 17–21.

Steyn, A. F. (1993). Stedelike gesinstrukture in die Republiek van Suid-Afrika [Urban family structures in the Republic of South Africa]. *South African Journal of Sociology, 24*(1), 17–26.

Steyn, A. F. (1996). Values that support quality marital and family life. *South African Journal of Sociology, 27*(4), 143–148.

Steyn, A. F. (1997). *Marriage and family life in South Africa: Research priorities. Theme 8—Summary and research proposals.* Pretoria: Human Sciences Research Council Publishers.

Van der Vliet, V. (1974). Growing up in traditional society. In W. D. Hammond-Tooke (Ed.), *The Bantu-speaking peoples of Southern Africa* (pp. 211–245). London: Routledge & Kegan Paul.

Van Warmelo, N.J. (1974). The classification of cultural groups. In W. D. Hammond-Tooke (Ed.), *The Bantu-speaking peoples of Southern Africa* (pp. 56–84). London: Routledge & Kegan Paul.

Viljoen, S. (1994). *Strengths and weaknesses in the family life of black South Africans.* Pretoria: Human Sciences Research Council Publishers.

INDEX

Abandonment, 23–24, 271–272, 330
Abortion, 23–24, 110, 191, 287, 330, 366
Adoption, 22, 39, 66, 129, 229, 285, 334, 335, 339, 340
  informal (child-shifting), 318–319, 320–322
Aging, 6, 7, 9, 68–69, 78–80, 98, 133, 139, 143, 164, 218, 226, 231, 236, 243, 251–252, 262, 267–268, 286, 338, 356, 375, 376, 379
AIDS, 39, 111, 283, 366–367, 376

Birth intervals, 22–23, 247, 352
Bofi families (Central Africa), 347–361
  aging, 356
  autonomy in, 360
  birth intervals, 352
  childcare in, 355–361
  child neglect, 358
  communalism in, 360
  disciplinary practices, 355–357, 361
  divorce in, 353–355
  extended, 351
  household division of labor, 349–351, 355–356, 360
  Kopay (bride wealth), 353
  religious values, 353, 359–360, 361
Brazilian families, 330–341
  abandonment, 330
  abortion, 330
  adoption in, 334, 335, 339, 340
  aging, 338
  childcare in, 337, 340–341
  divorce in, 338–339
  employment effects on, 333, 336, 337
  extended, 333, 334–335, 337–338, 339
  female sterilization, 338
  feminist influence on, 331, 337, 339, 340
  functional polygyny, 338–339
  godparentage, 335
  household division of labor, 336
  nuclear, 336, 337
  religious values, 332, 336, 338
  single-parent, 331
  street children, 339–341
  structure of, 334–335

Caribbean families, 311–326
  African Caribbean, 315–321
  childcare in, 319–321, 323–325
  child-shifting in (informal adoption), 318, 319, 320–321, 322
  disciplinary practices, 317–319, 321, 323–325
  extended, 318, 322, 323
  filial piety, 317–318
  household division of labor, 314, 315–316, 317, 322–323, 325
  Indo Caribbean, 321–325
  nonmarital unions, 314–316, 319
  religious values, 316–318, 322–324, 325
  single-parent, 314, 315–316, 317
  structure of, 314–316, 321–322, 325
  unemployment effects on, 322
Central Africa. *See* Bofi families
Child labor, 112–113, 118, 158, 164
Child neglect, 23–24, 122, 125, 134, 143, 358
Chinese families, 51–60
  childcare in, 58, 60

Chinese families *(continued)*
    divorce rates, 53
    employment effects on, 53–55, 57
    extended, 52
    household division of labor, 54,
        58–59
    interethnic marriages, 52
    nuclear, 53
    religious values, 52
    single-parent, 53
    structure of, 53–54
Collectivistic cultures, 51, 52, 56,
    70–71, 80, 87, 92, 133, 173–174,
    278–279, 288, 360
Contraception, 191, 233, 287

Divorce rates, 6, 20, 34, 36, 53, 77, 87,
    155, 159, 161, 171, 184, 186,
    188, 195, 214, 221, 227, 232,
    248, 296–297, 300, 354, 368–369,
    376
Domestic violence, 11, 20, 22, 55, 75,
    133, 134, 143, 161, 165, 172,
    180, 198, 233, 272, 281, 325,
    338, 340, 351, 378

Education, 6, 8, 35–36, 52, 53, 55, 57,
    66, 74, 111, 112, 113, 117, 123,
    127, 131–132, 134–136, 139,
    143–144, 156–157, 158, 159,
    161–162, 163–164, 171–173, 175,
    178, 179, 185–197, 195–196, 210,
    236, 243, 246, 254–255, 266–267,
    279, 285, 313, 315, 317, 319,
    332, 337, 372–373, 375
Egyptian families, 151–166
    aging, 164
    childcare in, 157–158, 160
    child labor, 158, 164
    divorce in, 161
    divorce rates, 155, 159, 161
    employment effects on, 154, 157,
        159, 160, 162–164

family planning, 158
family services, 165
household division of labor, 159,
    160, 164
illiteracy, 161–162
marital adjustment, 160, 164
marriage, 154–157, 165–166
polygamy, 8, 160–161
religious values, 152–156, 157–158,
    166
structure of, 163–164
unemployment effects on, 162–163

Family. *See also* Marriage, Parenting,
    Religious values, Socialization
    childbearing, 6, 34–37, 40, 157, 191,
        300, 315, 333, 338
    childcare, 7, 8, 17, 21, 23–25, 34,
        41–44, 58, 60, 129, 130, 133,
        140, 141, 143, 157–158, 160,
        171–172, 175, 235, 236, 265–266,
        285, 302, 303, 305–306, 319–321,
        323–325, 337, 340–341, 355–361,
        373–376
    childrearing, 6, 7, 9, 10, 52, 56, 57,
        58, 70, 73, 79, 129, 130, 174,
        177–178, 233, 288, 300, 314, 316,
        317, 333, 355–361, 374
    cohabiting, 6, 34–37, 40, 143, 173,
        185, 191, 197, 220, 232, 270–271,
        272, 274, 296, 300–303, 306, 315,
        319–321, 322, 323–325, 333, 334,
        371
    common-law, 5, 197, 314, 315, 322
    domestic violence in, 11, 20, 22, 55,
        75, 133, 134, 143, 161, 165, 172,
        180, 198, 233, 272, 281, 325,
        338, 340, 351, 378
    ecological perspective of, 15–26
    employment effects on, 7, 8, 35–36,
        38–39, 41, 43, 44, 53–55, 57, 69,
        74, 75, 80, 111, 133–134, 141,
        154, 157, 159, 160, 162–164,

171–172, 185–186, 194–197, 228–232, 233–237, 247, 261–263, 273, 279, 302, 333, 336, 337, 351, 365, 371, 372–374, 375, 376, 379

extended, 6, 7, 9, 18, 21, 25, 37–39, 41, 52, 68, 88–89, 90, 92, 104–105, 108, 110, 114, 118, 120–123, 127, 128, 130, 133, 138, 143, 171, 185, 195, 207, 211–217, 219–222, 228, 230, 262, 265, 266–268, 272, 273, 275, 318, 322, 323, 333, 334–335, 337–338, 339, 351, 368, 369–370, 376

familism, 8, 67, 185–197

filial piety, 6, 52, 56, 65, 66, 317–318

functions of, 124–125, 128–131, 211–213, 332–333, 371

household division of labor, 5–8, 21, 34, 41, 54, 58–59, 65, 70–74, 76–78, 81, 91, 111–113, 125, 129, 141, 159, 160, 164, 172, 174–176, 185–186, 195, 213–214, 215, 221, 247, 287–288, 300, 301–302, 314, 315–316, 317, 322–323, 325, 336, 349–351, 355–356, 360, 365, 368, 372–374, 379

inheritance patterns, 17–20, 23, 25, 66, 144, 138, 174, 180, 210, 212, 228, 334

lesbi/gay, 5, 6, 9, 11, 33, 34, 37, 41–43, 184, 197, 249–250, 301

nuclear, 6, 7, 25, 33, 36, 37–38, 53, 68, 69, 80, 87, 88, 97, 105, 110, 118, 120–121, 122–123, 127, 128, 130, 133–134, 138, 140, 141, 185, 196–197, 207, 211–212, 217–218, 220, 221–222, 228–231, 237, 246–248, 266–268, 272, 273, 336, 337, 369–370

reconstituted, 6, 227, 232, 273–274

single-parent, 6, 9, 16, 19, 34, 36, 53, 68, 87, 186, 198, 211, 214, 221, 227, 228, 231, 232, 248–249, 255, 268, 271, 273, 275, 278, 296, 305, 306, 314, 315–316, 317, 331, 365, 369–370, 373, 376

structure of, 8, 15, 34, 40, 42, 51, 53–54, 65–69, 72, 75, 79, 81, 86–89, 127–128, 137, 163–164, 184, 196–197, 212–213, 222, 226, 228–234, 236, 268, 298, 314–316, 321–322, 325, 334–335, 369–370, 378

technological influences on, 39–40, 101, 142, 248, 266

transsexual, 42–43

unemployment effects on, 36, 162–163, 194, 199, 264, 281, 322

Family policy, 8, 11, 14–15, 44–45, 54, 110–111, 163, 179–180, 197–198, 227, 239, 273, 279, 284, 325, 376–378

one-child policy (China), 11, 54, 59

Fertility rates, 6, 7, 17, 20, 22, 23, 34, 35, 44, 53, 67–68, 81, 110, 152, 157, 170, 175, 184, 186,188, 195–196, 214, 227, 233, 243, 247, 251, 282, 297, 306, 314, 338, 351–352, 366

French Polynesia (Marquesas Islands), 120–124, 136–144

child neglect, 122

employment effects on families, 141

extended families, 120–123, 138, 143

healthcare, 138

household division of labor, 141

nuclear families, 120–121, 122–123, 138, 140, 141

structure of families, 137

Gender roles, 6, 8, 43–44, 52–53,
    54–55, 58, 63–64, 70–75, 76–77,
    89–91, 111–113, 125, 129–130,
    142, 153–155, 157–159, 172–179,
    185, 189–190, 195–199, 213, 215,
    234, 236, 251, 286, 287–288, 300,
    302, 306, 316, 318–320, 322,
    324–325, 330–331, 332, 334,
    335–336, 337, 341, 349–351,
    355–356, 360, 365, 372–374
German families, 242–255
    aging, 243, 251–252
    birth intervals, 247
    divorce rates, 248
    employment effects on, 247
    feminist influence on, 250–251
    household division of labor, 247
    immigrant families, 252–253
    nuclear, 246–248
    religious values, 245–246
    single-parent, 248–249, 255
Globalization, 4, 7, 8, 97, 99–101, 118,
    159, 193–194, 221, 222, 268
Greek families, 207–222
    aging, 218
    bilinear inheritance (Karpathos), 212
    divorce in, 210
    divorce rates, 214, 221
    ecocultural framework, 209
    extended, 207, 211–217, 219–222
    family values, 215–217, 220–222
    household division of labor,
        213–214, 215, 221
    modernization theory, 221
    nuclear, 207, 211–212, 217–218,
        220, 221–222
    religious values, 210–211
    single-parent, 211, 214, 221
    structure of, 212–213, 222

Household division of labor, 5–8, 21,
    34, 41, 54, 58–59, 65, 70–74,
    76–78, 81, 91, 111–113, 125, 129,
    141, 159, 160, 164, 172, 174–176,
    185–186, 195, 213–214, 215, 221,
    247, 287–288, 300, 301–302, 314,

315–316, 317, 322–323, 325, 336,
    349–351, 355–356, 360, 365, 368,
    372–374, 379

Indian families, 85–101
    aging, 98
    extended, 88–89, 90, 92
    Hindu caste system, 92–94
    household division of labor, 91
    nuclear, 87, 88, 97
    religious values, 88, 90, 92–97,
        98–99, 101
    rites of passage, 93
    single-parent, 87
    structure of, 81, 86–89
Individualistic cultures, 9, 11, 17, 80,
    87, 92, 174, 185–188, 194, 199,
    288, 302–303
Indonesian families, 104–118
    abortion, 110
    AIDS, 111
    child labor, 112–113, 118
    Chinese, 115–117
    employment effects on, 111
    extended, 104–105, 108, 110, 114,
        118
    household division of labor,
        111–113
    mahar (bride price), 107, 112–113
    marriage regulations, 110, 117
    nuclear, 105, 110, 118
    premarital sex, 109, 118
    refugees, 117–118
    religious values, 104–112, 114–115
    STDs, 109–111
Infanticide, 23–25
Israel, 184–199
    abortion, 191
    androgyny, 187
    contraception, 191
    divorce, 185, 189–190
    divorce rates, 184, 186, 188, 195
    employment effects on families,
        185–186, 194–197
    extended families, 185, 195
    familism, 8, 67, 185–197

family honor killing, 190, 191
gender segregation, 187, 190
household division of labor,
185–186, 195
monogamy, 189
neomodern families, 196–197, 199
nuclear families, 185, 196–197
polygamy, 189–190
postmodern families, 197
religious values, 185, 186, 189–192,
195–199
single-parent, 186, 198
structure of families, 184, 196–197
ultraorthodox families (Haredi
families), 196
unemployment effects on families,
194, 199
Italian families, 225–239
adoption, 229
aging, 226, 231, 236
childcare in, 235, 236
contraception, 233
divorce rates, 227, 232
employment effects on, 228–232,
233–237
extended, 228, 230
illegitimate births, 227, 248
nuclear, 228–231, 237
religious values, 233
single-parent, 227, 228, 231, 232
structure of, 226, 228–234, 236

Japanese families, 63–81
adoption in, 66
aging, 68–69, 78–80
divorce rates, 87
employment effects on, 69, 74, 75,
80
extended, 68
familism, 67
filial piety, 65, 66
household division of labor, 65,
70–74, 76–78, 81
ie, 66–67
nuclear, 68, 69, 80
"parasite singles," 75, 81

religious values, 64, 65–66, 69–70
single-parent, 68
structure of, 65–69, 72, 75, 79, 81

Marriage
arranged, 6, 8, 54, 75–77, 79, 94,
108, 174, 190, 196, 283, 322,
334, 337, 339, 369, 370, 372
bride wealth, 8, 20, 24–25, 107,
112–113, 353, 370–371
customary, 370–371
dowry, 20, 90, 154, 174, 210, 222
endogamy, 25, 94
exogamy, 25, 350
extramarital sexual relationships, 35,
55, 77–78, 159, 338–339, 371,
372, 375
ilobodo (bride wealth), 370–371
interethnic, 52, 69, 79, 107, 155,
192, 252–253
Kopay (bride wealth), 353
mahar (bride price), 107, 112–113
monogamy, 7, 15–19, 20, 21, 25,
189, 284, 332, 336, 371
polyandry, 16–21, 25, 33
polygamy, 8, 160–161, 189–190,
284, 370, 371
polygyny, 15–18, 25, 33, 338–339,
352, 353
postponement of, 6, 7, 34–35, 68,
109, 226, 228, 246, 300, 306
premarital sex, 8, 109, 118, 154,
155, 159, 283, 300, 338, 353, 371
rates, 6, 35–36, 155, 171, 184, 186,
188, 214, 226, 284, 296, 301,
306, 315
regulations, 110–117
systems, 5, 16–19, 330
Mating systems, 16–17
Micronesian families, 120–124,
125–136, 143–144
adoption in, 129
aging, 133, 139, 143
childcare in, 129, 130, 133, 140,
141, 143
child neglect, 125, 134, 143

Micronesian families *(continued)*
  employment effects on, 133–134
  extended, 120–123, 127, 128, 130,
    133, 143
  healthcare, 126, 127, 131, 143
  household division of labor, 125, 129
  nuclear, 120–121, 122–123, 127,
    128, 130, 133–134, 138
  prevention and resolution of
    conflict, 130
  structure of, 127–128
Migration, 6–9, 38–39, 40–41, 89,
    97–98, 134, 139, 140–141, 142,
    155, 160, 170, 176, 208, 229,
    249, 262–263, 266–267, 269, 277,
    293, 312–314, 322, 331–332, 333,
    365, 368, 371, 372, 375, 376
Mortality rates, 22–23, 110, 123, 158,
    170, 228, 229, 243, 247, 282–283,
    297–298, 314, 338, 352–353,
    366–367

Norwegian families, 259–276
  abandonment, 271–272
  aging, 262, 267–268
  childcare in, 265–266
  divorce in, 271, 274
  employment effects on, 261–263,
    273
  extended, 262, 265, 266–268, 272,
    273, 275
  forced-sex situations, 271
  immigrant families, 263–264
  nuclear, 266–268, 272, 273
  postmodern, 268–269, 272
  religious values, 262, 265, 267
  silences stories, 269–270, 271
  single-parent, 268, 271, 273, 273,
    275
  social class differences, 261–264
  structure of, 268
  unemployment effects on, 264

Out of wedlock births, 6, 19, 35, 36,
    184, 185, 188, 270, 284–285, 297,
    303, 305, 368, 371, 376, 377

Parenting
  adoption, 22, 39, 66, 129, 229, 285,
    334, 335, 339, 340
  attachment, 19, 70–73, 91, 153, 175,
    340
  authoritarian, 8, 56, 58, 113, 118,
    304, 317–319, 321, 323–325,
    355–357, 361, 373
  authoritative, 304
  childcare, 7, 8, 17, 21, 23–25, 34,
    41–44, 58, 60, 129, 130, 133,
    140, 141, 143, 157–158, 160,
    171–172, 175, 235, 236, 265–266,
    285, 302, 303, 305–306, 319–321,
    323–325, 337, 340–341, 355–361,
    373–376
  childrearing, 6, 7, 9, 10, 52, 56, 57,
    58, 70, 73, 79, 129, 130, 174,
    177–178, 233, 300, 314, 316, 317,
    333, 355–361, 374, 388
  disciplinary practices, 178, 288, 303,
    317–319, 321, 323–325, 355–357,
    361, 373
  godparentage, 335
  permissive, 304, 325, 361
  step-parents, 21–22, 25, 33, 36
Pathogen stress, 18, 20, 25

Religious values, 5, 6, 8, 34, 35, 40,
    52, 64, 65–66, 69–70, 88, 90,
    92–97, 98–99, 101, 104–112,
    114–115, 152–156, 157–158, 166,
    172–179, 185, 186, 189–192,
    195–199, 210–211, 233, 245–246,
    262, 265, 267, 283–284, 286, 293,
    299–300, 303, 316–318, 322–324,
    325, 332, 336, 338, 353, 359–360,
    361, 365, 368–369, 371–372, 373,
    376–377, 378, 379
Rites of passage, 93, 262, 324, 360,
    374–375
Russian families, 277–288
  abortion, 287
  adoption in, 285
  aging, 286
  AIDS, 283

childcare in, 285
child homelessness, 285
contraception, 287
disciplinary practices, 288
divorce in, 284
employment effects on, 279
family planning, 286–287
healthcare, 285–286
household division of labor,
287–288
religious values, 283–284, 286
single-parent, 278
unemployment effects on, 281

Social class differences, 115, 171, 331,
333–341, 369–370
Socialization, 5, 6, 9–11, 17, 52,
56–60, 67, 69–75, 79, 87–92, 95,
96, 98, 101, 108–109, 128–131,
140–142, 158–160, 163–164,
173, 175–179, 216, 218–222,
236, 237, 245–246, 253–255,
265–266, 272–273, 279, 288,
300, 304–306, 315, 317–322,
323–325, 335, 349–351,
355–361, 372–376
South African families, 363–379
abortion, 366
aging, 375, 376, 379
AIDS, 366–367, 376
Apartheid, 362–365, 368, 375, 376,
378
childcare in, 373–376
customary marriage, 370–371
disciplinary practices, 373
divorce in, 368, 369, 376, 377, 378
divorce rates, 368–369, 376
employment effects on, 371,
372–374, 375, 376, 379
extended, 369–370, 376
household division of labor, 365,
368, 372–374, 379
ilobodo (bride wealth), 370–371
illegal births, 371
interracial marriage, 364
joint families, 369

migratory labor, 365, 368, 371, 375,
376
nuclear, 369–370
religious values, 365, 368–369,
371–372, 373, 376–377, 378, 379
single-parent, 365, 369–370, 373,
376
structure of, 369–370, 378

Teen suicide, 122, 135–136, 143, 325
Turkish families, 169–180
childcare in, 171–172, 175
conflict in, 175–177
disciplinary practices, 178
divorce rates, 171
employment effects on, 171–172
extended, 171
gender segregation, 176
household division of labor, 172,
174–176
religious values, 172–179
transitional extended, 171

United States, 34–45, 87, 293–306
adoption, 39
African American families, 35–36,
293, 306
Asian families, 294, 306
childcare, 34, 41–44, 302, 303,
305–306
disciplinary practices, 303
divorce, 299–301, 302–303, 304,
305, 306
divorce rates, 34, 36, 296–297, 300
employment effects on families,
35–36, 38–39, 41, 43, 44, 302
extended families, 37–39, 41
household division of labor, 34, 41,
300, 301–302
Latino families, 35, 38–39, 294, 306
marital satisfaction, 302
marriage patterns, 300–303
Mexican families, 293–294
Native American families, 293, 306
no-fault divorce movement in,
302–303

United States *(continued)*
   non-custodial fathers in, 305–306
   nuclear families, 33, 36, 37–38
   parent effects perspective, 304
   parenting, 303–306
   religious values, 34, 35, 40, 293,
      299–300, 303
   single-parent families, 34, 36, 296,
      305, 306
   structure of families, 34, 40, 42, 298
   teen marriages, 303
   unemployment effects on families,
      36